8961

P9-EDF-103

(Continued on back endsheets)

Seventeenth-Century British Nondramatic Poets

Second Series

Seventeenth-Century British Nondramatic Poets

Second Series

Edited by
M. Thomas Hester
North Carolina State University

A Bruccoli Clark Layman Book
Gale Research Inc.
Detroit, London

Printed in the United States of America

Published simultaneously in the United Kingdom
by Gale Research International Limited
(An affiliated company of Gale Research Inc.)

The paper used in this publication meets the minimum requirements
of American National Standard for Information Sciences—Permanence
Paper for Printed Library Materials, ANSI Z39.48-1984. ∞™

Library of Congress Catalog Card Number 92-42318
ISBN 0-8103-5385-7

10 9 8 7 6 5 4 3 2 1

Table of Contents

Plan of the Series

. . . Almost the most prodigious asset of a country, and perhaps its most precious possession, is its native literary product — when that product is fine and noble and enduring.

Mark Twain*

The advisory board, the editors, and the publisher of the *Dictionary of Literary Biography* are joined in endorsing Mark Twain's declaration. The literature of a nation provides an inexhaustible resource of permanent worth. We intend to make literature and its creators better understood and more accessible to students and the reading public, while satisfying the standards of teachers and scholars.

To meet these requirements, *literary biography* has been construed in terms of the author's achievement. The most important thing about a writer is his writing. Accordingly, the entries in *DLB* are career biographies, tracing the development of the author's canon and the evolution of his reputation.

The purpose of *DLB* is not only to provide reliable information in a convenient format but also to place the figures in the larger perspective of literary history and to offer appraisals of their accomplishments by qualified scholars.

The publication plan for *DLB* resulted from two years of preparation. The project was proposed to Bruccoli Clark by Frederick C. Ruffner, president of the Gale Research Company, in November 1975. After specimen entries were prepared and typeset, an advisory board was formed to refine the entry format and develop the series rationale. In meetings held during 1976, the publisher, series editors, and advisory board approved the scheme for a comprehensive biographical dictionary of persons who contributed to North American literature. Editorial work on the first volume began in January 1977, and it was published in 1978. In order to make *DLB* more than a reference tool and to compile volumes that individually have claim to status

*From an unpublished section of Mark Twain's autobiography, copyright by the Mark Twain Company

as literary history, it was decided to organize volumes by topic, period, or genre. Each of these free-standing volumes provides a biographical-bibliographical guide and overview for a particular area of literature. We are convinced that this organization — as opposed to a single alphabet method — constitutes a valuable innovation in the presentation of reference material. The volume plan necessarily requires many decisions for the placement and treatment of authors who might properly be included in two or three volumes. In some instances a major figure will be included in separate volumes, but with different entries emphasizing the aspect of his career appropriate to each volume. Ernest Hemingway, for example, is represented in *American Writers in Paris, 1920–1939* by an entry focusing on his expatriate apprenticeship; he is also in *American Novelists, 1910–1945* with an entry surveying his entire career. Each volume includes a cumulative index of the subject authors and articles. Comprehensive indexes to the entire series are planned.

With volume ten in 1982 it was decided to enlarge the scope of *DLB*. By the end of 1986 twenty-one volumes treating British literature had been published, and volumes for Commonwealth and Modern European literature were in progress. The series has been further augmented by the *DLB Yearbooks* (since 1981) which update published entries and add new entries to keep the *DLB* current with contemporary activity. There have also been *DLB Documentary Series* volumes which provide biographical and critical source materials for figures whose work is judged to have particular interest for students. One of these companion volumes is entirely devoted to Tennessee Williams.

We define literature as the *intellectual commerce of a nation:* not merely as belles lettres but as that ample and complex process by which ideas are generated, shaped, and transmitted. *DLB* entries are not limited to "creative writers" but extend to other figures who in their time and in their way influenced the mind of a people. Thus the series encompasses historians, journalists, publishers, and screenwriters. By this means readers of *DLB* may be aided to perceive literature not as cult scripture in the keeping of intellectual high priests but firmly positioned at the center of a nation's life.

DLB includes the major writers appropriate to each volume and those standing in the ranks immediately behind them. Scholarly and critical counsel has been sought in deciding which minor figures to include and how full their entries should be. Wherever possible, useful references are made to figures who do not warrant separate entries.

Each *DLB* volume has a volume editor responsible for planning the volume, selecting the figures for inclusion, and assigning the entries. Volume editors are also responsible for preparing, where appropriate, appendices surveying the major periodicals and literary and intellectual movements for their volumes, as well as lists of further readings. Work on the series as a whole is coordinated at the Bruccoli Clark Layman editorial center in Columbia, South Carolina, where the editorial staff is responsible for accuracy of the published volumes.

One feature that distinguishes *DLB* is the illustration policy – its concern with the iconography of literature. Just as an author is influenced by his surroundings, so is the reader's understanding of the author enhanced by a knowledge of his environment. Therefore *DLB* volumes include not only drawings, paintings, and photographs of authors, often depicting them at various stages in their careers, but also illustrations of their families and places where they lived. Title pages are regularly reproduced in facsimile along with dust jackets for modern authors. The dust jackets are a special feature of *DLB* because they often document better than anything else the way in which an author's work was perceived in its own time. Specimens of the writers' manuscripts are included when feasible.

Samuel Johnson rightly decreed that "The chief glory of every people arises from its authors." The purpose of the *Dictionary of Literary Biography* is to compile literary history in the surest way available to us – by accurate and comprehensive treatment of the lives and work of those who contributed to it.

The *DLB* Advisory Board

Introduction

This volume of the *Dictionary of Literary Biography* comprises entries for the second generation of seventeenth-century British nondramatic poets: those born after the English defeat of the Spanish Armada in 1588 and before the start of the Thirty Years' War in 1618. Two-thirds of the poets discussed were born after the death of Queen Elizabeth I in 1603 and died after the execution of King Charles I in 1649. All of them outlived the first Stuart king, James I (died 1625), and half of them lived to see the Restoration of the monarchy with the accession of King Charles II in 1660. The octogenarian Joseph Beaumont even survived to see the Glorious Revolution and exile of King James II in 1688 and the beginning of the reign of William III and Mary II in the following year. With the notable exception of George Herbert (1593–1633), Rachel Speght (1597–after 1630), and Thomas Randolph (1605–1635), who along with Thomas Carew (1594 or 1595–1640) and Sir John Suckling (1609–1641?) alone among this group were spared the experience of the civil wars (1642–1648), these poets wrote the majority of their works during the reign of Charles I (1625–1649), although many continued to compose significant poems during the Commonwealth rule by the Council of State (1649–1653), by Lord Protector Oliver Cromwell (1653–1658), and by his son, Richard Cromwell (1658–1660) during the Puritan Interregnum. As Caroline poets these authors thus composed the majority of their nondramatic poems during one of the most turbulent and violent periods of change in English history, an age that would in significant ways radically change forever the political, civil, and ecclesiastical landscape of the nation as it moved from the medieval to the threshold of the modern world.

After the luxury of (apparent) stability from outside threats was achieved by the defeat of the Spanish Armada in 1588, the nation began a sort of internecine struggle over royal prerogative that was to dominate the next century. Tensions between Elizabeth and her Parliaments increased as the Puritans (primarily Presbyterians) increased their demands for more reformation in religious matters and the Parliaments strove to assume a greater voice in financial and foreign affairs. Largely through a policy of astute management and conservative compromise, however, Elizabeth maintained until the last years of her rule the dominant hand in national affairs. James I rejected such an approach in favor of the assertion of the "divine rights of kings." He proceeded to levying customs duties beyond those prescribed by law, and, under the sway of the rakish George Villiers, first Duke of Buckingham, granted monopolies indiscriminately and widely. Parliament finally limited the royal sale of monopolies (1624), and followed with the assertion of its authority to impeach the king's ministers. Arguments fostered more arguments, protestations more protestations. So it is perhaps not surprising that when James's son, Charles I, came to the throne in 1625 he decided to stabilize his royal authority primarily by ruling without Parliament. Supported by the established Anglican church under the eventual leadership of Archbishop William Laud, whose Arminianism (with its Catholic-like stress on the free will) directly contravened the Calvinistic Puritanism (with its doctrine of the depravity of the will) of many Parliamentarians, encouraged and supported judicially by the able manipulations of Thomas Wentworth, first Earl of Strafford, the autocratic King Charles I returned to Parliament only to acquire necessary funds. As Henry Melvill Gwatkin phrases it, if James had "a genius for getting into difficulties," he yet was "not without a certain shrewdness in stopping just short of catastrophe. If he steered the ship straight for the rocks, he left his son to wreck it" (*Church and State in England,* 1917).

In some ways Gwatkin's quip is not fair to Charles I. After all, his court did not flaunt the corruption characteristic of that of his father or of his son, Charles II (even though enemies and some supporters saw Charles I's choice of a French Catholic for his queen to be much worse than to be dominated by the duke of Buckingham, as was his father, or by a Nell Gwyn, as his son would be – these, after all, were not the same as marriage to an extravagant mistress of the Catholic Antichrist). But if

Charles I did bring a command of decorum and an insistence on royal propriety to the world of the court, he was still not the astute administrator that his father, the so-called Britain's Solomon, was — and, from hindsight, Charles did not enjoy the advantage his own son would have by coming to power in 1660, as the Restoration of harmony and peace after the decades of civil war and military dictatorship. Unlike his father, Charles I brought war to the nation, and through his own religious policies managed to fracture the fragile harmony of a united Britain which James I (who was also James VI of Scotland) had achieved. But from a broader perspective, despite his many shortcomings, especially his error in assuming an aloofness from his nation and his taking literally a principle of "divine rule" which had already been severely questioned, it is possible to see that the first planks of the scaffolding outside Whitehall Palace where Charles would be executed in 1649 had been provided decades before — by the general revolt against authority by the Reformation itself. Following Martin Luther's devout but, in the root sense of the word, profane (*pro,* "outside"; *fanus,* "temple") posting of his demands for religious reform outside Wittenberg Cathedral, the grounds of secular authority and its medieval structures had been irreparably shaken. Having once ended the authority of the successor of King Solomon and Saint Peter (the pope) over God's English temple, it was certainly not inconceivable to oust the successor of James I from his earthly throne. It was as the enemy of the antiauthoritarian Reformation, in fact, that Charles I was painted by his Puritan and Parliamentarian foes. Indeed, as Andrew Marvell later phrased it, Charles "nothing common did, nor mean, / Upon that memorable stage" of his reign; but he was not sufficiently equipped with the skill, or perhaps even the luck, to be able to counter or to avoid "the war's and Fortune's son[s]" (both Puritans and Parliamentarians) opposed to his authority; in Marvell's terms, unlike the Puritan leader Oliver Cromwell, Charles I was unable to exhibit those "arts that did gain / A pow'r [and which] must it maintain" in the postmedieval world ("An Horatian Ode"). He may have been the greatest connoisseur and patron of the arts ever to rule England; but that characteristic itself might be emblematic of his distance from the forces of secular modern politics and of his misfortune of having come to the throne at the very time that the ideal of the Renaissance prince as a model of aristocratic taste and elitist decorum was becoming an object of contempt. It is not merely coincidental that the figure of Time dominates the court poetry of the age, that "carpe diem" is a consistent theme, or that one of the central concerns of that poetry is the pursuit of a world of artifice and art to counter the onslaught of "*Times trans-shifting.*"

If Charles was at the helm when the ship of state crashed into the rocks of civil disorder and cultural change, he yet had help, of course. His rule saw and accelerated the clash between the "antique" aristocratic wealth of the landed and the "new" wealth of middle-class trade, and the discord of increasingly adamant religious disputes about the character of English "reformation"; and his rule was greatly affected by the growing ideological "atomism" at his own court with its wide swings from an insistently enthusiastic cult of royalty and a poetic of debased "platonic love" to a rakish naturalistic cynicism and an aggressive hedonism. In fact, Sir Henry Wotton's wry comment that "*Disputandi pruritus fit Ecclesiarum scabies*" (translated in George Herbert's *Outlandish Proverbs,* 1640, as "The itch of disputation will prove the scab of the Church") turned out to be true of the nation at large as it moved from the height of national celebrations and apparent unity under "good Queen Bess" (Elizabeth I) to the disaster of the civil wars and eventually to the legal execution of King Charles I outside the ornately decorated memorial to Stuart "glory," Whitehall Palace.

One cause of the rapid deterioration of any semblance of national unity during the Stuart reign of James I and Charles I was simply that the court no longer reflected the balance of feudal and bourgeois energies that Elizabeth I had forged into a national "compromise," just as the Church of England, especially under Laudian principles, no longer reflected the wide range of interpretations of Protestantism in the country that Elizabeth had allowed. Her "Settlement" had already begun to decline during her waning years, of course, and it could not be sustained by the first two Stuart kings. They seemed not to understand that it could not be formalized by rigorous defenses of a theory of the "divine right of kings" nor maintained by the insistent performance of a sort of daily royal "masque" which obtained only the illusion of medieval political theology. Neither James nor Charles was able to inspire the personal confidence and devotion that had helped Elizabeth shape England — through the aid and genius of her chosen counselors and advisers, of course — into a confident, international state proud of its traditions and image. The offensive absolutism of James's divine-right theory, which lacked any basis in English custom and any appeal to the increasingly restless gentry and commercial classes – much less to the Puritans whom James told he would "harry out of the country" or to the radical sectarians (the Catholics?) who had engineered the Gunpowder Plot – was muted by the muddling moderation of his policies, the endless befuddlements of the "Spanish Match," in which James tried to arrange a marriage between his son and a Spanish princess (and thus bring peace to Europe). After the failures and melancholic results of James's rule, the effort of Charles to make the divine-right theory into a reality on the Gallic model was simply a recipe for disaster – especially when the increasing nonconformity in worship was met by the "crypto-Catholic" rigors of Archbishop Laud. Rapid disintegration followed, even during the long periods when Charles managed to run the country (or at least to orchestrate the court) without the advice or support of Parliament. For as he and his court retreated deeper into the remote indulgences and privileges of their own insulated "stage," they increasingly refused to confront in a timely fashion the national and international changes the world was undergoing, and they also framed an aesthetic that was increasingly distant from the Christian humanist traditions from which the Tudor successes had drawn their strength.

Social, political, and cultural change was not the goal of the majority of the generation of Caroline poets represented in this volume of literary biographies. (Rachel Speght's defense of female equality, especially in education, is a notable exception, of course; but even her project might be seen as a call for a return to the practice of the Sir Thomas More household.) Indeed, from the Low Church emblematist, Francis Quarles (whose emblem books ironically proved second in popularity only to the Bible among those Puritan readers he so detested) to the High Church George Herbert (whose emblem poems first illustrated the strengths of that medieval device as a vehicle for religious meditation), from the irreverent and risqué courtier poets Thomas Carew and Sir John Suckling to the rural neoclassicist Robert Herrick, from those perfectors of the closed couplet, Edmund Waller (early a moderate Parliamentarian who turned Royalist in 1643) and Sir John Denham (an Irish nobleman who gave new form to the genre of the topographical poem) to the Stuart poet laureate William Davenant, from the Laudian (and eventually Roman Catholic) poet Richard Crashaw and the Anglo-Catholic Joseph Beaumont (who was expelled with Crashaw from Cambridge University for "Catholic leanings") to the poet who carried the Metaphysical conceit nearly to the level of dialectical decadence, John

Cleveland, all these poets – from the "School of Donne" or from the "Tribe of Ben" Jonson – were *Royalists*.[*]

Indebted primarily to the example of the neoclassicism and plain style of the (unofficial) Jacobean poet laureate, Ben Jonson – coupled often with the sort of Spenserian nostalgia descended through Michael Drayton – most of these second generation Stuart poets still evince significant traces of the meditative, Metaphysical style of the "monarch of wit," John Donne – especially the strong lines, the epigrammatic concision shared with Jonson, and the fondness for satire and paradox. This influence of Donne is evident if only in their occasionally fervent denials of the libidinous emphases of that late Elizabethan poet's early love poems, as perhaps most fully exemplified in William Habington's *Castara* (1634–1640) or Henry More's Spenserian stanzas of Platonic philosophizings. Indeed, two of the most famous poems of the age announce the enduring example of the two masters, Donne and Jonson. Herrick's crisp and exquisite control of the epigrammatic precision exemplified by Jonson (with more than a touch of anti-Puritan hectoring added in the playful hagiography) evinces the effective use the Caroline poet could make of this classical Latinate vehicle:

> When I a Verse shall make,
> Know I have praid thee,
> For old *Religions* sake,
> Saint *Ben* to aide me.
>
> 2. Make the way smooth for me,
> When I, thy *Herrick*,
> Honouring thee, on my knee
> Offer my *Lyrick*.
>
> 3. Candles Ile give to thee,
> And a new Altar;
> And thou, Saint *Ben,* shalt be
> Writ in my *Psalter*.

("His Prayer to Ben. Johnson")

In the same spirit is Thomas Carew's attempt to capture the vigorous texture and colloquial voice of the Donnean style, while once again suggesting that such a poetic instrument would prove most useful in these times when the "Garden" of the Stuart

---

*It is not inappropriate, then, that the greatest Puritan poet, John Milton – even though he was born in 1608 and his first collection of poems was printed in 1645 – be allowed to appear in the third series of *Seventeenth-Century British Nondramatic Poets,* among those poets whose major works, like his own *Paradise Lost* (1667), *Paradise Regained,* and *Samson Agonistes* (both 1671), appeared during the Puritan Interregnum and the Restoration.

world was beginning to be threatened by forces just starting to feel their strength at the time of Donne's death in 1631:

> The Muses garden with Pedantique weedes
> O'rspred, was purg'd by thee; the lazie seeds
> Of servile imitation throwne away,
> And fresh invention planted, Thou didst pay
> The debts of our penurious bankrupt age;
> . . . .
> Thou hast redeem'd, and open'd Us a Mine
> Of rich and pregnant phansie, drawne a line
> Of masculine expression
> . . . .
> Thou shalt yield no precedence, but of time,
> And the blinde fate of language, whose tun'd chime
> More charmes the outward sense;
> . . . .
> Since to the awe of thy imperious wit
> Our stubborne language bends[.]
> . . . .
> Let others carve the rest, it shall suffice
> I on thy Tombe this Epitaph incise.
>
> *Here lies a King, that rul'd as hee thought fit*
> *The universal Monarchy of wit[.]*
>
> ("An Elegy upon the death of the Deane of Pauls, Dr. Iohn Donne")

As indicated by the aggressive language of Carew's elegy, who would himself fall more frequently under the direction of Jonson's than Donne's style, and by the ostentatious hagiography of Herrick's "Prayer," these conservative Caroline poets (like "Saint Ben") would strive to see themselves as defenders of that view of poetry as the architectonic master-teacher of English culture institutionalized by the major English Renaissance war hero, Sir Philip Sidney. And in the spirit of Sidney's characterization of poetry as the major servant-soldier, armed with Renaissance eloquence to battle the forces of darkness, so these Royalist poets often figure their situation as a battle for the survival of civilization.

One of the poets who was killed in action against the Parliamentarian army, for instance, is eulogized primarily as an enemy of Sidney's *mysomousoi* (poet-haters) – "murthered by those men that professed to destroy Wit and Learning" ("On Sidney Godolphin"). And one does not have to turn to the hyperboles of Owen Felltham's figuration of King "*CHARLES* the *First*" as "*CHRIST* the *second*," his description of the Parliamentarian general Oliver Cromwell as Judas, or his denunciation of the presider over the court that convicted the king (John Bradshaw) as Pontius Pilate, in order to hear

these poets characterize the Civil War and the cultural changes sought by their enemies as assaults on the literary as well as the social and political foundations of English life. Such tropes are native, of course, to the rhetoric of civil strife and political propaganda, but these are striking in one way for their compelling and insistent focus of attention on the seventeenth-century conflicts as a test of the literary ethos of the nation, specifically, their insistence that the health of the English civilization could be measured by the health of its literature. Denham suggests that the king's adviser (Strafford) had to die because "He's not too guilty, but too wise to live" in an age in which the forces of "Eloquence" are losing to those of "Rage." The disillusioned Royalist poet Alexander Brome decries

> the thick darkness of these *verseless* times,
> These *antigenius* times, this boisterous age,
> Where there dwell nought of Poetry but rage,

and Jasper Mayne, in mourning another Royalist casualty of the war (William Cartwright), assails these

> Times which make it Treason to be witty,
> Times where Great Poets do walk abroad by stealth,
> And Great Wits live in *Plato's* Commonwealth.

In one sense these poets link the Puritan "war against poetry" with the Parliamentarian assault on the monarchy; thus they record the identification of their foes with those enemies which these Royalist poets' Renaissance model and exemplar (Sidney) had identified as the major threats to the English Protestant project – the *mysomousoi*. The symbolic stag that is slain in Denham's 1642 georgic *Coopers Hill,* for instance, is not just Strafford (or the king in the 1655 version of the poem) but the essence of English culture – "Wit, Learning, and Poesy." Parliament, then, is not just "thirty fools and twenty knaves," as one wit phrased it, but "a Monster [that] doth rule thee" (according to Brome). It is led by anti-Creators such as John Pym and John Hampden, whose "evil spirit moved o'r this mighty Frame / O' the British Isle, and [of] this Chaos came." Hampden, said Abraham Cowley, "taught Confusion's Art" and the "Black Design Hell thought most fit," and was "cursed by *too good a Wit.*" (And this is not even to mention the full assault on the Puritans by Samuel Butler in his later *Hudibras,* 1662–1677.) As instruments of a national confusion threatening the very order of the universe – the terrible realization of William Shakespeare's "universal wolf, . . . seconded with will and power," that would "include itself in power / Power into will, will into appetite" (*Troilus and Cressida,* 1609), and the confirmation of Donne's warnings about a world in which "all just supply, and all Relation: / Prince, Subject, Father, Sonne are things forgot" ("The First Anniversary") – the Puritan Parliamentarians are seen by these Royalist poets as a chaotic assault on English civilization itself. As the stately heroic couplets of Denham contend, in terms recalling John of Gaunt's patriotic hymn in *Richard II* (1597), to challenge this "best of Kings" is to call into question "the harmony of things." Or, as Henry King insists in his mocking recollection of the Puritans' promise to make Charles "a great and glorious king" if he would relent to their demands, that when they executed the king, "In this last Wrong [they] did Him greatest Right, / And (cross to all You meant) by Plucking down / Lifted Him up to His Eternal crown" – wittily recalling, in fact, the monarch's own final words about his death: "If I must suffer a violent death with my saviour, . . . I go from a corruptible to an incorruptible crown." As John Dryden was to insist later, "never Rebel was to Arts a friend" (*Absalom and Achitophel,* 1681).

Such allegorical and apocalyptical machinery is not relegated to the verse of the Royalists alone, of course. The pugnaciously "prophetic" – and seemingly indestructible – George Wither, for instance, relies on the same lexicon of righteous contempt and cultural outrage to offer verse that often rises above the "popular" forms favored by the Puritan and Parliamentarian rhetors. Denham might sneer that the imprisoned Wither should not be hanged because while he lived Denham "should not be the worst poet in England," but Wither's attempts to counter the establishment's Arminian view of history and its assault on the "wicked angels" of Parliament with his support of the Puritans' view of history's providential determinism actually conscripts the same allegorical vocabulary on which Denham relied. The Royalist poets are the enemies of "God's elect," says Wither, and

> . . . For wicked ends
> Have the *Castalian Spring* defil'd with gall;
> And chang'd by witchcraft, most Satyricall,
> The bayes of *Helicon,* and myrtles mild,
> To pricking hawthornes, and to hollyes wild.

It was not just a political structure that was at stake in these conflicts, but an interpretation of "divine history" itself. And the nearly unanimous portrait of their foes as the enemies of civilization does not mean that the Royalists themselves did not offer

criticism and advice to the court, for whether one emphasizes their "political" stance as members of Charles's regime in designating them as "Caroline" poets or their social position as "Cavaliers," these poets yet sought to maintain the Renaissance definition of the courtier-poet as the *adviser* as well as the *servant* of the prince. Sir William Davenant's mock epic "Jeffereidos, Or the Captivitie of Jeffery" (1648), as Michael Parker has shown (in Claude Summers and Ted-Larry Pebworth, eds., "*The Muses Common-Weale,*" 1988), was largely a burlesque of the king's peace negotiations with Spain and his refusal to assume a more aggressive foreign policy through alliance with France. Although not entirely dangerous politically, because of the support this view had at court from Queen Henrietta Maria, the political satire in Davenant's hilarious account of the capture of the queen's dwarf (Jeffrey Hudson) by Dunkirkers while returning from France (and his hilarious battle with a turkey) is but one of the more delightful examples of criticism of royal conduct by the Caroline poets (in this case criticism of the Treaty of Susa, 14 July 1629, which Peter Paul Rubens had negotiated with Charles). But despite the light mockery of Davenant's criticism (to which one should add the early warnings of Cartwright, the anxieties of Denham, and the dire prophecies of Herbert's "The Church Militant"), the dominant mode of the Caroline ethos – even when the Caroline court no longer existed – encouraged the reader to see the court as the divine form framed by Providence to thwart threats to Christian civilization.

Whether one explains this allegorical hagiography as the product of these poets' endorsement of the Sidneian-Spenserian-Draytonian view of the poet as civilizer, or as the sum result of the Stuart propounding of the strictest readings of a hierarchical theory of the divine rights of kings, or even as the response to the grasp of the reins of power by what they saw as the forces of republican factionalism, classless appetite, and religious fanaticism at their most rapacious, there remains a considerable strain in these figurations. And it is not just a strain that comes from the English aristocratic world's being turned upside down by the victory of the Puritan Parliamentarians, but a strain deriving from the commitment of religious imagery and the energies of spiritual devotion to the "service" of a "policy" and "art" of a court increasingly unresponsive to and (in its extravagant isolationism, narrowing elitism, and self-indulgent remoteness) increasingly alienated from its own time and its own traditions.

In many ways, as articulated by the court poets at least, such language intimates an attempt, indeed what often reads like a desperate attempt, to return to the "paradise" of Elizabethan harmony. Even though probably printed as a critique of the Stuart court, the panegyrics of Queen Elizabeth in Diana Primrose's *A Chain of Pearle* (1630) register the extent of this impulse during the period. Its characterization of the "divine" Eliza in terms of the "heroick" virtues, underscored by embedded applications of the rich allegorical textures of the Song of Solomon, harkens back to the "cult of Elizabeth" which had endorsed the cultural foundation of the project of national stability and international respect that she and her adept advisers had so successfully undertaken – and which poets such as Edmund Spenser in *The Faerie Queene* (1590, 1596) had so successfully supported. (In fact, Speght's earlier, biblical representation of an egalitarian vision of the "family" might also imply a critique of the Stuart court, especially of its view of the state as an absolutist family as first insisted upon by James I.) But one needs only turn to the deification of his father which Charles I had Rubens portray in bold allegorical hyperbole (and at great expense) on the ceiling of the Banqueting Hall, or to recall the steady allegorical hyperbole which dominated the "stage" of his court in the form of the masques, plays, and poetic contests such as the *Cœlum Britannicum* (1634, for which Carew had supplied the libretto), or the poet laureate Davenant's extravagant *Salmacida Spolia* (1640) with its figuration of Charles as "Philogenes or Lover of his People" and his French Catholic Queen Henrietta Maria as a gift "sent down from Heaven by Pallas as a reward of his prudence" to sense what often seems like a near desperation to figure the insulated Caroline court as heir to the internationally successful Elizabethan project. As Graham Parry phrases it, many people in the period did respond to "the mysterious divinity of kingship as feelingly as other men did to the reality of religious power in their lives" (*The Seventeenth Century,* 1989). It is a keen observation, for the cult of the king often seemed to serve as a substitute for religion. The *Eikon Basilike* (1649) published a few days after Charles's death, in fact, presents a revealing subtitle: *the Pourtraicture of His Sacred Majestie in His Solitudes and Sufferings.* From the first days of his reign, in fact, the anagram of his name – *Charolus Stuartus = Christus Salvator* – set the tone and terms for what became an elaborate cult of worship. It is often a bit too much; and not just because the tensions that accompanied these poets' attempts to endorse the "court of love" involved them in the uncomfortable position of applying all lyrical and allegorical machinery to a *French* courtly model being revived by a *Catholic* devotee. Such an endeavor, in fact, only inclined to support the Puritan claim that the ecclesiastical reform instituted by Archbishop Laud was little more than a rejection of the Protestant Reformation; and it did nothing to dissuade the king's Parliamentarian enemies that his refusal to commit English forces to support the Protestant League against the militant Catholicism of Emperor Ferdinand II in the Thirty Years' War evinced a dangerous Catholic favoritism on his part. There is more than merely a trace of tension at the heart of the Caroline aesthetic itself. It is more often a note of disillusionment, in fact, a sort of disenchantment that at times approaches nostalgia but yet endorses finally a disengagement with the cultural project that is only accentuated by the fulsome and strained *sprezzatura* (the affected nonchalance) with which it is endorsed and celebrated.

This sense of strain and disillusionment might be most evident in what A. J. Smith has called the "failure of love" (*The Metaphysics of Love,* 1985) in Caroline court poetry. As he explains, the transcendental and "eternal" verities which the Elizabethan and Jacobean poets had inscribed when used by these poets of Charles's court manage only to "cut love down to the measure of a civilized social activity," achieving a sort of "urban equipose" that seems framed to counter an aggressive Hobbesian "nature" that disallows any commitment or transcendence. Even the relationship of the "divine" royal couple becomes explicable only in erotic terms that are relegated to the rules of a primitive nature: King Charles, writes Carew, "only can wilde lust provoke." And even the view of Queen Henrietta as the gift of Pallas is based on her power to "choke" Charles's "impurer flames": "where he scatters looser fires, / [She] turn'st them into chast desires" ("To the Queene"). Building on the example of Donne's witty and frank exploration of the character of male desire, these poets seem to have felt authorized to take Donne's anatomy to its more desperate conclusion, even while claiming to operate on Platonic assumptions. However much these poets may have in fact been merely "gentlemen who wrote with ease" (Alexander Pope, *The First Epistle of the Second Book of Horace Imitated,* 1737) and who managed to divorce their civic and their poetic activities, they yet repeatedly iterate what might be the central motif of the entire period, politically and poetically, the condition trumpeted in the title of the major poem of the age – *Paradise* [is indeed] *Lost.* Amidst some of the most precise artistry and most delicate harmonies ever achieved in English literature – poems whose crystalline brilliance and exquisite elegance, whose pristine mannerisms and evocative embodiment of the essence of the lyric moment, "forms of art which survive the ashes of political disaster" (as the poems of Carew and his friends are termed by Louis L. Martz in *The Wit of Love,* 1969) – there is the haunting presence of the powers "that negate or undermine love, from change and death to man's first disobedience and the concupiscence of Adam and Eve" (in Smith's terms). "Ask me no more," says Carew's lyricist, "whether love doth stray, [among] The golden Atomes of the day" ("A Song"). "The Roses in the bosome of" William Habington's Castara shall

> In those white cloysters live secure
> From the rude blasts of wanton breath,
> Each houre more innocent and pure,
> *Till you shall wither into death.*

One of the consistent paradoxes in the thousands of poems simply titled "Song" during the period (poems with which Henry Lawes was so successful in bringing out their finely tuned textures) is the view that the love lyric is a song of death. In the same vein, the masques and plays of the court enabled a myth of innocence amid a world at ideological and actual war, often blurring the borders of theater and reality – again, *desperately* rewriting the national mythology of that "glorious" period when England managed to be the only nation in the sixteenth century to undergo the Reformation without a war, furtively skirting the borders of blasphemy in order to devise a sort of artistic, stylized insulation against the "noise" which had led the king to suspend Parliament. And the Caroline love poetry, at least that composed at or for the court, enacts the same type of myth, even while attempting to defend its fragility and hence its virtues (or the appeal of its style) against the very real forces of Nature which would inevitably erase it. Whether the achievement of their greatest poems is a remarkable act of *avoidance* or a *gesture* of acceptance of the fragility of all is difficult to say.

Whether one sees the Caroline lyric as "well-wrought urn" or as mannerist gesture, then, the tensions endemic to these poems do suggest that the Caroline courtly project remains a sort of radical, nonmetaphysical extension of Jacobean melancholy. Their paradoxy yet suggests a basic note of disillusionment, a sort of loss of confidence that they strive above all to overcome but, in their intimate gestures of denial, only serve to accentuate. One might conclude, in fact, that the Caroline lyric,

unlike the dialectical hyperdetermination of the Donnean poem and the Jonsonian epigram, actually goes nowhere. And indeed, where could it go, given its basic estimation of the naturalistic basis of human desire, and its inability to endorse that thoroughly objectionable alternative outside the court? Only the *gesture* remains in a dying culture. It is highly ironic, then, that the advice of the poet most opposed to the Stuart hegemony might best evoke the turn which the Caroline poets took when, after his angels have explained the terms and nature of divine history, Milton's Adam is instructed: "not [to] be loath / To leave this Paradise, but [to seek to] possess / A paradise within thee, happier far." The court poets strove to find the "virtues" of that "Paradise" literally *within* the court of Charles and Henrietta, to a large degree, even while most conscious of its irreparable loss. One wonders if the entire Caroline pageant might be seen, in fact, as an elaborate, very stylish and stylized dance of death boldly enacted by an aristocratic troupe much too intelligent to believe with confidence in its ultimate viability. Even the "careless" verse of Suckling's libertine cynicism, John Shawcross suggests, intimates an unhappiness, a sense of frustration, and doubts about the Caroline ethos. Whether or not such inscriptions are to entertain the same sort of allegorical hyperbole which these masquers would have appreciated, it remains evident that the poetry of the period does, in fact, project a self-conscious loss of confidence that led to various forms of retreat into versions of an earthly paradise, or, in the case of the strongest poets in the period (Herbert and Crashaw), a retreat from the false paradise of the Caroline court, from the arena of political and civil pageantry altogether, in order to engage in a meditation on the power of Grace to effect "A paradise within . . . happier far." The forms of retreat which this loss of confidence brought about can be seen in representative poems of Carew, Herrick, and Herbert. The revisions of the "line of wit" of Donne and Jonson bequeathed to them as vatic "servants" of Stuart civilization by this courtier, this would-be courtier, and this former or non-courtier offer primary examples of the major contours of the *Caroline disenchantment* of their generation.

Sidney, England's most renowned Renaissance courtier, the author of the influential presentation of the frustration and "madness" of sexual desire (*Astrophel and Stella,* 1591) as well as that fundamental treatise on the need for the "right poet" to educate the nation through models for moral imitation (*Apologie for Poetrie,* 1595), was also the author (with his sister, Mary Sidney Herbert, Countess of Pembroke) of a versification of the Psalms. In response to this work, John Donne had asked why could

> a whole State present
> A lesser gift than some one man hath sent?
> . . . .
> We thy Sydnean Psalmes shall celebrate,
> And till we come th' Extemporall song to sing,
> . . . .
> . . . may
> These their sweet learned labours, all the way
> Be as our tuning; that, when hence we part,
> We may fall in with them, and sing our part.
>
> ("Upon the translation of the Psalms by Sir Philip
> Sydney and the Countess of Pembroke his sister")

But here is the response to this challenge by Carew, the most representative court poet in the 1630s:

> I Presse not to the Quire, nor dare I greet
> The holy place with my unhallowed feet;
> My unwasht Muse, polutes not things Divine,
> Nor mingles her prophaner notes with thine;
> Here, humbly at the porch she listning stayes
> . . . .
> Sufficeth her, that she a lay-place gaine,
> . . . .
> Who knowes, but that her wandring eyes that run,
> Now hunting Glow-wormes, may adore the Sun[.]
>
> ("To my worthy friend Master Geo. Sands, on his
> translation of the Psalmes")

In terms that recall the opening poems of Herbert's *The Temple* (1633) while borrowing the erotic sophistry of Donne's "Loves Warre," Carew says that his "restlesse soule" "may . . . Perhaps" "no more / In moulds of clay [his] God adore." But the vow remains hesitant, equivocal, a bit self-pitying — and largely unfulfilled in his poetic canon. His final admission that he "Perhaps . . . no more shall court the verdant Bay, . . . and rather *strive* to gaine from thence one Thorne, / Then all the flourishing wreathes by Laureats worne" (italics added) does capture the same note of hesitancy and disillusionment and doubt that exceeds (or at least covers the absence of) any penitential vow. As he submitted in "A divine Mistresse," his "faire love"

> hath every beauteous line:
> Yet I had beene farre happier,
> Had Nature that made me, made her;
> . . . .
> Shee hath too much divinity for mee,
> You Gods teach her some more humanitie.

Herbert, in fact, identified "Sin" in "The Church Militant" section of *The Temple* as a gallant and poet who "would serve / His pills of sublimate in that conserve." That gallant-poet could well have been (again in the emblematic terms of the age) Carew, who might have inclined towards such an identification. This response to the strains of Caroline disillusionment, self-doubt, and tense anxiety is also voiced in Carew's elegy on Donne, in his answer to Aurelian Townshend's request for him to pen an elegy for the king of Sweden, and in his two Jonsonian (but ethically un-Jonsonian) country-house poems, which also bespeak a sort of metaphysical hole at the center of the Caroline court project that its elaborate artifice and artistry could not cover or fill.

The elegy on Donne (1633) is Carew's most successful and perhaps his most significant poem. As Martz urges, the poem justifies (even more than his more frequent imitations of Jonson) Carew's success as an incredibly gifted "mannerist" able to fulfill the court aesthetic of posing and masking (without necessarily conveying the content or "moral" of the model, of course). Carew's mannerism is confirmed here in his own evoking of the vigorous cadences and colloquial expressiveness of what Donne himself called his "masculine perswasive force":

> The Muses garden with Pedantique weedes
> O'rspread, was purg'd by thee; The lazie seeds
> Of servile imitation throwne away;
> And fresh invitation planted, Thou didst pay
> The debts of our penurious bankrupt age;
> . . . .
> Thou hast redeem'd, and open'd Us a Mine
> Of rich and pregnant phansie, drawne a line
> Of masculine expression,
> . . . .
> Since to the awe of thy imperious wit
> Our stubborne language bends, made only fit
> With tough-thick-rib'd hoopes to gird about
> The Giant phansie, which had prov'd too stout
> For their soft melting Phrases.
> . . . .
> But thou art gone, and thy strict lawes will be
> Too hard for Libertines in Poetrie.

Capturing the complexities of the Metaphysical conceit and the concision of the epigrammatic line so typical of Donne, Carew offers a keen reading of the textures and achievement of Donne's witty poetry. But the Donne poem most recalled by the elegy is not a lyric or a love elegy but *An Anatomy of the World* (1611), in which Donne wittily framed the death of the fourteen-year-old Elizabeth Drury (a figure for the Virgin Mary, Wisdom, Queen Elizabeth, or Virtue, some readers urge) as the cause of a "Lethargie" by which the world has "speechlesse growne":

> Shee, shee is dead; shee's dead,
> . . . .
> And new Philosophy cals all in doubt,
> The Element of fire is quite put out;
> The Sunne is lost, and th'earth, and no mans wit
> Can well direct him, where to looke for it.
> . . . .
> 'Tis all in pieces, all cohærence gone;
> All just supply, and all Relation:
> Prince, Subiect, Father, Sonne, are things forgot,
> For euery man alone thinkes he hath got
> To be a Phoenix[.]
> . . . .
> The art is lost, and correspondence too.
> For heaven gives little, and the earth takes lesse,
> And man least knowes their trade, and purposes.
> . . . .
> Shee, shee is dead; shee's dead; when thou knowst
>   this,
> Thou knowst how drie a Cinder this world is.
> And learnst thus much by our Anatomy,
> That 'tis vaine to dew or mollifie
> It with thy Teares, or Sweat, or Bloud: no thing
> Is worth our trauaile, griefe, or perishing,
> But those rich ioyes, which did possess her hart,
> Of which shee's now a partaker, and a part.

In Carew's poem Donne himselfe has become a Caroline version of Elizabeth Drury. But the example and "pattern" of his wit — figured as a sort of divine Word of poetic "riches" which "redeem'd" the language and the culture — are *not* likely to be regained. Donne's bleak elegy asserted amid its candid contempt for the world, even in his use of correspondence to convey the "loss of correspondence," that "there's a kinde of World remaining still":

>   a glimmering light,
> A faint weake loue of vertue and of good
> Reflects from her, on them which vnderstood
> Her worth; And though she haue shut in all day,
> The twi-light of her memory doth stay;
> Which, from the carcasse of the old world, free,
> Creates a new world[.]

And poetry, Donne concluded in this the only verses he allowed to be published during his lifetime (along with *The Second Anniversary,* 1612), "hath a middle nature: heauen keepes soules, / The graue keeps bodies, verse the fame enroules." But Carew (even if his own achievement herein might undercut his assertion), from the opening series of questions which indict the failure of his age to respond to Donne's example, asserts that "Thy strict lawes will be too hard" for his own age. Indeed, given the spiritual foundations on which Donne had placed his faith in the creation of "a new world," it may not be surprising that Carew doubts that the "light" of Caroline poetry, especially that of "Libertines in Poetrie," will prove to be the "Phoenix" arising from the ashes of cultural decline around him. Perhaps, then, even though he did not live to see the eventual "death" of his way of life (perhaps because he saw its decay even as he wrote it) the tense insecurity which resounds throughout his elegy is less the anxiety of influence and knowledge of the inimitable character of Donne's poetry than it is, as the last lines of the poem might intimate, his realization that the poetic example of Donne will not long survive in the political arena either – "*Here lies a King, that rul'd as hee thought fit* / *The universall Monarchy.* . . ." Given the cult of Charles that continued to animate the allegorical language of his poets, that is, one is led to wonder if Carew's brilliant elegy for "the Monarch . . . of wit" might also insinuate a loss or questioning of his faith in and his awareness of the limited powers of the temporal "Monarch" he served.

Perhaps Carew was correct in his forlorn prophecy about the absence of any worthy successor to Donne in the age (Herbert, Crashaw, and Milton, notwithstanding, although none of them is a court poet); and perhaps Sir John Suckling's (mock) elegy for the other grand master of the age, Ben Jonson, in his witty "A Sessions of the Poets," might indicate why. For before turning the entire issue of poetic lineage and the vatic role of the poet into an absurdist comedy of manners, and eventually having his facetious Apollo name an anonymous stingy alderman as poet laureate, Suckling takes time to chide Carew for taking too much care with his poetry. Such attention to the importance of poetry, he says, is a fault "That would not well stand with a Laureat; / His Muse was hard bound, and th'issue of's brain / Was seldom brought forth but with trouble and pain." Suckling's characterization of himself as one who "loved not the Muses so well as his sport" might best summarize, in fact, the specter that Carew feared would prove the mortal blow to Donne's "glimmering light." (It is perhaps relevant to recall, in fact, as the critics of the court never tired of pointing out, that the poet laureateship vacated by the death of Jonson was filled by a playwright/poet with syphilis who proclaimed himself as an illegitimate son of Shakespeare.)

The same sense of strain and disillusionment is fundamental to Carew's most renowned political poem, "In answer of an Elegiacall Letter upon the death of the King of Sweden from Aurelian Townsend, inviting me to write on that subject." Townshend's prompt for Carew to enlist his talents in that last great religious war in Europe, in this case by elegizing the Protestant martyrdom of King Gustavus Adolphus, who was killed at Lutzen in 1632, is first met with the conventional poetic pose of humility, which claims that not even the combination of Virgil, Lucan, and Torquato Tasso, nor "*Donne,* worth all that went before, / With the united labour of their wit / Could a just Poem to this subject fit." This rhetorical dodge is then followed by the stern suggestion that the Swedish king actually participated in a sort of European holocaust that had turned "the whole *German* Continents vaste wombe" into a "Tombe," and then by the reprimand that Townshend himself should rather

> use the benefit
> Of peace and plenty, which the blessed hand
> Of our good King gives this obdurate Land,
> Let us of Revels sing, and let thy breath
> . . . .
> gently inspire
> Thy past'rall pipe, till all our swaines admire
> Thy song and subject, whilst they both comprise
> The beauties of the *SHEPHERDS PARADISE* [.]

Carew then alludes to several other masques performed at the Caroline court before concluding that the poets should forsake comment on the religious wars and "sing / To rurall tunes":

> Tourneyes, Masques, Theaters, better become
> Our *Halycon* dayes; what though the German Drum
> Bellow for freedome and revenge, the noyse
> Concernes not us, nor should divert our joyes;
> Nor ought the thunder of their Carabins
> Drowne the sweet Ayres of our tun'd Violins;
> Beleeve me friend, if their prevailing powers
> Gaine them a calme securitie like ours,
> They'le hang their Armes up on the Olive bough,
> And dance, and revell then, as we doe now.

Michael Parker's astute reading (*John Donne Journal,* 1, 1982) of the Virgilian precedents for the political uses of pastoral notwithstanding, Carew's response seems to carry the Caroline fascination with game-playing and sophisticated insulation beyond what the poet's own articulation of its terms will allow, if in no other way than in the tremendous pressures this rhetorical performance places on the precarious tenure of its last clause — "as we doe now." And surely Carew must have known the distance from

the courtly ideals of the English Renaissance that his illusory and illusive defense carried him. (The *Shepherd's Paradise* [1633], in fact, was composed by a Roman Catholic, Walter Montague.) Once again, the strain of credulity, accentuated in a poem so packed with conditional clauses, suggests a Caroline disillusionment with the project it "strains" to endorse, even in its evocation of those classical codes Parker has shown to be at work here.

What was a "strain" for the court poets was, of course, the cause of apocalyptic consternation for their opponents. But from the perspective of Carew's equivocal defense it is clear why William Prynne's one-thousand-page assault on the moral, aesthetic, and political code of the court, *Histriomastix* (1632), singled out the masque and the play as primary examples of the degeneration that the Puritans saw moving from the court to sweep over the entire nation. Perhaps only the sight of Suckling's expensively costumed troop of Cavaliers, decked out in white doublets, and scarlet pants, coats and fulsomely feathered hats, being led into battle in the First Bishops' War by the outstanding "gallant" of the age, could more fully confirm for their enemies how far the fantasy and self-indulgent mythology of Charles's regime had taken it from the major concerns and mores of the nation at large. Carew's response to Townshend and, in a more ostentatious and cynical manner, Suckling's theatrical approach to the war in the North might endorse the court's vision of a Caroline Golden Age impenetrably remote, but, as P. W. Thomas phrases it, to their enemies "it looked a thoroughly carnal kingdom, more like Babylon than the New Jerusalem" (in Conrad Russell, ed., *The Origins of the English Civil War,* 1973). It might even be, in fact, that an intimation of that view underlies both the strain of Carew's apologia and the ostentatiousness of Suckling's Cavalier histrionics.

Other examples of this strain and this sense of disillusionment in Carew's poetry can be seen by a comparison of "A Rapture" with its generic model, Donne's *Elegy 19* ("Going to Bed"). Donne manages to base his Ovidian wit on a "seriously" blasphemous juxtaposing of religious ecstasy and sexual ecstasy (perhaps even with a dangerous glance at what he saw as the religious hypocrisy of Queen Elizabeth and Sir Walter Ralegh's New World project). Carew's explicit eroticism, on the other hand, never rises to the level of blasphemy because of the inherent absence of any serious questions about the virtue of its subject. Equally revealing would be a closer look at how Carew's lyrics (like those of Suckling) in their own pursuit exclusively of instant gratification erase the tension between virtue and desire which animated the conflict of the English Petrarchan sonnet. But fuller examples of the strain which the Caroline project places on the poetic program it inherited are Carew's two country-house poems, especially when seen in relation to the Jonsonian models of the genre, "Upon Penshurst" and "To Sir Robert Wroth." Opening with an inscription of the cult of Caroline royalty —

> Sir,
> Ere you passe this threshold, stay,
> And give your creature leave to pay
> Those pious rites, which unto you
> As to our household Gods, are due

— which then accommodates the devotional paeans of Petrarchan convention to the monarch —

> In stead of sacrifice, each brest
> Is like a flaming Altar, drest
> With zealous fires, which from pure hearts
> Love mixt with loyaltie imparts

— Carew's 1620s poem, "To the King, at his entrance into Saxham, by Master Io. Crofts," in its initial publication in 1640 might have read like a response to the opening figures of Herbert's *The Temple*. In its generic directive (inherited from the poems of Horace, Martial, and Jonson to which it alludes) to show its subject to be the emblematic embodiment of civilization, the poem does, in fact, call on biblical parallels to support its case, describing the sacrificial reverence with which even the birds, fearing another "deluge," "The Pheasant, Partiridge, and the Lark / Flew to the house, as to the Arke," and even "The willing Oxe" and the sacrificial "Lambe, / And every beast ... thither" come forth "to be an offering." But the sum in the poem of this sumptuous eucharist of Laudianesque love of eating is "nothing but good fare ... fit to waite / Vpon the glory of [the king's] state" — a sort of Caroline *Babette's Feast* politicized.

Similarly, in his last poem, "To my friend G. N., from Wrest," written on the poet's return from the armed struggle against the Scots in Berwick in the early summer of 1639, Carew's expression of the exemplary character of the Caroline ideal (as in his "Answer" to Townshend) recommends a sensuous earthly paradise as an alternative to the "barbaric" enemies of the court. Composed a few months before Carew's death and a little over a year before Charles would be forced to reconvene Parliament after the eleven years of "*Halcyon*" insulation (the Long Parliament that would absolutely

destroy the king's authority), Carew's poem shows fully how his Caroline adaptation of Jonson's Christian classicism deviates from its model. Indebted as a verse epistle "To Sir Robert Wroth" but framed more precisely after the example of "To Penshurst," Carew's praise of the Bedfordshire country house of the earls of Kent invites comparison to Jonson's model. The poem opens with an address to "sweet Ghib" (perhaps Gilbert North, an official in Charles's court), in the mode of Jonson's Wroth epistle:

> I breath ... the temperate ayre of *Wrest*
> Where I no more with raging stormes opprest,
> Weare the cold nights out by the bankes of Tweed,
> On the bleake Mountains, where fierce tempests breed,
> And everlasting Winter dwells[.]

But, as conveyed in its primary characterization of its subject as "built for hospitality," where

> No sumptuous Chimney-peece of shining stone
> Invites strangers eye to gaze upon,
> . . . .
> No Dorique, nor Corinthan Pillars grace
> With Imagery this structures naked face,

its major debt is to Jonson's description of the Sidney estate:

> Thou art not, *Penshurst,* built to envious show,
>   Of touch, or marble; nor canst boast a row
> Of polish'd pillars, or a roofe of gold;
>   Thou hast no lantherne, whereof tales are told;
> Or stayre, or courts; but standst an ancient pile,
>   And these grudg'd at, art reverenc'd the while[.]
>
>   ("To Penshurst")

Carew's poem then turns to descriptions of the estate as evidence of Nature or God's plentitude, where

> steep'd in balmie dew, the pregnant Earth
> Sends from her teeming wombe a flowrie birth,
> And cherisht with the warme Suns quickning heate,
> Her porous bosome doth rich odours sweate;
>
>   ("To my friend G. N., from *Wrest*")

just as in Jonson's attention to where even the "blushing apricot, and woolly peach / Hang on the walls" to be reached by "every child" ("To Penshurst"). Both poems then move on to descriptions of the human genius which rules the place. Wrest Park, unlike those "prouder Piles," has as the "sole designe / Of our contriver, . . . things not fine, / But fit for service":

> *Amalthea's* Horne
> Of plentie is not in Effigie worne
> Without the gate, but she within the dore
> Empties her free and exhausted store.

"Thus I enjoy myself," Carew concludes exuberantly,

> and taste the fruit
> Of this blest Peace, whilst toyl'd in the pursuit
> Of Bucks, and Stags, th'emble of warre, you strive
> To keepe the memory of our Armes alive.

Perhaps, Martz suggests, such an ideal might have lived had the court not separated its life and its art as "a life apart" from the *non*-emblematic forces of liberty, freedom, and reality, whatever their evential consequences. But recollection of the directive of Carew's model intimates that the (self-conscious) strain of immersion in artifice and retreat at the end of Carew's encomium and suggests that it is more than an obdurate social irresponsibility that underpins and undercuts the Caroline fantasy. For noticeably absent in the final, inward turn of Carew's epistle is Jonson's focus on what "*dwells*" at Penshurst: its embrace of a vision beyond the cadences of classical self-fulfillment, its devotion to a world in which

> Each morn and even they are taught to pray,
> With the whole household, and may, every day,
> Read in their virtuous parents' noble parts
> The mysteries of manners, arms, and arts.
> Now, Penshurst, they that will proportion thee
> With other edifices, when they see
> Those proud ambitious heaps, and nothing else
> May say their lords have built, but thy lord dwells.

("To Penshurst")

If in a substantive sense the Renaissance does mark the Western movement from a basically medieval to a modern world, then Carew's representative *omission* of the creed of classical-Christian conduct that was evoked by Jonson might not only mark the grounds for the Puritan and Parliamentarian refusal to accept the Caroline version of the creed. It might also intimate one source for the sense of Caroline disillusionment and cultural strain which is embedded in the 1640 *Poems. By Thomas Carew Esquire. One of the Gentlemen of the Privie-Chamber, and Sewer in Ordinary to His Majesty*.

Similar to the strain within Carew's mannerist artifacts of Caroline fancy printed at the conclusion of what the Parliamentarians called the "Eleven Year Tyranny" are the paradoxes and crises which punctuate that collection of over a thousand poems by the generation's most thoroughgoing Jonsonian classical stylist – poems mostly composed during the "*Halycon*" days but published for the first time in 1648, one year after its author had been deprived of his ecclesiastical living at Dean Prior because of his Royalism, less than one year before the Parliamentarian forces of "*Times's trans-shifting*" ("The Argument of his Book") executed the "divine" king *legally* after having defeated the political, religious, and social forces with which Robert Herrick identified. But, then, it is the entire problem of *identity* with the Royalist cultural theater that seems most troubling in the exquisitely polished and delicately balanced verses of Herrick also. A devoted Jonsonian, but without Jonson's urbanity or his unswerving (or arrogant) moral self-assurance, Herrick's is finally an attenuated verse in several ways. One conflict within it stems from his distance from his desire to be an active member of that Stuart poetic coterie. A more telling strain attends his attempts to compose a courtly pastoral poetry of delicate artifice which most often manages a fine ethical commentary of Stoic moderation but which does not capture the vigorous moral cadences of his beloved "saint Ben." Without questioning the earnestness or the commitment of Herrick's careful application of the literature of "tears" in the *Noble Numbers* in order to record and to mourn the travesties heaped on the established church by the Puritan Parliamentarians (as explained by Claude Summers in "Tears for Herrick's Church," *George Herbert Journal,* [Fall-Spring 1990–1991]) and without qualifying the significance of the poet's validation of the Laudian position in religious issues in *Hesperides* (as shown by Achsah Guibbory in "*The Muses Common-Weale*"), it remains the case that the poems of his 1648 edition exhibit traces of the same sort of Caroline disillusionment that marks Carew's 1640 collection. Poised at the very precipice into which the Caroline establishment was to fall, it is not surprising that *Hesperides* seems framed above all to transform the artifacts and objects of that world into delicate poetic rituals which might survive their author's disappointment and their age's revolution. While ranging from an enduring nostalgia for a world of Elizabethan charm to a sort of ostentatious account of the vulgarity Herrick saw overwhelming his world, *Hesperides,* in its mixture of pagan and Christian customs, might well be seen as a sort of lyrical (and elegiac) companion to the court masque, relegated to Dean Prior, framed by Herrick out of a determination to maintain the world of Carew's "one continued festival" before the crudely "precise" *mysomousoi* took over. A "poet of sentiment," Herrick indeed is deeply troubled that he is "being abandoned by his mother country" (Jonathan F. S. Post, "Herrick: A Minority Report," *George Herbert Journal,* [Fall-Spring 1990–1991]).

Looking at *Hesperides* from the perspective of its publication in 1648 – from the vantage of the author's imagining its reception at the time of his decision to have it published (and as an oeuvre whose poems remain difficult or impossible to date individually), it is clear that one primary strain in Herrick's verse is local. In spite of all his efforts in poems such as "A Country Life," "The Wake," and "The Hock Cart" to consecrate the Caroline program of "pastoralized" nationalism initiated by James and supported by Charles I (by which the nobility would return to their manor houses in order to guide the people to a fuller appreciation of the Stuart monarchy), Herrick seems to have most wanted to be a Stuart courtier poet fashioning his "Poetic Liturgy" into a "Pillar of Fame" in defense of English state and church within the literary metropolis of London, at those "*Lyric* Feasts, / Made at the *Sun,* / The *Dog,* and the Triple *Tunne*" taverns ("An Ode for [Jonson]"). The "rude River in Devon, by which sometimes he lived" knows only a "people . . . churlish as the seas; / And rude (almost) as rudest Salvages," he bemoans ("To Deanbourn"); his "Mirth" has been "turn'd to mourning" by his "banishment / Into the loathed West" ("His Lachrimæ or Mirth, turn'd to mourning"); "Devonshire" is "dull" and "loath'd so much" ("Discontents in Devon"), for "London my home is: though by hard fate sent / Into a long and irksome banishment" and "the dull confines of the drooping West, / . . . / For rather then I'le to the West return, / I'le beg of thee first here to have mine Urn" ("His returne to London"). As in his dedication of the volume to Prince Charles II and his many encomia throughout to King Charles I as the "brave Prince of Cavaliers" and "best of Kings" ("To the King") whose misfortune in war "makes the Poet sad" ("The bad season . . . "), Herrick *can* manage a fulsome praise for the "Sweet Country life" as lived by Endymion Porter. But that poem remains unfinished. His efforts to present "His content in the Country" as the classical good life seem strained – he blesses his fortunes only when he sees "Our own beloved privacy"; and his attempt to figure "His Grange, or private wealth" as a pastoral paradise is

qualified by the concluding description of his "rural privacie" as merely "*some ease/Where . . . slight things do lightly please.*" And that poem itself is undercut by its companion riddle poem, "The Grange," which surmises that only a brown mouse could be "well contented in this private *Grange.*" His splendid song in praise of the ritualistic worship of the harvest hock-cart at the estate of Mildmay Fane, second Earl of Westmorland, is almost totally overturned by the somber reminder at its conclusion that the celebration of the "Sons of Summer, by whose toile, / We are the Lords of Wine and Oile," is actually only a pleasure which "is like raine, / Not sent ye for to drowne your paine, / But for to make it springe againe" ("The Hock-cart, or Harvest home"). The warmest praise for "this dull *Devonshire,*" in fact, is restricted to his "confession" that "I ne'r invented such / Ennobled numbers for the Presse, / Then where I loath'd so much" ("Discontents in Devon").

Herrick, it seems, feels himself forced to find delight in disorder, within the world of his own discontent. Exiled from the "Roman" court, he nevertheless attempts to support the ethos and aesthetic of that lost world by composing a sort of Caroline mannerist verse which can transform the "Garden" of poetic kinds into Laudian ceremonies of poetic ritual that will somehow transcend or, at the very least, offer a rebuff to the forces of "*Times trans-shifting*" that have relegated him to the country where he must be "content" and which now threaten – in the shape of a Puritan antipoetry that is "too precise in every part" ("Delight in Disorder") – to leave all of England "lost in an endlesse night" ("On Himself"). As he informed his readers in the first poem of *Hesperides,* his mission as an epic (that is, patriotic) poet of English civilization is to

> SING of *Brooks,* of *Blossomes, Birds,* and *Bowers:*
> Of *April, May,* of *June,* and *July*-Flowers,
> . . . of *May-poles, Hock-carts, Wassails, Wakes,*
> Of *bride-grooms, Brides,* and of their *Bridal-cakes,*
> . . . and have Accesse
> . . . By these, to sing of cleanly-*Wantonnesse.*
> ("The Argument of His Book")

But he will also "sing of *Times trans-shifting*" and "write of *Hell.*" He will "sing (and ever shall) / Of *Heaven*"; but like his qualified portrait of his pastoral "content" in "dull" rural Devon, his songs become largely a sort of lyrical *anatomy of* the dying of *the* Caroline *world* in which "delight," "content," and "The holy incantation of a verse" ("When He Would Have His Verses Read") are but moments he hopes to save from the harvest of all-powerful

Time by the delicate patterns and enduring euphonies of classical poetic ritual.

Indeed, in *Hesperides* Time "cut'st down all"; "all things decay with time"; all men and women eventually "shall wear / Such frost and snow in [their] hair"; all lovers will be "left alone" ... to number sorrow by / The departures [of their mistresses], and die." For man has "short time to stay," like the daffodils, and will be left like the meadows "here to lament [his] poor estates, alone, just as blossoms "glide into the night": "Putrefaction is the end / Of all that Nature doth attend." In fact, just as the light and delightful opening octave of the first poem of the volume ("The Argument of His Book") is countered by the emergence and finality of "*Time*" and by the cold acceptance that one must "write of *Hell*," so the volume overall – framed by poems celebrating the power of poetry, punctuated at its precise numerical middle (A. B. Chambers notes in *Transfigured Rites in Seventeenth-Century English Poetry,* 1972) by the poem on Herrick's "losse of his Finger" – falls in its concluding poems to a noisy, ugly, often bitter series of epigrams on the inevitability of decay and death and the eventuality of the "*Hell*" of "*Times trans-shifting*" through every sphere of the mortal world. From this perspective, then, it is clear that it is not any sort of cultural revival that the poet invokes in his celebration of native traditions and customs such as the maypole games; rather, it is an attempt to "Trust to good verses" which "onely will aspire, / When Pyramids, as men, / Are lost i'th the funerall fire," to capture in those "Numbers sweet" which "With endless life are crown'd" ("To live merrily, and to trust to Good Verses") those *wild* "civilities" that are on the verge of being erased by the troops of "Zelot." It is perhaps an indication of his desperate fear that the country will not sufficiently oppose the Puritan onslaught that his Corinna never manages to "get up" and participate in the national holiday despite seventy lines of warnings that they may "die / Before we know our liberty" ("Corinna's going a Maying"). Just as he sought in the neoclassicism of the Jonsonian model of civic poetry a form to withstand the winds of change and dislocation, so Herrick's carpe diem poems, especially those focusing attention on English habit and custom, seem posed to resist the tide of change and disorder he must have seen all around him in the last two decades of the Caroline reign.

Confronted, then, by forces that would allow no more "erring Lace," "Cuffe neglectful," "tempestous petticote," "carelesse shooe-string" – and certainly no "delight" growing out of any "Sweet disorder" or "wantonnesse" ("Delight in Disorder") – Herrick mocks the rigor of the Puritan program with an array of Ovidian carpe diem poems of the type composed by the Caroline city and court poets he wished to join – "I am a free-born Roman" ("His return to London"). These poems which directly challenge the directives of those fastidious warriors against poetry, especially those poems which frame the celebrations of those ancient "pagan" rites such as the maypole to be "Devotion," recall in many ways Richard Corbett's touching "Farewell" to those "fairies ... of the old profession" who "now, alas, ... all are dead, / Or gone beyond the seas, / Or further for religion fled" ("A Proper New Ballad, Intitled the Fairies' Farewell").

In fact, Herrick turns his volume (as Roger B. Rollin shows in his *Robert Herrick,* 1966) into a program of "secular religion." Clothing his verse in the language of Laudian anti-Puritan rituals – but rituals whose doctrinal content Herrick seldom emphasizes, using religious materials, in William Oram's words, to "serve purposes of an ordering that is more artistic than religious" ("Herrick's Use of Sacred Materials," in Rollin and J. Max Patrick, eds., "*Trust to Good Verses,*" 1978) – he packs *Hesperides* full of the very ceremonies, rituals, church furniture, ecclesiastical clothing, books of worship, and social and civic attitudes and stances to which the Puritans most strenuously objected. Indeed, Jonson's Penshurst becomes Herrick's "Fairie Temple" (not "rich for in and outward show") of "mixt Religion, ... Part Pagan, part Papisticall," where the secular priest "lowly to the Altar bows / ... / Hid in a cloud of *Frankincense*" ("The Fairie Temple"). Herrick's charmingly "Elizabethan" *Hesperides* with its blend of pagan rite and Christian custom becomes a sort of secular version of Herbert's *The Temple* in which the parodic references to anti-Puritan strictures increase as the volume nears its "timely" conclusion amid an onslaught of brutal epigrams on disease, death, and disaster, punctuated by warnings about "Warre," "A King" who is "No King," "Plots [being] not still Prosperous," "Flatterie" to a king, desperate men and "Distrust," before a final series of poems which endeavor to protect the only instrument he sees surviving – his poetry.

However, the "*Sacred Grove*" Herrick promised "To the Queene," the "*great Realme of Poetry*" he promised "To the King" – even the "Poetick Liturgie" that he promised "Mistresse Penelope Wheeler" would transform her into "a Saint" – still shares the limitations endemic to the Caroline aesthetic it sought to engage and "Canonize" ("To Mistresse Penelope"). A bit like the theater of the court and its mannerist poets with their nearly exclusive focus of attention on the command of the styles they assumed, Herrick's plentiful generic "garden" of epigrammatic pastoral verse yet remains a delicately balanced "song" about the end of a way of life – a way of life whose essential artifice and "play" was not to sustain it in the face of the forces of "*Times trans-shifting*" which confronted it. Herrick's poetic "Pillar of Fame" continues to ensure that "Poetry perpetuates the poet" even as it conveys a vivid swan song about the aesthetic he wanted to perfect.

Thus, the most un-Donnean of the "Tribe of Ben" concludes his own anatomy of his world with "A Pillar of Fame," a poem that, even as it recalls Herbert's "The Altar," affirms the conclusion of Donne's "First Anniversary": "verse hath a middle nature: heauen keepes soules, / The graue keeps bodies, verse the fame enroules." Herrick, his court and country, his mistresses, his codes, and even his maid Prue, do remain engraved in the verse of *Hesperides* as a record of the "strict" authority of "*Time's trans-shifting*." It is a "glittering" song about the essential "liquefaction" of the fallen world, which manages at its supreme moments (as in the harmony of Anglo-Saxon and Latinate, physical and ideational language of poems such as "Upon Julia's Clothes") to transform the particles of *concordia discors* into "*Pyramids*" of "Fame" that enroll the precious fragility of mortal being. "For old *Religions* sake," he'll offer candles, "a new Altar" and the words of "Saint *Ben*" in his poetic "*Psalter*" ("His Prayer to Ben. Johnson"), performing "Funerall Rites [for] the Rose," "*Ceremonies* for Candlemasse Eve," "for Candlemasse day," "for Christmas," mingling the "Churching" of Julia with the plea for Corinna to join the ancient maypole celebrations, inviting them to go "to the *Altar of perfumes*" in the temple ("To Julia in the Temple") of his "Poetic Liturgie" where he strives to enshrine "*eternall Images*" ("To his Honoured Kinsman, Sir Richard Stone"). But inevitably, as he strives to "leave this loathed Country-life, and then / Grow up to be a Roman *Citizen*" and to spend his "mites of Time" where cities shall "love thee" ("Upon Himself"), the strain of doubt about this alternative vision leads him to apply the rudiments of a Laudian form of devotion to merely the creation of "Good Verses" and to attempt to establish what is essentially a personal, secular immortality of poetic fame. "*No lust theres like to Poetry*" ("His age"), he assures himself; and in one of his eight poems entitled "Upon himself," he endeavors to confirm that

Thou shalt not All die; for while Love's fire shines
Upon his Altar, man shall read thy lines;
And learn'd Musicians shall to honour *Herricks*
Fame, and his Name, both set, and sing his Lyricks.

Like the mythological masques and Christic iconography of the Stuart court, Herrick finally searches for an "Art above Nature" ("To Julia") that can move him beyond the grasp of a country and an "art" that are "too precise" ("Delight in Disorder"). He may hope that the king can "cure the Evill" and that a national faith in the mysterious powers of Charles, his "Adored *Cesar*," can vanquish "The bad season" that "makes the Poet sad," but, as the last poem of *Hesperides* asserts emblematically, it is finally only to the "Altar" of secular poetry that he turned his (representatively Caroline) disenchantment with the world's "*trans-shifting*."

Herrick's pastoral vision places a tremendous burden on the companion verses, his *Noble Numbers,* to bring more than pious tears and the assertions of "nobility" (in which the Easter story is a *play* entitled "*Rex Tragicus*") to confront "*Time's trans-shifting*." It is perhaps a fitting tribute to the strength of Herrick's ceremonial (and secular) art and an indication of the deeply conflicted, even inherently disillusioned sense of its own strengths that it is his record of Time's triumph in *Hesperides* and not his attempt to confirm the "nobility" of Caroline piety in *Noble Numbers* that yet "taketh" us. *Noble Numbers* never matches, for example, Donne's response to the *contemptus mundi* program of his *Anatomy of the World* that is "sung" in his *Second Anniversary,* significantly subtitled "The Progress of the Soul." Perhaps, indeed, Herrick's appearance of ignorance of the most famous collection of poems in the age (Donne's 1633 *Poems*) is indicative of his refusal – as a Royalist, as a would-be courtier, as a Caroline poet – to accept the model of "Jack" Donne transfigured into "Dean" Donne inscribed by his age; adherence to the tenets of the Caroline court aesthetic might well instruct even as talented a poet as Herrick to turn from the meditative, sacred, otherworldly vision of Donne's "Progress" in defense of the essentially secular vision of the "pastoral" court and its own "divine" king and queen, and, when all coherence *is* gone and "all witt / In utter darkenes did, and still will sit, / Sleeping the lucklesse Age out," to place his (desperate) faith in the "Resurrection" ("Upon M. Ben. Jonson") of a classical "Pillar" of poetic ritual which can "withstand the blow / Of overthrow / . . . / Tho Kingdoms fal" ("The pillar of Fame"). Like a good Caroline pastoral mannerist, Herrick offers a plenteous "garden" of varieties of the epigram and lyric and panegyric, even though he does not always bring the moral fervor or vigor of the epigrams of a Crashaw or a Herbert – or for that matter even that of a Jonson – to his poems. Even as the poems of a "country parson," his work reflects his Caroline culture and its courtly sensibility – and its disenchantment with or doubts about its own project.

For George Herbert, on the other hand, the "*universal Monarchy of wit*" left vacant by the deaths of Donne and Jonson, the "*two flamens*" which influence his verse, called not for an endorsement or poetic defense of the Caroline aesthetic but the meditative record of "*the true God's priest*" (Carew, "An Elegie upon the death of the Deane of Pauls, Dr. Iohn Donne") and of "the many spiritual conflicts that have passed betwixt God and my soul before I could subject mine to the will of Jesus my Master, in whose service I now have found perfect freedom" – a "picture" of "The Progress of the Soul" in God's service. As "Religion" stood "tip-toe in our land, / Ready to pass to the American strand" and Herbert followed Donne's vision of "what a thing is man devoid of grace" ("The Church Militant"), he turned his version of the Caroline poetic into a tripartite "Sacrifice" to the "*King of Glory, King of Peace*" ("L'Envoy"). While Carew strove to imitate poetically the wild passions of Sidney's Astrophel in his courtly fantasies of desire and Herrick strove to counter the wild "noise" of Puritan aggressions with the "sweet" songs of a secularized Laudian "Poetic Liturgie" in the hopes of finding a Caroline "Paradise" within the Caroline aesthetic, Herbert offered (as Marion Singleton phrases it in *God's Courtier*, 1987) "a sacred alternative that the Cavaliers seldom consider[ed] in their celebration of this world" when he, as *God's Courtier*, strove to find "perfect freedom" within the "Temple" through the devout service of the imitation of Christ.

Even more than Carew (whose successful entrance into the court came through his being offered a secretaryship by Herbert's brother, Edward, Lord Herbert of Cherbury) and certainly more than Herrick (the fourth son of a goldsmith whose short-lived success at the court ended with the assassination of Buckingham, whom he had served as a chaplain for little more than a year), George Herbert had early and easy access to the circle of power and authority in the Stuart court. Descended from a Welsh prince and connected through marriage (when his widowed mother married Sir John Danvers) to the citadel of secular power, he had personal contacts with the Sidney family, with Sir Francis Bacon and

Bishop John Williams before their being forced from the court, and with Sir Henry Wotton before that friend's decision to retire to Eton as provost. He was, in Charles Cotton's terms, "in education, / Manners, and parts, / . . . fitted for a Court" (Izaak Walton's *Lives,* 1675), thoroughly qualified by nature and nurture to realize his brother's code that a courtier, as Singleton notes, is one who always observed "the Rules of Conscience, Vertue, and Honour." In two early sonnets (1610) to his mother, however, he asserted an anticourt stance which remained constant in *The Temple*:

My God, where is that ancient heat towards thee,
Wherewith whole showls of *Martyrs* once did burn,
   Besides their other flames? Doth Poetry
Wear *Venus* Livery? only serve her turn?
Why are not sonnets made of thee, and lays
   Upon thine Altar burnt?
    '. . . cannot thy *Dove*
Outstrip their *Cupid* easily . . . ?
. . . .
Sure, Lord, there is enough in thee to dry
Oceans of *Ink,* as the Deluge did
   Cover the Earth, so doth thy Majesty;
Each Cloud distills thy praise, and doth forbid
Poets to turn it to another use.

After the seventeen-year-old's aesthetic assertion in these two sonnets, he seems to have come to believe he could serve that ideal within the world of the Stuart court, eventually becoming Public Orator at Cambridge University (while completing his divinity studies) and then assuming a seat in the 1624 Parliament. However, immediately after that Parliament, like his friend Nicholas Ferrar, whose dismay at the dismantling of the Virginia Company led him to leave Parliament and to move towards the establishing of his "Arminian Nunnery" at Little Gidding, Herbert was thoroughly convinced of the wisdom of his earlier stance, but totally disenchanted with the possibility of pursuing that sacred "Call" within the world of the Stuart court. Primarily disillusioned by the successful efforts of Prince Charles and the duke of Buckingham (who had been rebuffed in their efforts to achieve the Spanish Match) to get King James to dissolve the treaty of peace with Spain, Herbert took his first steps toward Bemerton, where he would spend he last years of his life working (among attempts to reconstruct literally a church) on putting his poems into the collection which Ferrar saw through the press two years after the poet's death. In a sense, then, *The Temple* – as a work revised, completed, and published during the Caroline realm, and as one of the major efforts which Herbert undertook as a direct result of his disillusionment with the policies of the bellicose Charles and the rakish Villiers one year before the death of James — was consciously constructed in its 1633 arrangement to offer an alternative to the Caroline sensibility.

Herbert's spiritual courtesy-book is framed as an enchiridion of "service" within the calendar and liturgy of the Anglican church — a form of service coming under increasing assault by the Puritans, the type of devotional formula which led to the Bishops' Wars when Laud tried to institute it in Scotland, in fact. On one level, the "enormously rich and complex didacticism" of *The Temple,* as John N. Wall has shown (in his *Transformations of the Word,* 1988, and in his edition of *George Herbert: The Country Parson; The Temple,* 1981), locates the life of the humble mediator "in the context of the Church, [which] is seen as the mediator of divine grace and the community in which that grace empowers growth, . . . as caught up in God's larger plan, that working out of salvation which leads the Church onward toward [what the last lines of "The Church Militant" identify as the] 'time and place, where judgement shall appear.' " Within this liturgical framework (in accordance with Herbert's Arminian emphasis on the powers of the fallen will to participate with grace in one's salvation) and as prominently indicated by the epigraph from Psalm 29 on its title page — "In his Temple doth every man speak of his *honour*" — one consistent motif of the "picture" of Christian devotion as an exemplary alternative to the Caroline pattern of debased hagiography and cynical artifice is the return to the medieval Christian ideal of "courteous" service to "*My God, My King*" ("Jordan [I]"). As Malcolm M. Ross points out, this "Anglo-Catholic nostalgia for a world in which Christian and practical values seemed for a while to commingle" (*Poetry and Dogma,* 1954) — at least in the imagination of seventeenth-century authors — is succinctly voiced in Nathaniel Richards's *The Celestiall Publican* (1630):

> O blest performance, Noble race of men,
> Worthy the praise of an Immortal Pen
> Your famous deeds, past stars, recorded stand
> For ever and ever, written by the hand
> Of Sacred Truth, to the Eternal shame
> Of the sin-branded Vicious Courtier's Name.

In Herbert this alternative pattern is established in the opening "Church Porch" section of *The Temple* as an endorsement of the Sidneian vatic role by which "A verse may find him, who a sermon flies." A series of sententious moral adages is presented as a poetic response to an "England . . . full

of sin, but most of sloth [where] Thy Gentry bleats, . . . the most / Are gone to grass, and in the pasture lost," and which concludes in terms that would apply the courtly code to the devotional sphere: "In brief, acquit thee bravely; play the man; / . . . Defer not the least virtue" ("Perirrhanterium"). The "courtly" perspective of this devotional preparation is maintained throughout the central "Church" section of Herbert's emblematic "Temple" of "Sacred Poems and Private Ejaculations." Reflecting on the "frailty" of the meditator as evinced in his past failures to overcome the collar/choler of selfishness which distracts him from service to God, these central poems return repeatedly to how his presence has revised, altered, or rewritten Herbert's lapses of humility. Essentially, these poems dramatize a "reprising" of the Stuart world. "Jordan (I)," Anthony Low points out (*Criticism,* 14, 1972), attacks the groundless authority on which the favored pastoral and allegorical modes of court poetry base their masques:

> Who sayes that fictions onely and false hair
> Become a verse? . . .
> . . . .
> May no lines passe, except they do their dutie
>   Not to a true, but painted chair?

To these the speaker offers a moral option in his transformation of the sophistry of Astrophel's poetry of carnal desire (and sexual idolatry) into a vehicle of divine praise and service, as in "Jordan (II)":

> Thousands of notions in my brain did runne,
> Off'ring their service, if I were not sped:
> I often blotted what I had begunne;
> This was not quick enough, and that was dead.
> Nothing could seem too rich to clothe the sunne.
> . . . .
> But while I bustled, I might heare a friend
> Whisper, *How wide is all this long pretence!*
> *There is in love a sweetnesse readie penn'd:*
> *Copie out onely that, and save expense!*

The (quasi-autobiographical) "Affliction (I)" traces the speaker's "calling" from the "Time when thou didst entice to thee my heart, / I thought the *service* brave," emphasizing how his "birth and spirit rather took / The way that takes the town"; and concludes that his courtiership will not allow him to "change the *service,* and go seek / Some other master out": "though I am clean forgot, / Let me not love thee, if I love thee not." Here again Herbert transforms the mode of the countless Stuart poems addressed to royalty into religious meditation, love lyric into versified prayer, courtly decorum into spiritual propriety. In "Affliction (III)" Herbert's griefs become "a *scepter* of [God's] rod" and Christ's life makes it "A point of *honour,* now to grieve in me."

Meditations on the "Authority" of the court, on the other hand, discover a providential "designe" in which "great places and thy praise [of God] / Do not so well agree" ("Submission"). Only "Farre from court" does "Wine become a wing at last" ("The Banquet"). Poetry is

> not a crown,
> No point of honour, or gay suit,
> No hawk, or banquet, or renown,
> Nor a good sword, nor yet a lute;
> . . . .
> It is no office, art, or news,
> Nor the Exchange, or busie Hall.
>
> ("The Quidditie")

It is valuable only by how far it takes the meditator away from the court of man to the presence chamber of God. The "brags of life" are little more than "the fumes that spring / From private bodies, [which] make as big a thunder / As those which rise from a huge King" ("Content"); and "Wit and Conversation" are but "quick" and "short" from the perspective of "the houre of [God's] designe" ("The Quip"). When he "spies" "a gallant flower, / The crown Imperiall," he sees "a worme devoure / What show'd so well" ("Peace"). And even the "perfect lineaments" of Herbert's "dearest Mother," the Church – "whose meane thy praise and glorie is, / And long *may* be" ("The British Church") – is endangered by the Puritan "pratler" who "Not a fair look, but thou dost call it foul: / Not a sweet dish, but thou dost call it sowre: / Musick to the thee doth howl." The Rose of Sharon has been "cast . . . in the dirt / Where Pagans tread" ("Church-rents and schismes"). So Herbert turns from the "precise" extremes of the Puritans' response to the court model to a re-formation of its code of civil courtesy into divine "service," endeavoring to transfigure the "broken Altar" of his self, his history, and his church (through God's grace) into an image of the holy "SACRIFICE" which the Feast of the Lamb commemorates. As he says in "The Pearl," "I know the wayes of learning,/ . . . Yet I love thee," and

> I know the wayes of honour, what maintains
> The quick returns of courtesie and wit:
> In vies of favours whether partie gains,
> When glorie swells the heart, and moldeth it
> To all expressions both of hand and eye,
> Which on the world a true-love-knot may tie,

> And bear the bundle, wheresoe'er it goes:
> How many drammes of spirit there must be
> To sell my life unto my friends or foes:
>   Yet I love thee.

Figured throughout "The Church" by his transforming the courtly "virtues" into Christian humility, this celebration of his service as God's courtier is finally achieved in the splendidly courteous ritual of "Love (III)." A eucharistic poem which applies the love language of Renaissance lyric to its biblical origins, in its concluding vision of the timely (and sacramentally timeless) conversation by which fallen man responds "courteously" to the grace that civilizes his doubts, fears, and anxieties in a communion of harmony, this final meditation in "The Church" identifies the model for Herbert's poetic courtiership when "Love" says to the humble but doubtful believer, "I will serve." The speaker's response – "You must sit down, sayes Love, and taste my meat: / So I did sit and eat" – offers Herbert's final vision of the Banquet of Christian Civilization he sought in his retreat from the opportunities and pulls of the Caroline court to become "The Country Parson" of Bemerton. Jonson's classic, classical poem of English civilization, "Inviting a Friend to Supper," is refigured as Herbert's "Love (III)."

His faith in the eternality (or eventuality) of the Feast of the Lamb did not eradicate or lessen Herbert's disenchantment with the Stuart court and church, however. "Love (III)" is followed immediately by "The Church Militant," where the *contemptus mundi* tenor of Donne's *Anniversaries* predicts the demise of the Caroline world:

> Religion stands tip-toe in our land,
> Ready to pass to the *American* strand.
> When height of malice, and prodigious lusts,
> Impudent sinning, witchcrafts, and distrusts
> (The mark of future bane) shall fill our cup
> Unto the brim, and make our measure up;
> . . . .
>
> Then shall Religion to *America* flee:
> They have their times of Gospel, ev'n as we.
> . . . .
> Yet as the Church shall thither westward fly,
> So Sin shall trace and dog her instantly:
> They have their period also and set times
> Both for their virtuous actions and their crimes.
> . . . sin the Church shall smother.
> . . . .
> Thus also Sin and Darkness follow still
> the Church and sun with all their power and skill.

Herbert offers, in effect, a devastatingly prescient view of the future of the Caroline world. He does not alter his opening assertion in the poem – that it is eventually "Not the decrees of power, but bands of love" that determine the future of civilization, for he concludes that the Son does indeed outrun the sun and sin in God's "designe." As the closing lines of "The Church Militant" and the "L'Envoy" following them suggest, Herbert's poem looks beyond the Church Militant to the Church Triumphant (fully in agreement once again with Donne's *Anniversaries* with their balance of *contemptus mundi* directive and faithful vision of "an euerlastingnesse" by God's "Proclamation"). But, at the same time, such an eschatological perspective cannot obviate Herbert's powerful "picture" of a Caroline disenchantment even deeper than that of Carew and Herrick. For the inevitable collapse of the contemptuous world which Herbert prophesies is, again, framed in terms of his consistent contrast of the contrary uses of courteous "service" in the kingdoms of Caesar and God. In his final vision of a universal double "Progress" of religion and sin, in which the English state and church are "smother[ed]" by "Sin and Darkness," he reiterates that "Sin" is best "understood" as "a gallant [who] would serve / His pills of sublimate [that is, poison]. / . . . Glory was his chief instrument of old: / Pleasure succeeded straight, when that grew cold." Even the refrain which Herbert uses to divide his poem into the five sections conventional to an epithalamic meditation on (the Virgin Mary as) the Spouse of Christ (as used also in Donne's *First Anniversary*) seems (in 1633 at least) to sound over and over a stern rebuke to the hyperbolic royal iconography of the cult of King Charles I: "*How deare to me, O God, thy counsels are! / Who may with thee compare?*" And the words of the prayer of the "L'Envoy" which concludes Herbert's collection – that God "make warre to cease" – not only recall the specific origins of Herbert's retreat from the Stuart court after that 1624 Parliament in which Charles and the "gallant" Buckingham gained a momentary "conquest," but they also remind that God, not Charles, had finally the power of love sufficient to be not only the "King of Glorie" but also the "King of Peace" who alone deserves Herbert's "courteous" worship.

Except for the near unanimity of what Alistair Fowler has called "the epigrammatic revolution" among this generation of poets, this group is indeed, as he says, "difficult to put into focus" (*A History of English Literature,* 1987). This is true in one sense because of the general diffuseness of the verse and the absence of a poet of the stature or influence of a Donne or a Jonson (Stanley Stewart's illustration of a "School of Herbert" notwithstanding). But this difficulty is due also in large part to their being a generation in many ways out of focus *as a generation.* Owing to the poets' varying and various objections to or qualifications of the court model, the range of their doctrinal positions and attitudes across the widening spectrum of English Anglicanism, and their disparate interpretations of the role of the poet that the major models of Donne and Jonson bequeathed to them, this second generation of seventeenth-century British nondramatic poets – at least the group of Royalists represented in this volume – might share only the anxiety and strain (which sometimes developed into a discernible disillusionment, disenchantment, or disengagement) with which they faced the major cultural crisis of the age, anxious that "Paradise" was indeed lost despite the efforts of court artists to refigure it there, unsure that it could ever be regained as their world turned upside down. The magnificence of their poetic expressions of that crisis does, however, remain.

– *M. Thomas Hester*

Acknowledgments

This book was produced by Bruccoli Clark Layman, Inc. Karen L. Rood is senior editor for the *Dictionary of Literary Biography* series. Henry Cuningham was the in-house editor.

Production coordinator is James W. Hipp. Projects manager is Charles D. Brower. Photography editors are Edward Scott and Timothy C. Lundy. Layout and graphics supervisor is Penney L. Haughton. Copyediting supervisor is Bill Adams. Typesetting supervisor is Kathleen M. Flanagan. Mary Scott Dye is editorial associate. Systems manager is George F. Dodge. The production staff includes Rowena Betts, Steve Borsanyi, Barbara Brannon, Joseph Matthew Bruccoli, Teresa Chaney, Patricia Coate, Rebecca Crawford, Margaret McGinty Cureton, Denise Edwards, Sarah A. Estes, Joyce Fowler, Robert Fowler, Brenda A. Gillie, Bonita Graham, Jolyon M. Helterman, Ellen McCracken, Kathy Lawler Merlette, John Myrick, Pamela D. Norton, Thomas J. Pickett, Patricia Salisbury, Maxine K. Smalls, Deborah P. Stokes, and Wilma Weant.

Walter W. Ross and Samuel Bruce did library research. They were assisted by the following librarians at the Thomas Cooper Library of the University of South Carolina: Jens Holley and the inter-library-loan staff; reference librarians Gwen Baxter, Daniel Boice, Faye Chadwell, Cathy Eckman, Rhonda Felder, Gary Geer, Jackie Kinder, Laurie Preston, Jean Rhyne, Carol Tobin, Virginia Weathers, and Connie Widney; circulation-department head Thomas Marcil; and acquisitions-searching supervisor David Haggard.

Seventeenth-Century British Nondramatic Poets
Second Series

Joseph Beaumont

(13 March 1616 – 23 November 1699)

Lorraine M. Roberts
Saint Mary's College, Minnesota

BOOKS: *Psyche: or, Loves Mysterie in XX. Canto's: displaying the intercourse betwixt Christ, and the soule* (London: Printed by John Dawson for George Boddington, 1648; enlarged edition, edited by Charles Beaumont, Cambridge: Cambridge University Press, 1702);

Some Observations upon the Apologie of Dr. Henry More for his Mystery of Godliness (Cambridge: Printed by John Field, 1665);

Remarks on Dr. Henry More's Expositions of the Apocalypse and Daniel, and Upon his Apology: Defended Against his Answer To Them (London: Printed by T. M. for the author, 1690).

Editions: *Original Poems in English and Latin, with an appendix. Containing a dissertation, &c. and some remarks on the Epistle of Colossians. By Joseph Beaumont . . . To which is prefixed An Account of his Life and Writings,* edited by John Gee (Cambridge: Printed by J. Bentham, sold by W. Thurlbourn, 1749);

The Complete Poems of Dr. Joseph Beaumont (1615–1699), 2 volumes, edited by Alexander B. Grosart (Edinburgh: T. & A. Constable, 1880);

The Minor Poems of Joseph Beaumont, D. D. 1616-1699, edited by Eloise Robinson (London: Constable, 1914).

Joseph Beaumont is remembered primarily for the composition of one of the longest poems in English, *Psyche: or, Loves Mysterie* (1648), and for his association with the poet Richard Crashaw. Like

Joseph Beaumont (engraving by W. J. Alais after a portrait by R. White)

Crashaw, Beaumont was a fellow of Peterhouse, a college of Cambridge University and the center of

High Church or Laudian beliefs and practices during the 1630s and 1640s. Loyal supporters of King Charles I, Beaumont and Crashaw were officially banished by the Puritans in 1644 from their sinecures at Peterhouse. Crashaw fled to the Continent, became a Roman Catholic, and died before the Restoration. Beaumont, however, remained in England, retiring to his country home for the duration of the Commonwealth. He remained faithful to the High Church and, after the ascension of King Charles II in 1660, was honored with titles and positions.

Although Beaumont's poetry is of limited merit, his verse continues to be read because its subject matter, themes, imagery, and style are representative of Laudian spirituality and interests. Reminiscent of yet inferior to much of Crashaw's poetry, Beaumont's work is remarkable for showing that what is often thought to be Roman Catholic in Crashaw's work is actually representative of Laudian interests.

Joseph Beaumont's father, the Royalist John Beaumont, a clothier and sometime chief magistrate of the town of Hadleigh in Suffolk, was related to the famous dramatist Francis Beaumont and his brother, Sir John Beaumont, the poet of *Bosworth-field* (1629). John Beaumont's wife, Sarah Clarke Beaumont of East Berghdt, gave birth to Joseph Beaumont on 13 March 1616. Beaumont attended Hadleigh Grammar School under the tutelage of William Hawkins, priest and poet. Beaumont later contributed commendatory Latin verses to a 1634 volume of Hawkins's own Latin verses, *Corolla Varia*.

In November 1631 when he was fifteen years old, Beaumont entered Peterhouse, Cambridge, receiving the B.A. degree in 1634. He was elected to a fellowship at Peterhouse in the same year as Crashaw, 1636, and both received M.A. degrees in 1638. On 13 March 1643 Beaumont wrote a birthday poem entitled "Natalitium" (1914), which describes his early years and announces that at Peterhouse he finally gave up worldly learning: "Ambitious only not to be a foole / In that, which Saints and Angells draws to Schoole."

While in his early twenties Beaumont contributed an elegy to the collection *Justa Edouardo King* (1638), which lamented the death of a student at Cambridge. It was in this collection that John Milton published "Lycidas." Ruth Wallerstein describes Beaumont's elegy as a conventional lament, but having Marinistic, emblematic, paradoxical, and devotional aspects that become features of his later style. This slight poem successfully blends

Latin attitudes, personal religious intensity, and Anglican ideals of social order, a combination that reappears in Beaumont's *Psyche*.

A prodigious student of languages, Beaumont read Hebrew, Latin, Greek, Italian, Spanish, and French (although his editor Alexander Grosart was unimpressed with Beaumont's Latin). According to John Gee, master of Peterhouse and Beaumont's first biographer, Beaumont "exhausted all the fountains of Greek and Roman learning," and was thoroughly familiar with the subjects of oratory, poetry, and philosophy. During his Cambridge years and in his later retirement from public life, Beaumont studied the Bible in Hebrew, examined the state of Christianity from its beginning to the current day, and read the church fathers. He composed enough critical commentaries on some of these subjects to fill twenty-five volumes; but they were never published and are in large part traditional and essentially uninspired. He wrote daily on the lives of saints and martyrs, figures that later appeared in his shorter poems. He wrote a defense of miracles that occurred after the time of the apostles (a position that drew criticism from the Puritans) and a description of the Roman Empire under the sons of Theodosius, paralleling its misfortunes with the impending English Civil War.

In a Latin speech (translated by Paul Grant Stanwood) delivered in 1638 to the students at Peterhouse under his charge, Beaumont sought to advise them on a plan and method of reading. In it he extols the subjects of philosophy, rhetoric, and the classical and modern languages. From the classical world he singles out Plato, Homer (Homer's English translators as well), Virgil, and Cicero in addition to writers of history, tragedy, and comedy. Among the English he praises Francis Bacon; from the Italians, Petrarch, Giambattista Marini, and Torquato Tasso (indeed, saying he prefers Tasso's Jerusalem to Homer's Troy); from the French, Pierre de Ronsard and Guillaume de Salluste, Seigneur Du Bartas; and from the Spanish, Saint Teresa of Avila, of whom he speaks rapturously, commenting to his audience that Saint Teresa is "a name unheard by you, . . . more familiar to the angels than to our men." His mention of Saint Teresa appears to be the first public reference to her made by an English writer. (Although Teresa was canonized in 1622, the first English translation of her life, Sir Tobie Matthew's *The Flaming Heart*, did not appear until 1642.) Beaumont says in conclusion, "Thus allow yourselves to become learned, allow your names and your labors and your total selves to be consecrated to eternal honors through the multiplicity of languages, through the splendor of eloquence, and through the dignity of philosophy."

In 1641 Puritans came to Cambridge to look into what they thought were abuses in matters of religion and civil government. This investigation marked the beginning of the end of Beaumont's life of study at Cambridge. Allan Pritchard notes that manuscript 7011 in the British Library, No. 11 (fols. 52–93), undated but belonging to the early months of 1641, includes an extended survey of the activities of the Laudian party in Cambridge and lists practices that the Puritans condemned. Some of these practices were used in the trials against Archbishop William Laud and former Peterhouse master John Cosin. Peterhouse, the college, as well as Beaumont and Crashaw, were singled out for special attention. In particular, Beaumont was attacked for criticizing John Calvin in a sermon given at the church next to Peterhouse, Little Saint Mary's; for saying in a sermon on St. Peter's feast day that the saint had the keys to heaven and hell; for commending stories about the virtue of the Cross; and for suggesting in an address on 5 November 1640 that the Scots were more wicked than the perpetrators of the Gunpowder Plot.

Even though Beaumont was not formally ejected from Cambridge before June of 1644, he had returned to Hadleigh early in 1643. While in retirement, he wrote almost all of his poetry, which, in addition to *Psyche*, consists of two collections of short poems. The first collection was probably written between early 1644 and June 1652; the second collection, called "Cathemerina," after Prudentius's fourth century *Cathemerinon*, was probably written between 17 May and 3 September 1652. Only the first of the two collections survives in toto.

The manuscripts of Beaumont's short poems – in two hands, probably the other being John Gee, the editor of the selective *Original Poems in English and Latin* (1749) – comprise 177 poems, 30 of which were published with large omissions in Gee's edition. Eleven of these poems were from the second collection. Besides these English poems, Gee printed 17 Latin poems and 32 pages of Latin prose, which consisted of a treatise on miracles and critical notes on Saint Paul's Epistles. Many of the poems were marked for a musical setting, a few bearing the initials R. C. (perhaps Richard Crashaw) and T. T. (perhaps Thomas Traherne).

Like many of the religious poets before him – Robert Southwell, George Herbert, and Crashaw, to name a few – Beaumont eschewed secular subjects, deliberately choosing instead to write about Jesus, the "Worlds Sweet King," as he indicates in "Loves Monarchie." An overview of the other titles of his poems published in Gee's edition suggests as well the influence of these same poets, along with John Donne. Titles such as "Love," "Affliction," "H. Sacrament," "Christmasse Day," "Goodfryday," "S. Mary Magdalen's Ointment," "Epiphanie Carol," "Virtue," "The Garden," and others place Beaumont firmly in the company of the metaphysical poets. His subjects are likewise reminiscent of the great baroque painters of the Continent, for some poems concern saints such as Peter, Paul, Stephen, John, Andrew, Thomas, Joseph, Mary, and Mary Magdalene, to name a few. Beaumont often highlights a dramatic act of a saint's life, as the baroque painters did, striving for a sensory effect. His poem to Saint Matthew that begins "O Love Thou Art Almighty!" imitates Crashaw's first Teresa poem, and his poem on Saint Gregory of Nazianzus, to whom he compares Crashaw in *Psyche*, demonstrates his interest in devotion and mysticism.

In addition to "Easter," "Ash Wednesday," "Trinitie Sunday," and "Ascension," poems that recall liturgical feast days, there are other poems of moral persuasion or exemplum such as "The Sluggard," "Fasting," "Avarice," and "Self-Love," some of which are personal in example and application. A few poems address the sacrifice Beaumont felt in a life of retirement and describe what spiritual comfort he took from his situation. For example, in "The Check" he "checks" himself against grief, counseling himself to subordinate his will to God's; in "House and Home" he records his thoughts about the place of absolute freedom – his own heart where God dwells; in "Patience" he prays for virtue that will sustain him and help him gain a type of victory over those who may win without being in the right; in "Loves Monarchie" he sees in Christ a means to join all men together and for himself to be subsumed into God's will.

Other characteristics of Beaumont's shorter poems are a very regular rhythm, mostly iambs; a fondness for short lines (two-thirds are trimeters, dimeters, and monometers); an occasional pattern poem; a use of imperfect rhyme and many compound words suggestive of Crashaw; some classical allusions; and an abundance of puns, antitheses, and paradoxes. Most importantly, Beaumont's poetry is an echo of many of his contemporaries, as his editor Eloise Robinson demonstrates.

Poetry provided hours of amusement for Beaumont while in retirement from an active life. He considered his studies on Ecclesiastes and the

Pages from the diary Beaumont kept in Latin while he was master of Peterhouse College (Peterhouse College, Cambridge University)

Pentateuch to be his serious work. In addition to writing, he performed the Liturgy daily in his father's house and preached on Sunday. While Gee and Grosart suggest this indicates Beaumont had taken deacon's orders before he left the university in 1644, Robinson declares two Latin poems indicate a date of 27 February 1647.

During this retirement, Beaumont was under the patronage of Bishop Matthew Wren of Ely, who had been master of Peterhouse during Beaumont's early years there. An ardent Laudian, Wren was committed to the Tower of London on 1 September 1642 for a period of eighteen years; yet Beaumont got many benefices through Wren at this time, such as canon of Ely in 1646 as well as domestic chaplain to Wren in 1650. Beaumont married Wren's wealthy stepdaughter, Miss Brownrigg, in 1650, and both retired to Tatingston, her inherited estate.

Written before his marriage, from 1645 to the spring of 1648, *Psyche*, a poem of nearly forty thousand lines, is Beaumont's most important work. Beaumont's prefatory comments are reminiscent of the preface to Crashaw's *Steps to the Temple* (1646), a preface sometimes attributed to Beaumont. In *Psyche*, Beaumont writes that his intent is to "prompt *better Wits* to believe, that a *Divine Theam* is as capable and happy a *Subject* of *Poetical Ornament*, as any *Pagan* or *Humane Device*" while charming his "Readers into any *true degree of Devotion*." Of particular interest is canto 4 in which he stops his narrative to pay tribute to classical and Continental poets such as Pindar, Homer, Tasso, and Marini, as well as

Herbert (stanza 102), Saint Gregory (stanza 106), and Crashaw (stanzas 107–108), the three who constitute a poetic lineage for him.

Because Crashaw was on the Continent during the composition of *Psyche*, Beaumont expresses regret in canto 4, stanza 108 at the loss of that poet's critical judgment: "Fair had my *Psyche* been, had she at first / By thy judicious hand been drest and nurst." This reference seems to document the opinion of Robinson and L. C. Martin, Crashaw's editor (1927), that the similarities between Crashaw and Beaumont's poetry are due to the major influence of Crashaw on Beaumont. They both used poetry as a form of devotion, responded intensely to the Incarnation, showed an interest in New Testament saints, incorporated pleasing musical aspects into their verse, and depended on what is often deemed extravagant language and imagery. Further, Beaumont and Crashaw were more than kindred poetic spirits, as the preceding passage in *Psyche* suggests:

> And by this heart-attracting Pattern *Thou*
> *My only worthy self,* thy Songs didst frame:
> Witness those polish'd *Temple Steps*, which now
>   Stand as the Ladder to thy mounting fame;
>   And, spight of all thy Travels, make't appear
>   Th' art more in *England* than when Thou wert
>   here.

> More unto others, but not so to me
> Privy of old to all thy secret Worth:
> What half-lost I endure for want of *Thee*,
> The World will read in this mishapen *Birth.*

Elsie Elizabeth Duncan-Jones has argued on the basis of these expressions of friendship that Crashaw's only surviving autograph letter was intended, not for the Collett family as is usually thought, but for Beaumont.

The major reasons that *Psyche* is important are that it reflects the crisis in mid-seventeenth-century England in politics and religion while offering a representative example of English literature as it was being written by High Anglicans of the time. Many of the digressions in it express aspects of royalism and Laudian Anglicanism. For example, in canto 5, stanza 188, Beaumont expresses his opinion about the consequences of the Civil War:

> What strange and hideous monsters Kingdoms grow,
> Where *Law* and *Sovereignty*, the life and health
> Of every heav'n-descended State must bow
> To vile plebeians' wills! What Commonwealth
>   Can justify its Name, where Subjects may
>   Command, and Princes dare not but obey.

Behind Beaumont's royalism and Laudianism is a love of order and tradition and a dislike of dissension and change, positions that inevitably lead him to reject Puritanism and its conventicles, preaching, and lack of rituals.

To Beaumont the High Church participated in a history and an ecumenism that should have been promoted to produce order and peace. Thus he strove to revive the traditions and rituals of this historic past and in doing so he emphasized what were also themes in Continental Catholic literature and art: vision and ecstasy, legends of the Blessed Virgin and the saints, the sacraments, and the paradoxes of death and martyrdom. Not only the subjects but his methods as well were similar, for like the Counter-Reformation artists, he sought to render doctrine palpable and immediate. He had a fondness for oxymora (especially such ideas as death in life, life in death; sweet wounds of love; the antitheses of fire and water, light and dark), as did those writers he admired – Crashaw, Marini, and the Spanish mystics, as well as the composers of the Bible.

Henry Molle, university orator, and Edward Martin, ejected president of Queen's College, Cambridge, and once chaplain to Archbishop of Canterbury William Laud, praised *Psyche* and suggested it be published. Beaumont, however, was afraid he was too harsh on the Puritans and therefore suppressed some of what he had written; the second edition of 1702 (consisting of twenty-four rather than twenty cantos) is much more violent in its attacks on Puritans.

The subjects of *Psyche* are the vicissitudes of a soul that longs for union with God but must first overcome sins of lust, vanity, pride, and impatience through penance and acts of mortification; a history of Creation, the Fall, and Christ's life and death, with emphasis on the Incarnation, his miracles, Holy Eucharist, and his Martyrdom; a rebuke of ancient and modern heretics, especially Puritans; a eulogy of the poet's dead wife; and a paean for poets old and new, from Horace, Homer, and Virgil to Edmund Spenser and Crashaw.

The influences on Beaumont's allegorical epic are many. Specifically, Beaumont drew on Tasso for the prototype of his Christian hero. From Spenser and Giles and Phineas Fletcher he drew models of allegory. From William Shakespeare's *Venus and Adonis* (1593) he may have borrowed the six-line stanza format rhyming *ababcc*. From Marini and the Spanish saints, especially Saint Teresa, Beaumont studied the language of paradox and elaborate conceits, although closer to home was also the example of Crashaw. Beaumont no doubt was also familiar with Ludovico Ariosto, Du Bartas, and Marco Girolamo Vida. This amalgam of influences produced a curious blend of English didacticism and Continental devotional style. The only other poem in English like *Psyche* is Edward Benlowes's *Theophila, or Love's Sacrifice: A Divine Poem* (1652).

Paul Grant Stanwood sees in the unfolding of the narrative of *Psyche* a reference to the traditional steps to mystical union with Christ: the Purgative, Illuminative, and Unitive steps. Stanwood also sees in Psyche the figure of Saint Teresa, although never by direct reference. Within the three steps, Stanwood also sees the four distinct degrees of contemplation that Saint Teresa called "waters" in her *Vida* (written 1562-1565) and "mansions" in *El castillo interior* or *Las moradas* (written 1577).

In canto 1 of the second edition, the guardian angel of Psyche, Phylax, a Greek word for watchman or sentinel, relates the story of Joseph resisting Potiphar's wife as an instructive caution to Psyche, who is the target of Satan. In canto 2 Satan, disguised as a courtly lover, attempts to seduce Psyche, but with Phylax's help, she resists Satan's false charms. After hissing serpents, representing "unclean delight," are cast from Psyche's heart, Phylax tells her the story of Susannah and the Elders. Psyche falls asleep and dreams of a stately procession where Christ, as the King of Chastity, regards her. In canto 3 Phylax gives Psyche a "love-token" from God, a girdle whose rich embroidery depicts the life of Saint John the Baptist. When she wears it, she feels guilt, to such an extent that she has to fight disillusionment. In canto 4 she tries to adopt an ascetic life, but her senses and her passions rebel, take Reason a prisoner, and win the support of the Will as well. When in canto 5 Psyche is given a mirror to gaze at herself, she becomes full of pride and self-love and resents Phylax for wanting her to look in the mirror of conscience. In canto 6, after witnessing the conversion of another who had been shot with shafts of Love, Psyche is humbled. Full of remorse, she smites her breast, whereupon poison comes out. Phylax tells her the story of Creation, the Fall, and the birth of Jesus. When Phylax takes her to the scene of Nazareth in canto 7, Psyche is overcome with contrition at the story of Christ's birth. Cantos 8 to 16 then tell the full story of Christ's life on earth, his death, his resurrection, and the descent of the Holy Spirit. The result is that Psyche is overcome with a desire to be united with Christ.

Canto 17 offers a roll call of Christian heroes and a digression on the Civil War. While Phylax retreats from her, Psyche goes to Calvary and is seduced by one of Satan's cohorts. Canto 18, which eulogizes Beaumont's wife, also includes a debate on the Virgin Birth, the God-Man concept, and the Triune God. Because of her sinfulness Psyche drinks bane and sinks in woe, but Phylax returns to set her aright again. In canto 19 Phylax takes Psyche to the Gates of Heaven, where she sees Penance, who controls the key to its entrance. Psyche enters the hall where all the limited "truths" are, and where the Presbyterian god called Covenant is castigated. Then she is brought to Queen Ecclesia, the Bride of Christ, who is attended by all the virtues. Truth, who stands naked at the queen's right hand, rescues Psyche from Error's Net. Canto 20 digresses on Beaumont's removal from Cambridge and on the Restoration of King Charles II. It also praises fasting, silence, control of passions, and works of charity as means of mortification and edification. In cantos 21 and 22 Psyche successfully resists Satan by herself, but afterwards suffers a dark night of the soul, recorded in canto 23. Finally in canto 24, wounded by Love's arrows, Psyche prays for union with God in heaven; her prayer is answered, and she dies with "Love" on her lips.

If the poem were not so long, one could read it with ease and be charmed by its rhythms and instructed by its attitudes toward contemporary politics and religion and by its advocacy of Continental devotional methods. Samuel Johnson's comment on Milton's *Paradise Lost* (1667), however, also applies to Beaumont's *Psyche*: "No one ever wished it longer." On the positive side, the epic reveals the extent of Beaumont's reading, for many of the lines are echoes of the poets he admires, and they afford the reader the pleasure of recognition.

With the Restoration of Charles II, Beaumont's fortunes in the new society improved. He was appointed one of the royal chaplains to Charles II and resided at court. On 28 July 1660 the king had him created doctor of divinity. He proceeded to Sacrae Theologiae Professor (Professor of Sacred Theology) on 18 August 1660 and probably took orders the following 16 February. In 1661 he moved to Ely again at the request of Wren. His wife died 31 May 1662 and is buried behind the altar at Ely. A eulogy Beaumont incorporated into *Psyche* records that the Beaumonts' first two children died but that four more were born to them. In an essay entitled "A Portrait of Stuart Orthodoxy," Stanwood notes that three of the Beaumont children lived to adulthood. Shortly before his wife's death, Dr. Wren had obtained for Beaumont the mastership at Jesus College; this was to be a temporary position, however, for on 24 April 1663 Wren appointed Beaumont to be master of Peterhouse, after the death of Dr. Bernard Hale, its former master.

In that position Beaumont entered into a controversy with Dr. Henry More on the doctrines More had espoused in *An Explanation of the Grand Mystery of Godliness* (1660), for which Beaumont received the thanks of the university. Believing More to be dangerously heretical, Beaumont wrote *Some Observations upon the Apologie of Dr. Henry More for his Mystery of Godliness* (1665) as well as *Remarks on Dr. Henry More's Expositions of the Apocalypse and Daniel, and Upon his Apology: Defended Against his Answer To Them* (1690). According to Grosart, Beaumont did not sufficiently understand the argument of More, "and More crushes him, as one might crush a limpet shell, in his iron grasp and strangely piercing though mystical logic."

Beaumont's final prestigious elevation was his appointment to Cambridge as regius professor of divinity on 30 March 1674. He filled the chair for twenty-five years, reading public lectures in Latin twice a week that explained difficult passages in Paul's Epistles (especially Romans and Colossians), but these were never published. Seven collected autograph sermons exist in the Peterhouse library. The sermons and scriptural exegesis together fill twenty-five folio volumes. He died 23 November 1699 and is buried in the antechapel of Peterhouse.

Today Beaumont is remembered more for the times in which he lived and the company he kept than for the success of his own poetry. Nevertheless, all readers would have to be impressed with the sheer volume of his work. While it partakes of the themes and style of his greater contemporaries in seventeenth-century poetry such as Donne, Herbert, Crashaw, and Henry Vaughan, his verse lacks their wit, their originality, and their craft. Yet Beaumont has through time had readers who appreciated his work: James A. Means, for example, has seen in the final stanza of John Keats's "Ode on Melancholy" the influence of canto 1, stanza 162, of Beaumont's *Psyche*. Philip Herzbrun has also noted that the work most quoted in Joseph Spence's commonplace book is the 1648 *Psyche*; furthermore, Spence used the pseudonym of Sir Henry Beaumont in all three of his last major works and when he was moralizing. Today one reads Beaumont not for devotion, as he had wished, but for what he tells us about his age and his friends.

References:

A. B. Chambers, *Transfigured Rites in Seventeenth-Century English Poetry* (Columbia: University of Missouri Press, 1992);

Elsie Elizabeth Duncan-Jones, "Who Was the Recipient of Crashaw's Leyden Letter?," in *New Perspectives on the Life and Art of Richard Crashaw*, edited by John R. Roberts (Columbia: University of Missouri Press, 1990), pp. 174–179;

Philip Herzbrun, "Joseph Beaumont's *Psyche* and Joseph Spence as 'Sir Harry Beaumont,' " *Notes and Queries*, 30 (February 1983): 43–44;

Natalie Maynor, "Joseph Beaumont's *Psyche* in the Seventeenth-Century Context," Ph.D. dissertation, University of Tennessee, 1978;

Eleanor McCann, "Oxymora in Spanish Mystics and English Metaphysical Writers," *Comparative Literature*, 13 (Winter 1961): 16–25;

James A. Means, "Keats's 'Ode on Melancholy' and Beaumont's *Psyche*" (1648), *Notes and Queries*, 32 (September 1985): 341;

Allan Pritchard, "Puritan Charges Against Crashaw and Beaumont," *Times Literary Supplement*, 2 (July 1964), p. 578;

Malcolm Mackenzie Ross, *Poetry and Dogma: The Transfiguration of Eucharistic Symbols in Seventeenth-Century English Poetry* (New Brunswick, N.J.: Rutgers University Press, 1954), pp. 154, 162–174, 218, 228, 234;

Paul Grant Stanwood, "Joseph Beaumont's *Psyche: Or Loves Mysterie* (1648): Canto XIX, 'The Dereliction,' A Critical Edition," Ph.D. dissertation, University of Michigan, 1961;

Stanwood, "A Portrait of Stuart Orthodoxy," *Church Quarterly Review*, 165 (January–March 1964): 27–39;

Stanwood, "St. Teresa and Joseph Beaumont's *Psyche*," *Journal of English and Germanic Philology*, 62 (July 1963): 533–550;

Ruth Wallerstein, *Studies in Seventeenth-Century Poetic* (Madison: University of Wisconsin Press, 1950), pp. 97–99, 119, 121, 135, 384.

Papers:

All of Beaumont's unpublished papers are at Peterhouse College, Cambridge University. They include Latin speeches (MS 459), sermons (MS 448), and twenty-five volumes of theological works copied from the autograph by Thomas Richardson, D.D., master of St. Peter's College from 1699 to 1733 (MSS 49–73).

Edward Benlowes

(12 July 1602 – 18 December 1676)

Charles A. Huttar
Hope College

BOOKS: *Lusus Poëticus Poëtis* (London: Printed by G. Miller, 1634); republished in Francis Quarles, *Emblemes,* includes complimentary verse by Benlowes (London: Printed by G. Miller, 1635);

Sphinx Theologica sive Musica Templi, ubi Discordia Concors (Cambridge: Ex Academiæ celeberrimæ typographeo, 1636);

Papa Perstrictus (Echo) Ictus (London: typus Jacobis junii, 1645 [i.e., 1646]);

A Poetick Descant upon a Private Musick-Meeting (London, 1649);

Theophila, or Loves Sacrifice. A Divine Poem (London: Printed by R. N., sold by Henry Seile & Humphrey Moseley, 1652);

The Summary of Wisedome (London: Printed for Humphry Mosely, 1657);

A Glance at the Glories of Sacred Friendship (London: Printed by R. D. for Humphrey Moseley, 1657);

On St. Paul's Cathedrall represented by Mr Dan. King [and] *Threnodia Ædis Paulinæ de Seipsâ* (London: Sold by John Overton, 1658);

Threno-Thriambeuticon (London, 1660);

Oxonii Encomium (Oxford: Excudebat H. Hall, Academiis Typographus, 1672);

Oxonii Elogia [and] *Echo Veridica Joco-seria* (Oxford: Printed at the theatre, 1673);

Magia Coelestis (Oxford: Excudebat Lichfield, 1673).

Edition: "Theophila," "The Summary of Wisdom," and "A Poetic Descant upon a Private Music-Meeting," in *Minor Poets of the Caroline Period,* volume 1, edited by George Saintsbury (Oxford: Clarendon Press, 1905), pp. 305–483.

OTHER: Johann Gerhard, *A Golden Chaine of Divine Aphorismes,* translated by Ralph Winterton, includes complimentary verse by Benlowes (Cambridge: Printed by T. Buck & R. Daniel, printers to the University of Cambridge, 1632);

Winterton, ed.,' Ιπποκρατους του μεγαλου οι αφορισμοι. *Hippocratis . . . aphorismi,* includes complimentary work by Benlowes (Cambridge: Printed by T. Buck & R. Daniel, 1633);

Phineas Fletcher, *The Purple Island, or the Isle of Man: Together with Piscatorie Eclogs and Other Poeticall Miscellanies,* includes a commendatory poem by Benlowes (Cambridge: Printed by T. Buck & R. Daniel, printers to the University of Cambridge, 1633);

Richard Sibbes, *The Soules Conflict with It Selfe,* second edition, includes complimentary verse by Benlowes (London: Printed by M. Flesher for R. Dawlman, 1635);

Francis Quarles, *Hieroglyphikes of the Life of Man,* includes complimentary verse by Benlowes (London: Printed by M. Flesher for John Marriot, 1638);

Joannes Sictor, *Panegyricon inaugurale,* includes "De celeberrima & florentissima Trinobantiados Augustæ civitate" by Benlowes (London: Ex chalcographia T. Harperi, 1638);

Robert Ward, *Anima'dversions of Warre,* includes verse by Benlowes (London: Printed by J. Dawson, T. Cotes & R. Bishop, 1639);

Payne Fisher, *Marston-Moor,* includes complimentary verse by Benlowes (London: Printed by Thomas Newcomb, 1650);

Thomas Fuller, *The Church-History of Britain,* includes a poem by Benlowes (London: Printed for J. Williams, 1655);

Fisher, *Epinicion,* includes complimentary verse by Benlowes (London, 1658?);

Edward Sparke, *Scintillula Altaris,* second edition, includes complimentary verse by Benlowes (London: Printed by W. G. and R. W., 1660).

Edward Benlowes is significant equally for his patronage of the arts during the reign of Charles I and for an ambitious "heroic" poem on the ascent of the devout soul to God, which, despite its real merits, has been found difficult to take seriously because of obscure organization and stylistic extravagance; yet Henry Vaughan, Andrew Marvell, and John Milton were among the poets he influenced. At his best Benlowes had a capacity for both ecstatic utterance and telling satire. He could deploy the devices of Metaphysical wit with great effectiveness but could also egregiously overdo them. Anthony Wood, who befriended Benlowes during his final years in Oxford, epitomized him as "much noted in his time, but since not, for the art and faculty of poetry." Samuel Butler ridiculed him as a "small poet"; Alexander Pope in *The Dunciad* (1728) blasted his judgment as a patron ("propitious . . . to blockheads"); and, despite the judicious appreciation of George Saintsbury, George Williamson, Douglas Bush, and others, the poet's reputation has never fully recovered.

Edward Benlowes was born in 1602 into a wealthy Catholic family. At eleven, on his grandfather's death, Edward inherited the family estates in northern Essex and an annual income upward of one thousand pounds. He died in Oxford, in his seventy-fifth year, a pauper. The first third of his life brought him well on the way to conversion to what would be a bitterly antipapist Anglicanism; the second third was devoted to the life of a country gentleman, patron, and poet; and in the last third disasters of various sorts brought him eventually to debtor's prison and, finally, to a quiet contentment, in spite of privation, on the fringes of university culture.

Earlier than the sixteenth century his ancestry is unknown. His great-grandfather Sergeant William Bendlowes (died 1584) achieved high reputation and commensurate wealth and became known both as a legal authority and as a generous benefactor. The anagram Benevolus, cherished by Edward, reflects a family tradition of generosity. William's son, who possessed a fine medieval illuminated choir psalter that survives in the Bodleian Library, signed himself William Bendlowes Armiger. His son Andrew was fined for refusing to attend the state church, married Phillip (Phillippa) Gage, the daughter of another recusant family, and had five sons, of whom Edward was the eldest. At least two of these sons were sent abroad to receive a Catholic education, but Edward as heir was tutored privately at home. He was only nine when his father died; two years later, on the death of William, Edward became the master of Brent Hall, near Finchingfield.

Exposure to the larger world – he went to Saint John's College, Cambridge, in 1620, and on to

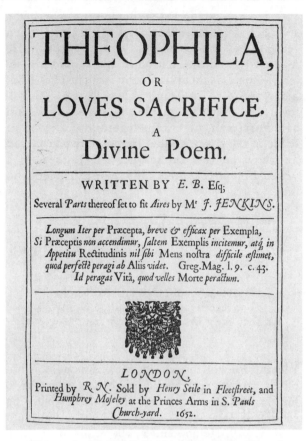

Title page for Edward Benlowes's epic poem describing the ascent of the devout soul to God

Lincoln's Inn in 1622 – resulted finally in his turning Anglican. Details of the early years are obscure: for example, an event in London in 1623 was made the subject of an anti-Catholic poem that appeared in Thomas Fuller's *Church-History of Britain* in 1655, but how early Benlowes wrote it is unknown. From 1627 to 1630, accompanied by a tutor, Benlowes took the grand tour. In Belgium he acquired a servant, a printer named John Schoren, and thus began a lifelong association of codependency that would finally, through embezzlement and lawsuits, contribute to his ruin. In Venice he contracted smallpox and was (according to Schoren's story) nursed back to health by his servant, who got him, when near death, to make confession to a priest. On the whole, however, exposure to Catholic Europe tended to confirm Benlowes's movement from Rome to the Church of England. In both Italy and the Low Countries he took especial interest in imprese and emblem books; though their European context was Catholic, usually Jesuit, their religious and aesthetic appeal to him obviously transcended sectarian differences.

Home again in Essex, Benlowes established a style of living that reflected not extravagance but a sense of his responsibility as a man of wealth. He made a splendid donation of books and art objects – some of them no doubt brought back from his travels – to his Cambridge college, in this following his father's example. Having acquired skill as a horseman, he became captain of a troop of horse in the Essex militia. He possibly considered marriage (at this or another time): there is a veiled hint in *Theophila* (1652) of a fiancée who died:

> T'have been affected by a *Virgin Heir,*
> Rich, young, and chast, wise, good, and fair,
> Was once his first Delight, but HEAV'N restrain'd that Care!

> Thou, *Providence,* dist both their Wills restrain;
> Thou mad'st their Losses turn to Gain;
> For Thou gav'st *Heav'n* to *her,* on *him* dost *Blessings* rain!

Whether or not this can be viewed as autobiography, Benlowes remained a bachelor; a reference to him as celibate, a comment by "M.G." following canto 8 of *Theophila,* is reinforced by a hint in canto 6, stanza 19. He appointed Schoren bailiff to manage his worldly affairs and devoted himself to spiritual duties, artistic pursuits, and friendships.

One of his friends was the Spenserian poet Phineas Fletcher, whose still-unpublished verse Benlowes could have known while at the university, though the older man had left Cambridge before Benlowes's time there. Encouragement from Benlowes could even have helped Fletcher decide in 1627 to publish the militantly Protestant poem *Locustæ, vel pietas Jesuitica,* on which he had been working for years. What is certain is that when Benlowes settled at Brent Hall, Fletcher was rector at Hilgay some thirty miles to the north, and soon the two were working together to bring out the allegorical poem *The Purple Island* (1633), which Fletcher had begun more than twenty years before. Benlowes's role of patron involved not only persuading Fletcher to publish but preparing gift copies inscribed "Benevolus" and lavishly adorned with emblematic engravings, probably from the private press at Brent Hall.

Another friendship cultivated by Benlowes was with Francis Quarles, author of several books of narrative and devotional poetry, to whom Benlowes showed two Antwerp emblem books with the suggestion that Quarles adapt them for Protestant England. "You have put the *Theorboe* into my hand; and I have played," Quarles said in dedicating to Benlowes his *Emblemes* (1635); local tradition claims Brent Hall as the place where they were written. Very likely Benlowes put money into Quarles's hand too, for the seventy-eight plates in *Emblemes* were expensive. One of them shows a globe marked with the locations of Finchingfield, Hilgay, and Quarles's village of Roxwell.

Commendatory verses written by Benlowes and books dedicated to him during this period and on through the 1650s give some idea of the range of his benevolence and patronage. His beneficiaries included the Cambridge scholar Ralph Winterton, the Puritan preacher Richard Sibbes, the Bohemian Protestant refugee Joannes Sictor, the reactionary controversialist Alexander Ross, and the Royalist men of letters Thomas Fuller, James Howell, and Sir William Davenant, the last two languishing in Puritan prisons.

Apart from the commendatory poems, Benlowes's own literary productions before 1649 were in Latin. There were the "Quarleis" and other verses published in 1634 under the title *Lusus Poëticus Poëtis* as an advance puff for his friend's *Emblemes* and then attached to the end of *Emblemes* when it was published. Included was a passage in praise of London, perhaps aimed at attracting for Quarles some employment there; this he revised and published in 1638 as "De celeberrima & florentissima Trinobantiados Augustæ civitate" in a similar endeavor on Sictor's behalf. His *Sphinx Theologica sive Musica Templi, ubi Discordia Concors* (1636) was much more elaborate in its scheme. In the title Benlowes alludes to George Herbert's *The Temple* (1633), as would the poets Richard Crashaw and Christopher Harvey a few years later; also reminiscent of Herbert is the explicit dedication of poetry to the service of piety; but the scale of Benlowes's plan is far removed from Herbert's cultivated simplicities, and the devotional purpose overwhelms the aesthetic. Benlowes projected thirty parts in three books, but only the first decade was ever published. These ten parts deal with religious concepts such as faith, the Trinity, and the Eucharist and with stages of divine revelation from the Creation to the Gospel miracles. In each a poetic section is sandwiched between a prose collage of Scripture texts and a prose meditation. Together with his earnestness Benlowes mingled fanciful toys, such as the chronogram on the title page that enables us to date the book. A decade later he published in broadsheet form, again with a chronogram, an echo poem entitled *Papa Perstrictus (Echo) Ictus* (1646), a diatribe against the pope.

By this time he was busy on his magnum opus, *Theophila,* which shows Benlowes equally opposed to the Puritan cause. He lamented "Schism, *and pervicacious* Heresie," the "*uncivil Pray'r*" of "Presters [Presbyterians], *rudely fierce*," the "*six-hundred-sixtie-six-word*-Covenant" of and the abolition of Christmas by those he called, in a witty coinage, "Proteustants." He scorned timeservers as "Vicar *Any Thing*"; "Worst *Atheist* from corrupted *Churchman* breeds," he thought.

> *Ah, could* dissembling Pulpeteers *cry't* Good
> *To wade through* Seas *of native* Blood,
> *Break greatest* Ties, *play fast and loose, beneath* Smects Hood!

That one of the Smectymnuan authors here castigated was Stephen Marshall, the vicar of Benlowes's own parish church, shows something of the strain under which Benlowes lived during the civil unrest. "Our National *Crimes* have extorted from thy JUSTICE National *Judgements*," he grieved in "The Author's Prayer" in *Theophila*. "*Cross-biasnesse to Grace* our Ruine spinn'd," so that "*Edge-hill* with Bones lookt white, with Blood lookt red" and

> *Our Sea-girt* World (*once* Fort'nate Isle, *O, Change Deplorable!*) *t'* It self *seems strange;*
> *Unthrifty* Death *has spread where thriving* Peace *did range.*

He lamented, too, those who escaped the battlefield only to die in prison. He longed chiefly for peace and the successful avoidance of extremes, praying that the Church might be "Steer[ed] ... safe amidst the *Rocks* and *Quicksands* of *Schism* and *Heresie*, *Superstition* and *Sacriledge* into the fair *Havens* of PEACE and TRUTH." Truth for him meant catholic orthodoxy, but without Rome or any High Church notions that savored of Rome.

He rejoiced that "in this general *combustion* of *Christendom*, THOU hast vouchsafed me a little *Zoar*, as Refuge"; but though he stayed aloof from the fighting, his monarchist loyalties cost him heavily in fines and levies as a wealthy landowner in Parliamentarian Essex. Finally in 1648 he did briefly see action, in the abortive campaign described in Milton's sonnet "On the Lord General Fairfax" ("new rebellions raise their hydra heads"). This quixotic decision made him even more vulnerable to retributive taxation. The *Dictionary of National Biography* errs in assigning to him Payne Fisher's broadside against the execution of the king, but Benlowes would later contribute commendatory lines to another book by Fisher (*Marston-Moor*, 1650), and his own attitude to the regicide may well be expressed in a line in *Theophila* which links "*Majestie*" and "*Martyrdome*." One of his neighbor-

hood friends, contributor of a testimonial to *Theophila*, was the royal ghostwriter John Gauden.

Composing *Theophila* was a major preoccupation during these years. "In war" can Virtue "yet use her lyre?" he asked. "Yes. She's unmov'd in earthquakes, tun'd in jars." He valued his "safe *Repose*" amid the "Rage of War"; "For Fields of *Combate*, Fields of Corn are here, / For Trooping-*Ranks*, *Tree*-ranks appear."

Music meant a good deal to him also, and in 1649 he published a short account of a concert, *A Poetick Descant upon a Private Musick-Meeting*, which wittily comments on women's and men's social roles and uses sound imagery to distinguish the various instruments. According to Benlowes, music enables "the enthusiastic soul" to "soar," but poetry can do it "without instruments." In this work was the first of several references in his writings to Famianus Strada's famous story of the nightingale, which Crashaw had just retold in "Musicks Duell" (1646, though surely Benlowes knew it in the original from 1617). Here also first appeared in print the unique stanza he had developed for *Theophila*, lines of ten, eight, and twelve syllables rhymed as a triplet. In 1652 the great work itself was finally published, lavishly decorated with engravings. He also commissioned a prominent composer, John Jenkins, to set parts of it to music (none of which has survived).

The heavy expenses of the war years left Benlowes with debts but still considerable wealth, until a series of setbacks in the 1650s severely reduced his estate. Brent Hall was destroyed by fire in 1653. What furnishings could be saved from the fire were sold, under the supervision of Schoren, who absconded with the proceeds of the sale. Benlowes felt honor-bound to maintain the charitable endowments established by his forebears and to furnish his niece, Phillippa, with a dowry commensurate with her rank – no matter that she and her betrothed, Walter Blount, were staunch Catholics. He mortgaged his estate to pay debts and bestow on her six thousand pounds. He then decided to recoup his cash assets by selling the property to a London merchant – who cheated him and, after years of litigation, finally was required to pay only about half of the original selling price of twenty-two thousand pounds; and most of that went for legal fees.

Now dwelling in London, Benlowes published a broadsheet poem on friendship (1657), another lamenting the decay of Saint Paul's Cathedral (1658), and, when the Interregnum came to a close, one celebrating the Restoration (*Threno-Thriambeuticon*, 1660). There was to be no restoration of his fortune, however, which was further impaired when Schoren sued for payment of the arrears of a handsome lifetime annuity that Benlowes in more affluent days had promised him, and Schoren's widow eventually won a judgment for more money than Benlowes had. Bankrupt, he was forced to leave his London lodgings for the Blounts' home in Mapledurham, near Reading, to find refuge from process servers: not successfully, for eventually he was arrested and held in prison in Oxford for a few weeks or months, until Blount paid the debt.

Benlowes took lodgings in Oxford and for nearly a decade was able to fulfill a dream of at least fifteen years' standing, pursuing a quiet existence among academic friends and reading in the Bodleian. Oxford gave him happiness, which he repaid with eulogies in Latin and English. Included in his *Oxonii Encomium* (1672) was "On Oxford, the Muses Paradise," and it represented a major change in Benlowes's style. Written as an ode in irregular rhymed stanzas, its labored classical allusions and poetic diction suggest that he had absorbed newer fashions in poetry. He published other things, including an echo poem, *Echo Veridica Joco-seria* (1673), essentially a reworking of the 1646 diatribe *Papa Perstrictus*. He had little money – a small annuity in Walter Blount's will was paid irregularly – and when he died, in the cold December of 1676, his friends took up a collection to bury him.

Theophila, his major work, begins traditionally enough with "The Author's Design," in both Latin and English versions – ten couplets offering a quasi-epic statement of theme ("Of CHRIST, and of the SPOUSES *Sighs,* I sing, / And of the *Joyes* that from Those *Ardors* spring"), an exorcism of evils reminiscent of Milton's "Il Penseroso" ("Blinde *Lust,* pack hence, / Hence *Pride, . . . Wealth . . . , Envie, . . . / . . . / . . . Calumnie,* / And . . . *Discord, . . . / . . .* with all *Sins Troop*"), and an appeal to Jesus to be "PATRON to my present *Cause.*" The "Spouse" is the God-loving soul Theophila, the heroine of the entire work; she is a literary descendant of Herman Hugo's (and Quarles's) Anima. Her spiritual adventures are evidently intended to move especially the "Ladies," to whom the next unit of eight triplets is addressed. The advice that they should

> Survey THEOPHIA; her *Rules* apply,
> That You may *live,* as You would *die:*
> VIRTUE enamels *Life;* ' Tis GRACE doth *glorifie*

suggests that Benlowes is thinking of his work within a tradition of spiritual direction that would

include, for example, Crashaw's poem to Susan Feilding, Countess of Denbigh.

After this opening the book comprises 1) a core of nine cantos – eight titled as a group "Theophila's Love-Sacrifice," introduced by "The Prelibation to the Sacrifice" – some twenty-eight hundred lines in all plus a prose "Summary" and "Prayer" following the introductory canto; 2) two supplementary units of two cantos each (numbered 10 to 13); and 3) miscellaneous pieces in verse and prose before, after, and interspersed, plus nineteen full-page and six smaller engravings.

The core cantos have the same general pattern of 100 numbered tercets in the unusual stanzaic form described above, with an "Argument" preceding in both Latin and English and a Latin quatrain at the end; but there are exceptions. For example, stanza 100 of "The Prelibation," where Benlowes describes his poem as "Loves Offering," is 10 lines within an architectural altar design. The first 180 lines of canto 4 are in groups of 6 (5 pentameters and a closing Alexandrine), but each group gets two numbers so as to maintain the stanza count of 100 for the canto. Canto 9 has 100 pentameter distichs – and a parallel version in Latin.

The "Prelibation" establishes the Christian Platonic poetics of the work: though the soul is held in *"pris'ning* Clay" the Fancy may "mount . . . to GLORIES Sphere," but poetry of wanton love or drunken reveling belongs rather to the bestial than the spiritual side of man. Better to reject the "cheating *World* " and Sin (personified in stanzas 48–52), tuning "the *Souls Theorb'* " to the "grave *Dorick Epods*" of "th' *Enthusiastick* MUSE." There follows a long passage in praise of religious poetry, weaving in bits from Herbert and John Cleveland:

> *Hymns* ravish those who *Pulpets* fly;
> Convert dull *Lead* to active *Gold* by LOVE-CHYMIE.

> As *Natures* prime *Confectioner,* the BEE,
> By her Flow'r-nibling *Chymistrie,*
> Turns *Vert* to *Or:* So, VERSE gross *Prose* does rarifie.

Art is worthless, however, without good deeds, through Grace to "aid" us "strugling under this sad Load of Clay."

Benlowes proceeds, in "The Summary of the Poem," to set forth a neat triadic structure for the narrative to follow: humility, zeal, contemplation, or the purgative, illuminative, and unitive ways of the mystical ascent, characterized by sincerity, fervency, and ecstasy, respectively. This outline becomes obscured, however, by the greatly different lengths of the three parts of the narrative – one canto, two, and four; by a long digression in canto 3 on the present state of England; by a tendency to circle back to favorite topics; and by too little difference in poetic tone between the "Fervent" part of the narrative and the "Extatical" part. It would be a mistake, however, to dismiss Benlowes's organization as nonexistent.

Canto 2 is "The Humiliation," the purgative way. A quick summary of the Creation and Fall leads to the stanza,

> Still in our Maw that *Apples* Core doth stick,
> Which they did swallow, and the thick
> Rinde of forbidden *Fruit* has left our Nature sick.

The effects of sin and the torments of hell, describable only in a series of paradoxes, set the stage for a call to repentance "Now." The urgency calls forth an arsenal of rhetorical devices: anaphora setting out a series of conceits (with a heavy debt for imagery to Benlowes's friend James Howell) –

> Before the *Suns* long Shadows span up Night;
> E're on thy shaking *Head* Snowes light;
> E're round thy palsy'd *Heart* Ice be congealèd quite;
>
> E're in thy Pocket thou thine *Eyes* dost wear;
> E're thy *Bones* serve for Calender;
> E're in thy *Hand*'s thy Leg, or Silver in thy *Hair;*

the shock tactics of charnel imagery as in the description of the Last Judgment when "queazie-stomackt *Graves* disgorge Worms fatning Chear"; or the dry, academic wordplay of "*Death* is a *Noun,* yet not *declin'd* in any *Case.*" "Unhing'd with Fear," Theophila repents, weeps for her lack of tears, "runs *Faiths* Course; breaks through *Despair,* / O'retakes *Hope,*" is stirred to grief by the inner sight of the incarnate and crucified God, and begins to pray. Theophila, of course, being the projection of the poet's own spirit, is carefully Protestant: "To Angel-Intercessor, I'm forbid / To pray." At length "the loud Volleyes of her *Pray'rs* begin / To make a Breach," the fortress of sin is overcome and "HEAV'N, storm'd by Violence, yields." Theophila has become regenerate.

Cantos 3, "The Restauration," and 4, "The Inamoration," make up part 2 as set forth in the "Summary," the second degree in Theophila's "ascen[t] to her BELOV'D," zeal (the illuminative way); but first there is a new invoking of the "Muse." The poet would emulate "noble *Du-bartas*" dancing "in a high-flown *Trance,*" reject the snares of worldly val-

ues, and claim the *furor poeticus* (poetic frenzy) "struck with Enthean Fire."

Theophila's new life begins: "GRACE dawns when *Nature* sets." Her beauty is no longer "rottenness skin'd o're," but "HEAV'NS brighter LOVE brighten[s] this *lovely Dame,*" and a catalogue of comparisons suitable for the most sensuous of Elizabethan epithalamia is required to describe her attractions. The fictitious ("wit-feign'd") beauty of Pandora is as far inferior to that of the virtuous soul as moonlight to the sun: "Thee, THEOPHIL, *Dayes* sparkling *Eye* we call." She has become a "*Feast*" for "sacred *Poets,*" who not only celebrate her fame with "Soul-ravishing" music but inspire Theophila herself to the quest for "HEAV'N *on* Earth" through music-nourished ecstasy.

Is such private fruition possible in the midst of a society torn by civil strife? Theophila in reply laments the current state of England and expresses a longing for peace, then breaks off in tears, "flowing *Rhet'rick*" by which "to GOD *She* would her *Heav'n-ascending Raptures* rear." The poet is persuaded to believe that individual piety may even help to heal the nation's wounds:

> If, THEOPHIL, thy LOVE-SONG can't asswage
> The *Fate* incumbent on this *Age,*
> No Time to *write,* but *weep;* For we are ripe for *Rage!*

Perhaps to "assuage" is what he conceives his role to be in these years of crisis.

The "Love-Song" referred to comes in canto 4 but is preceded by "Theophila's Soliloquie" in which she prepares to sing by meditating on the desired union of divine and human spirits, the reconciling power of divine love, and the longed-for consummation when faith, hope, and time – elements of earthly experience – give way to vision, fruition, and eternity. Then in the song itself a celebration of the name of Jesus unfolds into a longing for union with the heavenly "SPOUSE," in language borrowed from the Song of Songs and other traditional expressions of erotic spirituality. Both these segments of the canto have used the six-line groupings described above, but in the last forty stanzas Benlowes returns to his tercets. He narrates how "this Inamor'd VOT'RESSE" dreams of Christ coming to her and whispering, "*Come, come away,*" and wakens to offer prayers "more passionate, than *witty*" until finally

> *She* swound;
> O'recome with *Zeal,* She sunk to th' Ground:
> Darts of intolerable *Sweets* her *Soul* did wound.
>
> She lay with flaming LOVE empierc't to th' *Heart:*

Frontispiece to canto 5 of Theophila, *depicting the title character, who points to a symbol of herself being carried to heaven, while the author looks on*

Wak't, As *She* bled, *She* kist the *Dart;*
Then sigh'd. *Take all I am, or have! All, All* THOU *art!*

Benlowes is here at his most Crashavian. Theophila's prayers are granted: she will proceed to the unitive stage, to ecstasy.

Cantos 5 to 8 make up part 3, Theophila's ecstatic vision, marked off by a fresh prayer for divine aid:

Clear-sighted FAITH, point out the Way; I will
Neglect curl'd *Phrases* frizzled *Skill:*
Humble DEVOTION, lift *Thou* up my flagging *Quill.*

"Can squeaking *Reeds*," he adds, "sound forth the *Organs* full delight?" Human "dwarf-words" cannot "scan" heaven; "since *Time* began, / What constitutes

a *Gnat* was ne're found out by *Man.*" Benlowes rings changes of his own on the unanswerable questions put to Job in a passage that anticipates Pope's in the *Essay on Man* (1732–1734) but without Pope's scorn. No sooner has the poet concluded that this task requires an angel than his own vision begins and he is "*dazled*" by "a FORM ANGELLICK," which turns out to be "glorify'd THEOPHILA" describing with "*Voice-Musick*" her ecstatic experience. In the rest of canto 5, "The Representation," she narrates her upward progress through the atmosphere ("*I spare t'unlock those* Treasuries *Of* Snow; / *Or tell what paints the rainy* Bowe") and the Ptolemaic spheres. Her precise account of the distance of the primum mobile – a millstone dropped from there would take 120 years to reach Earth – reflects Benlowes's rather naive fascination with astronomical numbers (see also stanza 49). In stanza 56 she enters "HEAV'NS Suburbs," far brighter than the Sun: "Eyes, *till* glorify'd, *cannot the same behold.*" An attempt is made to define heaven in precise philosophical terms (purely spiritual, outside the universe but part of the creation, changeless), but this is seen to be inadequate:

> Who can THEE *fully state?*
> *For clearer knowledge* Man *must wait;*
> *First shoot* Deaths *Gulf. . . .*

At this point the poet listening to Theophila's account is so bursting with "zeal" that he interrupts for four stanzas, borrowing from Milton to speak of "BLISSE, / That with an individual *Kisse* / Greets Thee for ever" and abruptly adding, "Pardon this *Parenthesis.*" Hardly has Theophila resumed than the poet interrupts again, this time to pray for a heart

> Of WISDOM to attempt, proceed, and end
> What never Was, Is, Can be penn'd!
> (May *Spots* in *Maps* (dumb *Teachers*) *Empires* comprehend?[ )]

The attempt to describe heaven's dazzling glory, compared to which the stars are more dim than July's "*hairy* Worms *that glow,*" and from which even Saint Paul "did . . . recoyl," leads Theophila herself to reflections on the inadequacy of human language:

> Sense *knows not 'bove* Court-Triumphs, Thrones, *or*
>   *Kings,*
>   Gems, Musick, Beauties, Banquetings,
> *Without such* Tropes *it can't unfold* Spiritual Things.

Even with such tropes, however heightened in the imagination, "*one may t' a* Glimps, *None to a* Half *can rise.*" The experience of souls thus "*made* divine" and "*super-radiant . . . / From th' ever-flowing* SPRING *of the* refulgent TRINE" is "*beyond* Report *of high'st* Discourse" and "*'bove all* Art." Only by paraphrasing the Apocalypse can Theophila describe the heavenly city, and she exclaims, "HEAV'N *may be* gain'd *on* Earth, *but never* understood!"

   The distinction between the two speakers becomes increasingly difficult to maintain, for the heroine Theophila is not a generic human soul but the poet's own. Thus at the beginning of canto 6, "The Association," it is not fully clear which one goes on to describe the inhabitants of heaven, beginning with the martyrs and apostles. Paul, John, and Mary Magdalene are accorded a stanza each, and an allusion to Augustine is the occasion for a remarkable baroque conceit about tears:

> Parcht *Africks* GLORY, born in's Mothers Eyes,
>   (An happier *Offspring* of her *Cries,*
> Than of her *Womb*) here to ecstatick LOVE does rise.

This leads to stanzas in praise of divine love, and the roll call of the blessed continues with the virgins, in particular Saint Mary, in whose honor an "*Ode*" is inserted, consisting of many of the traditional Marian tropes and paradoxes. Mary responds in a single stanza based on the Magnificat. The poet then gives up the attempt to "anatomize the glorious *List*" of the saints: "*Silence* most *Rhet'rick* hath." He goes on to describe the particulars of their blissful state, culminating in their music — led by King David, here given a song of sixteen stanzas which combines the language of psalm paraphrase with that of philosophic discourse. The rest of the canto is devoted to the other inhabitants of heaven, the "bright-harnessed INTELLIGENCIES" whose "Ninefold QUIRE" makes such music as to "over-pow'r the *Windings* of a mortal *Ear.*" (For all his allegiance to a medieval cosmology, Benlowes was also interested in the anatomical inquiries of his time; he speaks elsewhere of dissection.) The narrator comments,

> Who MUSICK hate, in barb'rous *Discord* rowle;
>   In HEAV'N there is not such a Soul;
> For, there's *All-Harmony.* SAINTS sing, the *damned* howl.

   "May a *Creature,* its CREATORS GLORY write?" are the final words of canto 6. In canto 7, "The Contemplation," Benlowes struggles to do so, but not before the longest invocation yet. His starting point must be the inconceivability of eternity and the other infinite attributes of deity. Once again the only possible metaphor for the divine is light, and Benlowes reaches beyond his previous efforts in seeking a comparison for God's splendor. If all bright things in the universe, "all *Eyes* of *Earth, Skie,* HEAV'N" could be "combin'd, / And to one *Optick* point confin'd," God's splendor "would ev'n strike *That* blind!" Although "best *Eloquence* is *languid*" and "*Wit*" and "*Language* fail," Benlowes will "that GRACE implore, W^ch may *this* GLORY *show.*"

   It may be done in part with negatives ("Unbegun," "*sprung of* THY SELF, *or rather no way sprung*") and paradoxes ("*at once the* Plentitude *of All, and yet but* ONE") , in part with an account of the relation between God and all else ("PARENT *of* Beings, *Entities sole Stud*") , in part by a combination, again, of philosophical and biblical language. Benlowes recognizes the frequently metaphorical quality of the latter: "*Whole* Natures *six Dayes* Work *took up but six* Words *place.*" There is a strongly Platonic cast to his concept of Creation:

> *The optick Glass we of thy* PRÆSCIENCE *may*
> *Call th'* Ark, *where all* Idæas *lay,*
> *By which each* Entitie THOU *dost at first pourtray!*

Paradox again must express the relation of God to time and space and to the free will of creatures. The latter topic leads to presenting once again the Incarnation, the life of Christ, his passion and victory, and the Holy Spirit. The ecstasy builds. God is understood as himself the "BEATITUDE / *Which swallows us, yet swim we in this* LIVING FLOUD."

Canto 7 was to have been the last, but one hundred tercets proved insufficient for the subject. So the poet-speaker proceeds with canto 8, "The Admiration," significantly addressing Theophila as "Projection *to my* Soul" and begging her to tell now "*of* GODS *hid* NATURE." She rebukes him for not realizing that the "ABYSSE" is, by definition, unfathomable, but then proceeds to answer his request by taking up a final theme, the mystery of the Trinity. She begins by discoursing on the unity and "SELF-LIFE" of God; once that is firmly established, "All's ty'd in this *Love-knot:* JEHOVAH's LOVE," she says, and out of that, following Saint Augustine, the doctrine of the Trinity unfolds. First there is the slim evidence of biblical texts, then the language of theological abstraction, in the course of which a second "Mysterie," the Incarnation, is expounded. Finally, as an accommodation to human intellect –

> What *Soul* will have this TRIAD for his *Book,*
> With *Faith* must on the *Back-parts* look,
> For, with HIS glorious FACE, blind are ev'n SERAPHS
> strook!

– Benlowes offers the traditional analogies of a sort of triunity in "*Sols* Substance" and in the human mind: intellect, memory, will.

The ecstatic vision completed, what remains is to return to earthly life. Theophila advises that this wholly self-contained deity is, for all creatures, the absolute source of all good, apart from whom "*Caitives* [in Hell] pine, yet still their *Tortures* grow." "These *Esaus* sold their BLISSE," ironically, "for *Sin,* that worse than *Nothing* is." The mention of particular sinners, including Dives in Christ's parable, leads to an attack on the contemporary neglect of the homeless and hungry by those who have the role of "GODS Steward" – a role that Benlowes as a man of wealth took quite seriously. This in turn prompts the cry, "Love, Disengage *us* of our *selves*!," followed by a lyric on spiritual love that describes

union with God in terms of melted ice becoming one with the ocean. She recommends prayer, fasting, and faith as means through which to contemn the attractions of the world and pursue heavenly ends. Recommending, finally, a life of retirement and contemplation, she leaves the narrator to follow her example and "re-act her Part."

Theophila's story is now finished, but Benlowes cannot stop writing. He concludes the "Love-Sacrifice" with "Hecatombe IX" in one hundred Latin distichs, makes an English version – canto 9, "The Recapitulation. And Pourtrait of a Heav'nly breathing Soul" – based loosely on the Latin, and includes both, side by side, prefaced with a pair of odelike stanzas, twenty-five lines in all, each irregular in line length and unrhymed save for a final couplet. Benlowes here thinks of himself as "a holier *Ovid,*" celebrating a love which, though it begins "feebly" in one's regard for working associates and grows in the domestic sphere and toward country and king, becomes intense only when directed "to GOD" and, "ravisht with *Ecstasie,* It self *transcends.*"

The organization of the canto proper is the most difficult yet to detect, in part because the form, in pentameter distichs, tends to give us often independent units disjoined from one another in imagery. It does not strictly recapitulate the first eight cantos in abridgment or abstract form; rather it moves through some half-dozen themes also found there, bringing into slightly sharper focus the notion of arousing others by means of Theophila's story to follow her example. There is, first, an address to the "MUSE" which is essentially a prayer to God, declaring the poet's "ZEAL" (*Eros*) to convey in poetry his experience of divine love and his utter dependence on Christ to be able to do so. He would offer now *his* love-sacrifice, "This Verse-*Hecatomb,*" rejecting "*Springs* prophane" in favor of Siloam. "Trampling vain *Labours,* with loose *Wits* defil'd, / The Hallow'd BRAIN brings forth a *Spritely* [*spirituale*] *Childe.*" These thoughts lead to a passage on the rejection of worldly values in favor of spiritual, a passage markedly gnomic in style somewhat in the fashion of Herbert's "Church Porch." Included is a brief lament for a nation where through the church's neglect the "*Flocks* are pin'd"; but "the JUDGE in Time will come / Unthought of," and the poet prays to Christ for peace, joining his voice with those of other agrarian Royalist poets in the plea, "Let not that Hand bear Arms, that sowes the Earth." Then at length Theophila appears, "burn[ing], pierc't . . . with firie Dart," who is urged to "be *Bellows*" also: "As thy *Flames* grow,

Let those *Flames* Others fill." The poet turns over to her his tools of "*Wit*" and "*Judgement*" to effect moral reformation in the audience. Then comes the promised portrait of Theophila, beginning and ending with her virtues but made up largely of a reprise of the lyrical celebration of the heroine's physical beauties first encountered in canto 3, stanzas 26 to 35 (though verbally quite independent of that passage). Herself a vessel of divine love, she is an "*Elixir*" that he prays will "convert to *Gold* the worthlesse *Dross* in me"; and after three distichs offering emblematic images for such alchemical conversion, the poet-speaker turns again to his own role: "THOU shew'dst the *Way,* I'll prosecute the *Same.*" Beginning with a celebration of Christ's "*Pledge* of LOVE" in the Eucharist — "Is GOD both *Meat* and *Lover?*" — he responds by offering himself wholly to Christ and expressing, in traditional language of mysticism derived partly from the Song of Songs, a yearning for union with God and dying to earthly things.

Two appended poems complete *Theophila,* "The Vanitie of the World" and "The Sweetness of Retirement," each in two cantos with subtitles after the pattern of the previous nine: "The Abnegation" and "The Disincantation" for "Vanitie"; "The Segregation" and "The Reinvitation" for "Retirement." This pattern suggests that Benlowes thinks of the whole *Theophila* as unified. Indeed "Vanitie" and "Retirement" repeat some themes of "Theophila's Love-Sacrifice," the rejection of the world and a yearning for union with God — no longer, however, under the image of a personified human soul but in propria persona. The narrative of Theophila's journey, which occupied the core cantos, has become part of a larger implied narrative, that of the poet's progress through the labor of composition.

"Vanitie" (cantos 10 and 11) follows the established structure of one hundred tercets per canto. Prefacing the whole are Owen Felltham's poem "Upon the Vanitie of the World"; a Latin prose passage with a translation into English blank verse (Benlowes's only known use of that form); and a Latin poem of twenty-eight lines, "Mundo immundo." Benlowes announces that his "sharpned *Muse*" will now take up "Scourges of *Satyrick Vein,* / To lash the *World.*" "Sound *Reason*" will be his guide, "not sleight *Wit.*" He attacks first the "*World,*" personified as a "*Jugler*" and deceiver; this goes on for eighteen stanzas. He has an eye for irony: "*Gluttons,* who make themselves *Spittles* of each *Disease.*"

Deaths *Serjeant* soon thy courted *Helens* must
    Attach, whose *Eyes,* now *Orbs* of *Lust,*
The *Worms* shall feed on, till they crumble into *Dust.*

Now that the war is over, he is disturbed over the city's pursuit of wealth, "where still more *Noise* than *Sense* they vent, / And, *now* as much to *Gold,* as *late* to *Battles* bent." "I'll countercharm thy *Spells,*" he says, and in stanzas 25 to 47 he offers precepts and similes to expose the world's pretense. A fine description of a storm at sea is followed by the characterization of World as "Lifes Storm."

Benlowes now adopts the character sketch as a satiric device. The sin of ambition is described under the character of Aspiro, and the emptiness of ambition is stated in these lines:

Ev'n *That* to which *Prides* touring *Project* flies,
    When graspt, soon by *Fruition* dies:
Great *Fears,* great *Hopes,* great *Plots,* great *Men* make Tragedies!

In contrast, the true way to rise is by falling and by conquering sin. The miser Avaro is next — "as void of *Grace,* as stor'd / With *Gold,* the GOD his *Soul* ador'd" and having no pity for the poor. Ironically, Avaro's "*Dropsie* breeds *Consumption* [a pun] in [his] Heir" — whose very unfilial words are then imagined. Again, the section ends with a positive exhortation, to "cast over-board" "the dismall *Fraught* of sinking *Sins.*"

The heir, Avaro's son Volupto, occupies two-thirds of canto 11, and the behavior and manners of this "spruce *Gallant*" — starting with horse racing in Hyde Park — give an interesting picture of fashionable city life. Volupto dances, acts in questionable entertainments, is "modish" in his grooming — here the moralist in Benlowes interrupts the portrait to comment:

How blazing Tapers waste Lifes blink away
    In Socket of their mouldring Clay!
How powder'd Curls do sin-polluted Dust bewray!

As *Prudence* fram'd Art to be Natures Ape,
    So *Pride* forms Nature to Arts shape:
Corrupted Wine is worst that's prest from richest Grape.

The mention of wine inspires a passage on the epicurean vices, with such vivid imagery as in the line, "The Gluttons Teeth their Graves prepare." The social aspect of ethics is prominent in the charge that "on Tenants Sweat feeds rampant Waste" and "thou ... / Grind'st 'twixt thy Teeth the starving Poor"; but equally, "the Spark" himself suffers, has "tumultuous Dreams," and grows

cropsick. Post for *Physicks* Skill;
Phlebotomize he must, and take the *Vomit* Pill.

Doctor, the Cause of this Distemper state us.
  His Cachexie results from Flatus
Hypocondrunkicus ex Crapulâ creatus.

Ridiculously decked out by his tailor, Volupto is the victim of his prosperity, prizing, like the popular stereotype of a Roman cardinal, "Paris [the allusion may be to the French king Henry IV] . . . 'bove Paradise." He is the victim also of "pomp" and its attendant code of honor, and in five stanzas Benlowes expands on Hamlet's satiric remarks on those easily inflamed to fight duels. "Fierce *Balaam,*" he writes, "hold thy Hand, and smite no Asse / But him i'th' Saddle"; but Volupto, after being successively ape, swine, and peacock, has become a tiger. The moralist's comment:

They'r gross, not Great, who serve wild Laws of
    Blood;
  Such, only *Great,* who dare be *Good:*
GRACE buoies up *Honor,* which, without It, sticks in mud.

To cure him would be as difficult as squaring the circle or finding the Northwest Passage. "Idle Sloth" is a sort of death-in-life, the fate of those who, "for Lifes circumstance, the *Cause* of living wa[i]ve." Benlowes paraphrases the opening of the Westminster *Shorter Catechism* (1647):

Now, to what End can we conceive Mans Frame,
  Save to the *Glory* of GODS Name,
And his eternal *Blisse,* included in the Same.

Volupto, now renamed Nymphadoro, is thoroughly taken in by a "*Dame* of Pleasure" who is described at length. On this "*Courtesan*" he lavishes his wealth, "to gain the Shade of Joy, which, soon as gaind, decayes." Even were she an heiress, the young man should avoid her: "O, Joyes unsound / From light-bred *Daughters,* though they weigh ten thousand pound." Nymphadoro is left "to bebrine [his] Woes," but unfortunately the tears are not ones of repentance – a theme which takes up the rest of the canto:

Never too late does true *Repentance* sue;
  Yet, late *Repentance* seldom's true:
Who would not, when they might, may, when they
    would, It rue.

Benlowes's Metaphysical wit achieves a remarkable strength of expression in a few good lines in this section:

Men in their Generations live by turns;
  Their Light soon to its Socket burns;
Then to converse with *Spirits* they go, & None returns.

Tomb-pendant Scutcheons, pompous Rags of State,
  Those gorgeous Bubbles but relate
The thing that was, nere liv'd: 'Tis *Goodness* gildeth
    Fate.

Grace outlasts marble Vaults: *That* crowns Expense;
  Brass is shortliv'd to *Innocence:*
Times greedy Self shall one Day find its Præter-
    tense.

When *Heav'ns* that had their Deluge-dropsie, shall
  Their burning Feaver have; When All
Is one Combustion; when *Sol* seems a black burnt Ball:

When *Nature's* laid asleep in her own Urn;
  When, what was drown'd at first, shall burn;
Then, Sinners into quenchless Flames, Sins Mulct,
    shall turn!

Nere shall a cooling Julep Such appease,
  Whom Brimstone Torrents without Ease
Enrage, i'th dungeon of dark flames, and burning Seas!

In Center of the terrible Abysse,
  Remotest from supernall Blisse,
That horrid, hideous, gloomy, endlesse Dungeon is!

The poet returns to address the world; if hell is "the Upshot" of its offers – "Vanish beneath my scorn. Goe, *World,* recant, amend."

The second of the two appended poems, "The Sweetnesse of Retirement, or The Happinesse of a Private Life," comprises cantos 12 and 13, though the exact title seems not to have concerned Benlowes, for in 13 it appears as "The Pleasure of Retirement." Unable finally to limit himself to 100 tercets, he gave each canto 120. "Retirement" belongs, as Maren-Sofie Røstvig has shown, to a Christianized *beatus ille* (happy man) tradition adapted from Augustan poets. It is especially indebted to the Neo-Latin Jesuit poet Casimire Sarbiewski and, for descriptions of the landscape, to Milton's "L'Allegro." A twenty-eight-line Latin "Argument" states the theme, "Quies Animæ, sanctusque Recessus," and presents a sylvan scene described in detail as a temple. The poem itself begins with a link to "Vanitie," the companion piece – "Waste not an other Word on *Fools*" (followed by seventeen stanzas of satire against the "vain *World*" with its pursuit of "comb'rous Gain" and its religious corruption and strife, in contrast to the "humble *Goodness*" of "fraudlesse Swains"). Heavenly "discourse" must replace "fools Chat"; the recipe for happiness in solitude includes spiritual nourishment from Scripture and contemplation and the company of "a *Friend,* who gilds Delight." History, nature, and Scripture offer examples of the value of retirement; "sweet *Secesse*" will "nurse ... Happinesse" and guide one to virtue, with sense kept in subjection to reason. "Religious *Maries* Leisure" is to be emulated, as well as violets and strawberries, "*Emblem* of sweet *Blisse,* which low and hidden lies." "We rule our conquer'd Selves"; the Golden Age has returned.

The remainder of "Retirement" is built around three passages of sensuous nature description set at dawn, noon, and evening. The morning walk is filled with bird songs that are heard as "hoarse Laments" and evoke a sympathetic response in the "melting *Eyes*" of the strollers as they recall the devastation of civil war. This leads in turn to expressions of personal penitence and reflections on the efficacy of tears, which are seen in conceit as a salty sea bearing pilgrims to Heaven. The line "But whether stray'st thou, *Grief*?" ends the digression, and the description of landscape resumes, with moralizing interlarded. For example, a "curled *Stream*" is "meandring underneath the Hill: / Thus, Stream-like, glides our Life to *Deaths* broad Ocean still." Close observation of nature produces a wonder born of unusual perspective ("More than at Tusks of Bores we wonder at / This *Moths* strange Teeth" – a quotation of Hugo of Saint Victor); moral commonplaces (analogies between a beehive and a state); and the "abstruser Depths" of revelation: "By Observation GOD is seen in all wee see." Benlowes follows a well-established tradition of meditating on the book of creatures (nature). Rock, stream, or sea calls to mind the Exodus miracles; flowers, the brevity of life, and thus, yet again, the vanity of the world. Such reflections are Theophila's lingering legacy to the poet-speaker. "*Troy*'s gone"; even "vast *Pyramids*" and "ambitious *Obelisks*" have passed away; only the redeemed soul is immortal. The "mental Buds we from each Object take" inspire to ecstatic hymns in God's praise, especially for the abundance of his providence in nature: bath, drink, food, clothing, fuel, and the panacea tobacco. By stanza 120 it is time to pause in the journey and be refreshed; "with next rising *Sun*" is promised a final, "closing *Lay*."

The last canto begins by recounting adventures in paradise at blazing noon, in a context of rural labor. The spectators' detachment makes even open country a *hortus conclusus* (enclosed garden). "We" watch the mower at work, with his "big-swoln Veins" (an anticipation of Andrew Marvell), go fishing in "a Brook of liquid *Silver*," visit "harmlesse *Shepherds*" and

imitate them by tending, with "internal Vigils," the "disperst Flocks of our rambling Minde."

The spectators observe a shearing, hear (in language reminiscent of "L'Allegro") "the merry Hamlet Bells chime *Holy Day*," then turn and see the cattle grazing or plowing and the ripening grain, "dry Seas, with golden Surges." Then it is harvest time, and the sound of gnats replaces that of grasshoppers, and orchards are more than paradisal, bearing "fruit that from Taste of Death is free, / And such as gives Delight with choice Varietie." Yet a garden of such delight is only the setting for the greater delights of the "thriving *Minde*," content with little and therefore "rich at an inestimable Rate":

> He in Himself, Himself to rule, retires;
>   And can, or blow, or quench his Fires:
> All *Blessings* up are bound in bounding up *Desires.*
>
> His little *World* commands the Great....

Instead of the May Day activity of "London Gallants ..., / Coacht through Hide Park, to eye, be ey'd, / Which *Dayes* vain Cost might for the Poor a *Yeer* provide," the sequestered person walks with Christ in a garden which is also a "Bride-room," with Scripturia the soul's bride who both produces "*Soul-Elevations*" and directs how they may be maintained. "On *Feast-Dayes* from that *Bowr* to *Church* we haste, / Where HEAV'N dissolves into *Repast*" in the eucharistic banquet, the ecstasy of which abolishes "all Creature Love." He prays never to be deprived of that feast. He meditates on the values of affliction, using emblematic images and the example of Queen Elizabeth, and cries out with Augustine for a sacrificial union with God, though it be by death. The Christian Platonism often associated with this poetic tradition is, however, firmly overridden by an affirmation of bodily resurrection:

> Forbid the Banes [banns] 'twixt *Soul* and *Body* joyn'd,
>   The *Corps* but falls to be refin'd,
> And re-espous'd unto the Glorifi'd high *Minde.*

These thoughts carry the reader to twilight, when

>   the *Whislers* knock from *Plough*;
>   The droiling *Swineheards* Drum beats now;
> *Maids* have their *Cur*[*t*]*sies* made to th' spungy-teated
>   Cow.

All things go to rest, the speaker also to his cottage, "By *Innocence* protected, not / By *Guards.*" It is time for evensong, and a passage celebrating the value of prayer begins with an appositive series reminiscent in its rhetoric (though in none of its language) of Herbert's "Prayer" sonnet. This concludes with the thought that prayer, as the means by which the poor requite "Alms receiv'd," "beatifies" the "Grange" of the more well-to-do – who, in turn, have an obligation of charity. Thus is the Stoic sentiment of the contempt of fortune given a New Testament coloration:

> Enricht, lets darn up Want; what *Fortune* can
> Or give, or take away from Man,
> We prize not much: HEAV'N payes the good *Samaritan.*

Life so governed is a preparation for death and an anticipation of Heaven. "*Sequestration*" forgoes worldly "*Rumour*" in favor of true fame, that is, "HEAV'NS *Paroll*." Death is the "*Saints* Birth-day," the "Womb" of "IMMORTALITIE." The poem ends with a prayer for pardon and for grace to live indeed in this fashion and with a renunciation of poetry now that his task is finished: "My slender Pen to th'World I give; / My only study shall be how to *live, to live*."

Theophila* as it was published includes, besides the illustrations which are also part of the design, a third layer of literary material. It goes quite beyond the usual front matter for such a work, the author's preface and eleven commendatory poems by friends and admirers including a very laudatory Davenant. Following the preface are a list of "The severall Cantos" (which includes at the end one canto, "The Termination," that is not part of the finished book); a section, part prose and part verse, called "Pneumato-Sarco-Machia: or Theophila's Spiritual Warfare," which introduces an entirely different metaphor for the narrative to follow – an image that is then promptly dropped; and two other introductory poems by the author. Later, just after the commendatory verses, is an epigram (in both Latin and English versions) modestly disclaiming their adulation and insisting that God is rather to be praised. This is followed by two epigrams on the advantages of the sacred over the secular muse. At last we are ready for "The Prelibation"; and after that first canto comes a prose "Summary," "The Authors Prayer," and, arranged in pedestal shape, a dedication of the following work to the praise of Christ.

In the last third of the book several additional shorter pieces in Latin verse and prose are scattered between cantos – perhaps sometimes just to fill blank half-pages – and three translations into Latin verse of earlier cantos are offered: the "Prælibatio" translated by Benlowes's friend Alexander Ross and

canto 3 by an unidentified hand, inserted between "Theophila's Love-Sacrifice" and "The Vanitie of the World," and canto 7 translated by Jeremy Collier the Elder, appended after canto 13. This is followed by "Peroratio Eucharistica," a Latin poem in which Benlowes speaks of his European travels. On an engraved plate at the end there is another Latin poem, possibly by him, an intricate acrostic on the passion and resurrection of Christ written in the ancient medieval *carmina figurata* (figured poems) tradition which was enjoying a revival in the Continental baroque. The initial letters of the lines read vertically *Ardeo amore tui, mundi Saluator Iesu* (I burn with love for thee, Jesus, Savior of the World); the final letters read, *Mors tua uita mea est; ardeo amore tui* (Thy death is my life; I burn with love for thee); and internal letters one above another within a design of three crosses quote the dying Christ and the two thieves.

Even after publishing he was still not satisfied. Five years later he attempted to distill *Theophila* in a poem of one hundred tercets called *The Summary of Wisedome* (1657). This consists of selected stanzas rearranged and heavily reedited, with a few new tercets to link them, and a Latin version on the facing pages. Most of it comes from the last four cantos of the larger work; their *contemptus mundi* (contempt for the world) attitude doubtless helped Benlowes cope with his growing financial woes. One new stanza comments pessimistically on current affairs:

> No Christian kings win by each other's loss;
> What one gets by retail, in gross
> All lose; while still the Crescent gains upon the Cross.

The last two words of *The Summary of Wisedome* are a typical pun on "the end."

Benlowes's concept of the creative process and the way *Theophila* outgrew his original conception are revealed in this stanza written as he neared completion of his core poem. Included is a note to himself on future work:

> While *Pride* of *Life,* and *Lust* o'th' *Eye* do quite
> Dazle the *World,* SAINTS out of Sight
> Retire, to view their BLISSE: On which some *Canto's* write.

That Benlowes should publish *Theophila* without removing from it such marks of the writing process (here several have been noted but by no means all) certainly contributes to an impression that the organization is chaotic, but this charge is tempered by the observation made above that Benlowes's epic has a dual narrative focus, the mystical journey and (together with other epic poets) the process of com-

Latin poem around the crosses at Calvary, at the end of Theophila

position. The digressions, sudden inspirations, difficulty in maintaining a putative design that was too neat, parenthetical asides, struggles with the inadequacy of human wit and "curl'd *Phrases* frizzled *Skill*" – all contribute to the second narrative.

Benlowes's preface for *Theophila* amply reveals, however, the attention he paid to the poetics of his task and to contemporary critical theory. The question of defining excellence in heroic poetry is newly in the air: Benlowes claims that "if *Actions* . . . advancing moral Vertue merit the title of *Heroick,* much more" must Theophila's spiritual combat. Benlowes has absorbed Thomas Hobbes's very recent pronouncement that "wit" includes fancy and judgment together, not fancy alone, and indeed he considers "pleasures of the *Understanding*" a higher achievement in poetry than those of sense. He cannot, however, join the materialist philosopher in dispensing with fancy altogether, committed as he is to the reality of a spiritual realm and therefore to the poet's reliance on a divinely inspired furor – "the internal Triumph of the Mind, rapt with S. *Paul* into the third Heaven, where She contemplates Ineffables" beyond the reach of philosophy. Benlowes would cultivate "*Divine Poesie* . . . the sacred Oracles of Faith put into melodious Anthems that make Musick ravishing, no earthly Jubilation being comparable to It." He explicitly values the "sublime" – a term that would not generally interest English critics for another generation, even though the first English translation of *On the Sublime* had been made by John Hall in 1652.

Benlowes's theory was better than his practice, however. Making all due allowance for the succeeding age's discomfort with enthusiasm, we must still acknowledge that Benlowes's judgment fell far short of balancing fancy in his poetry making. He valued "sound *Reason*" above "sleight *Wit*," yet slight wit offered temptations hard to resist, and an excuse was always at hand in the transcendence of his theme.

" 'Tis *Judgement* begets the Strength . . . of a Poem," he wrote, echoing Hobbes; but Hobbes had written, "Judgment begets the strength and structure." The omission is significant. Benlowes cared little for structure on any large scale. He had epic ambitions but lacked the necessary architectonic sense. In the preface he places Theophila's heroism in her spiritual warfare, but hardly any struggle remains after her purgative stage in canto 2, and even there the heroine is not brought to life as a character. He then gets Theophila so quickly to a sufficient height of mystical experience that it becomes very difficult to differentiate all that follows; it is possible with effort to discern narrative progress, but there is little variety in tone, except by the violent contrast of satirical digressions. That such digressions occur bears witness to the casual and associative, rather than architectural, nature of the book's structure.

To put the matter more favorably, Benlowes's best effects are in a phrase, a line or two, or at most a few stanzas. He was a man who loved words: unusual words with Hellenic authority, such as "enthean" and "epinician"; words that could fill a whole line, such as "incomprehensibility," or almost do so, such as "transcendently restorative"; words yoked together in combinations never heard before or since, such as "love-chemy," "ear-minstrels," "eye-tribute," "nose-carbuncles," "strutting-uddered"; brand-new words such as "discardinate" and "fulgurance" and dozens of others which the *Oxford English Dictionary* traces back, if at all, no farther than Benlowes. "*Poets*," he explained in a parenthesis, "have *Legislative Pow'r* of making *Words.*" He reveled as well in other poets' coinages and pretty turns of diction, freely borrowing to a degree even beyond the fashion of his age. There are a few places where one has to agree with the critics' frequent charge of "piracy," but often the echoes are merely an enthusiast's tribute to poets who have pleased him; and often he improves what he borrows.

Butler's epigram about Benlowes in his "Character of a Small Poet" (published posthumously in *The Genuine Remains,* 1759) – "Bar him the Imitation of something he has read, and he has no Image in his Thoughts" – goes too far. *Theophila* shows that Benlowes will let his fancy play with words and sometimes produce a tersely telling line – "Who wasts his Time, as Time wasts him" – a suggestive conjunction of ideas – "World, ev'n thy name a *whirling* Storm implies" – or a contrast made pointed by verbal similarity – "*the* Deiform'd *Soul* deform'd *by Sin.*" The play on "watch" in the following quotation neatly finishes a wittily satirical comparison:

> Swayns, by thresholds Sight,
> Observe, as well as Lords by Clocks of Gold, Times flight.
>
> Whose Crystal Shrines, like Oysters, gape each hour,
> Discov'ring Time by Figures Pow'r:
> That is the nobler *Watch,* foreshowes the threatning Shour.

He can use the various classical figures of repetition to good effect, he can turn out freshly thoughtful oxymora, and now and then he can produce a coinage worthy of James Joyce: "Hypocondrunkicus," "Proteustant," "deluge-dropsy."

The trouble is that he is constantly attempting such ornaments, and to try to follow the dance of his fancy can prove tiring; but sometimes in addition the footwork is too clumsy, or too perfunctory, to be called a dance. For the failure of Benlowes's judgment is also seen in a weak sense of proportion or of what is fitting and in his inability to quit when he has said enough or to prune his work so that only the best remains. A poem is judged by "Vigour not Length," he said in his preface, but he disregarded his own counsel.

Another smaller-scale effect that occupied him was the conceit. Here, again, he was capable of a vivid and memorable picture, such as that of Death coming along with a voider when the banquet of life is over, or a concise and witty phrase: death as "*the* Body *brought a bed* o'th' SOUL." He could also echo, however, what had become Metaphysical clichés – Theophila's repentant "*Grief*" that "draws up *Mysts* to fall in weeping *Rain*" – or, equally well, go back to the more Spenserian idiom by which he praises Theophila's beauty in cantos 3 and 9: these two passages are remarkably similar, yet the stock of Elizabethan conceits is sufficiently large that Benlowes need never repeat himself. He was more at home in the older style of conceit; he goes less often to the abstruse or mundane fields of discourse associated with the Metaphysical style; but two common features in his imagery give it a baroque flavor with a hint as well of the medieval. His taste for hieroglyphics is one, seen in the abundant use of comparisons found in emblem literature (occasionally alchemical, but he has at most a casual interest in hermetic philosophy), in the carmen figuratum on the last page of *Theophila,* and in typographically shaped material (fairly rare: on this, Butler has proved quite misleading). The other is the mystical-erotic imagery found throughout, perhaps most intensely in Theophila's soliloquy and the ensuing stanzas.

Also Metaphysical is his taste for strong, packed lines: "CHRIST's *Spice . . . Light, Triumph, Praise* to me; / *Music, Wine, Feast, Fame, Crown,* GOD; *All* to Thee." He goes overboard, however. Again, he knew sound principles: "O may our *Numbers* in sweet Musick flow; / Nor the least Harshnesse of *Elisions* know"; but in practice, awkward contractions are the price he often pays for his always exact syllable count. Moreover, he used ellipsis in English poetry as if he were writing Latin:

> This *World*'s the Field, GOD sows, his WORD the Seed,
> *Satan* the Thief, the *Good,* Corn, th' *Ill,* the Weed.

> Thou, *Light, Way, Life*; who *sees, walks, liveth* by
> That *Flame, Path, Strength,* does not *fall, fail,* nor *die.*

These examples are more difficult than most, the extreme application of a tendency to compression and rational order which often works quite effectively –

> Who CHRIST for *Spouse,* His *Cross* for Joynture has;
> His *Hand* supports, where's Rod doth passe:
> The LORD of *Angels,* He the KING of Suff'rings was

– especially when coupled with a rhetorical figure or two, schemes being much more characteristic for Benlowes than tropes: "Fall to prevent / Thy Fall"; "Who studie Death, ere dead, ere th' Resurrection rise";

> *Amazing!* Most *Inexplicably* RARE!
> O, if, but *Those* Who *Worthy* are,
> None may This LIGHT declare; None may This LIGHT
> declare!

Like Herbert, Benlowes has a particular fondness for gnomic expression: "*Waitings,* which ripen *Hopes,* are not *Delayes*"; "The best *Securitie* is ne're to be *secure.*"

At work in *Theophila* is an always active intellect, interested in metaphysics not as a source for witty conceits but as a subject for exploration and passionate discovery. Some of his most theological passages employ simile and analogy but little metaphor, yet they convey intense feeling. Sometimes the cosmic scope of his imagination strikes a poetic spark:

> *Chime out, ye* Crystal Sphears, *and tune your* Poles;
> Skies, *sound your* Base; *ere ye to Coals*
> *Dissolve, and tumble on the* Bonfire World *in Shoals.*

It happens often enough to reward the sympathetic reader.

Biography:

Harold Jenkins, *Edward Benlowes, 1602–1676: A Biography of a Minor Poet* (Cambridge, Mass.: Harvard University Press, 1952).

References:

Elizabeth Jane Bellamy, "Edward Benlowes' Theophila's Love-Sacrifice: The Paradox of the Mystical Poet," Ph.D. dissertation, Duke University, 1982;

Elizabeth Cook, *Seeing through Words* (New Haven & London: Yale University Press, 1986), pp. 24–33;

Elsie E. Duncan-Jones, "Benlowes and Alexander Brome," *Notes and Queries,* 201 (November 1956): 477;

Duncan-Jones, "Benlowes, Marvell, and the Divine Casimire: A Note," *Huntington Library Quarterly,* 20 (February 1957): 183–184;

Duncan-Jones, "Benlowes's Borrowings from George Herbert," *Review of English Studies,* new series 6, no. 22 (1955): 179–180;

K. G. Hamilton, *The Two Harmonies* (Oxford: Clarendon Press, 1963);

Richard Helgerson, *Self-Crowned Laureates* (Berkeley, Los Angeles & London: University of California Press, 1983);

Christopher Hill, "Benlowes and His Times," *Essays in Criticism,* 3 (1953): 143–151; revised in *The Collected Essays of Christopher Hill,* 3 volumes (Amherst: University of Massachusetts Press, 1985-1986), I: 197-203;

Harold Jenkins, "Benlowes and Milton," *Modern Language Review,* 43 (April 1948): 186–195;

Richard F. Kennedy, "Allusions to Herbert in John Spencer and Edward Benlowes," *George Herbert Journal,* 12 (Fall 1988): 45–47;

C. F. Main, "Benlowes, Brome, and the Bejewelled Nose," *Notes and Queries,* 202 (June 1957): 232–233;

Gerald W. Morton, "An Interesting Benlowes Allusion," *Notes and Queries,* 231 (September 1986): 392;

Robert H. Ray, *The Herbert Allusion-Book*, Texts and Studies, Studies in Philology, 83 (Fall 1986);

H. J. L. Robbie, "Benlowes: A Seventeenth-Century Plagiarist," *Modern Language Review,* 23 (July 1928): 342–344;

Edouard Roditi, "The Wisdom and Folly of Benlowes," *Comparative Literature,* 2 (Fall 1950): 343–353;

Maren-Sofie Røstvig, "Benlowes, Marvell, and the Divine Casimire," *Huntington Library Quarterly,* 18 (November 1954): 13-35;

Røstvig, *The Happy Man: Studies in the Metamorphoses of a Classical Ideal 1600–1700,* Oslo Studies in English, no. 2 (Oslo: Akademisk Forlag / Oxford: Blackwell, 1954);

George Saintsbury, "Edward Benlowes's 'Theophila,'" *Bibliographer* (New York), 2 (January 1903): 3–14;

Kitty Scoular, *Natural Magic: Studies in the Presentation of Nature in English Poetry from Spenser to Marvell* (Oxford: Clarendon Press, 1965);

Robert Lathrop Sharp, *From Donne to Dryden* (Chapel Hill: University of North Carolina Press, 1940);

George Williamson, *The Donne Tradition* (Cambridge, Mass.: Harvard University Press, 1930).

Papers:
Located at the Bodleian Library are an exercise book by Benlowes (MS. Rawlinson D. 278), an illuminated fourteenth-century psalter owned by William Benlowes, Jr. (MS. Douce 131), and pedigree and biographical notes on the Benlowes family by William Holman (MS. Rawlinson Essex 1). Two letters by Benlowes are extant. One letter, dated 1643, is at the British Library (MS. Egerton 2647, fol. 312), and the other, dated 1676, is at the Public Record Office (S.P., Dom., Charles II, 381/203). Numerous legal papers dealing with property transactions from 1636 to 1657 and chancery proceedings from 1657 to 1669 involving Benlowes are at the Public Record Office.

Samuel Butler

(February 1613 – 25 September 1680)

Linda V. Troost
Washington and Jefferson College

See also the Butler entry in *DLB 101: British Prose Writers, 1660-1800, First Series.*

BOOKS: *A True and perfect copy of the Lord Roos, His Answer to the Marquesse of Dorchester's Letter written the 25 of February 1659* (London, 1660);

Hudibras: The First Part. Written in the time of the late Wars (London: Printed by J. G. for Richard Marriot, 1663 [i.e., 1662]);

Hudibras: The Second Part. By the Authour of the First (London: Printed by T. R. for John Martyn & James Allestry, 1664 [i.e., 1663]);

To the Memory of the Most Renowned Du-Vall. A Pindarick Ode. By the Author of Hudibras (London: Printed for H. Brome, 1671);

Two Letters; One from John Audland a Quaker, to William Prynne; The Other, William Prynne's Answer. By the author of Hudibras (London: Printed for Jonathan Edwin, 1672);

Hudibras. The First and Second Parts. Written in the time of the Late Wars. Corrected and Amended, with Several Additions and Annotations (London: Printed by T. N. for John Martyn & Henry Herringman, 1674);

Hudibras: The Third and last Part. Written by the Author of the First and Second Parts (London: Printed for Simon Miller, 1678 [i.e., 1677]);

The Plagiary Exposed: or an Old answer to a newly revived calumny against the memory of King Charles I. Being a reply to a book entitled King Charles's Case, formerly written by John Cook of Gray's Inn, Barrister (London: Printed for Thomas Bennet, 1691).

Editions: *Hudibras: In Three Parts. Corrected, with several additions and annotations* (London: Printed by W. Rogers, 1684);

Hudibras (London: Printed by T. W. for D. Browne, J. Walthoe, and others, 1726);

Hudibras, 2 volumes, edited by Zachary Grey (Cambridge: Printed by J. Bentham for W. Innys & seventeen others, London, 1744);

Samuel Butler (miniature by Samuel Cooper; Collection of the duke of Buccleuch and Queensberry, K.T.)

The Genuine Remains in Verse and Prose, 2 volumes, edited by Robert Thyer (London: J. & R. Tonson, 1759);

Hudibras (Troy, N.Y.: Printed by Wright, Goodenow & Stockwell, 1806);

Hudibras, edited by A. R. Waller (Cambridge: Cambridge University Press, 1905);

Characters and Passages from Note-Books, edited by Waller (Cambridge: Cambridge University Press, 1908);

Satires and Miscellaneous Poetry and Prose, edited by René Lamar (Cambridge: Cambridge University Press, 1928);

Samuel Butler: Three Poems, edited by Alexander C. Spence, Augustan Reprint Society Publication, no. 88 (Los Angeles: William Andrews Clark Memorial Library, 1961);

Hudibras, edited by John Wilders (Oxford: Clarendon Press, 1967);

Samuel Butler, 1612–1680: Characters, edited by Charles W. Daves (Cleveland, Ohio & London: Press of Case Western Reserve University, 1970);

Hudibras, Parts I and II and Selected Other Writings, edited by Wilders and Hugh de Quehen (Oxford: Clarendon Press, 1973);

Prose Observations, edited by de Quehen (Oxford: Clarendon Press, 1979).

OTHER: "Cydippe, Her Answer to Acontius," in *Ovid's Epistles Translated by Several Hands* (London: Jacob Tonson, 1680);

"To the Honorable Edward Howard," in *Examen Poeticum* (London: Printed by R. E. for Jacob Tonson, 1693);

"Butleriana," edited by Henry Southern, *London Magazine,* 3 (September 1825): 136–140; 3 (November 1825): 425–430; 4 (January 1826): 94–98; 4 (March 1826): 401–406; 6 (October 1826): 225–232; 6 (November 1826): 396–401.

Samuel Butler, known largely in the late twentieth century (if at all) as the author of *Hudibras* (1663–1678) and whom librarians and students confuse with a late-Victorian novelist, was in his day a favorite writer with kings and clergymen alike. *Hudibras,* a staunch attack of the Parliamentarians, won favor with King Charles II, who presented several copies of his favorite book as gifts. Butler, the poet who popularized burlesque verse in English, found a devoted follower in Jonathan Swift, whose own burlesque poems are written in the form Butler made famous: "hudibrastics."

Biographical details about Butler's early life are slim. The fifth of Samuel and Mary Butler's eight children, he was baptized on 14 February 1613 in Strensham, south of Worcester, and was named after his father, a clerk to Sir John Russell and an occasional church warden. Samuel Butler, Sr., descended from prosperous yeoman farmers, was a devout Anglican and man of learning, no doubt bringing his son up to be the same. In Strensham the Butlers lived on a farm leased from Sir John called "Butler's Cot," still standing as late as 1870. In 1621 the family was living at Barbourne in the parish of Claines, where the youngest child was born, and later near Strensham in Defford, where his father rented more land from Sir Russell.

Samuel Butler, Sr., died in 1626, at which time Mary Butler and her children probably returned to the Butler property consisting of twenty acres and a house in Claines called "Butler's Tenement." Samuel Butler, Sr., bequeathed to his namesake the free tenancy of the property as well as his books on law, logic, rhetoric, philosophy, poesy, physic, and all other books in Greek and Latin, a fact that suggests young Samuel had shown potential as a scholar.

Although no records survive, young Samuel probably attended the King's School in Worcester until 1628, when he was fifteen. Here he apparently first acquired his great contempt for useless formal learning, an attitude that would appear in several of his satires. Blocked perhaps from attending either Oxford or Cambridge because of financial limitations, Butler probably spent the time between 1628 and 1637 first managing Butler's Tenement and, during the 1630s, serving as a secretary or attendant to several notable personages, among them Leonard Jeffrey's son, Thomas, a justice of the peace in Worcestershire, from whom Butler could have received early legal training. Butler apparently took up painting while with the Jeffreys at Earl's Croome Court: two portraits by him are in the local church's vestry. In 1637 he surrendered Butler's Tenement, a free tenancy, to the owner, suggesting his abandonment of farming.

According to John Aubrey in his *Brief Lives* (1813), Butler went to Wrest Park, Bedfordshire (no longer standing), to serve Elizabeth Grey, the widowed countess of Kent. There he met Samuel Cooper, the miniaturist who later painted his portrait, and John Selden, the learned antiquarian and legal historian. Butler did translation work for Selden, and this association may have given Butler a distaste for conspicuous display of erudition.

After 1645 Butler seems to have left Bedfordshire for London, perhaps studying law at Gray's Inn, and certainly consorting with John Cleveland while residing in Holborn. The 1704 biography of Butler attributed to Sir James Astry erroneously claims that Butler served Sir Samuel Luke, a Presbyterian member of Parliament living in Cople, Bedfordshire, whose Puritan views inspired Butler to create his knight-errant, Hudibras. However, in a 19 March 1663 letter from Butler to Sir George Oxenden, Butler claims that an unnamed West Country knight lodging in the same house with him in Holborn was the model for Hudibras. This unnamed knight most likely was Sir Henry Rosewell of Forde Abbey, Devonshire.

Although Butler's name appears nowhere in the registry of admission to Gray's Inn, his work reveals an intimate knowledge of English law, legal language, and lawyers, and one of his early editors, T. R. Nash, claimed to have seen an abridgment of Sir Edward Coke's *Commentary on Littleton* (1628) in Butler's hand. His negative experiences with his various employers provided him with ammunition to use in his "Characters" (first published in *The Genuine Remains of Mr. Samuel Butler,* 1759) and in *Hudibras,* a work that mocks both legal manipulation and dishonorable justices of the peace.

It was in London during the late 1650s that Butler started writing the first part of *Hudibras* and most likely found employment as a Royalist pamphleteer and propagandist. The anonymity of publication clouds details on his pamphleteering career, but he probably wrote at this time the pro-Royalist tract that was printed after his death as *The Plagiary Exposed* (1691).

His first two poems, each titled "A Ballad," seem to date from his early London career. Neither of these was printed until Robert Thyer edited Butler's unpublished manuscripts as *The Genuine Remains* (1759). The first ballad is a satiric catalogue of the features of a demon sporting from its rump a long tail that can be seen in the city. Early commentators suggest that Butler is describing Oliver Cromwell, but members of the Rump Parliament might also serve as the answer to this riddle. The other ballad, describing in debasing terms Parliament as a goose attempting to hatch a king, clearly refers to the debate about offering Cromwell the crown in the spring of 1657.

Also dating from the late 1650s are several prose works, such as speeches (also first published in Thyer's collection) that reveal strong Royalist and satiric traits. Although the attribution is doubtful, Anthony Wood in his *Athenæ Oxoniensis* (1691, 1692) also ascribed to Butler *Mola Asinaria* (1660), a prose satire written in the voice of Puritan barrister William Prynne that foreshadows the Menippean satire of *Hudibras,* on which Butler was working at the time. The broadside *Lord Roos, His Answer to the Marquesse of Dorchester's Letter* (1660), more confidently attributed to Butler, also displays Butler's adeptness at parodic verbal mimicry.

After the accession of Charles II to the throne in 1660, Butler left London to serve as the steward of Richard Vaughan, Earl of Carbery, at Ludlow Castle, Shropshire, throughout 1661, his principal job being to make the castle habitable after the ravages of the civil wars. During his stay in Ludlow he finished the first part of *Hudibras.* He may also have married here, since he mentions a wife in an undated letter to his sister, although no record of such

a wedding exists. Aubrey claims that Butler's wife was a wealthy widow named Morgan: Astry links Butler with a spinster named Herbert. Butler probably stayed in Ludlow for another year, perhaps as the earl's secretary, since Butler acknowledges in a letter that he was not present in London when part 1 of *Hudibras* was printed.

Although Richard Marriot, the publisher, dated it 1663, the poem was entered in the Stationers' Register on 11 November 1662 and made available in bookshops shortly thereafter. Samuel Pepys, always eager to be au courant, bought a copy on 26 December for two shillings, sixpence, but recorded in his diary that he found it "so silly an abuse of the Presbyter-Knight going to the warrs, that I am ashamed of it; and by and by meeting at Mr. Townsends at dinner, I sold it to him for 18d." The poem proved so great a success that Pepys had to buy himself another copy a few weeks later on 6 February, "it being certainly some ill humour to be so set against that which all the world cries up to be the example of wit." Although Pepys wrote in his diary that he could never bring himself "to think it witty" (28 November 1663), many other Londoners, including King Charles II, thought it immensely witty.

Nine editions of the first part of the anonymous *Hudibras* appeared in 1663, five authorized and four pirated, attesting to the work's immense popularity. Within a few months the secret of authorship leaked out, and the poet received the sobriquet "Hudibras Butler." He also must have received some considerable profit from the success, since no records exist of his being employed during the remainder of the 1660s.

The first part of *Hudibras* (in three cantos) concerns the adventures of the title character, a Presbyterian knight-errant, and Ralpho, his squire, during the civil wars, "When *civil* Fury first grew high." Most of canto 1 describes the two principal characters at considerable length. Sir Hudibras, a justice of the peace, fancies himself a great intellect, formally trained in Greek, Latin, Hebrew, logic, rhetoric, mathematics, philosophy, and religion. His principal interest is revealed in his clothing: it is stuffed with a vast assortment of food, and his weapons are used largely for serving or preparing the food, some of it (such as black pudding) specifically forbidden by the Puritans. In this character Butler satirizes two types: first, the learned pedant devoted to an abstraction that perverts the intellect and, second, the hypocritical and zealous Puritan who professes piety and abstemiousness but practices the opposite.

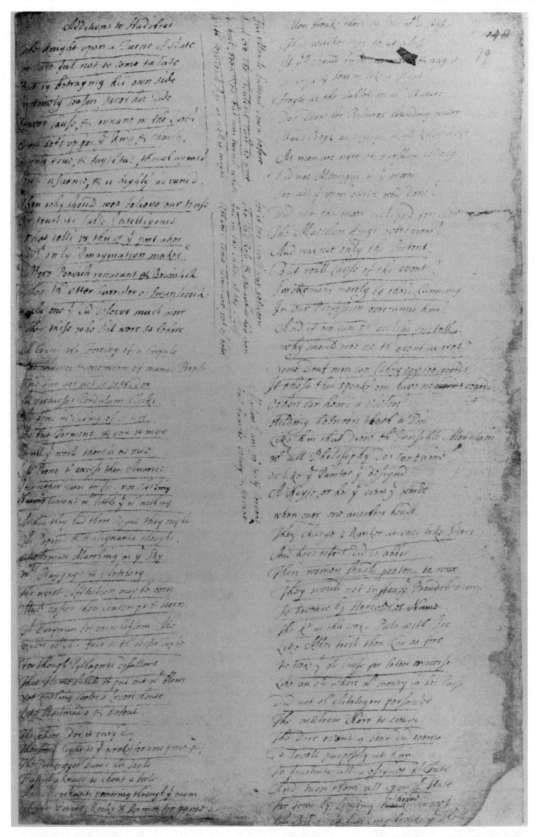

Pages from the additions to Hudibras *in the collection of papers that Butler left to William Longueville (British Library, Add. MS. 32625, f. 79ʳ and f. 139ʳ)*

To this Brave Man the Kt Repaires
for Counsil in his Law Affaires,
And though the Sage were not at Home
Were Led into an Inward Room:
His told, He should have Speedy Advice,
To wait upon em, in a Trice,
Mean while the Clerk flew out in Hast
And lock'd the Dore upon them fast.
And left the Kt & Sq, once more,
In Durance Closer then before.

The Lawyer was that morning gone,
Some Miles off to a Market-Town
Where He was wont to Ply for fees,
And Regulate Enormities & Rehy Breaches of ye Peace
To vend his Trumpery-Opinions
With Turnups, Cabbages & Inions
And in the Market put to Sale,
Recognisance, & Comon Bale.
But when his Clerk had found him out
And told him what he came about
How long his two New Clients had
For his Advice & Counsil stayd
Three howers at least, to Pay their fees,
Or Easier Earne Gratuitys To execute ye
Why then, Quoth he, tis ten to one,
The Birds before this time, are Flown.
Flown? Quoth the Clerk. Th'are fast enough
Ile warrant em from Getting of
I have em under Lock & Key
Soo well Secure to Run away
That's Right, Quoth he, But not ye Games
Wch are like to have outrey the Pames
Wch are such, as neare as I could Guess
That seldom faile to Pay their fees,
True Virtuosos & Lief-holders
Of Suits in Law, among their Neibours
They Love well, though the Letterds
Are fain to Spare in all things els

130

139

For when the Circulation of the Blood
Tho one so easy was not understood
How should the world expect things most hard
Should ever be Discover'd afterward
Like him that Concern'd Queen Elsabeth
So many Scores of years before her Death
And tho a Caius or an Antiquary
In such a vulgar Error to Miscarry
So that, that Led the rout, or Art to Indite
As fast as several Escrivans could write,
Twas only Comon Places of Transssents
To cleare obstructions in their Comesitions
And the the Famoussest of Antiquaries
Left such a Blemish on her Comentaries
They call Suedlox As the old Declamor
Describes the Antig Custome, & the manner
That like our Modern Curious virtuosos
That only knocking at the Dores of Hous
But by the Sound unroode the Just Sum
How many Persons are in any Rooms
As Naturally as De Seudery
Int Agypt Saylor men down the Bathy Sea
And what was first but Insolence, & Laughter
Any greater Anger had turnd to Blood & slaughter
The Devil was his to get termd by those
But charge I wonts before be an Exorcist
Was one Descendie of the Antig know
Begot by Stonis, that had been cast behind

The best the such as Pass with ble
The Cuning Shrine men wth ye Rabbit
And virtuosos out dost believe yeh
there propre for the trade wee onely
Th'are such quilts as that undersid
In my conceit, the Comon Road
Of Petty fogging — True Lutholders
Of suits in Law among their elders
That fee not —

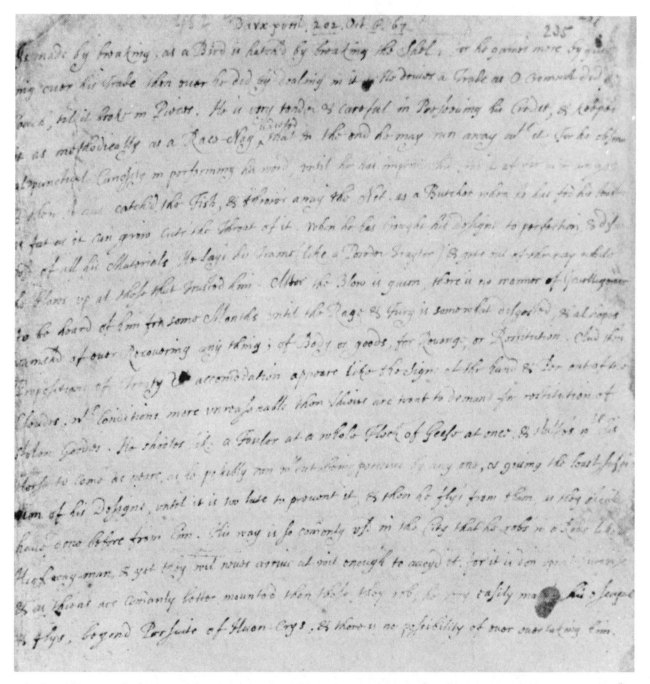

Butler's "Character of a Bankrupt," from the manuscript he left to William Longueville (British Library, Add. MS. 32625, f. 235ʳ)

His squire, Ralpho (or just "Ralph" when the meter demands it), represents a rival force in the Parliament of 1648, the less formally educated Independent. Ralpho's arguments and prophecies receive direct inspiration from inward light, "A Liberal Art, that costs no pains / Of Study, Industry, or Brains"; the squire's arguments are as ridiculous as those of his master. Hudibras and Ralpho's opposing stands on key matters such as church authority allow them to partake of several unresolvable Menippean dialogues on their way to the halting of a scheduled bearbaiting at a nearby inn (bearbaiting had been outlawed by Parliament in June 1647).

After an elaborate mock-epic fight in canto 2 that pits the two chivalric figures with rusty weapons against enemies armed with stout cudgels (including Crowdero the fiddler, Orsin the bearward, and the bold virago, Trulla), Hudibras manages to win the first two skirmishes and imprisons Crowdero in the stocks. In canto 3, however, Hudibras loses the third and final battle to Trulla. Hudibras and Ralpho now replace Crowdero in the village stocks, where they chop logic and create parodies of Biblical *exegesis*. After a lengthy debate on "Whether *Bears* are *better* / Then *Synod-men*," the two prove by example that fools who have debased reason, whether Presbyterian or not, belong on the great chain considerably below animals, who supposedly have no reason at all.

Butler had several models for his burlesque poem. Most obviously, Hudibras and Ralpho owe much to Miguel de Cervantes and his mock-chivalric romance characters Don Quixote and Sancho Panza. Butler's jog-trot octosyllabic couplets first appeared in 1648 in Paul Scarron's *Virgile travesti,* and Geoffrey Chaucer's mock-chivalric "Tale of Sir Thopas" could have offered Butler a model of middle-class knighthood. Butler's mockery of the epic tradition owes much to Scarron, and the religious-culinary satire echoes François Rabelais's *Pantagruel* (circa 1532) and *Gargantua* (1534). For Butler, the heroic literature that he so devotedly burlesques represented falsely grand ideas about human nature, reason, and even literary creativity. As he admits in his invocation, the muse these days inspires poets with "Ale, or viler Liquors," part of the decline of everything sacred. The choppy lines and strained rhymes echo the reduction of verse to mere sound and fury; the "hard words" and "*Babylonish* dialect" reveal the violence and chaos lurking behind the Puritan facade of spirituality and intellectuality.

The success of Butler's satire on the decline of human nature under the Puritan regime led to a spurious continuation of *Hudibras* during June 1663. Butler published a genuine continuation the following December, which must have been planned from the start. The work bears the date 1664, even though it was licensed on 5 November 1663 and in print by 23 November. Pepys was borrowing it from a bookseller on 28 November and buying it on 10 December. This time, Butler received a license for sole control over publication, which cut down on piracies. Two editions of part 2 appeared, both dated 1664.

Part 1 focuses on burlesquing the violence that epic glamorized while simultaneously attacking the hypocrisy of the Puritan; part 2 continues the attack on Puritans while mocking romance and love poetry. A rich widow, to whom Hudibras has unsuccessfully been paying court for three years, releases the knight-in-distress from the stocks on the condition that he later undergo a penitential whipping. The following morning Hudibras and Ralpho debate the nature of conscience and of oath-taking in order to find a way for Hudibras to evade his punishment, a debate that directly parodies the historical tendency of the Saints in Parliament to abjure oaths of allegiance. Ralpho argues that those illuminated with spiritual light are entitled to do anything they please and therefore need keep no oaths. The knight and the squire then visit an astrologer, Sidrophel, to see whether Hudibras's suit will prosper or whether the widow will detect his perjury. The visit ends with Hudibras's beating up the astrologer, ostensibly for his slander of the Presbyterians, but actually for his reminding Hudibras of his defeat at the hands of Trulla.

As in part 1, Butler uses the parodic inversion of having a woman get the better of Hudibras. Before the widow arranges for his release Hudibras and his lady debate the nature and power of love for several hundred lines. The knight takes a romantic tack, invoking several clichés of love poetry. The widow, however, suggests that money is the "real substance of the shadow" and forces Hudibras to reveal his actual motivation in courting her. She cynically attacks the Petrarchan conventions of love poetry:

Some with *Arabian spices* strive
T'embalm her, cruelly alive;
Or *season* her, as *French* Cooks use,
Their *Haut-gusts, Boullies,* or *Ragusts* [.]

To the widow, poets merely provide men with an attractive cover for self-interest. Their language conceals the predatory nature of man just as an artful cook conceals the animal origins of meat with

A page from the "Criticisms upon Books and Authors" section of the manuscript Butler bequeathed to William Longueville, with marginal notes by Longueville and crosses made during the 1750s by Robert Thyer to mark his selections for The Genuine Remains in Verse and Prose of Mr. Samuel Butler *(British Library, Add. MS. 32625, f. 202ᵛ)* to see Butler as more optimistic about the New Science: although he critiques poor scientific technique and mocks foolish experiments, he endorses properly skeptical Baconian science, as some of his prose writings reveal.

As both the scientific satires and the sketches in the Poetical Thesaurus attest, Butler abhors theory divorced from common sense, especially when it leads one to blind imitation. In "Repartees between Cat and Puss," he parodies the mindless paradoxes in the love scenes of heroic drama. "Satire Upon Plagiaries," probably an attack on Sir John Denham, ironically praises the resourcefulness of plagiarist poets who carry blind imitation a little too far. With logic worthy of Ralpho, Butler concludes the mock-ode with the observation that as the most successful banker deals in borrowed sums only, the most active plagiarist "May greatest Fame and Credit boast."

During the summer of 1677 Thomas Rymer published *The Tragedies of the last Age Consider'd and Examin'd by the Practice of the Ancients*, to which Butler wrote a verse response. In "On Critics Who Judge of Modern Plays Precisely by the Rules of the Ancients," Butler presents a brief demonstration of what such critics would do to popular entertainment such as puppet theater: Dick Whittington's cat must mew in Latin and "No Pudding shalbe suffer'd to be witty / Unles it be in Order to Raise Pitty." Evoking metaphors of scientific examination, Butler claims that Art cannot be calculated "to th' Hundreth Atom" or the air pressure on Parnassus measured with a barometer, "Torricellian Glasses." As Butler stated in the Poetical Thesaurus: "Rules / Were made for Novices, and Fools."

On 10 September 1677, Butler received a royal injunction granting him sole rights to the publication of all his poetry and, later in the month, an immediate gift of one hundred pounds together with an annual pension amounting to the same (which, however, did not appear until September 1678). Considering the king's fondness for Butler's work and unaware of the earlier gift of two hundred pounds, some (such as Aubrey) felt that the gift was inadequate and tardy. The final part of *Hudibras* (dated 1678 but on sale in November 1677) no doubt added to Butler's income but proved much less popular than the earlier two parts and had only three editions in three years.

The plot continues where part 2 left off. Unaware that Ralpho has revealed his deception, Hudibras approaches the wealthy widow to offer marriage and discredit his romantic rival, Sid-

Samuel Butler (portrait by Edward Lutterel; National Portrait Gallery, London)

rophel, through an elaborate lie. After a debate on the subject of marriage, the widow punishes his impudence by arranging for a terrifying antimasque in which hobgoblins attack him and punish him for having chosen "*that cursed Sin / Hypocrisie, to set up in*." The hobgoblins force Hudibras to confess all in a satiric inversion of a catechism.

The widow that Butler presented in part 2 stood largely for the voice of common sense. In part 3 she becomes an object of satire herself. The shift no doubt had to do with the changing relationship between the sexes in the 1670s. Hudibras adheres to the older view of marriage – men should rule women – but conceals much of his domination behind romantic clichés. The widow, at the other extreme, argues like a cynical libertine of the Restoration stage. In her view, women lose their liberty to men who are marrying them for money and power; therefore, women are better off single. In this case she may be right, for Hudibras's grand language conceals base motives.

The digression in canto 2 on the Saints in the Rump Parliament is not as unconnected as it seems. Butler presents the saints as a whole behaving just

a fancy sauce. Both cooks and poets, however, really cater only to common appetites: hunger and lust. The widow appears as one of the few characters not duped by manipulative language and false ideals, but the Amazonian and sadistic tendencies Butler gives her undercut his feminism.

Like the knight, the astrologer Sidrophel also conceals his true motives under elaborate language and conduct. He combines features of the quack astrologer and the Royal Society virtuoso, the latter a target of increasing interest for Butler. Since the Presbyterians had been attacking astrologers in a print debate during the 1650s, the physical attack that Hudibras launches on Sidrophel burlesques historical fact.

After the publication of part 2, Butler put *Hudibras* aside for several years, spending his time instead on the prose "Characters," written largely between 1667 and 1669, and several verse satires dating from 1668 to 1674. His collection of epigrams and fragments on subjects ranging from Astrology to Zeal, commonly called his Poetical Thesaurus (published in volume two of *The Genuine Remains*), probably dates from this time as well. On 19 July, Pepys invited Butler to dine with him, and on 14 October Butler made his single documented foray into theater by writing a fulsome prologue and epilogue (published in *The Genuine Remains*) for a revival of William Habington's *The Queene of Arragon* (published 1640) in honor of the birthday of the duke of York (later James II). From about 1669 to 1674 Butler served as secretary to the powerful George Villiers, second Duke of Buckingham, accompanying him on a diplomatic trip to France in 1670. Observations in his notebook suggest that he found the French as absurd as the English.

After his return Butler published anonymously in 1671 a mock-Pindaric ode in honor of a recently hanged French-born highwayman, Claude Duval. *To the Memory of the Most Renowned Du-Vall* attacks several of Butler's favorite targets. Duval leaves behind him a "great Example to Mankind," namely "how to hang in a more graceful fashion / Than e'er was known before to the dull *English* Nation." Duval's French background serves for a disquisition on that nation's preoccupation with clothing and fashion, a metaphor for Butler of deception. Duval's ability to find gold derives from his Hermetic skill, and his ironic robbing of cheating merchants receives mocking praise. Butler next compares the highwayman to a mighty conqueror who takes tribute from all,

even from the lawyer that "in his own allow'd Highway / Does Feats of Arms as great as his." The poem attacks both false values and deceptive literary modes such as heroic odes.

Several other of Butler's poems in *The Genuine Remains* attack social faults as well. Francophobia appears again in "Satire Upon Our Ridiculous Imitation of the French." Butler particularly criticizes the English for allowing the French to dictate what should be worn, even if the fashion goes contrary to common sense. Self-delusion is the real danger: for example, because of the fashion for gray wigs, the aged can fancy themselves as young as the youths who are also wearing gray wigs. The rage for French fashion also encourages the ignorant to judge solely by appearance instead of by substance.

Bad judgment in behavior derives not only from imitating the French but also by imitating fashionable vices. Butler may have thoroughly mocked the sanctimoniousness of the Puritan, but he likewise mocks the other extreme as well with satires on gaming and drinking. In his "Satire Upon the Licentious Age of Charles II," Butler lambastes the vices into which court society had fallen after freeing itself from the hypocrisy of the previous age. For Butler the present age is worse because inverted values make vice seem virtue. Again, ignorance is at the root of this moral miasma, which Butler seems to equate with a lack of sense and judgment rather than with a lack of reason or learning. Reason, in fact, only leads one further astray. Butler illustrates this clearly in *Hudibras* with Ralpho and Hudibras's manipulative verbiage.

An uncharacteristically serious poem, "Satire Upon the Weakness and Misery of Man," illustrates with copious examples how "Our Universal Inclination / Tends to the worst of our Creation." Rather than strive for the godly in themselves, people drag themselves down to the bestial. Any evil that Nature gives humankind is perpetuated; any good is spoiled. Even those who think they are escaping the trap by devoting themselves to the mind instead of the body paradoxically make themselves wretches by cracking their "Brains in plodding on / That, which is never to be known."

Education cannot be relied on to set humanity on the correct path and teach it its limitations. An unfinished poem that may be a response to Butler's days at the King's School, "Satire Upon the Imperfection and Abuse of Human Learning," exposes the uselessness of the educational system, which counteracts a child's natural intuition. Butler specifically attacks the method of language instruction, "the Curse of Babilon," which inculcates knowledge

First page of Butler's observations on France and the French, as transcribed by William Longueville in his commonplace book (Rosenbach Museum & Library, f. 2 [1]')

with "the Rod and whip" and teaches the child "to express / No sense at all, in Severall Languages." Butler recognizes that much of education serves only as display and that most scholars know little beyond the title pages in their libraries.

This satire makes explicit several points raised in *Hudibras*. Sir Hudibras had a formal education that gave him smatterings of knowledge and taught him casuistry. The product of English education, Hudibras learns only how to deceive the world and himself, thereby proving that a university degree has as much social significance as a fine suit of clothes from France, and about as much substance. Butler's lack of university training no doubt made him especially aware of the unjustified power such superficial intellectual display had.

The virtuosos of the Royal Society represented a similar intellectual abuse to Butler. Always concerned with setting limits on human knowledge, Butler satirized the scientific fellows of Gresham College, London, for exceeding what he felt to be natural intellectual boundaries. In revising the first two parts of *Hudibras* for publication in 1674, Butler fleshed out the virtuoso satire that he had hinted at in part 2 by adding "An Heroical Epistle of Hudibras to Sidrophel," 130 lines of abuse more in the style of the formal-verse satires he had written for the past several years than in the style of the *Hudibras* of 1662. A gift of two hundred pounds from the king's secret service funds in August 1674 no doubt supplied Butler with greatly needed income but did not prevent his satirizing one of the king's special interests, namely the Royal Society.

Butler's description of Sidrophel in part 2 associated him with several interests of the Royal Society (formally founded in 1662): optics, mathematics, the observation of the moon and comets through a telescope, silviculture, blood circulation in lice, the observation of maggots through microscopes, and so on. The "Heroical Epistle" enhances the satire by having Hudibras claim that all the discoveries of the Royal Society can do nothing to make Sidrophel a sensible person: blood transfusions cannot transfuse sense into a fool, nor can treatments for ailing trees "operate / Upon that duller Block, your Pate." Sidrophel's principal fault, however, lies in his self-deception. Hudibras berates the squire for setting himself up as a great dispenser of wisdom when he has picked up only a little knowledge:

'cause y' have gain'd o'th' *Colledge,*
A Quarter-share (at most) of Knowledge,
And brought in none, but spent Repute,

Y'assume a Pow'r as absolute
To Judge and Censure, and Controll,
As if you were the sole Sir *Poll*
And saucily pretend to know
More then your Dividend comes to.

Thyer identifies Sir Poll as Sir Paul Neile, an enth siastic member of the Royal Society; an earlier ed tor, Zachary Grey, notes that Neile offended Butl by claiming that *Hudibras* was not his work. T satire also applies to other Royal Society membe such as Robert Boyle, Robert Hooke, and Joh Evelyn. For Butler, the problem is not the pursuit knowledge; it is the self-delusion to which such quest leads.

"The Elephant in the Moon," a narrative th Butler wrote around the same time (published *The Genuine Remains*), treats the same theme. Me bers of a learned society are observing the mo through a telescope in order to make plans for p sible colonization. The chief virtuoso sees what pears to be a war being fought, and they all spe late on the sociology of lunar life. A second virtue looks into the telescope and observes an elephat which apparently has broken away from the fig ing. The virtuosos start writing up an exact nar tive for their next issue of the *Transactions* when of the footboys, looking through the telescope, i mediately concludes that a field mouse has crept side of it. After some debate, one of the grande (Boyle) rationalizes away the need to tell the tru Unable to decide on a version of the "truth," the s entists decide to check inside the telescope anyw and find not only the mouse, but a swarm of fl and gnats that they mistook for warring mo dwellers. Humiliated at their delusion, the scienti skulk away as the rational narrator's voice warns the dangers of seeing things "*Not as they are, but they seem.*"

Butler wrote this poem in two versions; first burlesque octosyllabic couplets and then in mo heroic couplets. The first version may have be written in 1666, a time when the Royal Society w particularly interested in lunar observation, wi the long version written some years later; most cri ics, however, choose 1676 as the date for the fir version because of topical references. Critics al split on how to read this poem. Some argue th Butler is criticizing science through the Royal Soc ety, portraying its members as delusive as the Pur tans had been a generation earlier. Claiming to "p rify" language, the New Scientists actually obfusca it and perpetuate lies. Their desire for person fame also leads them to deception instead of scien tific objectivity. More recently, critics have tende

like Hudibras, for they too swear false oaths and conceal their greed behind hypocritical masks. They even resort to the law to gain their "Profits" and "*Plunder*" and perform mock-exegesis on words such as *rump*. The approach of General George Monck and the city rabble's "*horrid Cookery*" of rump roasts in the street causes the assembly to disperse in terror. As the Puritan Hudibras finds himself vanquished by the libertine widow, so do the saints in Parliament find themselves vanquished by the coming of the Restoration.

The third canto, focusing on Hudibras's plan to sue the widow for breach of promise (and intimating that Sidrophel plans to sue Hudibras for the beating), shows again on the individual scale what has been happening on the national. Ralpho states that money-hungry lawyers who preside over such cases at the bar are in "a kind of *Civil War*." So the burlesque poem moves from national civil war to personal civil war. In the final exchange of epistles between Hudibras and the widow, the latter systematically demolishes Hudibras's rationalized myths about male superiority. The poem concludes by smashing almost all romantic ideas and replacing them with nothing except a sense that men and women will always remain in a state of civilized warfare.

Despite his pension, Butler's final year was spent in poverty, living in Rose Alley, Covent Garden (during Butler's residence here, John Dryden was ambushed and knocked unconscious in Rose Alley by hired assailants; Dryden was being punished for a poem mistakenly attributed to him). According to Aubrey, Butler spent most of the winter confined to the house with the gout. For artists such as Dryden and Thomas Otway, Butler's seeming neglect by the king who so loved *Hudibras* served as a cautionary tale (to be fair, the king had given Butler a gift of twenty pounds on 10 May 1680 in addition to the pension and earlier gifts). Butler died of consumption on 25 September 1680, at the age of sixty-seven, and was buried in the churchyard of Saint Paul's, Covent Garden, at the expense of his friend William Longueville, a lawyer. His pallbearers included Aubrey and Thomas Shadwell. Butler's final work, "Cydippe, Her Answer to Acontius" (1680), a serious translation of a romantic heroical epistle by Ovid (probably piecework written for ready money) serves as an ironic finale for the burlesque satirist who mocked the heroic, the learned, the idealistic, and the romantic, all of which, in his mind, led to self-delusion at its best and hypocrisy at its worst.

Bibliographies:

James L. Thorson, "The Publication of *Hudibras*," *Papers of the Bibliographical Society of America,* 60 (October–December 1966): 418–438;

Hugh de Quehen, "Editing Butler's Manuscripts," in *Editing Seventeenth-Century Prose,* edited by D. I. B. Smith (Toronto: Hakkert, 1972), pp. 71–93;

James L. Thorson, "Samuel Butler (1612–1680): A Bibliography," *Bulletin of Bibliography,* 30 (January–March 1973): 34–39;

George R. Wasserman, *Samuel Butler and the Earl of Rochester: A Reference Guide* (Boston: G. K. Hall, 1986).

Biographies:

Sir James Astry, "Life of Butler," in Butler's *Hudibras* (London: Sawbridge, 1704);

Treadway Russell Nash, "On Samuel Butler, Esq., Author of *Hudibras*," in Butler's *Hudibras* (London: Rickaby, 1793);

Samuel Johnson, "Samuel Butler," *Lives of the Poets,* 3 volumes, edited by George Birkbeck Hill (Oxford: Clarendon Press, 1905);

E. S. de Beer, "The Later Life of Samuel Butler," *Review of English Studies,* 4 (April 1928): 159–166;

Ricardo Quintana, "The Butler-Oxenden Correspondence," *Modern Language Notes,* 48 (January 1933): 1–11; 48 (November 1993): 486;

Norma E. Bentley, " 'Hudibras' Butler Abroad," *Modern Language Notes,* 60 (April 1945): 254–259;

Michael Wilding, "Samuel Butler at Barbourne," *Notes and Queries,* new series 13 (January 1966): 15–19;

Wilding, "The Date of Butler's Baptism," *Review of English Studies,* 17, no. 66 (1966): 174–177;

Wilding, "Butler and Gray's Inn," *Notes and Queries,* new series 18 (August 1971): 293–295.

References:

Josephine Bauer, "Some Verse Fragments and Prose *Characters* by Samuel Butler Not Included in the *Complete Works*," *Modern Philology,* 45 (February 1948): 160–168;

Richmond P. Bond, *English Burlesque Poetry: 1700–1750* (Cambridge: Harvard University Press, 1932);

Benjamin Boyce, *The Polemic Character: 1640–1661* (Lincoln: University of Nebraska Press, 1955);

Sv Bruun, "The Date of Samuel Butler's *The Elephant in the Moon,*" *English Studies,* 55 (April 1974): 133–139;

Bruun, "Who's Who in Samuel Butler's 'The Elephant in the Moon,'" *English Studies,* 50 (August 1969): 381–389;

Kevin L. Cope, "The Conquest of Truth: Wycherley, Rochester, Butler, and Dryden and the Restoration Critique of Satire," *Restoration,* 10 (Spring 1986): 19–40;

Cope, "The Infinite Perimeter: Human Nature and Ethical Mediation in Six Restoration Writers," *Restoration,* 5 (1981): 58–75;

A. D. Cousins, "The Idea of a 'Restoration' and the Verse Satires of Butler and Marvell," *Southern Review* (Adelaide), 14 (July 1981): 131–142;

Joseph Toy Curtiss, "Butler's *Sidrophel,*" *PMLA,* 44 (December 1929): 1066–1078;

Thomas R. Edwards, *Imagination and Power: A Study of Poetry on Public Themes* (New York: Oxford University Press, 1971);

Balz Engler, "*Hudibras* and the Problem of Satirical Distance," *English Studies,* 60 (August 1979): 436–443;

David Farley-Hills, *The Benevolence of Laughter: Comic Poetry of the Commonwealth and Restoration* (Totowa: Rowman & Littlefield, 1974), pp. 46–71;

Dan Gibson, Jr., "Samuel Butler," in *Seventeenth-Century Studies,* edited by Robert Shafer (Princeton: Princeton University Press, 1933), pp. 279–335;

Bruce Ingham Granger, "*Hudibras* in the American Revolution," *American Literature,* 27 (1956): 499–508;

Christopher Hill, *Writing and Revolution in 17th-Century England,* volume 1 of *The Collected Essays of Christopher Hill* (Amherst: University of Massachusetts Press, 1985);

William C. Horne, "'Between th' Petticoat and Breeches': Sexual Warfare and the Marriage Debate in *Hudibras,*" *Studies in Eighteenth-Century Culture,* volume 11, edited by Harry C. Payne (Madison: University of Wisconsin Press, 1982), pp. 133–146;

Horne, "Butler's Use of the *Rump* in *Hudibras,*" *Library Chronicle,* 37 (Spring 1971): 126–135;

Horne, "Curiosity and Ridicule in Samuel Butler's Satire on Science," *Restoration,* 7 (Spring 1983): 8–18;

Horne, "Hard Words in *Hudibras,*" *Durham University Journal,* 75 (June 1983): 31–43;

Ian Jack, *Augustan Satire: Intention and Idiom in English Poetry: 1660–1750* (Oxford: Clarendon Press, 1952), pp. 15–42;

Paul J. Korshin, *Typologies in England: 1650–1820* (Princeton: Princeton University Press, 1982), pp. 277–282;

Ellen Douglass Leyburn, "*Hudibras* Considered as Satiric Allegory," *Huntington Library Quarterly,* 16 (February 1953): 141–160;

Ward S. Miller, "The Allegory in Part I of *Hudibras,*" *Huntington Library Quarterly,* 21 (August 1958): 323–343;

Earl Miner, *The Restoration Mode from Milton to Dryden* (Princeton: Princeton University Press, 1974);

Nicolas H. Nelson, "Astrology, *Hudibras,* and the Puritans," *Journal of the History of Ideas,* 37 (July–September 1976): 521–536;

Ruth Nevo, *The Dial of Virtue: A Study of Poems on Affairs of State in the Seventeenth Century* (Princeton: Princeton University Press, 1963);

Marjorie Hope Nicolson, *Pepys' Diary and the New Science* (Charlottesville: University Press of Virginia, 1965), pp. 122–158;

Felicity A. Nussbaum *The Brink of All We Hate: English Satires on Women, 1660–1750* (Lexington: University of Kentucky, 1984), pp. 43–56;

Ricardo Quintana, "Samuel Butler: A Restoration Figure in a Modern Light," *ELH,* 18 (March 1951): 7–31;

Edward Ames Richards, *Hudibras in the Burlesque Tradition* (New York: Columbia University Press, 1937);

Ken Robinson, "The Skepticism of Butler's Satire on Science: Optimistic or Pessimistic?" *Restoration,* 7 (Spring 1983): 1–7;

Michael A. Seidel, "Patterns of Anarchy and Oppression in Samuel Butler's *Hudibras,*" *Eighteenth-Century Studies,* 5 (Winter 1971–1972): 294–314;

Seidel, *Satiric Inheritance: Rabelais to Sterne* (Princeton: Princeton University Press, 1979);

Alvin Snider, "A Babylonish Dialect: Samuel Butler's Polemics of Discourse," *Philological Quarterly,* 69 (Summer 1990): 299–317;

Snider, "By Equivocation Swear: *Hudibras* and The Politics of Interpretation," *Seventeenth Century,* 5 (Autumn 1990): 157–172;

Snider, "Hudibrastic," *Restoration,* 12 (Spring 1988): 1–9;

Susan Staves, *Players' Scepters: Fictions of Authority in the Restoration* (Lincoln: University of Nebraska Press, 1979);

Charles F. Totten, "Hypocrisy and Corruption in Four Characters of Samuel Butler," *Essays in*

Literature (Western Illinois), 2 (Fall 1975): 164–170;

Linda V. Troost, "Poetry, Politics, and Puddings: The Imagery of Food in Butler's *Hudibras,*" *Restoration,* 9 (Fall 1985): 83–92;

Jan Veldkamp, *Samuel Butler: The Author of* Hudibras (Hilversum: De Atlas, 1923);

David M. Vieth, "Divided Consciousness: The Trauma and Triumph of Restoration Culture," *Tennessee Studies in Literature,* 22 (1977): 46–62;

George R. Wasserman, "Carnival in *Hudibras,*" *ELH,* 55 (Spring 1988): 79–97;

Wasserman, "*Hudibras* and Male Chauvinism," *Studies in English Literature,* 16 (Summer 1976): 351–361;

Wasserman, "Samuel Butler and the Problem of Unnatural Man," *Modern Language Quarterly,* 31 (June 1970): 179–194;

Wasserman, *Samuel "Hudibras" Butler,* updated edition (Boston: Twayne, 1989);

Wasserman, "A Strange *Chimaera* of Beasts and Men: The Argument and Imagery of *Hudibras,* Part I," *Studies in English Literature,* 13 (Summer 1973): 405–421;

Michael Wilding, "The Last of the Epics: The Rejection of the Heroic in *Paradise Lost* and *Hudibras,*" in *Restoration Literature: Critical Approaches,* edited by Harold Love (London: Methuen, 1972), pp. 91–120.

Papers:

What remains of Samuel Butler's holograph manuscripts can be found in two collections. The British Library has two folio volumes, one of verse and prose in Butler's hand (Add. MS. 32625) and one a transcription by Robert Thyer (Add. MS. 32626) of papers no longer extant (portions are printed in *The Genuine Remains,* 1759). The British Library also has a copy of Butler's 1662 letter to Sir George Oxenden (Add. MS. 40711, fo. 34). The Rosenbach Library, Philadelphia, has a commonplace book that includes an uncompleted French-English dictionary in Butler's hand and transcriptions by William Longueville of manuscripts that Butler bequeathed to him.

Thomas Carew

(1594 or 1595 – March 1640)

Michael P. Parker
United States Naval Academy

BOOKS: *Cœlum Britanicum. A Masque at White-Hall in the Banqvetting-Hovse, on Shrove-Tvesday-Night, the 18. of February, 1633* (London: Printed for Thomas Walkley, 1634);

Poems. By Thomas Carew Esquire (London: Printed by I. Dawson for Thomas Walkley, 1640; enlarged, 1642; third edition, enlarged, London: Printed for Humphrey Moseley, 1651).

Edition: *The Poems of Thomas Carew with His Masque Coelum Britannicum*, edited by Rhodes Dunlap (Oxford: Clarendon Press, 1949).

OTHER: "To my Honoured friend, Master Thomas May," in Thomas May's *The Heire an Excellent Comedie* (London: Printed by B. Alsop for T. Jones, 1622);

"To my worthy Friend, M. D'Avenant," in Sir William Davenant's *The Ivst Italian* (London: Printed by T. Harper for J. Waterson, 1630);

"In Celias face a question did a rise" and "He that loves a Rosie Cheeke," in Walter Porter's *Madrigales and Ayres* (London: Printed by W. Stansby, 1632);

"An Elegie upon the death of the Deane of Pauls, D^r. Iohn Donne," in John Donne's *Poems* (London: Printed by M. F. for John Marriot, 1633);

"To the Reader of Master Davenant's Play," in Davenant's *The Witts: A Comedie* (London: Printed by A. Mathewes for R. Meighen, 1636);

"To my worthy friend Master Geo. Sands," in George Sandys's *A Paraphrase Vpon the Divine Poems* (London: Printed by John Legatt, 1638 [i.e., 1637]);

"To my much honoured friend, Henry Lord Cary of Lepington, upon his translation of Malvezzi," in Virgilio Malvezzi's *Romvlvs and Tarqvin*, translated by Henry Lord Cary, second edition (London: Printed by J. Haviland for J. Benson, 1638);

"To Will. Davenant my Friend," in Davenant's *Madagascar; With Other Poems* (London: Printed by J. Haviland for T. Walkley, 1638);

"Song. Conquest by Flight," in Samuel Pick's *Festum Voluptatis* (London: Printed by E. Purslowe for B. Langford, 1639).

Thomas Carew was the poetic arbiter elegantiae of the court of Charles I. He gave one last witty spin to the tradition of Petrarchan lyric, polishing and resetting the traditional conceits of love poetry for an increasingly sophisticated and aristocratic audience. Carew penned the most notorious erotic poem of the seventeenth century, "A Rapture," as well as what is generally regarded as the most accomplished of the Caroline masques, *Coelum Britannicum* (1634). His two contributions to the minor genre of the country-house poem, "To Saxham" and "To my friend G. N. from Wrest," are still frequently anthologized. In the final decade of his life Carew largely eschewed lyric for occasional and commendatory poems. His verses to Ben Jonson on the failure of *The New Inn* (performed 1629; published 1631) and his elegy (1633) on the death of John Donne are the most astute contemporary assessments of the two men's poetic legacies. Carew is, indeed, one of the great transitional figures of English poetry: although indebted to Donne and Jonson and deeply grounded in the literature of the high English Renaissance, he sketched out the lighter, more elegant style that has come to be known as Cavalier verse. His younger followers – Sir John Suckling, Richard Lovelace, Edmund Waller, Sir William Davenant, and in an entirely different mode, Andrew Marvell – dominated the literary scene at mid century and in turn foreshadowed the radical changes ushered in by the Restoration in 1660.

Thomas Carew was born between June 1594 and June 1595, probably at his parents' home at West Wickham in Kent, the third of three children. His father, Matthew Carew, a master in chancery, was descended from prominent Cornish gentry; his mother, Alice Ryvers Carew, was the daughter and granddaughter of lord mayors of London. His father, knighted about 1603, was already over sixty at the time of Thomas Carew's birth. Thomas Carew was enrolled in Merton College, Oxford, in June 1608, at which time he gave his age as thirteen. He took his degree on 31 January 1611 and on 14 February was admitted as a reader in the Bodleian Library. He was made a B.A. of Cambridge in 1612 and on 6 August of the same year entered the Middle Temple to begin his legal studies.

Carew was not, however, to persevere in his father's profession. According to Sir Matthew, Thomas studied his lawbooks "very litle." The Carew family, moreover, faced financial reverses. Sir Matthew's niece had married the diplomat Sir Dudley Carleton, who had recently been dispatched as ambassador to Venice, and in February 1613 Sir Matthew wrote the couple a plaintive account of his troubles. Carleton responded with a loan and with an offer to give young Thomas a position in Italy, presumably as his private secretary. Carew accepted and arrived in Italy sometime in late 1613.

We know very little of Carew's travels during this period. He did, however, meet Thomas Howard, Earl of Arundel, who was touring Italy after escorting Princess Elizabeth, daughter of James I, to Heidelberg following her marriage to Frederick, the Elector Palatine. In Arundel's train was Inigo Jones, who twenty years later would design the sets for *Coelum Britannicum*, and it is conceivable that Jones and Carew first met at this time. Carew returned with Carleton to England in December 1615; he had presumably given good service, for he was reengaged to accompany his patron on his next embassy, to the Netherlands, in March 1616.

At this point young Carew seemed well on the way to preferment; Carleton was a powerful man with friends at court. During the summer of 1616, however, Carew's relationship with his patron suffered an irreversible blow. Although the precise details still remain unclear, Carew apparently set several unflattering reflections on the character of Sir Dudley and Lady Carleton to paper. Sir Dudley found the paper but, instead of confronting Carew, merely advised him that he would have a better chance of preferment if he returned to England and sought the favor of a distant cousin, George, Lord Carew, who had recently been made a member of the Privy Council. Thomas Carew arrived back in London in August 1616, much to his father's surprise and displeasure. Over the next two months Sir Matthew dispatched anxious inquiries to Carleton

and to his agent, Edward Sherburne, and gradually the full story emerged. Sir Matthew, now in his early eighties, was furious with his wastrel son and urged him to reconcile himself to the Carletons; Thomas's efforts were seen as halfhearted, however, and the offended couple remained obdurate. Carew, nonetheless, apparently learned a valuable lesson from his indiscretion: in his later career he would prove himself the most circumspect of courtiers.

As he may well have surmised, Carew found no preferment from Lord Carew, but he nonetheless threw himself into the round of court ceremonial and celebration. He was an attendant at the creation of Charles as Prince of Wales on 4 November 1616; according to Carew's modern editor, Rhodes Dunlap, John Chamberlain singled Carew out as a "squire of high degree for cost and bravery." In October 1617 Sir Matthew Carew complained in a letter to Carleton that his son had been "mispending his time" and now lay languishing at home of "a new disease com in amongest us" – presumably syphilis – "by the which I pray God that he may be chastised to amend his lyfe." Carew's versification of nine of the Psalms may date from this period of illness and enforced idleness; the internal evidence of the pieces suggests that they are prentice work. Beset by financial worries and anxious about the future of his scapegrace younger son, Sir Matthew died on 2 August 1618 and was buried in the church of Saint Dunstan's-in-the-West.

It was presumably during these years in London that Carew first turned seriously to composing lyric and amatory verse. Many of these poems are addressed to a mistress named Celia: if she is a real person, her identity has never been discovered, but it is just as likely that she represents a composite of several women or is a wholly fictive creation. Carew's lyrics rest squarely in the tradition of English Petrarchanism. The poet employs all the traditional conceits and addresses the usual amatory situations; yet, through vivid diction, a penchant for the elegant variation, and an ability to give an old phrase a surprising turn, he makes the clichés witty and new. In "The Spring," for example, Carew upbraids his mistress for continuing to remain cold to his suit while all nature warms to the rays of the March sun. The trope is old, but Carew's exquisite diction tricks up the threadbare contrast between winter and spring:

Now that the winter's gone, the earth hath lost
Her snow-white robes, and now no more the frost
Candies the grasse, or castes an ycie creame

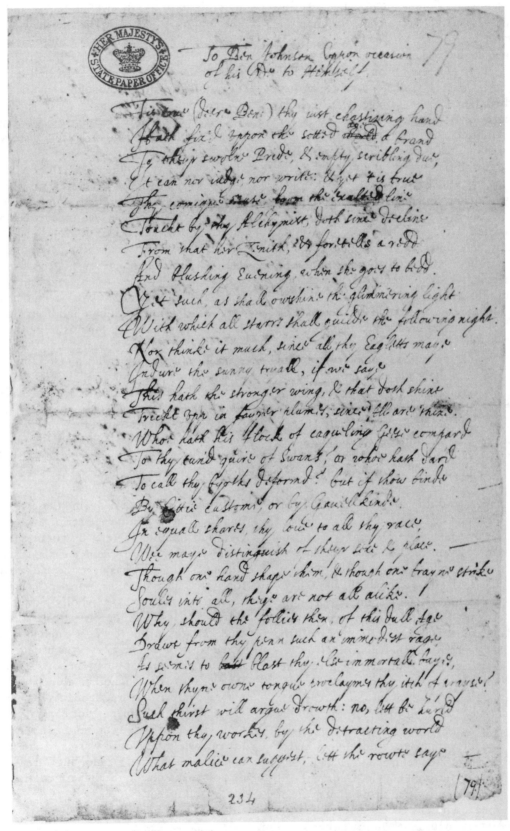

Manuscript for the poem Carew wrote to console Ben Jonson for the failure of his 1629 play The New Inn
(Public Record Office, S.P. 16/155, folio 79)

The running sands, that eer thou make a playe
Count the slowe minutts, might a Godwin frame
To swallowe when th'hast don thy shipwrackt name.
Lett them the deere expence of oyle vpbrayde
Suckt by thy watchfull Lampe, w. hath betrayde
To theft the bloud of martird Authors, spilt
Into thy inke, whilst thou growst pale w. guilt.
Repine not at thy taper thriftie wast,
That slickt thy labor'd poemes; nor is hast
Prayse, but excuse: & if thou ouercome
A knottie writer, bring the booty home.
Nor thinke it theft, if the rich spoyles so torne
From conquerd Authors be as trophies worne.
Let others glutt on the extorted prayse
Of vulgar breath, trust thou to after dayes:
Thy labour'd workes shall liue, when Time deuoures
Th'abortiue ofspring of thyr hastie howers.
Thou art not of thyr ranke, the quarrell lyes
Within thyne owne virge; then lett this suffize
The wiser world doth greater Thee confesse
Then all men else, then Thyselfe onely Lesse.

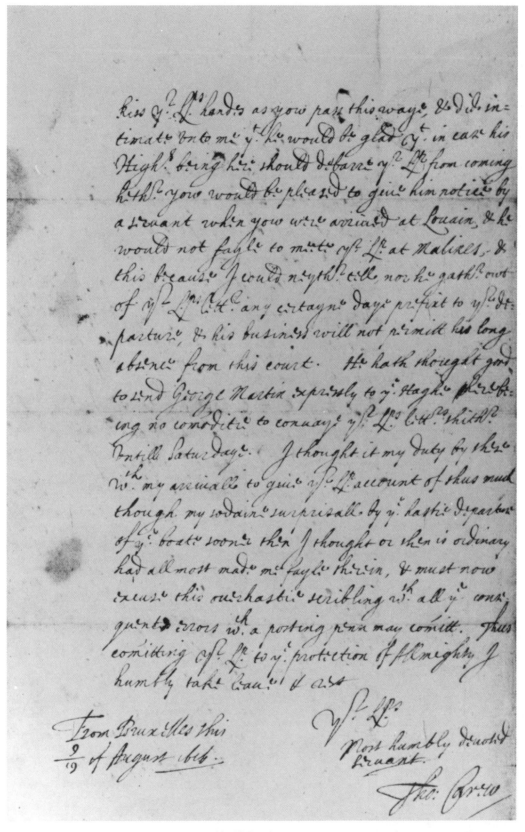

Second page of a letter written in Brussels from Thomas Carew to Sir Dudley Carleton (Public Record Office, SP 84/73/136ᵛ)

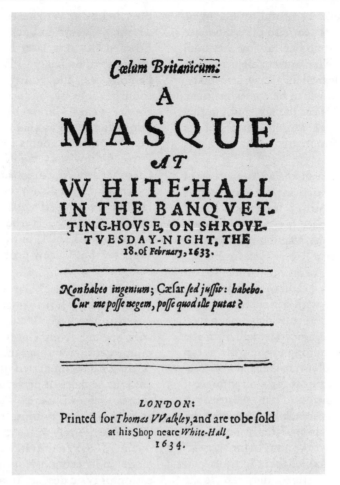

Coelum Britanicum:

A

MASQUE

AT

W HITE-HALL

IN THE BANQVET-

TING-HOVSE, ON SHROVE-

TVESDAY-NIGHT, THE

18. of *February*, 1633.

Non habeo ingenium; Cæsar sed jussit: habebo.
Cur me posse negem, posse quod ille putat?

LONDON:

Printed for *Thomas VValkley*, and are to be sold

at his Shop neare *White-Hall*,

1 6 3 4.

*Title page for the work that established Carew as a favorite in the
court of Charles I and his queen, Henrietta Maria*

Vpon the silver Lake, or Chrystall streame:
But the warme Sunne thawes the benummed Earth,
And makes it tender[.]

The striking chiasmus of the final lines of the poem —

         all things keepe
Time with the season, only shee doth carry
Iune in her eyes, in her heart Ianuary

— nicely conveys Carew's tight stylistic control
over his subject. In lyrics like these he is at heart a
bricoleur who manipulates the elements of a tradition
in novel and unexpected ways in order to make that
tradition his own.

The range of amatory situations that Carew
addresses in his lyrics is broad. "To A. L. Per-
swasions to love" is a fast-moving, closely argued
suasoria that makes its case with compelling urgency:

Oh love me then, and now begin it,
Let us not loose this present minute:
For time and age will worke that wrack
Which time or age shall ne're call backe.

"A Pastorall Dialogue," on the other hand,
demonstrates the pleasures of merely playing at
love, as a shepherd and a nymph, finding the deserted bower in which a pair of real lovers has spent
the night, reenact not their lovemaking but their
parting in an artistic aubade. "Good Counsel to a
young Maid" advises a girl not to yield too quickly
to a suitor while "Boldnesse in love" takes the
opposite tack, explaining to a "fond Boye" how
"moving accents" and self-confidence will cause
his mistress to receive him "With open eares, and
with unfolded armes." In "Ingratefull beauty
threatned" the poet admonishes Celia when she
scorns him: the lady should remember that "
'Twas I who gave thee thy renowne" and that the
poet can unmake what he has made. Conversely,

in "To A. D. unreasonable distrustfull of her owne beauty," the speaker attempts to raise the confidence of a shy girl, explaining that no one can love her until she first learns to love herself. Carew exhibits in these lyrics an exquisite psychological and social sensibility. In the aristocratic circles in which he passes his time, love is a game played to "cheat the lag, and lingring houres." Carew is the *magister ludi*, the master of the game, and his poems demonstrate that he alone knows all the right moves.

As is the case with Marvell, the amatory verse of Carew often addresses more than love. A lyric such as "A divine Mistris" – "In natures peeces still I see / Some errour, that might mended bee" – touches upon critical issues of aesthetics with a light but sure touch. In "To my Mistris sitting by a Rivers side. An Eddy," the speaker reads the actions of an eddy which strikes from the current toward the neighboring bank as an emblem of his relationship with his mistress. If she will accept his invitation to perpetual play, to a never-ending round of poetic and amorous dalliance, she can avoid being carried headlong to the wide ocean where she will "lose" her "colour, name, and tast." Poetry offers immortality, rescuing those who embrace it from the rushing river of time. In "To my Mistresse in absence" the poet offers a more explicit theory of the separation yet ultimate union of body and soul: though parted, the lovers "worke a mystique wreath" of hearts and minds that enables them to transcend the sublunary world. Thus fortified, they can "looke downe . . . and smile" at the pain their bodies suffer in the world below. This yearning for transcendence and, more importantly, a confidence that through poetry men and women can achieve it, becomes a major chord in Carew's poetry over the next twenty years.

The inspiration for many of these lyrics lies in Donne, whose songs, sonnets, and elegies enjoyed wide manuscript circulation in London during the years in which Carew began to write. The younger poet borrows ideas, images, sometimes precise wording from his model; yet the ultimate effect is very different from Donne. Carew's syntax is utterly clear, his arguments easy to follow; what he sacrifices in dynamism and immediacy he gains in lucidity. He utterly ignores the satiric side of Donne. Many lyrics also evince a thorough knowledge of late-Renaissance syncretism and treatises on love; Carew's poetry may well have been instrumental in laying the groundwork for the vogue of "platonic love" that would sweep the court in the 1630s.

After the death of Sir Matthew Carew the family sold their house in London, and his wife and older son, Matthew, retired to an estate at Mid-

dle Littleton, Worcestershire. On 13 May 1619 Thomas Carew embarked in the entourage of Sir Edward Herbert, later Lord Herbert of Cherbury, on his great embassy to Paris. Among Carew's companions was the young John Crofts, who would soon become his boon companion; over the next twenty years Carew became an intimate of the Crofts family of Saxham Parva, Suffolk, and wrote nearly a dozen poems to its various members. In Paris, Carew may well have met the Italian poet Giambattista Marini, whom he imitates in several lyrics; he could also have used this opportunity to familiarize himself with the works of the Pléiade and its successors. Herbert remained intermittently in Paris until 1624, but the evidence of the poems suggests that Carew probably returned to London before this time.

"To Saxham," Carew's first essay in the genre of the country-house poem, undoubtedly was composed in the early 1620s. Sir John Crofts and his wife sprang from Carew's own social class, the minor gentry; with a family of twelve children, including nine unmarried daughters, the Crofts were anxious seekers of preferment and husbands at the court of James I. Carew's tribute to the family estate at Saxham clearly imitates Ben Jonson's praise of the Sidney family in his most famous country-house poem, "To Penshurst," but it diverges from the model in its economy, its abstractness, and its application of lyric devices to a wholly new genre. A related poem, "To the King at his entrance into Saxham," celebrates a visit by James I to the Crofts's estate in the early 1620s and serves as the prologue to a masque staged by the family on that occasion. "To the King" explores the relationship between the monarch and his subjects through an appeal to the Ovidian fable of Philemon and Baucis – the country house and its traditions of hospitality make it possible for that "little god," the king, to mix easily with common men.

During the mid and late 1620s Carew's reputation as a poet grew rapidly. He was increasingly associated with the circle of scholars and wits in which Edward Hyde, later Earl of Clarendon, moved while studying at the Inns of Court. Clarendon recalled that Carew "was a person of a pleasant and facetious wit, and made many poems, (especially in the amorous way,) which for the sharpness of the fancy, and the elegancy of the language in which that fancy was spread, were at least equal, if not superior to any of that time." It is to this period in London that we should probably ascribe the composition of "A Rapture," the most accomplished and most infamous erotic poem of the century. The

POEMS.

By

THOMAS CAREW

Efquire.

One of the Gentlemen of the
Privie-Chamber, and Sewer in
Ordinary to His Majefty.

LONDON,

Printed by *I. D.* for *Thomas Walkley,*
and are to be fold at the figne of the
flying Horfe, between Brittains
Burfe, and York-Houfe.
1640

*Title page for the first collection of Carew's poetry, hastily compiled
soon after his death*

poem opens as a *suasoria* in which the poet invites his mistress, Celia, to enjoy the delights of lovemaking; it rapidly modulates into a witty, sensuous, and to some readers shocking celebration of the female body. Carew depicts Celia as a landscape waiting to be explored and conquered – "Then will I visit, with a wandring kisse, / The vale of Lillies, and the Bower of blisse"; Celia herself lies passively "like a sea of milke" while the poet invades her with such a tempest "as when *Jove* of old / Fell downe on *Danae* in a storme of gold." What raises "A Rapture" above the meaner beauties of Renaissance erotica is not only the lush precision of its imagery but also its conclusion, in which Carew seriously addresses the issue of the sexual double standard, asking why that one word "Honour" should mean such different and apparently contradictory things for men and women. Carew's argument, perhaps, is not completely thought out, and the frank sexuality of the first part of the poem tends to overwhelm its final movement, yet the intellectual daring of the endeavor distinguishes him from most of his contemporaries, whose thinking on human sexuality rarely broached new frontiers.

"A Rapture" drew a great deal of censure – it was even denounced by name in Parliament – but it also made the poet's reputation and gained him attention at court. By the late 1620s Carew had become intimate with Kit Villiers, Earl of Anglesey, and brother of the royal favorite, George Villiers, first Duke of Buckingham. Carew composed a pair of elegies on Buckingham after his assassination in 1628. Anglesey himself succumbed to the ravages of fast living in early 1630, and Carew wrote an elegy on him that remains a powerful and attractive statement of the pleasures of the retired life. Returning to the image that he had used in "An Eddy," Carew explains how Anglesey

chose not in the active streame to swim,
Nor hunted Honour; which, yet hunted him.
But like a quiet Eddie, that hath found

Some hollow creeke, there turnes his waters round,
And in continuall circles, dances free
From the impetuous Torrent; so did hee[.]

At the moment when Carew was about to embark on the most active phase of his career at court, he still recognized the allure of freedom, self-sufficiency, and ultimately transcendence that the retired life promised.

The demise of Buckingham brought a change in the character of the court. Charles I, who had succeeded his father, James, in 1625, was determined to purge the royal household and expel the immoral and unsavory figures who had clustered around his predecessor; Charles's queen, the French princess Henrietta Maria, emerged as the critical figure in setting the artistic tone of the new court. Carew made the transition to this brave new world with surprising ease, perhaps in part due to his friendship with James Hay, first Earl of Carlisle, and his dazzling wife Lucy, the intimate friend of Henrietta Maria and a renowned beauty in her own right. Carew tacked to the new wind: in a poem addressed "To the Queene" he renounces the libertine leanings he had evinced in "A Rapture" and confesses his embrace of the cult of pure platonic love that Henrietta Maria had introduced at court. Preferment came at last on 6 April 1630 when Carew was sworn a gentleman of the privy chamber; about the same time he was granted the active post of sewer in ordinary to the king, which he gained despite vigorous competition from a Scottish rival. The duty of the sewer was to taste and pass dishes of the food to the king, and the position brought Carew into almost daily contact with the monarchs. He would maintain the post for the rest of his life.

Despite his official duties Carew retained and strengthened his ties with the literary circles in London and on the court's periphery. Had Carew written nothing else, he would have secured his critical reputation with his poems "To Ben Iohnson: Vpon occasion of his Ode of defiance annext to his Play of the new Inne" and "An Elegie upon the death of the Deane of Pauls, Dr. Iohn Donne" (1633). Carew was the one major poet to write appreciations of both men; in doing so, he was undoubtedly attempting to sort out the major influences on his own work and to define his relation to the two towering figures of early-seventeenth-century poetry. "To Ben Iohnson" consoles the aging poet and playwright over the failure of *The New Inn* on the London stage; at the same time, it takes him to task for sparring with critics who are beneath him. Carew clearly owed a great debt to Jonson, particularly in

his early lyric poems: the forms he attempts, his comparatively simple diction, and his utterly limpid syntax are all Jonsonian in inspiration. The only account of a personal relationship between the two men, however, comes from James Howell, who in his *Epistolæ Ho-Elianæ* (1645) recounts a dinner at which Jonson began "to vapour extremely of himself, and by vilifying others, to magnify his own Muse." At this point Carew whispered to Howell that "tho' Ben had barrelled up a great deal of Knowledge, yet it seems he had not read the *Ethics*, which, among other Precepts of Morality, forbid Self-commendation, declaring it to be an ill-favour'd Solecism in good Manners." The anecdote is of a piece with Carew's poem, which combines clear-sighted appreciation of Jonson's literary achievement with a recognition that he may be past his prime – "Thy commique Muse" is in "decline / From that her Zenith." The tribute with which the poem concludes sums up the paradox of Jonson's situation: "The wiser world doth greater Thee confesse / Then all men else, then Thy selfe onely lesse." The triumph of Carew's poem is his combination of real praise with tactful admonition and the implicit suggestion that perhaps it is time for Jonson to retire and let other men take up his poetic laurels. Interestingly, Carew's epistle is shot through with Jonsonian allusion and imitations of the master's characteristic devices; in out-Jonsoning Jonson, he has suggested his own worthiness as a successor.

Carew's elegy on Donne is no less accomplished; it is, indeed, a bravura performance. Carew sets himself the difficult task of assessing Donne's position in English poetry, and he uses the occasion to predict how the successors of Donne, "Libertines in Poetrie," will squander his legacy. The elegy opens with a series of rhetorical questions, the answers to which form its organizing principle; Carew's response to the most interesting of these questions – "Can we not frame one elegy for Donne?" – consumes the larger portion of the poem. Donne is the great original in English poetry, Carew argues, and as such no elegy is possible because none of his degenerate successors is capable of writing one worthy of the subject. Carew's style, however, suggests that there may be one exception to this generalization. As in the epistle to Jonson, Carew displays an extraordinary skill for pastiche, imitating the most salient features of Donne's style and incorporating them into his own verse. The sweeping enjambment and knotty vocabulary, combined with a string of precise allusions to Donne's poetry, attest to Carew's intimate knowledge of his subject and slyly undercut his own argument. The poem closes with an oft quoted epitaph that aptly sums up Donne's career as poet and clergyman:

> Here lies a King, that rul'd as hee thought fit
> The universall Monarchy of wit;
> Here lie two Flamens, and both those, the best,
> Apollo's first, at last, the true Gods Priest.

Louis Martz sums up the achievement of the elegy in the simple statement, "If we grasp the poem we grasp Donne."

The question of the relative influence of Donne and Jonson on the poetry of Carew has been a major object of critical scrutiny over the past century, and different critical models have been advanced in support of one position or another. Most recent criticism has focused less on the amount of the debt than on what Carew did with what he borrowed: as the epistle to Jonson and the elegy on Donne demonstrate, Carew was extraordinarily adept at imitating both poets when the need occurred, but he is equally skilled at employing his mimetic powers to pursue his own, very different artistic ends. Perhaps the most balanced assessment is that while Jonson was the formative influence on Carew's poetry, he also borrowed heavily from Donne in his early lyrics and then in the major poems of the 1630s, beginning with the elegy. The early borrowings were primarily substantive, those in the 1630s primarily stylistic. Following the elegy on Donne, Carew's poetry assumes a new power and assurance as he addresses the issues that the 1630s brought to the fore.

Carew comes into his own as a commentator on affairs of state and as an enunciator of Caroline aesthetic ideals in his first major poem after the Donne elegy – "In answer of an Elegiacall Letter upon the death of the King of Sweden from Aurelian Townsend, inviting me to write on that subject." The death of Gustavus Adolphus, King of Sweden, in November 1632 had thrown the Protestant forces in the Thirty Years' War into confusion; Townshend and a spate of other English poets had penned rousing elegies urging that Charles I take up Gustavus's sword in order to reclaim the Palatinate for his sister, the exiled Elizabeth of Bohemia, and her family. In a deft and illuminating response, Carew declines Townshend's offer, pointing out that England would be foolish to exchange its "peace and plenty" for the death and devastation that Germany had already suffered in what by 1632 seemed a never-ending conflict. Englishmen should instead enjoy the "Halcyon dayes" of Charles's beneficent rule and celebrate with "Tourneyes,

Masques, Theaters" their good fortune. Mid-twentieth-century critics found the poem distasteful: C. V. Wedgwood decried what she termed a "mood of make-believe and play-acting" and Joseph H. Summers lamented the "smugly insular assumption of prosperity and an eternal party" in Carew's response. More recent articles have noted the grounding of the poem in Virgil's pastorals and have pointed out how closely attuned Carew's interpretation of European events was to the policy of the king and his advisers, who favored employing diplomatic rather than martial means to recover the Palatinate. Carew's poem is propaganda for the king's position, but it also constitutes an important exposition of his theories about how art ennobles men and women, permitting them to behold virtue, make it their own, and in so doing transcend their earthly limitations.

The central passage of "In answer to Aurelian Townsend" is a detailed description of how such a moral transformation takes place through participation in a court masque. Carew put his close observation of the form to good use the following year in his own masque, Coelum Britannicum, which was performed at Whitehall on Shrove Tuesday, 18 February 1634. Carew borrowed the basic idea of his masque from Spaccio de la Bestia Trionfante (1584), a dialogue by the sixteenth-century philosopher and mystic Giordano Bruno describing the moral reformation of the Olympian gods and the subsequent expulsion of the constellations, the mementos of their misdeeds, from the zodiac. In Carew's reworking of the theme, the decision of the gods to mend their ways springs from their desire to emulate the moral perfection of Charles and Henrietta Maria, who by this time had thoroughly purged the Caroline court of the unsavory hangers-on that they had inherited from the reign of James I. The main action of the masque parallels the cleansing of Olympus with what had already occurred in the Caroline court. Mercury, the messenger of the gods, outlines the general process, but it is left to Momus, the classical god of folly, to provide the tantalizing particulars. Momus's account is witty, ribald, and thoroughly satirical: his presence suggests that the court, or at least the poet who celebrated it, could still laugh at the occasional excesses that the monarchs' zeal might have led them to.

Mercury vanquishes an antimasque of allegorical figures representing vice and proclaims the apotheosis of Charles and Henrietta Maria, whose "Royall vertues" have earned them a place in the sky as the new constellation "Carlomaria." The dramatic performance cedes to the revels, which include a dance of ancient Picts, Scots, and Irish against an allegorical tableau of the three kingdoms that was designed by Inigo Jones. The masque concludes with a view of Windsor Castle; a troop of fifteen stars, signifying the stellified British heroes, appears in the sky surrounding the image of a serpent swallowing its tail, a Renaissance emblem of eternity whose circular form recalls the eddy image of Carew's earlier poems. Sir Henry Herbert, the master of the revels, remembered *Coelum Britannicum* as "the noblest masque of my time," and Carew's failure to write another masque after this triumph is puzzling. It may be that the satirical quips of Momus took too much license with the court; it may be that Carew found the form of the masque uncongenial; illness, perhaps, had begun to sap his creative energy. Whatever the cause, after 1634 it was Carew's friend and protégé, Sir William Davenant, who emerged as the preferred writer of court masques. In a sense *Coelum Britannicum* marks the high point of Carew's career. Although he continued to produce occasional poems and commendatory verses, and although one of his most exquisite pieces, "To G. N. from Wrest," still remained to be written, his most productive years were clearly those of the first half of the decade.

By the mid 1630s Thomas Carew had achieved the status of Caroline arbiter elegantiae, the man who set the standard for poetic excellence at the court. He attracted a following of younger poets, particularly Sir William Davenant and Sir John Suckling. Carew's relationship with Davenant stretched back to 1630 when he wrote commendatory verses for the first edition of *The Just Italian* (1630); he followed this poem with contributions to Davenant's *The Witts* (1636) and to *Madagascar* (1638), a volume of his occasional and lyric poetry. *The Just Italian* was shouted down by an unappreciative audience on its first production in October 1629, and one might more properly term Carew's poem consolatory rather than commendatory; the poet attacks "the sullen Age," counseling his young friend that only "men great and good" are so treated by "the Rabble." The poem prefixed to *Madagascar* is extremely significant for the insight it gives into Carew's aesthetic concerns. The title poem of Davenant's collection was a dream vision describing how Prince Rupert, the king's nephew, would lead an expedition to the island of Madagascar and conquer a new kingdom of incomparable richness for the Stuarts. Due to lack of funds and a growing skepticism – Rupert's mother, Elizabeth of Bohemia, labeled the plan "a Romance" out of "Don Quixotte" – the expedition never left port,

and by the time of its publication Davenant's high-flying heroic poem was something of a bad joke. Carew's poem "To Will. Davenant my Friend" concedes that the expedition was abortive, but argues,

> What though Romances lye
> Thus blended with more faithfull Historie?
> Wee, of th'adult'rate mixture not complaine,
> But thence more Characters of Vertue gaine[.]

These lines constitute the most explicit statement of the epideictic ends of Caroline art: the heroic characters who swirl through the masques and dramas of the 1630s are patterns for emulation, not the literal truth, but their value is none the less for that. Carew's confidence in the power of art seems boundless, and he imparted that belief to the court; it was this very confidence, perhaps, that made the ideological, political, and military reverses of the Civil War years so hard to believe and so difficult to endure.

Carew's relationship with Suckling is more problematic. Although the names of the two poets were often bracketed during their lifetimes and immediately thereafter, Carew never mentions Suckling in his work whereas Suckling addresses the older man in three poems and a pair of mock-humorous letters on the advisability of marriage. Suckling's pasquinade, "Upon T. C. having the P.," uses the traditional Petrarchan images of fire and water to poke fun at the humorous situation of Carew, the poet of love, laid up with a bout of the pox, or venereal disease. In his dialogue "Upon my Lady Carliles walking in Hampton-Court garden," Suckling presents the two men admiring the passage of the reigning court beauty. While the romantic T. C. confines himself to a discreet swoon at the sight of the lady's charms, the bolder J. S. confesses how he mentally stripped her of all her clothes as she strolled by. When Tom chides him for his presumption, Jack responds, "What ever fool like me had been, / If I'd not done as well as seen" and goes on to suggest that the countess is nothing more than a glorified slut. T. C. comes off as a fool whose excessive romanticism has blinded him to the true nature of his idol. In both these poems the presentation of Carew is jocular, but the humor has an edge: Suckling seems to admire Carew, and he embraces him as a comrade, but he also wants to take him down a peg. Suckling's final comment on Carew in "A Session of the Poets," his humorous catalogue of the Caroline poets who might be contenders for the poet laureateship after the death of Jonson, is similarly ambivalent. Carew, he writes, might have made a good laureate were it not that "His Muse was hard bound, and th'issue of's brain / Was seldom brought forth but with trouble and pain." Carew was indeed a meticulous craftsman, but the accusation that he labored over his verses would hardly have been considered a compliment in a court that valued *sprezzatura,* or aristocratic nonchalance, exceedingly. The excremental image in which the comment is wrapped completes the impression of a young Suckling trying to throw off what at times may have seemed the stifling influence of the older poet's strong artistic achievement.

By this point in his career Carew's fame as a lyricist and as a major artistic figure at court may well have seemed overwhelming to younger poets. Even the usually affable Davenant in his one piece addressed to Carew jokingly complains that Carew's poems are so good they have inflated courtly compliment. Lesser versifiers have been driven to desperation in the vain attempt to keep up, and lovers all over London will celebrate when the author of "A Rapture" finally breathes his last. This is, indeed, compliment with an edge. Carew apparently met this veiled hostility with silence. As Aurelian Townshend noted, Carew wrote no "rough footed Satires," and he continued to be generous with commendatory verses for other, less gifted poets until the end of his life.

The year 1639 found Thomas Carew at Wrest Park, Bedfordshire, the country seat of Henry de Grey, sixth Earl of Kent, and his wife, Elizabeth; it was from this rural retreat that Carew wrote what was probably his last poem, "To my friend G. N. from Wrest." The poem is an epistle to a fellow courtier serving in Charles I's abortive Scottish campaign during the spring of 1639; Carew contrasts the hardships his friend suffers on the bleak northern border with the plenty, peace, and leisure he enjoys with the de Greys. Carew consciously places his description of Wrest Park in the tradition of the country-house poem charted by "To Penshurst," but he diverges from the Jonsonian model in his emphasis on the physical and on the private rather than the public. In Carew's poem, Wrest, "i' th' center plac'd," is not so much an expansive emblem of an ideal social order as a terrestrial paradise protected by its triple moat from the political chaos that loomed just several years in the future. In its imagery and overall structure "To G. N. from Wrest" recalls the Caroline masque that Carew himself did so much to perfect; several of his descriptions, in fact, closely resemble the sets Jones designed for the last masque of the period, Davenant's *Salmacida Spolia* (1640). On the eve of the English Civil War, the poet retreats from the court, bearing the best of its culture with him. In this last work Carew looks forward to the uncertain and transient beauties of the Interregnum world of Andrew Marvell's "Upon Appleton House" rather than back to the solid verities of Jonson.

Thomas Carew died in March 1640. His place as sewer in ordinary was given to William Champneys on 22 March; he was buried in Saint Dunstan's-in-the-West on 23 March. His funeral cost forty-eight shillings, a sum larger than usual. Izaak Walton relates a story of the poet's deathbed repentance in the notes he collected for a life of the clergyman John Hales, who was both a cousin of Carew and a fellow of Merton when the poet matriculated there. According to Walton, in a dangerous fit of illness Carew had sent for Hales and received comfort and absolution on the promise that he would amend his scandalous life. Once recovered, however, Carew returned to his libertine ways. In his final illness Carew called again for Hales; the clergyman came but refused to absolve him, and the poet died unshriven.

No portrait of Thomas Carew has survived. The figures in the double portrait by Anthony Van Dyck that were once believed to depict Carew and Thomas Killigrew have now been firmly identified as Killigrew and William, Lord Crofts, the nephew of Carew's friend John.

Although Carew was celebrated during his lifetime and much imitated in the years immediately following his death, his critical reputation slowly sank over the next two centuries, to the point that Alexander Pope could dismiss him as "a bad Waller." His star has risen again in the second half of the twentieth century: New Critics recognized him as a deft and sophisticated master of the lyric, and more recent scholars have emphasized his roles as a political commentator, literary critic, and consummate courtier. More than the works of any other writer of the period, the poems of Thomas Carew define the aesthetic values of the aristocratic circles of the court of Charles I.

References:

Joanne Altieri, "Response to a Waning Mythology in Carew's Political Poetry," *Studies in English Literature*, 26 (Winter 1986): 107–124;

Raymond A. Anselment, "Thomas Carew and the 'Harmlesse Pastimes' of Caroline Peace," *Philological Quarterly*, 62 (Spring 1983): 201–219;

Rufus A. Blanshard, "Carew and Jonson," *Studies in Philology*, 52 (1955): 195–211;

Edward Hyde, *The History of the Rebellion and Civil Wars in England: Also His Life Written by Himself* (Oxford: Oxford University Press, 1843);

Paula Johnson, "Carew's 'A Rapture': The Dynamics of Fantasy," *Studies in English Literature*, 16 (Winter 1976): 145–155;

John Kerrigan, "Thomas Carew," The Chatterton Lecture on Poetry, *Proceedings of the British Academy*, 74 (1988): 311–350;

Ada Long and Hugh MacLean, " 'Deare Ben,' 'great DONNE,' and 'my *Celia*': The Wit of Carew's Poetry, *Studies in English Literature*, 18 (Winter 1978): 75–94;

Louis Martz, *The Wit of Love* (Notre Dame: University of Indiana Press, 1969);

C. E. McGee, " 'The Visit of the Nine Goddesses': A Masque at Sir John Crofts's House," *English Literary Renaissance*, 21 (Autumn 1991): 371–384;

Michael P. Parker, " 'All are not born (sir) to the Bay': 'Jack' Suckling, 'Tom' Carew, and the Making of a Poet," *English Literary Renaissance*, 12 (Autumn 1982): 341–368;

Parker, "Carew's Politic Pastoral: Virgilian Pretexts in the 'Answer to Aurelian Townshend,' " *John Donne Journal*, 1, nos. 1–2 (1982): 101–116;

Parker, " 'To my Friend G. N. from Wrest': Carew's Secular Masque," in *Classic and Cavalier: Essays on Jonson and the Sons of Ben*, edited by Claude J. Summers and Ted-Larry Pebworth (Pittsburgh: University of Pittsburgh Press, 1982), pp. 171–191;

Lynn Sadler, *Thomas Carew* (Boston: Twayne, 1979);

Edward I. Selig, *The Flourishing Wreath: A Study of Thomas Carew's Poetry* (New Haven: Yale University Press, 1958);

Kevin Sharpe, "Cavalier Critic: The Ethics and Politics of Thomas Carew's Poetry," in *Politics of Discourse*, edited by Sharpe and Steven N. Zwicker (Berkeley: University of California Press, 1987), pp. 117–146;

Sharpe, *Criticism and Compliment: The Politics and Literature in the England of Charles I* (Cambridge: Cambridge University Press, 1987);

Joseph H. Summers, *The Heirs of Donne and Jonson* (London: Chatto & Windus, 1970), pp. 62–75;

C. V. Wedgwood, *Poetry and Politics under the Stuarts* (Cambridge: Cambridge University Press, 1960).

Papers:

Sir Matthew Carew's correspondence with Sir Dudley Carleton and his agent, Edward Sherburne, is in the Public Record Office, London. Manuscripts including texts of Carew's poems are scattered throughout the United Kingdom and the United States, the most important single repositories being the British Library, London, and the Bodleian Library, Oxford.

William Cartwright

(circa 23 December 1611 – 29 November 1643)

Charles Clay Doyle
University of Georgia

BOOKS: *The Royall Slave. A Tragi-Comedy* (Oxford: Printed by William Turner for Thomas Robinson, 1639);

To the Right Honourble Philip Earle of Pembroke (London: Printed for T. W., 1641);

November, or, Signal Days (London, 1647);

Comedies, Tragi-Comedies, With other Poems (London: Printed for Humphrey Moseley, 1651);

An Off-Spring of Mercy, Issuing Out of the Womb of Cruelty (London: Printed by A. M., sold by John Brown, 1652).

Editions: *The Life and Poems of William Cartwright,* edited by R. Cullis Goffin (Cambridge: Cambridge University Press, 1918);

The Plays and Poems of William Cartwright, edited by G. Blakemore Evans (Madison: University of Wisconsin Press, 1951).

PLAY PRODUCTION: *The Royal Slave,* Oxford University, 30 August 1636.

OTHER: "On His Majesties recovery from the small Pox," in *Musarum Oxoniensium Pro Rege Suo Soteria* (Oxford: Printed by J. Lichfield and William Turner, 1633);

"To the King, On His Majesties Return from Scotland" and "To the Queen on the same Occasion," in *Solis Britannici Perigaeum* (Oxford: Printed by J. Lichfield and William Turner, 1633);

"On the Birth of the Duke of York," in *Vitis Carolinae Gemma Altera* (Oxford: Printed by J. Lichfield and William Turner, 1633);

"Upon the Translation of Chaucer's Troilus and Creseide," in *Amorum Troili et Creseidæ,* translated by Sir Francis Kynaston (Oxford: Printed by J. Lichfield, 1635);

"On the Birth of the King's Fourth Child," in *Coronae Carolinae Quadratura* (Oxford: Printed by L. Lichfield, 1636);

"To the King, on the Birth of the Princess Anne," in *Flos Britannicus Veris Novissimi Filiola Carolo &*

Portrait of William Cartwright engraved as the frontispiece to his posthumously published Comedies, Tragi-Comedies, With other Poems *(1651)*

Mariae (Oxford: Printed by L. Lichfield, 1637);

"On the Death of the Right Honourable the Lord Viscount Bayning," in *Death Repeal'd by a Thankfull Memoriall Sent from Christ-Church in Oxford* (Oxford: Printed by L. Lichfield for F. Bowman, 1638);

"To the Queen after her dangerous Delivery," in *Musarum Oxoniensium Charisteria pro Serenissima Regina Maria* (Oxford: Printed by L. Lichfield, 1638);

"In the memory of the most Worthy Benjamin Johnson," in *Ionsonvs Virbivs* (London: Printed by E. Purslow for H. Seile, 1638);

"Upon the Birth of the Kings sixth Child," in *Horti Carolini Rosa Altera* (Oxford: Printed by L. Lichfield, 1640);

"Upon the Death of the most hopefull the Lord Stafford," in Anthony Stafford, *Honour and Vertue, Triumphing over the Grave* (London: Printed by J. Okes for H. Seile, 1640);

"A sigh sent to his Mistresse," in *Poems: Written by Wil. Shake-speare, Gent.* (London: Printed by T. Cotes, sold by J. Benson, 1640);

"On the Marriage of the Lady Mary to the Prince of Aurange his Son," in *Proteleia Anglo-Batava* (Oxford: Printed by L. Lichfield, 1641);

"To My Honour'd Friend Mr. Thomas Killigrew, On these his Playes," in Thomas Killigrew, *The Prisoners and Claracilla* (London: Printed by T. Cotes for Andrew Crooke, 1641);

"On the Queens Return from the Low Countries," in *Musarum Oxoniensium Epibateria Serenissimae Reginarum Mariae ex Batavia Feliciter Reduci* (Oxford: Printed by L. Lichfield, 1643);

"Upon the death of the Right valiant Sir Bevill Grenvill Knight," in *Verses on the Death of the Right Valiant Sr Bevill Grenvill, Knight* (Oxford: Printed by L. Lichfield, 1643);

"Upon the Dramatick Poems of Mr John Fletcher" and "Another on the same," in Francis Beaumont and John Fletcher, *Comedies and Tragedies* (London: Printed for Humphrey Robinson and for Humphrey Moseley, 1647).

Of the myriad minor poets writing in the middle third of the seventeenth century, none enjoyed a higher contemporaneous reputation than William Cartwright. Ben Jonson is said to have proclaimed, "My son Cartwright writes all like a man." When Cartwright died in 1643, King Charles I is reported to have shed a tear and dressed in black. Accompanying the posthumous publication of Cartwright's works in 1651 were a record fifty-four commendatory poems, including tributes by Henry Lawes, Henry Vaughan, James Howell, Izaak Walton, Alexander Brome, John Birkenhead, Jasper Mayne, Katherine Philips, and John Fell. Some historians of literature have relegated Cartwright to a "representative" role – exemplifying an eclectic blend of Metaphysical wit and Cavalier polish that charac-

terized the transitional interval between Jacobean refulgence and the dawning of the Restoration. However, anyone who patiently reads the quantities of verse published in the 1630s, 1640s, and 1650s will recognize Cartwright's talent as far exceeding the typical.

Cartwright was born about 23 December 1611 in the village of Northway, Gloucestershire. His parents, William Cartwright and Dorothy Coles Cartwright, seem to have been prosperous at the time. At some point they moved to Cirencester and kept an inn, which did not flourish. Young William, meanwhile, had enrolled in the free school, from where he proceeded to Westminster school on a king's scholarship, probably in 1623 or 1624. In 1628 he entered Christ Church, Oxford, as a "gentleman scholar," a mark of academic distinction as well as a financial benefit. The university would be Cartwright's home for the remaining fifteen years of his life. During those same years Oxford evolved into something like the second seat of the embattled Stuart monarchy. That circumstance had an immense effect on Cartwright's career and reputation.

In 1630 Cartwright became a published poet, with a set of Latin verses in *Britanniae Natalis,* a collection of poems by Oxonians (none of them writing in English) commemorating the birth of Prince Charles. During his career poems by Cartwright (nine in Latin, eleven in English) appeared in twelve of the thirteen such Oxford collections that were published, mostly on occasions involving members of the royal family. While Cartwright was at Oxford the commemorative collections started to include English verse, especially in the poems addressed to Queen Henrietta Maria, who lacked knowledge of Latin.

Cartwright's first English poem, "On His Majesties recovery from the small Pox," was in the 1633 collection *Pro Rege Suo Soteria,* which celebrated the king's return to health. Like John Dryden's "Upon the Death of the Lord Hastings" (1650), Cartwright's poem shocks and repels the modern reader in its youthful effort to decorate what now seems an intrinsically "unpoetic" subject; of the royal lesions,

> let us say
> They were small Starres fixt in a Milky way;
> Or faithfull Turquoises, which Heaven sent
> For a discovery, not a punishment[.]

Royal births offered more propitious – and more frequent – opportunities for the Oxford poets. From 1633 through 1640 Cartwright published five English poems in university collections on the births of James, Elizabeth, Anne, Catherine, and

Henry. Perhaps the most interesting feature of these poems is the gradual introduction of pointed topical commentary into panegyric, a kind of poetry that by convention would not admit of such. In his poem on the birth of Prince James (1633), Cartwright might be heard gently and obliquely warning the king:

> Although in Royal births the Subjects lot
> Be to enjoy what's by the Prince begot;
> Yet fasten, CHARLES, fasten those eyes You owe
> Vnto a People, on this Sonne, to show
> You can be tender too, in this one thing
> Suffer the Father to depose the King.

If those lines contain a plea for "tenderness" in his monarchy, King Charles paid no heed.

When he celebrated the birth of Princess Elizabeth in 1636, Cartwright (like other Royalist poets) ventured touches of satire – even burlesque – directed at the unruly rabble and at Parliament itself. The queen's fecundity had become a topic of merriment for the poets (and she was only half through childbearing in 1636). When Cartwright muses, "For, now that Royal Births doe come so fast, / That we may feare They'll Commons be at last," the witticism was more prophetic than the poet could have imagined. Parenthetically the poem offers a sensible warning to the king (again unheeded): "For silenc'd Preachers have most Hearers still."

In 1638 the occasion was the birth and death of the infant Catherine and the queen's survival of her dangerous confinement. By this time the precariousness of the Stuart monarchy was obvious to nearly everyone except the king. Naturally, the Royalist poets put the best possible face on circumstances: Henrietta Maria was doing her part to secure the lineage, and Cartwright's poem bravely parallels the danger from which the queen had been delivered with the danger from which the king must deliver himself:

> See how Your Great Iust Consort bears the Crosse!
> Your Safeties Gaine makes him oresee the Losse:
> So that, although this Cloud stand at the Doore,
> His Great Designes goe on still as before.

The last line can be construed as either a commendation or a rebuke.

The mixed style in which Cartwright paid tribute to the Stuarts and defended monarchy, Anglicanism, and the good old cause – while directing satire and burlesque at Parliament, the Puritans, and the people – often saves the performances from the unrelieved hyperbole and sentimentality to which panegyric verse is prone.

In a sense the poems in the Oxford commemorative collections were academic exercises – the scholars vying to exhibit their learning, wit, and craftsmanship, while currying royal favor for themselves and the university. In another sense, though, the poems were deadly serious engagements in a war of ideology and propaganda. They also offered a means by which the academicians might hope to communicate with royal personages – if any bothered to read the tributes (it is more likely the queen did than the fatally abstracted and aloof king).

Cartwright had received his B.A. on 5 June 1632 and commenced his studies for the M.A., which he received on 15 April 1635. In that year his first commendatory poem appeared, eighteen lines prefacing Francis Kynaston's translation (1635) of Geoffrey Chaucer's *Troilus and Criseyde* into Latin verse – so that (in Cartwright's words) "we / Read *Chaucer* now without a Dictionary."

Another aspect of Cartwright's literary career blossomed in 1636, when the last of the great royal progresses, so beloved of Tudor Englishmen, reached Oxford. To climax the university's extravagant entertainments and tributes to the king and his family, Cartwright's play *The Royal Slave* received its premier performance on 30 August. There were troupes of dancers, Persian costumes and exotic scenes designed by Inigo Jones, and lyric poems set to music by Henry Lawes. The audience's praise was unanimous and unstinting. The queen commanded a performance to be staged at Court – at her expense – a few months later. The play was printed in 1639 and again in 1640. William Cartwright had become an author of note.

The Royal Slave holds but limited interest for modern readers, and it has not proved stage-worthy since the seventeenth century. The basis of its appeal to Royalist circles probably extended beyond the audience's superficial love of spectacle; after all, the play was popular in print as well as in performance. The mode of romantic, Platonic comedy – or tragicomedy – itself spoke to the Royalist yearning for a time or place in which all conflicts could be resolved by ceremony, genteel behavior, and academic disquisition. The play's title character, Cratander, a baseborn Greek, is now prisoner of war at the mercy of the king of Persia. Selected (according to the Persian custom) to serve as mock king for three days before being sacrificed to the sun god, Cratander (contrary to the practice of Persia's previous victims) spends his time scrupulously exemplifying and studiously discoursing upon the ideal of monarchy, winning the admiration and (platonic) love of the queen and her ladies – and finally the respect of the king, who transcends his confusion, jealousy, and other shortcomings as a ruler and a husband. At the end the king of Persia makes Cratander a king in his native Greece.

It might seem that the play was impudently allegorizing the inadequacies of a hereditary monarchy. However, the intended audience appears to have been not King Charles so much as Henrietta Maria, who would have approved of the Persian queen's enlightened attitudes and of the prominence of women's roles in the play. Still, as in the occasional poems addressed to royalty, it is possible that Cartwright was obliquely advising King Charles against some of his policies and practices that were leading toward chaos in the realm and ensuring his destruction.

There is no way to be sure when Cartwright's other three plays were written; they were not published until the posthumous *Comedies, Tragi-Comedies, With other Poems* of 1651, and there is no good evidence that they were ever acted (though markings in certain copies of the 1651 edition show that *The Lady Errant* and *The Ordinary* were prepared for the stage after the Restoration). *The Lady Errant* and *The Siege, or Love's Covert* are romantic comedies, or perhaps tragicomedies, somewhat in the manner of *The Royal Slave* (though with more comic action and less discussion of kingship). *The Ordinary,* in contrast, is a pure comedy. There Cartwright follows the conventions of Jonsonian "humors" comedy (the greatest influence would seem to be *The Alchemist,* 1612) as he pens his menagerie of rogues, dupes, social climbers, Puritans, and quick-witted women who congregate at the boarding house to nourish, recreate, and enrich themselves. *The Ordinary* also anticipates certain features of Restoration comedy, and the play is by no means unreadable today.

Cartwright took holy orders in 1638; he was reported by Anthony Wood (*Athenæ Oxoniensis,* 1692) to have been "the most florid and seraphical Preacher at the University." That year Cartwright contributed, presumably by invitation, to *Jonsonus Virbius,* in which the most famous writers of the time (Edmund Waller, John Cleveland, John Ford, James Howell, William Habington, Owen Felltham, Thomas May – thirty poets in all) paid tribute to the poet laureate, who had died the year before. This was Cartwright's first work to be published outside of Oxford; his horizons were broadening.

Affirming his own membership in the Sons of Ben, Cartwright begins his poem, "*Father of*

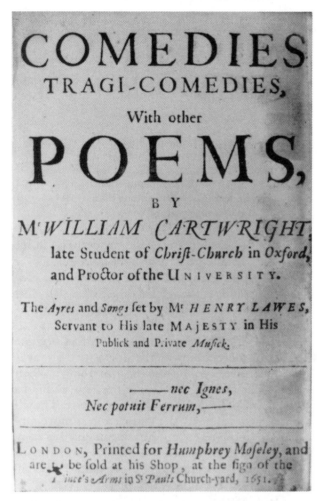

Title page for the first, posthumously published collection of Cartwright's works, whose appearance seven years after his death marks the height of his popularity, especially among Royalists who considered Cartwright a martyr to their cause

Poets. . . ." Unlike his poem on the Latin translation of Chaucer, an English poem (and one in Latin) on Thomas Killigrew's *The Prisoners and Claracilla* (1641), and two posthumously published tributes in the 1647 folio of Francis Beaumont and John Fletcher, Cartwright's poem of 184 lines on Jonson is not, strictly speaking, a "commendatory" poem, since it did not preface the publication of another author's work. However, in all other respects it exemplifies the commendatory poem at its best, comparing not unfavorably with Jonson's own verses on William Shakespeare, Thomas Carew's on John Donne, or John Birkenhead's on Cartwright himself. Commendatory poems do not, of course, offer literary criticism as such; rather, their business is to praise a poet, usually by delineating an ideal and asserting their subject's affinity with that ideal. Thus

Cartwright defines Jonson's success in achieving dramatic unity:

> No strange perplexed *maze* doth passe for *plot,*
> *Thou* always dost *unty,* not *cut* the *knot.*
> *Thy Lab'rinths* doores are open'd by one *thread*
> That tyes, and runnes through *all* that's *don* or *said.*

In a metrical tour de force, he commends Jonson's originality but even more his craftsmanship ("fancy" and "judgment," the seventeenth century would say):

> 'Tis easie to guild *gold:* there's small skill spent
> Where ev'n the first rude *masse* is *ornament:*
> *Thy Muse* tooke harder *metalls, purg'd* and *boild,*
> *Labour'd* and *try'd, heated,* and *beate* and *toyld,*
> *Sifted* the *drosse,* fil'd *roughnes,* then gave *dresse,*
> Vexing rude *subjects* into *comlinesse.*

Perhaps, with a pun on the word *subjects,* Cartwright was justifying the behavior of the king of England by praising the art of the king of poets.

Especially when a commendatory poem addresses a dead poet, the past era becomes idealized, in contrast with the present time of social decay and artistic diminution. So satire is easily incorporated into such poems:

> Though those *thy* thoughts, which the now queasie *age,*
> Doth count but *clods,* and refuse of the *stage,*
> Will come up *Porcelaine-wit* some hundreds hence,
> When there will be more *manners,* and more *sense;*
> 'Twas judgement yet to yeeld, and we afford
> *Thy* silence as much *fame,* as once *thy word* [.]

Events were approaching a crisis for King Charles, for Oxford, and for William Cartwright. In 1642 Cartwright was appointed reader in metaphysics to the university. That same year open hostilities broke out between Royalists and Parliamentarians. On 13 August the king issued a proclamation ordering the university to arm itself and to place the town in a state of defense. Cartwright was elected to a "Council of War" to facilitate the effort. In early October the parliamentary sympathizer William Fiennes, first Viscount Saye and Sele, took over the town, and Cartwright was imprisoned briefly for his activities. Shortly thereafter King Charles commandeered the town for his headquarters. When the king and the court repaired to Oxford after the Battle of Edgehill (the king took up lodging in Cartwright's college, Christ Church), Cartwright preached the "victory" sermon, the only sermon of his that survives; it was published in

1652 under the title *An Off-Spring of Mercy, Issuing Out of the Womb of Cruelty.*

In the summer of 1643 Cartwright wrote his last poem on a royal occasion, in an Oxford collection celebrating Queen Henrietta Maria's return from the Netherlands, where she had gone to solicit arms and funds from her Catholic kinsmen and allies to abet her husband's campaign against Parliament. The mission further eroded popular support for the royal cause. The king's principal minister, Thomas Wentworth, Earl of Strafford, had already been impeached, attainted, and executed by parliamentary decree ("the Crown-Martyrs blood so lately spilt"). Members of Parliament were accusing not only Archbishop William Laud but the queen herself of treason – against the office and the person of the king, according to the official metonymy that the Parliamentarians would shortly abandon, when they put the king's own person on trial for crimes against the realm. On disembarking in February 1643, the queen and her party were actually fired upon by parliamentary troops. In these straits Henrietta Maria seems to have behaved with considerable dignity and heroism:

> When greater Tempests, then on Sea before,
>   Receav'd Her on the shore,
> When She was shot at, *for the King's own good,*
>   By Villaines hir'd to Blood;
> How bravely did Shee doe, how bravely Beare,
> And shew'd, though they durst rage, Shee durst not feare.

That stanza was censored from some printings of the 1651 works. Not everything in the poem is sarcasm and satire. The following lines have been widely admired as a tribute that transcends both the conventions of the genre and the rancor of the times:

> Courage was cast about Her like a Dresse
>   Of solemne Comelinesse;
> A gather'd Mind, and an untroubled Face
>   Did give Her dangers grace.
> Thus arm'd with Innocence, secure they move,
> Whose Highest Treason is but Highest Love.

Cartwright's last poem that can be plausibly dated is an elegy on the death of Sir Bevil Grenville, a Cornishman who died in battle in July 1643, the same month the queen arrived at Oxford and received the collection of poems celebrating her return from the Continent. The university, probably hoping to cultivate the favor of Grenville's family, published a small volume to which only thirteen poets contributed, all of them writing in English. Such a tribute, as noted in the preface to the 1684 republication of the book (with a bit of exaggeration), was "a respect . . . never done before to any but the Royal Family." Predictably, the poems mix elegiac conventions with strident denunciations of the rebels. Though hardly a soldier himself, Cartwright certainly identified with Grenville's commitment to the cause:

> Whence, in a just esteeme, to Church and Crowne
> He offred All, and nothing thought his owne.
> This thrust Him into Action, Whole and Free;
> Knowing no Interest but Loyalty[.]

Those lines would have made a fair epitaph for Cartwright himself.

That autumn Cartwright, along with some other prominent Oxonians, fell sick with a new "camp disease" (perhaps dysentery, typhus, or typhoid). "The King and Queen enquired very anxiously of his health in his last sickness," according to David Lloyd's *Memoires* (1668). Cartwright died on 29 November and was buried in his beloved Christ Church, Oxford. No inscription identifies his grave.

Through the meanderings of literary history and the vagaries of canon revision, Cartwright has maintained a stable place among the second rank – or at least the third rank – of seventeenth-century poets. His martyrdom (so it was regarded) boosted his reputation to the zenith marked by the 1651 publication of his collected works, heralded by the fifty-four commendatory poems. The number of copies of that edition that survive today suggests that the book was widely owned and cherished, probably (among others) by nostalgic Royalists during the Interregnum. By 1700 more than a score of popular miscellanies and songbooks had reprinted individual poems by Cartwright. During the Restoration era and the eighteenth century, he was routinely grouped among noteworthy "modern" poets. In the nineteenth century several influential collections of poetry and biographical sketches of poets kept his name and reputation alive, if somewhat diminished. In the twentieth century renewed attention to Cartwright accompanied the general surge of interest in Metaphysical poetry. However, like other poets of his time, Cartwright has proved difficult to categorize; for instance, he is represented not only in Helen Gardner's *The Metaphysical Poets* (1957) but also in Hugh Maclean's *Ben Jonson and the Cavalier Poets* (1974).

It is as a lyric poet that Cartwright has been most valued in the present century. Thirty or so general and period anthologies include poems by him (from one to a dozen each). A few of those anthologies include one or two of Cartwright's "occasional" poems, but mostly they feature his lyric poems, including songs from the plays (of course, anthologies do tend to favor short poems). By far the poems most often anthologized are "To Chloe who wish'd her self young enough for me" and "No Platonique Love."

"To Chloe" is a gallant rhapsody of platonic love. It argues that a person's true age dates from the beginning of true love:

> There are two Births, the one when Light
> First strikes the new awak'ned sense;
> The Other when two Souls unite;
> And we must count our life from thence[.]

Such transcending of physical concerns also resembles the final resurrection of the body itself:

> Love, like that Angell that shall call
> Our bodies from the silent Grave,
> Unto one Age doth raise us all,
> None too much, none too little have[.]

In contrast, "No Platonique Love," coming from the pen of such a cloistered academician as Cartwright, author of poems and plays extolling platonic love, must have struck its early readers as hilariously paradoxical, beginning "Tell me no more of Minds embracing Minds." Less brilliantly than the persona of Donne's "Extasie" – but also more quietly, more smoothly, and much more briefly – the imagined speaker of Cartwright's four stanzas descends easily and guiltlessly to affections and to faculties:

> I was that silly thing that once was wrought
> To Practise this thin Love;
> I climb'd from Sex to Soul, from Soul to Thought;
> But thinking there to move,
> Headlong I rowl'd from Thought to Soul, and then
> From Soul I lighted at the Sex agen.

That stanza has hardly an image at all, much less a "metaphysical conceit"; yet it has genuine wit.

Perhaps most to be regretted about Cartwright's engulfment in the world of affairs – his commitment to a self-destructive cause and then his early death – is the loss to the world of more such elegantly good-humored lyrics.

Bibliography:

W. W. Greg, *A Bibliography of the English Printed Drama to the Restoration,* volume 3 (London: Bibliographical Society, 1957), pp. 1027–1031.

References:

Raymond A. Anselment, "William Cartwright's Commemorative Verse: A Reassessment," *Modern Language Studies,* 15 (Fall 1985): 232–244;

Anne Barton, "He That Plays the King," in *English Drama: Forms and Development, Essays in Honour of Muriel Clara Brad-Brook,* edited by Marie Axton and Raymond Williams (Cambridge & New York: Cambridge University Press, 1977), pp. 69–93;

G. E. Bentley, *The Jacobean and Caroline Stage,* volume 3 (Oxford: Clarendon Press, 1956), pp. 126–142;

Martin Butler, "Court Drama: The Queen's Circle, 1632–37," in his *Theatre and Crisis, 1632–1642* (Cambridge: Cambridge University Press, 1984), pp. 25–54;

Joe Lee Davis, *The Sons of Ben: Jonsonian Comedy in Caroline England* (Detroit: Wayne State University Press, 1967), pp. 159–162;

Charles Clay Doyle, "Nature's Fair Defect: Milton and William Cartwright on the Paradox of Woman," *English Language Notes,* 11 (December 1973): 107–110;

Willa McClung Evans, "Cartwright's Debt to Lawes," in *Music in English Renaissance Drama,* edited by John H. Long (Lexington: University of Kentucky Press, 1968), pp. 103–116;

D. F. Foxon, "The Varieties of Early Proof: Cartwright's *Royal Slave,* 1639, 1640," *Library,* 25 (June 1970): 151–154;

Edward LeComte, "Herrick's Corinna," *Names,* 33 (December 1985): 292–295;

James E. Ruoff, "Cartwright's Human Sacrifice Scene in 'The Royal Slave,' " *Notes and Queries,* 202 (July 1957): 295–296;

Kevin Sharpe, *Criticism and Compliment: The Politics of Literature in the England of Charles I* (Cambridge: Cambridge University Press, 1987), pp. 47–52.

Papers:

No Cartwright autograph papers exist today. It is possible (though far from likely) that surviving fragments of proof sheets for *The Royal Slave,* in the Bodleian Library, are corrected in Cartwright's hand. Numerous seventeenth-century manuscripts of individual poems and of *The Royal Slave* survive; most of these are in the British Library, the Bodleian Library, and the Folger Shakespeare Library (full descriptions appear in G. Blakemore Evans's edition of *The Plays and Poems of William Cartwright,* 1951).

John Cleveland

(June 1613 – 29 April 1658)

Daniel P. Jaeckle
University of Houston-Victoria

BOOKS: *The Character of a London Diurnall* (Oxford: Printed by L. Lichfield, 1644);

The Character of a London-Diurnall: With severall select Poems: By the same Author (London, 1647);

The Character of a Country Committee-man, with the Earmark of a Sequestrator (London, 1649);

Poems. By J. C. With Additions (London, 1651);

The Character of a Diurnal-maker (London, 1654);

J. Cleaveland Revived (London: Printed for Nathaniel Brook, 1659; second edition, enlarged, 1660);

Clievelandi Vindiciae; or, Clieveland's Genuine Poems, Orations, Epistles, &c., edited by Samuel Drake and John Lake (London: Printed by Nathaniel Brooke, 1677);

The Works of Mr. John Cleveland, Containing his Poems, Orations, Epistles, Collected into One Volume, With the Life of the Author (London: Printed by R. Holt for Obadiah Blagrave, 1687).

Editions: *The Poems of John Cleveland: Annotated and Correctly Printed for the First Time with Biographical and Historical Introductions,* edited by John M. Berdan (New York: Grafton, 1903);

The Poems of John Cleveland, edited by Brian Morris and Eleanor Withington (Oxford: Clarendon Press, 1967).

In his own day John Cleveland was one of the most popular living British poets. Between 1647 and 1687 there appeared at least twenty-five editions of his poetry, remarkable testimony to the wide appeal of his work. Contemporaries viewed him as a witty lyricist and brilliant satirist, as a genius in producing strong lines, and as a leading spokesperson for the Royalist faction in the dark days of the civil wars and their aftermath. An influence on many other authors, Cleveland most obviously affected Andrew Marvell and Samuel Butler. In the years after his death Cleveland's style was too extravagant for John Dryden, and Samuel Johnson in the eighteenth century chastised his conceits. In the twentieth century he has received attention as one of the last and most decadent of the Metaphysi-

Portrait of John Cleveland engraved as the frontispiece for his Poems *(1651)*

cal poets. In recent years Cleveland has also been treated as an important figure in the history of political satire.

The poet's father, Thomas Cleveland, graduated from Saint John's College, Cambridge, in 1609, and was sometime thereafter appointed assistant to the rector of the parish church in Loughborough, Leicestershire. In 1610 he married Elizabeth Hebbe. Their eldest son, John, was baptized on 20 June 1613, soon after birth. To supplement the family income, the poet's father assisted John Dawson at Burton's Grammar School. In 1621 Thomas was presented the vicarage in Hinckley, where he lived the rest of his life. At Hinckley young Cleveland studied under Richard Vines, a Puritan preacher of considerable reputation and influence. On 4 September 1627 John entered Christ's College, Cambridge, as a lesser pensioner. While a young undergraduate, he delivered a Latin oration welcoming the university's chancellor, Sir Henry Rich, first Earl of Holland, and his guest, the French ambassador. Probably near the end of his undergraduate studies, Cleveland was "Father" of the Cambridge revels, an annual burlesque of university life. In 1631 he received his B.A., and in 1635, his M.A. On 27 March 1634 he was elected to the Hebblethwaite Fellowship in Saint John's College, where he continued until at least 1642. His duties consisted largely of instructing undergraduates, among them Samuel Drake and John Lake, who were to edit his poems in 1677. Between 1635 and 1637 Cleveland was named Rhetoric Reader, and several of his Latin orations survive. In March 1642 he welcomed the king in a speech which so pleased Charles I that he asked for a copy to be sent to him as he continued his royal travels. Cleveland apparently did not seek sacred orders but, after his M.A., pursued the law line and perhaps the physic line.

At Cambridge, Cleveland contributed to two university collections of poems, the first published in 1638 on the occasion of Edward King's death, the second honoring Charles's return from Scotland in 1641. Although neither of the poems written for these occasions displays Cleveland at his best, both reveal his stylistic inclinations. The elegy for King may pale beside John Milton's "Lycidas" in the same volume, but it is notable for Cleveland's characteristically strong opening gesture: "I LIKE not tears in tune; nor will I prise / His artificiall grief, that scannes his eyes." If this opening promises a sincere reflection on the deceased, however, the poem fails to keep that promise. Cleveland elaborates themes common in the collection: King's learning and virtue, his death by water, and the task of the survivors to find meaning in this death. Conceits abound, as in these two couplets:

> I am no Poet here; my penne's the spout
> Where the rain-water of my eyes runs out
> In pitie of that name, whose fate we see
> Thus copi'd out in griefs Hydrographie.

The unusual polysyllabic word to end the second couplet is typical of Cleveland, as is the conceit of

his pen as rainspout for his tears in the first couplet. Cleveland does not always force conceits so, but labored figures are common in his poetic corpus.

The other poem written for a university collection, "Upon the Kings return from Scotland," is also characteristic of Cleveland's verse. The snappy opening – "RETURN'D? I'll ne'r believe't; First prove him hence" – displays the harshness and colloquialism of John Donne's most memorable first lines; but even more typical of Cleveland is the seemingly infinite variety of comparisons that fly with such speed through the poem. The ruling idea, that the king never left England though he was in Scotland, is likened to the ubiquity of the soul, the zodiac, trees sending down roots while branches rise, mythological Cacus's walking backward to steal cattle, a gun recoiling, and so on. Cleveland's exuberant invention is matched only by his ability to frame these witty figures in tight couplets.

These two poems introduce what John Dryden called "Clevelandism," a style occasionally imitated but not quite duplicated by Cleveland's contemporaries. Although Dryden was trying to clear ground for his own style by condemning Cleveland's penchant for catachresis, that is, in Dryden's words, the "wresting and torturing" of words out of their ordinary usages, Dryden's sense of decorum need not be applied to Cleveland, for Cleveland wrote in more troubled times, out of a different poetic impulse. The catachresis and the omnipresent conceits startle the reader into new ways of viewing his poetic subjects, serving especially well the frequent purpose of burlesque. By these means, too, when coupled with his unusual polysyllabic words and wide-ranging allusions, Cleveland manages to achieve the difficulty, strenuousness, and even obscurity that define what the age called "strong lines"; but he also exercised control over his lines by often working in tetrameter and pentameter couplets, frequently with a full grammatical stop at the couplet's end, and with a sharp antithesis in the second line of the pair. His poetry thus appears to be epigrammatical. When he is debunking his subject, he turns the epigrammatic couplet to humorous effect by closing it with a polysyllabic word whose primary stress is not on the final syllable. The resulting rhyme sounds unusual and so emphasizes all the more the long word by which it is achieved. The following four couplets from "The Rebell Scot" well exemplify this style:

> Had *Cain* been *Scot*, God would have chang'd his
>   doome,
> Not forc'd him wander, but confin'd him home.

Like Jewes they spread, and as Infection flie,
As if the Divell had Ubiquitie.
Hence 'tis, they live at Rovers; and defie
This or that Place, Rags of Geographie.
They're Citizens o'th World; they're all in all,
Scotland's a Nation Epidemicall.

Conceits such as "Rags of Geographie," the antithesis of the second line, the long word closing three of the four end-stopped couplets, and finally the speed with which he changes figures mark Cleveland's memorable style.

Scholars do not know when Cleveland wrote many of his poems. Moreover, because numerous poems by other authors were attributed to him or published with his works, the canon is difficult to establish. Nevertheless, a modest collection of lyrics and political poems is well attested, and scholars have generally agreed that the majority of those lyrics and some of the political pieces were written while the poet lived at Cambridge.

The lesser achievement, the lyric poetry, is not without charm. Of his amorous lyrics probably the best known is the frequently anthologized piece "Fuscara; or The Bee Errant." The poem devotes its eighty-two lines to the story of a bee leaving the fields of flowers to suck the sweetness of the poet's mistress. The bee moves from a vein to her palm, wrist, fingers, and arm before the King of Bees arrives to return the errant's allegiance to himself. Along the way Cleveland displays his constant ability to find unusual likenesses, the most well-known being his analogues for her palm – "So soft, 'tis ayr but once remov'd, / Tender as 'twere a Jellie glov'd." One of the best noncynical love poems is "Upon Phillis walking in a morning before Sun-rising." This gentle piece embodies the impulse behind pastoral hyperbole, the poetic figure that sees nature flourishing in the presence of the beloved and withering without her. The two couplets on the response of the trees to the appearance of Phillis suggest the poem's lyrical power, seldom matched in Cleveland's corpus:

The trees like yeomen of her guard,
Serving more for pomp then ward,
Rank't on each side with loyall duty,
Weave branches to inclose her beauty.

This same humanized nature stands behind much of Marvell's "Upon Appleton House." Moreover, from this poem Marvell may have learned something about how tetrameter couplets can serve lyric duty without monotony.

The most sophisticated of Cleveland's love lyrics is "The Hecatomb to his Mistresse." The piece opens by criticizing fellow poetic praisers of their mistresses as "beggers of the rhiming trade," intent on their superlative comparisons. Against their all too easy praise Cleveland fashions what might be called a negative poetic. Just as a negative theologian cannot describe God in positive terms, so the speaker cannot describe his mistress positively. He is reduced to saying that "she's not as others are," and can only be "known by ignorance." His final line most fittingly captures the essence of this poetic: she "makes the world but her Periphrasis." It has been suggested that this poem is an attack on the Metaphysical style; but if it is, it is also attracted to that which it burlesques.

"To the State of Love, or, The Senses Festival" begins as a visionary poem in words that recall Henry Vaughan or Thomas Traherne: "I SAW a Vision yesternight"; but Cleveland soon makes clear that this vision is not spiritual but carnal, for the poet sees a woman so beautiful that "You may break Lent with looking on her." As the stanzas progress, so does the encounter with this beauty, each move punctuated with conceits. In the second stanza the splendor of her face sunburns her cheeks. In the third stanza he embraces her, another Sir Francis Drake encircling the world. The fourth stanza dwells on the sweet taste of her kiss, the fifth on the perfume of her breath as she speaks. As always, the final stanza reaches a climax, in this case sexual fulfillment. The last line – "Who would not die upon the spot?" – uses the double sense of "die" so familiar in the period. The whole has an energy and playfulness that mark Cleveland's love lyrics.

One poem that has all the feel of a university setting is "Square-Cap." After an opening stanza sets the scene as a drinking bout, the speaker proceeds to describe a series of his competitors for the love of a Cambridge lass. He identifies each suitor by the type of hat that he wears. A soldier, a fashion-monger, a Puritan, a clerk, and a lawyer seek her favors, but she insists in a brief refrain that if ever she loves it will be a square cap, that is, a university graduate like the speaker. The poem is most delightful in capturing the spirit of the university drinking sessions, referring even to the field on which Cambridge men played football; but it also deftly dissects the square cap's rivals. The sketch of the Puritan is most successful for it associates an automatic piety with more carnal desires: "First he said grace, and then he kist her." Reading this poem, one can almost see the Cambridge men singing in the local inn, Cleveland in the lead.

Cleveland also has his share of cynical love poems. Of these "The Antiplatonick" is the best. After shaming the eternal male wooer for his hesitation, the speaker shames in turn the women who "Candy up" themselves, arguing that virtue in women is no more than a "green-sicknesse of the mind." The most memorable turn of phrase ends the second stanza: speaking of the resistance of women as if it were stone, the persona urges that "A Flint will break upon a Feather-bed." Cleveland's closest approximation to a carpe diem poem, "To Julia to expedite her promise," is built with rapidly shifting images that received the censure of Samuel Johnson. Some of the wit is genuine, however, as in the subtle distinction between the Julian and Gregorian calendars as analogue for the difference in life span between men and women. Moreover, Cleveland breaks the stream of difficult images with some that are transparent: "How can thy Fortresse ever stand / If't be not man'd?" These cynical poems, while not profound, entertain in the way of their kind.

Several editions of Cleveland's works include both "A Song of Marke Anthony," a love song recounting an evening which the speaker spends with his mistress, and its companion poem, "The Authours Mock-Song to Marke Anthony," in which the former poem is closely parodied in a nightmarish key. The first of these poems may not be Cleveland's, though the second is well attested. In the first work the three-line refrain of each stanza asserts that Mark Anthony never dallied more wantonly with Cleopatra than this lover does with his mistress. The parodic counterpart attempts to find a most revolting image with which to answer this wantonness:

Never did Incubus
Touch such a filthy Sus,
As was this foule Gipsie Queane.

The parodic piece has little to recommend it; it serves rather as proof that Cleveland could sustain a grotesque production.

Cleveland's nonpolitical, nonamorous lyrics include witty portraits of two interesting types of people, the hermaphrodite and the miser. "Upon an Hermophrodite" deploys image after image to capture this natural paradox. Some are predictable enough: Adams's unisex before the creation of Eve and the union of marriage. Others derive from classical myth, the most interesting being the allusion to the disguised Achilles before the Trojan War. Ulysses' trick of posing as a peddler and drawing out both needle and sword to trap Achilles would not work on the hermaphrodite, for he/she would reach for both. Some of the images play with the physical complexities of the subject more directly: the upper lip kisses the lower, the breasts are brother and sister. Taken together, these images display a range of allusion and a joy of invention that mark the poem as clever, if not insightful. Metrically, Cleveland's use of tetrameter couplets as the vehicle of the wit in this poem looks forward to Samuel Butler's *Hudibras* (1662–1677). Cleveland's other poem on the hermaphrodite was occasioned by the inclusion of the first poem in a collection of Thomas Randolph's poetry. Cleveland claims not to mind the honor of such a mistake, but he does need to express the new paradoxes of a double poetic pedigree for the hermaphrodite. As is often the case in Cleveland, the last line of the poem is the summit of the wit. Addressing Randolph's shade and alluding to Solomon, he writes: "Wee'l part the child, and yet commit no slaughter, / So shall it be thy Son, and yet my Daughter." The poem on the miser, less fun than that on the hermaphrodite, focuses on a feast that the stingy man gives. When the guests actually eat the food that the miser offers, Cleveland turns the eating of the meal into a simultaneous devouring of the man himself. So distressed is the miser that he soon dies a second time, now in his body, not through his goods. The final image, though more grotesque than what precedes it, nonetheless epitomizes the characterization of the man: "Should we, like *Thracians,* our dead bodies eat, / He would have liv'd only to save his meat."

While still at Cambridge Cleveland began his career as a political writer of both panegyric and satire, with special talent in the latter. His poetic satires are marked by their wit and extravagance, like the rest of his corpus, but one gets the feeling that this poet is in his element on the attack against the enemies of his world, the world of the established church, the Crown, and the university. His targets threaten that world by means of their zeal, their lack of erudition and courtesy, and their challenge to long honored lines of authority. In the early satires, no doubt because they were written early in the national conflict and because Cleveland was in the comfortable confines of his university, he wages his campaign with sophisticated glee. A sense of the superiority of his own party tinges the poems, and he feels no need to address issues in the conflict. The focus instead is on debunking his opponents.

"A Dialogue between two Zealots, upon the &c. in the Oath" is a highly fictional piece. The oath in question was written in 1640 by convocation and

J. Cleaveland Revived:

POEMS,

ORATIONS,

EPISTLES,

And other of his Genuine
Incomparable Pieces, never
before publiſht.

WITH
Some other Exquiſite Remains of
the moſt eminent Wits of both the
Univerſities that were his
Contemporaries.

Non norunt hæc monumenta mori.

LONDON,
Printed for *Nathaniel Brook*, at the
Angel in Corn-hill. 1659.

Title page for one of several unreliable posthumous editions of Cleveland's verse. He wrote only two of the thirty-seven poems in this book.

was to be subscribed by all clergy. The chief problem of the oath lay in an "&c." in a list of church offices to constitute the ecclesiastical government. Cleveland personally had no problem with the oath. On the contrary, his satiric game is to belittle the Puritan clergymen who did. To this end Cleveland invents Sir Roger, a Puritan divine, and his unnamed interlocutor, a sympathetic "Brother of the Cloth." In what follows, the speaker recounts and quotes their conversation on the "&c." Here Cleveland's skill at exaggeration works well, for it reveals the wild claims of the zealots. The "&c." becomes a monster:

The Brand upon the buttock of the Beast,
The Dragons taile ti'd on a knot, a neast
Of young *Apocryphaes,* the fashion
Of a new mentall Reservation.

Cleveland pokes fun at what he considers to be the excessive biblical wrenching and the claims of revelation of the Puritans; but he also manages to accuse the anti-&c. tribe of receiving part of their inspiration and energy from drinking: "So they drunk on, not offering to part / Til they had quite sworn out th'eleventh quart." The whole has a lightness of touch and sense of play that must have delighted the Cavalier party.

The other major satire probably written while Cleveland was at Cambridge is "Smectymnuus, or the Club-Divines." The fun here involves the amalgam "Smectymnuus" itself. Created from the names of five Puritan authors who penned a controversial pamphlet in 1641, the name drives Cleveland to strive after numerous analogies for this multiple entity in one. It also elicits several difficult questions, for example, "Who must be *Smec* at th' Resurrection?" Finally, he envisions the absurd possibility of a marriage between Smectymnuus and the "*Et cætera*" of the oath, with all kinds of possible offspring — a vestry, synod, conclave, or conventicle. After that idea plays out, the poet lets the subject go, not because all possibilities have been exhausted, but because, he says, he will leave them to "another's dressing." No high ecclesiastical politics, but good high jinks carry the day.

Cleveland's life after leaving Cambridge became increasingly involved in the politics of his nation. The evidence indicates that he was still at Cambridge in June of 1642, but sometime thereafter, probably in the spring of 1643, he left Cambridge for the Royalist stronghold of Oxford, where he probably resided until 1645. In *Athenæ Oxoniensis* (1691, 1692) Anthony Wood records that at Oxford Cleveland "was the first Champion that appeared in verse for the King's Cause against the Presbyterians" and that he "was much venerated and respected not only by the great Men of the Court, but by the then Wits remaining among the affrighted and distressed Muses, for his high Panegyrics and smart Satyrs." During this period at Oxford, Cleveland increased his writing of satires, both in poetry and in prose. His most famous prose piece, the stinging tract titled *The Character of a London Diurnall*, circulated in 1644. Although the first editions were probably printed at Oxford, in February 1645 Cleveland may have visited London to oversee a printing of the tract in the city. The subject of Cleveland's tract, the diurnal, was a forerunner of the newspaper and publicized much of the political turmoil of the period. Because those of London tended to take the parliamentary side in the conflict, Cleveland felt compelled literally to belittle these publications. The character opens with this sentence: "A *Diurnall* is a puny Chronicle, scarce pin-feather'd with the wings of time." What makes Cleveland's character so interesting for the history of prose satire, however, is its tendency to attack individual persons in the opposition, for example, Oliver Cromwell: "O brave *Oliver!* Times voyder, Sub-sizer to the Wormes; in whom Death, that formerly devoured our Ancestors, now chewes the Cud." This incisive analysis continues to score palpable hits for several more sentences, including comments on Cromwell's nose. Thus, not only does the tract reveal Cleveland's ability to identify early in the conflict the chief foes of the king, but it also enters into the history of the times in the most direct way, by naming names.

Cleveland penned two other prose characters, their dates of composition unknown. In *The Character of a Country Committee-man, with the Ear-mark of a Sequestrator* (1649), he draws the character of a committeeman, a person with the legal power to sequester estates of Royalists. Cleveland finds these persons unnatural, for their very label confuses the group with the individual: "a Committee-man is a Noun of Multitude.... Thus the Name is as monstrous as the Man." In the other prose character, *The Character of a Diurnal-maker* (1654), Cleveland diminishes the diurnal writer by attacking the belief that such scribbling can be called writing. The diurnal writer is as much an author as a "North-country Pedlar is a Merchant-man." The diurnal itself contributes to the decay of learning by encouraging the literate to waste valuable reading time on frippery. In all three of his prose characters, Cleveland combines wit with a satiric vein in the hopes of belittling his opponents and of exposing their ills simultaneously.

Cleveland wrote many poetic satires and panegyrics about the time that he moved to Oxford and while he continued there. Indeed, three of his most mature and accomplished works were probably written between late 1642 and 1644. The first of these poems, "To P. Rupert," intricately combines praise for Prince Rupert, the warrior nephew of the king, with satire of Parliament, its army, and its supporters. Cleveland ties the two projects together by contrast between the prince and his foes, and by speaking of the difficulty of encomium in a world in which truth is to be had only by reading against the letter. Among the satiric targets are the parliamentary general Robert Devereux, third Earl of Essex, whom the poet attacks as impotent, and the legislator John Pym, against whom Rupert's dog "holds up his Malignant leg." Given that the praise of Rupert seems strained, the introduction of the dog as a means of satirizing Parliament is a refreshing move. Cleveland envisions Parliament's taking action against the dog for barking "against the sense o' th House." More than good fun, the passage indicates the degree of difference between the Royalists and their opponents, a difference so great that the poet fears he does wrong writing of both within the same work: "Pardon, great Sir; for that ignoble crew / Gaines, when made bankrupt, in the scales with you." This is the kind of party poetry that leads directly to Marvell's "Last Instructions to a Painter" and, with greater permutation, to Dryden at his satiric best.

Among his poetic satires "The Mixt Assembly" is one of the most effective. It treats the Westminster Assembly called by Parliament to reform the church. This assembly, which began its work in 1643, was doubly mixed, with clergy and laity and with men of various ecclesiastical preferences. Cleveland wittily assaults this mixture with references ranging from the biblical story of Jacob's speckled flocks taken from Laban to "Linsie-Woolsie" cloth; but the early conceits weaken when compared to the last section of the poem, in which Cleveland figures the assembly as a jig, and specifies who dances with whom. The personal attacks get vicious, but the work maintains its wit throughout. The poet envisions a union between the five members whom the king tried to arrest in Parliament in 1642 and the five men whose names made up Smectymnuus. Should these two pairs of fives mate, the poet suggests, the issue would not be a child, but the emptying of the prisons, a "Gaole-Deliverie." Clearly, Cleveland thinks no more highly of the assembly than he does of Parliament.

If Cleveland had disdain for the assembly and Parliament, he was enraged by the Scots for siding against the king. In "The Rebell Scot," written around the time of the Scottish invasion in January 1644, Cleveland expresses his rage, providing his most explicit statements on satire. He asserts that "A Poet should be fear'd / When angry," and apostrophizes both keen iambics, the satiric measure, and satirists, asking the latter to imp his rage "With all the Scorpions that should whip this age." Making exceptions for the Scottish ancestry of Charles, a few good Scots, and the presence of the Anglican church in Scotland, Cleveland brutalizes the "Land that truckles under us." He sees the northerners as wolves repopulating England with their invasion. He mocks their poverty and lack of refinement. He even envisions Scotland as England's hemorrhoids, both the medical problem known under that name and a serpent whose bite causes unstoppable bleeding. It is not a pretty poem, nor was it meant to be. Cleveland remains civilized, but barely so, as he demeans these "demonic" people so inferior, by his lights, to the English.

On 10 January 1645 Archbishop William Laud, the hated opponent of the Puritans, was executed, an event that Cleveland commemorated in "On the Archbishop of Canterbury." Not unlike the elegy for Edward King, this poem begins with a discussion of how poets are to lament. According to Cleveland, it is not by study: "Who ever sob'd in numbers?" Lament in numbers he does, however, as he pictures the death of Laud as the death of the English church. The poem directly addresses the injustice of this execution, claiming that both Thomas Wentworth, first Earl of Strafford, and Laud were guilty of treason by prophecy, meaning that they offended against laws Parliament made after these men committed their allegedly offensive acts. Cleveland's conclusion is that great men must now lay low, "For worth is sin and eminence a crime." In 1645 the world that Cleveland inhabited was crumbling both civilly and ecclesiastically, and he knew it.

In February 1645 Cleveland was expelled from his fellowship at Saint John's; but he was quickly given a post by the Royalists as judge advocate of the garrison at Newark. The *Weekly Intelligencer* of 27 May 1645, calling him "that grand malignant of Cambridge," described his duties as collecting rents to support those dismissed from Cambridge; he was probably responsible for judging cases arising between the military and civilian populations. In any case, shortly after Charles left Newark in November 1645, a Scottish force laid siege to the city. Cleveland wrote the official rejection of the call for surrender, the key sentence of which reads, "Otherwise I desire you to take notice, that when I received my Commission for the Government of this place, I annex'd my Life as a Label to my Trust." Charles's cause, however, was rapidly becoming desperate. In April and May of 1646, the king wandered in disguise for eight days before surrendering to the Scots, an event which prompted Cleveland to write "The Kings Disguise." His most anguished work, this poem bespeaks Cleveland's recognition of the peril facing his world when a king is forced to travel incognito. For Cleveland the immediate future did not improve. After the king gave himself up, the Scots demanded the surrender of Newark. Cleveland was in the city when it capitulated. An eighteenth-century account of his trial at the hands of the Scots, and his dismissal by their commander David Leslie as a harmless versifier, is probably inaccurate.

For over nine years after Newark, Cleveland's life is a mystery. Being a well-known member of the defeated party and without means of his own, he lived with help from more fortunate Royalists. Helen Duffy and Paul S. Wilson have provided an interesting possibility for Cleveland's movements immediately after the surrender. Officers of the garrison were permitted to leave in honor if they had a clear destination. One of the other officers, an Edmund Thorold, was cousin to the Edmund Thorold who was a fellow student of Cleveland's at Christ's College. The former Edmund was also brother to Katharine Thorold, the woman whom the Osborn manuscript identifies as the lady of Cleveland's poem "To Mrs. K. T. who askt him why hee was dumb." Perhaps Cleveland accompanied his fellow officer to the Thorold estate nine miles from Newark. Since Edmund was a widower with children, it is not inconceivable that Cleveland stayed on for a while as tutor.

Another conjecture concerning Cleveland's activities in the years after Newark's fall comes from S. V. Gapp, who marshals evidence to suggest that in 1647 and 1648 Cleveland may have been residing in London, writing for the Royalist mercuries, especially *Mercurius Pragmaticus*. Although this kind of underground political activity is consistent with what is known of Cleveland's talents and beliefs, the evidence, like that associating him with the Thorolds, is currently insufficient to permit confident statements about his whereabouts and means of livelihood in the late 1640s.

One major poem, "The Hue and Cry After Sir John Presbyter," perhaps dates from 1646 or 1647. In this piece, Cleveland objects to the destruction of the Anglican prelacy and to its replacement by a Presbyterian ecclesiastical system. His complaint is straightforward: the Presbyterian arrangement is more imperious than the bishops had been, and yet the men and the morals of the new regime are inferior to those of the former system. Cleveland wishes for a return to the Book of Common Prayer and for the defiance of this false governance; but the poet was not destined to see the restoration of the Anglican prelacy.

The early 1650s are an even cleaner biographical slate than the late 1640s. What is known of Cleveland's activities before his arrest on 10 November 1655 comes from the letter sent on this date by the Norwich men who had taken Cleveland into custody to Secretary to the Council of State John Thurloe. According to this letter, Cleveland had confessed to having come to Norwich from London about a year previously. During that year he had lived in the house of Edward Cooke, had assisted in Cooke's studies, had seldom ventured into the city, and only once had gone into the country. The letter adds this commentary on the house in which Cleveland resided in Norwich:

> mr. Cooke's is a family of notorious disorder and where papists, delinquents, and other disaffected persons of the late king's party do often resort more than to any family in the said sity or county of Norfolk, as is commonly reported.

That Cleveland was living on the generosity of Royalists is clear from another article in the letter; Cooke allowed the poet thirty pounds a year, and two other unnamed gentlemen contributed twenty pounds annually to his maintenance.

The reason for Cleveland's arrest, besides the fact that he had been active against Parliament during the war, is given in the last article of the letter: "Mr. Cleveland is a person of great abilities, and so able to do the greater disservice." After three months in the Yarmouth prison, Cleveland wrote to Cromwell to ask for his release on grounds that, if he were not poor (a condition for which Cromwell's victory was responsible), he would never have been imprisoned. Cleveland admits that he had remained faithful to Charles, but he ingeniously argues that his former fidelity to the king should assure Cromwell of his fidelity to the current government. He received the clemency he requested and was released.

Cleveland's movements after his release are unclear. According to John M. Berdan, by the fall of 1657 he was living in Gray's Inn, London. He was maintained by a benefactor, perhaps John Onebye of Hinckley, who was a member of Gray's Inn. John Aubrey's *Brief Lives* (1813) suggests that during this period Cleveland and Samuel Butler met nightly in a club. Unreliable as Aubrey often is, this association of the two satirists may be factual.

Cleveland's stay in prison may have weakened him, for he died on 29 April 1658 of an intermittent fever at the age of forty-four. He was buried on 1 May in the parish church of Saint Michael Royal, London. Rev. Edward Thurman performed the service, Dr. John Pearson delivered the sermon, and many Royalists are said to have attended. The church containing his remains was destroyed by fire in 1666. Never having married, Cleveland left no known direct descendants.

No collection of Cleveland's poems in his own hand is known to exist. Moreover, he probably had little, if any, direct role in the printing of his poems; but his work saw many editions. In 1647 appeared six editions and two reissues, under the title *The Character of a London-Diurnall: With severall select Poems: By the same Author*. Later editions added poems and so indicated by addenda to the title. Seventeen editions of Cleveland's works appeared between 1651 and 1669 under various titles, the first of which is *Poems, By J. C., With Additions*. Again, the contents of these editions vary, and the later ones include many poems not by Cleveland. *J. Cleaveland Revived* (1659) has thirty-seven poems, but only two by Cleveland. The rest are by his contemporaries. A confusing preface by E. Williamson does indicate that all these works were not penned by Cleveland. Little is known about this Williamson, who claims to have been a friend of Cleveland. Later editions of *J. Cleaveland Revived* add other poems, perhaps none of which are by Cleveland. A 1677 edition entitled *Clievelandi Vindiciae; or, Clieveland's Genuine Poems, Orations, Epistles, &c.* has an interesting preface by Cleveland's former pupils John Lake and Samuel Drake. Although they claim to have purged earlier editions, this one too is not above question. In 1687 this collection was republished as *The Works of Mr. John Cleveland*, with many other poems previously (though falsely) attributed to Cleveland appended.

This collection was reissued in 1699 and again in 1742.

After his death Cleveland remained popular for a time, but the critical tide soon turned against him. In *Of Dramatick Poesie* (1667), Dryden accused Cleveland of often giving us "a hard Nut to break our Teeth, without a Kernel for our pains." He proceeded to contrast the satires of Donne and Cleveland: "That the one gives us deep thoughts in common language, though rough cadence; the other gives us common thoughts in abstruse words." In the eighteenth century Samuel Johnson exemplified overwrought conceits by quoting Cleveland, among other Metaphysical poets. The twentieth century has seen critics urge that Cleveland's wit eventually undoes him, but a renewed interest in his panegyrics and satires as responses to social turbulence has led others to see Cleveland as a significant bridge to Restoration satire. This focus of attention on the political poems has not raised Cleveland to the first order of poets nor revived widespread interest in his work, but it does suggest that the history of poetic satire in the seventeenth century cannot overlook him. His wit, though not for all seasons, can serve as a measure of a difficult time for British poetry in the troubled Civil War era.

Bibliography:

Brian Morris, *John Cleveland (1613–1658): A Bibliography of His Poems* (London: Bibliographical Society, 1967).

References:

Alfred Alvarez, *The School of Donne* (New York: Pantheon, 1961), pp. 133–144;

John M. Berdan, Introduction to *The Poems of John Cleveland*, edited by Berdan (New York: Grafton, 1903), pp. 9–49;

Harold F. Brooks, "English Verse Satire, 1640–1660: Prolegomena," *Seventeenth Century*, 3 (Spring 1988): 17–46;

A. D. Cousins, "The Cavalier World and John Cleveland," *Studies in Philology*, 78 (Winter 1981): 61–86;

John Dryden, *Of Dramatick Poesie: An Essay*, edited by James T. Boulton (London: Oxford University Press, 1964), pp. 38, 59–60;

Helen Duffy and Paul S. Wilson, "A Note on John Cleveland's 'To Mistress K. T.,' " *Notes and Queries*, 22 (December 1975): 546–548;

S. V. Gapp, "Notes on John Cleveland," *PMLA*, 46 (December 1931): 1075–1086;

Lee A. Jacobus, *John Cleveland* (Boston: Twayne, 1975);

John L. Kimmey, "John Cleveland and the Satiric Couplet in the Restoration," *Philological Quarterly*, 87 (October 1958): 410–423;

Paul J. Korshin, "The Evolution of Neoclassical Poetics: Cleveland, Denham, and Waller as Poetic Theorists," *Eighteenth-Century Studies*, 2 (December 1968): 102–137;

Harry Levin, "John Cleveland and the Conceit," *Criterion*, 14 (October 1934): 40–53;

Brian Morris, "Satire from Donne to Marvell," in *Metaphysical Poetry*, edited by D. S. Palmer & Malcolm Bradbury, Stratford-Upon-Avon Studies, 11 (London: Arnold, 1970), pp. 211–237;

Ruth Nevo, *The Dial of Virtue: A Study of Poems on Affairs of State in the Seventeenth Century* (Princeton: Princeton University Press, 1963);

K. K. Ruthven, *The Conceit* (London: Methuen, 1969), pp. 47–51;

Cicely Veronica Wedgwood, *Poetry and Politics under the Stuarts* (Cambridge: Cambridge University Press, 1961), pp. 42–47, 56–61, 191–193;

George Williamson, *The Donne Tradition: A Study in English Poetry from Donne to the Death of Cowley* (Cambridge: Harvard University Press, 1930), pp. 169–175;

Williamson, *Seventeenth Century Contexts*, revised edition (Chicago: University of Chicago Press, 1969);

Eleanor Withington, "The Canon of John Cleveland's Poetry," *Bulletin of the New York Public Library*, 67 (May 1963): 307–327; (June 1963): 377–394.

Richard Crashaw

(1612 or 1613 – 21 August 1649)

Maureen Sabine
University of Hong Kong

BOOKS: *Epigrammatum Sacrorum Liber* (Cambridge: Printed by T. Buck & R. Daniel, 1634);

Steps to the Temple. Sacred Poems, With other Delights of the Muses (London: Printed by T. W. for Humphrey Moseley, 1646); second edition, enlarged, published as *Steps to the Temple, Sacred Poems. With The Delights of the Muses* (London: Printed for Humphrey Moseley, 1648);

Carmen Deo Nostro, Te Decet Hymnvs Sacred Poems, Collected, Corrected, Avgmented, Most humbly Presented. To My Lady The Covntesse of Denbigh By Her most devoted Servant. R.C. In hearty acknowledgment of his immortall obligation to her Goodnes & Charity (Paris: Printed by Peter Targa, Printer to the Archbishope of Paris, 1652);

A Letter from Mr. Crashaw to the Countess of Denbigh, Against Irresolution and Delay in matters of Religion (London, 1653);

Richardi Crashawi Poemata et Epigrammata (Cambridge: Ex Officina Joan. Hayes, 1670).

Editions: *The Poems, English, Latin, and Greek, of Richard Crashaw,* edited by L. C. Martin (Oxford: Clarendon Press, 1927); second edition, revised, 1957);

The Complete Poetry of Richard Crashaw, edited by George Walton Williams (Garden City, N.Y.: Doubleday, 1970).

The intense and intimate depiction of Richard Crashaw that prefaces his English volumes of poetry (*Steps to the Temple,* 1646, enlarged 1648) is also a candlelit window that opens on his soul. To look through this window is to discover Crashaw in the state of unruffled devotion which is presented as the hub of his poetic genius.

Reader, we stile his Sacred Poems, Stepps to the Temple, *and aptly, for in the Temple of God, under his wing, he led his life in St. Maries Church neere St. Peters Colledge: There he lodged under Tertullian's roofe of Angels: There he made his nest more gladly then David's Swallow neere the house of God: where like a primitive Saint, he offered more prayers in the night, then others*

usually offer in the day; There, he penned these Poems, Stepps *for happy soules to climb heaven by.*

Whoever the *"Authors friend"* may be who wrote this "Preface to the Reader," his portrait made a deep impression on early-seventeenth-century biographers of Crashaw such as David Lloyd and Anthony Wood. Present-day readers need to appreciate once more that Crashaw's poetry was first admired as an extension of his prayer life and as the testimony of one who dwelt in the presence of God. Yet few were the "happy soules" who could turn away from the dramatic tragedy of the seventeenth century and look inward, as Crashaw does, at the "life hid with Christ in God" (Colossians). In his finest contemplative verse, he would reach out from the evening stillness of the sanctuary to an embattled world that was deaf to the soothing sound of Jesus, the name which, to his mind, cradled the cosmos.

> How many unknown WORLDS there are
> Of Comforts, which Thou hast in Keeping!
> How many Thousand Mercyes there
> In Pitty's soft lap ly a sleeping!
> Happy he who has the art
>   To awake them
>   And to take them
> Home, and lodge them in his HEART.
>   ("Hymn to the Name of Jesus")

Despite his artistic efforts to awaken spiritual understanding in men, Crashaw remains perhaps the most misunderstood of seventeenth-century English poets. Though he happily set out to follow in the steps of George Herbert, whose collection of sacred English poems was titled *The Temple* (1633), Crashaw is usually regarded as the incongruous younger brother of the Metaphysicals who weakens the "strong line" of their verse or the prodigal son who "took his journey into a far country" (Luke), namely the Continent and Catholicism. With a mind open to many influences, Crashaw did indeed write poetry rich with "many WORLDS" ("Hymn

71

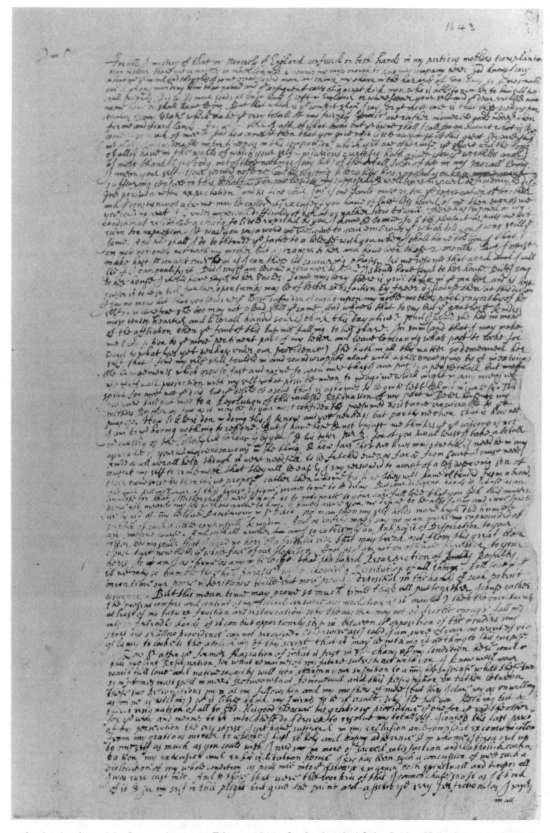

Crashaw's only surviving letter, written on 20 February 1644, after Crashaw had fled to Leiden, Holland, to avoid persecution
by the Puritans for his religious and political beliefs (University Library, Cambridge)

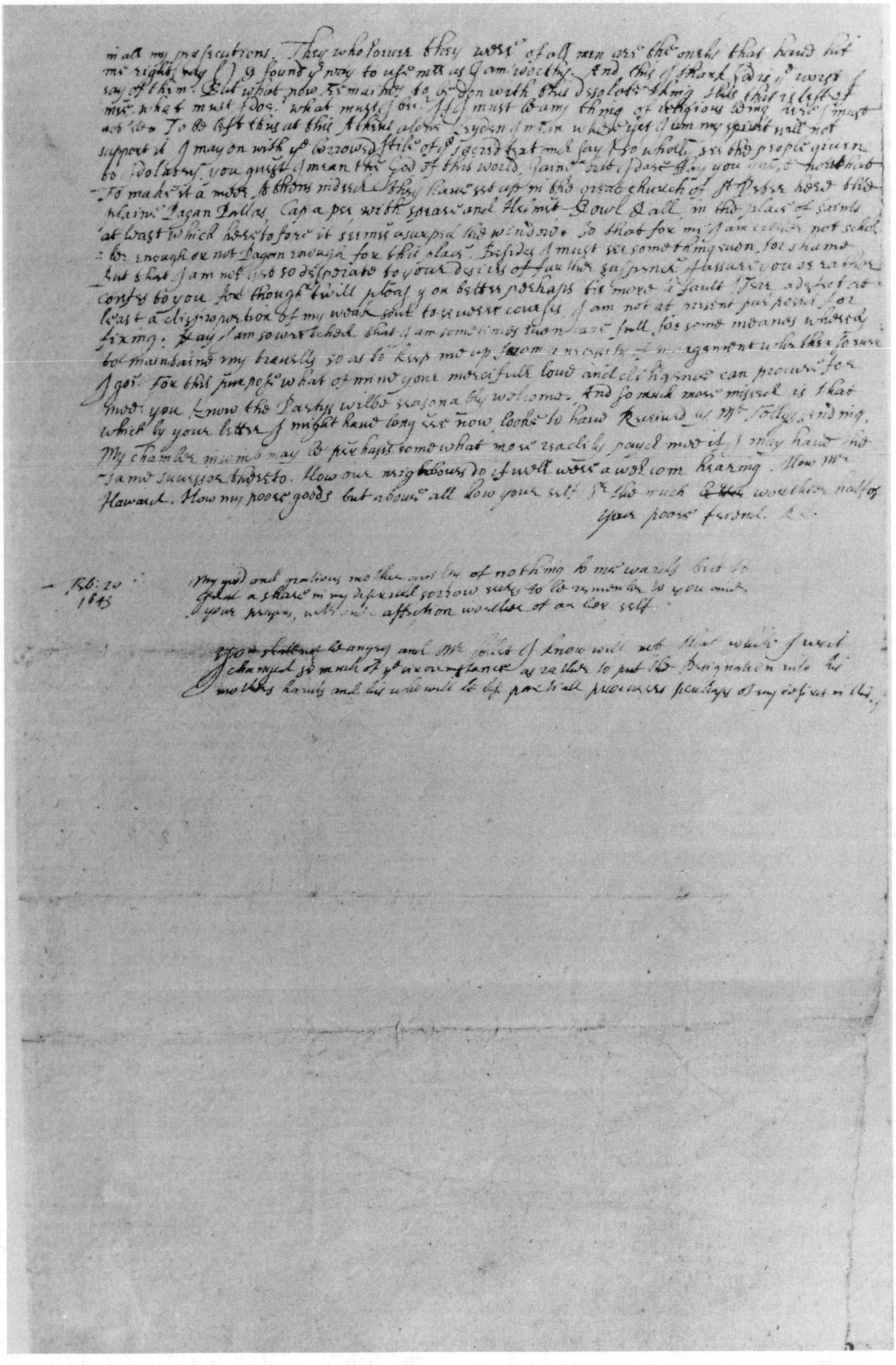

to the Name of Jesus"); but the most singular journey that he takes is not abroad — it is the inner journey toward that stationary center of human activity so memorably captured in the "Preface to the Reader."

If a fuller appreciation of Crashaw must address the centering activity that goes on in his poetry, it must also explore further the volatile gender states that paradoxically decenter his verse. Already feminist-inspired criticism has upset the conventional wisdom which deplored Crashaw's "feminine" sensibility, that is to say, his ardent devotion to women and his partiality for sweet, soft, or maternal images in his verse. The male critical preference for the tougher and supposedly more virile stance of a poet such as John Donne has been challenged by readers who sense that the weak man's feminine ways may contain hidden power. The deeply unsettling changes of gender perception which Crashaw encourages are crucial to an understanding of the spiritual intention of his poetry, which is to "unman" the narrow, orthodox mind, "narrow and low, and infinitely lesse / Then this GREAT mornings mighty Busynes" ("Hymn to the Name of Jesus"), which offers resistance to God and so permits his "Bright Joyes" to flood the soul.

Joy is the base note of Crashaw's poetry; exaltation the promised spiritual effect of his verse. Yet, early in life, Crashaw realized that we are born "dark Sons of Dust and Sorrow." Just when is not clear; nor, for that matter, is the exact date of his birth. From the devotional as well as literary importance of the Nativity in his poetry, it is conceivable that Crashaw was born on either side of the Christmas season — the Advent period of 1612 or the Epiphany period of 1613. Of his mother no trace survives. There is no way of knowing whether she lingered long enough to shape his primary memories or died during or soon after his birth, inspiring a lifetime of wishful mother thinking. The imprint of loving maternal care at the breast and in the warm nest of a woman's body, however, can be strongly felt in his poetry. Of the stepmother who showed "singular motherly affection to the child of her predecessor" there is a record, largely thanks to the funeral tributes which were written in 1620 on her death in childbirth. These tributes were printed together as *The Honour of Virtue,* reprinted in Katherine Usher Henderson and Barbara F. McManus's *Half Humankind* (1985). The "Matchless Mistress" Elizabeth Skinner Crashaw died at the age of twenty-four, when the poet was about eight, and after a brief seventeen months of marriage to a man twice her age, William Crashaw. Amid the lifeless

tributes to her accomplishments as a Christian gentlewoman and new wife, Elizabeth Crashaw emerges as a kindhearted soul who, like her stepson, "was belou'd by all; dispraysed by none" (Thomas Car's "Anagramme" prefacing Crashaw's *Carmen Deo Nostro,* 1652). According to the funeral sermon in *The Honour of Virtue,* though "young, healthful and living in great content and with a husband after her own heart," Elizabeth's pregnancy seems to have been clouded by foreboding that childbirth would prove "both the baptism of the son and burial of the mother." She correctly prophesied her own death but had not foreseen that her newborn son would soon follow her. Humbling consciousness of being "a dear-bought son," indeed, the only surviving child of loving parent figures, never left Crashaw as an artist. Neither did his sense of awe and obligation to the mothers who steeled themselves for sacrifice and were willing to face the dual ordeal of birth and death for the sake of another. The poet would complete his development in an exclusive male environment where strong fathers such as William Crashaw dominated the institutions of state. According to Victor Turner's *The Ritual Process* (1969), where patrilineality is the basis of society, as in Stuart England, the individual may form a more disinterested concept of "human-kindness," joining men together in a community of greater good through the mother and, by extension, through other women and femininity. In his mature verse, Crashaw's poetic vision of community would reach through the Virgin Mother and female saints up to the company of heaven and down to an unremembered chain of women on earth. Though weakened by labor, cut down to size by the world, and stifled by premature death, these women provided what Turner called the crucial "human bond, without which there could be *no* society," and it is to his credit that Crashaw never forgot this basic fact.

At the time of his stepmother's death it was marveled that Elizabeth Crashaw could have felt such a strong "strange affection to her husband." William Crashaw was a middle-aged Anglican divine from a long-established northern family. Some of the modest income from his early parish work in the Inner Temple, London, in Yorkshire, and finally at St. Mary Matfellon, Whitechapel, which he ministered from 1618 until his death in 1626, undoubtedly subsidized his passion for book collection; but a widower with a substantial library and a lonely son seemed no match for the "young gallants and rich heirs" who hoped to join their inheritance with Elizabeth Skinner's estimated "great estate." It is hard to believe that William Crashaw's fiery diatribes against popery or his reputation as a Puritan sympathizer could have wooed this gentle lady; but her mourners remarked on her admiration for the profession of clergy, her zeal for pastoral work, and the encouragement that she gave her husband to introduce the morning service from the Book of Common Prayer into his parish. These vestiges of the canonical day offices said in the medieval church would become the nucleus of meditative exercises in Crashaw's poetry. Indeed, the magnificent invocation at the close of one of his greatest poems recalls the "Litany of General Supplication" that follows morning prayers and begins: "By thine Agony and bloody Sweat; by thy Cross and Passion; by thy precious Death and Burial. . . ." In "The Flaming Heart," Crashaw's poetic entreaty to Saint Teresa, he consecrated all the devotion shown by women like his stepmother and joined it to Christ's Offering on the Cross.

Between his stepmother's death in 1620 and his admission to Charterhouse School in 1629, Crashaw underwent that educational regimen calculated to turn youngsters into precocious sages modeled on the boy Christ, who discoursed to his elders in the temple. Yet if Crashaw's classical scholarship bears the stamp of humanist learning, he developed no penchant for that hostility to women or denial of a kindhearted maternal world that, according to Richard Helgerson in *The Elizabethan Prodigals* (1976), characterized traditional English pedagogy; for this he had no less surprising a figure than his own father to thank. Though William Crashaw was a furious disputant of Catholicism and of its ardent devotion to Mary, the Mother of God, his passion in the pulpit softened to tenderness in the home. At his father's encouragement Crashaw may have composed his early verse rendition of "Psalme 23." This juvenile exercise, written no later than 1630 and possibly before his father's death in 1626, is an important link between Crashaw's childhood, about which we know so tantalizingly little, and the creative life which now began to unfold to him in poetry. The Psalms gave profound instruction to Jesus himself and so were second only to the Gospels in providing Christians edifying meditations and literary inspiration. Psalm 23 was particularly good material for a schoolboy keen to please and perhaps console the father who had been left his sole guardian. "The Lord is my shepherd; I shall not want" has been the traditional comfort of those who face bereavement and who pray for the serenity and the strength to look beyond death to God's everlasting life. In contrast to the somber six verses of the original psalm, however, Crashaw composed an ornate

and exuberant paraphrase of over seventy lines which begins, "Happy me! O happy sheepe! / Whom my God vouchsafes to keepe." The poem does not begin with the Lord who is the shepherd but with the sheepish, slightly ridiculous figure that Crashaw himself cuts in the world. As an aspiring poet, Crashaw had also begun to experiment with the expanded epigrams that are a hallmark of the Metaphysical poets; but whereas the Metaphysicals are noted for the controlled economy they bring to this form, Crashaw already shows an inclination to luxuriate in rather than compress his material. He makes the green pastures and still waters of the original psalm pulse with the creative energy of God, which he recognized as his own source of creativity and the one "that points me to these wayes of blisse." In the "cheerefull spring" of his poetic art, Crashaw had begun to employ ebullient, fanciful, outré imagery, such as that of "the blubb'ring Mountaine" which "Weeping, melts into a Fountaine." It would be a mistake, however, to conclude simply that he had picked up bad habits early in his artistic development or that these habits were learned from his father, who showed an excess of zeal in his own religious writings and whose *Manuall for True Catholickes* (1611) can be felt as an influence in "Psalme 23." As T. S. Eliot was among the first to appreciate, "there is brainwork" behind the seeming perversity and outrageousness of Crashaw's language.

What is crucial to a real as opposed to a formally argued appreciation of Crashaw is a recognition that he deliberately reveled in his own weakness, for his weakness taught him to turn inward to Christ for strength and outward to the many guardians, his father chief among them, whom he would depend upon to shepherd him over the course of his life. The poet who continued to babble away in his mature verse was thus not afraid to depict the speaker in "Psalme 23" as hopelessly ill equipped to fend for himself. God must "point" him in the right direction, must rescue him when he in "simple weaknesse strayes, / (Tangled in forbidden wayes)." The unquestioning faith which alienates modern readers of his devotional verse reflects an early intuition that he had found the path of his own bliss and that both friends and foes would show the "Way for a resolved mind." The Psalms were composed by David the shepherd boy. The confidence and the trust in Crashaw's psalm paraphrase suggest that in his own childhood the poet may have felt David's primitive sense of closeness to God. Certainly, there is no fear of God or trepidation at the prospect of dying in his poem, though his own family life could

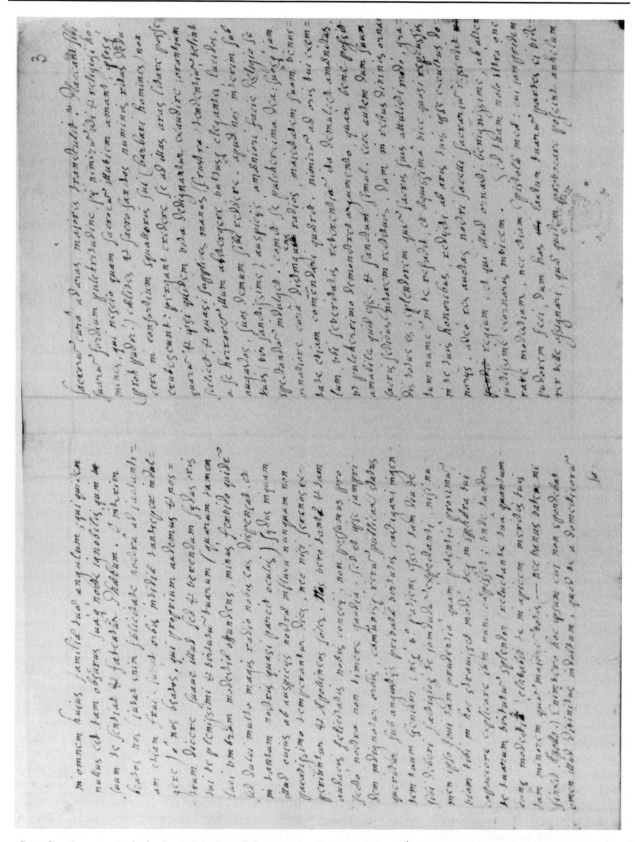

Pages from the manuscript for Crashaw's dedication to Epigrammatum Sacrorum Liber. *The dedication, apparently in the poet's hand, is quite different from the published version (British Library, Add. MS. 40176, ff. 2ᵛ and 3ʳ).*

not protect him from the hurt of bereavement. Nor does his speaker seem burdened by sin, though this has been interpreted as incognizance by hostile readers. When one considers that the speaker depicts himself as a silly sheep, or a foolish, wayward child, it becomes evident that Crashaw did not see sin as wickedness so much as another form of weakness. In the most original move of "Psalme 23," he depicts God not only as the Good Shepherd but also as the Good Mother who first "sings my soule to rest"; who later feeds him in Holy Writ and in the Eucharistic bread as earlier "at her brest"; and who finally welcomes him with open arms in death. The movement of this poem prefigures not only the shape of Crashaw's art but the direction of his whole life.

It is hard to believe that Crashaw would have shown this precocious awareness of the feminine core of the Lord's goodness to man had he not seen in his father something of the motherhood of God. It is known for a fact that in William Crashaw's extensive theological library his son had access to the accounts of female mystics and visionaries of the medieval church, and perhaps there this dreamy young man first seriously reflected on the idea of Christ as protomother. The poet's later involvement at Cambridge in the Laudian restoration of the Anglican church, in Marian devotion, and in Catholic-looking observances has been readily perceived as a conscious denial of his father's crusade against the Church of Rome. According to E. I. Watkin, however, William Crashaw's passionate concern that Anglicanism should embody the purity of the primitive and medieval church suggests that the poet's feminine-sounding faith was rather the completion and liberation of his father's emotional religious views. When his father died in 1626, Richard Crashaw, now entering his teens, became the charge of the lawyers Sir Henry Yelverton and Sir Randolph Crew. Three years later he was admitted to the distinguished Charterhouse School, where he bloomed under the indulgent eye of its Royalist head, Robert Brook, who was later expelled from this position around the time Crashaw fled from Cambridge in 1643. At Charterhouse Crashaw perfected the rigorous discipline of the classicist and epigrammatist. Every Sunday he was obliged to compose four Greek and four Latin verses on the New Testament reading at the second lesson of matins, a practice he continued on a Watt scholarship to Pembroke College, Cambridge, from 1631 to 1634. He produced his first volume of poetry at Cambridge in 1634, the *Epigrammatum Sacrorum Liber,* a collection of his classical epigrams on the morning service

Frontispiece to the enlarged edition (1648) of Crashaw's poems, which follow in the tradition of George Herbert's The Temple *(1633)*

which had so moved his stepmother. These verses reveal new springs of tenderness as he became absorbed in a Laudian theology of love, in the religious philanthropy practiced by his Pembroke master, Benjamin Laney, and preached by his tutor, John Tournay, and in the passionate poetic study of the Virgin Mother and Christ Child.

Crashaw's reputation as "the chaplaine of the virgin myld" (Car's "Anagramme") would be cemented at Peterhouse where he was elected to a fellowship in 1635. In secular verses from his undergraduate days such as "Wishes to his (supposed) Mistresse," however, he salutes the lady of his ardent imagination. The most brilliant of these exercises, "Musicks Duell," brings together his academic interest in translating Jesuit Neo-

Latin verse with an altogether more worldly knowledge of Thomas Carew's bold erotic masterpiece, "A Rapture." It would be wrong, then, to conclude from Car's posthumous allusion to "his virgin thoughtes and words" that Crashaw was indifferent to the force of sexuality. But by the time he took holy orders and was appointed to the Peterhouse curacy of Little St. Mary's around 1638, he had chosen to live as he would die "in th'virgines lappe"; and in this maternal framework his supreme development took place. According to Allan Pritchard, even the Puritan informers who kept the High Church rituals of Peterhouse under surveillance could sense the spiritually charged atmosphere that pervaded the sanctuary as Crashaw "turned himselfe to ye picture of the Virgin Mary . . . and used these words 'Hanc adoramus, colamus hanc' " (We adore her, we worship her). Indeed, one of Crashaw's early English epigrams, translated from a Latin exercise commemorating the Annunciation in 1632, is often depicted as a poetic reproduction of the religious paintings in which the Virgin adores the child seated on her lap. However, in this epigram, Mary is not richly adorned but represented unassumingly, and more to the point of Crashaw's title, "On the Blessed Virgins bashfulnesse," indirectly. No sentimental allusion to the Virgin's maiden shyness is being made in the title of his epigram which begins, "That on her lap she casts her humble Eye," and ends, " 'Twas once *looke up*, 'tis now *looke downe* to Heaven." Mary's face is hidden from the reader because it is fixed on Christ, who is the true focus of the poem. In an understated way Crashaw was refuting his detractors who accused him of idolizing the Virgin or who regarded Marian veneration as an arrogation of the honor due to Christ alone. Crashaw was also declaring his solidarity with Anthony Stafford's Laudian promotion of Mary in *The Femall Glory,* published in 1635:

> Yet would I not idolatrize thy worth,
> Like some, whose superstition sets thee forth,
> In costly ornaments, in cloathes so gay,
> So rich as never in the stable lay.
> . . . .
> I cannot thinke thy Virgin bashfulnesse
> Would weare the Lady of Lorettos dresse.

From the explicit reference to Stafford's citation of "Virgin bashfulnesse" in the title of Crashaw's own epigram, it may be concluded that he wrote this poem soon after his arrival at Peterhouse; but the ceremonial ostentation of Laudian practices there and the devotional excess of the Italian shrine of Our Lady of Loreto, where Crashaw would die in 1649, have often obscured the important ways in which the Virgin simplified his faith even as she inspired more sophisticated expressions of his art. If Peterhouse was the "little contenfull kingdom" (letter written at Leiden, Holland, 20 February 1644) in which he polished his poetry and purified his prayer life from 1635 until 1643, "On the Blessed Virgins bashfulnesse" is the "contentfull Cell" ("Description of a Religious House") epitomizing his later development. Like the proverbial mustard seed of the Gospels, the epigram hides the great truth of the Incarnation within its small, eight-line form: " 'Tis Heav'n 'tis Heaven she sees, Heavens God there lyes." At the Annunciation it had been revealed to Mary that she would become the mother of "Heavens God"; but as Crashaw contemplated what this feast meant to him, first in Latin and then in English verse, he saw that at the heart of the mystery of the Incarnation lay Christ's promise that the kingdom of Heaven is within everyone. It was the "least of your least," as Crashaw realized when he signed himself "Tuorum minimorum minimus" in the "Epistle Dedicatory" to the *Epigrammatum Sacrorum Liber,* who would inherit this kingdom because they alone were willing to minimize the self in importance. The difficulties that critics have with Crashaw's poetry and their almost invariable preference for Donne's religious sonnets, in which the human and divine ego are locked in a power struggle, indicate how highly self-consciousness is prized among readers. Yet, to read Crashaw's epigram, we are obliged to quiet the designing mind that clamors to be the center of attention. Foes who branded Crashaw "the chaplaine of the virgine myld" saw him rapt in prayer before the icon of the Virgin in Peterhouse College chapel. What this poem suggests, however, is that he learned to pray by contemplating her reflection on Christ.

Mary showed Crashaw his way forward in prayer and in poetry. Both are disciplines demanding periods of silence, self-abandonment, and solitude; and they thus require of the man or woman considerable courage, a courage observed in the Virgin at the Annunciation, who was prepared to "go it alone" as a mother. As Crashaw's devotion to Mary grew at Peterhouse, so did his readiness to put himself at risk politically as well as poetically. Indeed, Paul A. Parrish shows how Crashaw's life and art demonstrate a fidelity to feminine virtues that are opposed to a masculine world of power, domination, and control. It would be a mistake to see these as cloistered virtues, though they were, no doubt, fostered by prolonged prayer "in the Temple of God." From his nightly vigils before the altar of Little St. Mary's, Crashaw emerged like the medieval knight who vowed to serve the weakest members of his society. In his final days at Pembroke he had come out in support of his tutor, Tournay, who preached against the Puritan emphasis of faith at the expense of love. In a concurring Latin poem, "Fides quæ sola justificat," Crashaw depicted "this Faith *alone* so sadly, so desolately alone," like an aging widow, devoid of family and friends and bereft of their charity. When he first came to Peterhouse, the poet became further embroiled in the theological controversy raging at Cambridge between Puritans and Laudians when he wrote a preface in verse, "Upon the ensuing Treatises," for Robert Shelford's *Five Pious and Learned Discourses* (1635) and reiterated Saint Paul's warning to the Corinthians: "though I have all faith, so that I could remove mountains, and have not charity, I am nothing." In this remarkable poem Crashaw made it his radical "masculine theme" to create a feminine environment in which religion was no longer the blunt instrument of political power but the generous outpouring of the "tame and tender heart," "meek and humble eyes" like those of the bashful Virgin. His speaker reaches out in love to the "poore," the homeless, and, astonishingly, to the pope himself: "In summe, no longer shall our people hope, / To be a true Protestant, 's but to hate the Pope." In expressing his Christian love for all men, even the archenemy of his father and most English Protestants, Crashaw began to feel what it was like for Christ to be a stranger in his own land. Taking Shelford's words in his "First Discourse" to heart – "in God's service we must neither see father nor mother, brother nor sister . . . nor our own selves neither" – Crashaw would begin to let go of the past and become dispossessed like the Mother and Child.

The "Hymn in the Holy Nativity," which may have been drafted as early as 1637, was the first of three Christmastide hymns that would eventually appear as a trio in the *Carmen Deo Nostro*. In this first hymn Crashaw was inspired by the Nativity Gospel of Luke to emulate the song of joy which the shepherds improvised as they returned to their fields after beholding the Virgin and her newborn son in the manger. It is interesting to note that the first version of this hymn was placed almost immediately after "Psalme 23" in the 1646 *Steps to the Temple*. It would thus appear that this Nativity hymn was positioned to underline the poet's own identification not only with the stray sheep but with the

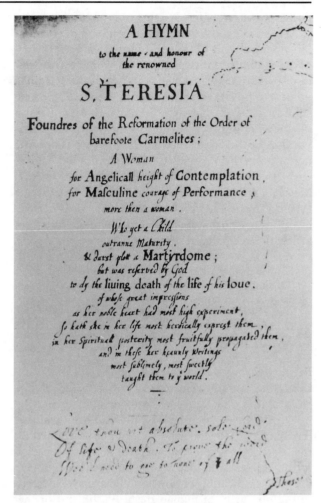

Title page, believed to be in Crashaw's hand, from the only complete manuscript for Crashaw's poem honoring Saint Teresa of Avila (Pierpont Morgan Library, MA 1385)

"poor Shepheards, home-spun things: / Whose Wealth's their flock; whose witt, to be / Well read in their simplicity" (1652 version of "Hymn in the Holy Nativity"). Moreover, as all eyes of the shepherds are on the infant Jesus asleep at the warm breast of his Mother, we can once again see how Crashaw used the Virgin and Child as an icon which focused his poetic attention and clarified the meditative purpose of his art which was prayerful absorption in God. In his final version of the hymn published in *Carmen Deo Nostro*, the sensuous stanza, in which Mary quiets her child with a mother's tender breast and lullaby, would be eliminated. For some the image of the woman openly breast-feeding her child is either too sentimental or too unseemly. The only image in Crashaw's poetry which exceeds that of the Virgin exposing her breast and offering it to her crying baby in its vulnerability is that of Christ stretched on the Cross, his breast exposed to the centurion's lance.

Crashaw was not afraid to show his "feminine" sensitivity to the most vulnerable members of society. His poetic rituals of vulnerability are a declaration of the opening of the heart to God which transpires in prayer. The lyrical stanza in which the Virgin's voice can be heard above that of the shepherds as "She sings thy Teares asleepe, and dips / Her Kisses in thy weeping Eye" would be cut from the 1652 version of the hymn. Given the poet's passionate devotion to the Virgin Mother, it cannot have been easy for him to sacrifice these lines "And let the MIGHTY BABE alone. / The Phœnix builds the Phœnix' nest. / LOVE's architecture is his own"; but no more authentic step could he have taken to affirm the necessity of self-surrender:

> To thee meeke Majesty! soft KING
> Of simple GRACES and sweet LOVES.
> Each of us his lamb will bring
> Each his pair of sylver Doves;
> Till burnt at last in fire of Thy fair eyes,
> Our selves become our own best SACRIFICE.

In this closing stanza the most powerful image of the hymn is fully released. It is the image of the child as the new light source to replace the sun, a mystical concept Crashaw would explore in all its terrible beauty in the Epiphany hymn. For much of the Nativity hymn, however, the fearsome energy of the child was hidden by the body of his mother, an adroit indication of how God incarnated himself in the obscurity of human flesh. At the end of the hymn, however, the shepherds no longer make the Old Testament sacrifice of burnt offerings. Imitating the divine child, who will become both their Good Shepherd and their Paschal Lamb, they are set alight with love as they gaze "in fire of Thy fair eyes."

What Crashaw was trying to suggest about the direct encounter with God in prayer is clarified by his august companion piece, "Hymn in the Glorious Epiphanie," which commemorates the Adoration of the Magi celebrated on 6 January as the feast in which Christ was made manifest to the Gentiles. The poem begins where the Nativity hymn left off, depicting the child mystically as the "Bright BABE! Whose awfull beautyes" disinherit the sun; and it examines the adjustments in perception that must be made if the world is to live and grow in the light of Christ, the *Lumen de Lumine*. Like the shepherds and their sheep, the wise men too "strangely went astray," not through slowness or stupidity, but the intellectual brilliance that is often at work in Metaphysical wit or contemporary criticism. As the poet reviewed a long human history of mistaken beliefs,

clever conceits, specious theories – all personified by pagan sun worship – he was aware that every age has its "Bright IDOL." According to Pritchard, when the Puritan investigators sought evidence in 1641 of popish image worship in the Laudian church services of Peterhouse, Crashaw himself would be cited for Mariolatry and for his superstitious practices of "diverse bowings, cringeings" and incensing before the altar. In turn, Crashaw saw the Puritan's religious intolerance and dogmatic iconoclasm as forms of self-idolatry. Idols reveal the susceptibility of all parties – Laudian, Puritan, Catholic, Protestant – to make themselves and not their God the center of life. In the final section of the Epiphany hymn the Crucifixion is represented as the portentous moment when mankind will be freed of its idols. Yet the Three Kings insist at the outset that the Christ child is the whole point of the poem – "All-circling point. All centring sphear. / The world's one, round, "Æternall year" – that Christ is mother as well as child: "O little all! in thy embrace / The world lyes warm, and likes his place." Only near the end of the hymn does it become possible to introduce the concept of the *via negativa* (negative path) conceived by Dionysius the Areopagite after he reportedly witnessed the ominous eclipse of the sun when the Son of God died on the Cross. The concept, that God can only be described in terms of what he is not, is only conceivable if the centering activity integral to prayer occurs and life no longer revolves around the sun or the self but Christ: "Thus shall that reverend child of light, / By being scholler first of that new night, / Come forth Great master of the mystick day."

Given the sensuous development of his poetic devotions, critics have wondered whether the Epiphany hymn represents "some attempted and never consummated change in the character of Crashaw's religious life and his poetic method." Indeed, Austin Warren suspects that he was temperamentally unsuited to pursue any further poetic experiment with the *via negativa*. Almost all of Crashaw's poetry, however, is some form of meditative exercise, the aim of which is to guide the reader toward the light of vision turned wholly on God. Crashaw's poetry takes us to the brink, the moment to which all prayer leads, the moment of apophatic wisdom when everything to do with the conscious self must be abandoned – images, ideas, words – and fall away before God. His dilemma as a poet was acute: he depended on artful language and thought and yet was striving to capture the non-conceptual, self-disregarding state of pure contemplation. Rather than burn his poetry, as other Renaissance poets did, Crashaw chose to follow the ardent path of the shepherds leading to ecstatic self-sacrifice, or the more taxing example of Mary which was unsung self-effacement. Neither course has been looked at sympathetically by his modern critics. If they do not read sexual sublimation or, worse, perversion into what William Butler Yeats might have called "the uncontrollable mystery" of Crashaw's work, they feel that he concentrates an abnormal amount of his poetic energy on a woman who is meek, mild, and mindless.

In his own day the poet's devout raptures were seen as the fruit of the intensive prayer program devised by his master at Peterhouse, John Cosin, or practiced by the spiritual community of Little Gidding. This was the first and only religious house to be formed after the traumatic dissolution of the monasteries during the Reformation. Little Gidding was founded in 1625 by Nicholas Ferrar, close friend of George Herbert and the original editor of his *Temple*. The devotional adherence at Little Gidding to older forms of piety such as round-the-clock prayer vigils and to relics of the old religion such as crucifixes or madonnas obviously attracted Crashaw, who was involved in similar practices and adornments at Peterhouse. Both he and the Ferrar family would also attract the unwelcome attention of the Puritans, who branded Little Gidding an "Armenian nunnery" and leveled it to the ground in 1647. Crashaw's intimate association with the Ferrar community dates from at least 1636, when the nephew of Nicholas Ferrar, Ferrar Collet, became his pupil at Peterhouse. It is possible, however, that the poet was introduced to the family as a boy by his own father through an early association with the Virginia Company. Indeed, his youthful poetic exercise "Psalme 23" could have originated from the psalm readings which were so important a feature of the daily worship at Little Gidding. If Richard Crashaw was not acquainted with Little Gidding from the time of its inception, he certainly showed a lifelong devotion to its members. After his flight abroad to Leiden, in 1644, he was anxious to see his college fellowship transferred to Ferrar Collet and to uphold the honor of Ferrar's chaste sister, Mary Collet, the "gratious mother" for whom he had strong feelings.

In "Description of a Religious House," first published in 1648 alongside Latin tributes to Peterhouse, Crashaw extolled the monastic life practiced at Little Gidding. This georgic poem of aching beauty enunciates his commitment to prayer as life in which he is conscious of God's presence in daily work – "Hands full of harty labours; Paines that

pay / And prize themselves; doe much, that more they may" – and sees his redemption at work even in "the sweat of this daye's sorrows." In the opening of this poem Crashaw emphatically disclaims "roofes of gold," "riotous tables shining," "endlesse dining," and "tyrian silk proud pavements sweeping" as "tumultuous joyes" and "false showes of short and slippery good." For the soul who loves God more than the world, the quality of life cannot be separated from the quiet practice of prayer:

> Silence, and sacred rest; peace, and pure joyes;
> Kind loves keep house, ly close, and make no noise,
> And room enough for Monarchs, while none swells
> Beyond the kingdomes of contentfull Cells.

In the letter that he wrote while in exile, probably to the Ferrar family, Crashaw would express his longing to return to the "little contenfull kingdom" of Peterhouse, a longing which no doubt included the "contentfull Cells" of neighboring Little Gidding. The longing for home is deeply imprinted in Crashaw's poetry and psychic makeup. He sought this home in an undifferentiated community like Little Gidding open to men and women; welcoming Protestants and Catholics; exhibiting "feminine" qualities, "soft" and "sweet," and masculine virtues, "hard" and "harty." He saw this home in the heaven that the Virgin made for her son in her womb, lap, and bosom. He ultimately finds it in the closing line of his poem when "the self-remembering SOUL / ... / ... meditates her immortall way / Home to the original source of LIGHT and intellectuall Day." Once again, Crashaw depicted his art as one of meditation, a repeated, rapturous discovery that God has made his home and his heaven in the center of every soul.

Crashaw's decade or so of piety at Cambridge, from 1631 until the end of 1642, was the most idyllic period of his short life. He experienced not only the depth but the height of Christ's love, and Crashaw's spiritual joy is evident in "O Gloriosa Domina," his paean to Mary as generatrix of goodness, not sin. With the support of his college friend and fellow poet, Joseph Beaumont, whose Laudian piety would also scandalize Puritans, Crashaw celebrated the "Glorious Assumption" of the Virgin. Though the Assumption was not formally recognized in the seventeenth century as an article of either Anglican or Roman faith, it allowed Crashaw to pursue his spiritual conviction that Christ stirs within the depths of our humanity and calls us to rise to his divine height. According to David Lloyd's *Memoires* (1668), Crashaw's church services were thronged with Christians eager for this message in sermons "that ravished more like Poems, than both the Poet and Saint . . . scattering not so much Sentences [as] Extasies." In fact, the appreciative editor of Crashaw's *Steps to the Temple,* who could well have been Beaumont, promised in the preface that the poet's verse would have much the same effect and "lift thee Reader, some yards above the ground." It was certainly Beaumont who in 1638 broadcast word of an elevated woman whose name and works were unheard of in English – the mystical Saint Teresa of Avila. Crashaw's three poems in her honor – "A Hymn to Sainte Teresa," "An Apologie for the fore-going Hymne," and "The Flaming Heart" – are, arguably, his most sublime works; they have earned him a new following among contemporary readers. These three poems form a triptych to the woman saint, representing three stages of faith: the institutional, critical, and mystical; three phases of human attachment: child, adult, and parent; and three expressions of gender: feminine, masculine, and androgynous. Just as Christians have difficulty in conceiving that there are three persons in one God, so they cannot see how in faith and in love they themselves approximate the Trinity. Indeed, the triune God is the prototype for Teresa's spiritual achievement, which is to embody all humanity in her "Flaming Heart."

The full title of "A Hymn to Sainte Teresa" describes Teresa as "A WOMAN for Angelicall heigth of speculation, for Masculine courage of performance, more then a woman. WHO Yet a child, out ran maturity, and durst plott a Martyrdome." According to Parrish, Teresa remains throughout the poem the child-woman who confounds all those of greater maturity. At the beginning of the hymn, she plans the first of her great escapes at age six, running away from home to bring Christian salvation to the Moors and win the martyr's instantaneous admission to heaven. Her role models are the Spanish conquistadores, such as her own brother: "old Souldiers, Great and tall, / Ripe Men of Martyrdom" who defend the doctrinal traditions and institutional history of the church militant. Teresa's spiritual growth involves unlearning their instruction to her in childhood and listening with a mystical wisdom, which has nothing to do with age, to the God who communicates directly to her from within:

> SWEET, not so fast! lo thy fair Spouse
> Whom thou seekst with so swift vowes,
> Calls thee back, and bidds thee come
> T'embrace a milder MARTYRDOM.

Stripped of male heroics, the martyr is simply one who bears witness in life to Christ. Socially prevented in childhood and by womanhood from the masculine conquest of new worlds, Teresa is gently turned to the conquest that absorbed the poet, the conquest of that mysterious world of the inner self. The latter half of the hymn draws on Teresa's own ecstatic account of her mystical transverberation and on images throbbing with eroticism to write "Love's noble history." This is not a history of subjugation or indoctrination but of surrender to Christ's enlargement of the heart and to a love which stretches from the "mild / And milky soul of a soft child" to the milky way of heaven. In the second of his Teresa poems, "An Apologie for the fore-going Hymne," Crashaw turns from this inner vision of Christ's all-embracing love to question the social prejudices that divide the Church on earth:

> Forbid it, mighty Love! let no fond Hate
> Of names and wordes, so farr præjudicate.
> Souls are not SPANIARDS too, one freindly floud
> Of BAPTISM blends them all into a blood.

Crashaw makes no apology for the fact that as an Anglican poet he has taken a Spaniard, a woman, and a Catholic for his subject – but only that neither this nor the foregoing hymn can capture Teresa's eloquence. He exhorts his fellow Christians to make peace with one another, but both his poetry and Teresa's writings on prayer direct readers to find this peace, which comes from Christ, first within themselves. At the end of the poem he elevates the Eucharistic chalice that he was accustomed to handling as a celebrant at Little St. Marys. It is filled with a communion wine strong in love, the only cordial for the stricken seventeenth-century heart. "The Flaming Heart," which completes his Teresa trilogy, alludes to a 1642 English translation of her life. Added to the *Steps* in 1648, Crashaw's poem is the most intricate of his tributes. The poet opens with the commanding voice of church authority:

> Readers, be rul'd by me; and make
> Here a well-plac't and wise mistake,
> You must transpose the picture quite,
> And spell it wrong to read it right[.]

His initial dispute is with the painter who drew a crude and childish illustration of the saint pierced through the heart by the dart of the seraphim. As a poet, Crashaw upheld the traditional superiority of the word to the picture in conveying such inner mysteries; but, as a painter himself, he was praised in Car's "Epigramme" (1652) for the "holy strife" between his pen and pencil as to "Which might draw vertue better to the life." Crashaw thus proposes to correct the painter's misconstruction with his own writer's pen and, in particular, to address the gender misconceptions that have led the artist to mock "with female FROST love's manly flame" by painting "Some weak, inferiour, woman saint." In the second section of the poem, which begins around line 69, he strives to reproduce Teresa's flaming heart. This heart personifies that which he must bring about in his own "hard, cold, hart," a spiritual transformation of self described in Galatians as a transformation in which "there is neither male nor female," neither parent nor child, strong nor weak, active nor passive, "for ye are all one in Christ Jesus." In the magnificent entreaty that culminates the poem, Crashaw invokes not only "all the eagle in thee, all the dove" but the pious memory of his own parents. He also concedes that both the verbal and the visual image fade away before Teresa's indescribable communion with God: "By all of HIM we have in THEE; / Leave nothing of my SELF in me." Though, in conclusion, he effaced himself and his art before the woman saint, he did not wish to dwell on Teresa so much as on Christ, who dwelled in her heart.

Crashaw's remarkable Teresa trilogy is the product of an inclusive prayer life in which he made God his center and saw God as the source of a more harmonious knowledge of the self and of others. If these poems nudge readers to relearn and unlearn many assumptions about the shape of the spiritual life, Crashaw himself was now forced by the destruction of the Civil War to wean himself from the security and the bliss he had found at Peterhouse. His movements after his disappearance from Cambridge in early 1643 remain something of a mystery and suggest a life in painful disarray. He may first have fled to nearby Little Gidding before making his way to a friend in Lincolnshire, with whom he left a private manuscript of his poems. He is next heard of in Leiden, when, on 20 February 1644, he writes his only surviving English letter, either to the Ferrar family or Beaumont. Scandalized by the secularism of Dutch life, denied access to his spiritual mother in exile, Mary Collet, by her uncles, Crashaw beseeches the friends he has left behind: "what must I doe? what must I bee?" It is possible that shortly thereafter Crashaw made his way back to England and found temporary shelter at the Oxford court of Queen Henrietta Maria. Those who would aid him in his final distress were present here with the queen – Abraham Cowley, another Cambridge friend and poet, and Susan Feilding, Countess of Denbigh and First Lady of the Bedchamber. The queen and her entourage fled to Paris in July 1644, and Crashaw went to ground, perhaps on the run in England, perhaps adrift on the Continent. Eventually surfacing in Paris sometime in 1645, Crashaw confided in Thomas Car, the experienced confessor to English refugees. The poet's vagrant existence made a lasting impression on Car, as shown by "The Anagramme":

> He seeks no downes, no sheetes, his bed's still made.
> If he can find a chaire or stoole, he's layd,
> When day peepes in, he quitts his restlesse rest.
> And still, poore soule, before he's up he's dres't.

For much of his life Crashaw was content to prosper as the birds of the air or the lilies of the field "and seek not ye what ye shall eat, or what ye shall drink, neither be ye of doubtful mind" (Luke). On the Continent he still sought the kingdom of heaven but simply could not have survived without the material intervention of his new friends, especially when his old ones spoke of him in the "Preface to the Reader" as "this Learned young Gentleman (now dead to us)." The countess of Denbigh used her influence to persuade the queen in early September 1646 to recommend Crashaw to the pope. The poet expressed the ardent gratitude of the Roman convert by entrusting his poems to Car for a new Catholic volume of his verse, Carmen Deo Nostro, and by ensuring that this volume, which was published posthumously in 1652, would be dedicated to the countess "in acknowledgment of her Goodnes & Charity" and in hopes of her own imminent conversion. Yet there was a malicious report published in a volume titled Legenda lignea (1652) that Crashaw had attached himself to "deluded, vain-glorious Ladies, and their friends." In his poems of devotional instruction such as "Letter to the Countess of Denbigh" or "Ode on a Prayer-book," he did not hide the sense of failure as well as success, of frustration as well as sweetness, that dogs the spiritual life. These poems are flawed as human nature itself is flawed. The nervous, excited imagery in "Letter to the Countess of Denbigh" of a "Heav'n-beseiged Heart" that "Stands Trembling at the Gate of Blisse" but "dares not venture" inside is an honest reflection of the struggle both for discipline and for release in prayer. Crashaw's controversial epigram "Blessed be the paps which Thou hast sucked" is addressed not to Mary but to weaker handmaidens of the Lord. In meditating on scripture, these women pray that Christ may be incarnated in their hearts but discover a deep unwillingness to respond wholly to his word, a phenomenon further demonstrated by the strong critical resistance to this poem. Even in Crashaw's other notorious poem, "The Weeper," feminine imagery is used lavishly to surfeit and to shut down the mind. The repetition that mars this work as poetry functions as a mantric device to release the prayer that, with Mary Magdalene's tears, wells up to heaven from the heart.

Bolstered by the great hopes which the English Catholic community abroad had of him, Crashaw made his way as a pilgrim to Rome in November 1646. For the next year he struggled with poverty and ill health, and while waiting for some papal retainer, is reputed by Sir Robert Southwell to have complained that "if the Roman church be not founded upon a rock, it is at least founded upon something which is as hard as a rock." After renewed diplomatic entreaties to the pope in 1647, Crashaw secured a post with the virtuous Cardinal Palotto who was closely associated with the English College. Finally, in April 1649, the cardinal procured him a cathedral benefice at the Virgin's so-called Holy House and Shrine, the Santa Casa at Loreto. Weakened by his precarious existence in exile, Crashaw set out for Loreto in May and died there of a fever on 21 August 1649. This "poore soule" was only thirty-six. No one conversant with the last wretched stage of Crashaw's life can see his poetry as insulated from suffering. As he drew near to the fabled house in Loreto, which was reputed to be where Mary was born and where she received the Annunciation, Crashaw must have thought he was on the home stretch. In a manner of speaking he was; but like Mary in "Sancta Maria Dolorum" he would first have to endure the pain of the Cross and look death in the face:

> Before her eyes
> Her's, and the whole world's joyes,
> Hanging all torn she sees; and in his woes
> And Paines, her Pangs and throes.
> Each wound of His, from every Part,
> All, more at home in her owne heart.

In this unique reworking of the Latin hymn "Stabat Mater," he studies the mother heartsick with grief before her crucified son: "His Nailes write swords in her, which soon her heart / Payes back, with more then their own smart." Just as Saint Teresa's heart was pierced by the seraphim's dart, so here Mary is transfixed by a Metaphysical sword of sorrow which corresponds to Christ's pain, especially to the deathblow he received from the centurion's spear. As an Anglican cleric at Little St.

Mary's, he had often contemplated a picture of the Virgin Mother. According to Paul Cardile in an essay published in *Cristiana* (1984), such paintings were often hung over altar tables and depicted Mary's priestly role at the Crucifixion, Presentation in the Temple, or Nativity. Little Gidding was noted for its *mater dolorosas*. In his tribute to the mother of sorrows, the poet now asked Mary to teach him the meaning of sacrifice which lay at the heart of his own priesthood:

> By all those stings
> Of love, sweet bitter things,
> Which these torn hands transcrib'd on thy true heart
> O teach mine too the art
> To study him so, till we mix
> Wounds; and become one crucifix.

In her maternal compassion Mary showed Crashaw what Christ suffered because he took mankind's own suffering to heart. Crashaw spoke as an Anglican priest, and he was never ordained in the Roman Church. He died a mere "beneficiatus" responsible only for singing the office in the basilica and having no active share in the great offering he had depicted. His lesser part corresponded to that of the angels who often attended Mary in paintings depicting her priestly mediation. They were sometimes dressed in the vestments of minor orders that Crashaw would have worn and been buried in at Loreto. His worldly friend, Abraham Cowley, described how fitting such a death was for a poet who spoke with the tongues of men and of angels:

> How well (blest Swan) did Fate contrive thy death;
> And made thee render up they tuneful breath
> In thy great Mistress Arms; thou most divine
> And richest Off'ering of Loretto's Shrine!
> Where like some holy Sacrifice t'expire,
> A Fever burns thee, and Love lights the Fire.
> Angels (they say) brought the fam'ed Chappel there,
> . . . .
> Tis surer much they brought thee there, and They,
> And Thou, their charge, went singing all the way.

In "Psalme 23" Crashaw had expressed the juvenescent hope that his end would be his beginning "And thence my ripe soule will I breath / Warme into the Armes of Death." "Hope," Cowley had asserted in a poetic debate with Crashaw at Cambridge, "is the most hopelesse thing of all." Cowley might well have felt his point was proved when according to Wood's *Athenæ Oxonienses* (1691, 1692), he found his friend in Paris "a meer Scholar and very shiftless." Yet from childhood Crashaw had treasured hopes of heaven, not of earthly reward. In death he was honored by Cowley for his poetic intimation of a deeper and higher wisdom to life, which eluded the subjects of a more knowing world.

Bibliographies:

John R. Roberts, *Richard Crashaw: An Annotated Bibliography of Criticism, 1632–1980* (Columbia: University of Missouri Press, 1985);

Roberts, "A Selected Bibliography of Modern Crashaw Studies," in *New Perspectives on the Life and Art of Richard Crashaw,* edited by John R. Roberts (Columbia & London: University of Missouri Press, 1990).

References:

Robert Martin Adams, "Taste and Bad Taste in Metaphysical Poetry: Richard Crashaw and Dylan Thomas," *Hudson Review,* 8 (Spring 1955): 61–77; reprinted in *Seventeenth-Century English Poetry: Modern Essays in Criticism,* edited by William R. Keast (New York: Oxford University Press, 1962);

Alfred Alvarez, "Metaphysical Rhetoric: Richard Crashaw," in Alvarez's *The School of Donne* (London: Chatto & Windus, 1961; New York: Pantheon, 1962);

Joan Bennett, "Richard Crashaw," in her *Five Metaphysical Poets: Donne, Herbert, Vaughan, Crashaw, Marvell* (Cambridge: Cambridge University Press, 1963), pp. 90–108;

Marc F. Bertonasco, *Crashaw and the Baroque* (University: University of Alabama Press, 1971);

Steven Blakemore, "The Name Made Flesh: Crashaw's Celebration of 'The Name Above Every Name,' " *Concerning Poetry,* 17 (Spring 1984): 63–77;

Vera J. Camden, "Richard Crashaw's Poetry: The Imagery of Bleeding Wounds," *American Images,* 40 (Fall 1983): 257–279;

Robert M. Cooper, *An Essay on the Art of Richard Crashaw,* edited by James Hogg, Salzburg Studies in English Literature, Elizabethan & Renaissance Studies no. 102 (Salzburg: Universität Salzburg, 1982);

Cooper, ed., *Essays on Richard Crashaw,* edited by Hogg, Salzburg Studies in English Literature, Elizabethan & Renaissance Studies no. 83 (Salzburg: Universität Salzburg, 1979);

Walter R. Davis, "The Meditative Hymnody of Richard Crashaw," *English Literary History,* 50 (Spring 1983): 107–129;

T. S. Eliot, "Note on Richard Crashaw," in Eliot's *For Lancelot Andrewes: Essays on Style and Order* (London: Faber & Gwyer, 1928), pp. 117–125;

Frank Fabry, "Richard Crashaw and the Art of Allusion: Pastoral in a 'Hymn to . . . Sainte Teresa,' " *English Literary Renaissance,* 16 (1986): 373–382;

Patrick Grant, "Richard Crashaw and the Capucins: Images and the Force of Belief," in Grant's *Images and Ideas in the Literature of the English Renaissance* (Amherst: University of Massachusetts Press, 1979), pp. 89–128;

Elizabeth H. Hageman, "Calendrical Symbolism and the Unity of Crashaw's *Carmen Deo Nostro,*" *Studies in Philology,* 77 (1980): 161–179;

Thomas F. Healy, *Richard Crashaw,* Medieval and Renaissance Authors, 8 (Leiden: Brill, 1986);

Anthony Low, "Richard Crashaw: Sensible Affection," in Low's *Love's Architecture: Devotional Modes in Seventeenth-Century English Poetry* (New York: New York University Press, 1978), pp. 116–159;

Leah Sinanoglou Marcus, "The Poet as Child: Herbert, Herrick, and Crashaw," in Marcus's *Childhood and Cultural Despair: A Theme and Variations in Seventeenth-Century Literature* (Pittsburgh: University of Pittsburgh Press, 1978), pp. 94–152;

L. C. Martin, Introduction to *The Poems, English, Latin, and Greek, of Richard Crashaw,* edited by Martin (Oxford: Clarendon Press, 1927), pp. xv–xlii;

Louis L. Martz, "Richard Crashaw: Love's Architecture," in Martz's *The Wit of Love: Donne, Carew, Crashaw, Marvell* (Notre Dame & London: University of Notre Dame Press, 1969), pp. 113-147;

Michael McCanles, "The Rhetoric of the Sublime in Crashaw's Poetry," in *The Rhetoric of Renaissance Poetry from Wyatt to Milton,* edited by Thomas O. Sloan and Raymond B. Waddington (Berkeley, Los Angeles & London: University of California Press, 1974), pp. 189–211;

Paul A. Parrish, "The Feminizing of Power: Crashaw's Life and Art," in *"The Muses Common-Weale": Poetry and Politics in the Seventeenth Century,* edited by Claude J. Summers and Ted-Larry Pebworth (Columbia: University of Missouri Press, 1988), pp. 148–162;

Robert T. Petersson, *The Art of Ecstasy: Teresa, Bernini and Crashaw* (London: Routledge & Kegan Paul, 1970; New York: Atheneum, 1970);

Mario Praz, "The Flaming Heart: Richard Crashaw and the Baroque," in Praz's *The Flaming Heart:*

Essays on Crashaw, Machiavelli, and Other Studies in the Relations between Italian and Renaissance Literature from Chaucer to T. S. Eliot (Garden City, N.Y.: Doubleday, 1958);

Allan Pritchard, "Puritan Charges Against Crashaw and Beaumont," *Times Literary Supplement,* 2 July 1964, p. 578;

Maureen Sabine, "Crashaw and the Feminine Animus: Patterns of Self-Sacrifice in Two of His Devotional Poems," *John Donne Journal,* 4 (1985): 69–94;

Sabine, *Feminine Engendered Faith: The Poetry of John Donne and Richard Crashaw* (London: Macmillan, 1992);

Ruth C. Wallerstein, *Richard Crashaw: A Study in Style and Poetic Development,* University of Wisconsin Studies in Language and Literature no. 37 (Madison: University of Wisconsin Press, 1935);

Austin Warren, *Richard Crashaw: A Study in Baroque Sensibility* (University: Louisiana State University Press, 1939);

E. I. Watkin, "Richard Crashaw" and "William Crashaw and His Son," in Watkin's *Poets and Mystics* (New York & London: Sheed & Ward, 1953), pp. 136–163, 164–187;

Helen C. White, "Richard Crashaw: Little Gidding to Rome" and "Richard Crashaw: 'Poet and Saint,' " in White's *The Metaphysical Poets: A Study in Religious Experience* (New York: Macmillan, 1936), pp. 202–229, 230–258;

George Walton Williams, *Image and Symbol in the Sacred Poetry of Richard Crashaw* (Columbia: University of South Carolina Press, 1963);

George Williamson, *The Donne Tradition: A Study in English Poetry from Donne to the Death of Cowley* (Cambridge: Harvard University Press, 1930);

R. V. Young, Jr., *Richard Crashaw and the Spanish Golden Age,* Yale Studies in English no. 191 (New Haven & London: Yale University Press, 1982).

Sir William Davenant

(February 1606 – 7 April 1668)

Jack D. Durant
North Carolina State University

See also the Davenant entry in *DLB 58: Jacobean and Caroline Dramatists.*

BOOKS: *The Tragedy of Albovine, King of the Lombards* (London: Printed by F. Kingston for R. Moore, 1629);

The Cruell Brother. A Tragedy (London: Printed by A. Mathewes for J. Waterson, 1630);

The Just Italian (London: Printed by T. Harper for J. Waterson, 1630);

The Temple of Love: A Masque (London: Printed for T. Walkley, 1635);

The Witts. A Comedie (London: Printed by A. Mathewes for R. Meighen, 1636);

The Platonick Lovers. A Tragæcomedy (London: Printed by A. Mathewes for R. Meighen, 1636);

The Triumphs of the Prince D'Amour. A Masque (London: Printed by A. Mathewes for R. Meighen, 1636);

Britannia Triumphans: A Masque (London: Printed by J. Haviland for T. Walkley, 1637);

Luminalia, Or The Festivall of Light (London: Printed by J. Haviland for T. Walkley, 1637);

Madagascar; With Other Poems (London: Printed by J. Haviland for T. Walkley, 1638);

Salmacida Spolia. A Masque (London: Printed by T. Harper for T. Walkley, 1640);

The Unfortunate Lovers: A Tragedie (London: Printed by R. H. & sold by Francis Coles, 1643);

Love and Honor (London: Printed for Humphrey Robinson & Humphrey Moseley, 1649);

A Discourse Upon Gondibert. An Heroick Poem (Paris: Chez Matthieu Guillemot, 1650);

Gondibert: An Heroic Poem (London: Printed by Tho. Newcomb for John Holden, 1651);

The Siege of Rhodes, part 1 (London: Printed by J. M. for H. Herringman, 1656); part 1 (revised) and part 2 (London: Printed for Henry Herringman, 1663);

The First Days Entertainment at Rutland House, By Declamations and Musick: After the Manner of the An-

Frontispiece to The Works of Sʳ William D'avenant *(1673; engraving by William Faithorne after a lost portrait by John Greenhill)*

cients (London: Printed by J. M. for H. Herringman, 1657);

The Cruelty of the Spaniards in Peru (London: Printed for Henry Herringman, 1658);

The History of Sʳ Francis Drake . . . The First Part (London: Printed for Henry Herringman, 1659);

Poem Upon His Sacred Majesties Most Happy Return to His Dominions (London: Printed for H. Herringman, 1660);

Poem to the King's Most Sacred Majesty (London: Printed for Henry Herringman, 1663);

The Rivals: A Comedy, adapted from William Shakespeare and John Fletcher's *The Two Noble Kinsmen* (London: Printed for William Cademan, 1668);

The Man's the Master: A Comedy, adapted from Paul Scarron's *Maître Valet* (London: Printed for Henry Herringman, 1669);

The Works of Sr William D'avenant K^t Consisting of Those Which Were Formerly Printed, and Those Which He Design'd for the Press (London: Printed by T. N. for Henry Herringman, 1673) — comprises *Gondibert; Madagascar, with Other Poems; Poems on Several Occasions, Never Before Printed; Declamations at Rutland-House; Three Masques at Whitehall; Cœlum Britannicum* (by Thomas Carew, possibly with the assistance of Davenant); *The Temple of Love*, and *The Triumphs of the Prince D'Amour; The Siege of Rhodes*, parts 1 and 2; *Playhouse to Be Let, Containing The History of Sir Francis Drake*, and *The Cruelty of the Spaniards in Peru; The Unfortunate Lovers; The Wits; Love and Honor; The Law Against Lovers; The Man's the Master; The Platonick Lovers; The Tragedy of Albovine; The Just Italian; The Cruell Brother; News from Plymouth; The Distresses; The Siege; The Fair Favorite*;

Macbeth, A Tragedy, adapted from Shakespeare's *Macbeth* (London: Printed for P. Chetwin, 1674);

The Seventh and Last Canto of the Third Book of Gondibert, Never Yet Printed (London: Printed for W. Miller & J. Watts, 1685);

The Tempest, or The Enchanted Island. A Comedy, adapted by Davenant and John Dryden from Shakespeare's *The Tempest* (London: Printed by J. M. for Herringman & sold by R. Bentley, 1690).

Editions: *The Dramatic Works of Sir William D'Avenant, with Prefatory Memoir and Notes*, 5 volumes, edited by J. Maidment and W. H. Logan (Edinburgh: W. Paterson, 1872–1874) — comprises *Albovine, The Cruel Brother, The Just Italian, The Temple of Love, The Prince D'Amour, The Platonick Lovers, The Wits, Britannia Triumphans, Salmacida Spolia, The Unfortunate Lovers, Love and Honor, Entertainment at Rutland House, The Siege of Rhodes, Playhouse to be Let, News from Plymouth, The Fair Favorite, The Distresses, The Siege, The Man's the Master, The Law Against Lovers, The Rivals, Macbeth, The Tempest*;

The Tempest, in *Shakespearean Adaptations*, edited by Montague Summers (London: Cape, 1922);

Selected Poems of Sir William Davenant, edited by Douglas Bush (Cambridge, Mass.: Willow Press, 1943);

The Wits, in *Six Caroline Plays*, edited by A. S. Knowland (London: Oxford University Press, 1962);

Macbeth, in *Five Restoration Adaptations of Shakespeare*, edited by Christopher Spencer (Urbana: University of Illinois Press, 1965);

Salmacida Spolia, in *A Book of Masques*, edited by T. J. B. Spencer and Stanley Wells (Cambridge: Cambridge University Press, 1967);

The Law Against Lovers, introduction by A. M. Gibbs (London: Cornmarket, 1970);

The Rivals, introduction by Kenneth Muir (London: Cornmarket, 1970);

The Triumphs of the Prince D'Amour and *Britannia Triumphans*, in *Trois Masques à la Cour de Charles Ier d'Angleterre*, edited by Murray Lefkowitz (Paris: Editions Centre National, 1970);

Gondibert, edited by David F. Gladish (Oxford: Clarendon Press, 1971);

News from Plymouth [parallel English and Italian texts], edited by Maria Crino (Verona: Fiorini, 1972);

The Shorter Poems and Songs from the Plays and Masques, edited by A. M. Gibbs (Oxford: Clarendon Press, 1972);

The Siege of Rhodes, parts 1 and 2, edited by Ann-Mari Hedback (Uppsala: Acta Universitatis Upsaliensia, 1973);

The Temple of Love, Britannia Triumphans, Luminalia, and *Salmacida Spolia*, in *Inigo Jones: The Theatre of the Stuart Court*, edited by Stephen Orgel and Roy Strong (London: Sotheby Parke Bernet, 1973).

PLAY PRODUCTIONS: See *DLB 58*.

Although best known as a dramatist and theater manager, Sir William Davenant (or D'Avenant) also deserves notice as a poet. In 1638, when a stipend of one hundred pounds per annum came to him from the Crown, he received distinction as the poet laureate, succeeding Ben Jonson, and he continued until the end of his life producing poems of many forms and purposes, some of them based on innovative theoretical principles.

He was born in late February 1606 in Oxford, where his father, John, a vintner and innkeeper, served as mayor. Davenant's Christian name probably honors William Shakespeare, an admired friend of the family, who, according to reliable tradition, was the poet's godfather. Less reliable tradition even holds that Shakespeare, smitten with the beautiful and witty Jane Shepherd Davenant, was the poet's natural father, a prospect not offensive to Davenant in later life, when he liked, some said, to link his own creative fancy to Shakespeare's.

His early schooling took place at Saint Paul's School, Oxford, under Edward Sylvester, and he might have received brief instruction during 1620 and 1621 at Lincoln College, Oxford, but the deaths of his parents within weeks of one another in April 1622 terminated his formal education and sent him in search of a livelihood to London, where he first took appointment as a page to Frances Bindon Stuart, first Duchess of Richmond. With the death in 1624 of the duchess's husband, Ludowick Stuart, Davenant joined the household of Fulke Greville, Lord Brooke. There, probably as a clerk or amanuensis, he entered a significant literary ambience and nurtured friendships with two courtiers important to his own literary career, Endymion Porter, master of the horse to the duke of Buckingham, and Henry Jermyn, a favorite of Queen Henrietta Maria. Davenant continued in the service of Lord Brooke until 1628.

During his tenure with Brooke he wrote two dark revenge tragedies, *Albovine* (1629) and *The Cruell Brother* (1630), and he probably saw military service with George Villiers, first Duke of Buckingham, on the Isle of Rhé in 1627 and again in 1628 in actions giving rise to his third play, *The Siege,* a tragicomedy written in 1629. After leaving military service in 1628 he seems to have taken up lodgings with Edward Hyde in the Middle Temple and to have authored while there a proposal for destroying the powder magazines at Dunkirk. In any case, a "Mr. Davenant" of that address receives credit for such a scheme. He also busied himself at that time with a second tragicomedy, *The Just Italian,* which was licensed for presentation in 1629 (published, 1630).

Although Davenant was probably married by 1629 (certainly by 1632), a sexual indiscretion, possibly in 1630, infected him with syphilis, which severely degenerated his nose and would probably have taken his life but for the ministrations of the queen's own physician, Thomas Cademan. Thereafter the butt of jokes about his deformed nose, Davenant was long thought to have inflicted mortal sword wounds on one Thomas Warren, a tapster in Braintree, who, during the period of Davenant's re-

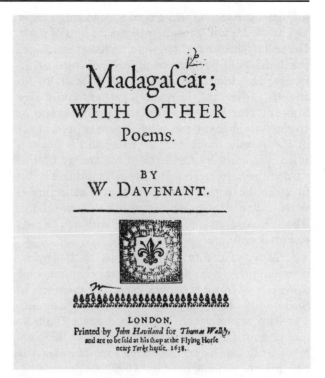

Title page for Davenant's first collection of verse. The title poem depicts an imaginary invasion of Madagascar by Prince Rupert, the nephew of Charles I.

cuperation, made one jest too many at the poet's expense. The story then has it that Davenant took refuge in Holland until promised a royal pardon in 1633, but findings now indicate that this fugitive refugee, a William Davenant quite different from the poet, was a resident of Halstead whose public records had long misled biographers not only into implicating the poet in the death of Warren but also into surmising that he had married and begotten a child before 1624.

While not literarily productive during the period of his illness, he returned to health with new creative vigor and composed six plays and four masques between 1634 and 1638. The full-length plays, which were performed by the King's Men at public theaters (Blackfriars or the Globe) and usually also at court, include two comedies, *The Witts* (performed, 1634; published, 1636) and *News from Plymouth* (performed, 1635; published, 1673); three tragicomedies, *Love and Honor* (performed, 1634; published, 1649), *The Platonick Lovers* (1636), and *The Fair Favorite* (performed, 1638; published, 1673); and one tragedy, *The Unfortunate Lovers* (performed, 1638; published, 1643). The masques include *The Temple of Love* (1635), *The Triumphs of the Prince D'Amour* (1636), *Britannia Triumphans,* and *Luminalia* (both published, 1637; performed, 1638).

Of these, the second was staged for the king's nephews at the Middle Temple with the designs of a Mr. Corseilles; the other three were staged at court with the designs of Inigo Jones and featured royal participants. No doubt assisted to royal favor by his friends Porter and Jermyn, Davenant could sign himself "Her Majesties Servant" by 1635, and he could sustain royal notice by the sheer persistence of his output, much of it adjusted to the queen's taste. Virtually by the force of his energy he had earned the laureateship in 1638, after adding to his fourteen theatrical pieces a substantial collection of verse called *Madagascar; With Other Poems* (1638). The volume appeared in February with dedications to Porter and Jermyn.

Most of the forty-two poems in *Madagascar* commend the lives, deaths, careers, characters, or prospects of eminent people, especially members of the nobility. The title poem, for example, promotes a scheme actually considered in the late 1630s to mount an invasion of Madagascar under the command of Prince Rupert, the king's nephew. Cast as a dream vision (enhanced by wine), the poem imagines Rupert a victorious conqueror receiving tribute from rulers who had rivaled him in his conquest of the island. He is assisted to victory by two mysterious champions who represent Porter and Jermyn.

Later in the collection Davenant's two patrons figure as Endymion and Arigo in a dialogue poem lamenting the supposed death of Col. George Goring, a hero of the siege of Breda, and in eight additional poems (one addressed to Jermyn and seven to Porter) the poet commends the generous services of his friends, who have supported and furthered him in his career and sustained him in his illness.

In three wedding poems the poet takes up his office as "Apollo's Priest" to flatter privileged young brides in their high prospects, and in seven elegiac poems he contrives ingenious means to console grieving widows, to celebrate lives well lived, to lament the loss of a poetic inspiration, to deplore the clamors of ambition, or to decry the rashness of dueling, which has cost a young worthy his life. A bit of elegiac whimsy even finds him reassuring a solicitous lady that he is not himself dead, and he certifies his vitality by sending her a gift of melons with his poem.

True to his identity as "Her Majestie's Servant," Davenant addresses five poems in the *Madagascar* collection to the queen. In one of them he recommends to her notice a fellow poet, F. S. In the others he celebrates her beauty and character and finds in them a sunlight capable of warming bleak places and of fostering hope for the future. The one

poem addressed to the king, a New Year's ode for 1630, commends him for his good judgment in concluding a new peace treaty with France, and it seems to counsel reinstatement of Parliament, which had been prorogued since 1628.

Perhaps the most ambitious poem of the collection is a mock-epic called "Jeffereidos," which recounts the misadventures of Jeffrey Hudson, the queen's dwarf, who was overtaken by privateers while under sail in 1629 from France, where he had gone to fetch a midwife for the queen's lying in. In the poem the privateers force Jeffrey to ride astride a French poodle; and, in a later humiliation, he must depend on the French midwife to rescue him from attack by a huge turkey.

Two poems in the collection evoke the camaraderie and high spirits derived from field sports in the Cotswolds, and three of them pay tribute to literary figures and achievements. One of these three admires the bright fancy of Thomas Carew; another honors a new edition of Jonson's poems; the third, possibly composed as early as 1620, memorializes Shakespeare in an affecting way. It advises poets who seek inspiration in the springtime to stay away from Stratford-upon-Avon, where all nature mourns and where the poor Avon has wept itself into a rivulet.

As these poems on literary subjects suggest, Davenant touches often in the *Madagascar* collection on his own life and profession. In evoking, for example, the agonies of his illness, he recalls the cruel isolation that had reduced him in size as in spirit and had hidden him from view like the tracks of a serpent. He expresses gratitude to his physician, Dr. Cademan, for restoring him to his friend Endymion, and he promises Endymion, whose example of moderation he respects, that he will never again "grow devout in a strange bed." A shadow of his illness even falls across one of the livelier poems – a mock-commiseration "To I. C.," whose servant has stolen his cloak – when the sudden arrival of an apothecary's bill chokes the muse to silence.

Other autobiographical hints in the collection relate to a protracted chancery dispute between Davenant and an "Ethnick Taylor" over exorbitant charges left unpaid, and a reference to the death of his first wife perhaps appears in one of the poems. His preoccupation with his role as a poet permeates the collection. At the outset, in "Madagascar," he claims a poet's laurels for writing the exploits of Prince Rupert because he has lived them vicariously in his own imagination. In recommending his colleague F. S. to the queen, he speaks of himself as the deputy of Orpheus; and, in another place, he characterizes poets as "Lords of Numbers." He invokes his muse in numerous contexts and acknowledges himself its servant. He values his status within the brotherhood of poets.

This status is reinforced by debts to John Donne and Jonson. In fact, Sir John Suckling takes occasion, in a dedicatory poem of the *Madagascar* volume, to observe of Davenant that since the death of Donne "no Man has ever writ / So neere him, in's owne way," a sentiment shared some decades later by Sir John Denham and Alexander Pope. In the last poem of the volume, "To Dr. Duppa, Deane of Christ-Church and Tutor to the Prince," Davenant himself acknowledges the "mighty Debt" he owes to Jonson, a debt he intends not to pay but to "keepe it to maintaine mee." In reflecting these two strong precedents, then, the collection displays scattered flashes of Donnean metaphor and concept, but it favors a metrical discipline and logical order rather more akin to Jonson than to Donne. Davenant selects regularized heroic couplets for virtually every poem, and, in the spirit of his mentor Thomas Hobbes, he grounds his poetic in logic and lucidity. In *Madagascar; With Other Poems,* he clearly builds transitions toward post-Restoration verse.

The years immediately following the 1638 volume found Davenant turning to theatrical management. His first managerial scheme, a new theater on Fleet Street, came to nothing, although formally approved by the Crown, but the second one secured him appointment as manager of the Cockpit theater in Drury Lane. Just months before assuming these managerial duties he had staged with Jones the last Caroline court masque, *Salmacida Spolia* (1640), in which the king had performed as Philogenes, the lover of his people. Very soon after beginning his career at the Cockpit, Davenant withdrew from it to enter military service in the Royalist cause. He no doubt took part in both Bishops' Wars (1639, 1640); he was arrested by Parliament in 1641 for treasonable conduct (in behalf of the queen) and threatened with execution; he served with the Royalist army in 1642 and 1643 and was knighted by the king at Gloucester in 1643. Between 1643 and 1645 he traversed the English Channel as a resourceful and successful munitions runner; and in December 1645, with the imminent collapse of the Royalist cause, he took refuge with the queen in Paris, where he rejoined his friends Porter and Jermyn and where he came into association with the great political philosopher Hobbes, with whom he consulted closely about his next poetic project, *Gondibert* (1651), an ambitious heroic romance.

A small portion of this poem, printed with a prefatory treatise addressed to Hobbes and with Hobbes's response to this treatise, appeared in Paris in 1650; and in 1651 the first two cantos of the poem, still accompanied by the prefatory essays, appeared in England in quarto and octavo editions. The poem, which was never to be finished, adds little luster to Davenant's reputation, but the preface holds a place of some credit in the history of literary theory.

At the outset the preface to *Gondibert* reviews the work of poets from Homer to Edmund Spenser, whose reputations rest wholly or importantly on epic poems. The inclinations of these poets to repeat one another's errors, especially in the introduction of supernatural actions, give rise to the general question of literary imitation and prompt from Davenant the observation that while imitation moderates excess in poetry it also stifles originality. Consequently, he says, he rejects slavish imitation in his poem and disallows supernatural actions. He proceeds then to explain the exotic setting of his poem (eighth-century Italy) by declaring that comic actions allow familiar settings while serious ones do not. Moreover, he argues, the best schools of morality for an epic poem, and consequently for *Gondibert,* are courts and camps, where love and ambition motivate exemplary conduct. He then announces that these values, love and ambition, provide the thematic conflicts of his poem, whose form, he adds, properly resembles the sequential movement of a tragedy, where expositions and complications in the first three acts lead to turns and counterturns in the fourth and to resolutions in the fifth. He explains that in the interest of music and stateliness he has rejected heroic couplets and has chosen instead for his poem a quatrain stanza rhyming *abab;* and he aspires, he says, to a noteworthy display of wit, which he defines as "the laborious and the lucky resultances of thought," the interplay of luck, effort, and mental agility. In the concluding sections of the preface he acknowledges the inspiration of friends such as Hobbes, he confesses that he writes to acquire fame, and he claims the authority of antiquity in insisting (despite Plato) that poets deserve fame because poetry is necessary to culture.

In the poem itself, Aribert, King of Lombardy, decides to resign his throne and to award it and the hand of his daughter, Rhodalind, to the worthier of two noble contenders, Gondibert and Oswald. In a deciding combat Gondibert emerges the winner but is driven by Oswald's followers to refuge at the

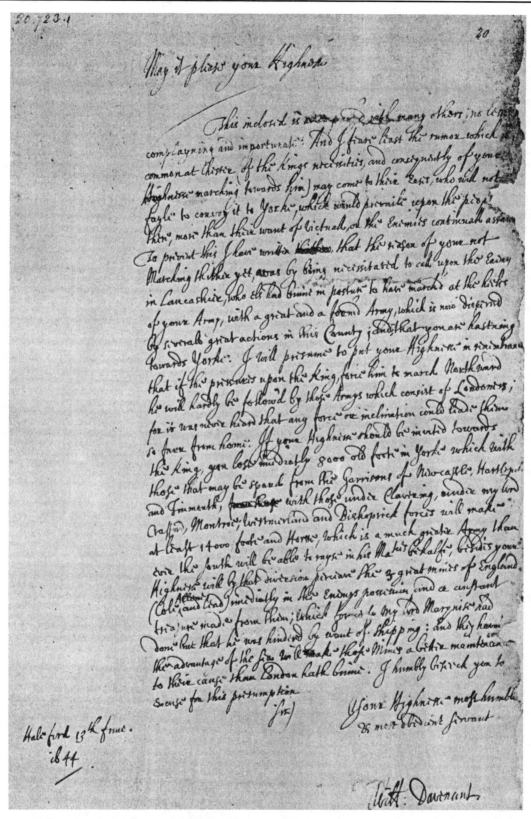

*Letter from Davenant (13 June 1644) to Prince Rupert in which Davenant offers advice on the conduct of the Civil War
(British Libary, MS. Addit. 20723, fol. 20)*

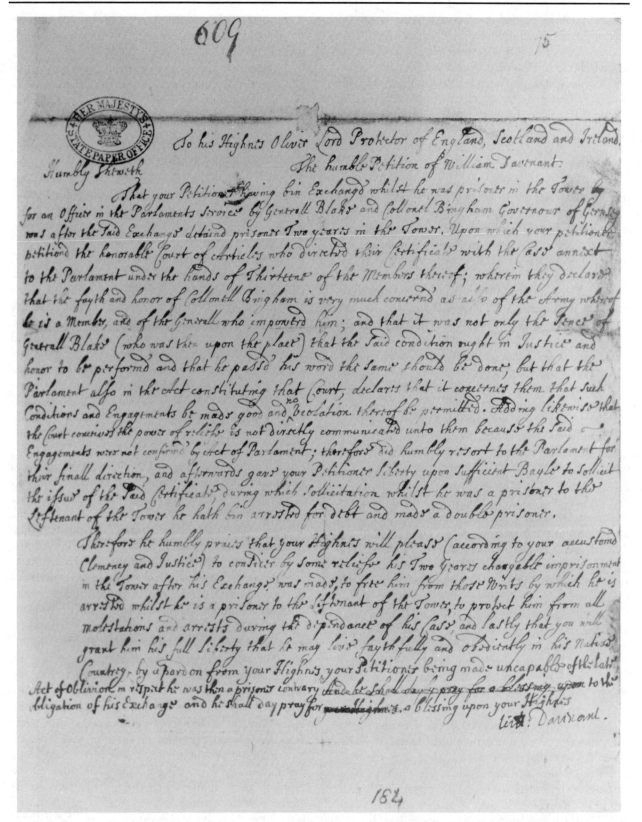

Letter to Oliver Cromwell (18 April 1654) in which Davenant, imprisoned for debt in the Tower of London, petitions for relief on the grounds that he has already spent two years (1650–1652) in the Tower because of his Royalist politics. He was released on 4 August (Public Record Office, SP. 18/69/75).

home of a sage named Astragon, whose daughter, Birtha, he comes to love. Despite his love for Birtha and his desire to live a retired life, Gondibert acknowledges, in a conflict between love and honor, his duty to Rhodalind and decides to marry her. He therefore proceeds, at the close of the fragment, to Verona, the place of this presumed marriage, and Birtha follows after him. Numerous lesser conflicts complicate this broad love-and-honor plot.

Some practices conventional to the classical epic emerge in the poem – a hunt, a funeral, a temple with murals, a duel between warriors – but the action more nearly resembles exemplary melodrama than heroic narrative. Certainly Gondibert, who longs to surrender authority and influence, makes few gestures at heroism, and his story, largely invented by Davenant, turns less on human dynamics than on abstract ideas. In some respects it allegorizes recent political events, the civil wars, the plight of the royal family, the cruelties of political ambition, and the consequences of misguided rule. More generally, however, it provides a platform for a vague rationalist doctrine. Rejecting supernatural interventions, it promotes the values of Astragon, a Baconian philosopher who supplants scholastic reasoning with inductive logic and empirical observation. While never really hostile to Christian orthodoxy, the poem acknowledges with sympathy the deistic principles of prayer, praise, and penitence.

After the sixth canto of the third book of *Gondibert*, Davenant explains in a postscript that he must cease his labors here at "an equal half of the POEM" because he is "threatened with Death." The government-in-exile of Charles II had commissioned Davenant governor of Maryland, to replace Cecilius Calvert, Lord Baltimore, but at the outset of his voyage to America in May of 1650, while crossing the English Channel, he was taken by privateers sympathetic to Parliament and imprisoned at Cowes Castle on the Isle of Wight. While there he composed the first half of the third book of his poem, but he begged leave then to desist, since "I am interrupted by so great an experiment as Dying." Eventually removed to the Tower of London, he continued a prisoner until October 1652, when he gained release on bail, possibly through the intercession of John Milton. He then married Anne Cademan, the widow of his physician, but he found little security in the modest estate of his new wife, and, during his brief marriage to her, he was more than once arrested for debt. After her death in March of 1655 he married Henrietta Maria du Tremblay, whom he had brought from France. By

then he had received full pardon for his Royalist activities and was able to resume his theatrical career, even in a cultural climate hostile to it.

To elude the statutes then in force against legitimate theater, he conceived in 1656 the notion of staging at his own residence *The First Days Entertainment at Rutland House, by Declamations and Musick: After the Manner of the Ancients* (performed, 1656; published, 1657). Later that year he introduced opera into England by staging *The Siege of Rhodes* (1656), a rhymed heroic play with dialogue chanted in recitative style. Another such play, *The Cruelty of the Spaniards in Peru,* appeared in 1658 and was performed daily in July at the Cockpit theater. Also presented at the Cockpit were *The History of Sr Francis Drake* (performed, 1658; published, 1659) and the second part of *The Siege of Rhodes* (published, 1663), the former of which raised some complaints from Parliament as a violation of the ban on plays. By maintaining a conciliatory posture with the Puritans, however, Davenant found means to provide theater in London during the late 1650s and to stand ready for the legitimation of theatrical activity after the Restoration.

He greeted the Restoration with three panegyrical poems, one of them addressed to Gen. George Monck, the other two to King Charles II. The one addressed to Monck, fifty lines in couplets, celebrates his dissolution of the Rump Parliament in February 1660 and applauds his defiance of the sectarians, who, according to Davenant, threaten the people with their bizarre doctrines and corrupt the language with their distortions of Scripture. When this poem was published in March of 1660 no one could divine Monck's intentions for the country, but Davenant obviously saw in the reinstatement of Parliament and in the reinforcement of Anglican unity developments favorable to Royalist prospects.

The first of the two panegyrics to the king, *Poem Upon His Sacred Majesties Most Happy Return to His Dominions* (August 1660), rhapsodizes on the character of the newly restored sovereign and presents it as a model of conduct for the entire kingdom. Issuing from the virtuous example of his parents, Charles's character demonstrates the clemency, judgment, magnanimity, valor, and strength by which the people might expiate the wrongs done against him in martyring his father. Under his exemplary new leadership, the nation will never again commit crimes in the name of religion and law. These kinds of effusions run to about three hundred lines in heroic couplets.

The second of the panegyrics to the king, *Poem to the King's Most Sacred Majesty* (1663), runs to 526 lines in couplets and focuses on the poet himself. Davenant complains that poets, who once shared with priests the responsibility of teaching moral reform, now share with them only poverty. His own case demonstrates that age robs poets of their influence and invention, and he grieves for the loss of his powers, but he finds in the young king a renewed inspiration, and he looks to him as a source of cultural regeneration. Already a generous patron of drama, the king must extend his favor to the entire realm of the mind; and poets, however enfeebled, will then embrace the privilege of celebrating his accomplishments. Davenant clearly represents himself in this poem as the neglected (and somewhat burned-out) laureate. The second Charles does not befriend him as warmly as the first had done.

In his theatrical career, however, Davenant fared quite well after 1660. By royal patent he had organized his own acting company, under the patronage of James, Duke of York, by November 1660; and, in the seven years remaining to him, he developed significant improvements in the techniques of theatrical production, including movable scenery and the proscenium stage. By strengthening production standards and refining the training of actors, he sustained the appeal of theatrical offerings and lengthened their runs, thus improving performances while reducing costs. Only two more plays came from his pen, a theatrical burlesque called *Playhouse to Be Let* (performed, 1663; published, 1673) and a Spanish intrigue comedy called *The Man's the Master* (performed, 1668; published 1669), but he had good success in the revival of his earlier work, and he adapted to the Restoration stage several of Shakespeare's plays (*Hamlet, Twelfth Night, Romeo and Juliet, Macbeth, Henry VIII, The Two Noble Kinsmen,* and *The Tempest*). In one daring venture, he undertook to combine *Measure for Measure* and *Much Ado About Nothing*. From Davenant's commitment to Shakespeare emerges one of his major legacies to literary history.

He died on 7 April 1668 and was buried grandly in Westminster Abbey under a tablet reading "O rare Sir Will. Davenant," an echo of the epitaph given Jonson, his predecessor in the laureateship. He was survived by his widow, Dame Mary, and their seven (or eight) sons, plus four stepsons who had been left to his charge at the death of his second wife, Anne Cademan.

In 1657 Davenant had entered in the Stationers' Register a collection of *Poems on Several Occasions,* but this publication did not reach print until 1673, when the poet's widow brought it out as part of a one-thousand-page issue of his collected works. Because the poems intended for the 1657 volume represent different parts of Davenant's life and cannot be dated with close accuracy, they say little about his development as a poet. Like the poems of the *Madagascar* volume, they acknowledge the lives, marriages, and deaths of eminent people; they pay tribute to noteworthy writers and literary achievements; and they adore the courage and beauty of the queen. They evince Donnean wit, Jonsonian order and scansion, and Cavalier insouciance. They distinguish themselves from the earlier collection, however, in their striking formal variety, their somewhat richer lyricism (in several instances), and their occasional political topicality.

If the earlier collection evokes senses of Davenant's life, *Poems on Several Occasions* reflects his times. One poem, for example, chides a "Northern prophet" for detracting bishops and courtiers and for predicting a "Successless" Parliament in 1630; another, "The Plots," possibly composed around 1655 (and unfinished), reviews British political history in the earlier seventeenth century; and the several poetic tributes to the queen depict her raising money and forces for the Royalist cause, serving as people's advocate before her somewhat intractable husband, and suffering generally reduced and harried circumstances.

The lyric character of the collection emerges in such pieces as "The Lark now leaves his watry Nest," which was set to music by John Wilson (1595–1674). It is one of ten pieces that are identified as "songs." (Another seventy-nine songs appear in Davenant's plays and masques, several of them also with extant musical settings.)

Formal varieties in *Poems on Several Occasions* occur in the stanzaic patterns that vary markedly from poem to poem and that prevail over the few instances of heroic couplets, which had dominated the *Madagascar* volume. Here, too, Davenant experiments a bit with dialect in a burlesque poem called "The long Vacation in London," and he finds himself drawn to dialogue forms in which philosophical or behavioral possibilities come under scrutiny. In one of them Olivia and Endymion Porter speculate on the afterlife and how they shall know one another there; in another a lover laments the lot of his dying mistress and debates with a philosopher the prospects of her spiritual destiny. Two others present the fate of the soul as seen first from the perspective of the philosopher ("The Philosophers Disquisition directed to the

Dying Christian"), then of the Christian ("The Christians Reply to the Phylosopher"). Thematically the most ambitious poems in the collection, these two seem to constitute a canceled canto from *Gondibert*. While nominally affirming Christian doctrine, they reflect Davenant's skeptical response to emergent conflicts between reason and faith.

Perhaps Davenant did not bring to his poetry a keenly sensitive ear or a highly resourceful invention, but he did bring to it a steady determination and a lively sense of his time. Situated at the center of culture and active in the processes of political change, he emerges in literary history as an authentically transitional figure. In pre-Restoration poetic output, he assimilated and reflected the subjects and idioms of his more gifted immediate forebears. While exiled with other Royalists in Paris, he set about adapting literary theory to the exigencies of his own day, and on the strength of this effort he rendered through a new rationalist aesthetic a new concept of heroic honor. Echoes of Jonson, Donne, and the Cavaliers clearly sound through his pre-Restoration verse, but the resonances of his poetry after 1660 (his three Restoration panegyrics) clearly associate him with the encomia of John Dryden, and in his identity as a transitional poet he yet asserts a legitimate claim to notice.

Bibliography:

Philip Bordinat and Sophia B. Blaydes, *Sir William Davenant: An Annotated Bibliography 1629–1985* (New York: Garland, 1986).

Biographies:

Alfred Harbage, *Sir William Davenant, Poet Venturer, 1606–1668* (Philadelphia: University of Pennsylvania Press / London: Oxford University Press, 1935);

Arthur H. Nethercot, *Sir William D'Avenant: Poet Laureate and Playwright-Manager* (Chicago: University of Chicago Press, 1938);

Mary Edmond, *Rare Sir William Davenant: Poet Laureate, Playwright, Civil War General, Restoration Theatre Manager* (New York: St. Martin's Press, 1987; Manchester: Manchester University Press, 1987).

References:

Philip Bordinat and Sophia B. Blaydes, *Sir William Davenant* (Boston: Twayne, 1981);

A. M. Gibbs, Introduction to *Sir William Davenant: The Shorter Poems, and Songs from the Plays and Masques* (Oxford: Clarendon Press, 1972);

David F. Gladish, Introduction to *Gondibert* (Oxford: Clarendon Press, 1971).

Sir John Denham

(1615 – 19 March 1669)

Elizabeth Skerpan
Southwest Texas State University

See also the Denham entry in *DLB 58: Jacobean and Caroline Dramatists.*

BOOKS: *The Sophy* (London: Printed by Richard Hearne for Thomas Walkley, 1642);

Coopers Hill. A Poeme (London: Printed for Thomas Walkley, 1642; revised edition, London: Printed for Humphrey Moseley, 1655);

The Anatomy of Play (London: Printed by G. P. for Nicholas Bourne, 1651);

On Mr. Abraham Cowley his Death, and Burial Amongst the Ancient Poets (London: Printed for H. Herringman, 1667);

The Second Advice to a Painter, possibly by Denham (London, 1667);

Poems and Translations. With the Sophy (London: Printed for H. Herringman, 1668) – includes "On the Earl of Strafford's Tryal and Death," "Natura Naturata," "The Passion of Dido for Aeneas," "The Progress of Learning," "Friendship and Single Life Against Love and Marriage";

Cato Major, Of Old Age. A Poem (London: Printed for Henry Herringman, 1669 [i.e., 1668]);

A Version of the Psalms of David, Fitted to the Tunes Used in Churches. By the Honourable Sir John Denham, Knight of the Bath (London: Printed for J. Bowyer, H. Clements, T. Varnum & J. Osborn, 1714).

Editions: *The Poetical Works of Sir John Denham,* edited by Theodore Howard Banks, Jr. (New Haven: Yale University Press/London: Oxford University Press, 1928; enlarged edition, Middletown, Conn.: Archon, 1969);

"The Second Advice to a Painter," attributed to Andrew Marvell, in volume 1 of *Poems on Affairs of State: Augustan Satirical Verse, 1660–1714,* edited by George deForest Lord (New Haven & London: Yale University Press, 1963), pp. 34–53;

Expans'd Hieroglyphicks: A Critical Edition of Sir John Denham's Coopers Hill, edited by Brendan O

Hehir (Berkeley & Los Angeles: University of California Press, 1969).

OTHER: "An Elegie Upon the Death of the Lord Hastings," in *Lachrymæ musarum: The Tears of the Muses,* edited by Richard Brome (London: Printed by Tho. Newcomb, 1649);

Certain Verses Written by severall of the Authors Friends; to be re-printed with the Second Edition of Gondibert, includes six satires by Denham (London, 1653);

Virgil, *The Destruction of Troy: an Essay upon the Second Book of Virgils Aeneis: Written in the year, 1636,* translated by Denham (London: Printed for Humphrey Moseley, 1656);

Poems. By the most deservedly Admired Mrs. Katherine Philips. The matchless Orinda. To which is added Monsieur Corneille's Pompey & Tragedies. Horace, With several other Translations out of French, second edition, scenes 6 and 7 of act 4, and act 5 of *Horace* translated by Denham (London: Printed by J. M. for H. Herringman, 1669).

The literary reputation of Sir John Denham – translator, playwright, poet, Royalist plotter, and Restoration public servant – today rests on his poem *Coopers Hill,* first published in 1642 and republished, extensively revised, in 1655. Admired both for its political sentiments and its versification, *Coopers Hill* directly inspired Edmund Waller's *Poem on St. James' Park* (1661), John Dyer's *Grongar Hill* (1794), and Alexander Pope's *Windsor Forest* (1713), as well as numerous other eighteenth-century descriptive poems. The quality of Denham's verse led Samuel Johnson to judge him "one of the fathers of English poetry," a writer who "improved our taste and advanced our language, and whom we ought therefore to read with gratitude." Although no modern critic shares Johnson's enthusiasm, recent research presents Denham as a model of the mid-seventeenth-century man of letters and links him with many important literary figures and practices of the day.

The only known likeness of Denham, depicting him at about age four, is the small figure at left on the monument, in Egham Parish Church, to Lady Cicely Denham (his father's first wife, right), Lady Eleanor Denham (the poet's mother, left) and the daughter with whom Lady Eleanor died in childbirth.

The progress of Denham's literary production is closely tied to the major event of his life – the English Revolution. His own family affiliated him with public life. He was born in Dublin in 1615, to the jurist Sir John Denham and his second wife, Eleanor, while his father was lord chief justice of the King's Bench in Ireland. The family moved to England in 1617. After his wife's death in 1619, the father never remarried. Thereafter, he and his son maintained an apparently uneasy relationship. The younger Denham matriculated at Trinity College, Oxford, on 18 November 1631, immediately showing signs of the compulsive gambling that followed him most of his life. He left Oxford in 1634 and on 25 June married Anne Cotton. In the same year he began studying law at Lincoln's Inn, where his companions included the future Royalist conspirator Allen Apsley and the fu-

ture regicide John Hutchinson, who married Apsley's sister Lucy. At this time Denham probably began his literary career. He may have written his short essay against gambling, *The Anatomy of Play* (1651), in 1636. Aubrey says he presented it "to his father to let him know his detestation of it." Further, there is evidence that Denham made his first effort at translation during the same year. His manuscript version of books 2 to 6 of Virgil's *Aeneid* appears in several places, including Lucy Hutchinson's commonplace book.

The last notices of Denham's early family life correspond to the period of growing tension between country and Crown. His father served as judge in John Hampden's Ship Money case in 1638, ruling with the minority in support of Hampden against the Crown, and died on 6 January 1639, shortly after delivering his opinion. Denham's wife gave birth to two sons in 1638. The first, John, died in infancy. The second, also named John, survived until after 1654. During the next five years Denham and his wife also had two daughters, Elizabeth and Anne, both of whom survived their parents. On 29 January 1639 Denham became a barrister, and his name began to be associated with moderate supporters of the king.

Denham made his first major appearance in the public record in 1641, when he served from 23 to 29 March as one of the few witnesses for the defense in the trial of Thomas Wentworth, first Earl of Strafford. This trial, which proved to be a rehearsal for the civil wars, provided parliamentary leaders an opportunity to attack the prerogative of the Crown and what they believed to be the exercise of arbitrary power by King Charles I. Denham himself appears to have been fairly ambivalent about the Royalist position. His first original poem, "On the Earl of Strafford's Tryal and Death" (1668), written some time during the summer of 1641, clearly sympathizes with Strafford and yet refuses to condemn wholly the opposition. Years later, as a committed Royalist, Denham revised the poem to eliminate any suggestion of error on Strafford's part, but in 1641 the poet was not yet a partisan of his future cause.

Denham's ambivalence about the conflict between king and Parliament may well have prompted his literary production, for it is during this period, from the summer of 1641 to the summer of 1642, that he began work on the two pieces for which he would be best known in his own lifetime: his play *The Sophy* and the first version of *Coopers Hill,* both published separately by Thomas Walkeley in August 1642. *The Sophy,* a tragedy about conflict resulting from evil counsel given to a king, sides neither with the sophy nor his opponents. A short poem written during the same period, "Elegy on the Death of Judge Crooke," takes a similar, moderate stance in its praise of Sir George Croke, who had joined Denham's father in ruling for the minority in Hampden's case.

Coopers Hill presents a more complex problem. Like most of Denham's work, the poem circulated in manuscript for many months before publication, undergoing numerous revisions as Denham brought its references up-to-date. The principal modern editor of *Coopers Hill,* Brendan O Hehir, dates draft 1 from perhaps March 1641; draft 2, which incorporates references to Waller's poem on Saint Paul's (in manuscript circulation at the time; published 1645), from 1641 to 1642; and draft 3,

the first published text, from 1642. Each stage represents a rethinking of the focus of the poem.

All drafts share eight sections. The poem opens with an invocation to Cooper's Hill itself, as the speaker defines the power of the poet to make Parnassus of the hill, that is, to transform what he sees into poetry. Further, the landscape is "More boundlesse in my fancie, then my eie," so the poem is not merely descriptive, but truly a creation of the poet. The second section moves the line of vision to Saint Paul's Cathedral and the city of London. Saint Paul's, preserved and restored by the king, stands as a representative of the kingly defense of religion, whether the cathedral is threatened by "Time, or Sword, or Fire, / Or Zeale." To emphasize the king's affiliation with Saint Paul's, Denham includes in drafts 2 and 3 an allusion to Waller's poem, "Upon His Majesties Repairing of Pauls." Despite royal protection, however, Denham's cathedral is surrounded by clouds and stormy weather. The city is also clouded. It is a place "where men like Ants / Toyle to prevent imaginarie wants." The activity of the citizens is mindless and destructive, both to themselves and the country.

The next two sections describe the hills surrounding the speaker, as the scene shifts from London, a model of discord, to Windsor, a model of harmony. Windsor Castle crowns the hill, and the speaker sees in it, "Thy Masters Embleme, in whose face I saw / A friend-like sweetnesse, and a King-like aw." The speaker then recounts the history of the castle, concentrating on Edward III, his founding of the Order of the Garter, and his choice of Saint George as patron saint of the order. The speaker sees the Garter as an emblem of England, and Edward the model for English kings. The fourth section reflects upon the meaning of an adjacent hill, Saint Anne's Hill, with its ruins of Chertsey Abbey. The ruins represent to the speaker the danger of unrestrained royal power, as embodied in Henry VIII. The speaker asks, "What crime could any Christian King incense / To such a rage?" The answer is both the church's slackness and Henry's greed: one extreme provoked the other.

The section on Saint Anne's Hill closes the first half of the poem. Denham connects this half to the next by following the movement of the Thames, his model of moderated power. It is royal, and yet it benefits the city of London. Its "faire bosome is the worlds Exchange," and its action is like that of a "wise King." The Thames flows past Windsor Forest, and a description of the forest comprises the sixth section of the poem. The forest shows the harmony intended by nature:

Wisely she knew the harmony of things,
Aswell as that of sounds, from discords springs;
Such was the discord, which did first disperse
Forme, order, beauty through the universe;
While drynesse moisture, coldnesse heat resists,
All that we have, and that we are subsists;
While the steepe horrid roughnesse of the wood
Strives with the gentle calmnesse of the flood.

In the middle of this calm scene, Denham places the stag hunt, one of the most famous sections of the poem. The action of this seventh section depicts *"our Charles"* pursuing a deer. The speaker focuses on the deer, giving it human qualities as he compares it to "a declining Statesman," abandoned by his former companions. Shot by Charles I, the deer dies like a hero.

Shifting his gaze to the neighboring Runnymede, the speaker then contrasts the pursuit of the stag by Charles I to the pursuit of the people's liberty by King John, who finally was forced by "armed subjects" to sign the Magna Charta. The speaker approves of the document, but reveals some hesitancy that the king was forced to sign. Under the Magna Charta the Crown renounced "Arbitrary power," thereby changing "Tyrant and Slave" into "King and Subject." Nevertheless, the speaker observes, the charter has failed. Kings gave away too much over the intervening centuries, and now subjects go too far in conspiring against royalty.

The poem closes with a return to the Thames, which appears this time as a warning. When the river is dammed too much it floods, devastating the surrounding land. The poem ends with an explicit working out of the analogy. When kings were too powerful, they needed to be restrained by the Magna Charta; now, subjects are aspiring to power and may provoke a violent response from the king. Each faction needs to balance the other. Royalty should keep "Within the Channell, and the shores of Law," and subjects should "obey."

The main critical question confronting modern readers of the poem is that of Denham's politics at the time of the poem's composition. He was a Royalist, but what kind of Royalist? The answer depends upon the dating of the poem. Earl R. Wasserman looks to the events of the summer of 1642 and finds evidence of Denham's sympathies in the stag hunt. Identifying the stag as Strafford, its voluntary death mirroring his, Wasserman sees an ambivalent Denham, anxious to defend the king's power without completely condemning Parliament. O Hehir supports Wasserman's reading, but gives the poem a much earlier date, during the trial of Strafford. He sees the poem as a warning to subjects: Denham supports their rights but believes they go too far and might compel the king to exercise his power against them to restore the essential balance of government. To this end, Strafford must be sacrificed, hence the voluntary death of the stag. John M. Wallace disagrees with the identification of the stag with Strafford and dates the poem from the conclusion of the Anglo-Scots treaty in the summer of 1641, arguing that the stag is not to be identified as a particular person; instead, it is a "symbol of arbitrary power," and in 1641 the arbitrary power is being exhibited by the Parliament, not the king, who is a peacemaker. Thus, Wallace sees Denham as a "new" Royalist: a member of a faction that formed around the king only after August 1641. Supporters of the parliamentary reforms of the early summer, the new Royalists felt that their leaders were now going too far, overstepping their natural boundaries. When the poem was finally published in 1642, it was, according to Wallace, "strictly royalist propaganda," but when it was written, it reflected Denham's hopes for a reconciliation of both sides.

By the summer of 1642 Denham had firmly sided with the king. His poem "To the Five Members of the Honourable House of Commons: The Humble Petition of the Poets," written before the outbreak of the war, is a satirical attack on Parliament, calling its declarations lies. Three subsequent poems of 1642 and 1643, "A Speech against Peace at the Close Committee," "A Western Wonder," and "A Second Western Wonder," lampoon Parliament's conduct of the war. The tone of the poems reflects Denham's own activity during the period. In the fall of 1642 he was pricked as sheriff for Surrey by the king and began to raise money for the Royalist cause at his home at Egham. His official position eventually brought him into contact with the poet George Wither, who was appointed parliamentary governor of the nearby Farnham Castle on 14 October. Upon the evacuation of the castle in mid November, Denham succeeded Wither as governor, only to surrender to Sir William Waller on 1 December and to be sent to London as prisoner. Denham's brief contact with Wither in 1642 was to have serious personal repercussions, as Wither vindictively pursued him through the courts between 1642 and 1656 in an effort to secure Denham's lands, already heavily indebted as a result of his continued gambling.

Released from prison sometime during the following spring, Denham served as a forwarding agent for Royalist correspondence and continued to participate in military activity. In January 1646 he was among those captured at Dartmouth by Sir Thomas Fairfax and was sent as a prisoner to London accompanied by the fanatical Puritan preacher Hugh Peters. Denham apparently established a friendship of sorts with Peters because, as Denham himself later wrote in the dedicatory epistle to his 1668 *Poems and Translations,* it was through the intervention of Peters in 1647 that Denham was able to visit the imprisoned King Charles I. Denham carried messages to the king from Queen Henrietta Maria, who may have contemplated using Denham as an intermediary in negotiations between Charles and the army that held him prisoner. Also, Denham took part in the conspiracy that enabled Charles to escape to the Isle of Wight on 11 November 1647. It is a mark of the confusion of the period that there are no records of either the births of Denham's daughters or the death of his wife, which occurred sometime between November 1645 and December 1647. Denham left Egham in 1642, never to return. He sold his house, "The Place," to John Thynne, member of Parliament, in January 1648 and left the country by the end of August.

From September 1648 to March 1653, Denham lived in exile on the Continent, mainly in The Hague. He served as special envoy to the future Charles II and as courier between him and Henrietta Maria. Further, from September 1650 to summer of the following year, Denham and William Crofts traveled to Poland to raise money for the Royalist cause from Scottish subjects living there, ultimately raising ten thousand pounds. Denham also composed several short poems during this period, including "An Elegie Upon the Death of the Lord Hastings," which appeared in *Lachrymæ musarum: The Tears of the Muses* (1649), in company with the first extant poem of the young John Dryden. Denham also wrote the philosophical reflection "Natura Naturata" (1668) and several humorous pieces on his experiences as an exile. Facing continued financial problems, Denham returned to England in March of 1653.

Upon his arrival Denham entered into the protection of Philip Herbert, fifth Earl of Pembroke, living at the earl's property at Wilton. Denham continued his work as a Royalist courier and agent but principally used his time to return to writing. At Wilton he wrote *The Destruction of Troy* (1656), his translation of book 2 of Virgil's *Aeneid,* and perhaps the translation "The Passion of Dido for Aeneas" and the Baconian "Progress of Learning," both of which appeared for the first time in *Poems and Translations* in 1668.

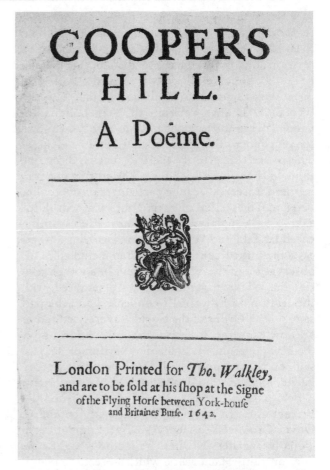

Title page for the work that inspired Samuel Johnson to call Denham "one of the fathers of English poetry" (courtesy of Henry E. Huntington Library and Art Gallery)

Denham's translations mark a significant departure from previous practice. As Paul J. Korshin shows, Denham's method makes an important contribution to literary theory by developing a system of nonliteral translation that, in Denham's own words, turns "Poesie into Poesie." Denham felt that the translator should make ancient texts comprehensible to contemporary readers: "If *Virgil* must needs speak English, it were fit he should speak not only as a man of this Nation, but as a man of this age." This preference for poetic merit over literal fidelity to the text produced translations that have not attracted much praise, but it profoundly influenced Dryden's work. As Dr. Johnson commented, "His versions of Virgil are not pleasing, but they taught Dryden to please better."

More important, at Wilton Denham also undertook his major revision of *Coopers Hill,* published by Humphrey Moseley in 1655. Because Denham included this text in *Poems and Translations,* it is this version of the poem on which his eighteenth-century reputation is founded. As O Hehir shows, this revision is in fact a total reworking of the 1642 text. Each of the eight sections of the poem is affected by revisions that reflect the changed political climate of England. The overall effect is to turn a polemical poem into a statement of universal truth.

In Denham's revision the stag hunt is expanded from thirty-eight lines to eighty-two, and the remainder of the poem is edited and condensed. The overall length of the 1655 text is about the same as that of the 1642 text. The editing generalizes and universalizes the particulars of the earlier version. The section on Saint Paul's Cathedral, for example, is replaced with six new lines uninfluenced by Edmund Waller's poem. Denham now recasts the cathedral as another hill to include it in his observation of the Thames valley. In another revision the Windsor Castle section is generalized, with the section on Edward III condensed and the passage on the Order of the Garter severely edited to acknowledge the society's discontinuation under the new government. In the new version of the passage on Saint Anne's Hill, Denham edits the language to echo the Instrument of Government, which, passed 16 December 1653, established the Protectorate. In so doing, he implicitly compares Oliver Cromwell to Henry VIII, calling both religious hypocrites. Further, he includes eight new lines on ruins of churches, which were more plentiful in the 1650s than in 1642.

The expanded stag hunt gives many more human characteristics to the stag, details that are not purely descriptive. Instead of being the hunter, Charles I is converted into the dying stag, and the hunt becomes an allegory of the events of the 1640s. The stag dies with guilt, remembering that he had abandoned a fellow stag to similar hunters. Charles himself died burdened with guilt over the death of Strafford. And just as the stag remembers scenes of his past life and pleasure, so Charles faced death on the scaffold in front of the Banqueting Hall at Whitehall, the scene of many court masques and entertainments.

Especially important for the subsequent reception of the poem, Denham added the famous Thames couplets:

> O could I flow like thee, and make thy stream
> My great example, as it is my theme!
> Though deep, yet clear, though gentle, yet not dull,
> Strong without rage, without ore-flowing full.

O Hehir comments that the Thames couplets are the key to the whole poem. The couplets picture the river as the image of harmony. Denham now balances this image by ending the poem with an image of the river in flood, a picture of uncontrolled power. The revised poem is, in O Hehir's words, "conceptual" rather than "visual," its end generalized to include Cromwell in an image of the world out of balance.

Following this brief period of literary activity, Denham participated in several of the major Royalist plots of the 1650s. The summer of 1655 found him under house arrest after the failure of Penruddock's Rising in March. Four years later he was communicating with his old associate Allen Apsley and taking limited part in Booth's Rising, which failed in August 1659. Between the two plots Denham traveled abroad twice and began an association with George Villiers, second Duke of Buckingham. In keeping with his complaisant nature, Denham communicated with both moderate Royalists and the fanatical supporters known as the Louvre faction, which was affiliated with Henrietta Maria. His dealings with the Louvrists were enough to earn him the suspicions of Edward Hyde, the future Earl of Clarendon. The coolness between the two persisted into the Restoration.

In March 1660 appeared *A Panegyric on His Excellency the Lord General George Monck*. It is a sign of Denham's subsequent reputation as a political poet that this poem was frequently attributed to him in the Restoration and afterwards. Theodore H. Banks, Jr., believes the evidence is sufficient to include the poem in the Denham canon, but more recently O Hehir has challenged the attribution. Certainly, the poem exhibits features that seem to have been associated with Denham. Written in closed couplets, it develops the traditional analogy between England and Troy, and Denham was known to have recently published *The Destruction of Troy*. Finally, the poet praises Monck for his moderation and emphasizes the need for mutuality in the settlement of the government in tones reminiscent of the 1642 text of *Coopers Hill*. The attribution is, if nothing else, a compliment to Denham's popularity as a Royalist poet. The poem "sounds like him," affirms Banks, and thus it gains attention by association with the author of *The Sophy* and *Coopers Hill*.

At the Restoration, in recognition of his service and in response to the petitioning of his cousin George Morley, Denham was made surveyor general of the king's works. While his tenure in the position was not as dazzling as that of his predecessor, Inigo Jones, or his successor, Christopher Wren, Denham nevertheless accomplished several important projects. He built Greenwich Palace, Burlington House, and Sir John Denham's Buildings in

Scotland Yard, which were his own property and served as his offices. Further, he embarked on many paving projects, supervised repairs to Windsor Castle, and granted licenses for building houses in London.

In recognition of his service to the Royalist cause, Denham was one of sixty-eight men made knights of the Honourable Order of the Bath at the coronation of Charles II on 23 April 1661. On 29 April he was elected to Parliament as burgess for Old Sarum, possibly through the influence of the earl of Pembroke. Denham remained an active member for the rest of his life, eventually serving on over nine committees. In May 1663 he was further honored with election as a founding fellow of the Royal Society.

Denham's successes, however, came relatively late in his life. His full public career truly began only after he turned forty-five. As with many of his generation, his life had been severely interrupted by the civil wars and revolution, and his first family essentially collapsed when Denham left home in 1642 to serve the king. These facts undoubtedly contributed to his notorious personal crisis, precipitated on 25 May 1665 by his marriage, at age fifty, to Margaret Brooke, age twenty-three. Prematurely aging and lame, Denham undoubtedly suffered from having a young and attractive wife at the court of Charles II. Lady Denham soon attracted the duke of York (later James II) and eventually became his mistress. Contemporaries said that this public affair caused Denham's attack of madness in April 1666.

Certainly, Denham did go mad. He had some kind of seizure on a visit to Somerset and subsequently developed a religious mania, believing, as he told the king, that he was the Holy Ghost. Denham was confined at the private asylum of a Dr. Lentall and apparently cured over the summer, since he was restored to his faculties at the time of the Great Fire on September 2. Since he never suffered a subsequent attack, Denham's madness was probably not caused by paresis, as some biographers have claimed, but rather what O Hehir calls a "psychological functional breakdown" as a result of his aging. O Hehir cites evidence that the affair between Lady Denham and the duke of York began during her husband's madness, and Denham himself tolerated it after his recovery. Whatever the cause of his madness, Denham's uncomfortable situation ended on 6 January 1667, when his wife died. John Aubrey and others gossiped that she was poisoned, perhaps by a jealous duchess of York (later

Queen Anne), but the cause of Lady Denham's death was probably appendicitis.

The year 1667 brought the publication of a significant political poem, *The Second Advice to a Painter,* an attack on the duke of York and the conduct of the Dutch Wars. This poem may be Denham's, and, if so, it represents the first of his renewed literary efforts, resumed after the death of his wife and the final settlement of his many debts. The poem is a thorough parody of Edmund Waller's *Instructions to a Painter* (1666), which fulsomely praises the duke of York. *Second Advice to a Painter* mocks everything about the earlier poem, from its subject and tone to its style. It calls into question the motives and characters of the chief English participants in the war. The duke of York is singled out for extensive criticism, along with his new wife, the daughter of Denham's nemesis Edward Hyde, first Earl of Clarendon, "whose transcendent paunch so swells of late / That he the rupture seems of law and state."

Denham's modern editors disagree whether the poem belongs in the Denham canon. Banks rejects it, judging principally from stylistic evidence. O Hehir, however, points to internal evidence to establish grounds for Denham's possible authorship. First, while the poem was written in 1666, the events it describes took place in the summer of 1665, except for the mention of Lady Denham's 1666 affair. Further, Waller's *Instructions to a Painter* was published in early March 1666. The time lag is covered by Denham's madness. Other evidence includes attacks in the poem on two minor figures, Henry Brunker and Sir William Coventry, both known to have been active in promoting the affair between Lady Denham and the duke of York. The author's hostility to the earl of Clarendon is also evident. O Hehir concludes that Denham's authorship is not unlikely, but denies Denham's involvement in the subsequent painter poems.

Whatever the authorship of *Second Advice,* Denham definitely did resume writing poetry in the summer of 1667, beginning with his elegy on an old colleague, *On Mr. Abraham Cowley his Death, and Burial Amongst the Ancient Poets* (1667). Denham characterizes Cowley's contribution to poetry by placing him in the line of great English poets. The poem begins with a catalogue of figures, from "Old *Chaucer,* like the morning Star," and "(like *Aurora*) *Spencer,*" to William Shakespeare, Ben Jonson, and John Fletcher. Denham praises Shakespeare and Fletcher for "Old Mother Wit" and "Nature," Edmund Spenser and Jonson for "Art," and commends Cowley for all three. He also notes Cowley's originality in lines later echoed by Jonathan Swift: "To him no

> ON
> ## Mr. ABRAHAM COWLEY
> *His Death, and Burial amongst the*
> *Ancient Poets.*
>
> By the Honourable Sir *John Denham.*
>
> **O**Ld *Chaucer,* like the morning Star,
> To us discovers day from far,
> His light those Mists and Clouds dissolv'd,
> Which our dark Nation long involv'd;
> But he descending to the shades,
> Darkness again the Age invades.
> Next (like *Aurora*) *Spencer* rose,
> Whose purple blush the day foreshews;
> The other three, with his own fires,
> *Phœbus,* the Poets God, inspires;
> By *Shakespear, Johnson, Fletcher's* lines,
> Our Stages lustre *Rome's* outshines:
> These Poets neer our Princes sleep,
> And in one Grave their Mansion keep;
> They liv'd to see so many days,
> Till time had blasted all their Bays:
> But cursed be the fatal hour
> That pluckt the fairest, sweetest flower
>
> *A*   That

Page from the elegy (1667) in which Denham placed Abraham Cowley in a line of poets extending from Geoffrey Chaucer to John Fletcher

Author was unknown, / Yet what he wrote was all his own." Denham anticipates the Augustans in admiring the partnership of Cowley's fancy and judgment and the purity and clarity of his "English stream" of verse.

The year 1668 saw the publication of *Poems and Translations. With The Sophy,* comprising most of the poems that Denham acknowledged as his. The collection opens with the 1655 version of *Coopers Hill* (which, as a result, became the accepted version of the poem), *The Destruction of Troy,* many short political poems, translations, and verse epistles. Also included were new translations of two Latin works by the fifteenth-century Italian poet Dominico Mancini, titled by Denham "Of Prudence" and "Of Justice." The collection does not include several

other poems known to be Denham's. The elegy on Judge Crooke existed only in manuscript until 1790. The elegy on Hastings and the satirical poems in *Certain Verses* (1653) also failed to appear. It is unknown why Denham excluded these poems.

Poems and Translations did not signal the end of Denham's literary career. His last efforts continued his interest in translation. He published *Cato Major, Of Old Age. A Poem,* an adaptation of Cicero's dialogue on old age, in November 1668. In the same year, he began his translation of the Psalms, *A Version of the Psalms of David, Fitted to the Tunes Used in Churches* (1714), although the text remained unpublished during his lifetime. The work includes a preface by Denham in which he discusses his principles of translation and versification. After acknowledging his "masters," Virgil and David, Denham praises the poetry of Horace and Cowley. Then he explains why it is easier for him to write as a mature man than as a youth: "It was much less difficult to suppress the Ebullitions of my Fancy, than I fear'd it wou'd have been; . . . a little Force serv'd my turn, to confine my self to such a proper Plainness as might not be contemn'd by the Learned, yet understood by the Vulgar." Denham's own critical standards anticipate those of the Augustans, for whom his verse was a model of good taste.

One of Denham's final efforts firmly links him to contemporary literary circles: he completed Katherine Philips's unfinished translation of Pierre Corneille's *Horace* (1640). This continuation appeared in the second edition of *Poems. By the most deservedly Admired Mrs. Katherine Philips. The matchless Orinda,* published by Henry Herringman in 1669. Since the first edition of Philip's *Poems,* printed in 1664 and reprinted by Herringman in 1667, includes only her incomplete version, Denham must have begun his work sometime later. Hence, the work was not collaborative. Nevertheless, Denham's work does connect him with Philips's circle, and he and Philips had a mutual acquaintance in Cowley, who contributed two dedicatory poems to the first edition of *Poems.* Thus, Denham continued to write up until the end of his life. After several weeks of failing health, he died at his office in Whitehall, probably on 19 March 1669. On 23 March he was buried in Poets' Corner, Westminster Abbey.

Denham's literary reputation was considerable, from his own lifetime until well into the nineteenth century. His activities link him to many of the important writers of his day, including not only Philips and Cowley, but Sir William Davenant, Dryden, Waller, Aubrey, and the diarists John Evelyn and Samuel Pepys. *Coopers Hill* was praised by Robert Herrick and Henry Vaughan and imitated by dozens of lesser poets. Denham's principal publishers – Humphrey Moseley, Henry Herringman, and, in the eighteenth century, Jacob Tonson – were three of the most prominent London printers and booksellers and printed all the major writers of the Restoration, including Dryden and John Milton. Herringman's shop appears many times in Pepys's *Diary* as one of the most important literary gathering places in London.

Denham's work continued to gain a critical reputation after his death. *Poems and Translations* proved to be a popular book, reprinted in 1671, 1684, 1703, 1709, 1719, 1769, and 1771. His poems appeared in twelve more collected editions

by 1857. His translation of the Psalms was edited by Heighes Woodford and dedicated to James Stanley, tenth Earl of Derby, whose wife was Denham's granddaughter, Mary Morley Stanley. Political poems continued to be attributed to Denham, most notably *The True Presbyterian Without Disguise: or, a Character of a Presbyterians Ways and Actions,* which appeared for the first time in 1680. The satire was reprinted in several of the editions of Edward Ward's anti-Whig tract, *The Secret History of the Calves-Head Club, Complt., Or, the Republican Unmask'd,* published in the early eighteenth century. Denham's political sympathies therefore carried considerable weight with some, even though readers were beginning to disengage the politics from his poems.

To eighteenth- and nineteenth-century critics, Denham deserved attention for his "improvement" of English verse, and *Coopers Hill* deserved admiration as a descriptive poem. Alexander Pope commended "Denham's strength" and, in *Windsor Forest* (1713), included his own description of Cooper's Hill and called Denham "Majestick." Dr. Johnson disliked the "digressions" and "morality" of *Coopers Hill* but endorsed it as the first example of English "*local poetry,*" calling Denham "an original author." Later eighteenth-century critics generally followed the anonymous Edinburgh editor who wrote in 1779 that Denham "may therefore be considered as one of those to whom we are originally indebted for that state of refinement, to which our poetry has since arrived." Nineteenth-century critics repeated the praise of Denham's versification but echoed Dr. Johnson's distaste for the political sentiments of *Coopers Hill,* finding, in the words of John Coleman, that "the desire to moralise is too frequently indulged in, and many of the digressions diverge too widely from the subject." The one notable dissenting voice is that of eighteenth-century critic John Scott. He not only disliked the political "digressions" of *Coopers Hill* but also dared to criticize the famous Thames couplets.

Thus critical practice in this period gradually eliminated Denham's overtly political poems from discussion and preserved *Coopers Hill* for its beauty rather than its sentiments. Critics preferred to discuss Denham's gambling rather than his public life. By the beginning of the twentieth century, both the poems and the man essentially lost their political dimension, and Denham faded along with the taste for local poetry.

Modern scholarship has tended to reflect this diminution. Of his minor poems, only five have prompted more than passing critical comment: *The*

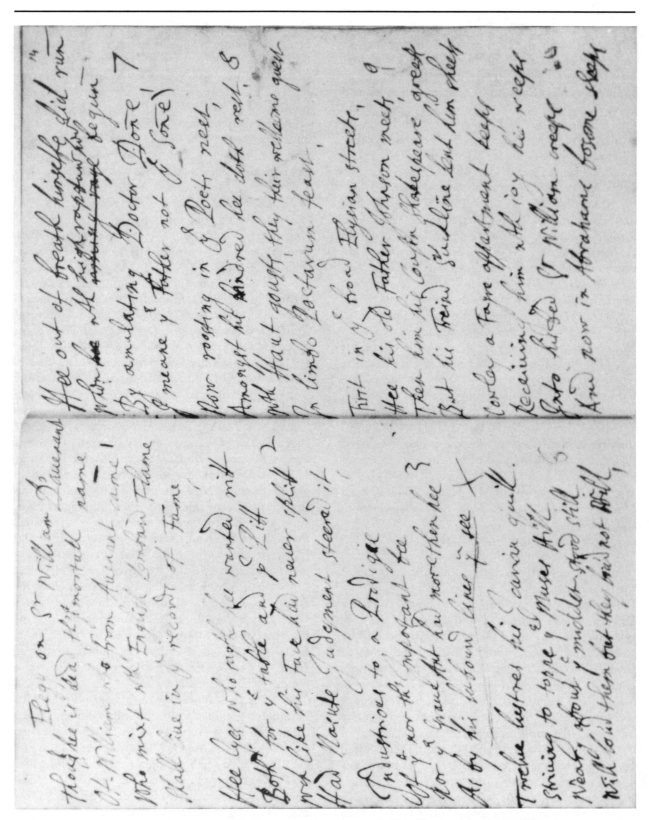

The last of nine poems Denham wrote in his own copy of Poems and Translations *(1668). These poems mocking Sir William Davenant are the only verses known to exist in Denham's hand (Yale University Library, Marie-Louise and James M. Osborn Collection).*

Destruction of Troy, "The Progress of Learning," "Natura Naturata," *On Mr. Abraham Cowley,* and "Friendship and Single Life Against Love and Marriage" (1668). Most scholarly attention has predictably been drawn to *Coopers Hill,* and interest has been divided between the political and descriptive qualities of the poem.

The recognition of *Coopers Hill* as a political poem revived in the late 1950s on publication of Rufus Putney's "The View from Cooper's Hill" (*University of Colorado Studies in Language and Literature,* 1957) and Wasserman's *The Subtler Language* (1959). Both give extensive analyses of the poem based on the political conditions of 1642. Wasserman identifies the organizing principle of *Coopers Hill* as *concordia discors* — "harmony-through-opposition." According to Denham, this principle is a universal law, so nature and therefore politics should reflect it. Thus, the king and Parliament both have vital roles to play in the governing of England. Each force balances the other and requires the other. The modern editor of the poem, O Hehir, locates Denham's method within the tradition of the emblem or hieroglyphic — the symbolic picture explained. Denham therefore "reads" the landscape for signs of God's universal truths contained in His creation.

Subsequent scholarship has generally agreed with and added to O Hehir and Wallace's interpretations of the politics of the poem. Robert Cummings supports Wallace's dating, arguing that Denham probably knew the medieval poem *Carolus Rex et Leo Papa* and drew from it his depiction of Charles I as a potential savior of the church from hostile mobs. James Turner, however, challenges both Wallace's dating and his characterization of Denham as a moderate Royalist. Turner maintains that "the doctrine of balanced opposites became part of the vocabulary of coarse royalism," and further sees Denham's process of revision as the charting of growing conservatism: the poet gradually eliminates suggestions of tension in the landscape in favor of symbols of sympathy and partnership. Thus, "balance" is a code word for the old order.

Recently several critics have returned to analyses of Denham's versification and literary artistry. W. Hutchings makes a strong case that description is in fact the organizing element in the poem, and that the description does not reflect *concordia discors* but a "synthesis" of arguments that Denham perceived as "universal truths" and beyond debate. David Hill Radcliffe argues that the poem influenced the rise of the georgic in the eighteenth century, noting in particular the affinities of *Coopers Hill* with the epigram and the formal meditation. Rad-

cliffe places the poem at the transition from meditation to georgic. Finally Robin Grove offers an analysis of the politics of Denham's style, seeing in his innovation of the closed couplet a verse form that is confined, restrained, and therefore conservative, providing "antithesis between high and low." Such a form attracted eighteenth-century writers and readers who valued education, sophistication, and separation from popular tastes.

Sir John Denham's poetry has not regained the popularity it commanded in the eighteenth century. Nevertheless, it justifiably retains interest for modern readers. Denham's literary activities ally him with many of the leading literary figures of his day, and his practice of circulating manuscripts, together with his continual revising, illuminates the practices of the coterie poet. His undeniable impact on the development of eighteenth-century taste and on the practice of translation makes his work significant to our understanding of Dryden, Pope, and other later poets. Further, Denham's work is important to the literary historian. Eric Rothstein emphasizes the creative properties of the unresolved tension of *concordia discors* in *Coopers Hill,* arguing that this aspect of Denham's poem in particular influenced subsequent descriptive poems. Turner sees the poem as a pivotal point in English poetry, as Denham transforms the *locus amoenus* poem into a landscape painting, fusing aesthetic, moral, and political values. Perhaps Denham's greatest value lies in illustrating the process of canon formation. Denham's poetry, even *Coopers Hill,* vanished from the libraries of educated readers before there was an established canon of English literature. Once admired for his verse and his sentiments, Denham lost his literary value when the political values that informed his poetry lost currency with readers who had once composed his natural audience.

Biography:

Brendan O Hehir, *Harmony from Discords: A Life of Sir John Denham* (Berkeley & Los Angeles: University of California Press, 1968).

References:

Theodore Howard Banks, Jr., Introduction to *The Poetical Works of Sir John Denham* (Middletown, Conn.: Archon Books, 1969), pp. 1–57;

Herbert Berry, "Sir John Denham at Law," *Modern Philology,* 71 (February 1974): 266–276;

John Coleman, *Historical Essays* (London: Thomas Hatchard, 1851), pp. 210–222;

Robert Cummings, "Denham's *Cooper's Hill* and *Carolus Rex et Leo Papa*," *Philological Quarterly,* 64 (Summer 1985): 337–346;

Robin Grove, "Nature Methodiz'd," *Critical Review,* 26 (1984): 52–68;

W. Hutchings, " 'The Harmony of Things': Denham's Coopers Hill as Descriptive Poem," *Papers on Language and Literature,* 19 (Fall 1983): 375–384;

Samuel Johnson, "Denham," in volume 1 of *Lives of the English Poets,* edited by Arthur Waugh (London: Oxford University Press, 1906), pp. 55–63;

Hilton Kelliher, "John Denham: New Letters and Documents," *British Library Journal,* 12 (Spring 1986): 1–20;

Paul J. Korshin, "The Evolution of Neoclassical Poetics: Cleveland, Denham, and Waller as Poetic Theorists," *Eighteenth-Century Studies,* 2 (December 1968): 102–137;

"The Life of Sir John Denham," in *The Poetical Works of Sir John Denham* (Edinburgh: Apollo, 1779), pp. viii–xvi;

Brendan O Hehir, "Introduction to *Coopers Hill,*" in *Expans'd Hieroglyphicks: A Critical Edition of Sir John Denham's Coopers Hill,* edited by O Hehir (Berkeley & Los Angeles: University of California Press, 1969), pp. 1–73;

Rufus Putney, "The View from Cooper's Hill," *University of Colorado Studies in Language and Literature,* no. 6 (1957): 13–22;

David Hill Radcliffe, "These Delights from Several Causes Move: Heterogeneity and Genre in 'Coopers Hill,' " *Papers on Language and Literature,* 22 (Fall 1986): 352–371;

Eric Rothstein, *Restoration and Eighteenth-Century Poetry 1660–1780,* edited by R. A. Foakes, Routledge History of English Poetry, 3 (Boston, London & Henley: Routledge & Kegan Paul, 1981);

John Scott, "On Denham's Cooper's-Hill," in *Critical Essays on Some of the Poems of Several English Poets* (London: Printed & sold by James Phillips, 1785), pp. 1–36;

James Turner, *The Politics of Landscape: Rural Scenery and Society in English Poetry 1630–1660* (Cambridge, Mass.: Harvard University Press, 1979);

John M. Wallace, "*Coopers Hill:* The Manifesto of Parliamentary Royalism, 1641," *ELH,* 41 (Winter 1974): 494–540;

Earl R. Wasserman, *The Subtler Language: Critical Readings of Neoclassic and Romantic Poems* (Baltimore: Johns Hopkins Press, 1959), pp. 35–88;

D. Wieser, "Bacon's Influence on Sir John Denham," *Notes and Queries,* new series 31 (September 1984): 335–337.

Sir Richard Fanshawe

(June 1608 - 26 June 1666)

Robert Thomas Fallon
La Salle University

BOOKS: *Il Pastor Fido, The faithful Shepherd. A Pastorall Written in Italian by Baptista Guarini, A Knight of Italie. And now Newly Translated out of the Originall* (London: Printed by R. Raworth, 1647; facsimile, edited by Nicoletta Neri, Turin: Giappichelli, 1963);

Il Pastor Fido. The Faithfull Shepheard; with An Addition of Divers Other Poems. Concluding with a Short Discourse of the Long Civill Warres of Rome, to His Highnesse The Prince of Wales (London: Printed for Humphrey Moseley, 1648);

Selected Parts of Horace, Prince of Lyricks, and of all the Latin Poets the Fullest Fraught with Excellent Morality. Concluding with a Piece out of Ausonius, and Another out of Virgil. Now Newly Put into English (London: Printed for M. M. Gabriel Bedell and T. Collins, 1652);

The Lusiad, or, Portugals Historicall Poem: Written in the Portingall Language by Luis de Camoens; and Now newly put into English by Richard Fanshaw, Esq. (London: Printed for Humphrey Moseley, 1655);

La Fida Pastora. Comœdia Pastoralis, Latin verse translation by Fanshawe of *The Faithful Shepherdess* by John Fletcher, including poems by Fanshawe (London: Printed by R. Daniels for G. Bedell & T. Collins, 1658);

Querer Por Solo Querer: To Love only for Love Sake: A Dramatick Romance. Represented at Aranjuez Before the King and Queen of Spain, to Celebrate The Birthday of that King By the Meninas: Which are a Sett of Ladies, in the Nature of Ladies of Honour in that Court, Children in Years, but Higher in Degree (being many of them Daughters and Heyres to Grandees of Spain) than the Ordinary Ladies of Honour, Attending Likewise that Queen. Written in Spanish by Don Antonio de Mendoza, 1623. Paraphrased in English, Anno 1654. Together with the Festivals of Aranwhez (London: Printed by William Godbid, 1670).

Editions: *The Fourth Book of Virgil's Aeneid, On the Loves of Dido and Aeneas, Done into English by the Right Honourable Sir Richard Fanshawe, Knight,* edited by A. L. Irvine (Oxford: Blackwell, 1924);

Luis de Camões, The Lusiads, in Sir Richard Fanshawe's Translation, edited by Geoffrey Bullough (London: Centaur, 1963; Carbondale: Southern Illinois University Press, 1964);

Sir Richard Fanshawe, Shorter Poems and Translations, edited by N. W. Bawcutt (Liverpool: Liverpool University Press, 1964);

A Critical Edition of Sir Richard Fanshawe's 1647 Translation of Giovanni Battista Guarini's Il Pastor Fido, edited by Walter F. Stanton, Jr., and William E. Simeone (Oxford: Clarendon Press, 1964);

Battista Guarini, Il Pastor Fido, The Faithful Shepherd, Translated (1647) by Richard Fanshawe, edited by John Humphreys Whitfield (Austin: University of Texas Press, 1976).

Sir Richard Fanshawe was an extraordinarily accomplished linguist, known chiefly for his translations from Italian, Portuguese, and Spanish and to and from Latin. His models were Horace, Virgil, and Edmund Spenser, the last particularly influential in his translation (1655) of Luiz de Camões's *Os Lusíadas* (1572). An ardent Royalist, Fanshawe alternated periods of intense service to a beleaguered monarchy with years of imprisonment, dislocation, and forced idleness, during which he produced the translations for which he is best known. His small collection of English poems places him in the Caroline courtly tradition; largely political in content, the poems were intended for the ear of Charles I and the young Prince of Wales (later Charles II), whom he served during the Civil War as mentor and minister. Fanshawe's loyalty was rewarded after the Restoration when he was appointed ambassador to Portugal and Spain and admitted to the king's Privy Council, duties which thoroughly engaged his energies, precluding any further literary pursuits.

Fanshawe was born in June 1608, the fifth son of Sir Henry Fanshawe of Ware Park,

Engraving from Original Letters of his Excellency Sir Richard Fanshaw *(1701; courtesy of Special Collections, Van Pelt Library, University of Pennsylvania)*

Hertfordshire, and Elizabeth, daughter of Thomas Smythe. His father died in 1616, and his mother undertook his upbringing and education. He attended the school of Thomas Farnaby in Cripplegate and in November 1623 was admitted to Jesus College, Cambridge, as a fellow-commoner. The prospects for younger sons being limited, he was intended for the law and entered the Inner Temple on 22 January 1626. Fanshawe had a scholarly bent, however, and left there the following year to travel abroad for language studies. He spent a year in Paris and then traveled to Madrid, where his skills came to the attention of Lord Walter Aston, the English ambassador, who engaged him as his secretary. Thus began his service to the Crown which was to end more than thirty years later with his death in that same city. When Aston returned to London in 1638,

Fanshawe was left to attend to English interests pending the arrival of the new ambassador.

The Fanshawe family had for generations held the post of king's remembrancer, and, upon Richard's return from Spain, his elder brother, Thomas, arranged for him to assume the position, on condition that he pay eight thousand pounds for it over a period of seven years. He had little opportunity to benefit from the office, which involved responsibility for Exchequer records, for the civil wars intervened and the king's court removed to Oxford. Fanshawe, a zealous Royalist, followed, beginning a career as courtier and diplomat in the cause of the monarchy.

In Oxford he met and, on 18 May 1644, married Anne Harrison, when she was nineteen and he was thirty-six. Anne's memoirs, written after her husband's death and first prepared by Sir Harris Nicolas and published in 1829, provide most of the known details of his life, giving a vivid picture of the trials of a devoted Royalist who endured exile, arrest, and imprisonment in the service of the king during the Interregnum. Anne was a spirited woman who refused to be separated from her husband during these years, accompanying him wherever he was sent, often in hazardous circumstances. On one occasion the couple lost all their baggage to thieves, and on another they survived a near shipwreck. It would seem, further, that she was almost continually pregnant. She bore six sons and eight daughters in twenty years, only five of whom survived childhood. The couple left children's graves in Madrid, Paris, London, and scattered English locations as grim landmarks of their wanderings. These deaths were the result of the often destitute conditions under which the Fanshawes were forced to live. Indeed, they christened three Elizabeths and three Richards before any so named survived. The description of her husband given in Anne's memoirs attests to the couple's devotion to one another:

> His conversation was so honest, that I never heard him speake a word in my life that tended to God's dishonour or incouragement of any kind of debauchery or sin. . . . He was the tendrest father imaginable, the carefullest and most generous master I ever knew . . . and though he would say I managed his domesticks wholy, yet I ever governed them and myself by his commands, in the managing of which I thank God I found his approbation and content.

At about the same time as the marriage, Charles I appointed Fanshawe secretary of war to the Prince of Wales. Fanshawe accompanied Prince Charles as he evaded parliamentary armies, retreating through Penzance, Land's End, and the Scilly Islands, finally joining his mother, Queen Henrietta Maria, on the Continent. Fanshawe returned to London, living there until 1648, when he was appointed treasurer of the navy under Prince Rupert.

It was during these years that he brought out his first publications, a 1647 translation of Battista Guarini's *Il Pastor Fido* (1590), with another edition the following year, to which he added some twenty-five of his poems. *Il Pastor Fido* is a long verse tragicomedy composed in the tradition of courtly love and obviously not intended for the stage. Fanshawe's first edition comprises the play, two poems addressed to the Prince of Wales, and an introductory letter explaining why the translation is dedicated to Prince Charles. The play, Fanshawe remarks, is set in times as troubled as his own, in which "a *gasping State*" is ravaged by "*A wild Boar (the sword),*" with "*Pestilence* unpeopling the *Towns*" and priests lamenting "their *owne* and the *common* Calamitie." The action concludes with peace renewed and the kingdom restored, a "miraculous change occasioned by the presaged Nuptials of two of Divine (that is, Royall) extraction." Fanshawe advises his master to choose his bride wisely so that the union will help restore peace to his land. "*So much,*" he concludes, "*depends upon the Marriages of Princes,*" for a "happy Royall Marriage" may serve to unite "a miserably divided people in a publick joy." Fanshawe offers the translation so that Prince Charles may reflect on it and make "a perfect *parallell*" between England and Arcadia, "with your self a great Instrument" for reconciliation.

Fanshawe's translation was greatly admired at the time. In dedicatory verses introducing the first edition, Sir John Denham praises the work highly:

> *That servile path thou nobly dost decline*
> *Of tracing word by word, and line by line.*
> *Those are the labour'd births of slavish brains,*
> *Not the effects of Poetry, but pains.*

The translation is to be admired, Denham continues, for

> *Wisely restoring whatsoever grace*
> *It lost by change of Times, or Tongues, or Place.*
> *Nor fetter'd to his Numbers, and his Times,*
> *Betray'st his Musick to unhappy Rimes.*

Denham's sentiments are somewhat puzzling, as Fanshawe is quite faithful to the original. The University of Texas Press edition of 1976, edited by John Humphreys Whitfield, with the Italian and the English on facing pages, shows the close parallel between the two, though Fanshawe's heroic couplets necessarily employ more words.

The two poems to the Prince of Wales, which appear at the end of the volume, are of interest in their reflection of Fanshawe's changing attitude toward the monarchy. The first poem, composed in 1645 and addressed to Prince Charles "At his going to the West," presents King Charles I as a model for his son and urges him to "make good / With all his worth the title of your blood." In the second, "Presented to His highnesse, In the West" the following year, Fanshawe seems to have abandoned hope for the king and placed all his expectations upon the heir. The prince will arise Phoenix-like from the ashes of the father, emerging "From his perfumed cradle (his Sires Urn)" and bringing "His Fathers honour'd ashes on his wings." He is urged to live

Engraving of the river god Alfeo, which appeared in the seventeenth-century editions
of Fanshawe's translation of Battista Guarini 's Il Pastor Fido

virtuously so as to prove himself worthy of his father, learning that " 'Tis not so much both Indies to command / As first to rule *himself,* and then *a Land.*" Fanshawe seems to be responding to the situation in 1646, by which time the fighting was over and Parliament triumphant; though the king was still very much alive, he had delivered himself a prisoner to the Scots.

The second edition of *Il Pastor Fido,* published in 1648, comprises the works included in the first with the addition of some twenty-five poems, both original and translations, reflecting the poet's eclectic interests: several sonnets translated from the Spanish; some Latin poems; the translation of a canto from *Progresse of Learning* by Thomas Carey (1597–1634) and book 4 of Virgil's *Aeneid;* a prose discourse on Rome's civil wars; and efforts at light Caroline verse on such traditional subjects as "A Rose," "The Ruby," "A Rich Foole," and "A Pic-

ture." For the most part, however, the collection focuses on political themes, reflecting the sentiments of a devoted Royalist during a time of troubles for the Crown. Fanshawe's earliest work, "An Ode Vpon occasion of His Majesties Proclamation in the yeare 1630. Commanding the Gentry to reside upon their Estates in the Country," is a variation of the traditional town-and-country poem. It opens with a recitation of the ravages of the Thirty Years' War, which, Fanshawe maintains, England has been spared through the care of the king. This peace is threatened, however, by the gentry who crowd the court and neglect their estates, whose bounty nourishes the nation:

The sapp and bloud o'th land, which fled
Into the roote, and choackt the heart,
Are bid their quickning pow'r to spread
Through ev'ry part.

"The Escuriall" praises a royal palace, albeit a Spanish one. The poem opens with an account of Philip II's vow to raise a structure to Saint Lawrence, whose shrine he had damaged in a siege. The palace is at once a convent, a college, and a royal residence to which the king "gave each part his due"; and Fanshawe applauds the concept, the plan, and the works of art that grace the walls of the three parts. In "On His Majesties Great Shippe lying almost finisht in Woolwich Docke Anno Dom. 1637, and afterwards called The Soveraigne of the Seas," the poet rather extravagantly celebrates the vessel, the "Escuriall of the Sea," and indirectly celebrates the king. Fanshawe finds it a microcosm of an ordered kingdom:

> The image of a perfect Government,
> Where, sitting at the helme the Monarch steeres,
> The Oares are labour'd by the active Peeres,
> And all the People distributed are
> In other offices of Peace and Warre.

The poem concludes with a fanciful apotheosis: the ship will not be wrecked or rot away, but "launcht a sayling Constellation" in the sky. Both "The Escuriall" and "On His Majesties Great Shippe" are rendered in English and Latin.

Many works arose from Fanshawe's experiences during the troubled 1640s. "On the Earle of Straffords Tryall" eulogizes the king's chief minister whose trial in 1641 ended in a parliamentary bill of attainder. Hoping to bring peace to the kingdom, Thomas Wentworth, first Earl of Strafford, is reputed to have urged the king to sign the bill of attainder, which indicted Strafford for crimes that would end in his execution. Several works obviously arose from Fanshawe's association with Prince Charles, to whom Fanshawe also dedicated the second edition. Intending the volume as a moral guide, Fanshawe assumed the role of elder counselor and mentor by offering a book in the tradition of the "Mirror of Princes." The fourth book of the *Aeneid* offers the example of a legendary hero who chooses to sacrifice his own interests and desires in order to achieve his destined role in history. Fanshawe renders the *Aeneid,* as he does Carey's *Progress of Learning,* in Spenserian stanzas, apparently experimenting with different verse forms. In the *Progress of Learning,* as James Turner observes, Fanshawe insists that a land will be fruitful only if it is subdued to order, not "shuffled in one Masse"; hence the monarchy and its aristocratic hierarchy must be restored if England is to be once more bountiful. The volume closes with two works associated with the Roman civil wars, obviously intended for Prince Charles's edification, the first a translation of two odes from Horace, the last a prose "Summary Discourse of the Civill Warres of Rome, extracted out of the best Latine Writers in Prose and Verse." In the latter, Fanshawe, translating Virgil's prediction of the coming of Augustus, holds that young emperor up as a model of dedication, moderation, and wise action, citing him as one who healed a nation after the devastation of civil broils. The dedication of the volume to the Prince of Wales was more than a courtly gesture to a royal patron, however, for Fanshawe obviously saw in the prince promise of a restored kingdom, which he fervently believed the only possible rule for the country. His devotion to that ideal is summed up in a striking couplet from the second poem to Charles: "Frank *Nature* never gave a better thing, / Nor ever will to men, then a good *King*."

Fanshawe left London in September 1648, initiating a period of almost continual travel, accompanied for the most part by his wife. He joined James Butler, twelfth Earl of Ormonde, in Ireland, consulted with Charles II in Holland, and in April 1650 joined Edward Hyde (later first Earl of Clarendon) in Madrid, where they sought financial aid for the Royalist cause. The mission was unsuccessful at a time when King Philip IV was actively supporting the English Republic in its war with Portugal; and the envoys proved distinctly unwelcome after June, when Royalists assassinated Anthony Ascham, Parliament's agent in Spain. In September Fanshawe returned to France, narrowly escaping shipwreck, proceeded to Holland, and finally joined Charles II in Scotland, where he served as secretary to the king. In the interim he had been granted a baronetcy (2 September 1650) in recognition of his service to the Crown.

Captured by Oliver Cromwell's forces at the Battle of Worcester on 3 September 1651, Fanshawe was imprisoned at Whitehall from 13 September until 28 November. His resourceful wife communicated with him regularly through a window in the prison, which she managed to visit undetected at four in the morning. Fanshawe fell ill with scurvy, which continued to plague him for years thereafter, and Anne, securing a doctor's certificate, presented it personally to the Council of State and with Cromwell's help received permission for her husband's release. He was set at liberty on a four-thousand-pound bond and took up residence at the estate of William Wentworth, second Earl of Strafford, in Tankersley Park, Yorkshire, from which he was forbidden by Parliament to travel more than five miles. The conditions of his bond were eventually relaxed, and the Fanshawes spent the next four years moving between lodgings in Chancery Lane and the homes of relatives. Finally released from the bond, he removed to Paris, where in 1659 he joined Charles II in the capacity of master of requests and secretary of the Latin tongue.

During this decade of dislocations he continued to work on translations; but though he remained resolutely loyal to the monarchy, his status under the Republic was so tenuous as to persuade him to devote himself to unprovocative literary pursuits. He published *Selected Parts of Horace* in 1652, *The Lusiad* in 1655, and *La Fida Pastora,* a Latin verse translation of John Fletcher's *The Faithful Shepherdess* (1609?) in 1658. The title page of *Querer Por Solo Querer,* published in 1670 after his death, indicates that it was "Paraphrased in English, Anno 1654." None of these works has the overt political tone and content of his publications in the 1640s. *The Lusiad,* for which he is best known today, is a loose translation of Camões's epic poem about the exploits of Vasco da Gama, who opened up the East to Portuguese trade in the early sixteenth century.

Denham's judgment that the translation of *Il Pastor Fido* "nobly dost decline / Of tracing word by word, and line by line" is perhaps more descriptive of *The Lusiad,* for Fanshawe's rendering of the Portuguese is very loose indeed. Geoffrey Bullough, the modern editor, suggests that Fanshawe's version is not a translation of the original at all, since there is some question as to the poet's mastery of the language of a country he did not visit until 1661. Drawing attention to the 1639 edition of Manuel de Faria e Sousa, in which each stanza of the original is followed by a prose translation in Spanish, Bullough demonstrates that Fanshawe surely used this volume. Fanshawe matches Camões's ottava rimas but takes considerable liberties with the text, rendering it in the style more characteristic of a Caroline love-poet than an epic bard, a bent which caused W. J. Mickle, a later translator, to complain about the "puns, conceits, and low, quaint expressions, uncountenanced by the original." Fanshawe's work, however, has stood the test of time. Sir Richard Francis Burton, who published a version of his own in 1870, acknowledges a debt to his predecessor, whom he praises for his "sprightly gallant style, the gay and lively lilt, the spring and swing of the verse," which Fanshawe could alternate, when the occasion demanded, with "stirring, dignified and dramatic" verse.

For the balance of Fanshawe's life he was so heavily engaged in public service as to leave little time for literary activities. He was knighted by

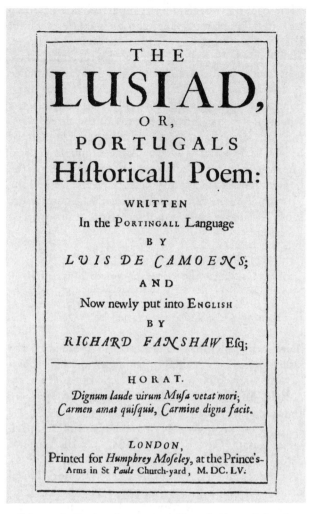

Title page for Fanshawe's most memorable work: his translation of an epic poem about Vasco da Gama

Charles II at Breda in April 1660, and the following month accompanied the king aboard the royal ship on his triumphal return to London. In assuming the duties of Latin secretary, he became the immediate successor of John Milton in that office, Milton having held the position for almost the entire period of the English Republic. Elected member of Parliament from Cambridge University on 11 March 1661, Fanshawe remained close to the king, who, perhaps recalling his earlier advice about royal marriages in the dedication of *Il Pastor Fido,* commissioned him to carry the royal portrait to Catherine of Braganza at Lisbon later that year. On 10 August 1662 Fanshawe was appointed ambassador to Portugal, and upon his return a year later he was honored by admission to the king's Privy Council on 1 October 1663. Fanshawe, who was ever a friend to Spain, was appointed ambassador to that country on 20 January 1664, with the mission of negotiating a commercial treaty between the two nations. He was able to conclude a highly favorable agreement but was forced to acquiesce to a provision stipulating that the protocol was to be ratified by Charles II within a fixed period of time, or else it would be withdrawn. When news of the provision reached Clarendon, the lord chancellor, he took exception to Fanshawe committing the king to such a limitation without first consulting the government. In March 1666, either as a consequence of Fanshawe's presumption or because of his own hostility to Spain, Clarendon ordered the ambassador withdrawn, to be replaced by Edward Montagu, first Earl of Sandwich. In June, while arranging for the transition, Fanshawe was stricken with ague and died on the twenty-sixth, just two weeks before he was scheduled to return to England.

Letters:

Original Letters of his Excellency Sir Richard Fanshaw, During his Embassies in Spain and Portugal (London: A. Roper, 1701).

Biography:

Lady Anne Fanshawe, *Memoirs of Lady Fanshawe, wife of the Right Hon. Sir Richard Fanshawe, bart., Ambassador from Charles the Second to the Court of Madrid in 1665. Written by herself. To which are added, extracts from the Correspondence of Sir Richard Fanshawe,* edited by Harris Nicolas (London: H. Colburn, 1829).

References:

Geoffrey Bullough, "The Early Poems of Sir Richard Fanshawe," in *Anglo-Americana,* edited by Karl Brunner, Weiner Beiträge zur englischen Philologie, 62 (Vienna: Braumüller, 1955), pp. 27–36;

Gareth Alban Davies, "Sir Richard Fanshawe, Hispanic Cavalier," *University of Leeds Review,* 20 (1977): 87–119;

John Loftis, ed., *The Memoirs of Anne, Lady Halkett and Ann, Lady Fanshawe* (Oxford: Clarendon Press, 1979);

Graham Parry, "A Troubled Arcadia," in *Literature and the English Civil War,* edited by Thomas Healy and Jonathan Sawday (Cambridge: Cambridge University Press, 1990), pp. 38–55;

James Turner, *The Politics of Landscape* (Cambridge: Harvard University Press, 1979);

J. H. Whitfield, "Sir Richard Fanshawe and The Faithful Shepherd," *Italian Studies,* 19 (1964): 64–82.

Papers:

Manuscripts for Fanshawe's English poems and his translations of Martial's epigrams are at the British Library (Add. MS 15228). Manuscripts for his translations of Spanish sonnets are at the Bodleian Library, Oxford (MS Firth c. 1). His diplomatic correspondence with the courts of Portugal and Spain is at Conington Castle, Peterborough. See *Report of the Manuscripts of J. M. Heathcote, Esq., of Conington Castle* (Norwich: Printed for the Historical Manuscripts Commission, 1899).

Owen Felltham

(1602? – 23 February 1668)

Claude J. Summers
University of Michigan – Dearborn

BOOKS: *Resolues Diuine, Morall, Politicall* (London: Printed for Henry Seile, 1623); enlarged as *Resolves A Duple Century, one new an other of a second Edition* (London: Printed for Henry Seile, 1628); enlarged again as *Resolves: The eight Impressiõ, With New, & Severall other Additions both in Prose and Verse* (London: Printed for Anne Seile, 1661);

Three Moneths Obseruations of the Low-Countries, Especially Holland. Containing A brief Description of the Country, Customes, Religions, Manners, and Dispositions of the People [pirated edition] (London: Printed for William Ley, 1648); authorized, unabridged edition published as *A Brief Character of the Low-Countries under the States. Being three weeks observation of the Vices and Vertues of the Inhabitants* (London: Printed for Henry Seile, 1652).

Editions: *The Poems of Owen Felltham,* edited by Ted-Larry Pebworth and Claude J. Summers (University Park, Pa.: *Seventeenth-Century News,* 1973).

Ted-Larry Pebworth, "An Anglican Family Worship Service of the Interregnum: A Canceled Early Text and a New Edition of Owen Felltham's 'A Form of Prayer,' " *English Literary Renaissance,* 16 (Winter 1986): 206–233.

OTHER: "To the Memory of immortall BEN," in *Ionsonvs Virbivs: Or, The Memorie of Ben: Johnson Revived By The Friends of the Muses* (London: Printed for Henry Seile, 1638), pp. 42–44;

"Against Ben: Johnson," in *Parnassus Biceps. or Severall Choice Pieces of Poetry, Composed by the best Wits that were in both the Universities Before Their Dissolution,* edited by Abraham Wright (London: Printed for George Eversden, 1656), pp. 154–156;

"When, Dearest, I but think on thee," misattributed to John Suckling, in *The Last Remains of Sᵣ John Suckling* (London: Printed for Humphrey Moseley, 1659), pp. 32–33.

Owen Felltham (or Feltham) is today remembered principally as the author of a single important work, *Resolves Divine, Morall, Politicall.* A collection of prose musings on religious, ethical, and social subjects, originally published in 1623, *Resolves* underwent extensive augmentation and revision both in the second edition of 1628 and in the eighth edition of 1661. As the formulaic "vow-like" resolves of 1623 matured into the freer and longer "excogitations" of 1628 and the personal essays of 1661, the collection provides a valuable portrait of an attractive individual's spiritual and intellectual growth over a period of thirty-eight years, as well as a fascinating record of generic and stylistic developments in seventeenth-century prose. Felltham was also the author of a humorous prose dissection of the Dutch, *A Brief Character of the Low-Countries* (1652), and of a small but impressive body of poetry. What Laurence Stapleton has noted in reference to *Resolves* is true of all of Felltham's work, especially his poetry: Virtue was Felltham's muse, but he also courted the Graces, those jealous custodians of artistic expression. Although Felltham is today only sparingly represented in modern anthologies of seventeenth-century poetry and is generally neglected by modern critics, he was recognized by Anthony Wood as one of the poets "which were the chiefest of the Nation" in the 1630s. Indeed, Felltham's poetic canon includes some stimulating and frequently moving tributes, elegies, epitaphs, and reflective poems, as well as distinctive love lyrics. He is a minor poet of genuine talent and considerable achievement.

Felltham was born sometime around 1602, probably at Mutford, a village near Lowestoft, Suffolk, the second son of a prosperous member of the landed gentry, Thomas Felltham, and his wife Mary Ufflete Felltham. Although he was later to have a poem included in *Parnassus Biceps* (1656), a collection of verse by alumni of Oxford and Cambridge, no record exists of his having attended either university. His was probably a squirearchical education, at the hands of tutors and his own hands. His

116

*Engraved title page by Robert Vaughan for an enlarged edition of Owen
Felltham's prose musings on religious, ethical, and social subjects*

self-education — as witnessed in the expansions and
revisions of *Resolves* by the increased breadth and
depth of his reading in modern and ancient, sacred
and secular authors — was a lifelong and fruitful
project. As a young man Felltham apparently
sought his fortune in London as a merchant. On 10
October 1621 he married Mary Clopton of
Kentwell Hall, Melford, Suffolk. A three-week trip
to Holland, made probably between 1623 and
1628, was the inspiration for *A Brief Character of the
Low-Countries,* but Felltham did not authorize its
publication until 1652. By 1628 he had left London
and the world of trade to become steward to
Barnabas O'Brien (after 1639 the sixth earl of
Thomond) and was chiefly responsible for oversee-
ing O'Brien's recently acquired manor at Great Bill-
ing, near Northampton. For the rest of his life,
Felltham remained in the service of the O'Brien
family as both a well-remunerated employee and a

trusted friend. When Barnabas died in 1657,
Felltham stayed on as steward to Henry O'Brien,
seventh Earl of Thomond, and to the Dowager
Countess Mary, dying in the latter's service at her
London townhouse on 23 February 1668. His wife
and any children they may have had must have pre-
deceased Felltham, for there is no mention of her or
of any offspring in his will.

When Felltham appended to the eighth edition
of *Resolves* (1661) the section entitled *Lusoria: Or Occasional Pieces. With a Taste of Some Letters,* which included forty-two of his poems, he cautioned in "To
the Reader" that "The Poems, the Character, and
some of the Letters, he looks upon as sports; that
rather improve a man by preserving him from
worse, then by otherwise any considerable profit."
This modest disclaimer reflects Felltham's conviction that his most secure claim to fame rested on his
large prose work, and it establishes his position as

an amateur rather than professional poet. Still, the poetry needs no apology. In addition to the forty-two poems included in *Lusoria* (several of which had circulated widely in manuscript or had been published in miscellanies), six fugitive poems survive (three as contributions to printed volumes and three attributed to him in manuscripts of the period). Considering the relative smallness of his poetic canon, Felltham's range is significant. Although, somewhat surprisingly, he wrote no religious lyrics, his poems include almost all the secular subgenres popular in the earlier seventeenth century, from the epitaph and elegy to the "instructions to the painter" poem. His range is evident even within the sixteen love lyrics, which include exercises written to an imaginary scornful young woman in the Petrarchan manner; witty variations on the cruel-fair theme; and a moving and personal sequence that explores Neoplatonic attitudes toward love in surprising and convincing depth. Several of these poems were set to music in the seventeenth century, including six settings by the Oxford music professor and songwriter John Wilson.

The subject matter of his occasional poems also reflects Felltham's breadth of interest. In addition to several epitaphs for little-known individuals, such as Francis Leigh, who died young, "Leaving quite widowed Handsomnesse and Truth," Felltham mourns the passing of public figures such as Henry de Vere, eighteenth Earl of Oxford, who became a national hero when he died in 1625 fighting in the Low Countries in the service of Frederick, the former elector Palatine; the scholar and antiquarian Sir Rowland Cotton, who "knew / More Tongues than were at *Babels* building new: / And in so many languages could write, / That he's learn'd now, that can but name them right"; Thomas, Baron Coventry, lord keeper of the Great Seal, whose integrity earned him fame equal to Sir Thomas More's learned wit and Sir Francis Bacon's "miracl'd Fancy"; the celebrated (and notorious) beauty Lady Venetia Digby, to whom death came "not like a Tyrant, on whose brow / A pompous terrour hung; but in a strain / Lovely and calm, / . . . / Gently he did embrace her into clay"; Archbishop William Laud, with whose beheading "the grandeur of the Kingdom, / the defence of the Cavaliers, / The tradition of the Church, / The freedom of the subjects, / And the safety of the British sphere / Are, for a season, buried together"; and, perhaps most infamous, King Charles I, who was "Inhumanely murthered by a perfidious Party of His prevalent Subjects." Felltham's poems on literary topics include both a witty rebuttal to one of Ben Jonson's

fits of pique and a moving tribute to the great man, as well as a sound critical estimate occasioned by the untimely death of Thomas Randolph, whose "play was Fancies flame, a lightning wit / So shot, that it could sooner pierce, then hit." Most of Felltham's poems share a highly developed sense of dramatic tension, arresting and beautiful imagery encased within an essentially plain style of strong lines and pointed aphorisms, and a tendency toward baroque virtuosity restrained by a tightly controlled sense of reality and decorum.

The portrait of Felltham that emerges in the successive revisions of *Resolves* is that of a charitable moralist, conservative in his politics, liberal in his theology, and Stoic in his philosophy. His undogmatic good sense humanizes his religious zeal, and his personal warmth gradually triumphs over youthful priggishness. Those same qualities are also apparent in his poetry, especially in the reflective and occasional works. The long, somewhat prosaic "True Happinesse," for example, locates Christian contentment in the via media of moderation and a Stoic acceptance of the vicissitudes of human existence. The same sense of moderation informs Felltham's "Considerations of one design'd for a Nunnery," where he endorses a balance between the ascetic and the carnal: "All spiritual is / too fine for flesh to live by; and too grosse / Is food corporeal all." In perhaps his best political poem, "On the Duke of Buckingham slain by Felton, the 23. Aug. 1628," Felltham's balanced perspective is also evident; and here it emerges as an interesting complexity of thought and feeling. This complexity is achieved by holding in suspension contrasting attitudes toward the unpopular George Villiers, first Duke of Buckingham, who as the chief minister of King Charles I had badly bungled the wars against Spain and France and whose assassination in 1628 stirred conflicting emotions on the part of many. Throughout the poem Felltham opposes Buckingham's greatness with his enemies' hatred for him, the duke's high estate with his assassin's resolve, finding in Buckingham a "great Example of Mortality" and sorrowing at his fall not because the duke was a worthy man, but because his fall was unworthy of his exalted station: "Can a knife / Let out so many Titles and a life?" Felltham examines in detail the extremism that can result in the fall of "so huge a pile / Of State" as Buckingham and resolves the tensions in the poem by indicating the reconciliation implicit in the bonds of Christianity common to all Englishmen. He consigns the assassin John Felton to a position in the underworld next to Brutus, where he shall "receive / Such Bayes as

Heath'nish ignorance can give," for "They oft decline into the worst of ill, / That act the Peoples wish without Laws will." The carefully sustained tension between the great heights that Buckingham had attained and the great hatred in which he was held, along with the thoughtful recognition of the moral and political complexities involved in the assassination, make the poem on Buckingham one of Felltham's most effective pieces.

Felltham's considered moderation in his poem on Buckingham should not obscure the fact that the poet was a fervent supporter of the Stuart monarchy and of the Church of England, positions that were to be increasingly reflected in his poetry during the religiopolitical turmoil of the 1640s, as the Parliamentarians and the Puritans, whom he detested, gained the ascendancy in the state and dismantled and disfigured his beloved Church of England. His poems prompted by the execution of Archbishop Laud, the abolishment of the celebration of Christmas, and the execution of King Charles I leave no doubt as to Felltham's political and religious sympathies. The epitaph on Charles I, for example, is anything but moderate. Infused with passionate indignation, it is also carefully controlled as it builds toward an outrageous but satisfyingly inevitable conclusion, progressing inexorably from divine right to divinity. Consisting entirely of clauses introduced by the anticipatory adverb "when," the poem begins by asserting Charles's ability and right to rule as sovereign of state and as head of the Anglican church and proceeds to the details of his humiliation and trial, and then to the regicide itself, where the king's death is depicted as a martyrdom equivalent to Christ's Passion. In terms of this analogy, Felltham identifies Oliver Cromwell with Judas Iscariot and John Bradshaw (the lord president of the court that condemned the king) with Pontius Pilate, and then sweeps to a hyperbolic yet inevitable climax:

> When it appear'd, He to this world was sent,
> The Glory of KINGS, but Shame of PARLIAMENT:
> The stain of th'*English,* that can never dye;
> The Protestants perpetual Infamy:
> When He had rose thus, Truths great Sacrifice,
> *Here CHARLES the First, and CHRIST the second lyes.*

In its excess, the poem is certainly an exaggeration, but an exaggeration in the direction of idealism. For all its flirtation with blasphemy, the epitaph succeeds by virtue of its rich tone of bitterness mixed with Stoic acceptance and by means of its impassioned yet tightly reined and narrowly focused rhetoric. The poem is a significant contribution to the literature of Royalist martyrolatry, a political and poetical strategy that in the event proved more successful than the rational justifications of the regicides. Felltham's loyalty to the Royalist cause found its recompense in the Restoration of the monarchy, about which he wrote ecstatically in the 1661 *Resolves*:

> let men see, how the Sacred wheel of Providence hath resurrection'd all our joys. How the Church recovers her late besmeared beauties. How the Tide of Trade returns. How brightned Swords have now a peaceful glitter; how Glory, Wealth, and Honour, with Loyalty, is return'd. How shouts of joy have drown'd the Cannons Roar; that till men come in Heaven, such joy on Earth can ne're again be expected to be seen.

If the epitaph on King Charles I is Felltham's most notorious poem, his best-known verse in his own day was probably his reply to Ben Jonson's "Ode to Himselfe," beginning "Come leave the lothed stage," which the playwright wrote in angry reaction to the failure of his 1629 comedy *The New Inn.* Jonson's tirade occasioned the responses of several poets, including Randolph and Thomas Carew, but Felltham's "Against Ben: Johnson" (1656; republished in *Resolves* as "An Answer to the Ode of Come leave the loathed Stage, &c.") is clearly the best – though the least laudatory – of the group. Closely imitating the form of Jonson's ode, Felltham's sharp and witty parody rebukes the dramatist's arrogance, accusing him not only of bad temper but also of loss of his powers ("Come leave this saucy way / Of baiting those that pay / Dear for the sight of your declining wit") and urging him to "Leave then this humour vain, / And this more humorous strain, / Where self-conceit and choler of the bloud / Eclipse what else is good." Although Felltham's response to Jonson's fit of pique punctured the playwright's pretentiousness, its wit and playfulness precluded any real ill-feeling even as it also clearly established Felltham's independence of judgment. Hence, it is not surprising that when Jonson died in 1637 Felltham wrote a generous and thoughtful elegy "To the Memory of immortall BEN." This seventy-four-line poem in heroic couplets was published in *Jonus Virbius* (1638), a volume of thirty-three elegies written about the dramatist by such poets and playwrights as William Cartwright; Lucius Cary, Lord Falkland; John Ford; Sidney Godolphin; James Howell; Henry King; and Edmund Waller. Felltham's poem recognizes the greatness of early-seventeenth-century drama, now widowed by the deaths of William Shakespeare and Jonson ("And now ... we well may say, / The Stage hath seene her glory and decay"); praises Jonson as lawgiver to the stage; celebrates the clarity and strength of Jonson's plain style ("Each line did like a Diamond drop distill, / Though hard, yet cleare"); and even turns Jonson's notorious slowness of composition into a virtue: "Admit his Muse was slow. 'Tis Judgements Fate / To move, like great Princes, still in state." A convincing and sincere tribute to the playwright, Felltham's poem ranks among the most distinguished memorials Jonson received.

It is singularly appropriate that Felltham should have written an elegy for Jonson since he was a great influence on Felltham's own poetry. Felltham learned from Jonson the chief elements of his own plain style: clarity of expression, urbane confidence, suggestive diction, aphoristic statement, regular form, and dramatic tension. Jonson's influence is sometimes quite obvious, as in the aphoristic formulation of this couplet in "On a Hopeful Youth": "Reading this know thou hast seen / Vertue tomb'd at but Fifteen," which echoes similar constructions among Jonson's epitaphs. The Jonsonian qualities of Felltham's verse are usually seen, however, in combination with elements to which Felltham is probably also indebted to the other great poetic innovator and influence of the period, John Donne. From Donne, Felltham probably inherited his fondness for ingenious comparisons (as when in "On the Lady *E. M.*" he compares the length of human life to that of various prose writings: "A sheet of *Bacon's* catch'd at more, we know / Than all sad *Fox,* long *Holinshead* or *Stow*"), paradoxes (as when in "Song: Cupid and Venus" he proves "That *Vulcan* onely is the god of Love"), and hyperbole (as in the elegy on Lord Coventry, where the elegiac convention that has nature mourning for the deceased is so extended that "Our *London* is turn'd *Venice*"). Although he is never as frankly erotic or libertine as Donne sometimes is and never partakes of the cynicism and despair of which Donne is capable, Felltham may also be indebted to Donne for his dominant attitude toward love, which is based on Neoplatonic theory tempered by experience in the direction of realism. While Felltham cannot be neatly categorized as either a "Son of Ben" or a student in the "School of Donne," he – like many minor poets of the period – learned from both great innovators.

The dual legacy of Donne and Jonson is especially apparent in Felltham's serious love lyrics, which celebrate spiritualized but erotic and mutually reciprocal relationships. Five of Felltham's poems – "The Cause," "The Vow-breach," "The Sympathy," "The Reconcilement," and "A Farewell" –

form a narrative sequence concerned with the union of lovers' souls. The dramatic situation is a familiar one: the male speaker attempts to convince a reluctant lady that his love is based on a deep spirituality that transcends (but does not exclude) the physical. The speaker of "The Cause" begins by denying physical attraction as the sole object of desire: "Think not, *Clarissa,* I love thee / For thy meer outside, though it be / A Heaven more clear than that men cloudless see." The greater attraction, he insists, is Clarissa's soul. The spiritual love that they share will, he argues, lead them upward "To clearer heights" until they "centre *Jove*" and mingle their souls so purely that gazers from below will think them a god. The pun on Jove as both a planet and a deity leads naturally to the striking metaphysical image on which the poem ends:

For when two souls shall towre so high,
Without their flesh their rayes shall flye,
Like Emanations from a Deity.

But insofar as "The Cause" is a seduction poem, it does not quite succeed, for in "The Vow-breach," Clarissa enigmatically confesses to a failure of faith, an obstacle that must be overcome before the lovers can be united. The third poem in the series, "The Sympathy," is carefully designed to purge Clarissa's "heretick thoughts" by proving that the lovers are "Two souls Co-animate." The central image of the poem is clever in the Donnean manner, yet wholly appropriate:

Two Lutes are strung.
And on a Table tun'd alike for song;
Strike one, and that which none did touch,
Shall sympathizing sound as much,
As that which toucht you see.
Think then this world (which Heaven inroules)
Is but a Table round, and souls
More apprehensive be.

An illustrative metaphor that functions similarly to Donne's famous comparison of lovers to a compass in "A Valediction: forbidding Mourning," this analogy reassures Clarissa of the exquisitely delicate sensitivity to which the lovers' souls are mutually attuned. The poem concludes with the speaker reminding Clarissa that, even in physical union, spiritual love can mix entwined hearts, thus allowing lovers to boast that no absence can affect their love.

In "The Reconcilement" the speaker pointedly invites Clarissa to join him in "Still water; close united Extasie," the goal toward which the entire sequence has been leading. Clarissa's "loose and wandring fears" have been purged by "penitential tears," and she is "new created." Hence the speaker entices her to a sensuous mingling of their souls (and bodies):

> Come then, and let us like two streams swell'd high,
> Meet, and with soft and gentle struglings try,
> How like their curling waves we mingle may,
> Till both be made one floud; then who can say
> Which this way flow'd, which that: For there will be
> Still water; close united Extasie.
> That when we next shall but of motion dream,
> We both shall slide one way, both make one stream.

This marvelous amalgam of natural, spiritual, and, especially, erotic signification in a single sustained conceit apparently convinces Clarissa, for in the final poem of the series, "A Farewell," the lovers are united. This poem explains how their union is such that no physical absence, not even death, can part them: "So absent think me but as scatter'd dew, / Till re-exhal'd again to Vertue; You." Felltham's Neoplatonic sequence illustrates well both his limitations and his considerable distinction as a love poet. The familiarity of the dramatic situation and the close resemblance of the individual poems in the sequence to better-known works by Donne and others may be evidence of a lack of originality. Yet the sequence is not merely derivative, for in its sincerity of statement, apt images, and tenderly restrained drama, it is wholly convincing. Felltham's distinction as a love poet, and as a poet generally, lies not in any uniqueness of thought, but in the beauty and pertinence of his expression.

Equally convincing is "When, Dearest, I but think on thee," Felltham's most frequently anthologized poem. The lyric seems to have circulated widely in manuscript during the seventeenth century, and a copy found among Sir John Suckling's papers after his death was included in his *Last Remains* (1659). In *Lusoria* Felltham calls attention to the mistaken attribution, but even twentieth-century anthologists have occasionally assigned the poem to Suckling and sometimes judged it to be one of that Cavalier's finest lyrics. The dramatic situation is the familiar one of the physical separation of lovers, but Felltham treats the old theme with freshness and vitality. Stressing the spirituality of true love and the impossibility of real absence, the speaker compares the memory of his love's beauty to "the grace of Deities, / Still present with us, though unsighted" and to sudden lights that awaken sleeping men. He reassures her that "No absence can consist with Loves, / That do partake of fair perfection: / Since in the darkest night they may / By their quick motion find a way / To see each other by reflection." Just as rivers can overflow their banks, so can love transcend the physical limits of time and space: "for that's an Ocean too, / That flows not every day, but ever." The poem is an excellent example of the blending of techniques and ideals associated with Donne and Jonson. The ingenious comparisons and idealistic attitude toward love are aspects of the poem that Felltham probably inherited from Donne, while the graceful clarity of expression, urbane restraint, and regular "singable" form are part of Jonson's legacy. Finally, however, "When, Dearest, I but think on thee" is interesting less for its lineage than for its own particular beauty of statement.

Felltham's poems are not all equally successful; a few are merely exercises and others are highly derivative. They reveal, however, the richness and diversity that mark Caroline poetry, and, as a body, they merit for Felltham more recognition as a poet than he has received. This seventeenth-century amateur of letters has no claim to status beyond that of minor poet, but such a ranking in a period as rich in poetry as his is not to be despised. His measure as a poet is not his originality but his ability to make fresh and personal poems that derive from so fertile and varied a milieu. Felltham merits the attention of modern readers not merely because he articulates the poetic idiom of his age, but because he does it so well.

Bibliography:
Ted-Larry Pebworth, "An Annotated Bibliography of Owen Felltham," *Bulletin of the New York Public Library,* 79 (Winter 1976): 209–224.

References:
Barbara E. Bergquist, "Owen Felltham: A Few Biographical Facts," *Notes and Queries,* new series 3 (May–June 1976): 233–235;

Ted-Larry Pebworth, *Owen Felltham* (New York: Twayne, 1976);

Jean Robertson, "The Poems of Owen Felltham," *Modern Language Notes,* 58 (May 1943): 388–390;

Laurence Stapleton, "The Graces and the Muses: Felltham's *Resolves,*" in her *The Elected Circle: Studies in the Art of Prose* (Princeton: Princeton University Press, 1973), pp. 73–92.

Sidney Godolphin

(January 1610 – 9 February 1643)

Graham Roebuck
McMaster University

WORKS: "Chronagramma" and "Insolita Angligenas," in *Carolvs Redvx* (Oxford: Printed by Iohannes Lichfield & J. Short, 1623);

"Ille dies quo Te cælum," in *Camdeni Insignia* (Oxford: Printed by Iohannes Lichfield & J. Short, 1624);

"Elegie on D.D.," in John Donne's *Poems, by J. D. With Elegies on the Authors Death,* enlarged edition (Printed by M. Flesher for J. Marriot, 1635);

"To my very much honoured Friend Mr. George Sandys upon his Paraphrase on the Poeticall Parts of the Bible," in George Sandys's *A Paraphrase Vpon the Divine Poems* (London: Printed by John Legatt, 1638 [i.e., 1637]);

"The Muses fairest light," in *Ionsonvs Virbivs: Or, The Memorie of Ben: Johnson Revived By The Friends of the Muses* (London: Printed by E. Purslowe for Henry Seile, 1638);

"An Epitaph upon the Lady Rich," in John Gauden's *Funerals made Cordials* (London: Printed by T. C. for Andrew Cook, 1658);

The Passion of Dido for Æneas. As it is Incomparably exprest in the Fourth Book of Virgil. Translated by Edmund Waller & Sidney Godolphin, Esq[rs.] (London: Printed for Humphrey Moseley, 1658);

"A Song by Sidny Godolphin, Esq; on Tom. Killigrew and Will. Murrey," in *Examen Poeticum: Being The Third Part of Miscellany Poems* (London: Printed by R. E. for Jacob Tonson, 1693);

"Song: Or love mee lesse, or love mee more," in volume 3 of *Specimens of the Early English Poets,* edited by George Ellis (London: G. & W. Nicol, 1801);

"Replye," in *Tixall Poetry,* edited by Arthur Clifford (Edinburgh: J. Ballantyne, 1813);

"The Poems of Sidney Godolphin: Now First Collected," in volume 2 of *Minor Poets of the Caroline Period,* edited by George Saintsbury (Oxford: Clarendon Press, 1906);

The Poems of Sidney Godolphin, edited by William Dighton (Oxford: Clarendon Press, 1931).

Praised in the warmest terms by his contemporaries for his exemplary character and his poetic skills, Sidney Godolphin is scarcely known for his work except to coterie aficionados. Only two collections of his small body of poems have been published, the most recent edition as long ago as 1931, and the earlier edition, a less complete compilation, in 1906. A few poems saw print in collections during his own lifetime, and several appeared in later miscellanies, while others have been wrongly attributed to him. There are also instances of his poetry being wrongly attributed to his nephew, Sidney, first Earl of Godolphin, lord high treasurer during Queen Anne's reign, who was not known as a poet. The rest of Godolphin's poetry remained in manuscript, accessible only to a few. His personal reputation is much greater than this slight literary recognition might suggest, a consequence of debate about his death in action during the English Civil War. This debate, closely related to the political events and philosophies of the mid seventeenth century, remains full of significance for modern times.

Sidney Godolphin was baptized on 15 January 1610 in the parish church at Breage, Cornwall, where his family had been prosperous and prominent since the eleventh century. Their name derives from the Cornish word Godolghan, meaning "white eagle," which was the device on their shield and coat of arms. Tin mining was the basis of the family wealth, with which they acquired lands and interests in Cornwall and in the Scilly Isles. They also acquired a reputation for loyalty to the Crown, a characteristic that was fully fledged in Sidney. After the battle of Naseby, near the end of the first civil war, Charles, Prince of Wales (later Charles II), may have been sheltered by the Godolphins in Cornwall. When he left the mainland, Charles is

SIDNEY GODOLPHIN.

Engraving by Clamp after a portrait by Harding (National Portrait Gallery, London)

known to have taken shelter in the Godolphin-governed Scilly Isles.

The parents of Sidney Godolphin, Thomasine Sidney Godolphin, from whom the poet received his Christian name, and Sir William Godolphin of Godolphin, Cornwall, died in 1612 and 1613 respectively. As the second of three sons, Sidney inherited an estate in Norfolk, which came into the family's possession as the dowry of his mother. He was brought up by his uncle Francis, who was the executor of the estate until the eldest son, also named Francis, reached twenty-one. The death of Sidney's younger brother in 1638 further contributed to his financial stability. Writing in his *Life* (1759), Edward Hyde, first Earl of Clarendon, recorded that Sidney was "liberally supplied for a very good education, and for a cheerful subsistence, in any course of life he proposed to himself."

His education seems to have been conducted by private tuition, since there is no record of his attending any of the notable schools, until at age fourteen he matriculated as a commoner of Exeter College, Oxford, on 25 June 1624, as did his elder brother, Francis. On 26 July he was admitted as a reader to the Bodleian Library. He went down from Oxford three years later without having taken a degree, expressing his gratitude to his college in the gift of a tankard, recorded in the college register as "Ex dono Sidney Godolphin hujus collegii commensalis et fillii Gulielmi Godolphin equitis aurati" (The gift of Sidney Godolphin commoner of this college and son of William Godolphin, knight). His connection with Oxford predates his matriculation, however, for a 1623 collection of Oxford poems, *Carolus Redux*, includes a clever Latin chronogram and two Latin lines on the unusual joy felt by the English people on Prince Charles's return from Spain on 5 October. Sidney's brother contributed a Latin ode to the same volume. In 1624 appeared a collection in memory of the renowned historian William Camden (who had died the year before), in gratitude for his founding a chair of history. This volume, *Camdeni Insignia*, includes an untitled eight-line verse by Sidney Godolphin.

To conclude his formal education, Godolphin may have attended one of the Inns of Court, as Anthony Wood's *Athenæ Oxonienses* (1691, 1692) attests, but of this there is no record. It is also uncertain when Godolphin undertook the travels mentioned by Clarendon in his *Life*: "he had spent some years in France and the low countries, and accompanied the Earl of Leicester in his ambassage into Denmark, before he resolved to be quiet and attend some promotion in the Court." It is unlikely that he spent twelve years abroad, as it has been asserted, for he must have spent sufficient time in London to have attended to his parliamentary duties – he was elected a member of Parliament for Helston, in his native Cornwall, on 6 March 1628 – and to have become known as one of the "Sons of Ben," and to have heard John Donne preach. Of all these activities, the politician's duties may have made the fewest demands, for the Third Parliament was dissolved in 1629, heralding the years of Charles's personal rule. Probably Godolphin was in Denmark while his kinsman, Robert Sidney, second Earl of Leicester, by a new creation in 1618, led an embassy to Christian IV, King of Denmark and Duke of Holstein from September to November 1632.

On 28 March 1640 Godolphin was elected to the Short Parliament, and in October to the fateful Long Parliament, in which, as earlier, he was unequivocally a Royalist, even a defender of the doomed William Wentworth, first Earl of Strafford. He was one of the last Royalists to leave the House at a time when warrants for the arrest of the king's supporters, termed "delinquents," were being issued. Volume six of the enlarged edition of John Somers's *Collection of Scarce and Valuable Tracts* (1811) mentions Godolphin's only recorded speech in the House, his valediction to the Commons:

> When the opposition was grown to this height, his majesty judged it fit that such members of both houses as had resolved against the parliament should withdraw themselves; and one of the last that continued sitting in the house of commons was Mr Sydney Godolphin, who, for a farewell, declared, "That by a war the parliament would expose itself to unknown dangers: for," said he, "when the cards are once shuffled, no man knows what the game will be;" which was afterwards found by parliament too true, when their own army became their masters.

It was after his first election, in the days of halcyon peace before the political storm gathered

(which, according to Clarendon, Godolphin foresaw more clearly than any man), that he made his abiding friendships with the men of the Great Tew circle, including its master, Lucius Cary, second Viscount Falkland, its "father," Jonson, and Clarendon (then Edward Hyde) and Thomas Hobbes. In *Private Men and Public Causes* (1962), Irene Coltman points out that Hobbes's favorite metaphor of chance and hazard in the political world was a game of cards. Clarendon's account of Godolphin, full of affection as it is, gives the character of one who stood somewhat apart from the company of friends at Great Tew in an isolation of his own desiring:

> Though every body loved his company well, yet he loved very much to be alone, being in his constitution inclined somewhat to melancholy, and to retirement amongst his books; and was so far from being active, that he was contented to be reproached by his friends with laziness; and was of so nice and tender a composition, that a little rain or wind would disorder him, and divert him from any short journey he had most willingly proposed to himself; insomuch as, when he rid abroad with those in whose company he most delighted, if the wind chanced to be in his face, he would (after a little pleasant murmuring) suddenly turn his horse, and go home.

It was in the period between Godolphin's appearance in London and the beginning of the Long Parliament that most of his small oeuvre was composed, for none of the extant poems seems to reflect direct experience of the actual political and military upheaval, although some may be read without undue straining of meaning as anticipating a gloomy foreclosing of the Caroline peace. This was the period, Clarendon wrote in his *Life*, when "England enjoyed the greatest measure of felicity that it had ever known" and stood in danger of nothing other than a surfeit of its happiness. Virgil's ironic line, adapted by Clarendon as an epitaph on that decade – "O fortunati nimium, bona si sua norint" (O exceedingly fortunate, if they but knew their own happiness) – was accepted by Godolphin and the Caroline poets as an abiding truth about human nature.

A skepticism about the availability of human self-knowledge and satisfaction in life pervades Godolphin's lyrical poetry. Although sometimes thought of as a Cavalier poet, he evinces a plangent and melancholic note, more serious and less ebullient than the verse usually associated with that label. The melancholy, in turn, is muted by a sense of sociability and decorum. This subtle mood is captured in a poem that seems finished (the more common state of Godolphin's poetry is incompletion), "Chorus." Godolphin's 1906 editor, George Saintsbury, remarks that the poem is "full of matter," but he does not elaborate his comment. "Chorus" begins with a striking variation on the commonplace theme of human vanity: the greatest happiness is no more than temporary alleviation of the given condition of life – deprivation:

> Vaine man, borne to noe happinesse,
> but by the title of distresse,
> Alli'de to a Capacitie
> of Joye, only by missery;
> whose pleasures are but remidies,
> and best delights but the supplies
> of what hee wantes, who hath noe sence
> but poverty and indigence[.]

Although Kurt Weber in *Lucius Cary, Second Vicount Falkland* (1940) refers to persistent doubt that Hobbes was a member of Great Tew, more recent studies such as J. C. Hayward's (*Seventeenth Century,* January 1987), which does not seek a firm definition of membership of the circle, suggest otherwise. Coltman sees Godolphin's poetry as being close to the views of Hobbes and cites the above lines as evidence. So it is, but contrary themes are also explored. Later lines, for instance, suggest the ideal of moderation, an ideal that has more kinship with Great Tew Anglicanism than Hobbism:

> Doeth not our Cheifest Blisse then lie
> Betwixt thirst and satiety,
> in the midd way? which is alone
> in an halfe satisfaction[.]

There is also in the same poem a ready recourse to Platonizing about love, which occurs often in Godolphin. Rather than invoking the Petrarchan tradition of Platonic love, Godolphin's treatment suggests a direct access to the Socratic arguments without the mediation of the poetic tradition:

> But Love is ever a mixt sence
> of what wee have, and what wee want,
> and though it bee a little scant
> of satisfaction, yet wee rest
> in such a halfe possession best.

If Godolphin goes directly to Plato, it is possibly because he shares some of Falkland's celebrated passion for the original philosophical texts. As Hayward has observed, Godolphin's poetry is "full of Platonic conceits." Yet the Great Tew circle was conscious of the need to combine the virtues of strenuous Roman political activity with Platonic passivity. The conclusion of "Chorus," however, supplies a remarkable figure, of a nautical cast, in which true love effortlessly achieves its goal, while the active passion is becalmed:

> They who love truly through the clyme
> of freesing North and scalding lyne,
> Sayle to their joyes, and have deepe sence
> both of the losse, and recompense:
> yet strength of passion doeth not prove
> Infallibly, the trueth of love,
> Shipps, which to day a storme did find,
> are since becalm'd, and feele no wind.

Sometimes Godolphin plays a subtle variation on the theme of the unavailability of human self-knowledge, and nowhere does he do so to better effect than in the "Song: Or love mee lesse, or love mee more." A lover, who would rather be rejected – and thus, paradoxically, restored to his liberty – by the beloved than remain in the ignoble torture between hope and fear, realizes how diminishing his indeterminate position really is:

> I see you weare that pittying smile
> which you have still vouchsaft my smart,
> Content thus cheapely to beguile
> and entertaine an harmlesse hart:
> But I noe longer can give way
> to hope, which doeth so little pay,
> And yet I dare noe freedome owe
> whilst you are kind, though but in shew.

Finally the lover withdraws even his pathetic demand to "love mee lesse," foreseeing the prospect of a yet more abject posture:

> But shew not a severer eye
> sooner to give mee liberty,
> for I shall love the very scorne
> which for my sake you doe put on.

The poem is a subtle, even exquisite, treatment of the theme of the availability of human self-delusion.

Another appeal to delusion, where self-flattery strives with unrequited love, is found in an untitled poem of twelve couplets, described by Saintsbury as belonging to the sequence of Elizabethan dream poems that started with the early sonneteers. Godolphin's poem opens with the speaker making a striking appeal to the figure of his scornful beloved as seen in a dream:

> fayre shadow stay, may I forever see
> thy beawty sever'd from thy cruelty,
> as in this dreame, doe not soe soone destroy
> soe deare to me, to you soe cheape a Joye.

In the deluding medium of dream the speaker imagines that, had his beloved been a little kinder, his self-flattery might have contented him, so that "my whole life had been / though without harvest, a perpetuall spring." This is Godolphin's most productive lyrical vein, his authentic voice. Love, unrequited, never supplies enough, and so must be augmented with fancy, flattery, and self-delusion. "When undeceiv'd," he writes in "Constancye," "love retires / tis but a modell lost." Of this clearly unfinished poem Saintsbury remarks, "it is not for children or fools," but is "an unusual document for the student of poetry," not only metrically, but also because "in point of thought he shows us more than a glimpse of the subtlety and depth which must have attracted Hobbes."

An untitled lyric that exploits with finesse Godolphin's self-deprecatory sense of his own small flame, reminiscent of the dream-poem, shows its quality in its first two stanzas:

> Noe more unto my thoughts appeare
>   att least appeare lesse Fayre
> For crazy tempers justly Feare
>   the goodnesse of the ayre;
>
> Whilst your pure Image hath a place
>   in my Impurer Mynde
> your very shaddow is the glasse
>   Wher my defects I finde.

Of this Saintsbury writes the most enthusiastic appraisal in print of any poem by Godolphin. So aware is he of his partiality, Saintsbury confesses that it might be due to his own lack of artistic restraint:

> Art should be quite contented with the almost complete mastery here shown of the form – with the throb and the soar of the common-measure flight, that 'common made' so 'uncommon.' If Godolphin wrote this, he may rest his claims on it *securus*. You cannot, if you have the due gift, read even into the second line without feeling that the *petite fièvre cérébrale* [slight touch of brain fever] is invading your imagination, that the *solita flamma* (old familiar flame) is caressing your heart. At least this is how some people are made; and the others may be sorry for them, or contemptuous of them if they like.

Godolphin has two ballads to his account; one of them is jocular and amused on the topic of his friends Thomas Killigrew and William Murray (later Earl of Dysart), who are cast as "Shepherds twain" in the 1693 *Examen Poeticum*. In the 1706 edition of the miscellany, they appear as "Shepherds Swains." The two versions differ greatly. Both men are in love with Pastora, who, preserving her honor, "gave no loose Encouragement / Yet kept Men from despairing." Such is her beauty's fame, Pastora is called to court, leaving Tom and Will deprived. The latter "broke his Pipes, and curst the day / That e'er he made a Ballet." The 1693 ascription to Godolphin seems to be the only authority. Even though it is not in his usual manner, it is not improbably his work. The verse letter, "When your knowne hand, and stile, and name" (about an obscure ecclesiastical dispute involving the bishop of Wells and the parishes of Britain and Pitcombe), although quite different in metrical form, is similarly spirited. Commenting on Godolphin's other ballad, Saintsbury notes that it is in the "triple time" meter of popular poetry, and he remarks, "Godolphin has not realized the fact that too many acataletic lines in the even places make the measure jolt." This seventy-two-line poem is based on the story of Cephalus and Procris from Ovid's *Metamorphoses*, an uncommon choice among the English poets. In Ovid's story too much happiness is the cause of Cephalus's eventual misery, as he, consumed by baseless jealousy, puts his faithful Procris to tests of her fidelity. Godolphin focuses on the last stage of the story only, in which Amarillis, Godolphin's version of Procris, spies on her shepherd-husband to see if he is unfaithful to her. Although the shepherd calls only to the breeze to refresh him, Amarillis believes he is addressing a lover. Mistaking his wife for a beast in hiding, the shepherd mortally wounds her with an arrow (in Ovid it is a special, unerring javelin). Godolphin's meter gallops to its conclusion:

> shee heares the mistake
> he curses his dart
> she dyes in her lymbs
> revived in her heart.

It might be that the story of one who is miserable from excess jealousy could be read allegorically for the condition of the Caroline peace and its destruction.

Edmund Waller, a considerable influence on Godolphin, may also have been his friend. Waller's extraordinary poetic fame was not secured until some time after his ignominious settlement with Parliament and the death of Godolphin. The two poets contributed to some of the same commemorative volumes, such as *Jonsonus Virbius* (1638). For their mutual acquaintance and sometime Great Tew companion, George Sandys, Waller and Godolphin wrote congratulatory verses for his *A Paraphrase Upon the Divine Poems* (1637). A poem by Waller entitled "Of Love," which starts "Unwisely we the

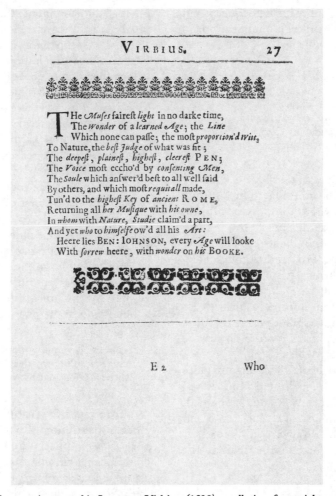

THe *Muses* faireſt *light* in no darke time,
The *Wonder* of a *learned Age*; the *Line*
Which none can paſſe; the moſt *proportion'd Witt*,
To Nature, the *beſt Judge* of what was fit ;
The *deepeſt*, *plaineſt*, *higheſt*, *cleereſt* P E N;
The *Voice* moſt eccho'd by *conſenting Men*,
The *Soule* which anſwer'd beſt to all well ſaid
By others, and which moſt *requitall* made,
Tun'd to the *higheſt Key* of *ancient* R O M E,
Returning all *her Muſique* with *his owne*,
In *whom* with *Nature*, *Studie* claim'd a part,
And yet *who* to *himſelfe* ow'd all his *Art*:
Heere lies BEN: IOHNSON, every *Age* will looke
With *ſorrew* heere, with *wonder* on *his* BOOKE.

E 2 Who

Godolphin's elegy on Ben Jonson as it appeared in Jonsonus Virbius *(1638); a collection of memorial poems by Jonson's friends*

wiser east," prompted a response from Godolphin. His "Replye" – "Unhappy East (not in that awe / you pay your Lords, whose will is law)" – seems to agree with Waller that the East is happy in the absolute power of its lords ("tyrants" in Waller) but unhappy in its treatment of women. Godolphin nicely disputes the presumed status and power of tyrannical, love-engendering women. Waller sees gallants in his society as bending to a female idol; Godolphin pleads the pleasures of enslavement to female beauty.

That Godolphin was nurtured by Jonson, both in his poetry and in his ethical understanding, is readily concluded from the elegy published in *Jonsonus Virbius*. In "The Muses fairest light," Godolphin describes the master as "The Voice most eccho'd by consenting Men." Godolphin's elegant sonnet is remarkable for a circumstance no doubt unforeseen by the author. On all extant copies of the 1638 edition, his name has been eliminated on page 27 (mispaginated) by a very heavy double line

of a printer's ornament which occurs nowhere else in the volume. The cause of this is unknown, and the question of how many copies of the 1638 printing were similarly treated is unanswered. Although his name is blotted out on page 27 of the copy owned by the British Library (c. 116.b.17), Godolphin's name is included in a contemporary manuscript list of contributors on the verso of the title page.

Whether Godolphin really knew Jonson personally or was sealed of the Tribe of Ben has been doubted, but even cautious Weber concludes that "it is indeed quite likely that Godolphin sat with the rest at the feet of Ben." Other evidence that supports Godolphin's membership in the Tribe (evidence judged to be dubious by Weber) is Falkland's own noble elegy in *Jonsonus Virbius*, "An Eglogue on the Death of Ben Iohnson, betweene Melybœus and Hylas," and Sir John Suckling's "A Sessions of the Poets." In the Falkland elegy Hylas, requested by Melybœus to commemorate Ben, protests, as Falkland might have done, not only his inadequacy, but his rusticity, and urges the superior qualifications of the urban and academic sophisticates:

> But from the *Academies, Courts,* and *Townes;*
> Let *Digby, Carew, Killigrew,* and *Maine,*
> *Godolphin, Waller,* that inspired *Traine,*
> Or whose rare *Pen* beside deserves the *grace,*
> Or of an *equall,* or a neighbouring *Place,*
> Answer thy *wish.*

This might be construed as referring to the city court of Ben, but Waller informed John Aubrey that, although he knew Falkland, Godolphin, Hobbes, and the others, he did not know Jonson. Jasper Mayne's sphere of influence centered on Christ Church College, Oxford. And although Falkland was inclined to stress his rural *convivium philosophicum* (philosophical circle), he was known to have met as a member of an informal club with Sir Francis Wenman, William Chillingworth, Waller, and Godolphin in London, as is reported by Percival Stockdale in his *Life* of Waller (1772).

In "A Sessions of the Poets" Suckling imagines a large gathering at which Apollo tries the wits of aspiring laureates. It includes Falkland, "gone with divinity," and some members of Great Tew, John Hales and Chillingworth, who were not known as poets. Jonson, of course, looms large. Among the many lesser pretenders

> in the court was hid
> One that Apollo soon miss'd, little Sid;
> And having spied him, call'd him out of the throng,
> And advis'd him in his ear not to write so strong.

The context allows, without certifying, the likelihood that "little Sid" was of the Tribe, though perhaps with an aura of isolation, of standing somewhat apart, just as Clarendon describes him with the Great Tew friends. William Dighton, reviewing the same instances as Weber, concludes more firmly, "we can be sure that Godolphin was one of the 'tribe of Ben.'"

What of Apollo's private advice to "little Sid"? If "strong" is understood as a property of the Donnean metaphysical line, its application to Godolphin is something of a mystery. If there is critical substance to Suckling's aperçu — rather than the adventitious rhyming of "throng" — it might be sought in contrast to Suckling's own "easy" versifying. In this respect Godolphin's poetry, despite its lack of bulk, is noteworthy for its metrical variety and, in some cases, its obscurity. The former is noted by Weber, who finds Godolphin's verse "sur-

prising" and comments that "he experimented felicitously with lines and stanzas of divers lengths and shapes." Comparing Falkland with Godolphin, Weber notices the latter's freer range. Hayward develops this theme, observing, "the technical achievements of Falkland's poetry have been correctly identified but overstressed, while those of Godolphin probably deserve more recognition."

Obscurity lurks in Godolphin's lyrics, sometimes because he proceeds in the most cerebral way, without recourse to imagery. The poet abstains from ornament; the picturesque is not part of his equipment. At other times Godolphin's obscurity may stem from the chronic incompleteness that commentators, especially Saintsbury, have noticed. One example, both incomplete and abstruse, as well as unmistakably imitating Donne, is the following second tercet of an untitled lyric on virtue and the woman (or, as Jonson might have said, the idea of woman) whom the poet addresses:

> if you are severall, you are severall soe
> that after subtle wordes A difference shew
> conceipts of one must into the other flow.

Among the Great Tew men there was a resistance to the notion of poetry as fancy, and to the *ut pictura poesis* (poetry and painting as sister arts). Godolphin demonstrates a reserve that seems to claim poetry as metrical philosophizing, in contrast to the Renaissance ideal of philosophy as poetry (or Plato as poet). Hayward sees that poetry was an element in Great Tew's wider intellectual agenda: "We can thus fairly appropriate Earle's *Microcosmographie,* most of Godolphin's poetry and some of Sandys's and Waller's, and almost the whole of Clarendon's writing."

Sandys's paraphrases express the Tew-Anglican sense of greater exegetical and topical freedom, as opposed to the stricter, more literal treatments of the Calvinist paraphrasers of the preceding decade. There are only two paraphrases of Psalms by Godolphin preserved in manuscript or print, and there is no suggestion that he attempted others. His version of Psalm 137 ("By the rivers of Babylon" in the Authorized Version) may be one of his last poems. Coltman felicitously describes the paraphrase as "the silence of poets in a desolate country" and suggests that Godolphin was voicing his foreboding.

In addition to expanding the sense of his source (probably the Authorized Version, although the Geneva version may have been consulted) almost to the point of incorporating commentary and exegesis, Godolphin's paraphrase elides some emphases. The central sense in the Hebrew psalm of captivity in Babylon is diverted into a sense of "our Ruin'd Countryes captiv'd state." Israel is not in Babylon; Babylon has erupted in Israel. Godolphin's paraphrase is close to being a contemplation on and an application of the Psalm, muting as much as possible its vivid retributory sentiments. Where, in the Authorized Version, he "that taketh and dashes thy [Babylonian] little ones against the stones" shall be "happy," Godolphin, without specifying the cause of it, sees Euphrates "purpled runn," and concludes, "thy childrens cryes will Fill the Ayre / and none shall pitty their despair."

His other paraphrase is of Psalm 141, which does not in itself suggest an occasion or a congruence with events in the poet's life such as Psalm 137 might. Although without known occasion, the paraphrase shows a different side of the poet. As if under George Herbert's influence (even though we know of no personal connection), the speaker of the psalm makes his heart a hallowed temple, and he expatiates on the "beawty of A synne" that might tempt him while, in a Platonizing vein, he differentiates himself from the "erring multitude." This phrase corresponds to the much more actively malign "men that work iniquities" in the Authorized Version. In Godolphin's version the psalmist is more likely to be misled, or beguiled, or diverted from the path, whereas in the source the wicked are a separate, present, and potently active force. Godolphin wishes to have a "ballast of just feare" — a sentiment without equivalent in the Authorized Version. The Old Testament depiction of stark confrontation is modulated in Godolphin to a suave sense of evil as residing in philosophical delusion, rather than evil as embodied in wicked men, workers of iniquity who lay snares and nets to capture him.

Godolphin was deeply concerned about paraphrasing the Bible, an activity charged with ecclesiastical and political significance. It is of interest that Godolphin commented in Sandys's *Paraphrase Upon the Divine Poems* on the absence from the volume of one of Sandys's attempts. Godolphin's poem of twenty-four triplets expressing his approbation includes three triplets (fifteen to seventeen) that refer to the suppression of the paraphrase of the Song of Songs:

Not in that ardent course, as where He woes
The Sacred Spouse, and her chast Love pursues,

With brighter flames, and with a higher Muse.
This Work had beene proportion'd to our Sight,
Had you but knowne with some allay to Write,
And not preserv'd your Authors Strength and Light

But you so crush those Odors, so dispense
Those rich perfumes, you make them too intense
And such (alas) as too much please our Sense.

That Sandys was censored at the command of Archbishop William Laud appears from the "Summa Approbationis" dated 7 November 1637 at Lambeth, which is printed in the midst of the verses of commendation in *A Paraphrase Upon the Divine Poems*. Godolphin's three verses occur in British Library MS Lansdowne 489 following a transcription of Sandys where they are titled "Y^e Judgm^{nt} off Sidney Godolphin On ye former worke not printed." It is a finely judged compliment to the senior poet.

A small number of poems appeared in published collections during Godolphin's life. To the second edition of Donne's *Poems* (1635), Godolphin contributed a worthy elegy that concentrates on Donne's preaching. In *The Making of Walton's Lives* (1958) David Novarr writes that Godolphin's elegy impressed Izaak Walton and helped to change his ensuing depictions of Donne the preacher. In 1658 *Funerals Made Cordials* appeared under John Gauden's name for the interment of Robert Rich, heir to the earldom of Warwick. In this volume Gauden, ever the opportunist, includes Godolphin's conventional, graceful, and accomplished "Epitaph upon the Lady Rich." From his earliest poetic excursions, Godolphin learned the sociable art of commemoration, which he practiced to the end of his brief career. He was never fulsome, always fastidious.

A sense of that fastidious spirit, which would turn back in a rain squall or doubt the power of love, might be conveyed by the following excerpt of an undated letter to Falkland from Godolphin, who apologizes for not being on time at a meeting with his friend, an apology hardly commensurate with the offense. It is transcribed here from Bodleian MS Locke c. 10, where it is written in a miniscule hand to the very edges of a tiny square of paper:

I meane yet to excuse myself at Burford [one of Falkland's Oxfordshire homes], but I feare least my offences w^c I pretend as ye reason of my comeing (to excuse them) will proue a secuent [sequent?] cause why I may not be soe happy as to come. I am confident I shall best excuse my self to you by waiting on [you] there, but my faults will be expiated in ye punishment: If I am constraind to stay here. If I come to you your favour will it may be giue me an innocence, If I doe not I shall satisfy ye utmost by ye torture of staying, & become innocent y^t unhappy way & noe other punishmnt can equall an offence ag^t you, but being banished from you, w^c is an unhappinesse [of] y^t nature, as it does not only disturb ye present time but recalls all y^t is past & armes our owne joys ag^t us to make us ye more miserable. But S^r since I can give oer to talk thus only by holding my peace, it seemes I make you a present of some value in resting

Your most humble servant
Sid: Godolphin

Easily the most substantial poetic work of Godolphin is his translation of book 4 of the *Aeneid*. It appeared in print first in 1658 (reprinted 1679) as *The Passion of Dido for Æneas* with Waller and Godolphin credited as the translators. Dighton, claiming more of the work for Godolphin than did Saintsbury, effectively shows that lines 1 to 454 (pages 291 to 311 in Bodleian MS Malone 13, which has no line numbers) are not, as has been supposed, the total of Godolphin's contribution. In a 1664 edition of Waller's poems, Waller's part is given as from line 455 to 585 (and subsequent editions do not claim more), after which follow 114 further lines. In the 1658 edition of *The Passion of Dido for Æneas* (unpaginated, unlined), there is simply a ¶ at the place where Waller begins and no further indicator. In a note to this edition, repeated in others, readers are informed that "this was done (all but a very little) by that incomparable person as well for virtue as wit, Mr. Sidney Godolphin, only for his own diversion." It goes on to excuse any carelessness on the ground that Godolphin had no intention of publication. In the Malone MS his name alone appears at the end. Dighton has reasonably conjectured that the whole was Godolphin's work, with one section of 113 lines reworked by Waller for publication. By 1658 Godolphin's virtue was a Royalist touchstone, and it is possible that Waller was giving thought to his political options.

Saintsbury praises the work for its heroic couplets and believes that it "ought to take much higher rank than it has usually done." There are other intrinsic values. Although book 4 of the *Aeneid* has always attracted translators for its profound pathos, it is also the locus classicus in Virgil of Epicurean philosophy as expounded in Lucretius, and therefore likely to appeal to Godolphin under the influence of Hobbes. What might seem unattractive to Godolphin is the vivid verbal painting of Virgil. Godolphin exercises his poetic translator's license precisely to diminish the picturesque and to accentuate the ethical dilemma. For instance, when Aeneas has left Dido alone in her great hall, Virgil's haunting treatment of the moon, weariness, and

sleep in "post, ubi digressi, lumenque obscura vicissim / luna premit, suadentque cadentia sidera somnos" (Afterwards, when they have parted, the moon, darkening in her turn, veils the light, and setting stars urge sleep) is rendered almost tritely as "But when the Prince (Nights darker ensignes spread, / and sleepy dew upon all mortalls shedd) doeth bid farewell." When, on the other hand, the fatal passion of Aeneas and Dido at the cave (ille dies primus leti primusque malorum / causa fuit) is rendered, Godolphin's couplet is perfect: "this was the hower which gave the fatall blow / the pregnant spring of all succeeding woe." The storm which occasions the cave scene is described by Virgil as "Interea magno misceri murmure caelum / incipit" (Meanwhile the heavens began to be confused with a great rumbling), but here Godolphin is not interested in matching Virgil's resonance: "Meane while the gathering cloudes obscure the Pole / they flash out Lightnings and in Thunder Role." Godolphin is little short of superb, however, when describing the figure of Rumor, imitating Virgil's emphatic reiterations:

> Shee (as tis sayd) was of that Monstrous birth
> the latest sister, which the teemyng earth
> producd to warr with Heaven, itt selfe alone
> surviving, all her Brothers over throwne,
> millions of Plumbs advance her easie flight
> as many eyes, enlarge her piercing sight,
> as many eares, to catch reports, and then,
> as many tongues, to spread those tales againe.

What Godolphin reads in Virgil is of the essence, and it speaks directly to what Coltman describes as Godolphin's sense of "the price of political purpose in private agony."

How close to the eruption of the Civil War Godolphin's translation was made is impossible to say. The work may express his own sense of duty, which was displayed in the crisis to come. On the other hand, his steady ethical resolve seems not to have waited on the climate of civil strife to bloom; rather it seems to have been the cast of his mature mind. Hobbes and Clarendon, while taking opposing positions on the war, both saw Godolphin as the perfect man. The virtuous man, Hobbes thought, possessed extreme courage, but also respected law, and therefore had no need of the threatening gallows, which for other men is the necessary apparatus to ensure civil quiet. Yet very few are born with such a morally generous nature. Hobbes's state is necessary as a condition in which such natures could flourish safe from stupid and random destruction. In the dedication of *Leviathan* (1651) to

Sidney's brother Francis, Hobbes succinctly puts his view:

> For there is not any vertue that disposeth a man, either to the service of God, or to the service of his Country, to Civill Society, or private Friendship, that did not manifestly appear in his conversation, not as acquired by necessity, or affected upon occasion, but as inhærent, and shining in a generous constitution of his nature.

Hobbes returns to this theme at the conclusion of *Leviathan*, arguing there is no

> repugnancy between fearing the Laws, and not fearing a publique Enemy; nor between abstaining from Injury, and pardoning it in others. There is therefore no such Inconsistence of Humane Nature, with Civill Duties, as some think. I have known cleernesse of Judgment, and largenesse of Fancy; strength of Reason, and gracefull elocution; a Courage for the Warre, and a Fear of the Laws, and all eminently in one man; and that was my most noble and honored friend Mr. *Sidney Godolphin;* who hating no man, nor hated of any, was unfortunately slain in the beginning of the late Civill warre, in the Publique quarrell, by an undiscerned, and an undiscerning hand.

As Coltman argues, Hobbes saw that Godolphin's death was the direct consequence of the liberal philosophy of the Great Tew members, notably Falkland and Clarendon with their love of constitutional monarchy, a "mixarchy," which led to inevitable war. Therefore, Coltman writes, Godolphin's death "lies at the heart of *Leviathan.*" Thus *Leviathan* is a sustained critique of Great Tew by one who, as much as they did, hated civil war. Yet Falkland and Godolphin stayed and were among those who paid with their lives, while Hobbes, with his more portable philosophy, was the first to leave.

Godolphin – lover of pure reason, soldier of justice and truth, and worthy to be loved – is commemorated again by Hobbes in his autobiography in Latin verse: "Godolphine jaces; puræ rationis amator, / Justitiæ et Vei miles amande, vale" (You lie here, Godolphin, lover of pure reason, a soldier in the cause of justice and truth, worthy to be loved, farewell). In this same account Hobbes recalls fleeing the country, his subsequent impoverishment, and his gratitude for a two-hundred-pound legacy from Godolphin.

The man who informed Hobbes of this bequest was Clarendon, who recalls the fact in his *A Brief View and Survey of the Dangerous and pernicious Errors to Church and State, in Mr. Hobbes's Book, Entitled Leviathan* (1676), in which he minutely and tenaciously disputes Hobbes's doctrines point by point.

Clarendon reminds Hobbes that it was he who introduced Hobbes to Godolphin, "whose memory he [Hobbes] seems most to extol." Clarendon concludes his book on *Leviathan* as Hobbes had in the original, with a tribute to Godolphin, just after he judges Hobbes guilty of "Sedition, Treason, and Impiety":

> And I would be very willing to preserve the just testimony which he gives to the memory of *Sidney Godolphin* who deserved all the Eulogy that he gives him, and whose untimely loss in the beginning of the War, was too lively an instance of the inequality of the contention, when such inestimable Treasure was ventur'd against dirty people of no name, and whose irreparable loss was lamented by all men living who pretend to Virtue, how much divided soever in the prosecution of that quarrel.

Then Clarendon, as he confesses, yields to the temptation of drawing a comparison:

> of all men living, there were no two more unlike then Mr. *Godolphin* and Mr. *Hobbes*, in the modesty of nature, or integrity of manners; and therefore it will be too reasonably suspected, that the freshness of the Legacy rather put him in mind of that Noble Gentleman, to mention him in the fag-end of his Book very unproperly, and in a huddle of many unjustifiable and wicked particulars.

Saintsbury remarks that to "be praised by Clarendon *and* Hobbes is indeed to have your name struck in double bronze."

Godolphin was slain in an early predawn skirmish on Wednesday, 9 February 1643, in the small town of Chagford in the West Country, where the parliamentary forces, which had earlier scattered at the approach of the Royalists, had regrouped. It was, as Clarendon put it, "by a too forward engagement" that Godolphin rode into musket fire and was mortally wounded. The 11 February entry of *Speciall Passages and Certain Informations from severall places* includes a report made by the parliamentary force at Exeter. The report describes the courageous resistance to the Cavaliers and records that one of the five or six killed was "Captain Cadolphin," who died a day after receiving his wounds. Clarendon reports him killed instantly. Godolphin was buried in the chancel of Okehampton Church on 10 February, but no memorial exists, and the church was burned down in the nineteenth century. In his *Life*, Clarendon elaborates the circumstances: "without saying any word more, than Oh God! I am hurt he fell dead from his horse; to the excessive grief of his friends, who were all that knew him; and the irreparable damage of the public." The Royalist commander Sir Ralph Hopton called him "a Gentleman never to bee forgotten ... as perfect, and as absolute piece of vertue as ever our Nation bredd." Soon after Godolphin, Sir Bevil Grenville was killed. The four notable Cornishmen lost in these early stages of the Western campaign are commemorated in an anonymous rhyme: "Grenville, Godolphin, Trevanion, Slanning slain, / The four wheels of Charles' wain."

In David Lloyd's *Memoires* (1668) is the following obituary:

> Col. *Sidney Godolphin*, descended of the most ancient Family both of Love and Wit; murdered by those men that professed to destroy Wit and Learning; and at that time when men were not allowed to wear Hair, much less Bays. A Gentleman that will live as long as Virgil, whom he hath translated; and as long as the best Times best Wit[s] [marginal note: "As Donne, &c."] whom he hath commended as elegantly as he was commended by them."

Such men, Lloyd concludes, are "Treasures of Arms and Arts; men equally fit for Colledge and Camp."

Though Godolphin left several legacies, including that to Hobbes, the largest was to Jane Berkeley – one thousand pounds, which he desired his brother to pay "with what conveniency he can." Aubrey records that she was "cosen german" to Godolphin and "also his mistresse. He loved her exceedingly."

References:

Elisabeth Dimont, *Godolphin Family Portraits, 1610–1781* (Salisbury: Dimont, 1987);

Hugh Elliot, *The Life of Sidney, Earl of Godolphin, K. G. Lord High Treasurer of England 1702 to 1710* (London & New York: Longmans, Green, 1888);

Edward Hyde, *The History of the Rebellion and Civil Wars in England*, 6 volumes, edited by W. Dunn Macray (Oxford: Clarendon Press, 1888);

Hyde, *The Life of Edward Earl of Clarendon*, 2 volumes (Oxford: Clarendon Press, 1857).

Papers:
The majority of Godolphin's lyrics and his Virgil are contained in the Bodleian Library MS Malone 13, which is a poetic miscellany in a good scribal hand, and in British Library MS Harleian 6917, a similar miscellany with poems by many contemporaries. The Harleian MS includes a poem not found in any other collection. A third collection, the Drinkwater MS (described in William Dighton's 1931 edition of Godolphin), is in the hand of the poet's nephew William. There are verses by Godolphin in British Library MS Lansdowne 489, and Bodleian MS Locke c. 10 includes a holograph letter.

William Habington

(4 November 1605 – 30 December 1654)

Raymond A. Anselment
University of Connecticut

BOOKS: *Castara. The first part* (London: Printed by Anne Griffin for William Cooke, 1634);

Castara. The second Edition. Corrected and Augmented (London: Printed by B. Alsop & T. Fawcet for William Cooke, 1635);

Castara. The third Edition. Corrected and augmented (London: Printed by T. Cotes for Will. Cooke, 1640);

The Queene of Arragon: A Tragi-Comedie (London: Printed by Tho. Cotes for William Cooke, 1640);

The Historie of Edward the Fovrth, King of England (London: Printed by Tho. Cotes for William Cooke, 1640); republished as *Praeces Principum, or The President of Illustrious Princes* (London: Printed & sold by John Place, 1659);

Observations Vpon historie (London: Printed by T. Cotes for William Cooke, 1641).

Editions: "The Poems of William Habington," in volume 6 of *The Works of English Poets, From Chaucer to Cowper,* edited by Alexander Chalmers (London: J. Johnson, 1810), pp. 437–482;

Habington's Castara, edited by Charles A. Elton (Bristol: J. M. Gutch, 1812);

William Habington. Castara. The Third Edition of 1640, edited by Edward Arber, English Reprints no. 22 (London: A. Murray, 1870);

The Poems of William Habington, edited by Kenneth Allott (Liverpool: University Press of Liverpool, 1948).

PLAY PRODUCTION: *The Queene of Arragon,* London, Whitehall, 9–10 April 1640.

OTHER: "*In Hymeneum Ingeniosissimi* Iacobi Shirley," in James Shirley, *The Wedding* (London: Printed by J. Okes for J. Grove, 1629);

"To his noble Friend, th' Author on his Tragedy of *Albouine,*" in William Davenant, *The Tragedy of Albovine* (London: Printed by F. Kingston for R. Moore, 1629);

"To my friend the Author," in James Shirley, *The Gratefull Servant* (London: Printed by B. Alsop & T. Fawcet for J. Grove, 1630);

"An Elegie upon the Death of Ben Johnson, the most excellent of English *Poets,*" in *Ionsonvs Virbivs; Or, The Memorie of Ben: Johnson Revived By the Friends of the Muses* (London: Printed by E. Purslowe for Henry Seile, 1638);

"To my Friend, *Will. Davenant,*" in William Davenant, *Madagascar; With Other Poems* (London: Printed by J. Haviland for T. Walkley, 1638);

"On Master John Fletchers Dramaticall Poems," in Francis Beaumont and John Fletcher, *Comedies and Tragedies* (London: Printed for Humphrey Robinson & Humphrey Mosely, 1647).

Among the many talented Caroline writers, William Habington no longer enjoys his seventeenth-century reputation. The eldest son of a Worcestershire family with significant Catholic loyalties, Habington married into a family with important London and court influences. His name may not have been among the wits of the 1630s singled out in Sir John Suckling's "A Sessions of the Poets"; but by the time this poem was written in 1637, two editions of Habington's *Castara* (1634, 1635) and his various commendatory poems had confirmed his position as an established and well-connected author. Before the civil crisis of 1642 dispelled the halcyon calm of Charles I's reign and curbed its growing toleration of Catholicism, Habington expanded another edition of *Castara* (1640), wrote a well-received play, and published two works of history. Together with his earlier poetry these pieces complete the development of a distinctive sensibility, one that reflects in varied form literary concerns central to the 1630s and 1640s.

Soon after his birth at Hindlip Hall on 4 November 1605, the day before Guy Fawkes was discovered amid the barrels of gunpowder intended to blow up the houses of Parliament, Habington's parents, Thomas and Mary, were caught up in the af-

Southeast view of Habington's birthplace, Hindlip Hall, as it appeared in 1776 (engraving by J. Ross). The house has since been destroyed.

termath of the Catholic conspiracy and their rural lives disrupted. The Habington estate, located on a rise about three miles northeast of Worcester, had long been among the Catholic sanctuaries in the Midlands. Thomas's father, John Habington, had rebuilt the manor house on land purchased in the 1560s, and within a decade this official of Queen Elizabeth's household made it the central residence for his family. Little is known about the middle son, Thomas, other than his attendance at Oxford and his study on the Continent and at the Inns of Court, until he was implicated with his older brother, Edward, in Anthony Babington's plot to assassinate the queen and to support Mary, Queen of Scots. Thomas escaped the fate Edward suffered on 20 September 1586 as a condemned traitor, probably because the evidence of his involvement was not as damning. As the heir to his father's diminished estates he resided at Hindlip Hall after six years imprisonment in the Tower of London. His marriage in 1593 to Mary Parker, the eldest daughter of Edward Parker, tenth Baron Morley, and the sister of William Parker, fourth Lord Monteagle, bound Thomas by marriage to those who would play central roles in the unfolding Gunpowder Plot; his residence at Hindlip

also involved him in the later events. The house had become a network of hiding places designed to conceal priests; and with the failure of the Gunpowder Plot to overthrow the government, Jesuit Superior Father Henry Garnett and others sought safety in Hindlip Hall. Their discovery after long, intensive search of the house once again implicated Thomas Habington in treasonable action.

Although Thomas narrowly escaped death a second time, his trial, sentence, and reprieve deeply affected this country family. His brother-in-law Lord Monteagle, who had brought to King James I the letter warning of the Gunpowder Plot, exerted considerable influence on Habington's behalf, and his life was spared. Under the terms of the reprieve Habington's lands were forfeited to the Crown for forty years, and his freedom to leave Worcestershire was restrained. Eventually the family regained the titles to the land, and Thomas Habington settled into a life of antiquarian studies, but his altered circumstances touched his five children. While not much is certain about William's childhood and early development, the position of the family among the recusants and their legacy of involvement in the intrigues of power may well have shaped the later conflict in his writing between engagement and withdrawal. And even if the young William ignored accounts of the crown-shaped grass that allegedly appeared quite miraculously on the grounds of Hindlip Hall after the execution of its hidden priests, he lived with the financial and social restraints that were the heritage of his family's association with the civil crisis.

The meager biographical evidence of William Habington's early years suggests an education heavily influenced by his family heritage. According to the seventeenth-century biographer Anthony Wood in the 1721 edition of *Athenæ Oxoniensis,* the young Habington received his formal education on the Continent, first in northern France at the Jesuit College of St. Omer and then in Paris. A paragraph and marginal note in James Wadsworth's *The English Spanish Pilgrime* (1629) corroborates Wood's suggestion that the priests at St. Omer tried unsuccessfully to enroll William in their order, though the bias so apparent in Wadsworth's portraits of the guileful Jesuits may qualify the accuracy of the account. After William allegedly escaped from his seductive teachers and spent an undetermined time in Paris, he returned to Worcestershire where, Wood reports, "being then at man's estate, he was instructed at home in matters of history by his father, and became an accomplish'd gentleman." A marginal entry in Wadsworth's book limits the son's tuition at Hindlip: "This Gentleman liues now in *England* at his Fathers house in *Holborne.*" The publication of Habington's first poems in 1629 among the commendatory pieces for James Shirley's *The Wedding* and William Davenant's *The Tragedy of Albovine* suggests that Habington by then had become a part of the London literary scene.

Shirley and Davenant were both associated with Gray's Inn, the same Inn of Court where Thomas Habington had earlier studied law; his son William may have followed his father's tradition. While no admission records place him at any of the Inns of Court, a later poem, "In praise of the City Life, in the long Vacation," implies an intimate acquaintance with the London world of law. Habington's first two poems, in any case, confirm the social and literary contexts that characterize the next decade of his writing. Neither of the poems, both brief and rather perfunctory, is distinguishable from the commendatory fare increasingly expected in the seventeenth century; both, however, link him with writers who would become through their masques, plays, and poems significant Caroline voices. Along with the other noteworthy commender Edward Hyde and perhaps in the company of the Gray's Inn group that included John Suckling, the Catholic country poet appeared comfortably established in the urbane literary and legal world of London. A year later in another commendatory poem, he confidently proclaimed "my friend" James Shirley, the author of *The Gratefull Servant* (1630), a worthy heir of Ben Jonson's dramatic muse.

Habington first pursued his own muse at length and anonymously with the 1634 publication of *Castara.* The author who prefaces the two-part collection of eighty-nine poems with the modest hope that his verses are "not so high, as to be wondred at, nor so low as to be contemned," disavows from the outset any apparent pattern in "what fancie had scattered in many loose papers." His is avowedly a chaste muse that refuses wanton strains and effeminate wit. "And though I appeare to strive against the streame of best wits, in erecting the self same Altar, both to chastity and love," the author insists, "I will for once adventure to doe well, without a president." Castara, or his chaste altar, is at once the object and the means of worship, the beloved and the loved. The rites of chaste love the poet-priest initiates in the opening sonnets to Castara celebrate the sacrifice and adoration of the heart in a new religion of love.

The transcendent, ineffable "starre" and "Queene of my love" paradoxically inspires a distinctly immediate celebration. The Castara celebrated directly and indirectly in all the eighty-nine sonnets, odes, dialogues, epistles, and elegies of the first edition assumes a biographical presence different from the Stellas, Amorets, Lucastas, and Sacharissas enshrined in Elizabethan and seventeenth-century love poetry. Despite the occasional oxymoron reminiscent of the conventionalized lover's plight, the hopes and fears of forced partings and an uncertain future reflect an actual courtship that ended with Habington's marriage in early 1633 to Lucy Herbert, a younger daughter of William Herbert, first Baron Powis. Though the beloved Castara and her suitor Araphill are never openly identified as Lucy Herbert and William Habington, other poems addressed to Endymion Porter, George Talbot, Lady Eleanor Powis, and Lord Powis express the joys and misgivings of the lyrical addresses to Castara. Early in the sequence epistles to Habington's friends exalt the wondrous nature of this unidentified Castara and concede the obstacles to a successful match. The poet also assures Castara that Hindlip Hall "(though not magnificent)" will become through her presence more fabulous than the mythic abodes of fiction, but subsequent dialogues recognize that the realities of wealth, social standing, and "Parents lawes" cannot be ignored. When Castara departs to "Faire *Seymors*," the manor house Lord and Lady Powis acquired in 1633, more than distance transforms the beautiful setting into "unkinde *Seymors*." The lament in another piece, "To Castara, Being debarr'd her presence," gives literal dimension to the poem's conventional hyperbole "Banisht from you" and to the complaint in the following sonnet about the "sad Fate" that denies "My prophane feete accesse." At greater length an address to Lucy Herbert's mother confronts the parental resistance implicit in the series, asserting the wealth of mutual love and disavowing any interest in family lineage or fortune. In the second part of *Castara* a similar poem – addressed to Lucy's father, affirming disinterest in "wealth or blood" and asking his blessing – implies Lucy married without Lord Powis's approval. The second part celebrates the mutual fulfillment of Araphill and Castara's first year together. Through Castara's ensuing sickness and a resulting awareness of mortality, husband and wife share a contentment that dispels earlier fears and uncertainties. Unlike the other Renaissance love sequences, which tend to leave relationships inconclusive or unfulfilled, the two parts of *Castara* resolve with unusual immediacy and conviction the social realities of unrequited love.

Its biographical dimensions give substance to the ideals embodied in the relationship between Araphill and Castara. In the guise of their characters as well as in propria persona Habington celebrates a spiritual love that challenges definition. In answer to the question posed in the poem "To Castara, Inquiring why I loved her," the speaker dismisses virtue, beauty, birth, and fortune; "something from above" transfixes him with its fire. Perhaps playing on the name Lucy, the poems liken Castara to light: she is the flame, the star that consumes, inspires, and guides. Hers is not the sorceress's magic or the rapture that enflames courtiers; heaven's "brightest Saint," she is the epitome of all that ambition yearns to possess. Often the "Deity of her sex" appears as the essential being of nature, a force that transforms harsh elements and instills new life. In the last poem of the first part Habington attempts to be more precise. "The Description of Castara" sketches in the abstract terms of virtue the portrait of a modest, reserved, and self-possessed woman obedient to wisdom and devoted to heaven.

United in matrimony, Araphill and Castara celebrate their transcendent fulfillment in the second part. He declares he would forsake Earth and in the ecstasy of their mutual fire shine unrivaled among the stars.

But as time-bound lovers who recognize their marriage will be perfected only in heaven, husband and wife become increasingly aware that "Love in himselfe's a world." Metaphors of sailing lead to the "blest Port" where the two lovers, anchored in virtue and safe from the storms of court, find in each other a new paradise. In this newfound land the lovers can withdraw from the toil of ambition and reign absolute in the "happiest Empire." The only tribute they require is the homage other couples pay on their day of marriage when they invoke in their ceremonies the way to similar bliss.

The rites in this religion of love are unmistakably offered at the "shrine of chastity." The lovers are chaste in the seventeenth-century sense of *caritas* (charity) and in the figurative sense of flames without "wanton heate." When the speaker insists that Castara's radiant soul would inspire the chaste moon to burn brighter or proposes that her chaste charms would turn Adonis into a "modest wanton in your armes," the understanding of "chaste desires" is neither oxymoronic nor priggish. The penultimate poem in the first part, "To Castara. Of the chastity of his Love," elevates the couple's passion above the desires of traditional love sonnets and likens the "zealous fire" to a celestial conjunction. In the second part chastity remains a welcome haven among the figurative islands of a blissful marriage whose fruitful union was hardly celibate. Habington recalls the innocence of a love distinct from that of "wilder youth, whose soule is sense." Near the end of the first edition, however, the poem "Against them who lay unchastity to the sex of Women" – a response to John Donne's "Goe, and Catche a Falling Starre" – expresses a broader interpretation of chastity. When Habington challenges "Who ever dare, / Affirme no woman chaste and faire" with the example of Castara, he conflates chastity and fidelity in his alteration of the Donnean line "Nowhere / Lives a woman true, and fair." He broadens his interpretation in a later piece that likens the couple's embrace to the union of angels, "For we no love obey / That's bastard to a fleshly touch." Elsewhere Habington recognizes that an angelic love without sense can be found only in the heavenly union of the mind; here he insists only that love not become subservient to the senses. Chastity in the view of the poem frees love from the mutable and marks its virtuous nature.

The sonnets to Castara opening the second part help clarify Habington's intention. The poems pair the love of Araphill for Castara with that of Charles I for Henrietta Maria: "Each wisely chuse, and chastely love a wife." The first edition of *Castara* in effect shows that "loyall subjects, must true lovers be." The poems reflect the rites of love elaborately celebrated in the Caroline masques. Several years before the publication of *Castara,* Ben Jonson's *Love's Triumph through Callipolis* (published, 1630; performed, 1631) and *Chloridia* (1631) initiated the praise of the king and queen that would inform the vision throughout the 1630s: "Love is the right affection of the mind / The noble appetite of what is best." The circle of love symbolizes in the royal couple's "world of chaste desires" a perfection celebrated in the tributes of later masques to the conjugal virtue that has made Britain "the Temple of Chaste Love." When Charles and Henrietta Maria took roles in the productions at the Banqueting House, the mythic and historical, the abstract and the real became in the magic of the spectacle indistinguishable. The embodiment of Habington's love similarly personalizes the ideal. Castara's mythic persona rivals the transcendence of her Whitehall counterpart: Habington's queen of love also becomes a wondrous force of change venerated through a similar adoration.

The Caroline rites of love that might appeal especially to a Catholic sensibility are not, however, the only source of Habington's vision; his faith in the miracle of mutual love remains very Donnean. Phrases from the earlier poet reveal Habington's knowledge of the Donne poems published posthumously in 1633, and the indebtedness to specific works is also apparent. In an epistle to his cousin Henry Parker the similarities to Donne's "The Canonization" suggest in particular the exaltation of love common in *Castara.* The lovers whose souls have become one merit in the miraculousness of the transformation the adoration Donne defiantly accords his saints of love who also turn away from mundane court ambitions and social gains. Even more emphatically than the earlier poet, Habington envisions for his married lovers the enclosed world that in Donne's "The Good-morrow" and "The Sunne Rising" defies an alien everyday existence. Though the celebration of Habington's first year of marriage in "Loves Anniversarie" falls short of Donne's "The Anniversarie," it and other poems in *Castara* espouse the same faith in an endless love indifferent to the threats of time.

The vision is developed, however, with little sense of Donne's Metaphysical wit; nor are the poems noticeably sensitive to earlier poetic influences. By the 1630s the sonnet was no longer a mainstay of love poetry, and Habington refused for the most part to be bound by its constraints. Only one of the fifty-four sonnets in the first edition develops a traditional rhyme scheme; the rest are couplets that tend to put a premium on a final turn. While their language betrays vestiges of Petrarchan diction and their limited epigrammatic closure plays with words, the similar images and rhythms are not characterized by witty intensity. The epistles develop the couplets in still looser fashion, catching occasionally a note of Ben Jonson's voice with none of his rhetorical and moral weightiness. Habington is most successful with shorter lines and varied forms, at times achieving the Caroline hallmarks of grace and ease. Often his touch is less deft, and usually he is more earnest, but a pair of poems on Castara's cheeks, for example, is as playful and delicately fanciful as Thomas Carew or Robert Herrick in a similar vein.

Seriousness is increasingly apparent in the second edition of *Castara,* which identifies the author for the first time in George Talbot's commendatory poem, "To his best friend and Kinsman *William Habington* Esquire." Four poems added near the end of the first section of this 1635 publication and eighteen new pieces before the final poem of the second part reinforce Habington's tendency toward introspection and disengagement. Each of the two parts now begins with an appropriate prose character, "A Mistris" and "A Wife," that embodies in specific terms the abstract ideals of womanhood. The companionship and security valued especially in the prose portrait of the desirable wife, who is "so true a friend" and "a safe retrying place," are reemphasized in the prose description of "A Friend," which precedes the concluding collection of eight elegies addressed to his kinsman George Talbot.

Though Castara no longer commands central attention in all the poems, the growing importance of withdrawal and contemplation enhances her value. The poet fated to the "humble quiet" of his shade welcomes the "sweete content" he and Castara enjoy in virtuous love and questions the vanity of ambitious struggles for glory. At their most abstract moments the poems celebrate a rarefied state of oneness beyond the lovers' understanding. Chaste virtue enflames a love elevated among the celestial lights, but a musing note gives philosophical weight to the celebratory tone. Time and mortality move the poet to contemplate the lost past and the certain grave. Against the inevitable and absolute, Habington asserts his faith in an "endlesse and intire" love that admits age but not decline. The last of the new poems to Castara, "What Lovers will say when she and he are dead," con-

*Engraved title page for the third edition of William Habington's
collection of love poems*

cludes that love must also die with the "chaste influence" achieved through "Loves Religion."

The poems addressed to others and not immediately preoccupied with love continue to express Habington's intensified awareness of vanity and mortality. With the exception of the poem to his wife's cousin Lucy Hay, Countess of Carlisle, which vies with many contemporary works in the praise of this influential court figure, Habington's epistles ponder the purposeful life and the threat of time. Perhaps the example of his father, Habington's marriage to Lucy, and his own experiences

in London encouraged a natural tendency toward introspection; certainly the reaction to court and the attraction of retirement reflect a humanist education deeply rooted in classical tradition. Habington embraces the serene life of contemplation Maren-Sofie Røstvig discusses in *The Happy Man* (1954): his epistles reflect the spirit of Horace in themes later common during the Civil War. The Horatian underpinnings are most evident in the tribute to Archibald Campbell, seventh Earl of Argyll. Later Richard Lovelace would turn to the same poem from Horace's second book of odes and its sailing imagery to counsel similar moderation to his brother. Habington recognizes the tension between engagement and disengagement that vexed both the Roman Stoics and the Renaissance humanists, but he instinctively prefers the private to the public life. With a Jonsonian authority not heard in his earlier poems, here and in other epistles of the 1635 edition he praises the "moderate minde, bounteous state," and "inward peace" found in the contentment of obscurity and solitude. The journey inward promises "a whole world within" safe from the rock and shelf that wreck the ambitious adventurer. Weighing the "dull solitude" of the country against the "busy cares" of the city, the best of the poems in this vein chooses the meditative solitude extolled in the epistle "To my noblest Friend, I. C. Esquire." Its desire "to grow all soule" is not a denial of reality but an ideal that inspires the enlightened mind to accept the inevitable journey through time.

The weight of mortality, which must have overwhelmed Habington with the death in 1634 of his closest friend and kinsman, George Talbot, is evident in these epistles and in the later poems to Castara. The series of eight elegies is not the poet's first effort in this genre. When the cousin of his wife's mother died in May 1633, Habington joined the painter Sir Anthony Van Dyck and many poets in commemorating the sudden death of Venetia Digby. Though the elegy consoling Castara on the death of her relative is far less ambitious than the sequence Jonson sent to Venetia's famous husband, the poem warrants the passing notice it receives in a modern biography of Kenelm Digby. The delicacy and gentleness that lessen the harshness of death distinguish the poem from perfunctory eulogy. The tone is less moving and the resolve more predictable in other elegies on the deaths of the ninth earl of Shrewsbury and Henry Campbell, the son of the seventh earl of Argyll. Habington refuses to pursue in the second poem questions raised with some feeling about the unjustness of death; the certainty of death, however, remains very much on his mind in the subsequent poem to Castara included with the elegy in the additions to the second edition. Habington struggles with the reality of death at length when he confronts the loss of his closest friend.

The eight poems express a numbing grief reminiscent of Donne's meditations on the death of Elizabeth Drury. The loss and emptiness in Habington's elegies are not developed through the witty hyperbole of *The Anniversaries* (1611, 1612), but the memory of the lost friend moves the mourner to a similar understanding of the virtuous

soul. Out of inexpressible sorrow emerges a tribute to virtue like that idealized in the earlier parts of *Castara*. George Talbot displaces Castara as the source of light and the star of guidance. The intimate friend who apparently died with Habington's name on his lips becomes the virtuous mind freed from a world that is lost in ambition and glory. In their resolution the poems ultimately turn to the hope that the light is not eclipsed in death and will illuminate the way for those who continue their journeys in the darkness of error. The elegiac consolation of the poem does not dispel, however, its poignancy; Habington recognizes that language neither expresses fully nor resolves completely his grief.

But the bereaved writer did not abandon poetry and withdraw into the solitude he cherished. Before he completed in 1640 the final edition of *Castara,* Habington seems to have been quite involved in the Caroline world. With the important influence of his wife's relative Philip Herbert, fourth Earl of Pembroke, Habington unsuccessfully competed in 1636 for the new position as Henrietta Maria's representative to the papal court. In 1638 he also contributed poems to the volume memorializing the death of Ben Jonson and to the edition of William Davenant's *Madagascar.* His contribution to *Jonsonus Virbius* has none of the critical acuity that occasionally distinguishes a poem such as the one contributed by William Cartwright. Habington instead grants Jonson the praise accorded Castara and Talbot: Jonson is the soul that guides the vessel of drama through now stormy seas. Habington's less exalted commendation of Davenant sustains a judicious personal tone not found in the verses Porter, Carew, and Suckling also wrote for the publication of *Madagascar.* Habington's celebration of the future poet laureate also compliments without the cutting, self-conscious wit of Carew and Suckling. It appears that Habington was at ease in the world of urbane camaraderie and not aloof from the centers of power. The publication in 1640 of both a new edition of *Castara* and a well-received play, *The Queene of Arragon,* confirmed his position.

Habington's final collection of verse expands the previous edition into a third part, a group of twenty-two new poems introduced by a prose character asserting that holiness is the only happiness. From the outset the prose characterization "A Holy Man" forthrightly proclaims that "Catholique faith is the foundation on which he erects Religion," but the religion of the holy man is not necessarily Catholic. Habington's prose discourages "private spirit" as well as "opinionated judgment" and acknowledges the obedience due the magistrate; rebellion even in the name of personal conscience is "neverthelesse high treason." An epistle to Sir Henry Percy approving his willingness to join the forces of King Charles I assembled in 1639 later states that the essential conflict remains the inward battle against the enemies threatening the soul. The holy man who triumphs spiritually possesses in the prose characterization the ideals of Stoicism and moderation lauded in the earlier editions; meditation and devotion are for him foremost, and death is an indifferent concern.

The meditative and devout tenor of the new poems sustains some of Habington's best poetry. Although the occasional epistle still warns against the vanities of ambition and counsels safety from the dangerous heights and tumultuous seas, the contemplation of time focuses with lyrical intensity on passages from the Bible and emblems from nature. The poet who would soar above the "humble flight of carnall love" and become one with the celestial finds in the rose or in a line from the Psalms renewed inspiration with which to combat a growing preoccupation with death. In the book of nature unfolded in Habington's "Nox nocti indicat Scientiam," the stars speak in silent wisdom about the impermanence of Earth. Exhorting his soul to imagine "thou and I" upon "our frighted deathbed," Habington vividly envisions in another meditation the fearful scene that he must one day enact before he is then forgotten. And turning in "Laudate Dominum de caelis" to the heavenly spirits already liberated by death, he longs for the celestial joy denied the fearful caught in the "sad length of Time." His fear is not merely that he will cease to be; the Psalms remind him of the eternal hell that may one day seize his soul. When Habington asks near the end of the collection "where have I wandred," he attempts to put his search for fulfillment into perspective. The phases of his life summarized in the stanzas of "Cogitabo pro peccato meo" recall the poet's early admiration for Edmund Spenser and Sir Philip Sidney, the verse sacrificed to his beloved, and his later interest in political advancement; all have led to an awareness of "How fraile is life, how vaine a breath / Opinion, how uncertaine death." The waste of time weighs heavily in the next poem, and tears of repentance are his only solace. In the end sober disdain enables him in "Cupio dissolvi" to embrace death as both a retreat from the delusions of time and the way to spiritual fulfillment.

The heavenly fires that will refine his soul are not the light celebrated in the first parts of the edition. The inward illumination of grace replaces the light of Castara, and she assumes no importance in the final part of the collection. Devotion to God and celestial love are not, however, completely distinct from temporal love. Although Habington never endorses a Platonic belief in the *scala d'amore* or ladder of love, he does suggest that the love for Lucy Herbert as well as the friendship and death of George Talbot have illuminated for him the essential value of existence. While Lucy's figurative light is not a substitute for the divine, its celebration expresses a religious yearning for the absolute.

Habington's other major literary work, *The Queene of Arragon,* reformulates for the stage issues central to *Castara.* The earl of Pembroke figured prominently in its publication; for if he did not, as Wood asserts, cause its publication "against the author's will," he provided the actors and paid for the elaborate staging at Whitehall on 9 April 1640. After a second performance for the king and queen, the play was produced at Blackfriars and appeared anonymously in print. The work described on the title page as "Tragi-Comedie" dramatizes a complicated variation of Lucy Herbert's conflict between the obligations to family and to self. Queen Cleodora, who resists the Aragonian subjects' attempts to choose her husband, finds the fate of her reign inextricably involved with her three suitors. The leader of the civil unrest, Decastro, challenges her private right to determine her marriage with her public obligation to the country. Though he has the support of the people, who fear the queen's involvement with a foreigner, his willingness to encourage civil rebellion compromises the selflessness of his avowed love. No taint of ambition motivates the general of the Castilian forces, Florentio, who repeats almost verbatim Habington's words to Lucy's mother when he assures the queen he is drawn to her virtuous person and not to her position. The attempt of the disguised king of Castile, Ascanio, to persuade the queen to see among men no distinction other than virtue also echoes Habington's earlier poems in its striking advocacy of nobility and contentment indifferent to artificial divisions of social class. On a lighter, satiric note the sharp tongue and wit of Cleantha, a lady at court, and the forced attentions of Sanmartino, a foppish cavalier, parody in the subplot the rapacity and vacuity of modish court behavior and its language of love.

Decastro and Ascania relinquish their suits and the queen is free to marry Florentino in a climactic scene that dramatizes Habington's concern with correct governance in affairs of state and heart. When Decastro pledges the loyalty of his supporters and the queen promises to honor his demands,

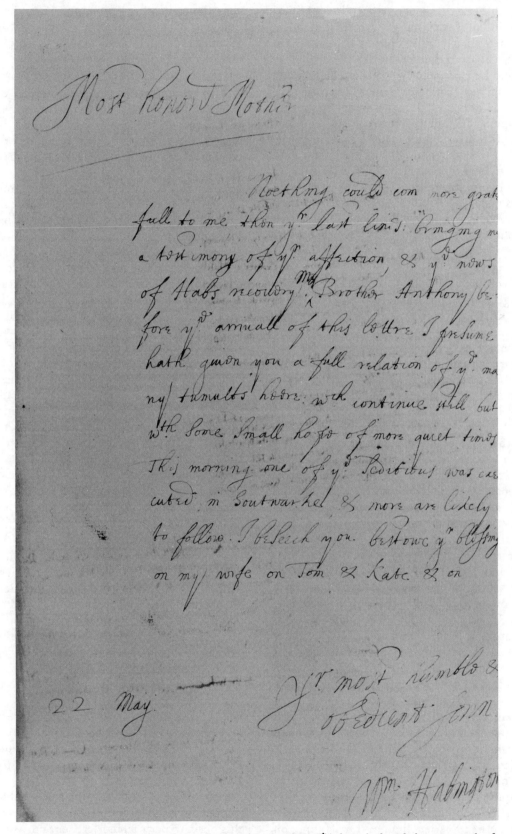

Letter from Habington to his mother, probably written in 1640. This letter is the only known example of the poet's handwriting (Library of the Society of Antiquaries, MS 145, item 33: f. 337ᵛ).

he returns to her a blank charter. Modern political interpretation of this exchange stresses the radical idea that the monarch rules only by the consent of the people. Cleodora does paradoxically ensure her freedom and independence when she seems willing to limit them, but Habington's later historical writing in no way endorses Decastro's contention that "The people's suffrage . . . inaugurates princes." The resolution of the play instead stresses in the public policy of state a mutual trust essential also to the private sphere of love. Decastro's willingness to abandon his suit also reflects Habington's growing misgivings about the worth of ambition. Ultimately Decastro's decision to follow his friend Ossuna into a life of solitude is not the action of a rejected lover; the wisdom of his retreat is among Habington's foremost beliefs.

The conflicts and conduct of government further engage Habington in a substantial work also published in 1640, *The Historie of Edward the Fourth.* No evidence supports Wood's claim that the book was written at Charles I's request and with the help of the elder Habington; nor is its style "florid" and "poetical." The dedication to the king contrasts the troubled unrest of the earlier monarchy with the uninterrupted peace of the Caroline reign, but the work itself is not a veiled parallel between the factions of the past and the Parliaments of 1640. Habington shares the contemporary view of Edward as a "most Magnificent and Majestick Prince," and he remains traditional in his insistence that "no injustice in a Soveraigne can authorize the subject to Rebellion." A skeptical and ironic note, in fact, qualifies the desire of Renaissance historians to trace a meaningful pattern in the providential course of time, for the narrative concedes that not all actions of the great are governed by deliberate policies or understood with any certainty. Habington's account of the civil strife between Lancastrians and Yorkists and of the later conflicts with Louis XI depicts Edward as a rightful heir and an effective monarch blessed by fortune and driven by necessity. The final sentence of the history concludes that Edward might have been an even greater monarch if he had valued glory more than pleasure, but the judgment is not harsh. Although passages cannot resist celebrating the virtue of chastity and denouncing "lust (the bastard of an idle security)," the book creates overall a sympathetic impression quite unlike the nineteenth-century image of a debauched and bloodthirsty king. From the distance and in the imperfect light of time Habington sees a flawed greatness shaped by forces of adversity and prosperity toward ends Edward had nei-

ther the leisure to contemplate nor the virtue to change. Throughout the pages of his history Habington understands that "We may by our endevors raise nature somewhat above her frailtie: but never triumph over her till death."

A second work of history completed the same year and published in 1641 contemplates the futility of triumph in the vicissitudes of time. *Observations Upon historie* is a series of six moments or "singular accidents" Habington considers to be arresting lessons about the frailty of human nature. Henry II's confrontation with his eldest son, Richard I's fateful last assault against the French, the battle in 1444 between the Hungarians and Turks at Varna, the fall of Constantinople, and the French nobles' discontent with Louis XI exemplify the greed, pride, and ambition that drive men to betray the closest bonds of family and nation. Habington's bleak lessons draw their moral most eloquently in the final narrative, Charles V's resignation of his crown. The holy Roman emperor and king of Spain who voluntarily retired to a religious order and then staged his own funeral epitomizes Habington's ideal of nobility. Neglected and disdained by his former subjects, Charles V dared to look beyond the shadow of his image: "For being now nothing but himselfe, he tooke justly his own height, and confest he was but man." Appropriately his triumph in life and over death is signaled by a comet that radiates the light that illuminates Habington's works; the comet disappears, in the last words of the book, "unable longer to shine, when this greater starre was darkned, from whom it derived its luster."

With the outbreak of the Civil War Habington withdrew with his wife and four children into his own Worcestershire solitude. The few details gleaned from the next decade indicate Habington lived as a recusant at Hindlip, held out against the king's opponents throughout the 1646 siege of Worcester, and suffered financially with the sequestration of the family estate. He appears to have written very little during these difficult years. Davenant's modern biographers agree that Habington may have been the W. H. who wrote the short prose dedication to the earl of Pembroke in Davenant's *The Unfortunate Lovers* (1643). The only other work from his pen, a poem commending Francis Beaumont and John Fletcher's 1647 folio, *Comedies and Tragedies,* praises the chaste flame of Fletcher's muse and lauds the playwright's view of monarchy. Nothing in the poem or in his life during this obscure period lends credence to Wood's cryptic conclusion that Habington "did run with the times, and was not unknown to Oliver the usurper."

He died on 30 December 1654 a Catholic and a loyalist; he was buried near his father in the Hindlip parish church.

A wooden plaque by the chancel of the church memorializes the coats of arms and history of the family; William Habington's poetry provides his personal memorial. In the 1640s and 1650s poets honored the anonymous recognition "Thy Muse is chaste and thy *Castara* too." Phrases from the poems were also adapted by Richard Lovelace in his celebration of the inspiring Lucasta, and Henry Vaughan's love poetry is both generally and specifically indebted to *Castara*. Habington's other major works similarly fared well. The original text and dedication of *The Historie of Edward the Fourth*, reprinted in 1648, appeared in 1659 as *Praeces Principum, or The President of Illustrious Princes*. With the revival of theater in the Restoration, a performance of *The Queene of Arragon* in the Guard Chamber of St. James's Palace honored the birthday of the duke of York (the future James II). Several days later Samuel Pepys admired another production on 19 October 1668 at the duke of York's playhouse, and the next day bought a copy to read aloud in the company of his wife. But Habington's fame as the author of *Castara* was not enduring: within ten years John Milton's nephew, Edward Phillips, acknowledged in *Theatrum Poetarum* (1675) Habington's reputation as a historian with the aside, "in respect of his Poems however they are now almost forgotten." Publications of *The Historie of Edward the Fourth* and *The Queene of Arragon* in eighteenth-century collections reflect a continued but limited interest in Habington's writing. The critical fortunes of *Castara* rose again in the early nineteenth century, and readers of "taste and feeling" found selections of his poetry and two new editions available (1811, 1812). The sweetness, warmth, and delicacy the Victorians admired had less appeal in the early twentieth century, and Habington's poetry merited only passing mention. Despite a fine modern critical edition of *Castara* and two musical settings of "Nox nocti indicat Scientiam" (1925, 1965), only the Horatian epistles and their interest in solitude have since received significant scholarly attention. Habington's play, however, has recently prompted serious study of its political importance, and the new interest in reassessing the Caroline years and redefining the relationship between literature and history may lead to further understanding and appreciation of *Castara*. Its author began these poems with modest expectations, and the three editions reinforced William Habington's status as a second-rank poet, but time has not yet justified his fear: "And when I'me lost in deaths cold night, / Who will remember, now I write?"

References:

Kenneth Allott, "Biography," in *The Poems of William Habington*, edited by Allott (Liverpool: University Press of Liverpool, 1948), pp. xi–xliv;

John Amphlett, "Thomas Habington," in volume 1 of Thomas Habington, *A Survey of Worcestershire* (Oxford: Worcestershire Historical Society, 1895), pp. 1–26;

Gerald Eades Bentley, *The Jacobean and Caroline Stage*, volume 4 (Oxford: Oxford University Press, 1956), pp. 520–525;

Martin Butler, *Theatre and Crisis 1632–1642* (Cambridge: Cambridge University Press, 1984), pp. 62–76;

Homer C. Combs, "Habington's *Castara* and the Date of His Marriage," *Modern Language Notes*, 63 (March 1948): 182–183;

J. B. Fletcher, "Précieuses at the Court of Charles I," *Journal of Comparative Literature*, 1 (April–June 1903): 146–149;

Alfred Harbage, *Cavalier Drama* (New York: Modern Language Association of America, 1936), pp. 122–124;

Barbara Lewalski, *Donne's Anniversaries and the Poetry of Praise* (Princeton: Princeton University Press, 1973), pp. 331–335;

Treadway Nash, *Collections for the History of Worcestershire*, volume 1 (London: Printed by John Nicholas, 1781), pp. 584–588;

Stephen Orgel and Roy Strong, *Inigo Jones: The Theatre of the Stuart Court*, volume 2 (Los Angeles & Berkeley: University of California Press, 1973), pp. 144–147;

R. T. Petersson, *Sir Kenelm Digby* (London: Cape, 1956), p. 105;

Maren-Sofie Røstvig, *The Happy Man: Studies in the Metamorphoses of a Classical Ideal 1600-1700*, volume 1 (Oslo: Norwegian Universities Press, 1954), pp. 160–176; revised (1962), pp. 88–99;

Albert H. Tricomi, *Anticourt Drama in England 1603–1642* (Charlottesville: University Press of Virginia, 1989), pp. 174–177.

Papers:

The Library of the Society of Antiquaries at Burlington House has Habington's only autograph work, a letter he wrote to his mother. Seventeenth-century verse miscellanies include transcriptions of poems from *Castara* copied by others.

George Herbert

(3 April 1593 - 1 March 1633)

Sidney Gottlieb
Sacred Heart University

BOOKS: *Oratio Qua auspicatissimum Serenissimi Principis Caroli* (Cambridge, 1623);

Memoriae Matris Sacrum, printed with *A Sermon of commemoracion of the ladye Danvers by John Donne . . . with other Commemoracions of her by George Herbert* (London: Philemon Stephens and Christopher Meredith, 1627);

The Temple. Sacred Poems and Private Ejaculations (Cambridge: Printed by Thomas Buck and Roger Daniel, 1633);

Herbert's Remains, Or, Sundry Pieces Of that sweet Singer of the Temple (London: Printed for Timothy Garthwait, 1652) – comprises *A Priest to the Temple: Or, The Country Parson His Character, and Rule of Holy Life* and *Jacula Prudentum Or Outlandish Proverbs, Sentences, &c.,* as well as a letter, several prayers, and three Latin poems.

Editions and Collections: *The Poetical Works of George Herbert,* edited by George Gilfillan (Edinburgh: J. Nichol, 1853);

The Works of George Herbert in Prose and Verse, 2 volumes, edited by William Pickering (London: W. Pickering, 1853);

The Complete Works in Verse and Prose of George Herbert, 3 volumes, edited by Alexander B. Grosart (London: Robson & Sons, 1874);

The English Works of George Herbert, 3 volumes, edited by George Herbert Palmer (Boston & New York: Houghton Mifflin, 1905; revised, 1907);

The Works of George Herbert, edited by F. E. Hutchinson (Oxford: Clarendon Press, 1941; revised, 1945);

The Latin Poetry of George Herbert, translated by Mark McCloskey and Paul R. Murphy (Athens: Ohio University Press, 1965);

The Selected Poetry of George Herbert, edited by Joseph H. Summers (New York: New American Library, 1967);

Major Poets of the Earlier Seventeenth Century, edited by Barbara K. Lewalski and Andrew J. Sabol (New York: Odyssey Press, 1973);

The English Poems of George Herbert, edited by C. A. Patrides (London: Dent, 1975);

George Herbert and Henry Vaughan, edited by Louis L. Martz, The Oxford Authors series (Oxford: Oxford University Press, 1986).

OTHER: "In Obitum Henrici Principis" and "Ulteriora timens cum morte paciscitur Orbis," in *Epicedium Cantabrigiense, In obitum immaturum Henrici, Principis Walliae* (Cambridge, 1612);

Luigi Cornaro, *A Treatise of Temperance and Sobrietie,* translated into English by Herbert, in *Hygiasticon* (Cambridge: Printed by R. Daniel, 1634);

Briefe Notes on Valdesso's Considerations, in *The Hundred and Ten Considerations of Signior Iohn Valdesso* (Oxford: Printed by Leonard Lichfield, 1638);

Outlandish Proverbs Selected by Mr. G. H. (London: Printed by T. P. for Humphrey Blunden, 1640);

Musae Responsoriae, in *Ecclesiastes Solomonis,* by James Duport (Cambridge: Printed for John Field, 1662);

The Williams Manuscript of George Herbert's Poems, edited by Amy M. Charles (Delmar, N.Y.: Scholars' Facsimiles & Reprints, 1977) – comprises early versions of some of the poems in *The Temple* as well as two collections of Latin poems, *Lucus* and *Passio Discerpta.*

Nestled somewhere within the Age of Shakespeare and the Age of Milton is George Herbert. There is no Age of Herbert: he did not consciously fashion an expansive literary career for himself, and his characteristic gestures, insofar as these can be gleaned from his poems and other writings, tend to be careful self-scrutiny rather than rhetorical pronouncement; local involvement rather than broad social engagement; and complex, ever-qualified lyric contemplation rather than epic or dramatic mythmaking. This is the stuff of humility and integrity, not celebrity. But even if Herbert does not appear to be one of the larger-than-life cultural monu-

George Herbert (portrait by Robert White; Houghton Library, Harvard University)

ments of seventeenth-century England – a position that virtually requires the qualities of irrepressible ambition and boldness, if not self-regarding arrogance, that he attempted to flee – he is in some ways a pivotal figure: enormously popular, deeply and broadly influential, and arguably the most skillful and important British devotional lyricist of this or any other time.

There is, as Stanley Stewart has convincingly demonstrated, a substantial School of Herbert cutting across all ages. Stewart focuses on the seventeenth-century poets who professed allegiance to Herbert and whose works are markedly indebted to his techniques, subjects, and devotional temperament. He comes up with an impressive list, including some admittedly minor poets, such as Henry Colman, Ralph Knevet, Mildmay Fane, Christopher Harvey, and Thomas Washbourne, and some considerably more talented poets, such as Henry Vaughan, Richard Crashaw, and Thomas Traherne. Extended through modern times, the School of Herbert includes Samuel Taylor Coleridge,

Ralph Waldo Emerson, Emily Dickinson, Gerard Manley Hopkins, T. S. Eliot, W. H. Auden, Elizabeth Bishop, Anthony Hecht, and, perhaps Robert Frost – although these later poets are far less simply derivative and single-minded in their devotion to Herbert than were his seventeenth-century followers.

Herbert is also important, especially in the seventeenth century, not only as a poet but as a cultural icon, an image of religious and political stability held up for emulation during tumultuous times. Much of his early popularity – there were at least eleven editions of *The Temple* in the seventeenth century – no doubt owes something to the carefully crafted persona of "holy Mr. Herbert" put forth by the custodians of his literary works and reputation. In the preface to the first edition of *The Temple,* published in 1633, shortly after Herbert died, his close friend Nicholas Ferrar established the contours of Herbert's exemplary life story, a story that not only validated but was also presumably told in the poems of the volume. In a few short pages Ferrar indelibly sketches Herbert as one who exchanged the advantages of noble birth and worldly preferment for the strains of serving at "Gods Altar," one whose "obedience and conformitie to the Church and the discipline thereof was singularly remarkable," and whose "faithfull discharge" of the holy duties to which he was called "make him justly a companion to the primitive Saints, and a pattern or more for the age he lived in." This is not only high praise, but praise with political as well as religious implications: in 1633 the church was a place of contention as well as worship, and Ferrar helped establish Herbert as a model of harmonious, orderly, noncontroversial devotion for whom faith brought answers and commitment to the social establishment, not divisive questions and social fragmentation.

By 1652, the time of the next major biographical statement about Herbert, the tensions of the 1630s had erupted into a devastating civil war: the army of King Charles I had been decisively defeated, and the king himself executed; the bishops had been disenfranchised from their high place in both church and state government; and the maintenance of peace depended on a coalition of parties — old and new landowners, merchants, religious enthusiasts, army commanders, and soldiers – with conflicting interests. Little wonder, then, that Barnabas Oley, a Royalist divine, envisioned Herbert as a "primitive . . . holy and heavenly soul" who could instruct a later generation living in much-deserved chastisement and exile. Herbert seemed to be a fit subject for nostalgia, one who lived and died in peace. In Oley's introduction to *Herbert's Remains* (1652), containing among other works *A Priest to the Temple: Or, The Country Parson,* Herbert's prose description of the ideal way a priest would serve his country parish (written during the last years of his life when he was a country parson at Bemerton), Oley pictures Herbert as one who embodies traits that the current age has left behind: a person of charity, a lover of traditional, time-honored worship, church music and ceremonies, and a master of "*modest, grave and Christian reproof.*" Oley's preface is apocalyptic throughout, and he frames Herbert's image in such a way that it may lead midcentury England to holiness and repentance, "Recovery, and Profit."

Izaak Walton, who wrote the first extensive biography of Herbert, follows the lead of Ferrar and Oley in shaping Herbert's life. Walton's *Life of Mr. George Herbert,* first published in 1670 and then revised in 1674 and 1675, does not have Ferrar's austerity nor Oley's urgency: by 1670 the king had been restored, the Anglican church was reestablished as the official religious institution of the country, and – despite inevitable exceptions – there seemed to be a growing respect for the advantages of toleration and accommodation rather than confrontation. Herbert was still needed, but not so much for reproof in perilous times as for gentle guidance in times of relative calm. For Walton, Herbert was not only a "primitive Saint" – that is, a throwback to the church of a simpler era – but a prefiguration of the ideal Restoration clergyman: wellborn but socially responsible, educated but devout, experienced in the ways of the world but fully committed to the ways of the church, and knowledgeable about both the pains and joys of spiritual life.

In Walton's hands Herbert comes alive, and it would be nice to believe everything he tells. But it would be safer to approach Walton's biography as one of the great works of seventeenth-century prose fiction. All subsequent examinations of Herbert inevitably rely on Walton: he is the source of much valuable information available nowhere else. But his story is picturesque, compelling, and more than occasionally unreliable. Some of the most memorable anecdotes he relates may not be untrue, but they are unverified and upon close examination seem to be stitched together from Herbert's own writings. Walton has a habit of treating Herbert's writings as literal and factually accurate autobiographical statements, and much of the *Life* seems to be a fanciful embellishment of such poems as "Affliction" (I), "The Collar," and "The Crosse" and the prose character-sketch *The Country Parson.* Like that of so many other biographers, Walton's logic seems to be that if certain events did not happen in his subject's life, they should have, and he therefore feels free to frame the life as he sees fit as long as he is faithful to his subject — especially if he is prompted by one of the subject's own works. (At one point Walton parenthetically describes an anecdote about Herbert rebuilding a church at his own cost – an event that is in fact documented by other sources besides Walton – as "a real Truth," as if to acknowledge that there are different levels of truth in his *Life.*) In addition, everything in Walton's story seems to be shaped according to a unifying theme: Herbert's disappointed "Court hopes" and his ensuing turn to the church. While this is unquestionably a key topic, as a frame for an entire life it is too restrictive. Herbert's life and work are much more varied, complex, and in some respects inscrutable than Walton or the other early biographers imagined.

George Herbert was born on 3 April 1593 at Black Hall in Montgomery, Wales. His family on his father's side was one of the oldest and most powerful in Montgomeryshire, having settled there in the early thirteenth century and improving and consolidating its status by shrewd marriage settlements and continuous governmental service. The surviving stories about the patriarchs focus, not surprisingly, on their bravery and valor as they fought to civilize the countryside, administer justice, and keep peace in an area that had a well-deserved reputation for wildness. Herbert no doubt grew up with these tales but could not have had much contact with the men themselves: his grandfather, evidently a remarkable courtier, warrior, and politician, died the month after Herbert was born; and his father, also an active local sheriff and member of Parliament, died when Herbert was three and a half years old.

Herbert may have spent his early years in a home without a strong father figure, but this is not to say that the household lacked a commanding presence. His mother, Magdalen, from the Newport family of Shropshire, was by all accounts an extraordinary woman, fully capable of managing the complex financial affairs of the family, moving the household when necessary, and supervising the academic and spiritual education of her ten children. There is evidence of Herbert's deep attachment to, and even identification with, his mother throughout his works: his earliest surviving poems, which attempt to outline his direction as a poet, were written and sent to her as a gift; he mourned her death (and celebrated her life) with a collection of Latin and Greek poems, *Memoriae Matris Sacrum* (1627); and *The Temple* is filled with images of childlike submissiveness and maternal love, devotion, and authority. John Donne's funeral sermon on Magdalen focuses quite a bit on her melancholy, and one wonders whether this too – not necessarily religious despair, but a kind of spiritual vulnerability and sadness – is a crucial part of her legacy to her son.

Magdalen did not keep the family long in Wales. Shortly after the birth of her last child, Thomas, in 1597, she moved the family first to Shropshire, then to Oxford – primarily to oversee the education of the oldest son, Edward – and then finally to a house at Charing Cross, London. This last move also facilitated the education of the other children. George was tutored at home and then entered Westminster School, probably in 1604, a distinguished grammar school that not only grounded him in the study of Latin, Greek, Hebrew, and music, but also introduced him to Lancelot An-

Magdalen Newport Herbert, the poet's mother, who inspired his Memoriae Matris Sacrum *(portrait possibly by Sir William Segar; Collection of the Earl of Bradford)*

drewes, one of the great churchmen and preachers of the time. From Westminster, Herbert went up to Trinity College, Cambridge, in 1609 and began one of the most important institutional affiliations of his life, one that lasted nearly twenty years.

At Cambridge, Herbert moved smoothly through the typical stages of academic success: he gained a B.A. then an M.A.; obtained a Minor fellowship then a Major fellowship, which involved increasing responsibilities as a tutor and lecturer; and was made university orator in 1620, a position of great prestige within the university that was often a stepping-stone to a successful career at court. The orator was the spokesperson for the university on a variety of occasions, making speeches and writing letters, and the little evidence that survives of Herbert's activities as orator indicates that he served in this capacity with both ceremonious wit and independent boldness. He was well able to offer the required fatuous compliments to the king: in a letter thanking King James I for the gift of his Latin works to Cambridge, he compared these volumes themselves to a library far grander than that of the Vatican or the Bodleian Library at Oxford. But he was also willing to dare to offer some unwanted advice when it was needed: in an oration on 8 October 1623 capping the university's celebration of the safe return of Prince Charles (later Charles I) and George Villiers, first Duke of Buckingham, from Spain, Herbert made a forceful plea for the value of keeping the peace, even though it was clear that the failure to marry off the prince to the Spanish Infanta made war with Spain more desirable and likely. It is unclear whether Herbert helped or hurt his chances for secular advancement by being both witty and principled.

During the Cambridge years Herbert wrote much of his poetry. He began, auspiciously enough, with a vow, made in a letter accompanying two sonnets sent to his mother as a New Year's gift in 1610, "that my poor Abilities in *Poetry,* shall be all, and ever consecrated to Gods glory." The sonnets are written at a high pitch of enthusiasm – there are nine astonished rhetorical questions in the first poem alone – as Herbert yearns to be a fiery martyr, burning with love of God, not women. Herbert was not alone in wanting to redirect poetry from Venus to God: Sir Philip Sidney, Robert Southwell, and Donne, among others, urged the same thing, and even King James helped encourage this kind of revolution by writing and publishing his own religious poems. But these two sonnets have the force of personal discovery behind them, and they are a preview of a cluster of later poems in *The Temple* that examine his willingness and ability to write religious verse. As in so many of his best poems, exuberance betrays a deep sense of disorder and nervousness.

These sonnets are disturbing declarations, filled with aching desire – "My God, where is that ancient heat" – but based on contemptuous dismissals of erotic love, love poetry, and women. As a present to his mother these verses are particularly curious. Magdalen Herbert was strikingly beautiful, if one can gauge this by her portrait and by contemporary accounts, and inescapably vital, with ten children and a dashing new husband half her age (she had married John Danvers in 1609). One wonders how Herbert expected her to respond to the anatomy of a woman that concludes his second sonnet:

Open the bones, and you shall nothing find
    In the best *face* but *filth,* when, Lord, in thee
    The *beauty* lies in the *discovery.*

Perhaps Magdalen would not have read the poem from the position of one of the women being so anatomized and would have simply appreciated the closing celebration of the Lord's beauty. Donne evidently trusted her as a reader not easily offended and capable of discerning the sincere motive of a poem. In sending her "The Autumnall," a poem presumably about her that contains some remarkably audacious and severe praise, Donne seems to have relied on certain qualities of her as a reader on which Herbert also counted. (Magdalen herself may have been a model for this kind of forthright and uncompromising directness: even as he writes her epitaph in *Memoriae Matris Sacrum* number 13, Herbert describes her as "seuera parens" [strict parent].) In any event, Herbert's earliest poems announce his dedication to sacred poetry in a startling fashion.

It is difficult to date most of Herbert's poems with certainty, but it is clear that not all his early poetic efforts were the kind of impassioned sacred lyrics promised by the sonnets he sent to his mother. His various occasional pieces – poems on the death of Prince Henry (oldest son of James I) in 1612 and Queen Anne (wife of James I) in 1619, to the queen of Bohemia in exile, to his friends Francis Bacon and Donne – show that Herbert, like his contemporaries, viewed and used poetry as a medium of social discourse, not just self-analysis and devotion. And even the bulk of Herbert's early religious poetry is public and didactic rather than introspective and meditative. His modern reputation rests almost exclusively on the devotional lyrics collected in "The Church," the middle section of *The Temple,* and while some of these lyrics may have been written as early as 1617, there is good reason to believe that most of them date from much later, from the mid 1620s to the last years of his life at Bemerton. But "The Church" is carefully positioned between two long poems, "The Church-porch" and "The Church Militant," both of which are early pieces much different from the later lyrics.

Amy M. Charles, Herbert's most thorough and meticulous biographer, suggests that "The Church-porch" was perhaps written as early as 1614 and that at least on one level it is a poem of advice addressed to his brother Henry, one year younger than George but already a man of the world and living in France. The two brothers shared a love of proverbs, and indeed what saves the poem from turning into a plodding collection of "thou shalt nots" is Herbert's ability to release the dramatic as well as the moral potential of some of these proverbs. In the context of *The Temple,* "The Church-porch" is intended as a kind of secular catechism instructing a young man in basic moral principles and

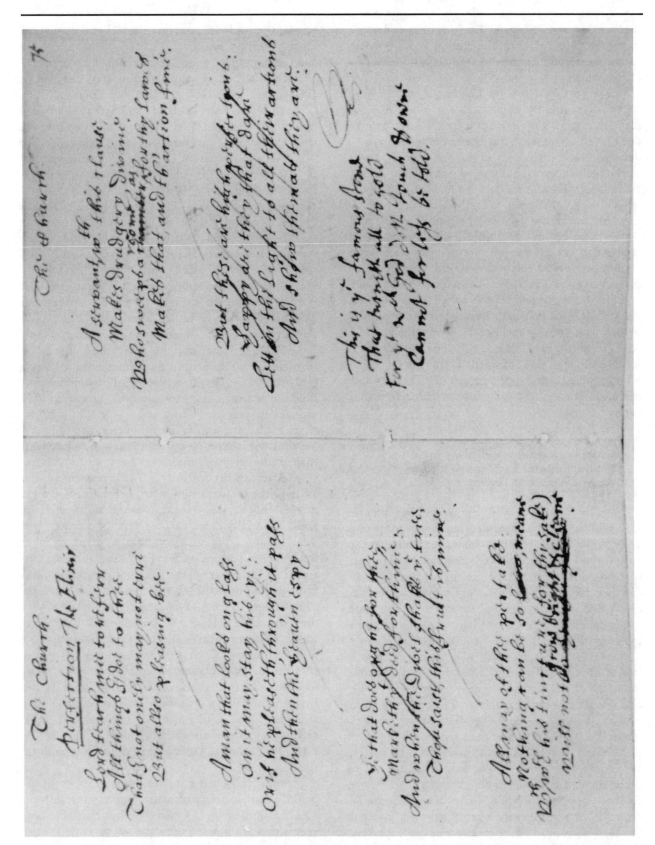

Pages from a manuscript volume – probably from Little Gidding – comprising scribal copies of English poems by Herbert and some of his Latin poems in his own hand. This scribal copy of "The Church" includes revisions and a final stanza added by Herbert (Dr. Williams's Library, London; MS. Jones B62).

manners to prepare him for life in society and, more important, entrance into the church, a place where he will encounter moral and spiritual problems of a different sort.

Herbert's premise, as he announces in two of his most frequently quoted lines, is that "A verse may finde him, who a sermon flies, / And turn delight into a sacrifice." But the poem would not be delightful at all if it only contained seventy-seven stanzas of prudential bullying: *Beware of lust, Lie not, Flie idlenesse, Be thriftie, Laugh not too much* and so on. What enlivens the poem is Herbert's ability to complement the moral tags with striking images and brief dramatizations (techniques that characterized the best, or at least the most appealing and effective, sermons of the time as well). "Drinke not the third glasse" is an abstract, easily disregarded bit of advice until it is capped by a vivid personal illustration: "It is most just to throw that on the ground, / Which would throw me there, if I keep the round." And Herbert's passionate apostrophe "O England! full of sinne, but most of sloth" is transformed from a forgettable traditional complaint to a memorable chastisement by a homely but stunning figure of speech:

> Thy Gentrie bleats, as if thy native cloth
> Transfus'd a sheepishnesse into thy storie:
>   Not that they are all so; but that the most
>   Are gone to grasse, and in the pasture lost.

"The Church-porch" has something in common with manuals of conduct that aim to prepare a young man not so much for moral behavior as for social advancement. Many of the traits that Herbert warns against are defects in the eyes of God but also disadvantages in the company of other men, particularly one's competitors and superiors. At this time in his life Herbert undoubtedly had high ambitions for himself, and it does not paint him as a mere placeseeker to suggest that he was shrewdly aware that a morally self-controlled and cautious person might gain both earthly and heavenly rewards. Still, one should not overemphasize the secular context of "The Church-porch." For all its descriptions of life in the social arena and comments on how to act in company, it concludes with advice about charity, prayer, and proper worship. The structure of the poem thus entices the imagined reader from where he lives to where he should live, from superficial concern for the pleasure of this world, a joy that "fades," to a much deeper awareness of holy joy that "remains." At this time Herbert may not have been ready to write the poems that describe the rhythm of pain and joy that define a spiritual life,

but he was well able to lead himself and his reader close to "The Church."

He was also ready to envision the corporate life of the church. In the broad plan of *The Temple*, the reader "sprinkled" by the "precepts" of "The Church-porch" and then transported by the twists and turns of faith in "The Church" still needs to see the fate of the institutional church, dramatized in "The Church Militant." This concluding section of *The Temple* is considered to be an early poem for several reasons: it is written in a combative, assertive tone like that which dominates much of Herbert's early Latin verse, and many of its satiric targets and topical allusions link it to other of his writings of the early 1620s that are vehemently controversial and impatient with a church establishment that is faulty and decaying but unable to heal itself. "The Church Militant," like his oldest brother Edward Herbert's satire *The State Progress of Ill* (1608) and Donne's *Second Anniversary: Of the Progres of the Soule* (1612), turns time into space and charts the historical development of the Christian church as a trip around the world, with Sin following close behind every move made by Religion. Like each individual believer, the church as a whole is bound to a rhythm of rising and falling, simple purity followed inevitably by excessive embellishment, wholeness turned into fragmentation.

After an invocation to God's beneficent creation of the church as an instrument of divine love, not earthly power – an outspoken political comment, especially during an age when the church was being counted on more and more as a subordinate but nevertheless vital ally of the king and administrator of his power – the poem is broken up into five main sections, each concluding with the lines "How deare to me, O God, thy counsels are! / Who may with thee compare?" Even though this psalm-based refrain captures the speaker's heartfelt submissive praise of God, these lines are ironic because they set up a model that the world at large is unable to follow. Despite the success that Christianity has in transforming pagan religion and culture into something beautiful and worthy of worship, sin is always capable of sneaking in to turn faith to "infidelitie," peace to controversy, and light to darkness.

Sin is imagined in broad terms as superstition, pride, and disorderly pleasure, but its most current and insidious form is Roman Catholicism. Herbert seems to align himself with the apocalyptic Protestant militants of late-sixteenth- and early-seventeenth-century England as he energetically and somewhat venomously satirizes the pope as Anti-

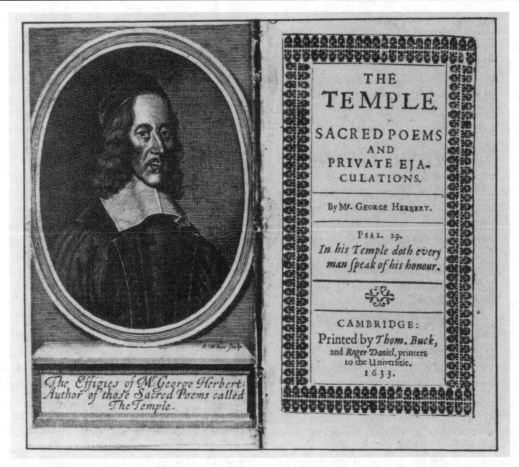

Frontispiece and title page for Herbert's best-known work. John Wesley adapted many of these sacred poems during the eighteenth century for use as hymns.

christ, Rome as "Western *Babylon,*" the Jesuits as the Devil's army, priests as crafty wizards, and Roman Catholicism in general as a religion of shameless glory rather than grace. And England is by no means a secure fortress: reformed though it is, the British church is all but ready to succumb to the darkness that has afflicted all previous churches.

Herbert's prophetic vision of the beleaguered true church poised and ready to depart England for America was quoted repeatedly by his seventeenth-century readers:

Religion stands on tip-toe in our land,
Readie to passe to the *American* strand.
When height of malice, and prodigious lusts,
Impudent sinning, witchcrafts, and distrusts
(The marks of future bane) shall fill our cup
Unto the brimme, and make our measure up;
When *Sein* shall swallow *Tiber,* and the *Thames*
By letting in them both pollutes her streams:
When *Italie* of us shall have her will,
And all her calender of sinnes fulfill;

Whereby one may foretell, what sinnes next yeare
Shall both in *France* and *England* domineer:
Then shall Religion to *America* flee:
They have their times of Gospel, ev'n as we.

For many these lines accurately predicted a new age of Protestant martyrdom and exile and the demise of the Protestant church in England at the hands of King Charles I; his French wife, Henrietta Maria, a Roman Catholic with a large entourage; and Archbishop William Laud, a High Churchman and anti-Calvinist (though not a Roman Catholic) with little taste or tolerance for Reformation theology or notions of church government. But for all Herbert's historical accuracy and prescience, his eyes were on the end of history, which promised a happy consummation of his "progress." Redemption, a final escape from the repetitive cycle of "vertuous actions" and "crimes," comes not in time but beyond time, on a day of judgment when the church and the sun overcome sin and darkness.

The two long early poems that frame "The Church" are thus substantially different from the lyrics that are Herbert's greatest achievement. But they serve an important function in the overall structure of *The Temple,* helping Herbert to present a multidimensional, comprehensive examination of moral, spiritual, and institutional history, and situating the persona (and reader) alternately in the world, in the church, and then finally in the midst of a macrocosmic struggle between religion and sin that begins in time but ends out of it. And in a curious way these two long poems do share something with the poems of "The Church." Like Herbert's most characteristic lyrics, they are "self-consuming," to use Stanley E. Fish's phrase: that is to say, the premises from which they begin are suspended by their conclusions. In "The Church-porch" adjustment to life in the social world of "plots" and "pleasures" is rendered if not inconsequential then at least of secondary importance by the concluding turn to life within the church, where "vain or busie thoughts have . . . no part." In "The Church Militant" outraged satire of the foolish spectacle of sin dogging the church is superseded by an abrupt but all-important vision of a day of judgment that takes us well beyond sin and satire.

During this time at Cambridge, Herbert also composed a substantial amount of Latin poetry. This, of course, should be no surprise: grammar school and university education was largely a matter of immersion in classical texts and repeated exercise in copying, translating, and imitating Latin authors. The Renaissance turn to distinctively national literature and the Reformation turn to vernacular Bible translations and church services by no means displaced Latin as the international language for diplomats and scholars and as the common vehicle for many types of serious disputation, religious devotion, and intellectual and poetic wit and playfulness. Writing Latin poetry was a natural development of Herbert's day-to-day activities at Cambridge and – because of the particular traditions of Latin and Neo-Latin literature that he knew intimately and the learned audience to which Latin works would be directed – allowed him to use different poetic voices than the ones he cultivated in his English lyrics.

Musae Responsoriae (1662) is a series of energetically witty and satiric "Epigrams in Defense of the Discipline of Our Church" meant to counter the attacks of Scottish Presbyterian Andrew Melville, whose poem *Anti-Tami-Cami-Categoria* pictured the British church as insufficiently reformed and still too beholden to Roman Catholic ceremonies, ritu-

als, and accompaniments to worship. The publication of Melville's poem in 1620 perhaps provided Herbert with an opportunity to assert himself as the newly appointed orator of Cambridge – the universities were, after all, under siege by Melville, who criticized both Oxford and Cambridge for not supporting Puritan reform – and an occasion to clarify his own notion of the ideal British church. As in "The Church Militant," Herbert was deeply critical of what he felt were the many excesses of Roman Catholicism, but he was not sympathetic to Melville's "vain fears of the Vatican She-wolf" and the puritanical drive to purge the church of music, traditional prayers, vestments, and bishops.

For Herbert, Roman Catholics and Puritans are brothers, twin dangers like Scylla and Charybdis between which the British church must navigate: the via media is best, a theme that he returns to in one of the poems in *The Temple,* "The British Church." *Musae Responsoriae* is filled with comic caricatures of abrasive Puritan preachers and disorderly worshipers; respectful addresses to King James, Prince Charles, and Lancelot Andrewes as custodians of the peace threatened by the Puritans; and satiric analysis of Melville's ridiculous desire to create a church of nakedness and noise to replace one of visual beauty and music. It is a witty volume aimed to tease and please, but it is also an integral part of Herbert's lifelong attempt to define his church – no mean feat, since neither Scylla nor Charybdis can or should be banished – and his place within it, as defender and worshiper.

Herbert's two other collections of Latin poems written during the early 1620s are comprised primarily of sacred rather than satiric and controversial epigrams. *Lucus* (a "Sacred Grove") is a somewhat loosely arranged miscellany that includes poems on Christ, the pope, the Bible, and several biblical episodes and figures, including Martha and Mary, and examines an assortment of topics such as love, pride, affliction, and death. Several of the poems, like those in *Musae Responsoriae,* use irony for satiric purposes.

The decrepit fate of Rome is ingeniously discovered in its very name, "Roma," which can be construed as an anagram depicting its decline from the glorious days of Virgil ("Maro") to the present day, when hate has banished love ("Amor"). But in most of the poems irony and paradox are used to convey the miraculous and mysterious power of Christ. Herbert's emphasis is not on careful, rational argumentation but bold, dramatic astonishment, as in the brief but dazzling lines "On the stoning of Stephen": "How marvelous! Who pounds rock gets fire. But Stephen from stones got heaven." The longest poem in the collection, "The Triumph of Death," indicts man's ironic misuse of intelligence to create weapons and other instruments of death, but the greater irony, revealed in the following poem, "The Christian's Triumph: Against Death," is that benign images of Christ – the lamb, the Cross – overwhelm even the most threatening spears, bows, and battering rams.

The twenty-one poems of *Passio Discerpta* are much more unified than those in *Lucus,* each focusing on some aspect of Christ's Crucifixion. Like Richard Crashaw's sacred epigrams, written some ten years later, these poems are intensely, even grotesquely, visual, but, unlike Crashaw's, Herbert's prevailing emotion is calm wonderment rather than ecstatic excitement. The description of the Passion of Christ is remarkably dispassionate: the poetic witness is not cold or distant but is moved primarily by the redemptive purpose rather than the melodramatic circumstances of the Crucifixion. He is transfixed and indelibly marked by what he sees – "I, joyous, and my mouth wide open, / Am driven to the drenched cross" – and he is well aware that the death of Christ crushes the world and, as he imagines it, grinds the human heart to powder. But these poems, as baroque and intense as they may seem to be on the surface, are written from the secure perspective of one who feels at every moment that the inimitable sacrifice of Christ "lightens all losses."

Though the Latin poems of *Musae Responsoriae, Lucus,* and *Passio Discerpta* are relatively early works in Herbert's canon and represent a distinctive stage in the development of his style and ideas, they are by no means mere apprentice work, disconnected from his later efforts. Thematically, these collections have much in common with the poems of "The Church" and illustrate that these later lyrics are the result of lifelong meditation on cert,ain themes, not spontaneous or occasional poeticizing. And, stylistically, the Latin poems, relying heavily on compression, paradox, wordplay, and climactic moments of understated surprise, are at least in some ways the foundation of what has been called Herbert's "metaphysical wit." Such poems as "The Agonie" and "Redemption" may be more finely crafted and powerful than any of the verses in *Passio Discerpta,* but they are deeply akin to them.

Poetry was not all that was on Herbert's mind at Cambridge. He was worried about money: not for any extravagant purposes, but simply to live on. His university position paid him modestly, and the yearly portion assigned him in his father's will was administered by his brother Edward and usually sent late and begrudgingly. He sought and probably got help from his stepfather, but, especially for someone who, as Ferrar describes him, valued his "independencie," financial insecurity was a great source of frustration. And he worried about his health. In several of his letters he tells of being sick, restricted to a very careful (and expensive) diet, and too weak to fulfill his daily duties. "I alwaies fear'd sickness more then death," he wrote to his mother, "because sickness has made me unable to perform those Offices for which I came into the world."

Ill health troubled him for his entire adult life, and although many of the "afflictions" he describes in *The Temple* are spiritual, his intimate knowledge of the precarious state of the human body makes such poems as "Church-monuments" and "The Flower" particularly moving. Though he sometimes felt the ravages of "Consuming agues" that left him "thinne and leane" ("Affliction" [I]), he turned himself into an emblem confirming that physical sickness need not be an impediment to spiritual health, as seen in "The Size":

> A Christians state and case
> Is not a corpulent, but a thinne and spare,
> Yet active strength: whose long and bonie face
> Content and care
> Do seem to equally divide.

The face that appears in Robert White's portrait of Herbert, copied from a lost original and printed in the first edition of Walton's *Life,* has these qualities: it is thin and spare, long and bony, and radiates both content and care.

However, Herbert's primary concern during the 1620s, more than health or money, was choosing his vocation, a recurrent theme in "The Church." Walton describes Herbert's path as a kind of involuntary conversion. His noble birth, upbringing, and education nurtured "ambitious Desires" for "the painted pleasures of a Court-life" and "the outward Glory of this World," but serious illness coupled with the death of his most influential friends at court led him to brood over his "many Conflicts with himself." "At last," Walton relates, "God inclin'd him to put on a resolution to serve at his Altar," and Herbert entered the church. Despite Walton's effort to praise Herbert's holiness and enviable commitment to church service, he stops just short of demonstrating that Herbert became a priest largely out of frustration and impatience.

Walton's analysis discounts the fact that well before the mid 1620s Herbert was preparing himself for a career in the church and believed that secular advancement was not necessarily antithetical to holy living. In a letter to John Danvers, dated 18 March 1618, he mentions his plans for a spiritual vocation as a long-acknowledged fact, not an agonizing crisis: "You know, Sir, how I am now setting foot into Divinity, to lay the platform of my future life." But this did not keep him from other pursuits: his public position as orator, which he defended as having "no such earthiness in it, but it may very well be joined with Heaven," and friendships with ambitious and powerful men at court and such as Francis Bacon and John Williams. These two men bolstered Herbert's hope that secular and sacred interests could be fruitfully reconciled: Bacon was lord chancellor and translator of *Certain Psalmes* (1625), dedicated to Herbert; and Williams was a holy bishop and a formidable power broker and patron at court and for a time Herbert's greatest benefactor.

Walton is right to note that after many early successes Herbert's chances for advancement began to falter. His highly placed friends died (Ludovick Stuart, second Duke of Lennox, in 1624 and James Hamilton, second Marquis of Hamilton, in 1625) or tumbled as a result of political infighting. (Bacon's fall into disgrace after going to trial for accepting bribes may have taught Herbert a great deal about the vagaries of power and the difficulty of reconciling morality and public greatness; and Williams went into retreat after losing battles with first Buckingham and then Laud.) His stepfather and his good friend Ferrar struggled in vain to save one of their pet projects and investments, the Virginia Company, formed to both colonize the New World and help spread the Gospel. After the king dissolved the corporation, Ferrar removed himself to a life of devotion at Little Gidding, while Danvers, much more volatile and angry, intensified both his gardening at his house in Chelsea and his political agitating. Two decades later he was actively fighting against Charles I and ultimately became one of the regicides, directly responsible for the king's execution.

The power and reputation of some of Herbert's influential friends and family members were thus certainly being challenged and weakened at this time, but Walton drastically oversimplifies Herbert's character by identifying thwarted ambition as his primary motivation in moving closer to the priesthood. Although we cannot know for sure, it is just as likely that Herbert was deeply influenced by firsthand experience of the world of business, political intrigue, and court maneuvering and discovered not so much that it did not offer him a place as

that it did not suit him. His youthful confidence that the sacred and the secular could be harmonized was not confirmed by the lives of those around him, and his attendance at the particularly tumultuous Parliament of 1624 more likely stifled than fanned any desire for a public political career. Years later, in *The Country Parson,* he recommended political service as a necessary part of the education of a gentleman: "for there is no School to a Parliament." But the lesson he learned there may be one stated simply in his poem "Submission," where he finds that worldly success and divine service are not easily blended: "Perhaps great places and thy praise / Do not so well agree."

Late in 1624 Herbert was preparing to take holy orders. Doing so would preclude any further service in Parliament and cut him off from many types of secular employment, but would be necessary for him to remain at Cambridge. (Fellows and other officials at the universities were required to take holy orders, normally within seven years of obtaining a master's degree, a vestige of the medieval origin of the university as primarily a training ground for church service.) But at this time Herbert was leaving both Parliament and Cambridge behind. He was largely absent from Cambridge and delegated most of his duties to others. He did not return even to deliver the funeral oration commemorating the death of King James on 27 March 1625, and though he was not officially replaced as the university orator until January 1628, he had basically begun his removal from the Cambridge community by late 1623.

Ordination as a deacon, which Amy M. Charles suggests occurred in late 1624, by no means resolved the major problems of Herbert's life and in fact may have coincided with a heightening of them. He was presented by Bishop John Williams with several church livings, one at Llandinam in his home county of Montgomeryshire in 1624 and another at Lincoln Cathedral in Huntingtonshire near Little Gidding in 1626, and these brought him at least modest income and required only a minimal effort of supervising some church functions and preaching once a year at Lincoln Cathedral. But this was not enough to support him, and between 1624 and 1629, with no house of his own, he stayed with a succession of friends and relatives: with "a friend in Kent," his stepfather and mother at Chelsea, his brother Henry at Woodford, and Henry Danvers, Earl of Danby (John Danvers's brother), at Dauntesey House in Wiltshire.

His financial condition improved substantially when in July 1627 a Crown grant made him part

Passio discerpta.   100

Monumenta aperta

Dum moreris, Mea Vita, ipsi vixere sepulti,
  Proq́ uno vincto turba soluta fuit.
Tu tamen, haud tibi tu moreris, quas vivis in illis,
  Asserit & vitam, Mors animata tuam.
Scilicet in tumulis, Crucifixum quaeritis, Vivit:
  Convincunt una multa sepulcra Crucem.
Sic, pro Maiestate, Deum, non perdere vitam
  Quam tribuit, verùm multiplicare decet.

Terra-motus

Te fixo vel Terra movet: nisi, cum Cruce, totam
  Circumferre potis; Sampson ut anti, fores.
Heu stolidi, primùm fugientem figite Terram,
  Tunc Dominus clavis aggrediendus erit.

Passio Discerpta, *one of the Latin poems that Herbert wrote in the manuscript volume from Little Gidding (Dr. Williams's Library, London, MS. Jones B62)* owner (with his brother Edward and Thomas Lawley, a cousin) of some land in Worcestershire, which was then sold to his brother Henry. The grant, about which little is known, may have assured Herbert that his family was not completely neglected (perhaps his estimate of his own current fate) nor out of royal favor (the frequent state of Edward, whose life as a courtier and diplomat oscillated between royal grace and disgrace), and the money he gained from the sale of the land was certainly welcome. Charles suggests that it allowed him to resign his position at Cambridge and gave him the wherewithal to turn toward one of the favorite projects of his later life, rebuilding churches, an activity he undertook not only at Leighton Bromswald but also at Bemerton. But the fact remains that at this time Herbert was still without a settled vocation.

Many of the poems of "The Church" focus on the problems of finding a proper vocation. Some, such as "Affliction" (I) and "Employment" (I) and (II), seem to be early meditations on Herbert's uneven progress toward finding a position that might satisfy both his and God's desires. Others, such as "The Priesthood" and "Aaron," are undoubtedly later poems reflecting on the specific implications of his decision to become a priest. "The Crosse," though, describes an intermediate stage, one at which Herbert was distressingly stuck in 1626, the probable date of this poem. The speaker seeks "some place, where I might sing, / And serve thee," but he comes to realize that the consequences of this desire are far more overwhelming than he had anticipated. "Wealth and familie," and indeed any sense that even the most dedicated believer brings something useful to Christ, prove to be irrelevancies and must be set aside. This "strange and uncouth thing," the Cross, completely disrupts one's normal life, and any potentially heartening illusions about "My power to serve thee" are replaced by an awareness that "I am in all a weak disabled thing."

One of the deepest ironies of the poem is that even when one's hesitancies about serving God are resolved, the basic impossibility of doing so still remains. As in so many of his other poems, Herbert finds himself on receding ground: God takes him up only to throw him down; devotion is not a release from physical and spiritual pain but an introduction to an even more devastating experience of "woe"; and the fulfillment of one's desire is never finally satisfying or peaceful — the speaker can "have my aim, and yet . . . be / Further from it then when I bent my bow." But, after trying so hard to plan his own life, the speaker finally discovers his role in a

life planned for him. There are various images and patterns of crosses in this poem, not the least of which is the intersection between man's choosing God and God's choosing him. The pains of life — "these crosse actions" that "cut my heart" — link one inextricably to Christ, particularly as a model of patient suffering and devoted service to man and God. Despite the plea "Ah my deare Father, ease my smart!" in the conclusion of the poem, Herbert is ultimately less concerned with escaping suffering than he is with finding meaning for it, and he does so by speaking Christ's words on the Cross, simultaneously letting Christ speak these words through him: "*Thy will be done.*"

As a logical conclusion, this will not do: Herbert fails to spell out exactly how one goes about following "thy will," details that would be especially important during a time of decision for him, such as the mid 1620s. But the last four words are a sign of devotional assent: a leap from, rather than a culmination of, rational analysis. This sudden imagination of the impossible — a characteristic movement in Herbert's most dynamic poems, such as "Prayer" (I) and "The Collar" — allows "The Crosse" to end with at least a momentary stay against confusion, as Frost might describe it. Weaving Scripture into his verses was an integral part of Herbert's attempt to forge a vocation as a servant of the Word of God, as both poet and priest. Here it allows him a sudden intuition into the blending of "mine" and "thine" as not one of the great problems, but one of the great joys, of religious experience. My will and thy will, my words and thy words, my voice and thy voice prove to be, as it were, intersecting beams in this poem about not the adoration, but the cooperative construction, of a cross.

Joseph H. Summers describes the years between 1626 and 1629 as "the blackest of all for Herbert," filled with anxious concern — conveyed in such poems as "The Crosse" — not only about his spiritual duties but also his physical health. In Walton's words Herbert was "seized with a sharp *Quotidian* Ague" in 1626 that required a full year of careful diet and convalescence. And not long after, in June of 1627, his mother died, an event that affected him in complex, even contradictory ways. The death of a parent — and in Herbert's case, of his one parent — can be an emotional shock that is both devastating and liberating, confusing and clarifying. Herbert indeed moves through this wide range of response in the nineteen Latin and Greek poems that make up *Memoriae Matris Sacrum*, registered for publication along with Donne's funeral sermon on

Magdalen Herbert on 7 July 1627, a month after her death. Mourning in general is highly ritualized, and such poems are usually formal and traditional rather than spontaneous and directly personal. One should therefore not expect these poems to record Herbert's unmediated feelings about the death of his mother, and one cannot know for sure when the poems are conventional exercises and when they are somewhat more telling autobiographical outbursts.

Even with these cautions in mind, *Memoriae Matris Sacrum* is an extremely revealing collection, giving important insight into his relationship with his mother and his corresponding sense of himself. Interestingly, it is the only collection of poems he published during his lifetime. (Although *Lucus, Passio Discerpta,* and the poems of *The Temple* were carefully copied out in manuscript, no doubt in preparation for eventual publication, they did not appear until after his death.) This may be explained by the prevailing norms of poetic practice for non-professionals at the time, which allowed for the publication of heroic, historical, and occasional poems, particularly of public celebration and mourning, but discouraged anything more than the circulation of other poems in manuscript, followed perhaps by posthumous publication. But Herbert's sense of himself as a poet was deeply intertwined with his relationship to his mother – as indicated by the early sonnets announcing to her his fiery poetic devotion – and not only writing but publishing *Memoriae Matris Sacrum* may have been part of a complex process of poetic self-assertion and self-definition as well as mourning.

It is common in elegiac and memorial poems to dwell on the impossibility of satisfactorily praising and mourning the person departed, but far more than this Herbert's poems examine the ways his mother both authorizes and threatens his poetry. "You taught me to write," he says in the second poem, and when he comes to write about important topics, such as her praise, "that skill, unloosed, / Floods the paper." And in the ninth poem he imagines himself in perennial communication with her, a "zealous child" sending her poems that she takes time off from her heavenly singing to read. She is integral to his fame: "For how can there be laurels for me, / How Nectar, unless with you / I pass the day in song?" But he also associates her with deep suspiciousness of language – "language being chaos since the time of Babel" – and complains that she failed to educate her children in a particular kind of verbal skill that might have made life easier: "manners' smooth / Mellifluous gift, the charm of words / To beat the lion back from us."

In the sixth poem Herbert confirms that poetry is his only remaining vehicle of contact with his mother and his only way of attempting to heal his deep distress, but the almost hallucinatory imagery conveys not only grief but also the intensity of Herbert's intertwined feelings about his mother and himself as a poet. After dismissing traditional medicine and suicide as possible sources of relief, he focuses on the act of writing in terms that are of great psychological interest. He pictures his arm swollen with the heat of "writing's fever," and anyone attempting to check his pulse would feel "the beating vein / My mother's residence." His swelling, setting aside its sexual suggestiveness, is both sickness and pregnancy, as his body now contains his mother, and his condition is, to say the least, precarious and unique: "Not sure my state: / My quality of flesh is not another's." But this same fever of creation is his best medicine, not an "Ill heat, but the only thing that heals the heart."

Memoriae Matris Sacrum is of course not exclusively about poetry. It includes many poignant expressions of sorrow and both directly and indirectly presents an interesting character sketch of Magdalen Herbert. Alongside conventional praise of her beauty, modesty, wide knowledge (especially in practical matters), charity, love of music, and fine penmanship, the reader catches glimpses of her somewhat more intimidating qualities: she "besieges" the Lord with "Sharp and fiery prayer," has a "Stern winsomeness," is a "strict mother," "Proud / and meek at once," and a "source of fiery contention / Of lord and commoner alike." Herbert's poems not only mourn and memorialize her but attempt to analyze and express the burden of a mother's love, a love that can both encourage and overwhelm, inspire and inflame. Not surprisingly, these dynamics recur in Herbert's later poems – despite his vow in the concluding poem that "This one time I write / To be forever still" – and the God that he loves and contends with in "The Church" is frequently not God the Father but God the Mother, at least as described in *Memoriae Matris Sacrum.*

It is sometimes difficult to determine what is a coincidence and what is a consequence, but in any event the death of his mother was followed by some decisive changes in Herbert's life. He separated himself finally from Cambridge (another of his mothers, alma mater) and went to stay at Dauntesey House in the countryside, where he recovered his health, probably wrote and revised some of the poems that would be gathered in "The Church," and got married. Walton tells a fanciful tale of how

Jane Danvers, his stepfather's cousin, wooed by her father's deep respect for Herbert, fell in love with him sight unseen. They first met only three days before their wedding, he says, "at which time a mutual affection entered into both their hearts, as a Conqueror enters into a surprized City, and made there such Laws and Resolutions, as neither party was able to resist."

The romantic overlay seems to be Walton's invention, uncorroborated by any other evidence and surprisingly dissonant with what we know of Herbert's emotional life from his own writings, but there is little reason to doubt Walton's fundamental assertion that the marriage was one thoughtfully negotiated and arranged, not uncommon during this time. Several sections in *The Country Parson* suggest that Herbert put a high value on companionate marriage, based on mutual love and shared work, and such a marriage with Jane Danvers at this time in his life may have served a variety of purposes: besides affording him emotional support, it perhaps also consolidated his relationship with the Danvers family, with whom he seemed to be very attached; eased his transition to life in Wiltshire, where he seemed to be gravitating; and allowed him to make practical plans for setting up his own household and accepting the vocation at which he had long aimed. Herbert and Jane were married on 5 March 1629, and although they lived for a year with her family at Baynton House, by the end of 1630 he was an ordained priest settled in the small parish of Bemerton, where he spent the few remaining years of his life.

Even after he had been presented with the living at Bemerton – probably through the influence of his relative William Herbert, third Earl of Pembroke, whose estate in Wilton was close to the tiny country parish of Bemerton – Herbert delayed entering the priesthood. He may have been, as Charles suggests, occupied with wrapping up bits of business of the life he was ready to leave behind: perhaps traveling to Lincoln Cathedral to deliver the last of his yearly sermons and to Little Gidding for a visit with Ferrar, something he might not have the luxury of doing once his full duties commenced at Bemerton. Or this may have been a final period of spiritual wrestling, with Herbert still needing to argue himself into a final conviction that he was worthy, willing, and able to be God's servant. Walton is frequently melodramatic, but some of the melodrama may be authentic: he describes Herbert on the day of his induction at Bemerton lying "prostrate on the ground before the Altar," devising rules for his own future conduct and making "a vow, to labour to keep them." His long-awaited ordination as a priest on 19 September 1630 surely did not mark the end of all his spiritual worries or sense of personal frailty, but it may well have signified a new accommodation of them, a deepened understanding of how weakness and worry (which in any event can never be erased from human experience) can be integrated into one's spiritual life.

While at Bemerton, Herbert was extremely busy with a wide range of activities. *The Country Parson* documents that for Herbert the priesthood was not only a spiritual vocation but a social commitment, and although this work was intended as an idealized portrait – "a Mark to aim at," he writes in the preface – rather than an autobiographical statement, Herbert undoubtedly was much like the parson he describes: charitable, conversant with his parishioners outside as well as inside the church, an arbiter of local squabbles, and a familiar example rather than a formal sermonizer. Walton tends to describe Herbert's life at Bemerton as a kind of intentional humbling of himself. He describes Herbert's first sermon as a learned and witty exercise that confounded his parishioners, but he concluded with a promise never to preach that way again: he would from that point on "be more plain and practical in his future Sermons."

This illustrates Herbert's dramatic conversion from university orator to parish priest. But while *The Country Parson* implicitly acknowledges that he had to make strenuous adjustments to enter into the life – and barns and houses – of common country people, there is little indication that he did this grudgingly. The model for condescension (literally "stepping down") is Christ, a model Herbert readily accepts. Throughout *The Country Parson* and in other poems (such as "Whitsunday," "Sunday," "Lent," and "The Elixir") he shows himself to be a sincere "Lover of old Customes," common charity, and daily labor quite unlike any he would have done at Cambridge or court.

This is not to say that life at Bemerton was a continual round of conversations with farmers and catechizing the uneducated. Wilton House was nearby, and Herbert was a confidant of Lady Anne Clifford, wife of his kinsman Philip Herbert, fourth Earl of Pembroke. Salisbury was also within walking distance, and some of Walton's most charming tales describe Herbert's love of music and his visits twice a week to evensong at the magnificent cathedral in Salisbury. Herbert was also busy directing the rebuilding of the church and rectory at Bemerton and entertaining guests, such as Arthur

Woodnoth, Ferrar's cousin and an important intermediary between him and Herbert.

As deeply involved as he was in the social life of the parish, Herbert still had time for private meditation and writing. *The Country Parson* is dated 1632 in his preface. At or near this time he was also annotating John Valdesso's *The Hundred and Ten Considerations,* a book of Catholic devotion sent him by Ferrar. In his "Briefe Notes," eventually included in an edition of Valdesso published in 1638, Herbert describes Valdesso as a "true servant of God," but one whose "defects" need correction. Herbert's careful attention to such a book indicates not his attraction to Roman Catholicism but his willingness to appreciate and learn from spiritual advice from a wide range of authors, a devotional openness that thwarts critics who try to define Herbert's theology too precisely. He was also engaged in translating *A Treatise of Temperance and Sobrietie,* by Luigi Cornaro, which shortly before his death he sent to Ferrar, who published it in 1634 as part of a larger work, *Hygiasticon.* Herbert's editor F. E. Hutchinson speculates that Bacon may have proposed the idea of translating this work, but no matter who set the task for him, the subjects of temperance, sobriety, and careful diet were of lifelong interest to Herbert. During this time Herbert probably also continued to work on another lifelong interest, his collection of proverbs, published as *Outlandish Proverbs Selected by Mr. G. H.* in 1640 and in an expanded version in 1652 as *Jacula Prudentum.*

More important, though, is his final work at Bemerton composing, revising, and structuring *The Temple.* According to Walton, Herbert described it as containing *"a picture of the many spiritual conflicts that have past betwixt God and my Soul, before I could subject mine to the will of* Jesus, my Master: *in whose service I have now found perfect freedom."* But this is an incomplete and misleading picture in several respects. First, it gives the impression that *The Temple* is primarily a miscellany of assorted poems on wavering faith, unstable devotion, and human resistance, problems at last securely overcome by strenuous efforts not described by the poems. On the contrary, *The Temple* dramatizes both "spiritual Conflicts" and the achievement of "perfect freedom." Second, Herbert's brief description sets up a simple division between the troubles of the past and the peaceful obedience of the present, a division that *The Temple* repeatedly undermines. Many of the troubled narratives and complaints in "The Church" ("The Collar," for example) are retrospective, presumably spoken from a position of strength or recovery, but the pains are conveyed with such vivid force and

immediacy that they infiltrate the present. The past rarely stays past for Herbert: "perfect freedom," obedience, peace, and joy are powerful realities in the poems, but they never become completely disengaged from the threats they overcome.

Herbert's understanding of this dialectical relationship between worry and assurance and his corresponding insight into the rhythms of the spiritual life remain somewhat veiled if one examines the poems randomly and individually instead of as parts of an intricately interconnected whole. It is clear that Herbert carefully planned the arrangement of the poems in *The Temple* and intended it to be read in its entirety. An early version of nearly half of the poems eventually printed in the first edition of 1633 appears in a manuscript copied probably in the mid 1620s, and this so-called Williams manuscript indicates that Herbert had not only outlined the basic structure of the volume by this time but also that he was constantly tinkering with it. Some of the poems in the manuscript are set in different places in the printed arrangement, and Herbert made changes in the texts and titles to fit these poems into their new positions.

Even a casual reader could hardly miss the many clues that *The Temple* is a carefully constructed artifact or sequence, but Herbert virtually announces his plans in one of the poems placed early in "The Church," titled "The H. Scriptures II." Here he not only praises the Bible for its penetrating insight into human life but notes that its wisdom may be somewhat mysterious unless one knows how it is structured:

> This verse marks that, and both do make a motion
>   Unto a Third, that ten leaves off doth lie:
>   Then as dispersed herbs do watch a potion,
> These three make up some Christians destinie.

Scriptural interpreters of the time stressed that the Bible is best understood as a unified work: difficult passages could be explicated by comparison with other places in the text, and in general the many repetitions and parallels written into the Bible linked not only the Old and New Testaments but the lives of all Christians. In this as in so many other ways, *The Temple* is modeled after the Bible.

There are many levels of structure in *The Temple,* some broad or obvious, others subtle or minute. The three main sections, "The Church-porch," "The Church," and "The Church Militant," of course indicate that the entire volume will move through stages of secular preparation, sacred initiation, and prophetic vision. Within "The Church" itself there is also a variety of clearly defined sequences of poems. The sense of temporal sequence is particularly strong in the first part of "The Church," perhaps because Herbert wants immediately to call attention to the fact that his poems trace out stages in a devotional life, but also perhaps because he wants to accustom his readers to a simple notion of poetic order before he goes on to more complicated patterns. "The Church" begins with a series of poems that concentrates on Easter week and dramatizes not only Christ's Crucifixion but the difficulties one faces in responding properly to this all-important event. Herbert starts his Christian calendar not with the birth of Christ, explored later in "The Church" in a two-part poem titled "Christmas," but with poems that describe Christ's death and how it allows his followers to live, including "The Sacrifice," "The Agonie," "Good Friday," "Redemption," "Easter," and "Easter-wings." And immediately after this sequence Herbert places another cluster of poems with a readily apparent linear plot. Even the titles of this group tell a familiar story: "H. Baptisme" (I) and (II), "Nature," "Sinne" (I), "Affliction" (I), "Repentance," "Faith," "Prayer" (I), and "The H. Communion."

Some of the sequences are not temporal narratives. For example, "Church-monuments," "Church-musick," "Church-lock and key," "The Church-floore," and "The Windows" are grouped together not so much because they describe a literal walk through the physical church but because each of these subjects prompts a meditation on interior qualities, a temple within. And other sequences allow Herbert to give sustained attention not to a plot but to a particular theme: the poems "Content," "The Quidditie," "Humilitie," "Frailtie," "Constancie," and "Affliction" (III) comprise a kind of anticourt sequence in which Herbert contrasts the sacred and secular worlds. No one poem could convey so well Herbert's complex understanding of the continuing allure of a life-style he sought to reject and the continuing difficulties and pains of a devotional style he sought to accept.

Just as it begins with a highly articulated temporal sequence, "The Church" ends with a series of poems that seems to confirm that all along Herbert has been tracing the life of an exemplary, though more than occasionally troubled, believer, and that at last these troubles are falling away. The final poems are filled with images of comfort and joy, and even potential worries are almost miraculously transformed into occasions for celebration. "Discipline" is an argumentative plea for God to

Page from the first edition of The Temple, *with one of the poems that was typographically structured to resemble its subject*

"Throw away thy rod," and its boldness betrays not lingering pride but confident intimacy with the God of Love. "The Invitation" issues a call to "Come ye hither All" to join with God in a splendid feast, a call answered in the following poem, "The Banquet." "The Posie," "A Parodie," "The Elixir," and "A Wreath" dramatize God's presence in dedicated human labor and in particular stress that poetry can be a fit vehicle for praise of God, a recurrent concern for Herbert.

The next four poems focus on the Last Things, but the traditional gloomy meditation on Death, Judgment, Heaven, and Hell becomes, in the best sense of the term, a comedy: Hell is not even mentioned; "Death" pictures not physical decay but the everlasting life made possible by Christ toward which one should rush at "Doomsday"; the day of "Judgement" is a time when human sins are accepted as "thine"; and "Heaven," written as an echo poem, describes a place of light, joy, pleasure, and leisure that calls out to us. Finally, the real Last Thing, first and last for Herbert, is "Love," and, in the third of the poems with this title in "The Church," Herbert dramatizes the persona's last resistance to God, acceptance of communion, and reception into the heaven promised by the God of Love.

In broad terms, then, the entire sequence of poems in "The Church" follows the spiritual progress of one who "groneth" to be "holy, pure, and cleare" ("Superliminare"), and although the path is difficult and uneven, the end is sure. But sometimes the groaning and the unevenness seem more prominent than the promised end. Unlike some of his followers – including Henry Colman and Christopher Harvey in the seventeenth century and John Keble in the nineteenth, who doggedly elaborate a Christian year or a physical church in their volumes and in the process flatten out the devotional life – Herbert's sequence is by no means simple and linear, and the path traversed by "The Church" is filled with interruptions, backslidings, and sudden rises and falls. Lessons need to be repeated and relearned, and in some respects linear progress throughout "The Church" is an illusion: the persona at the end of the sequence is still working on many of the same problems as at the beginning. The all-too-human but wrongheaded enthusiasm and evasiveness of the speaker of "The Thanksgiving," who does everything but look directly at his real task at hand – confronting the inimitable example of Christ – is akin to the shortsightedness of the speaker in "Miserie"; the forgivable boldness of the speaker in "Discipline," who tries to tell God what to do; and the stubbornness of the speaker in "Love" (III), who to the very end tries to resist the irresistible.

Nothing happens once and for all in "The Church," and every mood is transitory, liable to pass into its opposite. Sometimes this can be heartening. There are many moments of physical and spiritual recovery in the sequence, as one poem of worry is answered by another of wonderful consolation. "Church-monuments" relentlessly pictures the wearing away of the body to death and dust, but the next poem, "Church-musick," lifts the released, bodiless soul toward heaven. "Longing" is a prolonged poem of complaint by a tormented person who can hardly even imagine relief, but the opening line of "The Bag" announces a dramatic – though not final – end to all this: "Away despair! my gracious Lord doth heare." And, in one of the most remarkable instances of sudden healing and consolation in the entire collection, the accumulating worries, pains, and sorrows of "The Search," "Grief," and "The Crosse" give way to "The Flower" – "How

fresh, O Lord, how sweet and clean / Are thy returns!" – which turns even the cycle of joy and pain into a joy.

But joy, comfort, and recovery often seem to be as fleeting as pain and despair. "The Glimpse" opens with an emotional but not particularly surprised statement about the evanescence of comfort and assurance:

> Whither away delight?
> Thou cam'st but now; wilt thou so soon depart,
>   And give me up to night?

The "but now" could be a specific reference within the imaginary narrative constructed by the poems of "The Church": the preceding poem, "The Collar," ends with the sudden interruption of the consoling voice of the Lord calling to a rebellious child he claims rather than disowns, a "delight" that "The Glimpse" perhaps suggests is gone almost as soon as it is received. Even if "The Glimpse" is not responding directly to the experience of "The Collar," it describes a feeling of loss common in "The Church," one dramatized and interpreted in the paired poems titled "The Temper." The first of these poems ends with a vision of a universe of perfect unity and comfort, where God's "power and love, my love and trust, / Make one place ev'ry where." But the inevitable falling off happens in the short space between the end of the first and the beginning of the second poem, which opens in a voice that Herbert is a master of, blending astonishment and matter-of-factness: "It cannot be. Where is that mightie joy, / Which just now took up all my heart?"

These rises and falls, falls and rises, are apparently an inescapable and even a necessary part of the devotional life for Herbert. They torment – "O rack me not to such a vast extent" in "The Temper" (I) is a plea for release from an implement of torture – but also comprise part of a "tempering" process that ultimately tests and strengthens one: like metals heated to high temperatures and then suddenly cooled, the experience of emotional and spiritual extremes, no matter how painful, improves one. There is something to William Empson's provocative claim that Herbert's God, like John Milton's, is a savage God indeed if torment characterizes divine example and human fate. But the backslidings and nearly interminable emotional ups and downs in "The Church" are not indictments of a cruel God nor dramatizations of impossible devotional responsibilities. They are, though, reminders that spiritual progress is extremely complex, demanding, and in some ways unpredictable – terms that also provide an apt description of Herbert's artistry in arranging his poems to describe that progress.

This structural artistry is abundantly evident in the individual poems as well as in the plan of the entire collection. Herbert experimented constantly with poetic forms and meters: he shaped his poems carefully, rarely repeated stanzaic patterns or rhyme schemes, and frequently established patterns in order to break or vary them. This versatility may have been influenced by collections of poems such as the *Greek Anthology,* constantly consulted by Renaissance poets as a handbook of poetic practice, but the Bible also offered a model of stylistic diversity. The Book of Psalms in particular was frequently described as an encyclopedia of poetic genres and voices, and Herbert undoubtedly felt that the Psalms licensed and instructed him in his formal experimentation. Contemporary metrical translations of the Psalms, especially by Sir Philip Sidney and his sister, Mary Herbert, Countess of Pembroke, perhaps also played a great role in reinforcing Herbert's sense that the variety of religious experience requires a variety of poetic forms.

"The Church" is characterized not only by formal variety and experimentation but also by what may be called structural play: Herbert frequently relies on the form of a poem to embody and convey much of the meaning and effect. Some of the patterns are easily visible: "The Altar" is typographically shaped like an altar, and the two stanzas of "Easter-wings" look like angels' wings seen from behind. Later critics such as John Dryden ridiculed such poems, not only because they were unsympathetic to the visual dimensions of a verbal genre but also because they missed some of the complexities of what at first glance seem to be simple picture-poems. "The Altar" pictures not only an altar of poetic devotion but also a large "I," one of the great impediments to devotion. And the stanzas of "Easter-wings" look like wings only when they are turned on end: as the poem is read, the stanzas look like hourglasses. These poems are thus emblems or pictorial representations not so much of simple objects as of a complex process that recurs throughout "The Church": a shifting figure-ground relationship that confirms the instability of perception and interpretation. Because of this instability, Herbert's poems are frequently about reconsiderations — looking at, hearing, or otherwise evaluating or responding to something again. The first glance, figuratively speaking, is typically naive, insufficient, incomplete; the second is deeper, corrected, more properly informed.

Several of Herbert's pattern poems focus directly on this particular drama. "Jesu" pictures a broken "frame" — the human heart carved with the name of "Jesu" imagined as a printer's device holding individual letters — and describes the shifting stages of perception whereby a first glance of random letters turns to an awareness that they spell "*I ease you*" and then finally "JESU." (The fact that the letter *I* was used interchangeably with *J* at this time makes possible the pun at the heart of this poem.) And "Coloss. 3.3" literally embodies the "double motion" and double look it describes: the normal sequential reading of the lines must be supplemented by a separate reading of the statement embedded diagonally in the poem. The plodding and prosaic couplets are much in contrast with the italicized biblical quotation that is the dramatic revelation of the poem: "*My Life Is Hid In Him, That Is My Treasure.*"

Herbert's "hieroglyphic" patterns, to use Joseph H. Summers's term, do not always rely on direct pictorial or visual representation. Form creates or supports meaning throughout "The Church" in many ways. "Prayer" (I) is comprised of a tumbling together of apparently random epithets that have a disorienting effect and raise the suspicion that prayer may well be indefinable. But gradually the poem shapes itself as a sonnet, and the assertion of regular poetic form (there are two couplets, for example, in the last five lines) helps manage the extraordinary energy of the descriptions and allows for a peaceful conclusion: "something understood" is more the culmination of an emotional drama than a rational process of analysis and perhaps suggests that attempts to define prayer are subsumed by a sudden awareness of how prayer defines.

"The Collar" similarly uses a kind of free verse that is ultimately reined in by orderly and regular poetic form. The rebelliousness of the speaker is of course mirrored by the apparent disorder of his speech, a disorder that he flaunts: "My lines and life are free; free as the rode / Loose as the winde, as large as store." But the "fierce and wilde" complaints not only express but also exhaust this rebelliousness, and never far from the centrifugal energy on the surface of the poem is a substratum of order ready to emerge. The real plot of the poem is not the momentary flight from, but the inevitable movement toward, obedience and order, and this movement is underscored by the gradual achievement of structural stability culminating in the last four lines, a controlled, alternately rhyming quatrain. For all its formal pyrotechnics and structural play, though, "The Collar," like "Prayer" (I), is no mere five-finger exercise. These poems are devotional, not mechanical, fugues, and much of their extraordinary power comes from Herbert's ability to embody rather than merely describe dramas of faith and doubt, resistance and assent.

Herbert's structural artistry is matched by his verbal skill. His long-standing interest in rhetoric perhaps betrays not only his deep fascination with words but also his awareness of the connection between language and power, both secular and sacred. Verbal language is the primary, though not the only, vehicle of communication, exchange, and contact among people and between one person and God. In addition it may not be too much of an overstatement to say that the language of the self *is* the self, providing a necessary mode of construction as well as access and expression. For all that this proposition reeks of contemporary linguistic theorizing, one should note how closely it accords with Herbert's incarnational view of the world: an understanding of Christ as the Word made flesh undoubtedly reinforced Herbert's serious concern for the relationship between verbal expression and devotion and heightened his awareness of how his own self and the world he inhabited were, if not verbal artifacts, then at least inevitably shaped by words.

Herbert's wordplay, then, is often as philosophical as it is playful, and his poetic voice and style – really voices and styles – are not matters of convenience but careful devotional choices. He is most often praised for his simplicity, contrasted with William Shakespeare's tortuous ambiguity, John Donne's rugged obscurity, and Ben Jonson's learned allusiveness, but Herbert's simplicity is artful, studied, and less simple than it appears. He delights in the rich multiplicity of reference in words. "I like our language," he says in "The Sonne," not because words set up stable one-to-one relationships between signifier and signified but because they set up correspondences between the one and the many, which when properly traced out reveal a deeper one-to-one connection, between man and God. The word *son* refers not only to "parents issue and the sunnes bright starre" but ultimately to Christ, the Son of God and sun of our life – all of this neatly contained in a *sonnet*.

Key words in Herbert's poems often set off explosions of meaning, and this multiplicity frequently offers relief from, as well as a description of, the tensions and ironies of the human predicament. The "collar" in Herbert's poem of that name brings to mind a chafing yoke around the neck, rebellious anger ("choler"), and perhaps even the

"color" of rhetorical embellishment used to plead a difficult case forcefully, the speaker's exact situation here. It also sounds like "the caller," and in this way subtly foreshadows the climactic "Me thoughts I heard one Calling, *Child!* / And I reply'd, *My Lord.*" The first part of "Christmas" is a somewhat uneasy poem attempting to fathom the mystery of the Christ child, but the description of the baby's "contracted light" simultaneously increases the witness's awe at the spectacle of immensity made small and eases his worry about future "relief" by recalling the ineradicable contract between man and God. And in "The Crosse" one of the figures of speech that conveys the speaker's deepest depression – "To have my aim, and yet to be / Further from it then when I bent my bow" – imagines not only a bow and arrow helpless to shoot him closer to his target but also the bow of devotional obedience that concludes the poem, itself an imitation of Christ's bow on the Cross.

Herbert's art of plainness thus does not preclude purposeful ambiguity, and his wit thrives on assertions of multiple references for words. But as some of his poems about poetry indicate, he was deeply critical of showy and excessively self-assertive wit and obsessively concerned with the relationship between problems of style and problems of devotion. Poetry is a mode of holy service for Herbert and an index of spiritual health or affliction. Full recovery at the end of "The Flower" is imagined as a blend of organic rebirth, renewed sensuality, and poetic activity, the latter perhaps the most prominent:

> And now in age I bud again,
> After so many deaths I live and write;
>   I once more smell the dew and rain,
> And relish versing.

Behind these lines is the memory of another fact, visible in other poems, that despair is registered as a disruption of his ability to write: in "Deniall" distance from God breaks "my heart" and "my verse." Nearly all his devotional problems are analogous to stylistic problems: this reminds us that his poems on poetry are thus never about poetry alone. His worries cover a wide range. In "Grief" he wonders whether poetry is an adequate vehicle for his pain – "Verses, ye are too fine a thing, too wise / For my rough sorrows" – and in fact the poem ends with a dramatic assertion of the limits of poetry: his final sigh, "Alas, my God!," literally falls outside the poem, a sigh evidently too powerful to be contained by "measure, tune, and time."

He also frequently questions whether poetry can be an adequate vehicle for praise of God. The act of poetry is double-moated with irony for Herbert: it perhaps represents the best, even all we have to offer God, and yet it is still not enough; and even though it is all that we have, it too is not ours but a gift from God. Secular poets frequently play on these tropes – that even the highest praise is insufficient, and that it is derivative, not original, a return of beneficence already given by a lord who thus not only occasions, but in effect authors, the praise. With an infinitely more powerful Lord as his subject, this situation is potentially infinitely more humiliating for Herbert. As a poet and a worshiper he must face up to the devastating implications of the fact, stated most succinctly in "The Holdfast," that "nothing is our own."

Throughout "The Church" this assertion and variants of it threaten virtually to annihilate the self and in the process silence all poetry. The response of the persona in "The Holdfast" is typical: "I stood amaz'd at this, / Much troubled." But here and elsewhere such turmoil is the prelude to an all-important interpretive discovery: to say that "nothing is our own" or even that "to have nought is ours" disclaims sole ownership but not shared possession. The soothing voice of a friend at the end of the poem advises that the process of letting go is the best way of holding and being held fast: "all things were more ours by being his," kept by Christ. If one loses absolute independence by depending on Christ, one gains, in Ferrar's fine phrase describing Herbert, "independencie upon all others." One loses selfishness, not the self.

Many of Herbert's poems on poetry follow the same pattern as "The Holdfast," because while he feels the necessity of writing – "The shepherds sing; and shall I silent be?" he notes in "Christmas" – all writing is almost inescapably an act of self-assertion. The traditions and conventions of poetry reinforce this: a "good" poem is normally one that calls attention to itself by fine phrases; inevitable lies; false flattery; and indulgent wit, learning, or obscurity. Herbert attempts to reject all these qualities in such poems as "Jordan" (I) and (II), "A true Hymne," "The Posie," "The Forerunners," "A Parodie," and "A Wreath," but renunciation is always imperfect – poetic pride, like sin in general, is ineradicable and surfaces even in poems that aim to be simple and submissive – and even when it is momentarily successful, it raises further difficulties. What will take the place of all these banished qualities of conventional poetry?

The safest recourse is to construct poetry from God's words. Both "Jordan" poems end with advice to abandon a poetics of invention for one of quotation, ventriloquism, or direct imitation: one should "plainly say, *My God, My King*" (I) and humbly accept that "*There is in love a sweetnesse readie penn'd: / Copie out onely that, and save expense*" (II). And "The Forerunners" compresses a manifesto into a statement of rather strict limits: "For, *Thou art still my God,* is all that ye / Perhaps with more embellishment can say." Herbert's actual poetic practice indicates that he followed such advice both faithfully and creatively. Instead of weaving his "self into the sense," one of the dangers noted in "Jordan" (II), he attempted to weave the Bible into his poems, a process of literary allusion and devotional absorption studied in fine detail by Chana Bloch. In a powerful way the Bible created rather than stifled Herbert's poetic voice, stimulating him to find many ways to say "My God, My King." And despite his distrust of easily abused poetic fancy, he allowed himself the "embellishment" mentioned in "The Forerunners," decking the sense not to "sell" but to serve. For Herbert, devotion chastens but finally engages all human powers, and one sees the results of this in the art and the artlessness, the strain and the wondrously achieved calm, the prayer and the poetics of "The Church."

Herbert did not publish *The Temple* during his lifetime, although it is clear that he intended it to be published. Walton writes that when Herbert was on his deathbed, he gave his volume to a friend, Edmund Duncon, to deliver to Ferrar for publication, leaving these instructions: "*if he can think it may turn to the advantage of any dejected poor Soul, let it be made publick: if not, let him burn it.*" Literary fame was not on Herbert's mind. Still, *The Temple* was instantly well received: Walton noted in 1674 that "there have been more than Twenty Thousand of them sold since the first Impression." Herbert's immediate popularity cut across a wide range of readers, including Puritans, Anglicans, and Roman Catholics as well as Royalists, Parliamentarians, and republicans, but interest waned by the end of the seventeenth century. Early-eighteenth-century readers either avoided him or spoke respectfully of his piety but condescendingly of his false wit and grotesque imagery, and there was no new edition of his poems between 1709 and 1799.

Herbert's poems began to resurface in hymnals, primarily through the efforts of John Wesley, who adapted and rewrote many poems from *The Temple* and also published an edition of Herbert's selected sacred poems. Yet the real revival of interest came in the nineteenth century, buoyed by fine critical comments, allusions, and appreciations by such influential writers as Coleridge, Emerson, and John Ruskin. Several important editions of Herbert's complete works in the latter part of the century testified to and also helped spread the renewed interest, culminating in a dramatic twentieth-century revival of Herbert — as well as the other Metaphysical poets — led in part by T. S. Eliot, whose poems and critical writings illustrate his lifelong attraction to Herbert. Book-length critical studies of Herbert began to appear in the early 1950s and have continued unabated to the present day.

Many early analyses of Herbert — and some more current ones — draw his range much too narrowly, defining him in effect as the quintessential minor poet: extremely talented, but noticeably restricted. However, he is not nearly as limited as some imagine. His poems are of course deeply Christian, but contrary to what Coleridge and others suggest, one need not be a dutiful worshiper of the Anglican religion to find them powerful and relevant, and one not need be a Christian at all to respond deeply to many of his dramatizations of emotional loss, pain, joy, and recovery.

Herbert's simplicity has also been overstated, and while it has led some to view him as a refreshing contrast to Donne, it has tamed him too much. His formal simplicity is deceptive and challenging. Anyone who would speak of his temperamental simplicity is missing the variety in the poems, which includes near-hysterical worry, hallucinatory clarity (especially in visionary allegorical poems such as "Love unknown"), and both sweet acquiescence ("H. Baptisme" [II]) and sweet resistance ("Love" [III]). And although the lyric, Herbert's main genre, is sometimes thought of as too slight a form to sustain poetic greatness, Herbert stretches the form considerably not only by constant inventiveness but also by linking the individual lyrics into much broader patterns.

Perhaps more damaging to any attempt to amplify Herbert's stature is the perception that his poems are private and that they reflect a narrow range of interests and experience. The "spiritual Conflicts" of The Temple, though, are not Herbert's alone: they are deeply personal, even autobiographical, but also typical, shared; and the poems are acts of communion with a human as well as heavenly audience. Furthermore, the conflicts in The Temple are social and institutional as well as personal. Even in the devotional lyrics of "The Church," Herbert casts his eyes on the social and political as well as the religious turmoil of the early seventeenth century: this is most obvious in such poems as "The British Church," "Divinitie," and "Church-rents and schisms," which focus specifically on controversies of the day. Even though he is not a political poet in the way that Milton and Andrew Marvell are, many of his poems reflect his constant meditation on public affairs.

Finally, critics who feel that Herbert's range excludes secular issues also suggest that he is somewhat limited by lack of attention to secular love. For Donne we have not only sacred poems but also the Songs and Sonnets; for Herbert we have only sacred poems in "The Church," marked by the exclusion of and contempt for secular love and sexual attention to women. This unquestionably cuts him off from an important part of human experience. But he does give remarkably full expression to the erotic aspect of his relationship with God, a relationship marked by physical intimacy, patient wooing, and a sensation of "sweetness." Throughout "The Church" the persona is a lover, and the height of spiritual success is experienced as loving and being loved.

By most standards Herbert is both a major and a great poet. These standards involve the following qualities: a high level of analytical intelligence; a close but dynamic and innovative relationship to literary traditions and conventions; technical versatility; an ability to dramatize key crises of emotional and spiritual life; a distinctive style and voice; an extensive body of work; sustained popularity and influence; a strong sense of the physical nature of life; a sense of comedy (somewhat different from a sense of humor); and density of thought and expression.

To say that Herbert is one of the masters of the devotional lyric is high praise but may be misleading if that term qualifies as well as specifies his achievement. It is somewhat bolder but still justifiable to say simply that he is one of the great English poets. The Temple stands up to repeated readings and detailed analysis as a work that, as Ferrar felt it would, continues to "enrich the World with pleasure and piety."

Bibliography:

John R. Roberts, George Herbert: An Annotated Bibliography of Modern Criticism: Revised Edition, 1905–1984 (Columbia: University of Missouri Press, 1988).

Biographies:

Izaak Walton, The Lives of John Donne, Sir Henry Wotton, Richard Hooker, George Herbert, and Robert Sanderson (London: Oxford University

Press, 1927) [The life of Herbert was originally published in 1670];

Margaret Bottrall, *George Herbert* (London: John Murray, 1954);

Marchette Chute, *Two Gentle Men: The Lives of George Herbert and Robert Herrick* (New York: Dutton, 1959);

Amy M. Charles, *A Life of George Herbert* (Ithaca, N.Y.: Cornell University Press, 1977).

References:

Heather A. R. Asals, *Equivocal Predication: George Herbert's Way to God* (Toronto: University of Toronto Press, 1981);

Diana Benet, *Secretary of Praise: The Poetic Vocation of George Herbert* (Columbia: University of Missouri Press, 1984);

Chana Bloch, *Spelling the Word: George Herbert and the Bible* (Berkeley: University of California Press, 1985);

Ira Clark, *Christ Revealed: The History of the Neotypological Lyric in the English Renaissance* (Gainesville: University of Florida Press, 1982);

Donald R. Dickson, *The Fountain of Living Waters: The Typology of the Waters of Life in Herbert, Vaughan, and Traherne* (Columbia: University of Missouri Press, 1987);

T. S. Eliot, *George Herbert* (London: Longmans, Green, 1962);

Stanley E. Fish, *The Living Temple: George Herbert and Catechizing* (Berkeley: University of California Press, 1978);

Fish, *Self-Consuming Artifacts: The Experience of Seventeenth-Century Literature* (Berkeley: University of California Press, 1972);

Coburn Freer, *Music for a King: George Herbert's Style and the Metrical Psalms* (Baltimore: Johns Hopkins University Press, 1972);

Sidney Gottlieb, "The Social and Political Backgrounds of George Herbert's Poetry," in *"The Muses Common-Weale": Poetry and Politics in the Seventeenth Century* (Columbia: University of Missouri Press, 1989), pp. 107–118;

Gottlieb, ed., *George Herbert Journal,* 1977– ;

Patrick Grant, *The Transformation of Sin: Studies in Donne, Herbert, Vaughan, and Traherne* (Amherst: University of Massachusetts Press, 1974);

William Halewood, *The Poetry of Grace: Reformation Themes and Structures in English Seventeenth-Century Poetry* (New Haven: Yale University Press, 1970);

Barbara Leah Harman, *Costly Monuments: Representations of the Self in George Herbert's Poetry* (Cambridge, Mass.: Harvard University Press, 1982);

Barbara K. Lewalski, *Protestant Poetics and the Seventeenth-Century Religious Lyric* (Princeton: Princeton University Press, 1979);

Anthony Low, *Love's Architecture: Devotional Modes in Seventeenth-Century English Poetry* (New York: New York University Press, 1978);

Janis Lull, *The Poem in Time: Reading George Herbert's Revisions of "The Church"* (Newark: University of Delaware Press, 1990);

Mary Maleski, ed., *A Fine Tuning: Studies of the Religious Poetry of Herbert and Milton* (Binghamton, N.Y.: Medieval and Renaissance Texts and Studies, 1989);

Leah Sinanoglou Marcus, *Childhood and Cultural Despair: A Theme and Variations in Seventeenth-Century Literature* (Pittsburgh: University of Pittsburgh Press, 1978);

Louis L. Martz, *The Poetry of Meditation: A Study in English Religious Literature of the Seventeenth Century,* revised edition (New Haven: Yale University Press, 1962);

Edmund Miller and Robert Diyanni, eds., *"Like Season'd Timber": New Essays on George Herbert* (New York: Peter Lang, 1987);

A. D. Nuttall, *Overheard by God: Fiction and Prayer in Herbert, Milton, Dante and St. John* (London: Methuen, 1980);

William H. Pahlka, *Saint Augustine's Meter and George Herbert's Will* (Kent, Ohio: Kent State University Press, 1987);

C. A. Patrides, ed., *George Herbert: The Critical Heritage* (London: Routledge, 1983);

Robert H. Ray, ed., "The Herbert Allusion Book: Allusions to George Herbert in the Seventeenth-Century," *Studies in Philology,* 83 (Fall 1986): 1–182;

Mary Ellen Rickey, *Utmost Art: Complexity in the Verse of George Herbert* (Lexington: University of Kentucky Press, 1966);

John R. Roberts, ed., *Essential Articles for the Study of George Herbert's Poetry* (Hamden, Conn.: Archon, 1979);

Malcolm M. Ross, *Poetry and Dogma: The Transfiguration of Eucharistic Symbols in Seventeenth-Century English Poetry* (New York: Octagon Books, 1969);

Michael C. Schoenfeldt, *Prayer and Power: George Herbert and Renaissance Courtship* (Chicago: University of Chicago Press, 1991);

Robert B. Shaw, *The Call of God: The Theme of Vocation in the Poetry of Donne and Herbert* (Cambridge, Mass.: Cowley Publications, 1981);

Terry G. Sherwood, *Herbert's Prayerful Art* (Toronto: University of Toronto Press, 1989);

Marion White Singleton, *God's Courtier: Configuring a Different Grace in George Herbert's "Temple"* (Cambridge: Cambridge University Press, 1987);

Camille Wells Slights, *The Casuistical Tradition in Shakespeare, Donne, Herbert, and Milton* (Princeton: Princeton University Press, 1981);

Arnold Stein, *George Herbert's Lyrics* (Baltimore: Johns Hopkins University Press, 1968);

Stanley Stewart, *George Herbert* (Boston: Twayne, 1986);

Richard Strier, *Love Known: Theology and Experience in George Herbert's Poetry* (Chicago: University of Chicago Press, 1983);

Claude J. Summers and Ted-Larry Pebworth, eds., *"Too Rich to Clothe the Sunne": Essays on George Herbert* (Pittsburgh: University of Pittsburgh Press, 1980);

Joseph H. Summers, *George Herbert: His Religion and Art* (Cambridge, Mass.: Harvard University Press, 1954);

Mark Taylor, *The Soul in Paraphrase: George Herbert's Poetics* (The Hague: Mouton, 1974);

Richard Todd, *The Opacity of Signs: Acts of Interpretation in George Herbert's "The Temple"* (Columbia: University of Missouri Press, 1987);

Rosemond Tuve, *A Reading of George Herbert* (Chicago: University of Chicago Press, 1952);

Gene Edward Veith, Jr., *Reformation Spirituality: The Religion of George Herbert* (Lewisburg, Pa.: Bucknell University Press, 1985);

Helen Vendler, *The Poetry of George Herbert* (Cambridge, Mass.: Harvard University Press, 1975);

John N. Wall, Jr., *Transformations of the Word: Spenser, Herbert, Vaughan* (Athens: University of Georgia Press, 1988);

Bart Westerweel, *Patterns and Patterning: A Study of Four Poems by George Herbert* (Amsterdam: Rodopi, 1984);

Helen C. White, *The Metaphysical Poets: A Study in Religious Experience* (New York: Macmillan, 1936).

Papers:

There are two important manuscripts of Herbert's writings still in existence. The Williams Manuscript, held in Dr. Williams's Library, London, comprises an early version and arrangement of nearly one-half of the poems of *The Temple,* with some corrections in Herbert's own hand, and two Latin collections, *Lucus* and *Passio Discerpta,* written in Herbert's hand. The Bodleian manuscript, held in the Bodleian Library, Oxford, is the manuscript distributed to the licensers prior to the publication of *The Temple.* Other letters, orations, and records bearing Herbert's signature are located in the British Library, the Ferrar Papers at Magdalene College, Cambridge, Dr. Williams's Library, and the Salisbury Diocesan Registry. Izaak Walton reports that Herbert's widow preserved many of her husband's papers but that these were burnt during the English Civil War.

Robert Herrick

(August 1591 – October 1674)

Roger B. Rollin
Clemson University

BOOK: *Hesperides: Or, The Works Both Humane & Divine of Robert Herrick Esq.* (London: Printed for John Williams and Francis Eglesfield, 1648; facsimile, Menston, England: Scolar Press, 1969).

Editions: *Hesperides: or the Works both Humane and Divine of Robert Herrick, Esq.,* 2 volumes, British Poets, edited by F. J. Child (Boston: Little, Brown / New York: James S. Dickerson, 1856);

Poetical Works, edited by L. C. Martin (Oxford: Clarendon Press, 1956); revised as *The Poems of Robert Herrick* (London, New York & Toronto: Oxford University Press, 1965);

The Complete Poetry of Robert Herrick, edited by J. Max Patrick (Garden City: New York University Press, 1963).

Almost forgotten in the eighteenth century, and in the nineteenth century alternately applauded for his poetry's lyricism and condemned for its "obscenities," Robert Herrick is, in the latter half of the twentieth century, finally becoming recognized as one of the most accomplished nondramatic poets of his age. Long dismissed as merely a "minor poet" and, as a consequence, neglected or underestimated by scholars and critics, the achievement represented by his only book, the collection of poems entitled *Hesperides: Or, The Works Both Humane & Divine* (1648), is gradually coming to be more fully appreciated. While some of his individual poems – "To the Virgins to make much of Time," "Upon Julia's Clothes," and "Corinna's going a Maying," for example – are among the most popular of all time, recent examinations of his *Hesperides* as a whole have begun to reveal a Herrick whose artistry in the arrangement of his volume approximates the artistry of his individual works and whose sensibility is complex but coherent, subtle as well as substantive. In short, Robert Herrick, who was proud to be one of "the sons of Ben," has begun to be seen, along with his literary "father," Ben Jonson, as one of the most noteworthy figures of early-seventeenth-century British poetry.

Robert Herrick, baptized on 24 August 1591, was the seventh child and fourth son of a London goldsmith, Nicholas Herrick, and Julian (or Juliana or Julia) Stone Herrick. He was little more than fourteen months old when his father apparently committed suicide by "falling" from an upper story window of his house in Cheapside on 9 November 1592. His mother never remarried, and it seems more than a coincidence that father figures would loom large in the poet's *Hesperides*. One of that collection's best-known works, for example, is "To the reverend shade of his religious Father," in which Herrick resurrects his father by eternizing him in poetry: "For my life mortall, Rise from out thy Herse, / And take a life immortal from my Verse."

By age sixteen Herrick was apprenticed to his uncle, but apparently found either Sir William Herrick or the goldsmith trade incompatible, for the ten-year apprenticeship was terminated after six years. At the comparatively advanced age of twenty-two, Herrick matriculated at Saint John's College, Cambridge. Although his *Hesperides* would include a large number of commendatory poems to various relatives, none is addressed to Sir William. Extant, however, are fourteen letters from young "Robin" to his uncle: full of filial humility, all ask for money out of the nephew's own inheritance, which was apparently still controlled by Sir William. Limited means would eventually force Herrick to transfer to a less expensive college, Trinity Hall.

Between his graduation from Cambridge in 1617 and his appointment, twelve years later, as vicar of Dean Prior in Devonshire, tantalizingly little is known about Herrick's life. It is almost certain, however, that some of this time was spent in London, where the budding poet at last found a surrogate father who lived up to his expectations, Ben Jonson. Paterfamilias to "the sons of Ben," eminent

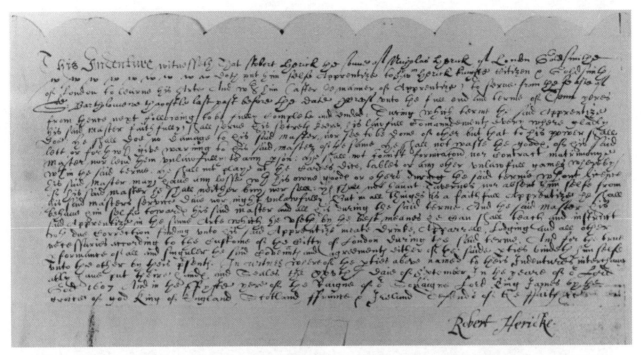

Indenture agreement (25 September 1607) by which sixteen-year-old Robert Herrick apprenticed himself to his uncle, Sir William Herrick, a goldsmith. This document, with the text in the hand of a professional scrivener, bears the earliest known example of Herrick's signature (Sotheby's auction catalogue, sale number 3506, 15 December 1988).

poet, dramatist, actor, man of letters, London's literary lion, Jonson became the subject of five of Herrick's poems. Although all of the poems praise Jonson as an artist, the first two to appear in *Hesperides,* "Upon Master Ben. Johnson. Epigram" and "Another," are not without ambivalence toward yet another "father" who has died (1637) and left his "son" behind. In the gently humorous "His Prayer to Ben Johnson," Herrick implicitly promises the kind of "life immortal" (through his poem) that he had explicitly promised Nicholas Herrick in "To the reverend shade of his religious Father." The poet's ultimate contentment in his role as a "son of Ben" finds expression in the formality of his epitaph "Upon Ben. Johnson" and in the intimacy and nostalgia of "An Ode for him."

The influence of Jonson, however, goes beyond these poetic tributes. More than any of the other "sons," Herrick follows Jonson's prescription for "writing well." For example, Jonson recommended reading "the best Authors," particularly "the Ancients," and Herrick has long been recognized for his more than nodding acquaintance with the works of classical writers such as the legendary Greek poet of wine, women, and song, Anacreon; and with Roman poets, especially Horace and Martial, but also Catullus, Tibullus, and Ovid (all of whom Herrick mentions, quotes, or borrows from). Although the ancients and the best moderns must

be employed as models, Jonson counseled, the aspiring poet's own sensibility should be imposed on the borrowed subjects, themes, and styles. This injunction Herrick also obeys – in "Anacreontike," for example – in scores of classically styled epigrams, epitaphs, odes, and lyrics, and even in imitations of Jonson himself such as "Delight in Disorder." Jonson was also a strong proponent of revision, and thus Herrick, in "His request to Julia," writes, "Better 'twere my Book were dead, / Then to live not perfected." Jonson finally admitted, however, that one cannot be a poet without endowments such as "nature," genius or talent, and "art," the kind of craftsmanship that can transform the stuff of human life into poetry. The endurance of Herrick's work and the growth of his reputation demonstrate that he possessed both.

In 1623 Herrick took holy orders, though there is no record of his being assigned to any particular parish. This step, at the mature age of thirty-two, may indicate that he was unable to find preferment elsewhere. As a poet, however, public recognition would come his way in the form of a generous mention in Richard James's *The Muses Dirge* (1625). Despite this tribute and Herrick's evident itch for literary fame, his name did not by any means become a household word during his long lifetime.

The next record of Herrick's activities is from 1627, when he became one of the several chaplains

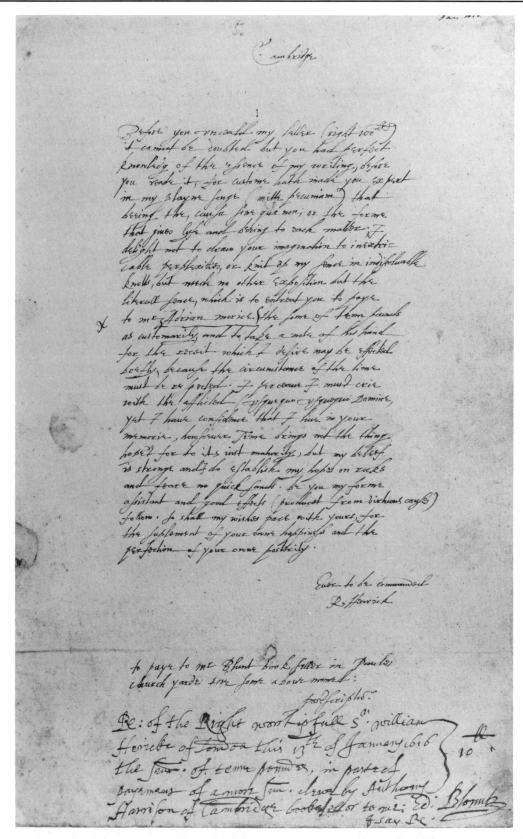

Letters written at Trinity Hall, Cambridge, in which Robert Herrick asks Sir William Herrick to pay booksellers. Cambridge bookseller Edward Blount wrote a receipt at the bottom of the letter above (Sotheby's auction catalogue, sale number 3506, 15 December 1988).

Cambridge: ij̄h̄ of
October.

Sr my deutie remembred to your
self and — the cause Essentiall
is this: That I would entreat you
to paye to this oringer to mr
Adrian marius book seller in
the black friers) the somke of
ε̄ᵗ: the which my Tutor hath
receaued, to be payde at London
I haue busines that drawes me
from prolixitie and I craue pardon.
for this rudeness still expecting
the sun-shine of your fauour
and the dayes of happiness. I end
with my prayers for your preser-
uation. and health the best terres-
triall good.   long by and
the affections of Heauen fall vpon you.

                    yours euer
                    obsequious
                    R Herrick.

The Parish Church of Saint George the Martyr, where Herrick was installed as vicar in 1630. His parsonage is on the right.

of George Villiers, first Duke of Buckingham, in a crusade to the Isle of Rhé to liberate French Protestants. A disastrous combination of illness among the troops, effective military action by the French, and a storm at sea while Buckingham's ships were retreating to England resulted in the loss of two-thirds of the expedition. Small wonder that shortly thereafter, in 1629, Herrick exchanged a life of danger for one of apparent safety by accepting a nomination to the vicarage of Dean Prior, a hamlet in Devonshire, far to the southwest of London.

He was installed as vicar on 29 October 1630. To become a country parson at age thirty-nine had to have been a radical change from Herrick's former life among literati, courtiers, and assorted military adventurers. The part of the West Country to which his new calling took him is even now largely rural: in the seventeenth century it was remote in the extreme. In 1630 the two nearest cities of size, Exeter to the northeast and Plymouth to the southwest, would both have been nearly a day's horseback ride away. The capital was a five-day journey. Herrick's church, of Saint George the Martyr (which still stands), though attractive, was modest, and the adjacent vicarage (portions of which have been incorporated into the existing dwelling) was more modest still.

Herrick may have expected this post to be temporary. He had, after all, highly placed friends such as Mildmay Fane, second Earl of Westmorland; Sir Clipsby Crewe; and an officer in the royal household, Endymion Porter. Moreover (although their dating is not certain), works of his such as "A Christmas Caroll" and "The New-yeeres Gift" would be set to music by the well-known musician Henry Lawes and sung before King Charles I. Herrick also cultivated the royal family with a series of flattering poems. Indeed, the king, though he was nine years younger than Herrick, emerges in *Hesperides* as yet another father figure. An occasional poem, "To the King, Upon comming with his Army into the West," precedes both Herrick's poem to his father and his first poem to Jonson in *Hesperides,* even though the event being celebrated took place only four years before publication of the collection. In this encomium, through a conflation of paternal archetypes, Charles is presented as a tutelary deity, a husband, and a conquering hero. The king's declining fortunes in the 1640s, however, must have made it difficult to sustain faith in his power and in his capacity to protect and nurture, to be a father to his subjects. As intimated by Herrick's body of religious verse, *His Noble Numbers* (published with *Hesperides*), the needs that his natural and other fathers were unable to meet he comes to find in his Heavenly Father.

Herrick served as vicar of Dean Prior for thirty-one years. That service was not, however, without interruption. Herrick was every inch the Royalist (as his panegyrics to Charles I, Henrietta Maria, and Charles, Prince of Wales, make evident) and, if his religious poems are any indication, a rather traditional Anglican, even though he resided in a part of the country strongly sympathetic to the Puritan cause and, during the Civil War, to the parliamentary forces. Such parsons were anathema to the victorious Puritans, and in 1647 the poet was among the 142 Devonshire clergymen expelled from their parishes for their convictions. Returning to his post during the Restoration, Herrick served for fourteen more years until his death at the end of harvest season in 1674.

About his expulsion Herrick must have had mixed feelings. He was, after all, a Londoner born and bred, university educated, and friend and acquaintance to some of the political and cultural powers of the land. In a poem with the explicitly autobiographical title of "To Dean-bourn, a rude river in Devon, by which sometimes he lived" (which may have been occasioned by his expulsion) Herrick rails, first, against the countryside, symbolized by this small stream:

Dean-bourn, farewell; I never look to see
MIDeane, or thy warty incivility.
Thy rockie bottome, that doth teare thy streams,
And makes them frantick, ev'n to all extreames;
To my content, I never sho'd behold,
Were thy streames silver, or thy rocks all gold.

Clearly, more than a river is on the poet's mind:

Rockie thou art; and rockie we discover
Thy men; and rockie are thy wayes all over.
O men, O manners; Now, and ever knowne
To be *A Rockie Generation!*
A people currish; churlish as the seas;
And rude (almost) as rudest Salvages.
With whom I did, and may re-sojourne when
Rockes turn to Rivers, Rivers turn to Men.

What the poem deplores is the primitiveness, not only of the countryside but of the people themselves, who represent nature unimproved by art – that is, by civilization and culture.

Another poem possibly inspired by Herrick's enforced departure from the West Country is "His returne to London." Here the emphasis shifts from the misery of time spent in "the dull confines of the drooping West" to the joys of London, "blest place

of my Nativitie!" London is England's Rome – "O *Place!* O *People!* Manners! fram'd to please" – and Herrick's "home." Herrick does not consider himself banished from Dean Prior; he was banished to it: "by hard fate sent / Into a long and irksome banishment." He would rather die than return to Devonshire, and he asks that his "sacred Reliques" be buried in London.

Either these poems represent the artistic advantages of poetic license or Herrick changed his mind: in 1660 he personally petitioned to be returned to his former vicarage in "the drooping West," and that petition was granted. There is a good deal of evidence that Herrick was in fact employing exaggeration for poetic effect in "To Dean-bourn" and "His returne to London." His attitude toward country life, like his attitudes on a wealth of topics (love and women, government, social class, even religion and poetry), was creatively ambivalent, as his well-known epigram "Discontents in Devon" demonstrates:

More discontents I never had
  Since I was born, then here;
Where I have been, and still am sad,
  In this dull *Devon-shire*:
Yet justly too I must confesse;
  I ne'r invented such
Ennobled numbers for the Presse,
  Then where I loath'd so much.

Musing on the mystery of creativity, on the relationship between milieu and productivity (as this most self-conscious poet does more than once), he has to conclude that for Robert Herrick the poet country life cannot be all bad. Even this grudging admission does not begin to suggest the vision of art and life that emerges from the more than fourteen hundred poems of Herrick's *Hesperides*. This fact, plus the very number and variety of these poems, as well as their arrangement (and thus their relationships to each other), make the issue of how Herrick's book should be approached a crucial one.

Today most readers encounter Herrick in anthology selections. That is, in a sense, how he was first read, in the days when a limited number of his poems circulated in manuscript. When he collected his oeuvre for publication, however, he clearly had something else in mind. He seems to have been the first poet – and still the only important poet – to gather practically all of his verses into one elaborately designed volume and see it through the presses. From the beginning of that volume Herrick makes it plain that he expects his audience to read his entire book, to read it in the order in which it is printed, and, above all, to read it with understanding and appreciation. Then as now, such an understanding and appreciation require that the reader develop some kind of approach to the text, and here Herrick volunteers his services.

Hesperides is the only major collection of poetry in English to open with a versified table of contents. This guide hints strongly at what type of poet Herrick thinks he is, and thus, by implication, how his book is to be approached. "The Argument of his Book" begins, "I Sing" – suggesting Herrick sees himself as a lyric poet – "of *Brooks,* of *Blossomes, Birds,* and *Bowers*: / Of *April, May,* of *June,* and *July-*Flowers" – suggesting he is also a pastoral poet. Pastoral poets, of course, valorize a life lived close to the beauties of nature (often opposing it to life lived in the decadent city) and idealize that life by focusing on the countryside in its most benign seasons. Elsewhere in *Hesperides* there is ample warrant for approaching Herrick as a pastoral poet, even though not all nor even most of his poems can be classified as bucolic.

Another approach to Herrick's collection, however, may be hinted at in succeeding lines of "The Argument of his Book": "I sing of *May-poles, Hock-carts, Wassails, Wakes,* / Of *Bride-grooms, Brides,* and of their *Bridall-Cakes.*" Maypoles and hockcarts (wagons in which the last fruits of the harvest are brought in) suggest English country life and, consequently, domesticated (rather than Greek, Roman, or biblical) pastoral. Love, of course, is also a common subject of bucolic poetry, but all of the images in these particular lines also have to do with ceremonies – special, often sanctified, events that figure importantly in human life and are fraught with significance as well as emotion. Poetry, or at least the reading of it, can be thought of as a kind of ritual, so perhaps Herrick is indicating here that he is a poet of ceremony and a ceremonial poet. Elsewhere in *Hesperides* there is warrant for taking this approach as well.

Lines 5 and 6 of Herrick's "Argument" begin with a different phrase, "I write" – less suggestive of a lyric poet – "of *Youth,* of *Love,* and have Accesse / By these, to sing of cleanly-*Wantonnesse.*" Although youth, love, and sex (Herrick's memorable phrase suggests sex without sin, something of a novel notion in the seventeenth century) have traditionally been subjects of lyric poetry, "I write" may hint at the hundreds of epigrams on amatory themes and the score of other subjects that are scattered throughout *Hesperides*. A productive approach to Herrick's collection must also accommodate these short, pithy poems that treat something other than bucolic or ceremonial themes.

In the remainder of "The Argument" Herrick indexes his other subjects – some natural, such as "*Dewes*" and "*Raines,*" "*Spice,* and *Amber-Greece,*" some philosophical, such as transiency ("*Times transshifting*"), and some supernatural, such as "the *Fairie-King.*" Herrick concludes by announcing that he is also a religious poet and a Christian man: "I write of *Hell*; I sing (and ever shall) / Of *Heaven,* and hope to have it after all."

Herrick's list is by no means exhaustive. He does not tell the reader that *Hesperides* includes political poems, ranging from flattering portraits of royalty and nobility to acerbic comments on government officials, practices, and policies. Nor does Herrick forewarn the reader that the collection also includes shockingly naturalistic, even scatological, epigrams. He also does not reveal that *Hesperides* is historically and morally grounded in numerous poems that pay tribute to an assortment of relatives, friends, and patrons (much as his "Father Jonson" so often did) by transforming them into representations of a Christian-humanistic ethos. In addition, Herrick only hints at the existence of his poems of the good life, works that, in the Cavalier tradition, celebrate friendship and sociability, the pleasures of fine food and drink, of conviviality in general.

The poet's more sober, philosophical vein, which surfaces in so many of the most important works in *Hesperides,* is signaled by the memorable phrase "*Times trans-shifting*" – the notion that everything that lives is subject to temporality and flux. The inexorable logic of time for humankind at least is the inevitability of decline and death. Though a Christian priest, Herrick is capable of contemplating death without transfiguration, seeing the grave as the end of all that is good, as ultimate oblivion, nothingness. He views this grim possibility with equanimity, with a poise that is intellectual as well as emotional. Like the classical Stoic, he responds to the prospect of his inevitable death by affirming life, but life lived modestly and taken as it comes, the bad with the good. Like the serious Epicurean, Herrick seeks to maximize pleasure and minimize pain by following the classical principle of moderation – "nothing in excess." Thus even the good life, in Herrick's vision, tends to be scaled down to modest expectations: love and friendship, good food and drink, ordinary pastimes, and, above all, poetry.

Although he is not always solemn, Herrick is often serious, and he takes "good verses" seriously indeed. No English poet of importance is so self-referential – so involved in writing poetry about poetry, about its readers, about poets, and about himself as a poet. For example, the next seven pieces following "The Argument of his Book" are "To his Muse," which implies he is a pastoralist who fears the "Contempts" that his verses may evoke from courts, cities, and critics; "To his Booke," which presents *Hesperides* as Herrick's "child" going forth into a precarious world; "Another," which comically skewers the hypocrisy of readers who publicly pretend to be embarrassed by his erotica but who privately take it in stride; another epigram by the same title, the first of many scatological poems that have unsettled Herrick's critics, curses with "*Piles*" anyone who has the effrontery to use the pages of his book for toilet paper; the next poem is a curse addressed "To the soure Reader" who works through the entire collection but still dislikes it; another epigram addressed "To his Booke" warns against intemperate readers; in the well-known "When he would have his verses read," however, Herrick proclaims that his poetry is not for reading on "sober mornings" but "when that men have both well drunke, and fed, . . . when the Hearth / Smiles to it selfe, and guilds the roofe with mirth" – in short, in Epicurean or Anacreontic moments.

Altogether, it is an extraordinary way to begin a collection of poetry – at once defensive, disarming, offensive, delightful, and instructive. Similarly self-referential poems interspersed throughout *Hesperides* are among the book's most memorable. Some are self-presentations: for example, "The bad season makes the poet sad" shows Herrick pondering why the Civil War has stifled his creativity, and "Upon his Verses" slyly declares that (unlike some poets) he is no plagiarist. At times Herrick waxes philosophical, contemplating the relationship between life and art metaphorically in "Delight in Disorder," for instance, or avuncular, as when he leaves to posterity his "Lyrick for Legacies."

Posterity, in fact, is much on Herrick's mind. Time and time again he reiterates his faith in "the eternizing power of poetry." This theme combines his poems about poetry with his neo-Stoical vein: since, as the title of one epigram proclaims, "Poetry perpetuates the poet," as well as the poet's subjects, Herrick can triumph over "*Times trans-shifting*" and live beyond death through his verses. *Hesperides* thus becomes his eternal monument, preserving his name and his fame forever:

> Trust to good Verses, then;
>   They onely will aspire,
> When Pyramids, as men,
>   Are lost, i'th' funerall fire.

The title of the poem in which these lines appear, "To live merrily, and to trust to Good Verses," has

sometimes been regarded as encapsulating the spirit of *Hesperides*. Such a view is too reductive to be entirely valid, but also too much in the neighborhood of the truth to be dismissed out of hand. Herrick exhibits an almost Roman gusto for the good life, and to such a life poetry is central. Poetry, however, is also connected with death, or with the denial of death.

For Herrick poetry becomes a secular religion and the symbolic foundation of *Hesperides*. The last work in the collection is a pattern poem in the shape of a classical column, "The pillar of Fame." On this pillar made of words Herrick's collected "humane works" symbolically rest, just as Herrick's art is grounded in the belief that it can secure eternal fame for him, be a monument "Out-during *Marble, Brasse,* or *Jet*." It is not an entirely misplaced belief: Robert Herrick, the obscure country parson and sometime poet, today is better known than most of the famous and infamous of his age.

The poetic base on which "The pillar of Fame" rests is an untitled epigram: "To his Book's end this last line he'd have plac't, / *Jocund his Muse was; but his Life was chast.*" This two-line poem does triple duty: it is intended to excuse Herrick for the off-color pieces in *Hesperides*, to act as a transition to the religious poetry of *His Noble Numbers* immediately following, and artfully to blur the distinctions between art and life, a frequent Hesperidean theme. Although "jocund" can accommodate a multitude of sins, what the poet probably had in mind are those works for which he is best known and probably most admired, his love lyrics.

Herrick never married, and literary gossips have reveled in speculations about the identities of the fourteen "mistresses" (in the seventeenth century, inamoratas, lady friends, or merely admired acquaintances) to whom he addressed 158 poems. Whether they were flesh and blood or, as modern consensus has it, pretty fictions is of little consequence: Herrick is only conforming to the common poetic practice of the time when he addresses his uniformly young and beautiful Julias, Corinnas, and Antheas. Where he does not conform is in his penning of romantic verses to identifiable women whose real names he supplies – for example, Elizabeth Wheeler, Lettice Yard, and Katherine Bradshaw. His poems to these flesh-and-blood, well-born ladies, however, tend to be more "cleanly" than "wanton."

Herrick's love poetry ranges from the bawdy ("The Vine") to the neo-Petrarchan ("To Anthea, who may command him anything"). That range, but also Herrick's normative representation of love, makes "cleanly-*Wantonnesse*" an apt phrase to characterize his amatory verses. The phrase suggests an accommodation between nature and civilization, between life and art, and between the romantic and the sexual that reflects Herrick's inclination toward the via media.

In addition to the love complaints and celebrations of the mistress so common to seventeenth-century love poetry, Herrick also treats subjects readers might think of as "modern." For example, one poem, invariably anthologized, is "Upon Julia's Clothes":

When as in silks my *Julia* goes,
Then, then (me thinks) how sweetly flowes
That liquefaction of her clothes.

Next, when I cast mine eyes and see
That brave Vibration each way free;
O how that glittering taketh me!

This small poem, merely two triplet stanzas, is grounded in the courtship ritual twentieth-century America calls "girl-watching." It turns on the joke that he who casts his eyes in a lady's direction may get hooked himself. "Upon Julia's Clothes" also glances at a mystery of sexual aesthetics: why someone can be more appealing in one particular garb than another. Indeed, sexual aesthetics – the question of the relationship between appearance and attraction – is a subject of particular interest to Herrick and has led to his being criticized by those who seem to believe that sex is chiefly hormonal.

Herrick also can bring his "invention" to bear upon more traditional forms of love poetry. For example, in "To Phillis to love and live with him," he avoids much of what had become the clichés of the invitation-to-love by shifting the scene of this pastoral subgenre indoors and having the lover woo the lady with citified gifts. Another pastoral invitation-poem with a difference, "Corinna's going a Maying," is also Herrick's most admired work. Here the lady is being seduced *out* of bed to join in the ceremonies of May Day, when the town goes into the country to gather greenery, thereby transforming the country into the town and vice versa. She is warned that lying in bed is a "sin" against the religion of nature: "Wash, dresse, be brief in praying: / Few Beads are best, when once we goe a maying." She is also reminded that she is missing romantic rituals associated with this day, from outdoor sex to courtship and betrothal: "And some have wept, and woo'd, and plighted Troth, / And chose their Priest, ere we can cast off sloth." What makes the poem most memorable, however, is its final stanza, where Herrick, with his customary Stoic realism, reminds

Corinna (and his reader) that, as creatures of nature, we are all subject to time, that time flies, and thus youth and love are not forever:

Come, let us goe, while we are in our prime;
And take the harmlesse follie of the time.
    We shall grow old apace, and die
    Before we know our liberty.
    Our life is short; and our dayes run
    As fast away as do's the Sunne;
And as a vapour, or a drop of raine
Once lost, can ne'r be found againe:
    So when or you or I are made
    A fable, song, or fleeting shade;
    All love, all liking, all delight
    Lies drown'd with us in endlesse night.
Then while time serves, and we are but decaying;
Come, my *Corinna,* come, let's goe a Maying.

It is but another step to the grim vision of Andrew Marvell's "To his Coy Mistress," which likewise denies that love can offer transcendence.

Critical consensus holds that Herrick is also particularly successful in the genre of the marriage poem. He wrote two of them, both for actual weddings, and they are among the longest and most ambitious of his efforts. Both are ceremonial works in a dual sense: they depict and elevate the rituals that follow the marriage service and, as ceremonial works themselves, they participate in those rituals. "A Nuptiall Song" is especially noteworthy for its intricate prosody, lush imagery, and humor combined with pathos. The poet who lived a single life and revealed in "No spouse but a Sister" that he could be more than a little cynical about wedded bliss –

A Bachelour I will
Live as I have liv'd still,
And never take a wife
To crucifie my life

– can wax eloquent about other people's weddings and even acknowledge the possibility of a "pleasing wife." The latter phrase comes from a poem entitled "His age," in which Herrick fantasizes himself not only old, but married, and with a son. He imagines his "young / *Iülus*" singing and reading his father's love lyrics, eventually leading "old" Herrick to conclude that, when all is said and done, "*No lust there's like to Poetry.*"

Herrick's invention is notable too in that poetic mode with which he most identifies himself, the pastoral. He can write the most conventional sort of Arcadian dialogue, such as "A Bucolick betwixt Two," complete with conventional Greek names for his shepherd and shepherdess (Lacon and Thyrsis) and conventional bathos. He is more likely, however, to take his classical models and English them, as he does in "The Country life." This poem, addressed to his high-ranking friend and patron, Endymion Porter, after drawing a conventional contrast between the "Sweet Country life" and the frantic existence to be found in "Courts, and Cities," goes on to follow Porter as he makes the rounds of his rural estate. Here classical images of "enameld Meads" (picture-perfect meadows) and piping shepherds are mixed with more familiar vignettes, such as a whistling plowman, and native English pastimes such as the "Morris-dance."

In the similarly titled "A Country life," another Anglicized pastoral, Herrick praises his older brother Thomas for being one who "Could'st leave the City, for exchange, to see / The Countries sweet simplicity." The poem, indeed, advises practicing rural simplicity and cultivating rural innocence, and it gradually develops an ethos of as well as a prescription for the good life. Herrick describes his brother as a person who possesses a good conscience, who understands and applies the principle of moderation in all things, including love. In aphorism after aphorism Herrick builds up the kind of portrait of the ideal person that his ethical epigrams and personal encomiums also paint. Such a person should be Stoical, like Thomas – "thou liv'st fearlesse; and thy face ne'r shewes / Fortune when she comes or goes" – and should be satisfied with what the countryside affords, for "*Content makes all Ambrosia.*" Amid such familiar English sounds as "singing Crickits by thy fire" and English sights such as a "green-ey'd Kitling" chasing a "brisk Mouse," Thomas realizes that "*Wealth cannot make a life, but Love.*" Such aphorisms, embedded in a pastoral-advisive poem, indicate how Herrick synthesizes his bucolic, ritualistic, and epigrammatic strains.

Most pastoral poets tend to be city types nostalgic for a golden age or for an impossible rural ideal. Herrick is appreciative of the native English country culture, but he is at the same time aware of its socioeconomic base. "The Wake," for example, catalogues the agreeable array of foods and entertainments at a typical annual parish festival but also observes that English rustics (unlike the swains of traditional pastoral) are prone to fighting and drunkenness. The gentleman speaker also notes in closing that the expectations these humble folk have about life are (by implication) more modest than his, but where there is less to lose, there is less to worry about:

> Happy Rusticks, best content
> With the cheapest Merriment:
> And possesse no other feare,
> Then to want the Wake next Yeare.

Herrick also explores relationships between social class and perception in the poem entitled "The Hock-cart, or Harvest home." This too is a ceremonial as well as a pastoral work, for not only is its subject a country ritual but the poem itself is structured like a ritual: as speaker, Herrick serves as the master of the revels for this celebration of the end of the harvest on the estate of his friend, the earl of Westmorland. Herrick calls together the farmhands, the "Sons of Summer," whose physical labors support their betters (like himself and Westmorland), and invites the earl to enjoy the sights and sounds of the various folk rituals. The poet then urges the "brave boys" into the great hall for a feast and a series of toasts – first, of course, "to your Lords health," then "to the Plough (the Common-wealth)," that is, the symbol of the agricultural economy upon which all subsist. In the very midst of the festivities, however, Herrick bluntly reminds these laborers that although they, like oxen, fatten up in this time of plenty, both men and animals must in the spring go back to working the land. In conclusion Herrick recalls to them the economic foundations of the master-servant relationship:

> And, you must know, your Lords word's true,
> Feed him ye must, whose food fils you.
> And that this pleasure is like raine,
> Not sent ye for to drowne your paine,
> But for to make it spring againe.

This is real-world pastoral in which landowners and laborers exist in a symbiotic relationship and holidays help insure that farm work ("your paine") will resume when springtime comes.

In two poems that bring pastoral down to an even more personal and private level, "His content in the Country" and "A Thanksgiving to God, for his House," Herrick further develops his unique domesticated vision of the good life close to nature. The first poem is another epigram that advances an ethos, centered typically on the classical virtue of moderation; given Herrick's sensitivity to the placement of his poems, it is probably no coincidence that it is located at the very center of *Hesperides*:

> Here, here I live with what my Board
> Can with the smallest cost afford.
> Though ne'r so mean the Viands be,
> They well content my *Prew* and me.

Herrick may be the only important English poet to refer to his housemaid in his poetry (and he does so more than once). Such things do not make the old Royalist a democrat, but they do say something about his sensibility, which it would be presumptuous to call "modern." He recognizes that ordinary people and ordinary life can be as much the stuff of poetry as great ones and glamour. The poem goes on to illustrate the principle "What ever comes" — whether it be garden vegetables, modest housing, freedom from debt, or sound sleep — "content makes sweet." The country life is a quiet and private life — "We blesse our Fortunes, when we see / Our own beloved privacie" — and, for this fame-struck poet, one of surprisingly agreeable anonymity: "[We] like our living, where w'are known / To very few, or else to none."

"A Thanksgiving to God, for his House" is likewise everyday pastoral, this time in the shape of an informal, rambling, and genial prayer. Herrick's vicarage alongside the Exeter-Plymouth road is a "little house, whose humble Roof / Is weatherproof; / Under the sparres of which I lie / Both soft, and drie." The idealized self-image he presents here is one that accords well with this house: he thanks God for his humility — "Low is my porch, as is my Fate" — for his charity and hospitality, for simple food such as "my beloved Beet," for "Wassaile Bowles to drink," and for a "teeming Hen" and "healthfull Ewes." One central domestic image of universal appeal sums up this poet's content in the country:

> Some brittle sticks of Thorne or Briar
> > Make me a fire,
> Close by whose living coale I sit,
> > And glow like it.

Herrick's images allow one to believe that this former university wit, man-about-London, military veteran, and friend of the great is genuinely thankful for his humble country living in Dean Prior:

> All these, and better Thou dost send
> > Me, to this end,
> That I should render, for my part,
> > A thankfull heart[.]

"A Thanksgiving to God, for his House" is to be found in Herrick's collection of religious poetry, *His Noble Numbers: Or, His Pious Pieces,* and an overarching pattern of that collection may help explain why, despite his own protestations, Herrick returned to his West Country vicarage after the Restoration. Although bound with the 1648 *Hesperides, His Noble Num-*

bers has its own title page bearing a 1647 date, which suggests that the work may have been intended to be printed earlier and separately. Whatever the reasons for deciding to combine the two books, the result was a happy one. Although it has been something of a critical cliché that this successful secular poet strangely fails as a sacred one, Herrick is one poet, not two, and his collections are linked thematically, stylistically, structurally, and by the author's "unifying personality." The neo-Stoicism of the secular verse had since the Middle Ages been seen as eminently compatible with a Christian ethos, and so it proves to be in both of Herrick's collections. Likewise, the pastoral stance of *Hesperides* reappears in *His Noble Numbers,* though less frequently. As might be expected in the case of religious verse, Herrick's epigrammatic and ceremonial modes predominate. His tendency to experiment with the length of his lines and to employ short lines (more than any other notable English poet) is almost as apparent in *His Noble Numbers* as in *Hesperides.* Like the latter, the former begins and ends with a set series of poems. Between these "framing" devices attention clearly has been paid to the arrangement of individual poems and of "poem clusters." The majority of the "Pious Pieces," like the poems in *Hesperides,* cannot be dated, but it is reasonable to assume that, just as Herrick wrote secular verse after he took holy orders, as a good Christian he probably wrote a certain amount of religious poetry before he became a priest. Moreover, it is the case that poems in *Hesperides,* especially those in the philosophical or meditative modes, can be viewed as pious pieces in the broader sense of that phrase.

In contrast to the originality and smooth assuredness of "The Argument of his Book," the opening poem of *His Noble Numbers* is the ritualistic "His Confession," which begs God to forgive all of Herrick's works of "wanton wit" — the poems, ironically, that would win him his fame. The next poem, "His Prayer for Absolution," repeats this refrain, begging pardon for his "unbaptized Rhimes" (which Herrick nonetheless printed) "Writ in my wild unhallowed Times." These retraction-poems express the tension many seventeenth-century writers experienced between their desire to write secular verse and their sense of obligation to their faith.

These two poems are followed by a series of seven epigrams in which Herrick assumes the role of theologian (interestingly enough, the vicar of Dean Prior never explicitly adopts the role of priest in this collection). These succinct poems paradoxically explore the nature but ultimate unknowability of God. Many of the sacred epigrams in the collection are theological in nature, some of them quite

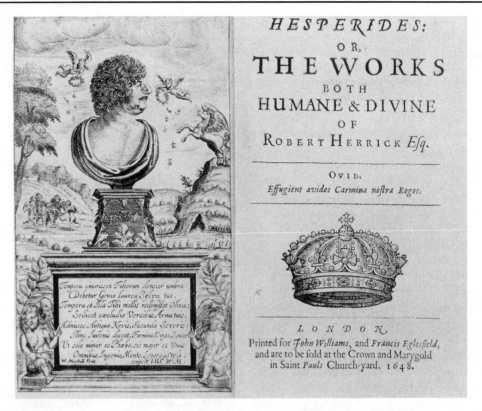

Frontispiece and title page for Herrick's only book. Behind the bust of Herrick are the Hill of Parnassus, the Spring of Helicon, the nine Muses, and their winged horse, Pegasus — all associated with poetic inspiration.

abstract and abstruse, thus disproving the view that Herrick's religion is "childlike." Everywhere, the figure of the deity is dominant. In the first third of *His Noble Numbers,* God tends to be a remote figure who is both threatening and benign. Poems in which the Heavenly Father punishes his wicked children far outnumber those in which he exhibits paternal love. Prominent among the latter, however, are "A Thanksgiving to God, for his House" and a nativity ode. The familiar Herrick of *Hesperides* and the Herrick of *His Noble Numbers* meet in "His Letanie, to the Holy Spirit," in which the speaker vividly envisions his own deathbed scene. The poet dramatically combines stanza-length scenes of pathos – "When I lie within my bed, / Sick in heart, and sick in head, / And with doubts discomforted" – with vignettes of morbid humor – "When the artlesse Doctor sees / No one hope, but of his Fees, / And his skill runs on the lees" – each followed by the anxious refrain "Sweet Spirit comfort me!" The initial third of Herrick's "Pious Pieces" also includes "His Creed," a poem that, because it sets forth the most basic Christian doctrine in sixteen terse lines – as any versified catechism should – has led critics who have failed to read carefully all of *His Noble Numbers* to characterize the poet's Christianity as "simplistic."

The second third of Herrick's sacred collection is marked by several ambitious lyrics on the infant Christ. Indeed, the Son of God figures more prominently in the middle section than in the first, and the effect is to soften the image of the Almighty as a punishing father. Consequently, the initial ambivalence about God expressed early in *His Noble Numbers* begins to dissipate. The most original poem in this group, however, "The white Island: or place of the Blest," exhibits a mood and tone that are mixed, even elusive. The image of heaven as a white island seems to have been Herrick's own, and not all readers will find it congenial. In contrast to existence on Earth (characterized as "the *Isle of Dreames*"), in "that *whiter Island*" above, "Things are evermore sincere; / Candor here, and lustre there / Delighting." The very abstractness of "Things," "sincere," "Candor," and "lustre" makes "Delighting" seem a doubtful choice of participles. Herrick goes on to describe heaven as a place where people will no longer require "calm and cooling sleep" but will remain forever with their eyes wide open. Readers may be forgiven if they find this prospect vaguely discomforting and the promise of abstract "Pleasures" and "fresh joyes" unconvincing. This poem is one of very few in which Herrick's intentions are unclear, reminding the reader, perhaps, how of the Earth, earthy, he is.

The final third of *His Noble Numbers,* like the rest of the collection, is made up mainly of sacred epigrams, almost any of which could serve as a kind of versified "text" on which a sermon could be based. Many of these epigrams, such as "Predestination," offer succinct explanations of Christian doctrine or, such as "*Almes,*" are advisory or admonitory in nature. In the latter vein is a lyric that explains how "To keep a true Lent" even as it shames hypocritical kinds of observance. More personal is an important work in this part of the collection, "His meditation upon Death," whose speaker sounds very much like the neo-Stoical Herrick of the secular poems – that is, one who professes to be "content" even if his earthly hours are numbered, and "indifferent" if a long life lies before him: living well, not long, is the key. Herrick vows to contemplate his own death every night when he retires, to "shun the least Temptation to a sin," and expresses quiet confidence that, if he dies, he will "rise triumphant in my Funerall." But what most marks this final group of religious poems is its emphasis upon a more human and humane deity. For example, one of several prayers entitled "To God" asks the Almighty to set aside the kind of "stately terrors" that evoked such anxiety from Herrick in the first third of the collection, urging God to "talke with me familiarly," to become the kind of nurturing father figure the poet has sought for so long. Similarly, the epigram "Christs Action" celebrates the deity's "Humane Nature," and yet another prayer "To God" speaks of "my *deare,* / My *mild,* my *loving Tutor, Lord and God!*" The poem that immediately follows (and bears the same title) serves in a sense as the valediction of Herrick's book. It begins, "The work is done," and goes on to ask his Heavenly Father to do what this poet has requested of a succession of friends, relatives, and patrons throughout *Hesperides* – to place a crown of "*Lawrell*" on his brow. "That done," Herrick concludes, "with Honour Thou dost me create / Thy *Poet,* and Thy *Prophet Lawreat.*" His final image of the sacred poet, then, is identical to that of John Milton – as one who not only writes religious verse but through whom God himself can speak.

His Noble Numbers is actually brought to a close, however, with a dramatic series of ten poems on the Crucifixion and its aftermath, described as if the speaker (and the reader) are actual witnesses of the events. The first of these, "Good Friday: Rex Tragicus, or Christ going to His Crosse," is one of Herrick's most ambitious sacred works, an internal

"dialogue of one" with this "markt-out man," who must "this day act the Tragedian," with the Cross for his stage. The Crucifixion scene is vividly evoked by theatrical metaphor, by Herrick's mordantly witty descriptions of the "audience," and through dramatic irony (the reader, for example, knows what part "that sowre Fellow, with his *vinegar*" will eventually play in this tragedy).

With similar artistic boldness, Herrick, in "His Saviours words, going to the Crosse," has Christ touchingly describe himself as "a man of misierie!" A pattern poem in the shape of a cross follows, and the collection concludes with three works in which Herrick continues his role as a biblical character, here an Everyman who seeks out "his Saviours Sepulcher," offers a "Virgin-Flower" there (recalling the many lyrics of *Hesperides* in which flowers are humanized and humans "flowerized"), and discovers, in "His coming to the Sepulcher," that "my sweet Savior's gone!" But instead of the predictable celebration of the Resurrection to climax the poem (and indeed the collection as a whole), Herrick portrays himself as bewildered by the absence of Christ's body, wondering, "Is He, from hence, gone to the shades beneath, / To vanquish Hell, as here He conquer'd Death?" Then, like a newly fledged hero of faith, Herrick vows, "If so; I'le thither follow, without feare; / And live in Hell, if that my *Christ* stayes there." The envisioned scenario is extraordinary and perhaps unprecedented. The poem itself, indeed the sequence which it concludes, is a tour de force, as striking an ending to Herrick's collection as "The Argument of his Book" and its self-referential successors are a beginning.

In the absence of much evidence, it is difficult to determine the kind of reception *Hesperides* received on its publication in 1648. The time, certainly, was far from propitious. Herrick's world, riven and exhausted by the Civil War, would be turned completely upside down with the execution, only a year later, of the king to whom he had been so devoted. What is certain is that his book did not explode upon the literary scene nor did it, during his lifetime, bring him the literary fame he so avidly desired. He lived for twenty-six more years and died a poor country parson, whom no fellow poet seems to have commemorated with a verse-epitaph, much less an elegy. Most remarkably, in that twenty-six years, he appears to have ceased to write poetry: no extant poem from that period can with absolute certainty be attributed to him. It is as if the composition of all of those 1,402 "Works Both Humane & Divine" and their painstaking arrangement had exhausted Herrick's creativity. He may have been embittered by his fate as a poet, and as a man, but one doubts it. Herrick was at once a realist about art and life and an optimist, one who knew all about careless readers and carping critics but who could still hope for a favorable judgment from time. That hope, of course, has been realized. Just as he predicted, Herrick's tombstone has vanished, but in the last one hundred years at least, his better monument, his poetry, has led to his becoming more widely loved and more profoundly respected than even he, dreaming of literary immortality in remotest Devonshire, might have imagined.

Bibliographies:

Ted-Larry Pebworth, A. Leigh DeNeef, Dorothy Lee, James E. Siemon, and Claude J. Summers, "Selected and Annotated Bibliography," in *"Trust to Good Verses": Herrick Tercentenary Essays,"* edited by Roger B. Rollin and J. Max Patrick (Pittsburgh: University of Pittsburgh Press, 1978), pp. 235–281;

Elizabeth H. Hageman, *Robert Herrick: A Reference Guide* (Boston: G. K. Hall, 1983).

Biography:

George Walton Scott, *Robert Herrick, 1591–1674* (London: Sidgwick & Jackson, 1974).

References:

Gordon Braden, "Robert Herrick and Classical Lyric Poetry," in his *The Classics and English Renaissance Poetry: Three Case Studies* (New Haven: Yale University Press, 1978), pp. 154–254;

A. B. Chambers, "Herrick and the Trans-shifting of Time," *Studies in Philology,* 72 (January 1975): 85–111;

Ann Baynes Coiro, "Herrick's 'Julia' Poems," *John Donne Journal,* 6, no. 1 (1987): 67–89;

Coiro, *Robert Herrick's "Hesperides" and the Epigram Book Tradition* (Baltimore: Johns Hopkins University Press, 1988);

Robert L. Deming, *Ceremony and Art: Robert Herrick's Poetry* (The Hague & Paris: Mouton, 1974);

A. Leigh DeNeef, *"This Poetick Liturgie": Robert Herrick's Ceremonial Mode* (Durham, N.C.: Duke University Press, 1974);

T. S. Eliot, "What Is Minor Poetry?," in his *On Poetry and Poets* (New York: Farrar, Straus & Cudahy, 1957), pp. 34–51;

Achsah Guibbory, "Robert Herrick: 'Repullulation' and the Cyclical Order," in her *The Map of Time: Seventeenth-Century English Literature and*

Ideas of Pattern in History (Urbana: University of Illinois Press, 1986), pp. 137–167;

John L. Kimmey, "Order and Form in Herrick's *Hesperides,"* *Journal of English and Germanic Philology,* 70 (Spring 1971): 255–268;

Kimmey, "Robert Herrick's Persona," *Studies in Philology,* 67 (April 1970): 221–236;

Kimmey, "Robert Herrick's Satirical Epigrams," *English Studies,* 51 (August 1970): 312–323;

Leah Sinanoglou Marcus, "Churchman among the Maypoles: Herrick and the *Hesperides,"* in her *The Politics of Mirth: Jonson, Herrick, Milton, Marvell, and the Defense of Holiday Pastimes* (Chicago: University of Chicago Press, 1986), pp. 140–168;

Marcus, "The Poet as Child: Herbert, Herrick, and Crashaw," in her *Childhood and Cultural Despair: A Theme and Variations in Seventeenth-Century Literature* (Pittsburgh: University of Pittsburgh Press, 1978), pp. 94–152;

Earl Miner, *The Cavalier Mode from Jonson to Cotton* (Princeton: Princeton University Press, 1971);

F. W. Moorman, *Robert Herrick: A Biographical and Critical Study* (London: John Lane, 1910; New York: Russell & Russell, 1962);

S. Musgrove, *The Universe of Robert Herrick,* Auckland University College Bulletin, no. 38, English Series, no. 4 (Auckland: Pelorus Press, 1958);

Roger B. Rollin, *Robert Herrick,* revised edition (New York: Twayne, 1992);

Rollin and J. Max Patrick, eds., *"Trust to Good Verses": Herrick Tercentenary Essays* (Pittsburgh: University of Pittsburgh Press, 1978);

Louise Schleiner, "Herrick's Songs and the Character of *"Hesperides,"* *English Literary Renaissance,* 6 (Winter 1976): 77–91;

Miriam K. Starkman, *"Noble Numbers* and the Poetry of Devotion," in *Reason and the Imagination,* edited by J. A. Mazzeo (New York: Columbia University Press, 1962), pp. 1–27;

Claude J. Summers, "Herrick's Political Counterplots," *Studies in English Literature, 1500–1900,* 25 (Winter 1985): 165–182;

Harold Toliver, "Herrick's Book of Realms and Moments," *English Literary History,* 49 (Summer 1982): 429–448;

Thomas R. Whitaker, "Herrick and the Fruits of the Garden," *English Literary History,* 22 (March 1955): 16–33.

Henry King

(January 1592 – 30 September 1669)

Gary A. Stringer
University of Southern Mississippi

BOOKS: *A Sermon Preached at Pauls Crosse, the 25. of Nouember. 1621. Vpon Occasion of that False and Scandalous Report (lately printed) Touching the Supposed Apostasie of the Right Reuerend Father in God, Iohn King, Late Lord Bishop of London* (London: Printed by Felix Kyngston for William Barret, 1621);

Two Sermons. Vpon the Act Svnday, Being the 10th of Iuly. 1625 (Oxford: Printed by John Lichfield and William Turner for William Turner, 1625);

A Sermon of Deliverance. Preached at the Spittle on Easter Monday, 1626 (London: Printed by John Haviland for John Marriot, 1626);

Two Sermons Preached at White-Hall in Lent (London: Printed by John Haviland, 1627);

An Exposition upon The Lords Prayer (London: Printed by J. Haviland, sold by J. Partridge, 1628);

A Sermon Preached at St Pauls March 27. 1640 (London: Printed by Edward Griffin, 1640);

A Groane at the Fvnerall of that Incomparable and Glorious Monarch, Charles the First (London, 1649); revised as *A Deepe Groane, Fetch'd at the Funerall of that Incomparable and Glorious Monarch, Charles the First* (London, 1649);

The Psalmes of David, from the New Translation of the Bible Turned into Meter (London: Printed by Ed Griffin, sold by Humphrey Moseley, 1651; enlarged edition, London: Printed by S. G., sold by Humphrey Moseley, 1654);

Poems, Elegies, Paradoxes, and Sonnets (London: Printed by J. G. for Richard Marriott and Henry Herringman, 1657); facsimile, edited by Eluned Brown (Menston: Scolar Press, 1973); enlarged edition (London: Printed for Henry Herringman, 1664); republished as *Ben Johnson's Poems, Elegies, Paradoxes, and Sonnets* (London, 1700);

An Elegy upon the Most Incomparable King Charls the I (London, 1659);

A Sermon Preached at White-Hall on the 29th of May (London: Printed for Henry Herringman, 1661);

A Sermon Preached at the Funeral of the R'Reverend Father in God Bryan, Lord Bp. of Winchester (London: Printed for Henry Herringman, 1662);

A Sermon Preached at Lewis in the Diocess of Chichester (London: Printed for Henry Herringman, 1663);

A Sermon Preached the 30th of January at White-Hall, 1664 (London: Printed for Henry Herringman, 1665).

Editions: *Poems and Psalms by Henry King D. D.,* edited by J. Hannah (Oxford: F. Macpherson, 1843);

The English Poems of Henry King, D. D., edited by Lawrence Mason (New Haven: Yale University Press, 1914);

The Poems of Bishop Henry King, edited by John Sparrow (London: Nonesuch, 1925);

The Poems of Henry King, edited by Margaret Crum (Oxford: Clarendon Press, 1965);

The Stoughton Manuscript, edited by Mary Hobbs (Aldershot: Scolar Press, 1990).

Though not a major poetic intelligence or innovator of the stature of John Donne, nor an exquisite artistic craftsman like George Herbert, Henry King produced a substantial body of high-quality verse. His poetry is consistently intellectually demanding and artful, and some of it is aesthetically superb. Employing principally (though not exclusively) the rhymed couplet, in poems ranging from 2 to over 500 lines, King wrote in many genres and poetic modes, producing commendatory verses to friends and patrons, translations from classical writers, poems commemorative of public events and notable achievements, denunciatory poems on figures of whom he disapproved, poems of religious meditation and philosophical reflection, narrative poems

Henry King, Bishop of Chichester (portrait by an unknown artist in the city-council chamber of the Chichester Council House)

chronicling his (usually outraged and despairing) reactions to the events of the Civil War, love sonnets (in a chastened Petrarchan vein), and, especially, formal funeral elegies and other elegiac verse. Indeed, with the frequently anthologized "An Exequy to his Matchlesse never to be forgotten Freind," written to mourn the loss of his youthful wife, King penned an elegy that many would rank among the best in the language, and some of his other poems achieve a similarly high standard. Though King's sermons are seldom read in our time and his translations of the Psalms are no longer employed in the liturgy, his poems continue to repay the attention of twentieth-century readers – not only because they are representative of many of the poetic trends, styles, and kinds in the seventeenth century, but also because they are worthwhile in their own right.

Born at Worminghall in Buckinghamshire in the room in which his father had been born, Henry King came from a family that was prominent in ecclesiastical and courtly affairs for about one hundred years during the reigns of the later Tudors and earlier Stuarts. Henry's grandfather Robert had been made bishop of Oxford in 1542; and Henry's father, John, was chaplain not only to Queen Elizabeth, but also to King James, who styled John "the King of Preachers" and advanced him in 1604 to the deanship of Christ Church, Oxford, and to the bishopric of London in 1611. John King intended all his five sons for the priesthood and sent Henry and the next younger son, John, to Westminster School, possibly because its inclusion of Hebrew in the curriculum seemed to promise superior preparation for training in divinity. Henry and John, separated in age by three years, evidently remained devoted to one another all their lives. They went up together to Christ Church, Oxford, in 1608, and together took the B. A. (19 June 1611), the M. A. (7 July 1614), and the D. D. (19 May 1625). They also named their eldest sons after one another and wrote poetry so similar that editors have frequently confused their work.

Henry left Christ Church in July of 1616 and, in accordance with the arrangement of his father (the bishop of London), assumed a prebendary at Saint Paul's, where he became friends with and enjoyed frequent contact with Dr. John Donne, of whose will King was made coexecutor in 1631. About 1617 Henry married Anne Berkeley, of the Berkeleys of Berkeley Castle, who bore him five children but died young and was buried on 5 January 1624. Henry was made canon of Christ Church on 3 March 1624 and became archdeacon of Colchester and chaplain to the court within a short time, but he did not become dean of Rochester until 6 February 1639, the tardiness of this step in his career perhaps reflecting the loss of the patronage of his father, who had died in 1621 and whose funeral sermon Donne had preached. King was consecrated as bishop of Chichester on 6 February 1642, the year in which the Civil War began, and Chichester fell to the Puritan army of Sir William Waller, driving King from his see. Later harassed and fined, King was not restored to his place until the Restoration.

In about a score of such popular seventeenth-century poetical miscellanies as *Wits Recreation* (1641), *The Academy of Complements* (1646, 1650), *The Harmony of the Muses* (1654), and *Parnassus Biceps* (1656), some twenty-seven printings of poems by King are included. The first collected edition of his *Poems, Elegies, Paradoxes, and Sonnets,* however, was not published until 1657, and then, if the publisher's preface is to be believed, without King's cooperation. Indeed, like many other poets of his time, Henry King was essentially a manuscript poet throughout most of his life, and this fact has important consequences for our understanding of his poems and of how he worked as a poet. Principally through the agency of a coterie centered at Christ Church, Oxford, manuscript copies of King's poems circulated widely among his contemporaries. In volume two of his *Index of English Literary Manuscripts* (1987), Peter Beal locates slightly over eight hundred manuscript copies of the eighty-three poems he lists, and some poems far exceed the ten-copy average. King's "Exequy" to his wife, for instance, was much beloved in his own day, surviving in thirty-three separate manuscripts; and of the highly popular "Boy's answere to the Blackmore" there are seventy remaining manuscript transcriptions.

Such figures indicate that a poet who eschewed the broad glory available through the medium of print might yet seek the great interest of a coterie of select readers, whose attentions would provide encouragement and gratification sufficient to keep the poet happily practicing his craft. As with other manuscript poets, the apparent targeting of a specific coterie audience frequently helps to explain King's choice and treatment of poetic subject matter. For example, King's 44-line "Upon the King's happy Returne from Scotland," written in 1633; his 144 lines "To my Noble and Judicious Friend Mr Henry Blount upon his Voyage," written soon after Blount published an account of his voyages in the Levant in 1636; and his seventeen-couplet "Salutation of His Majestye's Shipp The Soveraigne," penned soon after the vessel was launched in 1637, were not printed until 1657. Yet we may be assured that the intended (and most important) audiences for these poems received copies in good time and that King reaped the rewards of his efforts as surely as if these poems had appeared widely in print. The same is undoubtedly true of scores of other poems that remained unpublished until the 1657 edition or the enlarged edition of 1664.

The way in which King in particular managed his career as a manuscript poet allowed him substantial control over the shape of his canon. Once a manuscript copy of a given poem or group of poems had left his hands and entered the larger culture, of course, King could do nothing to preserve the accuracy of the texts or to ensure that they retained any intended associations with other poems. Unlike Donne, however, King apparently took pains to preserve the integrity of his work, maintaining a master manuscript (now lost) of his collected verse, which he periodically updated, corrected, and revised; according to Beal, during the 1630s King allowed some "fair copies" of his verse to be made "for use within a limited coterie." The six most important surviving such manuscripts, all closely related to King's personal master collection, comprise between fifty-six and seventy-eight poems each, and they show a great deal of agreement in content, in arrangement, and in the texts of individual poems.

The arrangement of the poems within these manuscripts is potentially of considerable interpretive significance, given the proximity of these documents to the author. Unfortunately, what King might have meant by his placement of a given poem within this manuscript context — where the poem fit into his own imaginative development or meaningful associations the poem might have had with surrounding poems — cannot be recovered from the printed editions. Whereas the major manuscripts intermix poems of various genres in what appears to be a rough chronological order, the poems in the

1657 edition were grouped generically according to the general scheme: songs and other secular poems, occasional poems (royal occasions first), and meditative and religious poems. King's reputation, unlike Donne's, did not need the recuperative sinner-turned-saint image reflected in this organization of the 1657 *Poems,* so the publisher may simply have seen a hierarchical organization by genres as a means of imposing order on the materials. Margaret Crum, editor of the current standard edition (1965), follows a similar impulse to categorize, presenting the poems under the two rubrics of "Occasional" and "Undated." Crum's edition, though generally organized chronologically within her two ruling categories, does not precisely indicate the original manuscript contexts of the poems. The physical sequencing of poems, however, can be as significant as the chronology of their composition or their generic associations.

The recent publication in facsimile of *The Stoughton Manuscript* (1990), one of the six major surviving manuscript collections of King's poetry, provides modern readers the opportunity to see how manuscript context affects a reader's response to poems. In the manuscript, copied in the same neat italic hand, appears the following sequence of poems: "An Exequy" ("Accept thou Shrine of my Dead Saint"), "An Elegy" ("So soone growne old? hast thou beene sixe Yeares dead"), and "On Two Children dying of one Disease and buryed in one Grave" ("Brought forth in Sorrow and bred vp in Care"). Crum, however, prints these poems in the order "An Exequy," "On Two Children dying," and "An Elegy" and emphasizes that the occasion of the poem on the two children cannot be real, since "it is impossible that any two of Henry King's children were buried at one time." In the cold medium of type, especially when accompanied by Crum's literalist caveat, these three poems are likely to seem severely detached from one another – the grief of "An Exequy" is followed by the "unreal" lament for the fictitious dead children, which is followed by a second dirge, some six years later, for the dead wife. In the manuscript's warmer, more credible medium of calligraphy, however, which connotes a deliberateness in the arrangement of the contents, it is almost impossible that a reader will not find significance in the ordering of these poems, detecting a kind of Jobean sequence of grief from the initial wretchedness at the death of King's "bride" ("An Exequy") to the commemoration of the sixth anniversary of loss ("An Elegy") to what will seem fate's crowning, unbearable blast at the distraught father – the deaths at a single stroke of two of the

children of the previously deceased mother. The truth of this sequence is of the imaginative order of poetry, not of the order of mundane reality, and it is a truth that is denied us in the printed editions. Bearing in mind the importance of original manuscript associations between and among poems, we may survey King's achievement as a poet by discussing specific poems within the major generic categories in which he worked.

King is perhaps most justly remembered as an elegiac poet, and not just because of what he achieved in "An Exequy." Apart from his versified Psalms, King left about thirty-nine hundred lines of verse in slightly more than eighty poems. At least twenty-six of his poems are occasional and thus datable with a high degree of precision. Eighteen of the twenty-six poems, comprising over seventeen hundred lines, are elegiac in nature. Beginning with Prince Henry in 1612, King poetically commemorated the deaths of many of the powerful and famous of his day, writing funereal poems on Sir Walter Ralegh (died 1618); Richard Sackville, third Earl of Dorset (died 1624); Dr. John Donne (died 1631); King Gustavus Adolphus of Sweden (died 1633); Ben Jonson (died 1637); Lady Anne Riche (died 1638); Robert Devereux, third Earl of Essex (died 1646); Sir Charles Lucas and Sir George Lisle (died 1648); King Charles I (died 1649); and Anne, Lady Stanhope (died 1654), who was the daughter of Algernon Percy, tenth Earl of Northumberland. He also lamented in verse the loss of personal friends and relatives, including his father, Bishop John King (died 1621); his son-in-law Edward Holt (died 1643); and his "Best Friend L[ady] K[atherine] C[holmondeley]" (died 1657). His elegiac impulse even extended to "An Elegy Upon Mrs. Kirk unfortunately drowned in Thames" (died 1641), a lady of the queen's bedchamber who died with "divers ladies" in a notorious barge wreck. King rose to the pinnacle of his achievement as an elegist – and, many would say, as a poet – with "An Exequy" (written 1624) and, as noted earlier, returned to the theme of his wife's death six years later in "The Anniverse. An Elegy."

The sheer number of King's obsequies on particular deaths suggests that he was of a sober turn of mind, and this impression is strengthened by the presence of many other doleful poems in his canon, including "The Woes of Esay," which versifies a portion of Isaiah; "An Essay on Death and a Prison," which compares the two topics at length; "Sic Vita," a 12-line lament on the transitoriness of human life that was popular in nineteenth-century

An Exequy

Accept thou Shrine of my dead Saint

Instead of Dirges this Complaint;

And for sweet flowers to crowne thy Hearse

Receiue a strew of weeping Verse

From thy grievd Friend; whome Thou might'st see

Quite melted into teares for Thee.

Deare Losse! since thy vntimely fate

My task hath beene to meditate

On Thee, on Thee. Thou art the Book,

The Library whereon J look

Though allmost blind. For Thee (Lov'd Clay)

J languish out, not Liue, the Day,

Vsing no other Exercise

But what J practise with my Eyes:

By wch wett glasses J find out

How lazily Time creepes about

To one that mournes: This, only this

My Exercise and businesse is:

So J compute the weary howres

With Sighes dissolved into Showres.

Not wonder:

Nor wonder if my Time goe thus
Backward and most preposterous;
Thou hast benighted mee, Thy Sett
This Eue of blacknesse did beget,
who wast my Day though overcast
Before Thou had'st thy Noone-tide past.
And if remember must in teares
Thou scarce had'st scene so many Yeares
As Day tells flowres: By thy Cleere Sun
My Soue and Fortune first did run;
But Thou wilt never more appeare
Folded within my Hemispheare.
Since both thy Light and Motion,
Like a fledd Starr is falne and gone,
And twixt mee and my soules Deare wish
The Earth now interposed is,
wth such a straunge Eclipse doth make
As nere was read in Allmanake.
         i could allow Thee for a time
To darken mee and my sad Clime,
Were it a Month a Yeare, or Ten,
i would thy Exile liue till then
                              And all.

anthologies; "My Midd-night Meditation," a poem popular in King's own day urging that "e'ry Spectacle" that "Ill busy'd Mann" looks upon "Presents and Actes" his "Execution"; "Being waked out of my Sleep by a Snuff of Candle which offended mee, I thus thought," which develops the conceit that "Man is a Candle," though with "the Diff'rence" that after man's light goes out, God rekindles it to "an Eternall Flame"; "An Elegy Occasioned by Sicknesse," which uses 108 lines to anatomize humankind's misery, proneness to sickness, and susceptibility to disease; and "The Dirge," a six-stanza poem that answers the question "What is th'Existence of Man's Life?" by developing six conventional conceits – "open Warr, or Slumber'd Strife," "a Storme," "a Flow'r," "a Dreame," "a Dyall," and "a weary Enterlude."

The sentiments and ideas in much of King's elegiac verse are likely to strike a modern reader as the conventional sort of thing that might be expected on a greeting card. Especially in elegies where he is inspired by a personal relationship with or special knowledge of the deceased, however, he is capable of expressing a sense of deeply felt grief in poetry – "That Art," as he graciously defines it in the late elegy "Upon my Best Friend L. K. C.," "wherewith our Crosses we beguile, / And make them in Harmonious numbers smile." The occasion of "An Exequy to his Matchlesse never to be forgotten Freind" surely provided King his greatest challenge to this artistic credo.

Beginning with the words "Exequy" and "Freind" in its title and continuing in the first couplet, "An Exequy" immediately announces itself as generically complex: "Accept, thou Shrine of my Dead Saint! / Instead of Dirges this Complaint." The poem is a lament for the dead, but it is also conceived as a lover's "complaint," and this generic intention informs much of the remainder of the poem. This funereal love song comprises 120 lines of tetrametric couplets marked off into a dozen verse paragraphs (eleven in Crum's edition) and falling into two basic parts. The first major division of the poem, concerned with registering the speaker's grief at his loss, concludes with the couplet of lines 79–80 – "So close the ground, and 'bout hir shade / Black Curtaines draw, My Bride is lay'd." Having thus yielded his "Bride" to the "Earth" as in preparation for the wedding night (the word "lay'd" is explicitly epithalamic, as in Donne's "Epithalamion . . . on St. Valentine's Day"), the speaker develops the remainder of the poem as a consolation; and he does so in a moving and somewhat unexpected way. From a Christian poet we expect the elegiac conso-

lation to stress the ultimate triumph of the deceased (and all the redeemed) over death – "So Lycidas sunk low, but mounted high," as John Milton puts it in a comparable case. King, however, has already touched this theme in the first half of the poem, warning "Earth" that an "Auditt" of "Each Grane and Atome" of the dust of his beloved will be required by God. The consolation King elaborates in the second half of the poem, spoken as though to his still-listening wife, consists in the assurance that he is steadily and certainly approaching her for a second nuptial in death, when "age, or grief, or sicknes must / Marry my Body to that Dust / It so much loves." This notion produces the best and most-often-quoted lines in the poem:

> 'Tis true; with shame and grief I yeild
> Thou, like the Vann, first took'st the Field,
> And gotten hast the Victory
> In thus adventuring to Dy
> Before Mee; whose more yeeres might crave
> A just præcedence in the Grave.
> But hark! My Pulse, like a soft Drum
> Beates my Approach, Tells Thee I come;
> And, slowe howe're my Marches bee,
> I shall at last sitt downe by Thee.

If lines 105 to 109 seem ironically to anticipate the words Adam speaks to Eve in *Paradise Lost* (1667) upon first feeling the effects of the forbidden fruit, King expresses the martial conceit of lines 111 to 114 so effectively that they can scarcely be imitated. The unexpected figuration of the pulse as a memento mori rather than as a sign of vitality is paralleled by the metrical irregularities of "like a soft Drum" and "Beates my Approach" (a trochee plus an iambus in each case), which seem perfectly suited to reflect an excited, irregular heartbeat that then settles back into an insistent, steady rhythm as the speaker marches inexorably toward the final consummation of his love.

Certain features of "An Exequy" reflect King's debts and credits in the history of seventeenth-century poetry as well as his individual achievement. The possibility that Milton echoes the poem in *Paradise Lost* has already been suggested. Conjoining the King poem's description of itself as a "complaint" with the topos of concession in lines 39 to 44 inevitably reminds us of Andrew Marvell:

> I could allow Thee for a time
> To darken mee and my sad Clime,
> Were it a Month, a Yeere, or Ten,
> I would thy Exile live till then;
> And all that space my mirth adjourne,
> So Thou wouldst promise to returne. . . .

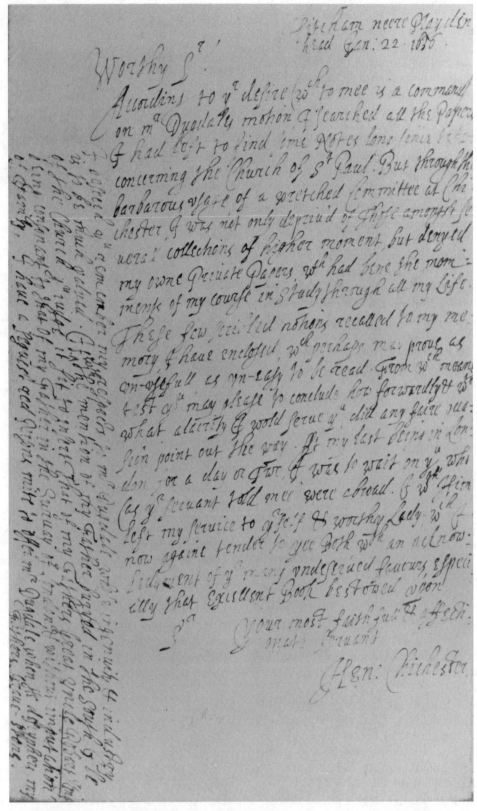

Letter from King to Edward Bysshe enclosed with notes describing the repairs made to Saint Paul's Cathedral in 1620 (Collection of Sir William Dugdale, Bt. M.C.). King sent the information for the use of antiquarian William Dugdale (1605–1686), who published his History of St. Paul's Cathedral *in 1658.*

The impulse to detect these lines lying behind the first paragraph of "To His Coy Mistress" is irresistible. In addition to the possible reference to the Saint Valentine's Day epithalamion, moreover, the poem also seems to echo Donne in other places – in the cosmographical conceit, which laments, "But Thou wilt never more appear / Folded within my Hemispheare"; in its reference to "a fierce Feaver" that "must calcine / The Body of this World"; in the nautical imagery of "At Night when I betake to rest, / Next Morne I rise neerer my West." The controlled tetrametric couplets in which the whole is written reflect a Jonsonian spirit.

King's "Upon the Death of my ever Desired Freind Dr Donne Dean of Paules" was published in 1632 with Donne's sermon *Death's Duell* and again in 1633 as the first of the thirteen elegies on the author included in the first collected edition of Donne's *Poems*. The elegy is one of King's finest poems, and it is an excellent poem by any measure. In these fifty-eight lines King rightly downplays the private grief he must have felt at the death of his mentor, friend, and benefactor, adopting instead the posture of a community spokesman called upon to make a public response to an event for which there is nothing adequate to say. Indeed, "I doe not like the Office," he exclaims; yet he acquits himself in this public performance every whit as admirably as he had in the more private circumstances of "An Exequy."

The poem is divided into four paragraphs and a concluding couplet, which successively commend Donne's eminence as a poet and explain how his death has devastated the art of poetry; praise *Death's Duell* as Donne's own funeral sermon and lament that he did not render the elegist's art unnecessary by similarly ringing his own "Elegiack Knell" in verse; protest King's distaste for an elegiac task that can only amount to Donne's "reborrow[ing]" from a "bankrupt" age the wit he lent the age in the first place; and finally, playing off the fact that King himself had been designated Donne's executor, invoke the paradox of naming Donne as his own "Executor" on grounds that "but Thy owne, / No Pen could doe Thee Justice." In language that is lapidary in both substance and form, the final couplet concludes the thought of the preceding paragraph and splendidly sums up the poem with a stunning conceit: "So Jewellers no Art, or Metall trust / To forme the Diamond, but the Diamond's Dust."

Several of King's other elegiac poems deserve wider attention in the present age. One such is "To my Dead Friend Ben: Johnson," which is interesting not only for its appraisal of Ben Jonson's learning,

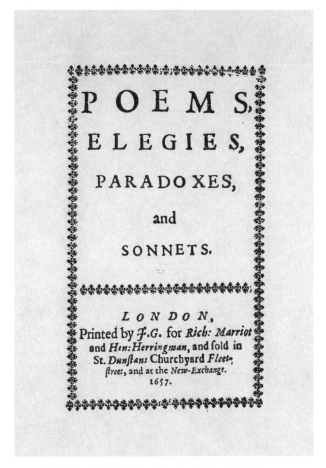

Title page for the first collected edition of King's poems

his enhancement of the English tongue (Jonson made English comparable to the "full Greek or Latine"), and reform of the stage, but also for insights it gives us into King's conception of his own identity as a poet. The elegies on Lady Stanhope and his "Best Friend L. K. C." will also repay study, the former showing a perfect control of decorum in the commendation of a twenty-year-old young lady whom King barely knew, the latter (like Donne's "Obsequies to the Lord Harrington") declaring the poet's performance of the "last Office" of his "broken Verse" so that he may "[him] Self become the Elegie."

The topic of love, of course, is not completely absent from King's elegiac verse, but he also left about three dozen poems that more specifically constitute a body of amatory verse. Though this work bears King's peculiar stamp, almost all of it can be located within the world of Petrarchan love poetry that had been developed and expanded by King's Elizabethan and early Jacobean predecessors; and, in various ways, it specifically reflects the influence of Donne and Jonson – the two towering poetic figures for whom King composed elegies. The Jonsonian influence is everywhere apparent in King's predilection for the rhymed couplet and the straightforward, plain style. Indeed, King abandons the couplet in only two or three instances, employing it even in the ten poems explicitly labeled "sonnets" in the manuscripts. The spirit of Jonson is evident, too, in the titles of such poems as "The Pink" and "To One demanding why Wine sparkles," which remind us of Robert Herrick and suggest that he was not the only scion of Ben. The Donnean influence appears less in style than in substance, and even in substance King realizes a tamer, less variegated experience of love than Donne. King has little of the metaphysical poet's knotty syntax, and he seldom elaborates the abstruse conceit. In some of his imagery, however, and especially in the topics he takes up – in the imagined moments or turns of event that form the basis of particular poems – he is reminiscent of Donne. King's use of the Petrarchan idiom as a medium of social interchange with lady friends, moreover, recalls Donne's practice in verse letters to women; and King's "Madam Gabrina, or the Ill-favoured Choice" seems directly indebted to Donne's "The Anagram." The two playful paradoxes – "That it is best for a Young Maid to marry an Old Man" and "That Fruition destroyes Love" – show King gratifying in verse an impulse that Donne satisfied in prose.

King wrote only one "sonnet" at the conventional fourteen-line length, "The Double Rock," preferring under this generic heading a poem of twelve lines – or at least of some multiple of six. Only in "Tell me no more how faire shee is" does he abandon the rhymed couplet, composing three six-line stanzas in alternating tetrameter and trimeter lines rhyming *ababcc*. Even "The Double Rock," though it shows an almost Herbertian metrical diversity, rhymes in couplets. In every way except stanzaically, however, King's sonnets are conventionally Petrarchan. This is evident even from a glance at the first lines of such typical sonnets as "Dry those faire, those Christall Eyes," "When I entreat, either thou wilt not heare," and "Were thy heart soft, as Thou art faire."

Though the sonnets are largely devoid of real affective power, King skillfully manipulates the Petrarchan idiom, and occasionally achieves something exceptional. The twelve-line "Goe Thou, that vainly dost mine eyes invite," for example, is a typical insomniac piece, recording the lover's answer to one who advised him to "coole the Feaver of my braine / In those sweet balmy Dewes which slumber

paine." The explanation for his sleeplessness comes in the second sestet of the poem:

> O! couldst Thou for a Time change brests with mee,
> Thou in that broken Glasse should'st plainly see,
> A Heart, which wasts in the slowe smoth'ring fire
> Blowne by Despaire, and fed by false Desire,
>   Can only reap such sleepes as Seamen have,
>   When fierce winds rock them on the foaming wave.

Much of the imagery of this sonnet – the "Feaver" of his brain, the "fire / Blowne by Despaire," the "broken Glasse" of the breast – is utterly predictable and familiar. This conclusion, however, elevates this poem above the ordinary through its artful syntax, by its surprising merger of two standard tropes, and by the delicate handling of the imagery of the last two lines. Casting the entirety of the stanza as a single, periodic sentence forms the basis of King's success here, and he could hardly have executed his design more adroitly – the reader's curiosity about where the sentence is going can simply not be satisfied until the very last word, "wave"; and there is a major surprise along the way. Driving toward syntactic completion, the reader traverses a chaos of imagery, passing from a wasteland of "smoth'ring fire" onto the wild, raging sea, and is enmeshed in the paradox that somehow the latter is supposed to help explain the former – and that is not all. An archetypal conceit, the surging sea is used everywhere in Petrarchan poetry to image human emotion. King handles it, however, with extreme skill here, not directly and predictably equating the sea with the welter of conflicted and implicitly libidinous feelings of the lover (this is about as sexy as King gets), but instead indirectly suggesting the lover's emotional state by linking the seaman's passion to the surging sea and then connecting the lover to the seaman by means of "sleepes" that may not even occur.

In a handful of poems bearing such titles as "The Defence," "The Farwell," "The Vow-Breaker," "The Retreit," "The Forlorne Hope," and "The Legacy," King treats many of the standard topics in the Petrarchan cosmos of love. Such poems are not presented as a coherent narrative sequence in the early sources, and it appears that King composed them sporadically throughout his career. Thus, though his language generally recalls a more ordinary vintage of Petrarchism, King's foundation of these poems on particular events or moments of a love affair – and especially his use of titles to label those moments – may invoke Donne's *Songs and Sonnets* as a backdrop for King's practice as a love poet. Indeed, some of these poems seem specifically indebted to particular Donne lyrics – "The Defence" to Donne's "The Canonization," for instance, and "The Farwell" to "Twicknam Garden." Poems that reveal a Donnean influence, however, are never merely derivative or imitative. King changes what he borrows to reflect his own sensibility and perhaps his social position.

A somewhat stark example of what that sensibility and position can produce is found in "Love's Harvest," cast in King's personal sonnet form. Under such a heading, we might expect a celebration of the joys of consummated love; what King in fact gives us is an admonition against reaping those joys prematurely:

> Fond Lunatick forbeare. Why dost thou sue
> For thy Affection's Pay ere it is due?
> Love's Fruites are Legall use; and therefore may
> Be only taken on the Marriage day.
>   Who for this Interest too early call,
>   By that Exaction loose the Principall.
>
> Then gather not those immature delights,
> Untill their riper Autumne thee invites.
> He that Abortive Corne cutts off his Ground,
> No Husband, but a Ravisher is found.
>   So those that reap their Love, before they Wed,
>   Do in effect but Cuckold their own Bed.

Rather than imitating an invitatory poem such as Donne's "The Flea" or Jonson's "Come, my Celia," King explicitly rejects the premise of such poems by invoking the moral norms of seventeenth-century Christian society. Though not completely without wit, "Love's Harvest" is not a particularly interesting poem, nor one of King's best. What it does with its avowed topic, however, shows a great deal about the canons of moral and imaginative decorum that result in a bookish and essentially bloodless Petrarchism in many of King's love poems.

Though it is not always easy with King to draw the requisite distinctions, all the poems on love topics mentioned above seem purely fictive. In many poems obviously rooted in his biography, however, King addressed various women friends, acquaintances, and would-be friends in much the same terms that he uses in the love poems, turning his brand of Petrarchism into a medium of social intercourse. The titles of such poems as "A Letter" (which praises the virtues of a "Freind" who, King says, "did assume / Mee to your Bosome") and the delicate "Upon a Braid of Haire in a Heart sent by Mris. E. H." suggest this social purpose; and other poems bearing such headings as "The Departure," "The Acquittance," and "The Forfeiture" function

similarly and are verse letters in effect. Indeed, early in this century, Lawrence Mason combined some of these poems with others on various love topics and the paradox "That it is best for a Young Maid to marry an Old Man" in arguing that King had cryptically embedded the autobiographical story of a wooing and second marriage in these poems. Despite the ultimate failure of Mason's argument to convince, it does testify to King's skill in realizing a credible experience of love in poems clearly based on the facts of his life.

Also in the vein of social verse, King wrote many of what Crum labels "presentation" poems, "Upon a Table-book presented to a Lady" and "To the same Lady Upon Mr. Burton's Melancholy" being examples. King has, in addition, a handful of epigrams based on or paraphrasing classical writers ("I would not in my Love too soone prevaile: / An easy Conquest makes the Purchase stale," for instance, translates a Latin original by Petronius Arbiter); and an epigrammatic spirit, the impulse to define in the well-polished phrase, also manifests itself in his general ability to finish poems memorably, a feature any reader is certain to recognize.

An ensconced member of the Jacobean establishment, King was of course theologically and politically conservative, and he espouses the Anglican, Royalist view in several of the poems on public figures and occasions already mentioned. His most sustained and overtly political poems, however, are the companion poems *A Deepe Groane, Fetch'd at the Funerall of that Incomparable and Glorious Monarch, Charles the First,* published in 1649, and *An Elegy upon the Most Incomparable King Charls the I,* also initially drafted in 1649, but not finished and published until 1659, when King might anticipate his own vindication along with that of the monarchy at the Restoration. The first of the two poems, comprising 236 lines of English couplets and a 7-line Latin epitaph, is almost equally divided between denunciation of Charles I's executioners and praise of the martyred monarch. Though King does not hit on a central, governing conceit or narrative framework that might have provided *A Deepe Groane* with the unity of Samuel Butler's *Hudibras* (1662–1677), his excoriation of the "Bloud-thirsty" Puritan "Tygars" is as unrelenting as Butler's, and some patches of his invective seem truly inspired:

> Ryot Apochryphall, of Legend breed;
> Above the Canon of a Jesuite's Creed.
> Spirits-of-witch-craft! quintessentiall guilt!
> Hel's Pyramid! another Babell built!
> Monstrous in bulke! above our Fancies' span!
> A Behemoth! a Crime Leviathan!

The satirical thrust continues in the 520-line *Elegy,* which lengthily narrates Charles's misfortunes and struggles from the early 1640s up to his defeat and execution, eventually finding formal (though not emotionally convincing) consolation in the paradox that Parliament, counter to its intentions, "by Plucking down / Lifted Him up to His Eternal Crown." Not only its relative length and its narration of a story that King found horrifyingly central in the history of the nation, but also certain structural features suggest that the *Elegy* self-consciously seeks to fulfill an epic purpose along with its other generic goals. It opens by invoking inspiration from "amazed thoughts" and "that Trump of Death the Mandrake's Groan" and announces the purpose of elevating Charles by comparing him to Josiah, "the best of Judah's Kings." It then suspends this purpose and digresses to enumerate and catalogue in meticulous detail the events leading up to Charles's execution, enforcing their horror with allusions to signal examples of apostasy from the Old Testament and earlier Christian history. The poem eventually returns explicitly to the theme of the king's heroic martyrdom and reiterates the parallel with Josiah as it raises a cynical doubt whether "God does not keep His Word / If Zimri dye in Peace that slew his Lord." King thus manages only a pattern of sporadic allusion. Had he been able to realize the consistent allegory that, for instance, John Dryden was shortly to achieve in *Absalom and Achitophel* (1681), which may owe something to King's poem, or otherwise been able to distance himself from the turbulence of his emotions, he might have left something that would have remained more vital to future ages. As it is, much of the poem's long, historical middle is tedious and prosaic, and we are likely to value King's intention above his accomplishment.

According to Ronald Berman, King's "contemporaries thought of him as a figure of real consequence as poet and translator," and Thomas Fuller's commendation (in *The Worthies of England,* 1662) of King's sermons "began a tradition of his excellence in the sermon which was perpetuated for two centuries." The eighteenth century, ignoring King's attacks on Puritanism, accepted his reputation for piety and ignored his secular poetry. He is not discussed in Samuel Johnson's *Lives of the Poets*

(1779–1781). Berman notes that the nineteenth century praised his "respectability" at the "expense of his artistry" and anthologized a few works that exhibited "pretty images" and "mournful thoughts." In the twentieth century King has received some scholarly attention, but most of it is bibliographical and/or textual in nature. Only Berman has published a full-length critical monograph, and it deals with the main body of King's poetry in a single thirty-six-page chapter, principally employing the interpretive tenets of the New Criticism. King's poetry deserves and would repay more scholarly attention than it has had, particularly from readers interested in genre, the interrelationships of literature and history (especially political history), and the ways various poems connect to each other in the realm of textuality. Such approaches will not establish King as a major poet of the seventeenth century, but they will help to pull him more into the light and permit us to appreciate what he did achieve.

Bibliography:

Geoffrey Keynes, *A Bibliography of Henry King D. D., Bishop of Chichester* (London: D. Cleverdon, 1977).

References:

Ronald Berman, *Henry King and the Seventeenth Century* (London: Chatto & Windus, 1964);

Margaret Crum, Introduction to *The Poems of Henry King,* edited by Crum (Oxford: Clarendon Press, 1965);

Lawrence Mason, "The Life and Works of Henry King, D.D.," *Transactions of the Connecticut Academy of Arts and Sciences,* 18 (November 1913): 227–289;

Rosemund Tuve, *Elizabethan and Metaphysical Imagery* (Chicago: University of Chicago Press, 1965).

Papers:

Manuscripts for King's poems are located at the Bodleian Library, Oxford; Corpus Christi College, Oxford; the British Library; and Cambridge University. For original letters by King see volume two of Peter Beal's *Index of English Literary Manuscripts* (1987), pp. 588–589.

Henry Lawes

(5 January 1596 – 21 October 1662)

Joan S. Applegate
Shippensburg University of Pennsylvania

and

James Applegate
Wilson College

BOOKS: *A Paraphrase Vpon the Psalmes of David. By G. S. Set to new tunes for private Devotion,* musical settings by Lawes of paraphrases by George Sandys (London: Printed by J. Legatt, 1638);

Choice Psalmes Put Into Musick, For Three Voices, musical settings by Lawes and William Lawes of paraphrases by Sandys (London: Printed by James Young for Humphrey Moseley and Richard Wodenothe, 1648);

Ayres and Dialogues for One, Two, and Three Voyces (London: Printed by T. Harper for John Playford, 1653);

The Second Booke of Ayres, and Dialogues (London: Printed by T. Harper for John Playford, 1655);

Ayres and Dialogues for One, Two, and Three Voices: The Third Booke (London: Printed by W. Godbid for John Playford, 1658).

Editions: *Ten Ayres by Henry Lawes,* edited by Thurston Dart (London: Stainer & Bell, 1956);

Hymns to the Holy Trinity, edited by Gwilym Beechey, Musica da camera, 8 (London: Oxford University Press, 1973);

Six Songs, edited by Beechey (London: Peters, 1979).

OTHER: John Playford, ed., *The Treasury of Musick,* includes work by Lawes (London: Printed by William Godbid for John Playford, 1669; facsimile, Ridgewood, N. J.: Gregg, 1966).

Henry Lawes was the preeminent songwriter among the musicians associated with the court of Charles I. He was especially valued and praised by contemporary poets because the style of early baroque monody, or continuo, song, which he devel-oped as a vehicle for lyric verse, gave the greatest possible exposure to the poetic text in terms of meaning, imagery, and verbal play – qualities that were often summed up as "wit." Lawes set to music poems by many of the poets of his time, and his prestige was such that contemporary printer-publishers such as Humphrey Moseley and Thomas Walkley included a reference to Lawes's settings on the title pages of volumes by John Milton, Thomas Carew, Edmund Waller, Sir John Suckling, and William Cartwright (as well as the more common attributions accompanying individual poems, used in the Robert Herrick and the Richard Lovelace editions). In turn, many of these and lesser poets provided commendatory poems to the published volumes of Lawes's songs, the most famous being Milton's sonnet, "To My Friend, Mr. Henry Lawes, on His Airs," which was first printed in Lawes's *Choice Psalmes* in 1648:

> Harry, whose tunefull and well measur'd song
> First taught our English Music how to span
> Words with just note and accent, not to scan
> With *Midas* eares, committing short and long,
> Thy worth and skill exempts thee from the throng,
> With praise enough for Envie to look wan;
> To after age thou shalt be writ the man
> That with smooth Aire couldst humour best our tongue.
> Thou honour'st Verse, and Verse must lend her wing
> To honour thee, the Priest of *Phoebus* Quire
> That tun'st their happiest Lines in hymne or story.
> *Dantè* shall give Fame leave to set thee higher
> Then his *Casella,* whom he woo'd to sing,
> Met in the milder shades of Purgatory.

Lawes, born on 5 January 1596, and his younger brother William (1602–1645), who was the pre-

Henry Lawes (portrait by an unknown artist; Music School Collection, Oxford)

eminent instrumental composer of the Caroline court, were the sons of Thomas Lawes and Lucris Shepherd Lawes of Dinton in Wiltshire. It is known that William at an early age was taught by Giovanni Coperario (John Cooper) in the household of Edward Seymour, Earl of Hertford. Henry's musical education probably began in the same way, though possibly in the household of the other great Wiltshire patron of artists, William Herbert, third Earl of Pembroke. In either house they also would have encountered Alfonso Ferrabosco, who, with Coperario and others, introduced the new Italian style of monody to Prince Charles's circle. These Wiltshire connections could also have been the Laweses' entrée to the aristocratic households of London, where Henry is known to have been living by 1615, when he was nineteen years old. He received royal preferment soon after the accession of Prince Charles to the throne in 1625. On 1 January 1626 Henry was granted a probationary post in the Chapel Royal, followed within two years by full appointment as gentleman of the chapel. Five years later, in January 1631, he also became "Musician for Lutes and Voices" in the secular arm of the court musical establishment, the King's Musicke. In both posts his primary duties were to perform (he had a high tenor, or countertenor, voice), but he was also called on as a composer.

During the Interregnum, Lawes supported himself primarily by teaching but continued to compose and permitted the publication of many of his songs. Personal allusions in commendatory poems and elsewhere depict Lawes as a sympathetic and convivial companion, and the number and quality of tributes to him by poets bespeak a genuine and widespread admiration. With the Restoration he was returned to his former court positions, and he composed one of the traditional coronation anthems, "Zadoc the Priest," for the coronation of Charles II; but he was no longer an active force, and he died within a very few years. His will mentions a "dear and loving wife Eleanor," who served as executrix; he left no known descendants.

The musical style with which Lawes's generation is associated stands in sharp contrast to that of the preceding generation, the so-called English school of lutenist songwriters, whose major figures were John Dowland and Thomas Campion. In their

Manuscript for one of the five musical settings that Lawes composed for lyrics in John Milton's Comus, *first performed at Ludlow Castle on 29 September 1634 (British Library, Add. MS. 53723, fol. 37)*

songs the solo voice was supported by a fully realized accompaniment to be played on the lute or, optionally, to be provided by other voices. While the texture of this accompaniment was most frequently that of a simple chordal homophonic style, at times – as with Dowland – it could bloom into a rich contrapuntal web with a considerable musical presence of its own. The song style of the new generation, on the other hand, sharply curtailed the accompaniment, typically providing only a bare bass line (the continuo) from which a lute or keyboard player would improvise simple background harmonies. The singer was urged, instead of conforming to the traditional decorum of the musical structures, to adopt the model of the orator and to declaim the text, using a somewhat free rhythmic delivery and adding "rhetorical shadings" – ornamental figures and variations in dynamics – calculated further to en-

hance the eloquence of the song. The deceptively slight musical substance of these songs in their printed form has led to their being undervalued by subsequent generations, although the songs had clearly enthralled their poetry-centered contemporaries. A detailed reconstruction of the conventions of performance, with attention to tempo, rhythmic detailing, ornamentation, expressive dissonance in the continuo background, and a personalized delivery, including some use of gesture, is needed for the modern performer, whose task is to convey the "charming negligence" that so delighted the original audience, an audience that could include connoisseurs as formidable but also as different as Milton and Carew.

Henry Lawes is noteworthy not only because of his stature as a composer of songs but also because of the range and variety of poets whose lyrics he set. His association with Milton is well documented, especially in relation to *Comus* (1637), though it is seldom noted that at the time of these collaborations Lawes, not Milton, was the well-established artist sponsoring a young unknown. Evidence of Lawes's personal association with other poets is sparse and inconclusive as to how long or how well he knew them. Nevertheless, it seems justifiable to think of him as – in the phrasing of the subtitle to Willa McClung Evans's biography (1941) – a "friend of poets," widely acquainted among the writers and wits of his time, working closely and fruitfully with some and on terms of long intimacy with a few. He worked almost entirely with the poems of contemporaries, and in the preface to the first book of *Ayres and Dialogues* (1653) he makes the explicit claim that he received copies of the verses directly from their authors. If he was being accurate, this claim alone would establish an acquaintance with twenty-eight poets, several certainly among the "chiefest of our time," as he describes them – Herrick, Carew, Lovelace, Waller, Sir William Davenant – as well as some considerable minor figures: Cartwright, William Herbert, Sir Thomas Killigrew, John Berkenhead, Aurelian Townshend, and Francis Quarles. If to these are added the authors whose credentials in the Table of Contents are primarily aristocratic or academic, Lawes's circle of acquaintances revealed by this volume alone is a fair cross section of the poets of the period. Other collections, including Lawes's large autograph manuscript (British Library, Add. MS. 53723), add to this already impressive number about forty more poets whom Lawes could have known personally, including Katherine Philips, George Sandys, Suckling, James Shirley, George Herbert, and Edward, Lord Herbert of Cherbury.

The earliest of Lawes's songs have been preserved in the autograph manuscript, which he probably began in the decade 1615 to 1625, between his coming to London and his first official court appointment, a period in which he probably performed a variety of musical services – teaching, performing, and composing – for one or more aristocratic patrons. The first thirty or so songs in the manuscript, which is roughly chronological, are apprentice works with clear lute-song features; they include settings of several texts by Sir Philip Sidney and John Donne, as well as Lawes's settings of light verse by the third earl of Pembroke and his circle.

Perhaps beginning from the time Lawes received his first court appointment as a chorister, sacred vocal compositions, mostly small in scale and intended for devotions in a private chapel or home, became a secondary but substantial segment of his production. His principal collaboration was with the courtier Sandys, for whose fashionable metrical paraphrases of the Psalms Lawes provided first a set of new psalm tunes (1638) and then, in the troubled decade of the 1640s, more-elaborate, three-voice settings of a selection of the texts which spoke to Royalist experiences of war, discouragement, and defeat – the *Choice Psalmes* of 1648.

During his appointment with the King's Musicke, Lawes would certainly have been involved as a performer in the great cycle of Caroline court masques that began in 1631. These masques functioned not only as entertainment for the court circle but also as propaganda, projecting an idealized image of an almost divine royal pair who provided a serene and secure life for their fortunate subjects. Only a small amount of the masque music has survived, and there is little evidence that Lawes was much employed in the role of composer for them, with the possible exception of Carew's *Cœlum Britanicum* (1634), for which no music survives. His major contribution to the masque genre is as composer for *Comus*, which was commissioned by John Egerton, first Earl of Bridgewater, to celebrate his appointment as lord president of Wales. A far more modest production than the court masques, *Comus* was performed far from London, at Ludlow Castle, by Lawes and three of the Egerton children, whom Lawes served as music master. The five solo songs which Lawes wrote for *Comus* nevertheless bear many of the typical stylistic traits of the court masque song: energetic rhythmic pacing and angular contours, which often suggest gesture.

Lawes's principal service to the court seems not to have been in the great public functions of the Chapel Royal and the King's Musicke but rather in the King's Private Musicke, where he composed and performed for the many small social gatherings that occurred, typically in the presence of Queen Henrietta Maria, herself a skilled performer, and her circle of ladies. It was for this audience, and for the private pleasure of his other aristocratic patrons and students, that Lawes composed the hundreds of solo chamber airs on which his reputation rests.

Lawes's solo songs to poems by Carew constitute the largest group of settings of any single author. Carew is associated with an ornate and highly sophisticated style of poetry, which represents, according to Louis L. Martz, "the ideals of the Cava-

Figure 1: Musical setting by Lawes for Thomas Carew's "A Prayer to the Wind"

Figure 2: Musical setting by Lawes for a variant text of Carew's "A divine Mistris"

lier world . . . graceful, elegant, perfectly crafted." Lawes set more than forty of Carew's poetic texts. He may have been attracted in part to the Italianate qualities in Carew's poetry; Carew's fascination with the verse of Giambattista Marini echoed the influence of Italian composers such as Giulio Caccini and Claudio Monteverdi on musicians of Lawes's generation.

Almost all of the texts set by Lawes appeared in Carew's posthumous *Poems* of 1640. The chosen texts are single stanzas as often as strophic poems. Metrically there is a preponderance of tetrameter, but, because of Carew's frequent use of enjambment and Lawes's commitment to following the "sense" (specifically, the syntax), the musical result is never a series of regular four-measure dancelike phrases (see Figure 1). Instead, the settings move in asymmetrical phrases and with a fluctuating internal pacing based on the rhetorical flow. The term "declamatory style" is used to characterize the Caroline songwriters because the overall effect is often oratorical or dramatic rather than lyrical (see Figure 2). In such songs the declamation can be intensified to the level of a dramatic scene, with the singer "acting out" the witty, seductive, highly personalized discourse of lover or beloved. The Carew settings are considered the peak of Lawes's artistic achievement, yet more than half of them never appeared in Lawes's printed song collections of the 1650s and 1660s, most surviving only in the autograph manuscript. Conceived for the cultivated court audience of the 1630s, the settings may well have seemed too precious for the rougher preoccupations of the decades which followed.

Lawes's special sensitivity to poetic structure and tone can be demonstrated by a comparison of his Carew settings with the settings for seventeen poems by Waller and sixteen poems by Herrick. Waller's love poetry is associated, like Carew's, with the court life of the 1630s, but his poetry was already cast in a direction that foreshadowed the Augustan poets of the next generation. Waller's celebrated qualities of smoothness and sweetness, which can seem bland in comparison with the more complex syntax and the nervous intensity of Carew's poems, are echoed in Lawes's settings, which often lack the dramatic force and the eccentricity of the Carew songs. Waller's strong preference for self-contained couplets, simple tetrameter, and multiple, shorter stanzas could be expected to be reflected in more tuneful settings, but in most of them Lawes mixes tuneful four-measure phrases with both more-compressed and more-extended ones. Further, the occasional run-on poetic line is

invariably reflected in the music, suggesting a conscious preference for asymmetry or at least for a more personal utterance.

For his setting of Waller's best-known lyric, "Go, lovely rose," Lawes devised a partially through-composed setting for the four five-line stanzas of the poem; that is, the continuous music for the first two stanzas is repeated for stanzas three and four (see Figure 3). Significantly, the irregular phrase lengths of the autograph manuscript version are revised in the version of *The Second Booke of Ayres, and Dialogues* (1655), changing internal emphases but still retaining the general principle of irregularity. Such revisions tacitly allowed the performer freedom in the realization of the pacing. It should be noted that the problem of which version the modern performer should prefer is complicated even more by the fact that this setting, like many others, is tailored in detail to the syntax and sense of verses 1 and 2 and consequently is a poor fit for the demands of verses 3 and 4. Contemporary evidence suggests that the performers themselves were expected to make the necessary adjustments by shortening or lengthening notes or by the insertion of appropriate rests.

Waller addressed a poem "To Mr. Henry Lawes, Who had then newly set a Song of mine in the Year, 1635." Lawes used it almost two decades later as a commendatory poem prefacing the first book of *Ayres and Dialogues*:

> Verse makes Heroick Vertue live,
> But you can life to Verses give.
> . . . .
> So in your Ayres our Numbers drest,
> Make a shrill sally from the Brest
> Of Nymphs, who singing what we pen'd,
> Our Passions to themselves commend,
> . . . .
> So others with Division hide
> The Light of Sense, the Poets Pride,
> But you alone may truly boast
> That not a syllable is lost
> The Writer's and the Setter's skill
> At once the ravish't Eare do fill.

The poem reveals not only the function of much Caroline song as adjunct to social entertainment and courtship but also the particular aesthetic that endeared Lawes to both poets and patrons, the full exposure of the meaning or sense of the text. Only nine of Lawes's seventeen Waller settings appeared in print; considering the popularity of the poems themselves (Waller's 1645 *Poems* went through several editions within a year), it is perhaps surprising that Lawes did not use more of his store.

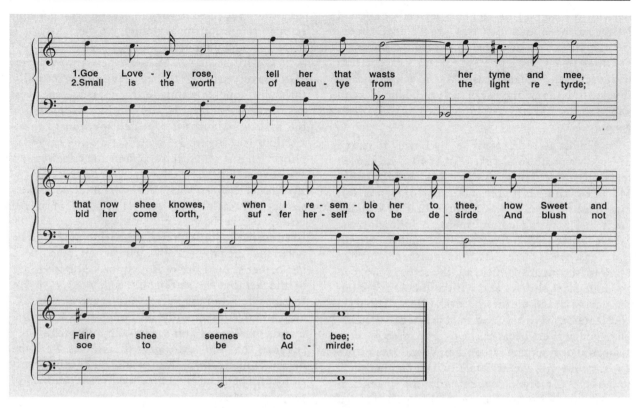

Figure 3: Musical setting by Lawes for Edmund Waller's "Go, lovely rose"

The other substantial group of Lawes settings for the lyrics of a major Caroline consists of the songs he made for Herrick. The exact length of Lawes's association with Herrick is not known, but it has been assumed to be of long standing, extending back to at least 1627, when both men were in London and before Herrick took holy orders. They were together again during Herrick's 1640 visit to London from Dean Priory, and Herrick's awareness of the death of Henry's brother can be shown by the elegiac poem, "Upon M. William Lawes, the rare Musitian."

Lawes may have set more of Herrick's poems, but only sixteen have survived, most of them only in the autograph manuscript. Like Waller and Milton, Herrick addressed a poem to Lawes, "To M. Henry Lawes, the excellent Composer of his Lyricks":

Touch but thy Lire (my *Harrie*) and I heare
From thee some raptures of the rare *Gotire* [Jacques
     Gaultier]
Then if thy voice commingle with the String
I hear in thee rare *Laniere* to sing;
Or curious *Wilson:* Tell me, canst thou be
Less than *Apollo,* that usurp'st such Three?
Three, unto whom the whole world give applause;
Yet their Three praises, praise but One; that's *Lawes.*

The Herrick-Lawes songs are very different in style from Lawes's settings of both Carew and Waller. The majority of the poems chosen are strophic and written in quatrains, their light, playful tone matched by an exuberant range of meters: tetrameter, common meter, trimeter, and even poulter's measure. Equally significant, Lawes chose to set eight of the fourteen solo songs in triple meter, with its strong connotations both of current court dances (such as the courante and saraband) and also of popular ballad and dance. In contrast, Lawes used triple meter for only one song each by Carew and Waller (aside from the occasional triple-meter conclusions). The little "dance songs" that result, however, are seldom the simple series of four-measure phrases that one might expect; in "One silent night of late," trimeter quatrains are compressed into only two phrases, each a surprising five measures in length and artfully designed to allow a variety of rhythmic emphases (see Figure 4). In another song, "Bid me but live," the 4/3 4/3 of common meter quatrains is set as 4/2 4/3, with the second line compressed into an artful hemiola. The tetrameter quatrains of "Amonge the Myrtles as I walk'de" are indeed set in four-measure phrases, but with a subtle variety of both straight and implied hemiolas that neatly accommodates the varied syntactical patterns and accentual demands of subsequent strophes (see

Figure 5). Most impressive are Lawes's settings of "Cupid as he Laye amonge roses," a long single stanza of fifteen lines, and "About the Sweet Bagg of a Bee," three short stanzas which Lawes has through-composed. Both settings become virtuoso exercises in triple-meter patterning, which balance the accentual and syntactic requirements of the declamation with a charming variety of dance-related musical echoes.

More than half of the Herrick settings were published, either in Lawes's own collections or in the popular John Playford miscellanies. Again the shorter, more tuneful songs were chosen; several of the finest – "Amarillis, by A springes . . . Murmeringes slept" and "Cupid as he Laye amonge roses" – have survived only in manuscript sources.

The masquing season of 1640 can be seen as marking the effective end of Caroline court culture. That year saw the calling and dissolving of the first Parliament in a decade, the disastrous second Bishops' War of King Charles I, and, in November, the beginning of the Long Parliament, which would sit through the Civil War and the defeat of the king, up to the very eve of his execution in 1649. The king's musicians, as members of the royal household, were eventually ordered, in March 1643, to leave London and join the king in Oxford, which became the de facto Royalist capital for the remainder of the war. Queen Henrietta Maria, who had gone to the Continent the previous year to attempt to raise money and support for the king's cause, also rejoined the court at Oxford. There was an attempt to create a semblance of normal court life in the following months with plays, masques, and probably many less formal entertainments. Many of Lawes's songs have themes strikingly appropriate for such occasions. Two of these are long, though poetically uninspired accounts of the queen's recent encounter with a violent sea storm, en route from Holland to England. "Amintor setting on a Rock Expecting Cloris" focuses on the joyful return:

See, See! my Cloris comes in yonder Barke:
Blow gently wyndes, for if yee Sinke that Arke,
You'le drowne the world with teares, and at One
     breath,
Give to us all, a universall death.
. . . .
See how the Syrenes Flock to wayte uppon her,
As Queene of Love, and they her maydes of Honer.

"A Sea Storme" recounts the terrors of the storm itself:

Help, help, o help! devinitye of Love,
Or Neptune will Commit a Rape
Uppon my Cloris.

Lawes's setting for each is written in an unusually free declamatory style, musically underlining both the colorful imagery and the excited tone of the narrator: "They Fight! they Fight!" or "Hold Boreas, hold! he will not heere; / The Rudder cracks, the mayne-mast falls."

Lawes's most ambitious attempt in this genre is his setting of Cartwright's poem of 102 lines on the Ariadne theme, "Ariadne deserted by Theseus, as She sitts upon a Rock in the Island of Naxos, thus complains":

Theseus, O Theseus, hark! but yet in vaine;
Alas deserted I complain;
It was some neighb'ring Rock, more soft than he,
Whose hollow bowels pitty'd me.
And beating back that false and cruell name,
Did comfort and revenge my shame.

Its general theme of desertion and despair would have suited the Royalist mood, echoing the spirit of the *Choice Psalmes* texts. The queen's favored pastoral language appears also in many short verses that use the Cloris and Amintor names and are centered on small incidents of grief, partings, reunions, and fears of deception – appropriate fare for court musicales, some perhaps performed by Henrietta Maria herself.

During the civil wars the king's musicians were given military roles, albeit somewhat protected ones, and accompanied the army into the field. It was thus that Lawes's brother William was killed, as the result of exposing himself to enemy fire during the siege of Chester in 1645. A group of eight musical elegies to William Lawes was included at the end of *Choice Psalmes,* one bearing the title, "A Pastorall Elegie to the memory of my deare Brother William Lawes." The text is presumably Lawes's own:

Cease you jolly Shepheards, cease your merry layes;
Pipe no more in medowes green,
. . . .
but tune your oaten Reeds with saddest notes,
with sadest notes to mourne:
For gentle Willy, you lov'd Lawes is dead.

The music, for three voices and continuo, is Lawes at his most eloquent. He also appended a grieving letter "To the Reader," which is printed after the bold dedication to the imprisoned king, who was within months of his own death. The combined

Figure 4: Musical setting by Lawes for Robert Herrick's "One silent night of late"

Figure 5: Musical setting by Lawes for Herrick's "Amonge the Myrtles as I walk'de"

weight of sorrow expressed in the elegies, the dedication, the letter, and the psalm texts themselves is still palpable after the lapse of three and a half centuries.

Among the mass of Englishmen dislocated by the eventual defeat of the king's party were, of course, the court musicians, now forced to find other musical employment in a new society that had sponsored the breaking of cathedral organs and the closing of theaters. In spite of Puritan attitudes against both elaborate church music and the public stage, there was in fact a widespread cultivation of music during the Interregnum, largely in private homes or semiprivate venues. Stemming in part from the entrepreneurial energies of the divested court musical establishment, this exceptional approval of music also reflected an attitude that saw it as not only a harmless pastime but a healing art for a troubled time – a sentiment expressed in Katherine Philips's poem "To the much honoured Mr. Henry Lawes":

> Live then (Great Soul of Nature) to asswage
> The savage dulness of this sullen Age;
> Charm us to sense; . . . .
> . . . .
> Be it thy care our Age to new create,
> What built a world, may sure repair a State.

One of the most compelling signs of musical activity during the Commonwealth was the revival of music printing (moribund since the 1620s) under Playford. Beginning in 1651 Playford began to publish small collections of instrumental and vocal music, largely by the erstwhile court musicians. Unlike the earlier generation of music printer-publishers, for whom the noble patron had prime importance, Playford aimed his books at a more general public. When, the following year, Playford produced his first miscellany of vocal airs, *Select Musicall Ayres and Dialogues* (1652), Lawes was one of four composers listed on the title page and addressed in Playford's complimentary preface. Most significantly, however, in 1653 Playford published the first of what would grow to be three volumes of Lawes's own compositions – *Ayres and Dialogues for One, Two, and Three Voyces*. Although Playford continued to publish expanded editions of the popular song miscellany, Lawes was the only composer honored with his own series.

In the 1653, 1655, and 1658 volumes the music scores consist, as they do in the autograph manuscript, of the voice line or lines and an unfigured bass from which a simple chordal accompaniment was to be improvised. The title of Playford's *Select Musicall Ayres and Dialogues* describes the practice: "For one and two Voyces, to sing to the Theorbo, Lute, or Basse Violl." Subsequent title pages within the volumes typically announce a separate section for the dialogues and a final section of light part songs: "short ayres or songs for three voyces, so composed, as they may either be sung by a voyce alone, to an instrument, or by two or three voyces." It was the solo airs, however, which dominated the songbooks, both numerically and artistically; this was especially true of the Lawes volumes of *Ayres and Dialogues*.

The first book of *Ayres and Dialogues* opens with one of Lawes's most extended works, his setting of Cartwright's "Ariadne." To many of his contemporaries it must have suggested an ambitious parallel with Claudio Monteverdi's "Lamento d'Arianna" (1608), which had a uniquely exalted reputation. Lawes's *Second Booke of Ayres, and Dialogues* appeared in 1655 and is of particular interest because it reveals the composer's association with a group of gifted women. The first volume had been dedicated to two women who were among Lawes's most long-standing patrons and, indeed, former students: Alice Egerton – the original Lady of *Comus*, now countess of Carberry – and her older sister, Mary, Lady Herbert of Cherbury and Castle-Island (her husband being the son of Edward, Lord Herbert of Cherbury, and nephew of George Herbert). The second volume is also dedicated to a woman who was a patron and student, Lady Unton Dering, and the volume included two of her songs with modest settings by her husband, Sir Edward Dering. The commendatory poems to this volume include verses by two other remarkable women: the distinguished singer Mary Knight, who was Lawes's pupil, and Philips, whose poem "Come, my Lucatia, since we see that miracles mens faith do move" appears in the volume. Philips cultivated a wide literary coterie mostly of ardent Royalists – former London school friends, who are commemorated in her poems and are well represented among the poets of the *Second Booke of Ayres, and Dialogues*.

Knight achieved a position of eminence after the Restoration when the use of professional women singers and actresses finally became an accepted practice on the English stage; entries in the diaries of both John Evelyn and Samuel Pepys allude to her formidable skill. She also became, for a time, mistress to King Charles II. The thin line between performing artist and courtesan would long complicate the lives of such women in England, as it had in Italy, where opportunities for women to become professional singers had developed almost a century earlier.

In view of the existence of official censorship, it is noteworthy that several songs in the volumes of *Ayres and Dialogues* express Royalist sentiments openly or through veiled allusions that no one could have missed. *The Second Booke of Ayres, and Dialogues* opens with "A Storme: Cloris at sea, neer the land, is surprised by a storm, Amintor on the shore expecting her arivall, thus complains" — a topical scene which comes close to being an overt political statement of loyalties. Several other short Cloris-and-Amintor ballads are included, as well as two songs with admiring references to Henrietta Maria's singing. The third book of *Ayres and Dialogues* shows even more clearly the increasing confidence of the Royalist party. The opening song is the other sea storm scene, "See, see, my Chloris," this time identified boldly as "on the Queens landing at Burlington." Many of the light airs that follow also include references, overt and concealed, to the absent king and queen. Songs that at an earlier stage in the Interregnum would have carried only nostalgia for a lost age, must now have been received as hopeful omens for the future; one song is, in fact, titled "Future Hope" and begins, "When shall I see my Captive heart / That lies in Chloris brest?"

Fewer than half of Lawes's known solo songs, dialogues, and anthems were published in his lifetime or soon after his death, and these cannot be assumed to be the "best" or "most important" or "most popular," even by contemporary standards. The publications occurred several decades after his peak period of composition, and they were directed to a wider, less sophisticated audience.

During the later years of the Interregnum, Lawes and several other former court musicians collaborated with Davenant in mounting a type of theater performance that evaded the official prohibition against stage plays. When *The First Day's Entertainment at Rutland House by Declamations and Music* (characterized by Edward J. Dent as little more than a "lecture-recital in costume") was tolerated in the spring of 1656, it was followed in autumn by a production far more ambitious, *The Siege of Rhodes*. Always described as the first English opera, the play consisted of five acts, or "entries," the first and last of which were composed by Lawes; the work is assumed to have been set to music throughout. Davenant's official description of the work was of "A Representation by the art of Prospective in

Scenes and the Story sung in Recitative Musick." None of the music for either production has survived, although *The Siege of Rhodes* enjoyed a long and continued success after the Restoration. Whether Lawes was able to summon fresh inspiration for such a major opportunity coming in his final years, or whether the music exhibited the decline suggested by the last score of songs in the autograph manuscript, will probably never be known.

Bibliography:

Pamela J. Willetts, *The Henry Lawes Manuscript* (London: Trustees of the British Museum, 1969).

Biography:

Willa McClung Evans, *Henry Lawes, Musician and Friend of Poets* (New York: Modern Language Association, 1941).

References:

Joan S. Applegate, "English Cavalier Dance-Songs: Henry Lawes and Robert Herrick," in *Dance History Scholars Proceedings* (Columbus: Ohio State University, 1983), pp. 71–83;

C. L. Day and E. B. Murrie, *English Song Books, 1651–1702* (London: Bibliographic Society, 1940);

Edward J. Dent, *Foundations of English Opera* (Cambridge: Cambridge University Press, 1928);

Eric Ford Hart, "Introduction to Henry Lawes," *Music and Letters,* 32, no. 3 (1951): 217–225; no. 4 (1951): 328–344;

Elise Bickford Jorgens, *The Well-Tun'd Word: Musical Interpretations of English Poetry, 1597–1651* (Minneapolis: University of Minnesota Press, 1982);

Murray Lefkowitz, *William Lawes* (London: Routledge & Kegan Paul, 1960);

Louis L. Martz, *The Wit of Love* (Notre Dame, Ind.: University of Notre Dame Press, 1969), pp. 101–102, 198;

John Playford, *An Introduction to the Skill of Musick,* facsimile (Ridgewood, N.J.: Gregg, 1966);

Ian Spink, *English Song: Dowland to Purcell* (New York: Scribners, 1974).

Papers:

Manuscripts for Lawes are located at the British Library (Add. MS. 53723, Add. MS. 11608, Add. MS. 29396), the Bodleian Library (MS Don. c. 57), and the New York Public Library (Drexel MS. 4041, Drexel MS. 4257).

Jasper Mayne

(November 1604 – 6 December 1672)

Dennis Flynn
Bentley College

BOOKS: *The Citye Match. A Comoedye* (Oxford: Printed by Leonard Lichfield, 1639);

The Difference about Church Government Ended: By taking away the Distinction of Government into Ecclesiasticall and Civill: and proving the Government of the Civill Magistrate onely sufficient in a Christian Kingdom (London: Printed by R. L. for William Leake, 1646);

A Sermon Against False Prophets. Preached In St. Maries Chvrch In Oxford, shortly after the Surrender of that Garrison (Oxford: Printed by Leonard Lichfield, 1646);

A Sermon concerning Unity & Agreement. Preached at Carfax Church in Oxford, August 9. 1646 (Oxford: Printed by L. Lichfield, 1646);

A late Printed Sermon Against False Prophets, Vindicated by Letter From the causeless Aspersions of Mr. Francis Cheynell (London, 1647);

Οχλο-μαχια. *or The Peoples War, Examined According to the Principles of Scripture & Reason, in Two of the most Plausible Pretences of it. In Answer to a Letter sent by a Person of Quality, who desired satisfaction* (Oxford: Printed by Leonard Lichfield, 1647);

The Amorovs Warre. A Tragi-Comædy (London, 1648);

A Sermon Against Schisme: or, The Separations of these Times. Preacht in the Church of Wattlington in Oxford-shire, with some Interruption, September 11. 1652. At a publick dispute held there, Between Jasper Mayne, D.D. And one _____ (London: Printed for R. Royston, 1652);

Certaine Sermons And Letters of Defence and Resolvtion, To Some of the late Controversies Of Our Times (London: Printed for R. Royston, 1653);

Concio ad Academiam Oxoniensem pro more habita inchoante termino, Maii 27. 1662 (London: Typis J. Grismond, & prostant apud R. Royston, 1662);

A Sermon Preached at the Consecration of the Right Reverend Father in God, Herbert, Lord Bishop of Hereford (London: Printed for R. Royston, 1662);

To His Royall Highnesse The Duke of Yorke. On our late Sea-fight (Oxford: Printed by Henry Hall for Richard Davis, 1665).

OTHER: *Epithalamia Oxoniensia. In auspicatissimum, potentissimi Monarchae Caroli, Magnae Britanniae, Franciae, et Hiberniae Regis, &c. cum Henretta Maria, aeternae memoriae Henrici Magni Gallorum Regis Filia, Connubium,* includes a Latin poem by Mayne (Oxford: Printed by John Lichfield & G. Turner, 1625);

Oxoniensis Academiae Parentalia. Sacratissimæ Memoriæ potentissimi Monarchae Iacobi, Magnae Britanniae, Franciae & Hiberniae Regis, Fidei Orthodoxae defensoris celeberrimi, &c. Dicata, includes a Latin poem by Mayne (Oxford: Printed by John Lichfield & G. Turner, 1625);

"On Worthy Master Shakespeare and his Poems," in *Mr. William Shakespeares Comedies, Histories, & Tragedies. Published according to the True Originall Copies. The second Impression* (London: Printed by Thomas Cotes for John Smethwick, William Aspley, Richard Hawkins, Richard Meighen, and Robert Allot, 1632);

Musarum Oxoniensum pro Rege Suo Soteria, includes a poem by Mayne (Oxford: Printed by John Lichfield & William Turner, 1633);

"On Dr. Donne's death," in John Donne, *Poems* (London: Printed by M. F. for John Marriot, 1633);

"Upon the *Kings* returne from Scotland," in *Solis Britannici Perigæum. Sive Itinerantis Caroli Auspicatissima Periodus,* also includes a Latin poem by Mayne (Oxford: Printed by John Lichfield & G. Turner, 1633);

Vitis Carolinæ Gemma Altera sive Auspicatissima Ducis Eboracensis Genethliaca Decantata ad Vada Isidis, includes two poems by Mayne (Oxford: Printed by John Lichfield & G. Turner, 1633);

Flos Britannicus Veris Novissimi Filiola Carolo & Mariæ Nata XVII Martii Anno. M. DC. XXXVI, includes a Latin poem and an English poem by

Mayne (Oxford: Printed by Leonard Lichfield, 1637);

"Upon the Death of the Lord Viscount Bayning," in *Death Repeal'd by a Thankfull Memoriall Sent from Christ-Church in Oxford, Celebrating the Noble Deserts of the Right Honourable, Paule, Late Lord Viscount Bayning of Sudbury. Who changed his Earthly Honours June the 11. 1638* (Oxford: Printed by Leonard Lichfield for Francis Bowman, 1638);

"To the Memory of *Ben. Iohnson,*" in *Ionsonus Virbius; Or, The Memorie of Ben: Johnson Revived By The Friends of the Muses* (London: Printed by E. Purslowe for Henry Seile, 1638);

Musarum Oxoniensium Charisteria pro Serenissima Regina Maria, Recens e Nixus Laboriosi discrimine receptâ, includes a poem by Mayne (Oxford: Printed by Leonard Lichfield, 1638);

Eucharistica Oxoniensia. In Exoptatissimum & Auspicatissimum Caroli Magnae Britanniae Franciae & Hiberniae &c. Serenissimi & Clementissimi Regis Nostri E Scotia Reditum Gratulatoria, includes a poem by Mayne (Oxford: Printed by Leonard Lichfield, 1641);

Proteleia Anglo-Batava Pari Plusquam Virgineo, Guilielmo Arausit, & Mariae Britanniarum, Academia Oxoniensi Procurante, includes a Latin poem and an English poem by Mayne (Oxford: Printed by Leonard Lichfield, 1641);

Musarum Oxoniensium Epibateria Serenissimae Reginarum Mariae ex Batavia Feliciter Reduci, includes a poem by Mayne (Oxford: Printed by Leonard Lichfield, 1643);

"Upon Mr. Fletchers Incomparable Playes" and "On the Works of Beaumont and Fletcher, now at length printed," in Francis Beaumont and John Fletcher, *Comedies and Tragedies* (London: Printed by Humphrey Robinson & Humphrey Moseley, 1647);

"To the Memorie of the most religious and virtuous Ladie, the Ladie Letice, Vi-Countesse Falkland," in John Duncon, *The Returns of Spiritual comfort and grief, in a devout soul* (London: Printed by R. Royston, 1649);

"To the deceased Author of these Poems," in William Cartwright, *Comedies, Tragi-Comedies, With other Poems* (London: Printed by Humphrey Moseley, 1651);

"A sheaf of Miscellany Epigrams. Written in Latin by J. D. Translated by J. Main D. D.," in Donne, *Paradoxes, Problemes, Essayes, Characters,* edited by John Donne, Jr. (London: Printed by Humphrey Moseley, 1652);

Epicedia Academiae Oxoniensis, in *Obitum Celsissimi Principis Henrici Ducis Glocestrensis,* includes a

Latin poem by Mayne (Oxford: Printed by Leonard Lichfield, 1660);

Part of Lucian made English from the Originall. In the Yeare 1638 . . . to which are adjoyned these other Dialogues . . . translated by Mr. Frances Hicks, includes pieces by Lucian translated by Mayne (Oxford: Printed by H. Hall for R. Davis, 1663).

Jasper Mayne was a Caroline academic – poet, dramatist, and translator – who during the English Civil War preached sermons and wrote pamphlets in the cause of Royalism; was expelled from Oxford University and deprived of his Christ Church benefices by Parliament; and after the Restoration was appointed a canon of Christ Church Cathedral, archdeacon of Chichester, and chaplain to King Charles II. Mayne has been best known for his plays, which are amusing, but his even more noteworthy poems and translations have on insufficient grounds been slighted, ignored as misattributions, or branded as forgeries. Though some of his work is mediocre, Mayne was capable and did on many occasions rise to poetry, as in his commendatory poems for William Shakespeare, John Donne, Ben Jonson, and William Cartwright.

Mayne's parents, Jasper and Mary Mayne, baptized him at Hatherleigh, an old market town in northwest Devonshire, on 23 November 1604. Perhaps his was the family of the first Catholic seminary priest executed under the Elizabethan penal laws, Cuthbert Mayne (died 1577), who came from Youlston, about ten miles from Hatherleigh. The Maynes were Catholic gentry; their property was gradually wasted in the first half of the seventeenth century. By 1648 Jasper's oldest brother, John, suffered sequestration of the family's estate and himself was listed with other Devon papists as "Delinquent, notorious, poor."

Mayne's family enrolled him at Westminster School in London where, despite his religious background, he did well enough to gain a place in 1623 as a servitor at Christ Church College, Oxford. Flourishing especially under deans Richard Corbett and Brian Duppa, Mayne was elected a student in 1627 and proceeded to take holy orders, graduating B.A. 1628, M.A. 1631, B.D. 1642, and D.D. 1646. According to Anthony Wood in his *Athenæ Oxoniensis* (1691, 1692), Mayne at Christ Church "became a quaint preacher and a noted poet." His fellow student at both Westminster School and Christ Church College was John Donne, Jr., son of the famous poet and preacher, whose preaching Mayne had earlier witnessed.

His other companion at both Westminster and Christ Church was Cartwright, with whom Mayne seems to have joined in an effort to preserve threatened privileges traditionally enjoyed by Westminster scholars at Christ Church, the so-called "Westminster suppers." With Cartwright, Mayne also contributed to most of the collections of Latin and English verse instigated by Corbett, Duppa, and other deans of Christ Church formally commemorating various events and personages – in memory of King James I; for the marriage of King Charles I and Queen Henrietta Maria; on the recovery of King Charles from illness; on the king's return from Scotland; on the birth of the royal couple's second son, James; and so on. In such trivial academic flattery Mayne showed himself no worse and sometimes better than other contributors.

Mayne applied his poetic talent to much better effect in several prefatory and commendatory poems contributed to editions of poetry by some of the finest English writers. Earliest among these was "On Worthy Master Shakespeare and his Poems," prefaced to the Second Folio edition of the plays (1632). Justly praised in *The Shakspeare Allusion-Book* (1909) for its "graceful melodious verse and mastery of language," this poem has at the same time (for no real reason) been doubted as too good to be Mayne's. Like Ben Jonson's tribute in the First Folio, Mayne's poem even in its opening words seizes on the timeless quality of Shakespeare's mind, "A Mind reflecting ages past." The first thirty-nine lines praise the playwright's power to "blow ope the iron gates Of death and Lethe," revealing the "physiognomie of shades," as if "*Plato*'s yeare and new Scene of the world / Them unto us, or us to them had hurld." This illusionary power of making the past seem real and present is the defining quality of Shakespeare's work for Mayne: "abus'd, and glad / To be abus'd, affected with that truth / Which we perceive is false." In the conclusion of the poem Mayne envisions Shakespeare wooed by the Muses, who weave and clothe him in a richly embroidered cloak of many colors – his verse – in which though dead he lives forever. Mayne's technique in these lines and throughout is to replicate prosodic effects and imagery characteristic of Shakespeare's own verse, to celebrate Shakespeare through parody and imitation.

"On Dr. Donne's death," for the 1633 first edition of Donne's *Poems,* similarly utilizes tropes and distinctive prosodic effects like those identified with Donne's own poetry, in a funeral poem for the foremost funeral poet in English. Mayne asks, "Who shall presume to mourn thee, *Donne,* unlesse / He could his teares in thy expressions dresse[?]"even as he begins to do precisely what he speaks of as being too difficult. The difficulty is that

> thy carelesse houres brought forth
> Fancies beyond our studies, and thy play
> Was happier, then our serious time of day.
> So learned was thy chance; thy haste had wit,
> And matter from thy pen flow'd rashly fit.

The poem thus constitutes as a whole an evocation of Donne's hyperbolic and self-referential wit, providing passages that both refer to and imitate Donne's funeral verse, his satires, and his love poetry. Like Donne's career as a writer, Mayne's elegy is divided between the concerns of poetry and sermons. Mayne recounts his personal experience of the effect of Donne's preaching:

> at thy sermons, eare was all our sense;
> Yet have I seene thee in the pulpit stand,
> Where wee might take notes, from thy looke, and hand;
> And from thy speaking action beare away
> More Sermon, then some teachers use to say.

Mayne goes on to contrast Donne's preaching to the newfangled preaching of Puritan divines, comparatively lacking in Donne's qualities of physical grace and temperance of utterance.

Another of Mayne's parodic elegies is his contribution to *Jonsonus Virbius,* the 1638 collection of poems by various hands after the death of Ben Jonson. "To the Memory of *Ben. Iohnson,*" far from being (as described in *The Shakspeare Allusion-Book*) "finger-counting doggrel" or "trashy," again skillfully incorporates stylistic allusions to Jonson's writing, especially its epigrammatic density, because (Mayne wittily explains) "tis too much / To write thy *Epitaph,* and not be such;" and "*Verses* on *Thee* / And not like *thine,* would but kind *Libels* be." For Mayne, a pithy classicism is the distinctive feature of Jonson's work, which constitutes in itself a sort of prefabricated antiquity. Mayne imagines Jonson's funeral monument ruined by time:

> Th'*inscription* worne out, and the *Marble* dumbe;
> So that 'twould pose a *Critick* to restore
> Halfe *words,* and *words* expir'd so long before.

Nevertheless, despite this anticipated ruin of Jonson's statue, his writings will have prevented the ravages of time and preserved him because of their runic toughness:

Thou'lt have a whole *Name* still, nor needst *thou* feare
That will be ruin'd, or lose *nose,* or *haire.*
Let others write so *thin,* that they can't be
Authors till rotten, no *Posteritie*
Can adde to *thy Workes*; th'had their whole growth then
When first borne, and came aged from thy *Pen.*

As in Jonson's own verse, the prosody is exact though compressed, and the meaning is clear though dense. Mayne goes on to defend Jonson against charges stemming from envy that his writing took too long, or was excessively worked over and revised, or was inspired by sack. He praises Jonson for compositions that reveal themselves anew with each reading or performance, because of the learning and intensity inherent in their conception. Jonson's writings were decorous, chaste, and wholesome by comparison to others. The use he made of classical sources was discriminating and original, and even without his learning his work would have

> beene as *rare*
> As *Beaumont, Fletcher,* or as *Shakespeare* were:
> And like *them,* from thy *native Stock* could'st say,
> *Poets* and *Kings* are not *borne* every day.

Uniquely having eulogized the three foremost poets of his time, Mayne in his middle thirties advanced into the most successful and yet the most disastrous decade of his career, in which the civil wars of England cramped and truncated his work as a poet, translator, and Oxford divine. In 1639 he published (anonymously) his play *The Citye Match,* which had been performed before King Charles I and Queen Henrietta Maria at Whitehall the same year; but his translation of Lucian's dialogues, eventually dedicated to William Cavendish, Marquess (later Duke) of Newcastle, was interrupted when Newcastle was forced to turn his attention from patronage of the arts to the conduct of civil war.

Though Mayne continued to publish occasional poems in Oxford collections of commemorative verse while proceeding in the 1640s to both bachelor and doctoral degrees in divinity, the disaster of civil war forced him more and more to withdraw from literature in order to take part in ideological struggle in the cause of Royalism. King Charles at this period was encamped at Oxford. After the summer of 1642 the university, surrounded by a hostile town, became a garrison. It is not clear whether, like Cartwright, Mayne formed part of the band of "loyal scholars" who took up training in arms for the defense of the university. (Cartwright, himself a leader of this group, became a casualty of the war, dying of camp fever in 1643.) However,

Mayne certainly engaged in the propaganda war. Several of his sermons of the period were published; and in 1646 and 1647 he also published pamphlets supporting Royalist church government and opposing "the Peoples War" against their king.

In 1648, as a hostile army and parliamentary visitors took control of Oxford, Mayne was successively summoned before the visitors, expelled from his scholarship at Christ Church, and ultimately ejected from his Christ Church benefice at nearby Cassington. Mayne retreated from Oxford to a more remote Christ Church living at Pyrton, Oxfordshire. Here he lived in comparative isolation until 1656, enduring at a distance the discomfiture of the defeat and decapitation of Royalism.

While at Pyrton, Mayne anonymously published a second play in 1648 – *The Amorous Warre,* a very complicated piece of plotting; apparently it was never produced on the stage. Moreover, in 1651 he published another of his commemorative elegies on deceased poets, this time for an edition of the poetry of Cartwright, his late fellow student at Christ Church. "To the deceased Author of these Poems" is as much a lament for Mayne's own career in literature as an elegy for Cartwright, who emerges here the incarnation of Mayne's own aspirations as a poet, scholar, and preacher. The poem includes rich and perhaps exaggerated appreciations of Cartwright's exemplary wit, fancy, art, learning, versatility, and eloquence in poetry and preaching. Included are some wonderfully satirical contrasts between Cartwright's preaching and the typical preaching of Puritan divines. The poem concludes with pathos on a personal note that expresses succinctly what Mayne felt, in the wake of his friend's death, about the condition of the poet-preacher in civil-war-torn England:

> The Wildness of the Place in which I dwell,
> The Desert of my unfrequented Cell,
> My want of quick Recruits made from the Citty,
> And Times which make it Treason to be witty,
> Times where Great Parts do walk abroad by stealth,
> And Great Witts live in *Plato's* Common-wealth,
> Have made me dull: my Friends with some remorse
> See me, who wrote ill alwaies, now write worse.
> The little fire which once I had is lost,
> I write, as all my Neighbours speak, in frost.

The desolation Mayne feels, surrounded by the evident demise of his own blasted career, is here assimilated to the death of Cartwright.

Mayne's predicament in the desert of the "Common-wealth" is illustrated by an incident from his Pyrton period, when about a year after publication of

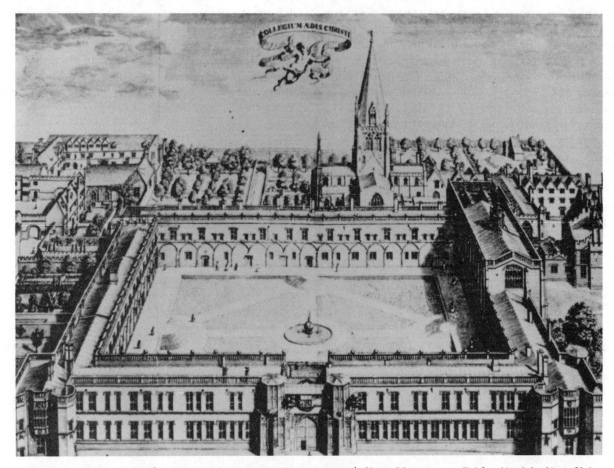

Christ Church College, Oxford (from David Loggan, Oxonia Illustrata, *1675); Jasper Mayne was expelled from his scholarship at Christ Church in 1648 because of his support of the Royalist cause.*

the Cartwright poem he engaged in a futile disputation at nearby Wattlington parish. In *Athenæ Oxoniensis,* Wood records that one John Pendarves, an Anabaptist "preaching in homes, barns, under trees, hedges, etc.," had provoked Mayne to preach at Wattlington to a mainly hostile congregation. Mayne's eloquent and learned sermon addressed the needs of that small portion of the auditory who felt inundated by the followers of Pendarves and craved the traditional ministrations of the Church of England. Mayne's sermon, however, was brutally interrupted by "a great party of anabaptists and the scum of the people." Nevertheless, Mayne published his full text, *A Sermon Against Schisme: or, The Separations of these Times,* reminiscent of the preaching style of Donne, wherein Mayne bemoans the damage caused by the Civil War to English society.

Also in 1652 Mayne published his translations of Donne's Latin epigrams in a volume of Donne's fugitive prose and poetry edited by Mayne's college friend John Donne, Jr. The Latin epigrams seem to have been translated earlier, probably before 1632, although no earlier edition of the poems is known.

Since the original Latin poems have been lost, Mayne's translations constitute our only record of Donne's earliest work as a poet. The translations suggest that the originals were written during Donne's early adolescence in imitation of the epigrams of Sir Thomas More.

In 1653 Mayne wrote a prose letter to preface Richard Whitlock's Ζωοτομια; *or Observations on the Present Manners of the English* (1654), explaining why Mayne declined to write prefatory verse for the work: "the *Rudeness* of the *place* where I dwell, and my weekly *Thoughts* compelled to *size themselves* to a plain *Countrey Congregation,* have abated much of that *Fancie* which should do honour, either to your *Book* or my self." He went on to complain in addition that "all my *publike Poetry* hath and still is, *objected* to me as a piece of *Lightnesse,* not befitting the *Profession* or *Degree* of" a vicar.

Finally deprived of his Pyrton living in 1656, Mayne seems to have retreated to Chatsworth, an estate of William Cavendish, third Earl of Devonshire, where he renewed his old acquaintance with the philosopher Thomas Hobbes. According to

Wood, "Between them there never was a right understanding," presumably in theological if not in political discussions. After the Restoration, Mayne was reinstated in his college benefices and also appointed canon of Christ Church Cathedral, archdeacon of Chichester, and chaplain in ordinary to the king. He could never reconcile himself to the changes a decade of parliamentary domination had brought to Oxford. In a Latin sermon of 1662 he blasted the faculty as dull, "*plumbeos aldermannos*" (leaden politicians). Nevertheless he supported the activities of students, such as a play of 1664 after which the actors seem to have caroused excessively with the encouragement of Mayne and some other dons. According to Wood in his *Life,* "Dr. Mayne spoke them a speech commending them for their ingenuity, and told them he liked well an acting student."

Mayne now became a rich man, and contributed money for restoring a building at Christ Church College. Nevertheless, at his death on 6 December 1672, though he willed a large sum for the rebuilding of Saint Paul's Cathedral and additional bequests to the poor people of his parishes at Cassington and Pyrton, he left nothing to Christ Church College, whose atmosphere and administration on the whole he had come to find offensive. A related gesture perhaps, reported by Wood in his *Life,* was Mayne's promise to one of his servants at the college of "something which would make him drink after his master's death." The bequest turned out to be a salted herring.

References:

E. T. Abell, "A Note on Jasper Mayne," *Reports and Transactions of the Devonshire Association,* 57 (1926): 257–265;

Montagu Burrows, ed., *The Register of the Visitors of The University of Oxford From A.D. 1647 to A.D. 1658* (London: Camden Society, 1881), pp. lxxx–cxiii, 30–31, 196, 489;

Andrew Clark, ed., *The Life and Times of Anthony Wood, Antiquary,* 5 volumes (Oxford: Oxford Historical Society, 1891), I: 441; II: 2, 90;

Clement M. Ingleby, Lucy Toulmin Smith, and Frederick J. Furnivall, *The Shakspere Allusion-Book,* 2 volumes, edited by John Munro (London: Chatto & Windus, 1909), I: 366–368, 414.

Henry More

(October 1614 – 1 September 1687)

George Klawitter
Viterbo College

BOOKS: ψυχ ωδια *Platonica; or, a platonicall song of the soul, consisting of foure severall poems; viz.* ψυχωξωια. ψυχαθανασια. Ἀντεψυχαπαννυχια. Ἀντιμονοψυχια. *Hereto is added a paraphrasticall interpretation of the answer of Apollo, consulted by Amelius, about Plotinus soul departed this life* (Cambridge: Printed by Roger Daniel, 1642);

Democritus Platonissans: or, an Essay upon the Infinity of Worlds out of Platonick Principles. Hereunto is annexed Cupids Conflict together with the Philosophers Devotion (Cambridge: Printed by Roger Daniel, 1646; facsimile, edited by P. G. Stanwood, Augustan Reprint Society 130, Los Angeles: Clark Library, 1968);

Philosophicall Poems (Cambridge: Printed by Roger Daniel, 1647);

Observations upon Anthroposophia Theomagica and Anima Magica Abscondita by Alazonomastix Philalethes (London: Sold by O. Pullen, 1650);

The Second Lash of Alazonomastix: Containing a Solid and Serious Reply to a very uncivill Answer to certain Observations upon Anthroposophia Theomagica and Anima Magica Abscondita (Cambridge: Printed by the Printers to the University of Cambridge, 1651);

An Antidote against Atheisme, Or An Appeal to the Natural Faculties of the Minde of Man, whether there be not a God (London: Printed by Roger Daniel, 1653; second edition, revised, London: Printed by James Flesher, sold by William Morden, Cambridge, 1655);

Conjectura Cabbalistica: Or, A Conjectural Essay of interpreting the minde of Moses according to a threefold Cabbala, viz., literal, philosophical, mystical, or, divinely moral (London: James Flesher, 1653);

Enthusiasmus Triumphatus, Or, A Discourse of the Nature, Causes, Kinds, and Cure, of Enthusiasme; Written by Philophilus Parresiastes, and prefixed to Alazonomastix His Observations and Reply: Whereunto is added a Letter of his to a Private Friend, wherein certain passages in his Reply are vindicated, and several matters relating to Enthusiasme more fully cleared (London: James Flesher, sold by William Morden, Cambridge, 1656);

The Immortality of the Soul, So farre forth as it is demonstrable from the Knowledge of Nature and the Light of Reason (London: Printed by James Flesher for William Morden, Cambridge, 1659);

An Explanation of the Grand Mystery of Godliness; Or, A True and Faithful Representation of the Everlasting Gospel Of our Lord and Saviour Jesus Christ, the Onely Begotten Son of God and Sovereign over Men and Angels (London: Printed by James Flesher for William Morden, Cambridge, 1660);

A Collection of Several Philosophical Writings of Dr. Henry More, Fellow of Christ's Colledge in Cambridge. As Namely His: Antidote Against Atheism. Appendix to the said Antidote. Enthusiasmus Triumphatus. Letters to Descartes &c. Immortality of the Soul. Conjectura Cabbalistica. The Second Edition more correct and much enlarged (London: Printed by James Flesher for William Morden, Cambridge, 1662; revised edition, London: Joseph Downing, 1712);

A Modest Enquiry into the Mystery of Iniquity, The First Part, Containing A Careful and Impartial Delineation of the True Idea of Antichristianism in the Real and Genuine Members thereof, such as are indeed opposite to the indispensible Purposes of the Gospel of Christ, and to the Interest of his Kingdome (London: Printed by James Flesher for William Morden, Cambridge, 1664);

Epistola H. Mori ad V.C. quae Apologiam complectitur pro Cartesio, quaeque introductionis loco esse poterit ad universam philosophiam cartesianam (London: Printed by James Flesher for William Morden, Cambridge, 1664);

Enchiridion Ethicum, praecipua Moralis Philosophiae Rudimenta complectens, illustrata ut plurimum Veterum Monumentis, et ad Probitatem Vitae perpetuo accomodata (London: Printed by James Flesher for William Morden, Cambridge, 1667); translated into English by Edward

Henry More in 1671 (engraving by David Loggan, after a portrait by Sir Peter Lely)

Southwell as *An Account of Virtue: Or, Dr. Henry More's Abridgement of Morals, Put into English, by 'K. W.'* (London: Printed for B. Tooke, 1690); facsimile published as *Enchiridion Ethicum* (New York: Facsimile Text Society, 1930);

Divine Dialogues, Containing sundry Disquisitions and Instructions Concerning the Attributes and Providence of God in the World. The First Three Dialogues, Treating of the Attributes of God and his Providence at Large. Collected and Compiled by the Care and Industry of Franciscus Palaeopolitanus (London: Printed by James Flesher, 1668);

An Exposition of the Seven Epistles to the Seven Churches; together with A brief Discourse of Idolatry, with application to the Church of Rome (London: Printed by James Flesher, 1669);

Philosophiae Teutonicae Censura (London: Printed by James Flesher, 1670);

Enchiridion Metaphysicum; sive, De Rebus Incorporeia Succincta & luculenta Dissertatio. Pars Prima: De Existentia & Natura Rerum Incorporearum in

Genere. In qua quamplurima Mundi Phaenomena ad Leges Cartesii Mechanicas obeter expenduntur, illiosque Philosophiae, & aliorum omnino omnium qui Mundana Phaenomena in Causas pure Mechanicas solvi posse supponunt, Vanitas Falsitasque detegitur (London: Printed by James Flesher for William Morden, Cambridge, 1671);

A Brief Reply to a Late Answer to Dr. Henry More his Antidote against Idolatry. Shewing that there is nothing in the said Answer that does any ways weaken his Proofs of Idolatry against the Church of Rome, and therefore all are bound to take heed how they enter into, or continue in the Communion of that Church as they tender their own Salvation (London: Printed by J. Redmayne for Walter Kettilby, 1672);

H. Mori Cantabrigiensis Opera Theologica, Anglice quidem primitus scripta, nunc vero Per Autorem Latine reddita. Hisce novus praefixus est de Synchronismis Apocalypticis Tractatulus, cum Luculenta demonstratione necessariae et inevitabilis Intelligibilitatis Visionum Apocalypticarum calci ejus-

dem Tractatus adjecta (London: Printed by J. Maycock for J. Martyn & Walter Kettilby, 1675);

H. Mori Cantabrigiensis Opera Theologica, Anglice guidem primitus scripta, nunc vero Per Autorem Latine reddita. Hisce novus praefixus est de Synchronismis Apocalypticis Tractatulus, cum Luculenta demonstratione necessariae et inevitabilis Intelligibilitatis Visionum Apocalypticarum calci ejusdem Tractatus adjecta (London: Printed by J. Maycock for J. Martyn & Walter Kettilby, 1675);

Remarks upon two late ingenious Discourses; the one, an Essay, touching the Gravitation and Non-gravitation of Fluid Bodies; the other, touching the Torricellian Experiment (by Sir Matthew Hale), so far forth as they may concern any passages in his Enchiridion Metaphysicum (London: Printed for Walter Kettilby, 1676);

H. Mori Cantabrigiensis Opera Omnia, Tum quae Latine, tum quae Anglice scipta sunt; nunc vero Latinitate Donata Instigatu et Impensis Generissimi Juvenis Johannis Cockshuti Nobilis Angli (London: Printed by J. Macock for J. Martyn & Walter Kettilby, 1679);

Henrici Mori Cantabrigiensis Scriptorum Philosophicorum Tomus Altera, Qui Suam Variorum Scriptorum Philosophicorum Collectionem primitus dictam complectitur (London: Printed by R. Norton for J. Martyn & Walter Kettilby, 1679);

Apocalypsis Apocalypseos; or, the Revelation of St. John the Divine unveiled. Containing A Brief but perspicuous and continued Exposition from Chapter to Chapter, and from Verse to Verse, of the whole book of the Apocalypse (London: Printed by J. Martyn for Walter Kettilby, 1680);

A Plain and continued Exposition of the several Prophecies or Divine Visions of the Prophet Daniel, which have or may concern the People of God, whether Jew or Christians; Whereunto is annexed a Threefold Appendage, Touching Three main Points, the First, Relating to Daniel, the other Two to the Apocalypse (London: Printed by M. Flesher for Walter Kettilby, 1681);

Tetractys Anti-Astrologica, or, The four chapters in the Explanation of the Grand Mystery of Godliness (London: Printed by J. Martyn for Walter Kettilby, London: 1681);

Two Choice and Vseful Treatises; the one Lux Orientalis; Or An Enquiry into the Opinions of the Eastern Sages Concerning the Præexistence of Sovls. Being a Key to unlock the Grand Mysteries of Providence. In Relation to Mans Sin and Misery. The Other, A Discovrse of Trvth, By the late Reverend Dr. Rvst, Lord

Bishop of Dromore in Ireland. With Annotations on them both, annotations by More (London: Printed for James Collins & Sam. Lowndes, 1682);

An Answer to Several Remarks upon Dr. Henry More His Expositions of the Apocalypse and Daniel, As Also upon his Apology. Written by S. E. Mennonite, And Published in English by the Answerer. Whereunto is annexed two small Pieces, Arithmetica Apocalyptica, and Appendicula Apocalyptica (London: Printed by M. Flesher for Walter Kettilby, 1684);

An illustration of those Two Abstruse Books in Holy Scripture, The Book of Daniel and the Revelation of S. John, by Continued, Brief but Clear Notes, From Chapter to Chapter, and from Verse to Verse: With very Usefull and Apposite Arguments Prefixt to each Chapter: Framed out of the Expositions of Dr. Henry More (London: Printed by M. Flesher for Walter Kettilby, 1685);

Paralipomena Prophetica; Containing Several Supplements and Defenses of Dr. Henry More his Expositions of the Prophet Daniel and the Apocalypse, whereby the impregnable Firmness and Solidity of the said Expositions is further evidenced to the World. Whereunto is also added, Philicrines upon R. B. his Notes on the Revelation of St. John (London: Printed for Walter Kettilby, 1685);

A Brief Discourse of the Real Presence of the Body and Blood of Christ in the Celebration of the Holy Eucharist: Wherein the Witty Artifices of the Bishop of Meaux and of Monsieur Maimbourg are obviated, whereby they would draw in the Protestants to imbrace the doctrine of Transubstantiation (London: Printed for Walter Kettilby, 1686);

Discourses on Several Texts of Scripture. By the Late Pious and Learned Henry More (London: Printed by J. R., sold by Brabazon Aylmer, 1692);

A Collection of Aphorisms. In Two Parts. Written by the late Reverend Dr. Henry More, Fellow of Christ's College in Cambridge (London: Joseph Downing, 1704);

Divine Hymns. Upon the Nativity, Passion, Resurrection, and Ascension of our Lord . . . Jesus Christ (London, 1706);

The Theological Works of the most Pious and Learned Henry More, D.D. Sometime Fellow of Christ's College in Cambridge. Containing An Explanation of the Grand Mystery of Godliness. An Enquiry into the Mystery of Iniquity. In Two Parts. A Prophetical Expositon of the Epistles to the Seven Churches in Asia. A Discourse of the Grounds of Faith in Points of Religion. An Antidote against Idolatry. An Appendix to the Antidote against Idolatry. To which are adjoin'd Some Divine Hymns. According to the Author's Im-

provements in his Latin Edition (London: Printed and sold by Joseph Downing, 1708).

Editions: *The Complete Poems of Dr. Henry More*, edited by Alexander B. Grosart (Edinburgh: Edinburgh University Press, 1878);

The Philosophical Writings of Henry More, edited by Flora Isabel MacKinnon (New York: Oxford University Press, 1925);

Philosophical Poems of Henry More, edited by Geoffrey Bullough (Manchester: Manchester University Press, 1931);

Henry More. The Immortality of the Soul, edited by Alexander Jacob (Dordrecht, Boston & Lancaster: Martinus Nijhoff, 1987).

In his own day Henry More was an important writer of prose tracts, read by many, and he was reputed by his eighteenth-century biographer Richard Ward to have been at one point in the Restoration the best-selling author in London bookstalls. His poetry, however, was popular mainly with his Cambridge students and, if one can believe his biographer, soldiers in the civil wars. More apparently never believed his poetry would elicit a large following, and to this day he has lacked even a small coterie of fervid readers who would, like John Donne's, fan embers of appreciation into flame. More also suffers because he wrote at the same time as John Milton, Robert Herrick, Richard Crashaw, and John Dryden. More's nineteenth-century editor Alexander B. Grosart suggested More's poems deserve more attention than they have received. Indeed, Cambridge Platonism cannot be adequately understood without an appreciation of the poems, because anyone who attempts to fathom seventeenth-century Neoplatonism through only the prose of Ralph Cudworth and John Smith loses vital access to content that only Henry More's allegorical poetry can elucidate.

Born the last of twelve children to Alexander and Anne Lacy More at Grantham, Lincolnshire, Henry More was baptized at the parish church, Saint Wulfram's, on 10 October 1614. The date of his birth is not recorded. The parents were staunch Calvinists, but More rebelled against the doctrine of predestination while at Grantham School. His religion and politics were Royalist throughout his life. At fourteen he was sent to Eton, and after three years there he enrolled in late 1631 at Christ's College, Cambridge. Here he would live for the rest of his life in a Neoplatonic milieu enriched by his colleagues Benjamin Whichcote, Cudworth, and Smith. He took his bachelor's degree in 1635, his master's degree in 1639, and was ordained in 1641.

He repeatedly turned down bishoprics and all academic preferments. Content to live as a scholar and teacher, he rarely left Cambridge except to visit his "heroine pupil," Lady Anne Conway of Warwickshire.

By 1641 More had contributed verses to the usual collections made by university students, but his great work began only when the lack of university employment during the Civil War afforded him the leisure to write his long poems. Although More was not the first poet to write Spenserian stanzas after Edmund Spenser (Richard Barnfield holds that honor for the nineteen-stanza poem "Cynthia") nor the first to write long strings of Spenserian stanzas (Robert Aylett published two sets of *Meditations* in 1622), More is the first poet to write almost exclusively in the form. He penned 1,029 Spenserian stanzas for his philosophical poems in an attempt to explain Platonic myths. ψυχωδια *Platonica; or, a platonicall song of the soul*, published in 1642, was reprinted with additions in *Philosophicall Poems* (1647). Although essentially one poem, it breaks down into four parts. Appendix poems were added to parts 2 and 3 of the enlarged 1647 edition. "The Life of the Soul" comprises 180 stanzas and "The Immortality of the Soul" comprises 422 stanzas. "The Infinity of Worlds," the first appendix poem, comprises 107 stanzas. "The Sleep of the Soul" has 132 stanzas, and "The Præexistency of the Soul," the second appendix poem, has 104 stanzas. The book ends with "The Unity of Souls" in 40 stanzas. "The Life of the Soul" and "The Immortality of the Soul" are the most accessible of the pieces; the later poems are almost entirely didactic and include little narrative reprieve.

"The Life of the Soul" begins with a Platonic trinity: in addition to his son Æon, Atove generates a daughter Uranore. Adorned with the quintessence (ether) which enables the senses in man to work with a "phansie," Uranore is the principle by which man can rise above himself and know Æon. In describing Uranore's four garments at the end of canto 1, More says he cannot explain them because his purpose is to allegorize what he has intuited as truth. The second half of "The Life of the Soul" begins in canto 2 with stanza 24, where More begins his account of a journey through Psychania, the land of souls. Geoffrey Bullough claims this episode is a description of More's own travels into mysticism, but the poetry is not really mystical in the manner, for example, of Saint John of the Cross; it reads more like John Bunyan's *Pilgrim's Progress* (1678, 1684) except that the place-names are pseudo-Platonic. The country of Psychania has two

Letter from More (18 April 1653) to his "heroine pupil," Lady Anne Conway of Warwickshire (British Library, Add. MSS 23, 216, f. 24)

Cupids Conflict.

Mela. Cleanthes.

Cl. MEla my dear! why been thy looks so sad
As if thy gentle heart were sunk with care?
Impart thy case; for be it good or bad
Friendship in either will bear equall share.
Mel. Not so; *Cleanthes*, for if bad it be
  My self must bleed afresh by wounding thee.

But what it is, my slow, uncertain wit
Cannot well judge. But thou shalt sentence give
How manfully of late my self I quit,
When with that lordly lad by chance I strive:
  Cl. Of friendship *Mela*! let's that story hear.
  Mel. Sit down *Cleanthes* then, and lend thine ear.

Upon a day as best did please my mind
Walking abroad amidst the verdant field
Scattering my carefull thoughts i'th' wanton wind
The pleasure of my path so farre had till'd
  My feeble feet that without timely rest
  Uneath it were to reach my wonted nest.

In secret shade farre moved from mortals sight
In lowly dale my wandring limbs I laid
On the cool grasse where Natures pregnant wit
A goodly bower of thickest trees had made.
  Amongst the leaves the chearfull birds did fare
  And sweetly carrol'd to the echoing air.

Hard at my feet ran down a crystall spring
Which did the cumbrous pebbles hoarsly chide
For standing in the way. Though murmuring
The broken stream his course did rightly guide
  And strongly pressing forward with disdain
  The grassie flore divided into twain.

The

First page of a poem in which More's poet figure rejects a call for ornamented verse praising earthly love (from the 1646 edition of Democritus Platonissans)

kingdoms: that of Autœsthesia, ruled by Dæmon (spouse of Duessa), and that of Theoprepy, ruled by Michael. Autœsthesia is subdivided into two provinces, Adamah and Dizoia. Adamah has a subprovince named Psittacuse Land (the Lesser Adamah), and Dizoia has two subprovinces, Aptery and Pteroessa. Adamah represents the corrupt natural life: it is here where the pilgrimage begins as the reader is introduced to a new narrator named Mnemon who tells about travels taken when "he was in youthfull state" and "mens natures gan to contemplate, and kingdoms view." Although told from the outset that the narrative is allegorical, readers will have difficulty from this point until the end of the poem remembering that they are not meeting actual people and seeing actual places.

In his later years More mentioned in a letter that he had been called a latitudinarian and did not know what that meant. His tone could be construed as playful, but More was very well aware of the dis-

dain he brought on himself for his tolerance of other religions. In "The Life of the Soul" one already finds the seeds of his religious tolerance when he writes of the rabble that inhabit Ida Castle: two dozen miscreants cataloged from "ireful ignorance" to "eager-slavering-after-hid-skill":

These and such like be that rude Regiment
That from the glittering sword of *Michael* fly:
They fly his outstretch'd arm, else they were shent
If they unto this Castle did not hie,
Strongly within its walls to fortify
Themselves[.]

As Mnemon wonders who will be able to overcome this fortress, he has a vision of Michael leading ten thousand saints on milk-white horses "to judge the world, and rule it with his rod." Unscathed by the castle guardians, Mnemon on a river bank sees the archangel Gabriel wooing a maid. This nymph is a wingless soul whose faith, emerging as Gabriel talks, becomes one of her wings; her love emerges as the other wing. A final trial before Mnemon can lead his travelers into Theoprepy is to pass through the Dale of Ain, which More defines as "nihil," nothingness. Surrounded by a wall of bland smoke (no thickness, no moisture, no smell), the Dale is terrible to anyone who has not given up self entirely. It is the mystical end to Mnemon's (More's) journey, a kind of *via unitiva* (unitive way), a reward merited by the narrator for his purgative journey.

"The Immortality of the Soul," the second section of More's epic, purports to be a proof for the immortality of the soul, but the opening stanzas elaborate the Horatian doctrine *poeta nascitur, non fit* (a poet is born, not made), and the entire first canto includes no argument for immortality. The argument, such as it is, begins with a definition of the rational soul and its contrast to vegetable and animal souls. More then bases an argument for immortality on the concept of kinesis which Plato uses in *Phaedrus*. This criterion of "self-moving" exhausts a major portion of canto 2. In canto 3 More narrates a vision which tells him he is immortal, but this experience is no logical proof of immortality. In fact, More often does not play fairly with logic. Leading his readers into accepting a priori statements (those for autokinesis) is not an isolated case of More's aggressively illogical argumentation. The closing stanzas of book 1, canto 2, of "The Immortality of the Soul" consist of elaborate mathematical problems, the purpose of which is to convince the reader that truth is slippery, that some truths are paradoxical and cannot be resolved by human discursive reasoning:

> But if't consist of points, then a Scalene
> I'll prove all one with an Isosceles:
> With as much ease I'll evince clear and clean
> That the crosse lines of a Rhomboides,
> That from their meeting to all angles presse
> Be of one length[.]

In manipulating mathematics, More presumes of his readers a rudimentary knowledge of geometry, but only enough familiarity with its terms so that he can illustrate the omnipotence of God, who exists above paradox.

The reader who expects a logical set of arguments proving the immortality of the soul is going to be disappointed, because More did not write a philosophical tract in the sense of a scholastic set of proofs. Too often critics, reading some of the poem, give up in disgust because they come to More's poetry under one of two misunderstandings, thinking they are going to read philosophy or thinking they are going to read poetry. Philosophy and poetry do make strange partners, each calling into focus different activities of the brain, the former requiring logic and ratiocination, the latter requiring imagination. Ancient poets, however, had succeeded in wedding poetry to natural science and agriculture. With examples of such "scientific" poetry in classical times as the *Georgics* of Virgil and *De rerum natura,* by Lucretius, More had every right to hope that he could blend poetry with philosophical proofs for immortality of the human soul.

In the preface to the 1647 edition of his poems, More specifies three objections to attempting discursive proofs of immortality. First, an incontrovertible proof might lead people, convinced they would never be annihilated, to attempt suicide as Cleombrotus did after reading Plato's *Phaedo*:

> For would it not be an overproportionated engine, to the again endangering of Cleombrotus neck, or too forcibly driving men to obedience if they had their immortality as demonstrable as; That the three angles in a triangle are equall to two right angles.

Such a remark, coming as it does from an ordained minister, seems very unusual since it ignores the Christian doctrine of eternal damnation. Linked to the suicide question, which More never touches in the poetry itself, the problem More raises next is that of free will, a problem dear to Calvinists. If people knew beyond a shadow of a doubt that they were immortal, they would have, says More, a circumscribed or forced obedience. For More, hostile to the Calvinists since his public school days, virtue not freely chosen is no credit to the human soul. Corollary to this idea of choice is More's second reason for avoiding discursive proofs of immortality:

> it would prevent that fitting triall of the soul, how she would be affected if there were nothing to come; whence she would not be able so sensibly to discover to her self her own Hypocrisie or sinceritie.

It is good that man is uncertain of his future, More reasons, because he can then merit knowledge of immortality by his own process of discovery. Finally, More suggests that demonstrable proofs of immortality would dissuade men from total reliance on God:

> that loving adherence and affectionate cleaving to God by Faith and divine sense, would be forestall'd by such undeniable evidence of Reason and Nature.

More advocates a blind leap into the arms of an all-providing God, urging an ultimate dependence on divine power, a dependence which to him does not conflict with his previous injunction that man should discover his own way to knowledge of immortality. There is no conflict, of course, if readers appreciate More's view that life is based on faith in the unknown; the reward for living on faith is the mystical appreciation of ideas that are above the ken of ordinary ratiocination. No conflict exists between faith and reason when faith supersedes reason. Ultimately More is more interested in the virtue of souls than in their immortality.

More is thus more interested in theories than in proof. At the close of book 1, canto 3, of "The Immortality of the Soul," he posits eight orbs of existence, seven of which do not decay. The eighth orb (Hyle) is corruptible and merits all of canto 4. Book 2, canto 1, reasserts the old theory that a soul debases itself by dipping down into matter, and canto 2 proves the unity of the soul but not its immortality. Canto 3 proves the soul is incorporeal. Book 3 begins by postulating three centers for the soul and claims, without proof, that the middle one survives. Canto 2 of book 3 then proves the soul's independence, and canto 3, a long digression on astronomy, proves nothing. The final canto of "The Immortality of the Soul" asserts that the just man simply knows he is immortal, and readers realize, if they have not already realized, that More is ultimately forced to base his immortality arguments on faith rather than on reason.

What "The Immortality of the Soul" lacks to relieve its tedium is the whimsy and narrative of "The Life of the Soul," which carried itself on a kind of Platonic science fiction of make-believe kingdoms and personalities. More nowhere apologizes for the dryness of "The Immortality of the Soul." In fact, in the preface to his *Philosophicall Poems*, More tells the reader not to expect a polished version of his earlier poems, referring not to the rhetorical decorations of the verse so much as to the order of the proofs: "true opinion is as faithful a guide as necessity and demonstration." He is aware of the fact that his philosophical arguments are helter-skelter, but he does not have the time to marshal them into good scholastic form, nor does he feel that it is important to do so:

> As for a more determinate decision of those many speculations which I have set on foot in these writings, though I made some kind of promise that way in my first, I must crave leave a while to defer it till I find the thing of more consequence and myself at better leisure.

It is possible, of course, that More made such a statement in order to cover his tracks, resisting the tedium of drastic revisions. More seems sincere, however, in the explanation of his poetic method.

What he was up against then, as much as he is today, are readers trained to expect syllogistic proofs in matters of philosophy. Proof by "demonstration" is bound to fail just as it failed, according to More, for René Descartes, who promised too much and delivered not enough. Although More corresponded with Descartes and admired the French philosopher enough to accept the theory of multiple universes, he later renounced Descartes before the 1647 edition of "The Infinity of Worlds." Proofs based on natural reasoning cannot compare to those quickened by what More calls the "sweet ethereall gale of divine breathing." Thus his poem-argument for the preexistence of the soul ends not with rational proofs but with appeals (through metaphor) to divine infusion:

> Like to a light fast-lock'd in lanthorn dark,
> Whereby, by night our wary steps we guide
> In slabby streets, and dirty channels mark,
> Some weaker rayes through the black top do glide,
> And flusher streams perhaps from horny side.
> But when we've passed the perill of the way
> Arriv'd at home, and laid that case aside,
> The naked light how clearly doth it ray
> And spread its joyful beams as bright as summer's day.
>
> Even so the soul in this contracted state
> Confin'd to these strait instruments of sense
> More dull and narrowly doth operate.
> At this hole hears, the sight must ray from thence,
> Here tasts, there smels; But when she's gone from hence,
> Like naked lamp she is one shining sphear.
> And round about has perfect cognoscence
> Whatere in her Horizon doth appear:
> She is one Orb of sense, all eye, all airy ear.

One of the advantages that More had in choosing not to construct his proofs in "The Immortality of the Soul" discursively is that, if his defenses prove false, they can still be vehicles for transmitting truth just as the truth of the divine hypostatical union is valid although the metaphor of light and colors used to teach it for hundreds of years was proven to be false.

"The Immortality of the Soul" is by far the longest of the epic segments, and to it More appended "The Infinity of Worlds" for the 1647 edition of his verses. The appended poem, first published separately (*Democritus Platonissans*, 1646), attempts to prove that the number of planets is infinite, an idea More had earlier repudiated in "The Immortality of the Soul" (book 3, canto 4) and would repudiate again in his *Enchiridion Metaphysicum* (1671).

The final poems of the collection are energetic but tedious in their subject matter. "The Sleep of the Soul" and "The Unity of Souls" argue for the union of the soul with God after death. The first poem denies the extinction of the soul:

> For sure in vain do humane souls exist
> After this life, if lull'd in listlesse sleep
> They senselesse lie, wrapt in eternal mist,
> Bound up in foggy clouds, that ever weep
> Benumming tears, and the souls centre steep
> With deading liquor, that she never minds
> Or feeleth ought. Thus drench'd in *Lethe* deep,
> Nor misseth she her self, nor seeks nor finds
> Her self. This mirksome state all the soul's actions binds.

The Unity of Souls stresses the absorption of the soul into God:

> For that one soul is judge of everything
> And heareth all Philosophers dispute;
> Herself disputes in all that jangling,
> In reasoning fiercely doth her self confute,
> And contradictions confidently conclude:
> That is so monstrous that no man can think
> To have least shew of truth. So this pursuit
> I well might now leave off: what need I swink
> To prove whats clearly true, and force out needlesse ink.

Both poems lack the dramatic color of "The Life of the Soul." They do not use narrative technique, have no dramatis personae, and read very much like prose paragraphs put into Spenserian stanzas. The second appendix poem, "The Præexistency of the Soul," carries an argument based on pious faith and stories of ghosts appearing after death:

> Ne may I passe that story sad of *Saul*
> And *Samuels* ghost, whom he in great distresse
> Consulted, was foretold his finall fall
> By that old man, whom *Endors* sorceresse
> Awak'd from pleasant vision and sweet ease,
> Straitning a while his wonted liberty
> By clammy air more close and thick compresse;
> Then gan the mantled sage *Sauls* destiny
> To reade, and thine with his, dear *Jonathan!* to tie.

> That lovely lasse *Pausanias* did kill
> Through ill surmise she ment him treachery;
> How did her angry spirit haunt him still
> That he could no where rest, nor quiet ly:
> Her wrongèd ghost was ever in his eye.
> And he that in his anger slew his wife,
> And was exempt by Law from penalty,
> Poore sorry man he led a weary life
> Each night the Shrow him beat with buffes and boxes rife.

More's attempt at rational argument becomes sensational rather than logical.

Since More published only one poem in book form (if the entire ψυχωδια *Platonica; or, a platonicall song of the soul* is considered a single poem) and republished it five years later with "The Infinity of Worlds" and "The Præexistency of the Soul," there is little development to trace in his short poetic career. Because he composed poems that depend on an interest in Platonism, Neoplatonism, mathematics, natural science, astronomy, metaphysics, and ghost stories, his verse does not have the homogeneity, for example, of Sir John Davies's *Nosce Teipsum* (1599). More's poetry, however, seems the freer for its convolutions, its outlandish mathematical "proofs," its fallacies, and its patina of Cambridge college life. Blending story with philosophy, More could better appeal to an audience who read to be entertained as well as educated, who needed to be prodded into thinking and discussing rather than handed proofs for immortality signed and sealed. More saw two intellectual needs in the few years he wrote verse: the earlier need, to educate undergraduates in Platonism, was blended into a utilitarian need, to prepare Civil War soldiers to face death with hope of an afterlife. His philosophical argument in verse, which avoided excessive moralizing on the one hand and pure ratiocination on the other, made More a mythomystic voice in his time. Today his poetry, still accessible, remains both ennobling and didactically invigorating, a unique filament in the web of seventeenth-century verse.

It is possible to reconstruct More's reactions to criticism of his first edition of poems and thus to see what More wanted poetry to be, what English society liked poetry to be in the early years of the first civil war, and what More thought of the taste of society. Most of the adverse criticism immediately following the 1642 edition apparently concerned More's vocabulary, not his lofty ideas (although Thomas Vaughan made sport with those). The many attacks More sustained throughout his life for the prose works on philosophy, witchcraft, and cabalism document his philosophical vagaries and are not concerned with his aesthetic of poetry.

The longest of the minor poems dealing with More's aesthetic is "Cupids Conflict," a poem in eighty-six stanzas framed as a dialogue within a dialogue between two men, Mela and Cleanthes:

> Mela my dear! why been thy looks so sad
> As if thy gentle heart were sunk with care?
> Impart thy case; for be it good or bad
> Friendship in either will bear equall share.
> *Mel.*: Not so; *Cleanthes*, for if bad it be
> My self must bleed afresh by wounding thee.

> But what it is, my slow, uncertain wit

Cannot well judge. But thou shalt sentence give
  How manfully of late my self I quit,
When with that lordly lad by chance I strive.
  Cl.: Of friendship, *Mela!* let's that story hear.
  Mel.: Sit down, *Cleanthes*, then, and lend thine ear.

The two men sit down, and Mela begins explaining why he is sad. Out walking in the fields one day, he stopped to rest in a bower. A naked swain with blue and purple wings alighted on the other side of a nearby stream and started shooting arrows at Mela, but they all fell short into the water. Cupid, finding his attack ineffective, switches to verbal arrows and chides Mela for being so ascetical, neglecting Nature, and not having a mistress. Mela replies if he had let Cupid guide his verses, he would call lust "love" and style vice as "vertue," and, pursuing one mistress in verse, he would ignore "all the whole world for one poore sorry wight." Resisting Cupid's style of love by eschewing a relationship with one woman, Mela has discovered that he has been able to expand his love to the whole universe.

Cupid, however, berates Mela for failing to praise a mistress in rhyme because earthly love would soften and make popular poetry that has been neglected. Cupid spells out the faults of Mela's verse: the lines are rough, the rhymes "unwelcome" (strange), and the diction, which uses uncommon words and repeats them too frequently, is barbarous:

Great hope indeed thy rhymes should men enlight,
That be with clouds and darkness all o'ercast,
Harsh style and harder sense void of delight
  The Readers wearied eye in vain do wast.
    And when men win thy meaning with much pain,
    Thy uncouth sense they coldly entertain.

  For wotst thou not that all the world is dead
Unto that Genius that moves in thy vein
Of poetrie! But like by like is fed.
Sing of my Trophees in triumphant strein.
    Then correspondent life, thy powerfull verse
    Shall strongly strike and with quick passion pierce.

The tender frie of lads and lasses young
With thirstie eare thee compassing about,
Thy Nectar-dropping Muse, thy sugar'd song
  Will swallow down with eager hearty draught;
    Relishing truly what thy rhymes convey,
    And highly praising thy soul-smiting lay.

Mela rejects Cupid's suggestion that he sing of earthly love, first because such love would close his soul to the greater joys of celibate love, and second because he uses his rough poetic language for a purpose, not wanting ornament to distract from sense. He defends his "rude," rugged, uncouth style as the fittest way to measure his tongue because he will "conjure up old words out of their grave / Or call fresh forrein force in if need crave" in order to get his meaning across in verse. All the modern poets who fly after fame are going to be sadly disappointed after their death, explains Mela. Cupid then wonders what moves Mela to write verse – could it be money?

Or is thy abject mind so basely bent
As of thy Muse to maken Merchandize?
(And well I wote this is no strange intent.)
  The hopefull glimps of gold from chattering Pies,
    From Daws and Crows, and Parots oft hath wrung
    An unexpected Pegaseian song.

Mela bristles at the suggestion and retorts that virtue is the only reward the soul needs. Cupid is not satisfied, so Mela tells him that the same thing moves him to compose as moves the lark to sing; if a few people receive light while reading his verses, Mela considers their reward his reward. Cupid replies sarcastically that harsh rhymes can hardly enlighten people if people are not delighted to read them in the first place. Therefore, Mela should lure young boys and girls to read his verses by sugaring the lines, making the poems palatable.

Since the world is dead to the true genius of poetry that moves in Mela's veins, Cupid explains, Mela would do better to wean people back to verse so "all Sexes, Ages, Orders, Occupations / Would listen to thee with attentive ear." Mela could win readers, in other words, by ornamenting his verse. Mela replies that the times, though bad, will not last long since "a three branch'd Flame will soon sweep clean the stage / Of this old dirty drosse." In preparation for this day Mela will throw his words into the air and let them be thawed in the future. Cupid finally leaves in a huff. Unlike Spenser, More could have nothing to do with traditional love ethos and saved his poetic fervor to sing the Platonic proofs for immortality and other qualities of the human soul.

Among More's minor poems is a short poem expressing sentiments similar to those in "Cupids Conflict" and bearing an interesting relation to that longer poem, a relation that sheds further light on More's aesthetic of poetry. In the 1647 edition the piece is titled "Ad Paronem." The critic addressed by More is attacked for having a "shallow mind," looking more for ornament and smooth wording than meaning. The critic is more concerned with the "rind" of verse than its "pith," and thus he is unable to pierce below the surface of the verse to where More's "profounder quill" works best. When he is only human, says More, and not transported by poetic frenzy, his own verses seem to him "a rude confused heap of ashes dead," and he faults himself for the use of three things: archaic words, coinages, and repetitiousness:

> A rude confused heap of ashes dead
> My verses seem, when that celestial flame
> That sacred spirit of life's extinguishèd
> In my cold breast. Then gin I rashly blame
> My rugged lines: This word is obsolete;
> That boldly coined, a third too oft doth beat
>
> Mine humorous ears. Thus fondly curious
> Is the faint reader, that doth want that fire
> And inward vigor heavenly furious
> That made my enrag'd spirit in strong desire
> Break through such tender cob-web niceties,
> That oft entangle these blind buzzing flies.

We recognize today that Spenser's love for archaic phrases was a mark of his regard for Chaucer; similarly, More's use was indicative of his regard for Spenser.

The aesthetic of Henry More is uniformly Platonic, but the divine frenzy of his earliest creations became tainted by 1647 through a need to spar, far away from heaven, with hostile critics on their own Platonic turf, Earth. Neither milieu, however, is unimportant in More's Platonic cosmology. Had More sustained an interest in writing poetry after his academic career was launched, he may have eventually penned an extended apologia for his rough lines, strange rhymes, and barbarous diction, but his mind soon engaged itself in prose polemic, and the poetry remained confined to a single volume. Glimmers of his aesthetic appear in several minor poems and the opening lines of "The Immortality of the Soul":

> So hath he rais'd my soul, and so possest
> My inward spright, with that unfainèd will
> He bears to *Psyche's* brood, that I nere rest
> But ruth or ragefull indignation fill
> My troubled veins, that I my life near spill
> With sorrow and disdain, for that foul lore
> That crept from dismall shades of Night, and quill
> Steep'd in sad Styx, and fed with stinking gore
> Suckt from corrupted corse, that God and men abhorre.

Tracing More's aesthetic between 1642 and 1647 gives, however, information of some value on the feelings pro and con toward academic verse in a period more intent on civil war than poetry, but a period not so far from the age of golden verse that some readers could object when a young poet attempted to foist rough and barbarous verses onto their golden sensibilities.

A few critics have written appreciatively of More's verse. Grosart's introduction to the poems contains a glowing analysis of his favorite More lines. Bullough's introduction to his own edition of the poems is more objectively critical. Ward's life of More has a second volume (which has never been published) devoted solely to a critical appreciation of More's work. Marjorie Nicolson tried to get More into the public eye with articles in the 1920s, an outgrowth of her dissertation. Since Nicolson's work, a handful of doctoral students have been interested in More's poetry, but he remains an unmined treasure.

Biography:

Richard Ward, *The Life of the Learned and Pious Dr. Henry More*, edited by M. F. Howard (London: Theosophical Society, 1911).

References:

Geoffrey Bullough, Introduction to *Philosophical Poems of Henry More* (Manchester: Manchester University Press, 1931);

Alexander B. Grosart, Introduction to *The Complete Poems of Dr. Henry More* (Edinburgh: Edinburgh University Press, 1878);

Les Haring, "Henry More's Psychathanasia and Democritus Platonissans: A Critical Edition," Ph.D. dissertation, Columbia University, 1961;

Alexander Jacob, "Henry More's 'A Platonick Song of the Soul': A Critical Study," Ph.D. dissertation, Pennsylvania State University, 1988;

George Klawitter, "The Poetry of Henry More," Ph.D. dissertation, University of Chicago, 1981;

Aharon Lichtenstein, *Henry More: The Rational Theology of a Cambridge Platonist* (Cambridge: Harvard University Press, 1936);

Marjorie Nicolson, *Conway Letters* (New Haven: Yale University Press, 1930);

Nicolson, "More's *Psychozoia*," *Modern Language Notes*, 37 (March 1922): 141–148;

P. G. Stanwood, Introduction to *Democritus Platonissans* (Los Angeles: Clark Library, 1968);

John Tulloch, *Rational Theology and Christian Philosophy in England in the Seventeenth Century*, 2 volumes (Edinburgh: Blackwood, 1872), II: 303–409.

Papers:

Letters by More are located at the Bodleian Library (MS Tanner Letters, 42, f. 38; MS Tanner Letters, 38, f. 115) and the British Library (Additional MS 23,216, Additional MS 4279 f. 156, Additional MS 4276 f. 41; MS Sloane. 235 f. 14–45).

Diana Primrose

(floruit circa 1630)

Kari Boyd McBride
University of Arizona

BOOK: *A Chaine of Pearle. Or, A Memoriall of the peerles Graces, and Heroick Vertues of Queene Eliza-beth, of Glorious Memory. Composed by the Noble Lady, Diana Primrose* (London: Printed by J. Dawson for Thomas Paine, sold by Philip Waterhouse, 1630).

A Chaine of Pearle (1630) is a panegyric to the virtues of Queen Elizabeth I, published during the reign of Charles I when the cult of the Virgin Queen was often coterminous with criticism of the excesses and failures of Charles's political and religious inclinations. The qualities ascribed to Elizabeth in *A Chaine of Pearle* are in accord with the picture that has survived to the twentieth century of a moderate and savvy ruler who reigned by carefully controlling the image of her personal and public life. The descriptions of the "pearles" of virtue show an unusual melding of the public and private aspects of each virtue, which, taken together, form a unique commentary on the notion of the monarch's "two bodies." Nonetheless, aside from minimal speculation in biographical dictionaries about the identity of the author and summary comments on the poem, there has been no modern critical work on the text of *A Chaine of Pearle.*

Information about the author of the work is only speculative, and there is reason to question even the existence of a Diana Primrose. All that can be said with some certainty is that the poem was written by a woman, since the author in "The Induction" refers to Elizabeth as "Empresse of our Sex." Thomas Park, editor of *The Harleian Miscellany* (1808–1813), which includes this "most rare" work in its entirety, concedes that "*Of the Lady-authoress, I cannot impart any information.*" Robert Harley, first Earl of Oxford (1661–1724), from whose manuscripts *The Harleian Miscellany* was compiled, recorded nothing about the author, though he was born only three decades after the publication of *A Chaine of Pearle.* Frederick Rowton in *The Female Poets of Great Britain* (1848) included an excerpt from Primrose's poem, calling it "an insufferably prosy tract" but offering no biographical information about the author.

Maureen Bell, George Parfitt, and Simon Shepherd in a *Biographical Dictionary of English Women Writers 1580–1720* (1990) suggest that Diana may have been the wife of the Protestant minister Gilbert Primrose (circa 1580–1642) and argue that this Diana used William Camden's *Annales rerum Anglicarum, et Hibernicarum, regnante Elizabetha* (1615) as her source, since she probably would not have had firsthand knowledge of Elizabeth. Gilbert Primrose, Scottish-born and educated, was a prominent Huguenot minister in France during most of the reign of James I. Later he became the minister of the French Church of Threadneedle Street, London, chaplain-in-ordinary to James I and Charles I, and author of several religious tracts. In no contemporary source that has come to light, however, is a Diana named as his wife. Indeed, mention of a wife is conspicuously absent in an extended entry in the *Dictionary of National Biography,* in which his mother's name is included; and in *Alumni Oxonienses* (1891, 1892), in which his sons are named. If Diana was this Gilbert's wife, she was probably either Scottish- or French-born (living with him in France from 1602 to 1624) and would have died before 14 December 1637, when Gilbert married Jeane Hersey. Another Gilbert Primrose of the same era was the surgeon of James VI in Scotland and later – as of May 1603, after James's accession to the English throne – sergeant surgeon to the king. Again, there is no evidence linking Diana Primrose to either Gilbert, or to any of the several other Primroses of James's court.

John Nichols (1745–1826), publisher and antiquarian, thought Diana Primrose to be a pseudonym for Lady Anne Clifford, Countess of Dorset, later Countess of Pembroke and Montgomery (1590–1676). In his *Progresses and Public Processions of Queen Elizabeth* (1788–1821), Nichols does not explain his reasons for the connection but merely lists

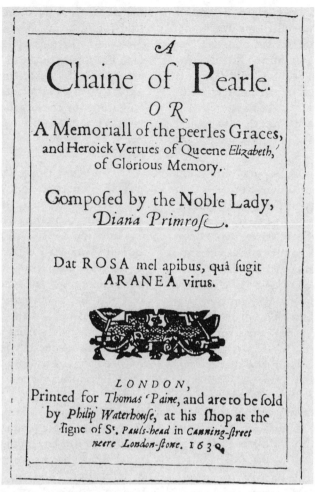

Title page for a panegyric to Elizabeth I published during the reign of Charles I
as implicit criticism of his methods of government

Clifford in the index as "author of a Chain of Pearl." At the end of *The Progresses,* he reprints *A Chaine of Pearle* along with laments written at the death of Elizabeth, and he notes the date of publication for the Primrose poem inaccurately as 1603, the year of Elizabeth's death. This mistake, perhaps nothing more than a typographical error, may have led Nichols to speculate that Clifford, who recorded an account of Elizabeth's last days (also included in *The Progresses*), was the author of the poetic encomium as well. On the other hand, Nichols may well have had corroborative data that would connect Diana Primrose with Lady Anne Clifford.

Indeed, the reference within the poem to the Pope's having "lately sent from Rome, / Strange Bookes and pictures painting out the Doome / Of his pretended Martyrs"; two references in marginal notes to events of the first year of James I's reign (one a cryptic aside about a court scandal); and the

lack of reference to any event beyond 1603 strongly suggest that the poem was written very soon after Elizabeth's death rather than in 1630, and by someone who knew the court intimately. Also, in a *Harleian Miscellany* footnote, Park argues that Dorothy Berry's prefatory verse includes "a poetical hint to our James the First": Elizabeth's "noble praise / Deserves a quill pluckt from an angel's wing / And none to write it but a Crowned King." It had been said that the king's pen was "made of a quill pluckt from an angel's wing." The presence in the poem of references to the goings-on at court during the first year of James's reign makes it doubtful that Diana Primrose the author was the wife of Gilbert Primrose the prelate: whether Scottish or French, Gilbert's wife would not have known court gossip nor have passed it on so mysteriously, as to an audience in the know. Further, she would not speak of seditious papal actions – which sound more like the religious difficulties of the early years of James's reign than events under Charles I – as having occurred "lately." Such points *may* support the theory that somebody like Lady Anne Clifford was the author of the piece. Nothing in Clifford's diary or letters, however, shows a connection to Primrose. If Clifford did write *A Chaine of Pearle* on the occasion of Elizabeth's death, she would have been a precocious thirteen or fourteen years old at the time.

There is justification for speculating that Diana Primrose is a pseudonym, for the first name evokes the mythology of the Virgin Queen. Further, the epigraph to the work – "*Dat rosa mel apibus, quâ sugit aranea virus*" (the rose gives honey to the bees, from which the spider sucks venom), a Latin proverb common to the Renaissance – includes uncommon reference to a specific flower, the rose, which may indicate a play on the, perhaps fictitious, author's name. The proverb may also be present to deflect royal criticism of the author's motives, implying that construction of the poem's meaning depends on the reader, not the author. Berry's prefatory verse also plays on the author's name – "Shine forth (*Diana*) dart thy Golden Raies"; "Thou, the *Prime-Rose* of the *Muses* nine." The absence of biographical data on the author may further suggest the book's pseudonymity.

Thus the evidence, while hardly conclusive, points to the poem having been written in or soon after 1603 by a woman, perhaps named Diana Primrose, who was intimate with court life. (This date of composition would preclude Camden's *Annales* as a source.) Publication in 1630 would imply criticism of Charles I not necessarily originally intended by the author; Charles is not mentioned in the poem, and James I is mentioned only in marginal notes. One marginal note states that information in the poem about a court scandal in 1603 was relayed by "the honorable Kt. and Baronet, Sir Richard Houghton of Houghton Tower." Since Houghton was not made baronet until 1611 (when the baronetage was created), the marginal notes must have been added after the composition of the original poem, if the theory of the poem's early composition is correct. The notes would most likely be added upon publication of the poem in 1630, to make sense of events no longer familiar to English readers. The scandal referred to is described by Leopold von Ranke in *A History of England* (1875) as the advances by "Taxis that great Don" (Juan de Tassis or Taxis, the Spanish ambassador to James's court in 1603)

toward a woman identified only as "That Noble Lady of the Court." It is possible that the story was "related by" Houghton to the author long after the fact, but this hypothesis seems unlikely, since there would be little reason for including such an obscure narrative in a composition of 1630. Thus the data still argue for composition in 1603 and suggest that Nichols had good reason for printing *A Chaine of Pearle* as a lament written on the death of Elizabeth.

Whoever the author may have been, if she was alive in 1630 she would probably have given her permission for the publication of the work and have understood the poem serving a function different from the one envisioned when it was composed. In 1629 Charles I had adjourned Parliament (with difficulty), beginning the eleven years of nonparliamentary rule preceding the Short Parliament of 1640 that eventually led to the Civil War. Although in 1630 the author could not have foreseen these events, she or her publishers might have been sufficiently alarmed by the king's high-handed ways to discover in her portrait of virtuous Elizabeth a scathing and fitting contrast to Charles.

The slim quarto book (entered in the Stationers' Register 15 January 1630), written entirely in rhymed iambic pentameter couplets (with the exception of the Latin epigraph, postscript, and marginal notes), begins with three prefatory verses: first a dedication "To All Noble Ladies, and Gentlewomen" followed by Berry's verse "To the Excellent Lady, the Composer of this Worke." "The Induction," addressed to "Great Eliza, Englands brightest Sun," calls Elizabeth greater than "the greatest Princes . . . / That ever scepter swai'd or Crowne did Weare," and states the author's intent to blazon the queen's "most Royall parts." This section is signed by "Thy Emperial Majesties eternall Votary, Diana." The text itself is divided into ten "pearles": religion, chastity, prudence, temperance, clemency, justice, fortitude, science, patience, and bounty.

The "heroick" virtues chosen by the author for enumeration represent a motley assembly of qualities. Four are the cardinal (or natural, or moral) virtues: prudence, temperance, justice, and fortitude. When Elizabeth had enumerated the qualities she thought most important for a ruler (in a 1586 response to Parliament included in Camden's *Annales*), she named "those prime capital Vertues, Justice, Temperance, Prudence and Magnanimity." She thought the first two "proper to men" rather than women but claimed her share of the latter two.

The author of *A Chaine of Pearle* omits the theological virtues, faith, hope, and charity, but adds six other virtues to make the unusual number of ten (rather than the more standard seven, as antidote to the seven vices). Religion is unusually cast here as a virtue, represented as a public, even political, accomplishment as well as a private grace; Elizabeth's personal religion was, by virtue of her being "Supreme Governor" of both spiritual and temporal matters, the religion of England. The presence of chastity in a paean to Elizabeth is not unusual, and, moreover, chastity appeared often in elaborated medieval and Renaissance catalogues of the Christian virtues. Clemency is related to mercy, a quality more often attributed to God than to human beings – perhaps a significant point in a poem that deifies "the English Goddesse." Science was, as Thomas Traherne called it in his *Christian Ethicks* (1675), an intellectual virtue. Bounty, or liberality, another virtue common to contemporary expositions on the virtues, Traherne called one of the "less principle" moral virtues. This conglomeration of various qualities is not unusual in itself; once the magic number seven is surpassed, any number of virtues might find their way into a treatise. What stands out is not the number or kinds of virtues included but that the author of *A Chaine of Pearle* understands Elizabeth's virtues functioning as both private graces and political gifts in a manner unique to a female monarch.

In the first pearl, "Religion," Elizabeth is praised as "Christs Glorious Ensigne," the promoter of "true religion" who at her ascension to the throne found the kingdom "infected much / With Superstition, and Abuses." Elizabeth's virtue here is in her reforming the English church without violence: "shee swaid the Scepter with a Ladies Hand," not forcing the reformed religion on the "Romists." The Pope is an inciter of treason whose actions, including the papal bull that declared Elizabeth heretical, forced her to make "stricter lawes / Against Recusants."

The second pearl, Elizabeth's "Chastity," is described as "Her impregnable Virginity," a weapon of state against the machinations of the Pope as embodied in the French and Spanish (Roman Catholic) contenders for Elizabeth's hand in marriage and, thus, for control of the English state and state religion. A parenthetical sermon counsels all women to guard chastity from "foule Desires" – whether they be virgins, wives, or widows – and states a Protestant position (reminiscent of Edmund Spenser's *The Faerie Queene*, 1590, 1596)

that, of the three types of chastity, "God respects / All equally." This section ends with a cryptic reference to the story of "That Noble Lady of the Court" (of the first year of James I) who refused the overtures of the Spanish ambassador and maintained her chastity.

The third pearl, Elizabeth's "Prudence," lies chiefly in her political wisdom: "though her Wit and Spirit were divine," she ruled by "Counsels" rather than by tyranny. In 1630 this comment could have been read as a criticism of Charles I, whose manner of government was anything but conciliar. The author argues that prudence, so rare in most women, is by contrast "more emminent" in Elizabeth.

Her "Temperance," the fourth pearl, is both her "selfe-governance" and her moderation in the governance of the state, another clever integration of public and private virtue in the monarch's "two bodies." Her "Clemency," a pearl related to her "Justice," reveals itself in her treatment of rebels and recusants. The author argues in "Justice" that the machinations of the Pope pushed Elizabeth to take untoward measures against "Villany" and "Disloyalty,"

> a Taske
> Unfit for Feminine hands, which rather love
> To write of pleasing subjects, then approve
> The most deserved slaughtering of any.

Elizabeth's measured response to papal provocation both tests and demonstrates her justice.

The section on "Fortitude" tells of the queen's speech at Tilbury, where "words deliver'd in most Princely sort / Did animate the Army, and report / To all the World Her Magnanimity" and "haughtie Courage." The author connects Elizabeth's courage to her "Science," here rhetorical skill: "Shee did with Atticke Eloquence controule / Her Speeches to our Academians," showing her superiority to those who "in rude rambling Rhetoricke did roule." Again this sign of Elizabeth's personal accomplishment is directly linked to her political skill:

> with what Oratory-ravishments
> Did Shee imparadise Her Parliament.
> . . . .
> Her Loyal Commons how did Shee embrace,
> And entertaine with a most Royall Grace.

This skill in wooing Parliament would form another painful contrast to Charles's troubles in 1630.

The paean to Elizabeth's "Patience" recounts her early imprisonment and attributes her release and escape from death to the hand of God. Here the author makes a tacit comparison of Elizabeth to Christ: "by her patient bearing of the Crosse, Shee reaped greatest Gaine from greatest Losse."

In the final section, the pearl of "Bounty," the author calls Elizabeth "England's Rose and Lillie" and cleverly evokes the imagery of the "song of songs" in a final commentary on the relationship between the public and private virtues of a queen. In this image, Elizabeth is both the beloved woman of the biblical love poem and the embodiment of the English church in the metaphoric reading of the poem that equates the lover with Christ and the beloved with the Church: Elizabeth is both woman and institution. The poem ends abruptly with a description of the poet's "adoring" muse. (The sense of the short passage is unclear because of the omission of at least one word.) The final Latin couplet seems to contrast the blissful rest of the poet's muse with those who near the horrifying grave shall weep eternally and insatiably over Elizabeth, turned to ashes.

The author of *A Chaine of Pearle,* while writing in the standard biographical tradition that grew up around Elizabeth even before her death, has manipulated the details of that tradition to make a unique commentary on the nature of the woman ruler. Rather than seeing the queen's gender as preventing her from exercising "heroick" virtues, the author instead finds Elizabeth's "two bodies" inseparable: her public virtues as a ruler are one with her private self, and the divinity inherent in monarchy is thus conferred on Elizabeth the woman.

Francis Quarles

(1592 – 8 September 1644)

Lorraine M. Roberts
Saint Mary's College, Minnesota

BOOKS: *A Feast for Wormes. Set Forth in a Poeme of the History of Ionah* (London: Printed by Felix Kyngston for Richard Moore, 1620; revised, 1626);

Hadassa, or The History of Qveene Ester: With Meditations thereupon, Diuine and Morall (London: Printed by Felix Kingston for Richard Moore, 1621);

Iob Militant: With Meditations Divine and Morall (London: Printed by Felix Kyngston for George Winder, 1624);

Sions Elegies. Wept by Jeremie the Prophet (London: Printed by W. Stansby for Thomas Dewe, 1624);

Sions Sonets. Sung by Solomon the King (London: Printed by W. Stansby for Thomas Dewe, 1625);

Argalus and Parthenia (London: Printed for John Marriott, 1629; revised, 1632);

Divine Poems: Containing the History of Ionah. Ester. Iob. Sions Sonets. Elegies (London: Printed by M. Flesher for John Marriott, 1630);

The Historie of Samson (London: Printed by M. Flesher for John Marriott, 1631);

Divine Fancies: Digested into Epigrammes, Meditations, and Observations (London: Printed by M. Flesher for John Marriot, 1632);

Emblemes (London: Printed by G. Miller, sold by John Marriot, 1635; enlarged edition, London: Printed by J. Dawson for Francis Eglesfield, 1639);

An Elegie Vpon the Truely Lamented Death of the Right Honorable Sir Julius Cæsar K^{nt}. (London: Printed by M. Flesher for John Marriot, 1636);

An Elegie Vpon my Deare Brother, the Jonathan of my heart, M^r. Iohn Wheeler (London: Printed by Thomas Cotes for Nicholas Alsop and T. Nicholes, 1637);

Hieroglyphikes of the life of Man (London: Printed by M. Flesher for John Marriot, 1638);

Memorials Vpon The Death of Sir Robert Qvarles, Knight (London: Printed by Thomas Cotes for Nicholas Alsop, 1639);

Enchyridion (London: Printed by Thomas Cotes, 1640; revised edition, London: Printed by Thomas Cotes for G. Hutton, 1641);

Sighes At the contemporary deaths of Those incomparable Sisters, The Countesse of Cleaveland, and Mistrisse Cicily Killegrve (London: Printed by Thomas Cotes for Nicholas Alsop, 1640);

Threnodes On the Lady Marsham late wife to Sir William Marsham of High Laver in the County of Essex B^{nt.} and William Cheyne Esquire (Printed by T. & R. Cotes for George Hutton, 1641);

Observations Concerning Princes and States, Upon Peace and Warre (London: Printed for John Sweeting, 1642);

Barnabas and Boanerges: or, Wine and Oyle for Afflicted Soules (London: Printed by Richard Bishop for Richard Loundes, 1644); authorized edition published as part 2 of *Judgement & Mercy for Afflicted Soules* (1646);

The Loyall Convert (Oxford: Printed by Leonard Lichfield, 1644);

The Shepheards Oracle: Delivered in an Eglogue (Oxford, 1644);

The Whipper Whipt (London, 1644);

The New Distemper (Oxford: Printed by Leonard Lichfield, 1645);

The Profest Royalist: His Qvarrell With The Times: Maintained In Three Tracts: viz., The Loyall Convert. New Distemper. Whipper Whipt. (Oxford, 1645);

Solomons Recantation, Entituled Ecclesiastes, Paraphrased (London: Printed by M. F. for Richard Royston, 1645);

Judgement & Mercy for Afflicted Soules, part 1 (London: Printed by Ric. Cotes for Richard Royston, 1646; part 2, Cambridge: Printed by R. Daniel for V. Quarles, 1646);

The Shepheards Oracles: Delivered in certain Eglogues (London: Printed by M. F. for John Marriot and Richard Marriot, 1646);

Francis Quarles (portrait attributed to William Dobson; National Portrait Gallery, London)

Hosanna, Or Divine Poems On The Passion of Christ
(London: Printed for John Benson, 1647);
The Virgin Widow. A Comedie (London: Printed for R.
Royston, 1649).

Editions: *The Complete Works in Prose and Verse of
Francis Quarles,* 3 volumes, edited by Alexander B. Grosart (Edinburgh: Constable, 1880);
John Horden, ed., *Hosanna, or Divine Poems on the Passion of Christ and Threnodes* (Liverpool: Liverpool University Press, 1960).

Francis Quarles is reputed to have been the
most popular writer of his day, and his attraction
continued well beyond the eighteenth century.
Today his work is valued less for its own merits
than for its influence, especially that of the *Emblemes*
(1635), on more-gifted poets of the earlier seventeenth century such as John Donne, George Herbert, and Richard Crashaw, as well as later writers
such as John Bunyan, Samuel Taylor Coleridge,
and Robert Browning. For *Emblemes* Quarles appro-

priated Continental engravings (sometimes modify-
ing them to suit his purposes) and accompanied
them with a motto, scriptural and patristic quotations, a poem, and an epigram, the whole to be used
as didactic and meditative aids. Quarles was a loyal
supporter of the Church of England and of the
king; yet, ironically, during his lifetime he was accused of being a Roman Catholic sympathizer, and
after his death his work became very popular with
Puritan readers.

Most of the information about Quarles's life
comes from "Short Relation of the Life and Death
of Mr. Francis Quarles, by Ursula Quarles his
Sorrowfull Widow," which was prefixed to *Solomons
Recantation, Entituled Ecclesiastes, Paraphrased* (1645).
The exact date of Quarles's birth is unknown, but
his baptism was on 8 May 1592. Born in Stewards,
Kent, he was the third son of Joan Dalton Quarles
and James Quarles, "a Gentleman both by birth and
desert," said his widow. When Francis was seven,
his father (who had been clerk of green cloth and

purveyor of the navy to Queen Elizabeth) died on 25 September 1599, leaving Francis an annuity of fifty pounds a year. He attended school at Romford in Essex while living in a "stately house" at Stewards. The chaplain, William Tichbourne, took an interest in him and his studies.

In 1606, seven years after the death of his father, Quarles's mother died; her will shows that she had previously been unable to forward to Quarles the full annuity his father had bequeathed him, giving him instead only fifteen pounds yearly for his education. Now, however, he was to receive the full sum, which he needed to attend Christ's College, Cambridge, having entered there in 1605 when he was fourteen. After being graduated B.A. in 1608, Quarles studied law at Lincoln's Inn but wished for a vocation of devotion and study rather than a public life. Nevertheless, he traveled abroad as part of the retinue of the daughter of James I, Princess Elizabeth, who would become the queen of Bohemia in 1619. From 1613 Quarles was cupbearer for her until his marriage on 28 May 1618 to Ursula Woodgate of Saint Andrews, Holborn. Together the Quarleses had eighteen children; their son John was the only one to achieve any measure of public fame, as a poet.

In the earliest years of the marriage the family lived in London, but in 1621 Quarles was in Dublin as secretary to James Ussher, the primate of Ireland and archbishop of Armagh; there Quarles wrote *Argalus and Parthenia,* which was published later in 1629. In 1630 Quarles lived at Bath, where he may have written the paraphrase *The Historie of Samson* (1631) and prepared for publication *Divine Fancies* (1632), a collection of four hundred short pieces. In the summer of 1633 Quarles returned to Essex to live at Roxwell, where he composed his best-known work, *Emblemes.* From 4 February 1640 until his death he held the office that was formerly held by Ben Jonson, that of chronologer to the city of London. Quarles's record of his duties, a manuscript entitled "Chronicle of the Citty of London," has since been lost.

By 1640 Quarles left Roxwell to live at Ridley Hall in Terling, another Essex parish. The move was perhaps economical, for his fortunes were declining, as well as problematic, for Terling was basically a congregational community, whose vicar, John Stalham, may have been one who accused Quarles of being a Papist. It was during this period that Quarles wrote *Enchyridion* (1640) and other prose pieces. His advocacy of King Charles I's cause in the pamphlets *The Loyall Convert* (1644), *The Whipper Whipt* (1644), and *The New Distemper* (1645)

led to the taking of his property, the burning of his manuscripts, and the assassination of his character. Quarles died 8 September 1644 and was buried in the Church of Saint Olave, Silver Street, London. His widow claimed he had not wished to live after being subjected to false allegations of being a Papist for defending the king's alliance with the Roman Catholics. She was referring to a petition in 1644 that was put forward against Quarles by eight men (only two of whom were known). While Quarles was cleared of all charges before he died, his disappointment led to his refusing the services of a Roman Catholic doctor to treat his illness.

In her "Short Relation of the Life and Death of Mr. Francis Quarles," the poet's wife defended his life in these words:

> In all his duties to God and Man he was conscionable and orderly: He preferred God and religion to the first place in his thoughts, his King and Country to the second, his family and studies he reserved to the last. As for God, he was frequent in his devotions and prayers to Him, and almost constant in reading or meditating on his Holy Word, as his *Divine Fancies* and other parts of his Works will sufficiently testifie. For his Religion, he was a true sonne of the Church of England; an even Protestant, not in the least degree biassed to this hand of superstition, or that of schisme, though both those factions were ready to cry him down for this inclination to the contrary.

Quarles's contemporaries mourned his death, one claiming that Quarles, "next to Bartas, sang the heavenliest lay." He died a pauper, leaving his wife and nine living children destitute. Ursula Quarles tried to support the family by publishing her husband's remaining manuscripts, but lawsuits she brought against two booksellers suggest that she was cheated by them.

During the Interregnum all Quarles's works remained popular, in spite of his support of a losing cause. Some critics of Quarles have considered him the unlearned or unsophisticated reader's Metaphysical poet (Milton's nephew Edward Phillips in *Theatrum Poetarum,* 1675, called Quarles the "sometimes darling of the Plebian judgments"), but his works were popular among the upper classes as well. While his position as a Church of England adherent was well known, he had numerous Puritan friends, including the family of his godfather, Sir Francis Barrington. The piety of his works accounted for their popularity among Puritans as well as Church of England readers and explains why he was later dubbed the "puritanical poet" by Anthony Wood. Quarles's disapproval of plays on Sundays, of drinking, and of ribald talk also aligned him with the Puritans.

His first work, *A Feast for Wormes,* was written and published in 1620, establishing the genre and style of much of his earliest work, biblical paraphrases in pentameter couplets. The paraphrases are intended to appeal to popular taste in their promotion of familiar biblical narratives, their offering of pious wisdom in the accompanying meditations, and their use of homely, familiar language. Dedicated to Robert, Lord Sidney, the full title of *A Feast for Wormes* indicates it is a poetic history of the biblical Jonah in thirteen parts, each followed by a meditation on the mercy of God toward human beings, who are merely "feasts for worms." Quarles concludes with "The Generall Use of this History," which says the poem is meant to promote a life of prayer; "A Hymne to God" and "Eleven Pious Meditations" end the work. Immediately following the poem in the 1620 and 1626 editions is *Pentelogia, or The Quintessence of Meditation,* comprising two groups of five meditations each: "Mors tua" (Thy Death), "Mors Christi" (Christ's Death), "Fraus Mundi" (The World's Temptation), "Gloria Cœli" (Heaven's Joy), and "Dolor Inferni" (Hell's Torment).

Hadassa, or The History of Queene Ester was published in 1621 and dedicated to King James I. Its organization, verse pattern, and didactic intent are similar to those aspects of his first work. In the twenty-sectioned paraphrase of Queen Ester's saving of the Jews from destruction by Haman, Quarles follows each part with a meditation meant to draw out the moral of the story and with pious thoughts on other tangential matters, as shown in "Meditatio tertia":

> *Since of a Rib first framed was a Wife,*
> *Let Ribs be Hi' rogliphicks of their life:*
> *Ribs coast the heart, and guard it round about,*
> *And like a trusty Watch keepe danger out;*
> *So tender Wiues should loyally impart*
> *Their watchfull care to fence their Spouses' heart[.]*

Written about the same time, while Quarles was living in Dublin, was his only romance, *Argalus and Parthenia,* a tale of steadfast love and ill-timed death extracted from Sir Philip Sidney's *Arcadia* (1590). Quarles's long narrative poem was not published until 1629, but then it had the enormous success of twenty-one editions before 1691, twelve before the Restoration. Dedicated to Henry, Lord Rich of Kensington, the poem addresses the reader in words that seem to belie any association with a Metaphysical style:

> In this discourse, I have not affected to set thy understanding on the Rack, by the tyranny of strong *lines,* which (as they fabulously report of *China-dishes*) are made for the third *Generation* to make use of, and are
>
> the meere itch of wit.

Thus, to be considered a poor man's Metaphysical seems to be another irony in Quarles's career.

Quarles expands Sidney's account of Argalus and Parthenia from four thousand to thirty-six thousand words, using every detail from Sidney with elaboration, as well as inserting new material such as the death by poisoning of Parthenia's maid. Called a "billow of mismetered lines, loose couplets, and a breathlessly dramatic style" by B. S. Field, Jr., the work inspired two accounts, *The Most Pleasant and Delightful History of Argalus and Parthenia* (1672) and *The Unfortunate Lovers* (circa 1700).

Quarles continued his biblical paraphrases, publishing in 1624 *Job Militant: With Meditations Divine and Morall* and *Sions Elegies. Wept by Jeremie the Prophet.* The former is dedicated to Prince Charles, the latter to William Herbert, third Earl of Pembroke. The paraphrase of Job adopts the structure of *A Feast for Wormes* by paralleling narrative and meditation; the paraphrase of Jeremiah begins with a poem to Christ, followed by four threnodia, each with twenty-two elegies consisting of six couplets. The first elegy begins with the letter *A,* and each letter of the alphabet is given in order by the succeeding elegies, a scheme based on the biblical original. The reason behind this technique, Quarles claims in his preface "To the Reader," is "*partly for Eloquence, partly for Memorie sake, meaning either literally thus, that it ought to be perfect as the Alphabet, in Memorie, or Hieroglyphically thus, that as the Alphabet is the Radix of all wordes, so the miseries of the Iewes, were the combination of all miseries.*" The poem concludes with Jeremiah's prayer for the distressed people of Jerusalem.

These two works are followed by *Sions Sonets. Sung by Solomon the King* (1625), which is dedicated to James, Marquis of Hamilton, and is a dialogue between the Bride and Bridegroom of "the song of songs." *The Historie of Samson* (1631), dedicated to Sir James Fullerton and structured with paralleled history and meditation in twenty-three sections, essentially completes the biblical paraphrases, most written during the time that Quarles served in Dublin under Archbishop Ussher. It is not on the strength of these works, however, that Quarles is remembered. Indeed, in 1656 Abraham Cowley expressed his dislike of the biblical narratives.

From 1625 to 1641 Quarles wrote many elegies to famous people, for example, *An Alphabet of*

Engraved title page for the first of eighteen seventeenth-century editions of Quarles's best-known book, based on the premise that all God's creatures are
"Hieroglyphicks *and* Emblemes *of His Glory"*

Elegies, upon the much and truly lamented death of that famous for Learning, Piety, and true Friendship, Doctor Ailmer, in which the first letter of each successive line of "The Epitaph" is the respective letter of the alphabet. This elegy was originally published with the 1630 collection called *Divine Poems* (which consisted of the histories of Jonah, Esther, and Job; *Sions Sonets;* and *Sions Elegies*) and was included with the numerous subsequent editions of the collection. He also wrote elegies to Sir Julius Caesar (1636), John Wheeler (1637), Sir Robert Quarles (1639), Sir John Wolstenholme (1640), Anne Wentworth, Countess of Cleveland, and Mrs. Cicily Killegrew (1640), and *Threnodes On the Lady Marsham . . . and William Cheyne* (1641). Elegies to a Doctor Wilson and to Mildred, Lady Luckyn, whose epitaph makes wings, were published with later editions of *Divine Poems.*

To Prince Charles and to his governess, Mary Sackville, Countess of Dorset, Quarles dedicated in

1632 his *Divine Fancies: Digested into Epigrammes, Meditations, and Observations,* a work that became recommended reading for upper forms in school as an aid in writing verse. In his address to his readers, Quarles states:

> I heere present thee with a *Hive of Bees;* laden, some with *Wax,* and some with *Honey:* Feare not to approach; There are no *Waspes;* there are not *Hornets,* here: If some wanton *Bee* should chance to buzze about thine eares, stand thy Ground, and hold thy hands: There's none will sting thee, if thou strike not first: If any doe; she hath Honey in her *Bagge,* will cure thee too: In playner tearmes, I present thee with a Booke of *Fancies* [.]

There are four books in this collection; the first three books have 100 poems each, while the fourth has 117. This very popular work was full of pious wisdom and moral maxims expressed in relatively short but varied epigrammatic stanzas.

The work on which Quarles's reputation rests today is the best-known English example of a genre that began on the Continent in the sixteenth century. *Emblemes* was first published in 1635 and was dedicated to Quarles's friend Edward Benlowes, the author of *Theophila, or Loves Sacrifice: A Divine Poem* (1652). The 1639 and 1643 editions of *Emblemes,* which together totaled five thousand copies, incorporated the *Hieroglyphickes of the life of Man,* first published in 1638. All further editions were composed of both works. At least forty-four editions appeared after the first one, eighteen before 1700, justifying Felix Schelling's calling it "altogether the most popular book of verse published during the century." No other English emblem book of the time attained even a second edition. The first emblem book in England was Geffrey Whitney's *Choice of Emblemes and Other Devices* (1586). Other later English writers interested in the emblem were Henry Peacham (*Minerva Britanna, or A Garden of Heroical Devices,* 1612), George Wither (*A Collection of Emblemes,* 1635), Christopher Harvey (*Schola Cordis,* 1647), John Hall, and John Bunyan.

Emblem literature – which combines a motto, a picture, and a poem to express a moral or ethical theme – was enormously popular in the Renaissance for its use of the new art of engraving along with the traditional art of poetry. The first Renaissance emblem book was *Emblematum liber* (1531), a Latin work by the Venetian lawyer Andrea Alciati. From the late sixteenth until well into the seventeenth century, the genre attracted English poets who made of it less a decorative art and more a serious literature.

In emblem literature a motto appeared above the picture as a label to announce the theme of the work, which might concern a virtue or vice or a classical tag or proverb. The picture was always symbolic rather than naturalistic and might depict anything from a single object or person to something complicated like a detailed landscape. The poem of the emblem was an epigram or sonnet that explained the picture, or applied a moral to it, or both. To Renaissance poets, nature itself was a kind of emblem book, as was history; both were inscribed by the Creator with meanings that human wit could discover. As Quarles explained in the preface to his *Emblemes:*

An *Embleme* is but a silent Parable. Let not the tender Eye check, to see the allusion to our blessed Saviour figured in these Types. In holy Scripture, he is sometimes called a Sower; sometimes, a Fisher; sometimes a Physician: And why not presented so as well to the eye as to the eare? Before the knowledge of letters God was

known by *Hieroglyphicks:* And, indeed, what are the Heavens, the Earth, nay every Creature, but *Hieroglyphicks* and *Emblemes* of His Glory?

Five books comprise Quarles's *Emblemes,* each with fifteen parts, a numerical scheme he took from Herman Hugo, whose *Pia Desideria* (1624) was the source of many of Quarles's illustrations. Each emblem begins with a quote from the Old or New Testament, followed by a relatively long poem. The poem is followed by quotes from the church fathers and a concluding epigram. The extracts from the Fathers are taken from Thomas Hibernicus's *Flores Doctorum* (circa 1497), a florilegium. Book 3 is dominated by quotes from Psalms and Job; book 4 by the Canticles and the Psalms; book 5 by the Psalms again and the Canticles. The traditional view of the relationship of the five books is that the first two books deal with a rivalry between human and divine love against the background of a fallen world; the last three books deal with the vicissitudes of the soul, whose progress is from anguish to joy.

The woodcut illustrations for the first five books are not original with Quarles; all but ten of seventy-nine plates come from other sources. Twenty-two of the thirty-two plates of books 1 and 2 (including frontispiece and invocation) come from *Typus Mundi* (1627), an emblem book published by the College of Rhetoric of the Jesuits at Antwerp; the other ten are new ones. The plates of books 3, 4, and 5 come from the Jesuit Hugo's *Pia Desideria.* At times lines from Hugo's Latin poems are paraphrased. In Quarles's original printing the engravings were carefully reproduced, primarily by William Marshall and William Simpson, with only a few departures. One engraving was done by John Payne.

The plates of *Pia Desideria* contain two doll-like figures of Anima (the human soul) and Amor (Divine Love); one editor called them "execrable," believing they ridiculed rather than revered religious themes. The figures are, in fact, heirs of cupids in secular emblem books. In a few instances Quarles had the emblems modified to suit his purposes – for example, altering the typography of a globe to highlight Roxwell (Quarles's home), Finchingfield (Benlowes's home), and Hilgary (Phineas Fletcher's home). These modifications encourage the belief that these two friends were responsible for Quarles's undertaking *Emblemes* in the first place. Quarles obviously respected the opinion of both and had praised Fletcher's *Purple Island* (1633).

Quarles's use of Continental emblems was unacknowledged by him, but noticed by Edmund Arwaker, who in 1686, making a new translation of *Pia Desideria,* said, "Mr. Quarles only borrowed his Emblems to prefix them to much inferior sense." Quarles's borrowing of lines of poetry, however, was minimal, and his allegorical interpretations and thematic emphases are his own. He was more interested in poetic form than those from whom he borrowed, using a wide variety of stanzaic and metrical patterns and indulging in dialogue and elaborate rhetorical figures to heighten the drama.

According to Rosemary Freeman, Quarles's symbols "represent the individual experience of the human soul in its search for sanctity, and their significance is psychological. Amor and Anima between them embody the subjects of religious contemplation, and the poems accompanying the emblems both explain the symbolism and explore the states of mind they suggest." In *The Visual in Metaphysical Poetry* (1981), Mary Cole Sloan points out that the reader's response enters the psychological drama as well, producing perhaps emblems of conflict. Ernest Gilman sees a tension between word and image; the allegorical picture fascinates but also conceals, in such a way that the picture needs correction by the words. Indeed, as Dale Randall shows, the emblems are interesting precisely because the text is not always accommodated to the image; Quarles "has achieved more than, quite literally, first meets the eye."

Like *Emblemes,* Quarles's *Hieroglyphickes* also has fifteen parts, each part introduced by pictures of light. Dedicated to the countess of Dorset, governess of Prince Charles and James, Duke of York, "The mind of the Frontispiece" reads, "This Bubble's Man: Hope, Fear, false Joy and Trouble, / Are those four Winds which dayly tosse this Bubble." The illustration on the engraved title page depicts wind that seems to blow directly at Quarles's name (see Figure 1), perhaps because it was a time of reduced circumstances for him. In his second address to the reader, Quarles says:

> If you are satisfied with my *Emblemes,* I here set before you a second service. It is an Ægyptian dish, drest on the English fashion: They, at their Feasts, used to present a Death's-head at their second course: This will serve for both. You need not fear a surfet: Here is but little; and that, light of digestion: If it but please your Palate, I question not your stomach: Fall too; and much good may it do you.

In *Hieroglyphickes,* Quarles compares man's life to a candle, which appears in each picture. For ex-

Figure 1: Engraved title page for the 1638 edition of Hieroglyphickes

ample, for the first hieroglyphic, there is an unlit candle (because the light of nature is inferior to divine light); in the second, the gift of light is given by a hand descending from a cloud; but the third presents blasts of nature that beset the light, which is meant to guide the soul through dangers that beset it; the sixth presents the figures of Time and Death arguing over their prey (see Figure 2); the last seven depict the Seven Ages of Man. In each the urn that holds the candle changes, until finally it represents a funeral urn.

Hieroglyphickes differs from *Emblemes* in being more static and less dynamic because the illustrations are less narrative. The scenes do not represent an allegorical tale of a struggle between Anima and Amor but are meant to serve as meditations on the symbolic concept of light. There is also a closer interaction of image and word than there is in *Emblemes,* perhaps because the illustrations were not borrowed before the idea was conceived. While only the last seven hieroglyphics have a firm, unifying concept – the Seven Ages of Man – they were perhaps the idea behind the whole. The formula for the seven candles seems to be the *System Aetates,* the Ptolemaic doctrine of seven planets that reign over the seven parts of man's life. Quarles probably got the concept from the 1633 edition of *The Differences of the Ages of Mans Life,* by Henry Cuffe. Two Flemish series of prints by Gerard de Jode, published at Antwerp, may have served as iconographic models for the planets, the occupations, and the symbolic animals. The Jesuit Hieremias Drexelius from Bavaria may have furnished skeletons, windblown trees, and astrological signs. According to Karl Josef Holtgen, "Quarles's second emblem book is the most important English rendering of the theme of the Ages of Man and an interesting offshoot of the hieroglyphical tradition."

The source of the popularity of Quarles's emblems and hieroglyphics has been variously ascribed. One explanation is the fact that Quarles did have genuine abilities as a poet, in spite of what his detractors claimed, and his subjects and pictures had an appeal of homely familiarity and accessibility to the less educated. In *Studies in Seventeenth-Century Imagery* (1964) Mario Praz wrote, "Quarles' *Emblemes* supplied the wider public with a cheap substitute for that Metaphysical wit which authors like George Chapman and John Donne provided for a more refined audience." Another reason for the popularity was that pictures, of great interest at that time, tended to obscure Quarles's defects as a poet, such as those of structure. Finally, his epigrammatic style and his use of every kind of rhetorical device – mostly to stretch out his thought – were in vogue; but, as Alexander B. Grosart commented about Quarles, "over and over he says and says, not because he has something to say, but in order to say something."

The eighth emblem of book 3 can serve as an example of Quarles's use of the genre. The picture itself has three parts. Its bottom is basically a fountain held up by fish on either side; on each of their backs is a globe with a cross on top. The center of the fountain has a heart that is spewing out liquid. The very top of the picture features urns on their sides, likewise spilling out liquid, but these urns are also eyes, in the midst of what appears to be a weeping willow. The middle of the picture looks like an altar or a monument with a circular frame on it outlined with hearts. Within the circle is Anima, crying in the midst of a disturbed sea. A globe with a cross on top is likewise in the sea.

The motto to accompany this picture is from Jeremiah: "*O that my head were waters, and mine eyes a fountain of tears, that I might weep day and night.*" This is followed by a forty-six-line stanza that is a prayer for tears of remorse to expiate sins. Then passages from Saints Ambrose, Gregory Nazianzen, and Je-

Figure 2: *Illustration for Hieroglyphic 6 (from the 1638 edition of* Hieroglyphickes)

rome appear. Nazianzen's quote is "*Tears are the deluge of sinne, and the world's sacrifice.*" The emblem concludes with the following epigram:

Earth is an Island ported round with fears;
The way to Heav'n is through the Sea of tears.
It is a stormy passage, where is found
The wrack of many a ship, but no man drown'd.

The influence of the emblem on a poem such as Richard Crashaw's "The Weeper" – with its motto (a quotation from Saint Francis de Sales), its picture (of a tearful Magdalene with a bleeding heart), and its epigrammatic stanzas that explore the meaning of Christian tears – is obvious to all readers of Metaphysical poetry. As a form in its own right, however, the emblem ceased to exist after Bunyan.

About the time Quarles became chronologer of London, he took to writing prose, publishing *Enchyridion* in 1640. The 1641 second edition comprises four books or centuries, each with one hundred chapters. Book 1 of the second edition, dedicated to Charles, Prince of Wales, consists of new material. The full title of the work expresses its subject and purpose: "Institutions Divine (Contemplative, Practicall) and Morall (Ethycall, Oeconomicall, Politicall)." In "To the Reader," Quarles declares his purpose is "to present these few *politicall Observations*" to the prince and to "ripen him in the glorious vertues of his renowned Father," looking to when the prince shall succeed the father as Charles II. Book 2 is dedicated to Mrs. Elizabeth Ussher, daughter of Archbishop Ussher. The work is filled with pithy expressions such as the following from century 4:

> Praise no man too liberally before his face, nor Censure him too lavishly behind his backe; the one savours of Flattery; the other, of Malice, and both are reprehensible: The true way to advance another's Vertue, is to follow it; and the best meanes to cry downe another's Vice is to decline it.

Many of Quarles's aphorisms are close borrowings from the 1632 edition of Francis Bacon's *Essayes* and from Edward Dacres's translations of *Machiavels Discourses. Upon the First Decade of T. Livius* (1636) and *Nicolas Machiavel's Prince* (1640). *Enchyridion* was very popular, also coming out in new editions in 1646, 1654, 1658, 1670, 1677, 1680, 1681, 1682, 1692, 1702, one spurious edition in 1695, and two in 1698. Even a Swedish translation appeared in 1696. While Quarles disclaimed that the work commented on the times, half of the aphorisms are concerned with war, and at least a third of them discuss the conduct of a king. All the rest refer in some way to questions of either church or government.

This work was followed in 1642 by another prose piece, *Observations Concerning Princes and States, Upon Peace and Warre,* which includes seventy-five maxims reprinted from century 1 of the 1641 *Enchyridion,* together with twenty-five new maxims drawn from Bacon and Niccolò Machiavelli. Quarles softens some of the sinister ideas of the latter. Again Quarles disavows he is talking about Charles I, but the work appeared in September just as the civil strife had begun. Although he did not believe in war, he sided with the king, writing three pamphlets in defense of his position: *The Loyall Convert* (1644), *The Whipper Whipt* (1644), and *The New Distemper* (1645). All three works were published together posthumously in 1645 as *The Profest Royalist: His Quarrell With The Times* with a dedication to King Charles I. Quarles was a strong defender of the divine right of kings, of established order and uniformity, but he was not blind to Anglican errors or to

Charles's faults. Nevertheless, his public declaration of support for the king was his personal undoing. His property was confiscated and his name proscribed by Parliament. He was treated with contempt by some literary contemporaries. When the monarchy was restored, Quarles's reputation was not; ironically he was referred to as "an old Puritanical poet." Hating extremism and fanaticism, Quarles wrote in *Observations Concerning Princes and States* (1642) that "the true *Protestant* Religion stands like a *vertue* between two *vices, Popery* and *Separatisme*"; and the true religion was the Church of England. He felt the Puritans would destroy beauty, learning, and manners, while the Laudians would force superstition on people. Both groups were united, he believed, in wanting to destroy a moderate and tolerant religion, which the Church of England was to him.

The first pamphlet, *The Loyall Convert,* decries the miserable state to which religious differences had reduced England. Quarles resorts to the Bible for guidance and finds many passages that defend sovereigns, even wicked ones. Quarles believes that kings are the Lord's anointed, and attributes attacks on the divine right of kings to the "abuse of Ceremonies." If iconoclasts meddle with doctrine itself, "Farewell our Religion." These comments offended parliamentary leaders, some of whom Quarles had attacked individually. He condemns as well the transgressions of Royalist forces and believes no one will ultimately win, because factions always exist. Only a king can bring peace and uniformity, he declares. In the preface to this work he denies being a Papist.

The Whipper Whipt was a reply to an anonymous pamphlet called *The Whip,* which attacked *The Fire of the Sanctuary,* by Dr. Cornelius Burges, a Parliamentarian and a moderate. In his introduction Quarles objects to the way that Burges's words have been twisted, so he sets up a debate using a Calumniator, a Replyer, and Burges's own words to try to undo the misrepresentations. The Calumniator is suspicious of all ceremony that seems Roman Catholic and disapproves of what he sees as "worshipping" the king. *The New Distemper* is a final plea for peace. It gives a history of the conflicts in the Anglican church, especially the "disease" of nonconformity. To Quarles the remedy is to "reduce her to her first Constitutions," which means to have everyone submit to an established church without banishing or killing anyone. The doctrine of faith is fine, for the distemper lies in church discipline and government. Quarles defends the Anglican liturgy and episcopacy. He believes the king has made concilia-

Figure 3: Frontispiece to a 1646 edition of The Shepheards Oracles

tory offers and the Parliament should accept them. There were two written responses to these opinions, one very abusive, but Quarles died before they appeared.

After the death of Quarles, his widow was left only with manuscripts, not money. The bookseller Richard Royston asked her to write a biography of her husband to be included with a collection of elegies on him. Adding the biography and a picture of Quarles to *Solomons Recantation* (1645), Royston printed five or six thousand copies with no compensation to the widow. Richard Lowndes had published *Barnabas and Boanerges* (1644), indicating he would publish other manuscripts as well. Dissatisfied with Royston and Lowndes, Ursula presented a court petition against both men on 9 June 1645, which listed, in addition to these two published works, manuscripts of "A Chronicle of the Citty of London," which probably dated from 1640 or later; "The Eglogue" (probably the manuscript for *The Shepheards Oracles,* 1646); "The Psalmes of David Putt and Composed into English Verses"; and other manuscripts (probably including *The Virgin Widow,* which Roysten pub-

lished in 1649), and a poem on Christ, which Thomas Bancroft alluded to in an epigram addressed to Quarles in 1639. On 5 June 1646 Ursula revived an old Chancery suit her husband had begun in 1641 against the booksellers Francis Eglesfield and John Williams, in order to get profits from the *Emblemes.*

The first of the posthumous works that appeared was *Solomons Recantation,* a paraphrase of Ecclesiastes that was probably written along with the earlier paraphrases and, like them, divided into presentations of the biblical narrative plus Quarles's own meditation. It was accompanied by Ursula Quarles's biography, "With a Short Relation of His Life and Death." This work was followed in 1646 by the two-part *Judgement & Mercy for Afflicted Soules.* The first part was dedicated to King Charles I and consists of twenty meditations, each describing a problem such as "The sensuall man's Solace," followed by "His sentence," "His proofs" (quotations from scripture and the church fathers), "Soliloquie," and "His Prayer." Part 2 (an authorized version of *Barnabas and Boarnerges*) comprises twenty meditations that emphasize mercy rather than judgment, but all except the second meditation have the same pattern. An appendix called "A Preface to the Reader," added in 1671, decries the decay of religion, piety, and civil and sacred discipline, expressing the hope that the meditations will be aids to prayer.

The Shepheards Oracles: Delivered in certain Eglogues also appeared in 1646, accompanied by a symbolic engraving. There are eleven eclogues between figures such as Gallio and Britannus, Vigilius and Evangelus, and Anarchus and Canonicus. The eleventh eclogue had been published separately and anonymously at Oxford as *The Shepheards Oracle* (1644). In it Quarles objected to Independents because he thought they were abandoning lawful government. He believed there would be no religious peace without uniformity of belief and practice. Although not blind to the faults of the English clergy, he objected to lay lecturers who tried to please people by preaching liberty, which was bad for authority and uniformity.

Eclogue 11 includes the "Song of Anarchus," a popular ballad frame that attacks Roman Catholics and Separatists. The first seven of eight stanzas in Quarles's ballad were first published as "The Round-heads Race" in the anonymous *Distractions of our Times* (1642). After Anarchus finishes his song and departs, the loyal shepherd assures his friend Philarthus that Parliament understands the ignoble motives of the Separatists. The body of Philarthus's speech is illustrated in the emblematic frontispiece engraved by William Marshall and prefixed to a 1646 edition (see Figure 3). A meek English bishop is piously watering the tree of religion, while a Roman Catholic prelate in cope and miter stands on the other side, scaling off the bark with his knife. Up above, two Separatists sitting in the tree are chopping at the branches of Obedience and Good Works, while a company of their fellows kneels on the ground, attacking the roots with shovels and pickaxes. One violent figure in a tub brandishes a pike on which the books of the Liturgy and the Canons are speared. At left, with sword uplifted, stands King Charles forbidding the impious assault on religion, while a hand from heaven holds forth another sword to confirm him. In "Francis Quarles in the Civil War," Gordon S. Haight suggests that the engraving was probably made prior to the war, while the Root-and-Branch Bill was before the House of Commons.

Hosanna, Or Divine Poems On The Passion of Christ appeared in 1647. This series of twenty-five poems concerns more than the Passion, encompassing biblical events from the Nativity to Pentecost. The modern editor of the work, John Horden, believes it may have been unfinished or unrevised. Unlike other poetry by Quarles, the verse in *Hosanna* shows restraint and plainness of diction accompanied by much stanzaic variety.

The Virgin Widow (1649) was actually written in 1620, but Quarles's only drama, a five-act comedy with only one scene in each act, was the last of his works to be published. Haight believes that the subplot discusses the religious questions of the time under a thin veil of allegory. Dr. Artesio represents the Church of England; the mountebank Quack, formerly Artesio's servant, represents the Roman Catholics. Quack had been licensed to practice in the kingdom by Queen Augusta and her son Bellarmo. In act 4 Quack's man, Quibble, makes a conventional speech about his master's skill, occasionally making fun of Roman Catholics. The opening scene of act 5 indicates the play was intended for performance late in 1640, when the victorious Scots army was still in England, receiving an allowance of about twenty-five thousand pounds a month. In the play, an ailing Lady Albion, after seeing a Scottish doctor who charged her exorbitantly for his advice, has her page call on Dr. Artesio. The page informs Artesio that the lady is in "a brown study," and Dr. Artesio says he must draw blood. Lady Temple, another patient, says she went to Canterbury and had too much *Duck* (the name of the Laudian chancellor of the London diocese). One day a "rude company" broke all her windows. She was so drowsy that her servant says "the common people think she is troubled with a *Liturgie.*"

In spite of the popularity of Quarles's work in the seventeenth century, especially his poetry, through the course of time it has mostly suffered from a negative critical press. By the end of his own century Quarles's name was associated with bad or uncouth verse. While his books may have sold in the earlier seventeenth century, John Oldham said in *Poems and Translations* (1683) that Quarles's books were "damned to wrapping Drugs, and Wares." In *Select Beauties of Ancient English Poetry* (1787), however, Henry Headley wrote that Quarles was mostly censured "from the want of being read." Alexander Pope went on to make Quarles's name a byword for dullness, but of course at a time when Metaphysical poetry was greatly out of fashion. Grosart surmises that Pope introduced Quarles into *The Dunciad* (1728) ("the picture for the page atone / And Quarles is sav'd by Beauties not his own") because his name rhymed with Charles. Dr. Samuel Johnson ignored him altogether, but Horace Walpole said Milton had to wait until the world had stopped admiring Quarles before it turned its attention to him.

There have undoubtedly been appreciative readers of Quarles. Almonte C. Howell has effectively argued that Augustus Toplady, the composer of the hymn "Rock of Ages," was influenced by *Emblemes* in general and emblem 12 of book 3 in particular. In the nineteenth century Quarles was read fondly by Robert Browning, who called *Emblemes* his "childhood's pet book" and referred to it in letters to his wife. The twentieth century has been interested in Quarles's work, not for spiritual reading, but for gauging the degree to which this popular literature of its day influenced the poetry of Donne, Herbert, Crashaw, and others. The result has been instructive readings not only of Quarles's poetry but of other Metaphysicals as well.

Bibliography:

John Horden, *Francis Quarles (1593–1664), a Bibliography of his Works to the Year 1800* (Oxford: Oxford University Press, 1953).

Biography:

Karl Josef Holtgen, *Francis Quarles: 1592–1644: Meditativer Dichter, Emblematiker. Royalist: e. biograph. u. krit. Studie* (Tübingen: Niemeyer, 1978).

References:

B. S. Field, Jr., "Sidney's Influence: The Evidence of the Publication of the History of *Argalus and Parthenia*," *English Language Notes,* 17 (December 1979): 98–102;

Rosemary Freeman, *English Emblem Books* (London: Chatto & Windus, 1948);

Ernest B. Gilman, "Word and Image in Quarles's *Emblemes*," *Critical Inquiry,* 6 (Spring 1980): 385–410;

Gordon S. Haight, "Francis Quarles in the Civil War," *Review of English Studies,* 12 (April 1936): 147–164;

Haight, "The Sources of Quarles's *Emblems*," *Library,* new series 16 (September 1935): 188–209;

Karl Josef Holtgen, "Francis Quarles's Second Emblem Book: *Hieroglyphikes of the Life of Man*," in *Word and Visual Imagination: Studies in the Interaction of English Literature and the Visual Arts,* edited by Höltgen, Peter M. Daly, and Wolfgang Lottes (Erlangen: Universitätsbund Erlangen-Nürnberg, 1988);

Almonte C. Howell, "Augustus Toplady and Quarles' *Emblems*," *Studies in Philology,* 57 (April 1960): 178–185;

Eleanor James, "The Imagery of Francis Quarles' Emblems," *University of Texas Studies in English* (1943): 26–49;

Mario Praz, "The English Emblem Literature," *English Studies,* 16 (1934): 129–140;

Praz, *Studies in Seventeenth-Century Imagery,* 2 volumes (Rome: Edizione di Storia e Letteratura, 1964, 1974);

Dale B. J. Randall, "*Phosphore Redde Diem:* Ancient Starlight in Quarles' *Emblemes*," *John Donne Journal,* 6, no. 1 (1987): 91–103.

Thomas Randolph

(June 1605 – March 1635)

Charles M. Kovich
Rockhurst College

See also the Randolph entry in *DLB 58: Jacobean and Caroline Dramatists.*

BOOKS: *Aristippus, or The Joviall Philosopher. . . . To Which Is Added, The Conceited Pedlar* (London: Printed by T. Harper for J. Marriot, sold by R. Mynne, 1630);

The Jealous Lovers (Cambridge: Printed by T. & J. Buck, printers to the University of Cambridge, 1632);

Cornelianum dolium. Comœdia lepidissima, attributed to Randolph and R. Brathwait (London: Printed by T. Harper for T. Slater & L. Chapman, 1638);

Poems with The Muses Looking-Glasse: and Amyntas (Oxford: Printed by L. Lichfield for F. Bowman, 1638);

A Pleasant Comedie, entituled Hey for Honesty, Down with Knavery (London, 1651);

The Drinking Academy, or The Cheaters' Holiday, edited by Hyder E. Rollins, *PMLA,* 39 (December 1924): 837–871; republished, edited by Rollins and Samuel A. Tannenbaum (Cambridge, Mass: Harvard University Press, 1930);

The Fary Knight; or, Oberon the Second, attributed to Randolph, edited by Fredson Thayer Bowers (Chapel Hill: University of North Carolina Press, 1942).

Editions: *Poetical and Dramatic Works of Thomas Randolph,* 2 volumes, edited by W. Carew Hazlitt (London: Reeves & Turner, 1875) – comprises *Aristippus, The Conceited Pedlar, The Jealous Lovers, The Muses Looking Glass, Amyntas, Hey for Honesty, Poems,* and *Oratio Praevaricatoria;*

The Poems and Amyntas of Thomas Randolph, edited by John Jay Parry (New Haven: Yale University Press, 1917) – includes *Praeludium;*

The Poems of Thomas Randolph, edited by G. Thorn-Drury (London: Etchells & Macdonald, 1929).

PLAY PRODUCTIONS: See *DLB 58.*

During his short but rather productive life, in the first part of the seventeenth century, Thomas Randolph (sometimes called Randall) achieved fame for his poetry and drama as one of the renowned "sons of Ben." Ben Jonson was the great literary leader of this time, the model for the Tribe of Ben, whose "sons" were special followers of the stylistic and innovative leads that he provided. Attaining a wide reputation in his own day for his literary productions in the tradition of Jonson, Randolph was called one of "the most pregnant wits of his age."

Born at Newnham-cum-Badby in Northamptonshire to William Randolph (steward to Edward, Lord Zouch) and his wife Elizabeth, Thomas was baptized on 15 June 1605. Supposedly he demonstrated his literary abilities early; around the age of ten he wrote a poem entitled "History of the Incarnation of our Saviour." He received his education as a king's scholar at Westminster School and, presumably on showing talent in academics, was elected to Trinity College, Cambridge University, in 1623. He graduated with a B.A. in January 1628 (his name was eighth on the list of bachelors). He was elected a Fellow of Trinity in September 1629 and received his M.A. in July 1631. He was also incorporated M.A. at Oxford University.

Wasting no time in deciding on his life's ambition, Randolph determined to find a way into Jonson's company. While yet an undergraduate, he paid a visit to London and to the Devil Tavern (near Temple Bar), where Jonson was known to entertain his Tribe. He peeped into the room where they were, and Jonson, seeing Randolph's shy manner and poor, academic attire, shouted out, "John Bo-peep, come in!" Happily the young man joined the company, who began to comment on his threadbare clothing and challenged him "to call for his quart of sack." Embarrassed by his poverty but demonstrating his poetic gifts, he composed this poem on the spot:

A nineteenth-century engraving of Randolph's birthplace at Newnham-cum-Badby in Northamptonshire

I, John Bo-peep,
To you four sheep,
With each one his good fleece;
If that you are willing,
To give me five shilling,
'Tis fifteen pence apiece.

In reply Jonson is reputed to have said, "I believe this is my son Randolph!" His place in the Tribe of Ben was thus assured by the master himself. This story, although sounding apocryphal, is generally considered to contain elements of truth. It is clear that Randolph admired Jonson's "adoption" of him greatly; his poem, "A gratulatory to Master Ben. Jonson, for his adopting of him to be his son," is evidence of his appreciation:

                  I will boast
No further than my father; that's the most
I can, or should be proud of; and I were
Unworthy his adoption; if that here
I should be dully modest; boast I must,
Being son of his adoption, not his lust.

Randolph's pride in being a genuine son of the Tribe of Ben comes through in every line of this poem. Jonson's plain style, epigrammatic qualities, lyrical songs, and devotion to classical doctrines of imitation were all influences that a university-trained student such as Randolph would appreciate readily.

It is also evident that Randolph was aware of the literary and cultural currents of his age. A poem from the earliest period of his literary career, "On the Passion of Christ," has the sound and sensibility of one whom Randolph followed in going to Westminster and Trinity College, George Herbert:

What rends the temple's veil, where is day gone?
How can a general darkness cloud the sun?
Astrologers their skill in vain do try,
Nature must needs be sick, when God can die.

Some think it unfortunate that this religious strain was not continued in the poet's career, especially after he fell under the influence of Jonson. The purity and simplicity of the lines coupled with deep feeling and biblical allusion point to a promise that Randolph never fulfilled.

Indeed, many believe lack of fulfillment to be the unhappy hallmark of Randolph's poetic career. In *English Literature in the Earlier Seventeenth Century 1600–1660* (1945), Douglas Bush writes of Randolph that "among the courtly and metaphysical poets he remained the precocious undergraduate." A follower, not a leader; a copier, not an originator — these were to be the customary literary lean-

240

The end of Thomas Randolph's "Of that Inestimable Content he enjoys in the Muses" and the beginning of "A gratulatory to Master Ben. Jonson, for his adopting of him to be his son" in the Rolfe Manuscript, a collection in the hands of two scribes, which includes fourteen poems attributed to Randolph (Sotheby's auction catalogue, sale number 2036, 21 July 1988)

On sixe Cambridge Lasses Bathings themselfes
by queenes colledge on the 25th of June
att night and espied by a scholer.

When bashfull daylight now was gone
And night, that Rides a Blush, came on.
Sixe Pretty Nymphes to wash away
The sweatinge of a Summers daye
In Chams fair streames did gently swim
And naked bathd each curious limbe.
O Who had this blest sight but seene
Would thinke they all had Clælia's bene.
A Scholer that a walke did take
Perchance for Meditation sake.
This blessed Object chanc'd to find
Straight all thinges else went out of mind
No studyes better in this life
For Practicke or Contemplatiue:
Who thought Poore soule that hee had seene,
Fair Dian and her Nymphes had bene.
And therefore thought in piteous frare
Actæons fortune was too nere.
Or that the Water-Nymphes they were
Together met to sport um there
And that to him such loue they bore
As to Iolas once before.

What could hee thinke but that his eye
Sixe VENUSSES at once did spie
Rise from the waues, or that perchaunce
Fresh = Water Syrens came to dance
Upon our streames with songes and lookes
To tempt Poore Scholers from their bookes.
Hee cannot thinke they Graces are
Unlesse their number doubled were.
Nor can hee thinke they Muses bee
Because alasse they wanted three.
I should haue rather guess'd that here
Another brood of Helens were
Begot by Ioue upon ye playnes
Hatchd by some Leda of the Swans.

Manuscript for Randolph's poem about "Six Pretty Nymphes" bathing nude in the Cam River by Queen's College, Cambridge. The piece was first published in the second edition of Poems with The Muses Looking-Glasse *(Oxford: Worcester College, MS. 346).*

The maydes [strayd] were in a fright
And blush'd (but twas not seene ith night.)
At last all by ye banke did stand
And hee, good harte lent them his hand.
    to her twas his blisse to feele all ore
Soft Paps, smooth thighes and somethinge more.
But Envious Night masqud from his eyes
The place where loue and pleasure lyes.
Guesse LOuers guesse, o you ye daze
What then might ere this scholers praier
That hee wist but a Cat to spye
Or had but now Tyberius eyes.

    Yet since this hope was all in Vaine
Hee helpes um don their cloths agayne.
Makes Promise they shall none bee shent
So with them to the Tauerne went.
    Where how hee then might sport or play
Pardon mee Muse I must not say
Guesse you that haue a mind to be
Whither hee were a Foole or no.

                                    T. Randolph.

ings of Randolph throughout his short life of a little less than thirty years.

Randolph does, however, sow genuine delight in his poetic subjects; his deep love of nature is one of the areas for which he has been noted. His poem, "A Pastoral Courtship," continues a tradition that went before him and continued afterward:

> Behold these woods, and mark, my sweet,
> How all the boughs together meet?
> The cedar his fair arm displays,
> And mixes branches with the bays!

Strains of Robert Herrick (who had made the acquaintance of Jonson) before him and Andrew Marvell succeeding him can easily be heard in this poem. Marvell, in fact, arrived at Trinity College only a year after Randolph left in 1632 and may have felt his influence. Some, for example, think that Marvell's masterpiece, "To His Coy Mistress," was influenced by Randolph's poem, "A complaint against Cupid, that he never made him in Love:"

> Give me a mistress in whose looks to joy
> And such a mistress (Love) as will be coy,
> Not easily won, though to be won in time;
> That from her niceness I may store my rhyme:
> Then in a thousand sighs to thee I'll pay
> My morning orisons, and every day
> Two thousand groans[.]

Randolph's university training was made quite clear in his attempts to produce poems using the Latin of his education but still employing poetic purity and directness in his own English translation of them:

> *Prima tibi soboles (dilecta Maria),*
> *Elufitque uterum mœsta Diana tuum.*
> *Tunc cœlo, nunc et terris fœcunda fuisti,*
> *Quœ potes et reges et peperisse deos.*
> The first birth, Mary, was unto a tomb,
> And sad Lucina cheated thy blest womb.
> To heaven thou then wert fruitful, now to earth;
> Thou canst give saints as well as kings a birth.
> ("In Natalem Augustissimi Principis Carloli")

Randolph's visits to London became more and more frequent after his 1628 graduation; among his friends and supporters he numbered Owen Felltham, James Shirley, and Sir Kenelm Digby. Until 1632 he spent a great deal of time in Cambridge, riding the crest of his popularity as writer of English and Latin verse and as organizer of dramatic performances of his own plays. His *Aristippus, or the Joviall Philosopher* (1630), for example, is prose interspersed with some verse and is done in the manner of Jonson. It is a satire of the university education that Randolph

knew so well and a high-spirited defense of drinking, which was sure to please the student audience. Other successes on the stage included *Hey for Honesty, Down with Knavery*; *Amyntas, or the Impossible Dowry*; *The Muses Looking-Glass* (performed, 1630; published, 1638); and *The Jealous Lovers* (1632), which was presented before King Charles I and Queen Henrietta Maria in March 1632 at Cambridge by the students of Trinity College. Randolph followed classical models in the tradition of Jonson in this drama while adapting them for the modern English sensibilities of his own age. The poetry interspersed throughout these plays is direct and made to service the plot and characters. For example, in *Hey for Honesty, Down with Knavery,* a character enters "drunk and singing" this piece:

> *I'll kiss the old hag no more,*
> *She has no moisture in her:*
> *If ever I lie with a lass ere I die,*
> *It shall be a youthful sinner.*

Unfortunately, Randolph is reputed to have lived the very dissolute life he presented so well in his plays. In two poems he describes the loss of one of his fingers after a drink fest with others. He was besieged by creditors, infected with smallpox, and afflicted with failing health. His continuing regard for Jonson (and continued love of theater) is evidenced by his delightful poem, "An Answer to Master Ben. Jonson's Ode, to persuade him not to leave the Stage," a call to the master not to be done in by the ignorant age:

> Ben, do not leave the stage,
> 'Cause 'tis a loathsome age;
> For pride and impudence will grow too bold
> When they shall hear it told
> They frighted thee. Stand high, as is thy cause;
> Their hiss is thy applause.

Thomas Randolph's life finally overwhelmed his art in March 1635, when the frailty of his body gave way, due to, in the words of Thomas Bancroft, drinking "too greedily of the Muse's spring." Thus ended Randolph's career in imitation of the classics he knew so well and in reflection of his adopted literary father, whose example sustained him in his compact but prolific life. His popularity has decreased through the years, but his dedication as a true disciple of his master is still admired by many.

Bibliography:
Samuel A. Tannenbaum and Dorothy Rosenweig
    Tannenbaum, *Thomas Randolph,* Elizabethan

Bibliographies, 6 (Port Washington, N.Y.: Kennikat, 1967).

References:

Jonas A. Barish, *Ben Jonson and the Language of Prose Comedy* (Cambridge, Mass.: Havard University Press, 1960), pp. 98–101, 112–113;

Frederick S. Boas, *An Introduction to Stuart Drama* (Oxford: Oxford University Press, 1946), pp. 408–409;

Georges Borias, "Randolph's *Praeludium:* An Edited Transcription Comprising a Short Introductory Note," *Cahiers Elisabethains: Etudes sur la Pre-Renaissance et la Renaissance Anglaises,* 29 (April 1986): 53–76;

Martin Butler, "The Auspices of Thomas Randolph's *Hey for Honesty, Down with Knavery,*" *Notes and Queries,* 35 (December 1988): 491–492;

John Cutts, "Thomas Randolph's *The Muses' Looking-Glass* and *The Battle of the Vices Against the Virtues,*" *Notes and Queries,* 32 (June 1985): 161–162;

Leonard Forster, "An Unnoticed Latin Poem by Thomas Randolph, 1633," *English Studies,* 41, no. 4 (1960): 258;

Alfred Harbage, *Cavalier Drama* (New York: Russell & Russell, 1964), pp. 127–130;

William Hilton Kelliher, "Two Notes on Thomas Randolph," *Philological Quarterly,* 51 (October 1972): 941–945;

Mina Kerr, *Influence of Ben Jonson on English Comedy 1598–1642* (New York: Appleton, 1912);

Gerard Langbaine, *An Account of the English Dramatick Poets* (New York: Burt Franklin, 1967), pp. 411–417;

Felix Emmanuel Schelling, *Elizabethan Drama 1558–1642* (New York: Russell & Russell, 1959);

George Nauman Shuster, *The English Ode from Milton to Keats* (Gloucester, Mass.: Smith, 1964), pp. 46–48;

G. C. Moore Smith, "The Canon of Randolph's Dramatic Works," *Review of English Studies,* 1 (July 1925): 309–323;

Claude J. Summers and Ted-Larry Pebworth, eds., *Classic and Cavalier: Essays on Jonson and the Sons of Ben* (Pittsburgh: University of Pittsburgh Press, 1982);

Phyllis Brooks Toback, "Thomas Randolph's *Hey for Honesty, Down with Knavery*: A Critical Edition," Ph.D. dissertation, New York University, 1971;

George Williamson, "Senecan Style in the Seventeenth Century," *Philological Quarterly,* 15 (October 1936): 321–351.

Papers:

The British Library has manuscripts for Randolph's *Aristippus* (MS Sloane 2531, fols. 124–1406), *The Conceited Pedlar* (MS Add. 27406), and *Praeludium* (MS Add. 37425, fols. 54–55).

Rachel Speght
(1597 – after 1630)

Meg Lota Brown
University of Arizona

BOOKS: *A Movzell for Melastomvs, The Cynicall Bayter of, and foule mouthed Barker against Evahs Sex. Or an Apologeticall Answere to that Irreligious and Illiterate Pamphlet made by Io. Sw. and by him Intituled, The Arraignement of Women* (London: Printed by Nicholas Okes for Thomas Archer, 1617);

Mortalities Memorandvm, with A Dreame Prefixed, imaginarie in manner, reall in matter (London: Printed by E. Griffin for Jacob Bloome, 1621).

Editions: "A Muzzle for Melastomus," in *The Women's Sharp Revenge: Five Women's Pamphlets from the Renaissance,* edited by Simon Shepherd (London: Fourth Estate, 1985), pp. 57–83;

Excerpts from "The Dreame," in *Kissing the Rod: An Anthology of Seventeenth-Century Women's Verse,* edited by Germaine Greer, Susan Hastings, Jeslyn Medoff, and Melinda Sansone (London: Virago, 1988; New York: Farrar, Straus & Giroux, 1989), pp. 69–78.

Rachel Speght, pamphleteer and poet, was an important voice in the gender polemics of the early seventeenth century. She was the first of many authors to respond in print to Joseph Swetnam's *Arraignment of Lewd, idle, froward and unconstant women* (1615). Her 1617 response, *A Mouzell for Melastomus,* is one of the first semireligious texts published by a woman in English. In addition, hers was the only female response that included her real name on the title page; all other pamphlets written by women in the Swetnam controversy were published pseudonymously. Four years later, in 1621, Speght published a long dream vision in verse, *Mortalities Memorandum.* The poem, also published under her own name, was her last publication.

Born in 1597 in London, Rachel was the daughter of James Speght. Her father (son of John Speght of Horbury, Yorkshire) graduated doctor of divinity from Christ's College, Cambridge, and was ordained in May 1591. He became rector of two churches in London, St. Mary Magdalene in Milkstreet, from 1592 to 1637, and St. Clement in Eastcheap, from 1611 to 1637. Two of James's sermons were published during his lifetime: *A briefe demonstration who have, and of their certainty of their salvation that have the spirit of Jesus Christ* (1613) and *The Day-Spring of Comfort* (1615; also published as *The Christian's Comfort,* 1616). Little is known of Rachel Speght's mother. She died before 1621, as Rachel describes her death in "The Dreame," prefixed to *Mortalities Memorandum.* Less than one month after the dream vision was entered in the Stationers' Register, James Speght married Elizabeth Smith. He died in early May 1637. Rachel's father is sometimes incorrectly identified as Thomas Speght, another Yorkshireman, who was a schoolmaster and editor of Geoffrey Chaucer's works (1598 and 1602). Although Thomas was not Rachel's father, he may have been a relative.

Rachel's godmother, to whom she dedicated *Mortalities Memorandum,* was Mary Hill Moundford, wife of Dr. Thomas Moundford. Mary was born in 1562 and died ninety-four years later in 1656. Both she and her husband were members of James Speght's parish. Thomas was a successful London physician who had been bursar of King's College, Cambridge, and who published *Vir Bonus* in 1622. Whether Rachel Speght had a formal education is not known, but that she was educated is certain, for her works demonstrate familiarity not only with the Bible, but also with Latin and a host of classical and contemporary philosophers and poets. She was also well connected socially.

On 2 August 1621, at the age of twenty-four, Rachel Speght married William Procter, a twenty-nine-year-old clerk; the marriage took place at St. Mary Woolchurch in London. Although it was not performed at James Speght's church, the wedding, according to a biographical note in *Kissing the Rod* (1988), did have the father's " 'consent'; this legal term usually implied that the couple had obtained a special license in order to dispense with the three-week reading of the banns." Residents in the parish of St. Bartolph's Aldersgate, the

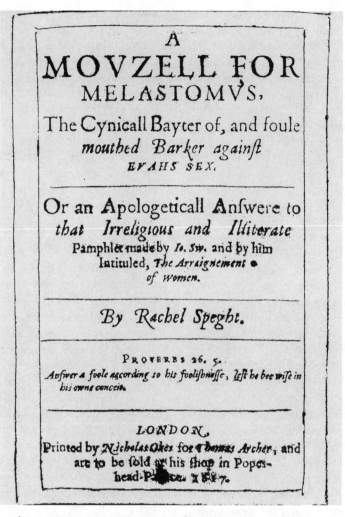

A

MOVZELL FOR

MELASTOMVS,

The Cynicall Bayter of, and foule
mouthed Barker againſt
EVAHS SEX.

Or an Apologeticall Anſwere to
that Irreligious and Illiterate
Pamphlet made by *Io. Sw.* and by him
Intituled, *The Arraignement*
of women.

By *Rachel Speght.*

PROVERBS 26. 5.
*Anſwer a foole according to his foolishneſſe, leſt he bee wiſe in
his owne conceit.*

LONDON,
Printed by *Nicholas Okes* for *Thomas Archer*, and
are to be ſold at his ſhop in Popes-
head-Pallace. 1617.

*Title page for Rachel Speght's response to Joseph Swetnam's attack on "Lewd,
idle, froward and unconstant women"*

couple christened a daughter, Rachel, in February 1626 and a son, William, in December 1630.

A Mouzell for Melastomus was entered in the Stationers' Register on 14 November 1616. Included in the pamphlet is a poem, "In praise of the Author and her Work," which describes Speght as "having not yet seen twenty years" when she wrote her response to Swetnam. Speght herself repeatedly refers to her "tenderness in years" and the "imperfection" of her age. Learned and articulate, *A Mouzell for Melastomus* is more restrained in tone and argument than Swetnam's scurrilous tract. Speght focuses on the dignity of women and of marriage. Although she describes man as "the stronger vessel," she insists that marriage is predicated on mutuality and interdependence. Men and women, she argues, were created "correspondent and meet each for the other." Both

were fashioned in God's image, Eve a "collateral companion" for Adam.

> For man was created of the dust of the earth (*Genesis* ii.7), but woman was made of a part of man after that he was a living soul. Yet was she not produced from Adam's foot, to be his too low inferior; nor from his head to be his superior; but from his side, near his heart, to be his equal: that where he is lord, she may be lady. . . . For as God gave man a lofty countenance that he might look up toward heaven, so did he likewise give unto woman.

Very little contemporary reaction to Speght's pamphlet has survived. *A Mouzell for Melastomus* was never reprinted, unlike Swetnam's tract, which appeared in 1615, 1619, 1628, 1634, 1645, 1690, and several times in the eighteenth century; his work was also published twice in Dutch. One of the pseudonymous respondents to Swetnam, Ester Sowernam, writes disparagingly of Speght in *Ester hath hang'd Haman* (1617). Sowernam identifies Rachel as "a Minister's daughter" and then quips, "I did observe that whereas the maid doth many times excuse her tenderness of years, I found it to be true in the slenderness of her answer." Other evidence of contemporary reaction to Speght's pamphlet is provided in the dedicatory epistle of her own *Mortalities Memorandum*. There she complains not only of the censure she has received for "my mouzeling Melastomus," but also of the public's maddening attribution of that work to her father and not to herself, "depriv[ing] me of my due."

Modern work on Speght has only recently begun. The modern editor of *A Mouzell for Melastomus*, Simon Shepherd, sees Speght as a protofeminist, and Mary Nyquist gives her prominence among biblical exegetes: "In deploying a linguistic stress on balance and mutuality to neutralize hierarchical oppositions, this young, early seventeenth-century Protestant may very well be the most important unsung foremother of modern liberal feminist commentators on Genesis and on *Paradise Lost*."

Speght's second and final publication, *Mortalities Memorandum*, was entered in the Stationers' Register on 18 January 1621. It was never reprinted, and it seems to have attracted little attention. The poem is 1,056 lines of iambic pentameter, 300 lines of which constitute "The Dreame"; the rhyme scheme of the six-line stanzas is *abcbdd*. Although no extensive study has yet been published of either *Mortalities Memorandum* or "The Dreame," the latter has attracted more modern critical attention than the former because of its protofeminist arguments. Speght's allegorical dream vision, a common genre in the *querelle des femmes* (quarrel of the women) from the Middle Ages through the Renaissance, follows the conventions that Ambrosius Theodosius Macrobius popularized in the fourth century: it begins with the *insomnium* (dream) as the disturbed dreamer is transported to the *locus amoenus* (place most pleasant to the eye), a lovely haven from her troubles, where she converses with personified virtues and emotions. As in Christine de Pizan's *Booke of the Cyte of Ladyes* (1521), all of the allegorical virtues are female, and there is a strong emphasis throughout on the importance of education for women.

Indeed, Speght may well have read de Pizan's dream vision, published in English translation by Bryan Anslye. Other sources she could have found in Thomas Speght's edition of Chaucer, which included no less than seven examples of the dream vi-

sion genre: a translation of Guillaume de Lorris and Jean de Meun's *Roman de la Rose;* three Chaucerian works, *The Book of the Duchess, The Legend of Good Women,* and *The House of Fame;* and three works incorrectly attributed to Chaucer, *The Assembly of Ladies, The Flower and the Leaf,*, and "Chaucer's Dreame," or "the Isle of Ladies." Typical of writers in the *querelle,* Speght substantiates her defense of women with lists of virtuous females from the Bible and from antiquity. According to the editors of *Kissing the Rod*, Speght's probable classical sources are "Plutarch's *Vitae* (translated into English by Thomas North in 1579 as *The Lives of the Noble Grecians and Romanes*), his *Moralia* (englished by Philemon Holland in 1603 as *The Philosophie, commonly called the Morals*), and Diogenes Laertius's *Vitae,* published several times in Latin during the sixteenth century, but untranslated until 1688."

"The Dreame" begins with a description of the female narrator, weary with daily cares. As she falls asleep, Thought appears and asks why she is unhappy. The narrator responds that her sadness is caused by her ignorance and that she does not know how to cure herself. Thought pities her and explains that they must enlist the aid of Experience, who in turn requires Knowledge. As the narrator converses with her benefactors, Disswassion intervenes and attempts to demoralize her with arguments about her lack of wit and memory, the difficulties of attaining Erudition, and the weaknesses of her sex and age. The narrator falters, discouraged, but Desire, Truth, and Industrie defend her against Disswassion. Truth presents a lengthy vindication of women, citing many biblical and classical examples of learned, accomplished, and virtuous females, and convinces the narrator to persevere in her search for Knowledge. In Erudition's garden, Truth instructs her charge about the nature of Knowledge: it is God's image in both men and women, enabling them to understand evil and to practice virtue. Indeed, Knowledge is the "mother" of Christian virtues. Even salvation depends on Knowledge (of God and Christ).

Desire kindles the narrator "To couet *Knowledge* daily more and more," but she is suddenly and mysteriously prevented from her education:

Till some occurrence called me away.
. . . .
And quenched hope for gaining any more,
For I my time must other-wayes bestow.
I therefore to that place return'd againe,
From whence I came, and where I must remaine.

While returning from Erudition's garden, the narrator sees a rabid beast (Joseph Swetnam) who fulminates against women. She attempts to muzzle the beast, but, according to a "selfe-conceited Creature" (Ester Sowernam), her skill in *A Mouzell for Melastomus* is not as strong as her emotion. After an allegorical account of the Swetnam controversy, the narrator encounters Death and wakes up weeping because her mother has died in the dream. Reality proves as dire as the dream: her mother is indeed dead. Doubly distraught by the loss because she is unprepared for it, the narrator ends the piece by resolving to write *Mortalities Memorandum,* a warning to others to prepare themselves for inevitable death.

Mortalities Memorandum is suffused with biblical references and conventional subjects of the *contemptus mundi* – the misery of the human condition, the evanescence of mortal pleasures, death as liberation into eternal life, the torments of hell, and the joys of heaven. Speght's arguments are tightly organized and often advanced in numbered catalogues. She enumerates, for example, three kinds of death, three advantages of death, three reasons to meditate on death, and seven advantages to preparing for death. The poem is liberally sprinkled with aphorisms and sometimes indulges in wordplay: "*Vile, Liue,* and *Euil,* have the selfe same letters, / He *liues* but *vile* whom *euil* holds in fetters." Despite the putative occasion of its composition, the poem does not convey the immediacy or personal intensity of its author's grief for her mother's death.

Beginning with an analysis of the advantages of death, Speght constructs some uncomfortable contradictions. "Tis true," she writes, "that life's the blessing of the Lord," and yet a governing assertion of the poem is that life is a vale of tears from which the pious death is a liberation:

> who is he, that will not wish to dye?
> And he whom God by *Death* doth soonest call,
> Is in my minde the happiest wight of all.
> . . . .
> When *Simeon* had embraced in his armes,
> His Lord, whom he had waited long to see,
> He of his Sauiour instantly desir'd
> A *nunc dimittis,* that he might be free
> From bitter bondage of unpleasant life,
> Where flesh and spirit alwayes are at strife.

Two hundred lines after her account of Simeon's exemplary plea for death, Speght draws back somewhat from her initial position. Of "the godly" she remarks, "though to *die* they dare not supplicate, / Yet for their dissolution they doe waite."

After arguing the advantages of death, Speght describes the loathsomeness of the body and the degradation and misery that constitute life. Our bodies are our prisons, repulsive and offensive constraints to the soul:

> What worse Bocardo for the soule of man,
> Then is the bodie, which with filth is fraught;
> Witnesse the sinkes therof, through which doe passe
> The excrements, appoynted for the draught.
> Euacuations, loathsome in their smell,
> Egested filth, vnfit for tongue to tell.

All pleasures of this world, the poem observes, are vain and evanescent. The senses are a source of suffering. All earthly good is vulnerable and potentially painful; all accomplishments, relationships, and pleasures cause distress. Following her anatomy of misery, Speght dwells on the ineffable joys of heaven. She then describes the horrors of death for the wicked, and she ends the poem with a long exhortation (over 300 of the 756 lines of the poem) to meditate on death daily.

Although Rachel Speght's works have received little attention since their publication, they are currently benefiting from the critical recovery of texts that has accompanied concerns with expanding the literary canon. *A Mouzell for Melastomus,* for example, has begun to serve importantly in discussions of the *querelle des femmes* and of gender relations in the Renaissance. Speght's works are beginning to be seen as cultural and literary "artifacts" and, as such, well worth attention and interest.

References:

Mary Nyquist, "The genesis of gendered subjectivity in the divorce tracts and in *Paradise Lost,*" in *Re-Membering Milton: Essays on the Texts and Traditions,* edited by Nyquist and Margaret W. Ferguson (New York: Methuen, 1988), pp. 99–127;

Betty Travitsky, *The Paradise of Women: Writings by Englishwomen of the Renaissance* (New York: Columbia University Press, 1989).

William Strode

(1603 – 10 March 1645)

Edmund Miller
C. W. Post Campus, Long Island University

BOOKS: *The Kings Majesties Speech, as It Was Delivered the Second of November Before the Vniversity and City of Oxford: Together with a Gratulatory Replication Expressed by That Learned Man Doctor W. Strode, Orator for the famous Vniversity of Oxford* (London, 1642);

Speech Made to Queen Mary at Oxon at Her Return Out of Holland (Oxford, 1643);

A Sermon Concerning Death and the Resurrection, Preached in St. Maries at Oxford, On Low Sunday, April the 28. 1644 (Oxford: Printed by Leonard Lichfield, 1644);

A Sermon Concerning Swearing, on Matth. 3, 37 (Oxford: Printed by Leonard Lichfield, 1644);

The Floating Island: A Tragi-Comedy (London: Printed by T. C. for H. Twiford, N. Brooke & J. Place, 1655);

A Sermon Preached at a Visitation Held at Lin in Norfolk, June the 24th Anno 1633. Being an Admonition to the Clergy to Remember and Keep Those Severall Oaths, Promises, and Subscriptions, Which They Solemnly Have Made at the Taking of Their Degrees (Oxford: Printed by W. Wilson for Samuel Brown, 1660).

Editions: "The Kings Majesties Speech," in John Somers, *Collection of Scarce and Valuable Tracts,* volume 4, edited by Walter Scott (London: Printed for T. Cadell, W. Davies & others, 1810);

Poetical Works of William Strode (1600–1645) Now First Collected from Manuscript and Printed Sources: To Which is Added The Floating Island: A Tragi-Comedy: Now First Reprinted from the Original Edition of 1655, edited by Bertram Dobell (London: Printed by the editor, 1908);

Four Poems by William Strode (Flansham, Bognor Regis, Sussex: Peartree, 1934);

A Collection of Poems by Several Hands; viz.: Duke of Newcastle, W. Strode, R. Whitehall, J. Dryden, T. Shadwell, Earl of Rochester, Sir T. Thornbill, S. Wesley, Jun., Walbeck Miscellany no. 2, edited by Francis Needham (Bungay, Suffolk: Printed by R. Clay, 1934) – includes "A Commendation of a Good Voyce" and "A Wassail" by Strode.

OTHER: *Academiæ Oxoniensis Funebria Sacra. Æternæ memoriæ reginæ Annæ dicata,* includes Latin verse by Strode (Oxford: Printed by J. Lichfield & J. Short, 1619);

Ultima Linea Savilii, includes Latin verse by Strode (Oxford: Printed by J. Lichfield & J. Short, 1622);

Carolus Redux, includes Latin verse by Strode (Oxford: Printed by J. Lichfield & J. Short, 1623);

Funerall Elegies, upon the most untimely death of Sir John Stanhope, includes Latin verse by Strode (London: Printed by G. Purslowe for R. Mab, 1624);

Camdeni Insignia, includes Latin verse by Strode (Oxford: Printed by J. Lichfield & J. Short, 1624);

Oxoniensis Academiae Parentalia. Sacratissimæ Memoriæ Jacobi, Regis, Dicata, includes Latin verse by Strode (Oxford: Printed by J. Lichfield & G. Turner, 1625);

Epithalamia Oxoniensia. In . . . Caroli, Regis, &c. cum Henretta Maria, Connubium, includes Latin verse by Strode (Oxford: Printed by J. Lichfield & G. Turner, 1625);

Britanniæ Natalis, includes "Valent Sotherton of Christ Church" by Strode and translations by Strode of poems attributed to Richard Corbett and Leonard Hutton (Oxford: Printed by J. Lichfield, 1630);

Ad Magnificum . . . virum Dominum J. Cirenbergium, Proconsulem Civitatis Gedanensis . . . Carmen Honorarium ad Cirenbergium, edited by J. Rous, includes Latin verse by Strode (Oxford: Printed by J. Lichfield, 1631);

Amores Troili et Cressidæ liber primus (secundus) Latinè versus, Geoffrey Chaucer's *Troilus and Criseyde* translated into Latin by Sir Francis Kynaston, includes Latin verse by Strode (Oxford: Printed by J. Lichfield, 1635);

Parentalia: Spectatissimo Rolando Cottono Equiti Aurato Salopiensi: Memoriæ & Pietatis Ergo, edited by E. Heigham, includes Latin verse by Strode (London: Printed by Augustine Mathewes, 1635);

Musarum Oxoniensium Charisteria, includes Latin verse by Strode (Oxford: Printed by L. Lichfield, 1638);

Horti Carolini Rosa Altera, includes Latin verse by Strode (Oxford: Printed by L. Lichfield, 1640);

Eucharistica Oxoniensia, includes Latin verse by Strode (Oxford, 1641);

Musarum Oxoniensium Επιβατηρια, includes Latin verse by Strode (Oxford: Printed by Leonard Lichfield, 1643);

Richardi Gardiner ex Æde Christi Oxon. Specimen Oratorium, includes Latin verse by Strode (London: Printed by Humphrey Moseley, 1653).

Although widely appreciated for his lyric touch in his own day and frequently included in anthologies and commonplace books, William Strode has never been a major poetic light. If Strode's place as a lyric poet is a lesser one, his poetic corpus is never inferior and always melodious, and of all the Cavalier poets he has perhaps the most original imagery. In addition, Strode's play *The Floating Island* (1655) has an important place in theatrical history and a minor one in political history.

The only son of Philip Strode and Wilmot Hanton Strode, William Strode was born near Plympton, Devonshire, and baptized 11 January 1603. He attended Winchester School and entered Christ Church College, Oxford University, on 1 June 1621. His interest in both drama and poetry was evident early in his university career. He played the role of Tarentilla in the student performance at Christ Church of Robert Burton's *Philophaster* on 16 February 1618. In 1619 he contributed an elegy to a collection of Latin verses, and he was to do so again on many other occasions throughout his career. Having received the B.A. on 6 December 1621 and the M.A. on 17 June 1624, he was in 1629 appointed proctor, a position of even more than the usual trust in light of a scandal touching that office in 1628. Later in 1629 he was also appointed public orator of the university.

His contributions to the 1630 collection *Britanniæ Natalis* throw some light on the decline of Latin as a medium of academic discourse. While Strode contributed a poem in his own name to the volume, he also seems to have been asked to produce the Latin versions of poems on the birth of Prince Charles ascribed in the volume to Richard Corbett and Leonard Hutton. Both were learned men, doctors at the university, and authors of Latin works, and yet the Latin versions of their occasional verses had to be provided by a ghostwriter. Indeed, it appears that even the English version of Hutton's poem was not his own but was by Corbett. Sometime during this period Strode married the daughter of Dr. Simpson, prebendary of Canterbury.

While continuing his academic career, Strode began a parallel career as a divine. He was awarded the degree of B.D. on 10 December 1631. After taking holy orders, he became chaplain to Corbett, who was bishop of Oxford. In addition Strode became the (presumably nonresident) rector of East Bradenham, Norfolk. He acquired something of a reputation as an eloquent but baroque preacher. As orator, he greeted King Charles I and Queen Henrietta Maria with a Latin oration during the royal visit of 1636.

For the same occasion his moralizing English play *The Floating Island* was produced on 29 August with the songs set to music by Henry Lawes. The courtiers thought it rather dull compared to two other plays performed during the visit, but the king liked it, and Strode's subsequent preferments can perhaps be attributed to the politic impression he made in his dual capacity as orator and playwright on the occasion of this royal visit.

It is not surprising that the king liked the content of Strode's play, since it is both a satire against Puritans and a plea for monarchical legitimacy. As in Ben Jonson's *Bartholomew Fayre* (1631), the anti-Puritan satire takes the specific form of counterattacking Puritan objections to the theater. William Prynne's antitheatrical diatribe *Histrio-mastix* had been published in 1633. A parenthetical reference in the index of that book to actresses as whores had been interpreted to the disadvantage of the queen, who was fond of appearing in masques, and after a sensational trial Prynne lost both his ears and his Oxford degrees. With not only the queen but also Archbishop Laud, Prynne's chief nemesis, in attendance, Strode produced, among other things, a *drame à clef* with a major character, Malevolo, an obvious portrait of Prynne. Malevolo is described as a person whose "pen / Hath scourged the stage." Of himself the character says, "Locks which I have scorn'd / Must hide my Eare stumps." In light of subsequent events, the play was perhaps both daring and prescient since in it the central character, a king named Prudentius and specifically said by the prologue to have been modeled after Charles, is toppled in a coup and then restored through no active

Manuscripts for poems by William Strode with annotations in the hand of William Fulman, who owned a collection of Strode's manuscripts during the late seventeenth century (Corpus Christi College, Oxford, MS. 325)

An Opposite to Melancholy.

Returne my ioyes & hither bring
A tony not made to speake but sing
A merry spleene, an inward feast,
A causelesse laugh, without a ieast.
A face which Conscience doth anoint
An Arme out of his ioynt
A sprightfull gate that leaues noe print
And makes a feather of a flint.
A heart thats lighter then the aire
An Eie still dancing in its sphere
Strong mirth which nothing shall controule
A Body quick as any of Soule;
Free wandring thoughts not tied to muse
Which on all things chuse,
Which come and so are gon.
These Life itselfe doth liue vpon.
Howto Care but to be iolly
to be more wretched than wee must, is folly.

For Business well don, for strife will
For debts dischargd, & life amended;
then act & thoughts

Returne
ut supr.

effort of his own when everyone has seen the folly of the misrule of Melancolico. Also, at the end the king banishes the conspirators to "th'suburbs, or new-England." In theatrical history the performance of Strode's play is also memorable as the occasion of the invention of several stage devices, including a mechanism for moving scenery without the visible aid of stagehands.

In 1638 Strode was awarded the degree of D.D. (6 July) and became a canon of Christ Church and vicar of Blackbourton, Oxfordshire. The following year he was made vicar of Badby, Northamptonshire, where he served until 1642.

Throughout his life Strode composed occasional poetry in both English and Latin. Because the bulk of his poetry in both languages consists of elegies, it has suffered oblivion together with most of the elegiac poetry of the seventeenth century. Strode's two English elegies "On Mistress Mary Prideaux" perhaps deserve a better fate. In "Strode's Longer Elegy," Harry Morris has noted the daring imagery Strode uses in saying that the dead child's deforming illness would have made her "not sure so loath to goe" and in addressing her as "more like a mother than a childe."

Given modern sensibilities, the English lyrics are now clearly his most important productions. They reward reading on many levels, they maintain a high level of musicality, and they give a special slant to the Petrarchan imagery that was the common heritage of the Cavalier poets. In "The Poetry of William Strode," Morris describes the particular virtue of Strode's lyrics as his litotic imagery. Such images produce surprising domesticity or modesty by attaching shrinking or lessening characterizations to the things described, for example "creeping wind" from "The Commendation of Music." A more attenuate illustration of the sort of litotes that Morris sees at the root of Strode's best and most characteristic imagery is the description of "The pleated wrinkles of the face / Of wave-swolne earth." The pleats domesticate the wrinkles of the face, and the pleats and wrinkles together reduce and domesticate the topographical image. The domesticity of much of Strode's imagery allies him to some extent to George Herbert. Strode's, however, is very much a unique voice. No other seventeenth-century English poet, except perhaps Prynne, had such a personally distinctive approach to imagery.

"On a Gentlewoman Walking in the Snowe," often known by its first line as "I Saw Faire Chloris Walke Alone," was printed twenty-three times during the seventeenth century and appeared in at least eighteen manuscript commonplace books. It was frequently reprinted throughout the eighteenth century as well, although never attributed to Strode. It is clearly and with justification Strode's most famous poem. The basic conceit of the poem is that a flake of snow, having fallen on the lady and been "overcome with the whiteness there," thawed into a tear and then (to quote the superior variant from Bertram Dobell's notes) "trickling down her garments hemme / To deck her freezd into a gemme." The litotic quality is clear in the general direction of the conceit but is also reinforced nicely by specific images such as the description of snow as "feather'd rayne" and the picture of it flying to the lady's "breast / Like little birds into their nest."

Many of Strode's surviving English poems are humorous in intent. While less musical than his other English poems, these have an advantage for modern readers not shared by much other seventeenth-century humorous writing of forbearing obscurity. Typical except in its extreme brevity is the two-line poem "On a Butcher Marrying a Tanner's Daughter": "A Fitter match hath never bin — / The flesh is married to the skinne."

Strode also has a few divine poems — surprisingly few considering his profession. Perhaps he felt that his characteristic litotic imagery was out of place with this subject matter. He can sometimes use such imagery with telling effect, as in "On the Life of Man" when he writes "Our graves that hide us from the burning sunne / Are but drawne curtaynes when the play is done." More often in these divine poems the litotes seem not so much to domesticate the mysteries of faith — as Herbert does so well — but to diminish them, for example when in "On a Register for the Bible" he praises such an index because "the Welchman well may bring / Himself to Heaven in a string" of pious index entries.

Having retired from his position as vicar of Badby, toward the end of his life Strode published a few sermons. He died at Christ Church College on 10 March 1645 and is buried in the divinity chapel there.

After his death his reputation suffered from the neglect shown by his literary executors in failing to produce a collected edition of his work. In the early twentieth century Dobell accomplished the difficult task of gathering together scattered individual poems in a modern edition of the English works. While this can no longer be regarded as complete, and while it also falls somewhat short of modern standards of scholarly editing, it did allow the literary establishment the first real opportunity to assess a body of Strode's work. Although Dobell tried enthusiastically to find Strode a place in the literary canon beside his other discovery, Thomas Traherne, Strode is not a major poet either in the quality or in the quantity of his work. On the other hand, the inadequacy of Dobell's edition has perhaps made Strode seem less striking than he is. In addition to excluding the Latin works on principle, this edition lacks nearly fifty English poems attested to by manuscript in Strode's own hand. The biggest drawback, however, is conservative editorial practices which led Dobell to choose just the most conventional of alternative readings. Nevertheless, even in Dobell's versions Strode's poems are always musical and are clearly as deserving of attention as those of Edmund Waller, Thomas Randolph, Francis Quarles, and others routinely anthologized.

Letters:

The Works of the Most Reverend Father in God, William Laud, D.D., Sometime Lord Archbishop of Canterbury, 7 volumes, edited by William Scott and James Bliss (Oxford: J. H. Parker, 1847–1860) – includes one letter identified as from Strode and others dating from the period of Strode's oratorship identified only as coming from the University of Oxford.

Bibliography:

John Ingle Dredge, *A Few Sheaves of Devon Bibliography,* 5 parts (Plymouth: Brendon, 1889–1896).

References:

Gerald Eades Bentley, "William Strode," in *Jacobean and Caroline Stage,* volume 5 (Oxford: Clarendon Press, 1956), pp. 1187–1195;

Willa McClung Evans, *Henry Lawes, Musician and Friend of Poets* (New York: Modern Language Association of America / London: Oxford University Press, 1941), pp. 122–127, 134, 146;

Ernest Godfrey Hoffsten, *The Floating Island by William Strode: Together with an Account of the Life of the Author and a Review of the University Drama in England, Chiefly after the Year 1600* (Saint Louis: Gottschalk, 1908);

C. F. Main, "Notes on Some Poems Attributed to William Strode," *Philological Quarterly,* 34 (October 1955): 444–448;

Harry Morris, "The Poetry of William Strode," *Tulane Studies in English,* 7 (1957): 17–28;

Morris, "Strode's Longer Elegy," *Renaissance News,* 12 (Summer 1959): 170–171;

C. L. Powell, "New Material on Thomas Carew," *Modern Language Review,* 11 (July 1916): 285–297;

H. K. Russell, "Tudor and Stuart Dramatizations of the Doctrine of Natural and Moral Philosophy," *Studies in Philology,* 31 (January 1934): 1–27.

Papers:

Corpus Christi Library MS. C.C.C. 325, a collection of Strode's poetry in his own hand, is described by Margaret C. Crum in volume 4 of the *Bodleian Library Record* (1953): 324–335. It includes forty-nine English poems not in Bertram Dobell's edition and twenty-three Latin poems not previously published. About half of the Latin poems and a third of the English are elegies. Three poems are translations into Latin by Strode of poems by Richard Corbett, and one poem is a translation into Latin by Strode of a poem by Leonard Hutton. The British Library also has Strode manuscripts, some of these filed under "Stroud." The Bodleian Library and the Harleain Library have additional materials, and the Folger Library has one of the two manuscripts used by Dobell (MS. 646.4).

Sir John Suckling

(1609 – 1641?)

John T. Shawcross
University of Kentucky

See also the Suckling entry in *DLB 58: Jacobean and Caroline Dramatists.*

BOOKS: *Aglaura* (London: Printed by John Haviland for Thomas Walkley, 1638);

A Coppy of a Letter Found in the Privy Lodgeings at Whitehall (London: Printed by John Dawson, 1641); republished as "To Mr. Henry German, in the beginning of Parliament, 1640," in *Fragmenta Avrea* (1646);

The Coppy of a Letter Written to the Lower Hovse of Parliament Touching Divers Grievances and Inconveniences of the State &c. London (London: Printed by John Dawson for Thomas Walkley, 1641);

Fragmenta Avrea. A Collection of all the Incomparable Peeces (London: Printed by Ruth Raworth for Humphrey Moseley, 1646; second edition, revised, London: Printed for Humphrey Moseley, 1648) – comprises *Poems, Letters, An Account of Religion by Reason, Aglaura, The Goblins,* and *Brennoralt;*

The Last Remains of Sr John Suckling. Being a Full Collection of his Poems and Letters (London: Printed by Thomas Newcombe for Humphrey Moseley, 1659); republished with *Fragmenta Avrea* (London: Printed for Humphrey Moseley, 1672?); republished as *The Works of Sir John Suckling* (London: Printed for Henry Herringman, 1676; revised edition, London: Printed for Henry Herringman and sold by Richard Bentley, Jacob Tonson, Thomas Bennet, and Francis Saunders, 1696).

Editions: *The Works of Sir John Suckling: The Non-Dramatic Works,* edited by Thomas Clayton (Oxford: Clarendon Press, 1971);

The Works of Sir John Suckling, the Plays, edited by L. A. Beaurline (Oxford: Oxford University Press, 1971).

PLAY PRODUCTIONS: See *DLB 58.*

A popular label for many poets in seventeenth-century Britain has been "Cavalier," and the person who usually comes first to mind is Sir John Suckling. The classification implies an allegiance to Charles I in his political and military battles against various Parliamentarian or religious groups during the later 1620s through his execution on 30 January 1649. Included thus are the poets Thomas Carew, Richard Lovelace, Suckling, and Edmund Waller. "Cavalier" also implies that these poets were of a gentlemanly social class, that they bore arms and indeed rode horses in battle when the civil wars raged from 1641 to 1648 (*cavalier* derives from the French word for horse, *cheval*), and that they were carefree gallants. Suckling, at least, was of the aristocratic class and often a part of the courtly world of the précieuse life ushered in by Charles's queen, Henrietta Maria, and her French retinue; he was a soldier and was involved in political intrigue; and he was notorious as a gambler and for his conquests of women. A poem like "A Soldier" reflects these matters and at the same time employs the punning wit associated with the poetic group:

> I am a man of war and might,
> And know thus much, that I can fight,
> Whether I am i'th' wrong or right,
>   devoutly.
>
> No woman under heaven I fear,
> New Oaths I can exactly swear,
> And forty Healths my brain will bear
>   most stoutly.
>
> I cannot speak, but I can doe
> As much as any of our crew;
> And if you doubt it, some of you
>   may prove me.
>
> I dare be bold thus much to say,
> If that my bullets do but play,
> You would be hurt so night and day,
>   Yet love me.

Sir John Suckling (portrait attributed to Sir Anthony Van Dyck; Frick Collection, New York)

Perhaps it should be pointed out that the "New Oaths" in this context are the protestations of true love in order to seduce the woman sexually, that the "forty Healths" are not only toasts of ale ("stout") but imply a lifetime ("forty") of such activity as well as bodily trials ("Healths") when combined with "bear," that "doe" means to have sexual intercourse and "bullets" also means ejaculation. The age-old motif of Venus and Mars, love and war, was a staple of the Cavalier poets.

In former critical views, "Cavalier" also denoted influence from Ben Jonson, not so much as a Son of Ben (like Thomas Randolph) or sealed of the Tribe of Ben (like Robert Herrick), but one not in the mold of John Donne, not a Metaphysical, and not devotional. Yet among the early poems (seldom reprinted and little known) are such epigrams as "Upon Christ his birth," "Upon Stephen stoned," "Upon the Epiphanie Or Starr that appear'd to the wisemen," and others. "Out upon it," with its employment of Donne and Donne's manner, gives the lie to another part of the critical cliché. Suckling's editor Thomas Clayton compares that poem with lines from Donne's "Farewell to Love," and one should note "The Undertaking" (which has the same metric form) and "Womans constancy" (where "Now thou hast lov'd me one whole day" becomes "I have lov'd / Three whole days together") and their mutual themes. Or another example is the third of Suckling's grouped sonnets beginning "Oh for some honest Lovers ghost," which borrows from Donne's line in "Loves Deitie," "I long to talke with some old lovers ghost."

The Jonsonian elements that appear in Suckling's poems are plain style, a frequent use of iambic pentameter or tetrameter, classical influences (though not Jonson's exacting classical rhythms), and occasion as impetus. An encomium such as "To his much honoured, the Lord Lepington, upon his Translation of Malvezzi His Romulus and Tarquin" (that is, Henry Carey) exemplifies those elements:

'Tis he that doth the Roman dame restore,
Makes *Lucrece* chaster for her being whore;
Gives her a kind Revenge for *Tarquins* sinne,
For ravish't first, she ravisheth againe.

(The immediately preceding line, "But like to Worlds in little Maps contriv'd," seems to owe, however, something to Donne's "Let Maps to others, worlds on worlds have showne" from "The good-morrow.") A different kind of case in point is the well-known lyric "Song: Why so pale and wan fond Lover?" from the play *Aglaura* (1638), spoken by the "antiplatonique" Orsames to the Ladies in answer to Orithie's "This modestie becomes you as ill, my Lord, as wooing would us women; pray, put's not to't." The satiric tone in its plain style is not far from the lyrics of Jonson's "A Celebration of Charis" or his "Another In Defence of Their Inconstancie," though the speaker's gender is different.

The namesake of his father and the elder son and second of six children, Suckling was a member of a prominent Norwich family whose last name, changed from Esthawe by his great grandfather, equates "Socling," a person holding an estate through tenant farming. Sir John Suckling, the father, held positions under various notable governmental officials, was a member of Parliament at different times from 1601 through 1626, was knighted by James I in January 1616, and served as a member of the Privy Council in 1622. He died on 27 March 1627. The poet's mother was Martha Cranfield, daughter of a prosperous merchant in London; she died on 28 October 1613. Born in Twickenham, Middlesex, Suckling was baptized on 10 February 1609. He seems to have been privately tutored and matriculated as a fellow-commoner from Trinity College, Cambridge, in Easter term, 1623. A short period at Gray's Inn in 1627 ended apparently because of his father's death and his inheriting almost all his father's extensive holdings. Later that year, the Thirty Years' War then being waged, he may

have been a member of the expedition of George Villiers, first Duke of Buckingham, to the Ile de Ré, and in 1629 he went to the Low Countries as a member of the regiment of Sir Edward Cecil, Lord Wimbledon. Suckling attended the University of Leyden briefly but had returned before 19 September 1630 when he was knighted at Theobald's Inn. From October 1631 through the spring of 1632 he was in Germany, being a member of the entourage of Sir Henry Vane, ambassador to Gustavus Adolphus, Sweden then controlling the Germanies.

Prior to this time he was linked romantically with various women, primarily his cousin Mary Cranfield. By the end of 1632 and for many years after, Suckling led a rather dissolute life with much gambling at bowling and cards, so much so that his inheritances were being sold off to cover debts. He engaged in a courtship of Anne Willoughby for possible monetary gain, and, in John Aubrey's words, "he was the greatest gallant of his time, and the greatest gamester." The Willoughby affair became complicated, with other suitors involved, opposition from her father, legal injunctions, duels, and a brief imprisonment in November 1634. The identity of the woman whose pseudonym titles his first play, *Aglaura,* has frequently been speculated on; many candidates have been offered, among them Mary Cranfield; her sister Frances Cranfield Sackville, Lady Buckhurst and Countess of Dorset (who invalidly was rumored to have born her son, the earl of Dorset, by Suckling); and Mary Bulkeley of Baron Hill, Beaumaris, Anglesey, who today is generally accepted as Aglaura. The play was written in 1637; produced in February 1638 by the King's Company at Blackfriars; given at court on 3 April with new prologues, fifth act, and epilogue; and published in 1638 with both versions included. The revision turns a tragedy into a tragicomedy.

Suckling wrote *An Account of Religion by Reason,* a Socinian tract, which he dedicated to Edward Sackville, fourth Earl of Dorset, in late 1637 (published in 1646 with *Fragmenta Aurea*) and may have revised the works of others around this time. On 20 November 1638 he became a Gentleman of the Privy Chamber Extraordinary, and with the outbreak of hostilities between the Scots Covenanters and Charles's forces in the North Country in January 1639 (the First Bishops' War), he became active in the army, allegedly outfitting his men lavishly, for which he was lampooned. A further threat from the Scots in 1640 saw Suckling commissioned as captain of a troop of carabineers. Soon after this Suckling lost in his first bid to become a member of Parliament and then on 30 April was elected mem-

Vpon Christmas

Haile welcome time, whose long expected date
The pining hearts of men doth liberate
Who from their toile cessations now require,
And live in warme Elysiums by the fire
Vpon whose sunny banks they take delight
To see the winged, and fowre-footed fight,
And charge each other in the flameing field's
With spitts for speares, & dripping-pans for shield's
Some little friends doe turne about, & play
Till seorcht with heat become to men a prey
And Schollers too prison-schoole set free
Proclaime aloud a goale deliverie,
Invoke the Gods of sports, nor feare y maine
By Plough-day writs to bee attacht againe
Will did our fathers when by Christ set free
Elect us thus to their fraternitie:
But shall those impious mouth's by new-fond lights
Inspir'd revile, & loath these sacred rites,
Whose festivalls w prayer, & almes allay'd
A time of Charitie, and gladnesse made
Shall they w poison-breathing slaunder staine
This time, and it abolish as profane?
Noe Noe: let's keepe it still whilst them wee see
With Christmas pull downe Christ Nativitie

Manuscripts, probably in the hand of a scribe, for two of Suckling's early poems, from the personal papers of Lionel Cranfield, first Earl of Middlesex, Suckling's uncle (Cranfield Papers, U. 269, F. 36, No. 37, f. 2ʳ and No. 38, f. 2ʳ; Collection of Lord Sackville of Knole)

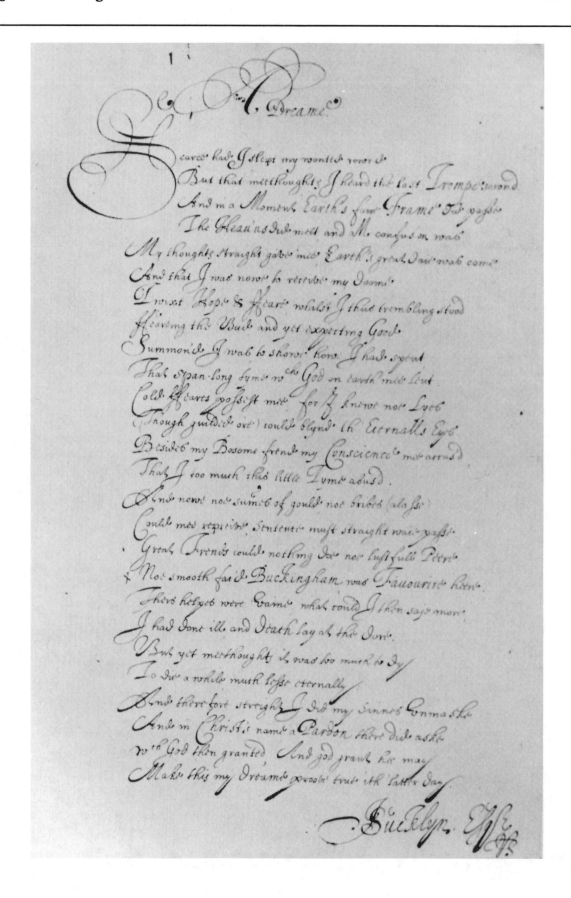

ber from Bramber, but this Short Parliament was soon dissolved. The ensuing short-lived Second Bishops' War seems to have engaged him but exactly how is not clear. His letter "To Mr. Henry German, in the beginning of Parliament, 1640 [old style]" (first published as *A Coppy of a Letter Found in the Privy Lodgeings at Whitehall,* 1641; republished in *Fragmenta Aurea,* 1646) offered advice to the king and brought Suckling into the political arena. His political involvement continued with his complicity in the Army Plot in 1641 (an attempt to free Sir Thomas Wentworth, first Earl of Strafford, adviser to the king and opponent of Parliament and the Scots), his subsequent flight to France, and apparently his death in 1641. Strafford, who had been condemned and imprisoned in the Tower, abortive schemes to free him having failed, was executed on 12 May 1641. On 6 May a writ for Suckling's arrest as well as that of Lord Henry Percy, Lord Henry Jermyn, Sir William Davenant, and Henry Billingsley was issued, but they had sailed to France from Portsmouth with Col. George Goring that same day. Landing at Dieppe, Suckling proceeded to Paris on 14 May. He was convicted of high treason by the House of Commons on 13 August.

The last unquestionable reference to him as being alive is 23 July 1641. Stories of his going to Spain and to the Lowlands are unsubstantiated, and later governmental references to him do not prove his still being alive. His relatives in 1664 reported 7 May 1641 as his death date; this may be the English form of the continental 17 May 1641, which is three days after Suckling arrived in Paris. According to Thomas May in *The History of the Parliament of England* (1647), he died soon after his arrival in France. Two accounts of his death exist; the second is given more credence. The first recounts a theft of his belongings by his servant, once they had reached France; the servant, knowing Suckling's quick temper, drove a nail into his boot so that he would not give pursuit, but Suckling did, apprehended the servant, took off the boot, having endured the great pain he felt, and saw himself all bloodied. The wound was so bad that a fever developed and caused his death only a few days later. On the other hand Aubrey presents a despondent Suckling, who acquired poison from an apothecary and proceeded to commit suicide. There are errors of fact and discrepancies in both accounts. If Aubrey's remarks are accepted, one nevertheless wonders whether Suckling was buried in a Protestant churchyard. The stories reappear with variations and are sometimes confounded. (Much of the information about Suckling in the years 1637 to 1641 derives from extant letters written by him and by others.) A portrait reputedly painted by Sir Anthony Van Dyck, in the Frick Collection in New York City, is the only authenticated one, all others — such as William Marshall's frontispiece to *Fragmenta Aurea* and eighteenth-century versions — deriving ultimately from it.

As with most seventeenth-century poets, the text and canon of Suckling's poems are not definitive. There are numerous poems included in the early editions that are clearly spurious, there are numerous versions of poems in nonauthorial manuscripts, and there are some incidental printings of works assigned to him that do not appear in any of the three basic collections, *Fragmenta Aurea, The Last Remains of Sr John Suckling* (1659), and *The Works of Sir John Suckling* (1676). It is most probable that Suckling did not collect his poems or have them collected, thus accounting for questions of text and canon which beset even the works of Jonson, who did collect and publish his verse. The arrangement of Suckling's poems in the editions is random, and dating of those that are not occasional is most uncertain.

"Song: I prithee send me back my heart," for example, printed in *The Last Remains* and found in several manuscripts, has now been dislodged from the canon. Clayton suggests that the poem may have been written by Dr. Henry Hughes. Yet it has similarities to other poems in the canon and derives from Donne's "The Message" as well as "The Broken Heart" in specific language, image, and content. On the one hand labeling poets such as Suckling non-Metaphysical is made suspect, and on the other the reading that is often advanced through such delimiting terminology is invalidated. While this poem does not depend on a conceit, it does work through a few standard metaphors explored in paradoxic expression. The "logic" of "Why should two hearts in one breast lie, / And yet not lodge together?" is not different from Donne's in his popular "The Flea." The poem, like such accepted poems as " 'Tis now since I sate down before," may revel in the frivolous lover's strategy and be an example of coterie poetry written for a male audience, but it also posits a psychology of the male anxious over his sexual attractiveness to the female.

The latter poem reflects an intertext with poems by Donne (for example, "The Dampe") and Thomas Carew (such as "A Rapture") in its pursuit of the love game, and its military imagery recalls Donne's "Loves Warre," even though biographical subtexts may impinge in both areas. Many of Suckling's poems present Petrarchan themes and language, as in "Profer'd Love rejected," or seventeenth-century developments from classical subjects, such as "The deformed Mistress," or the contrasting female poetic voice (found also in Donne and Jonson) turning the situation topsy-turvy, as in the two "Against Fruition" poems. The coterie aspects of such writing are evidenced in these verses of an older, experienced woman, trying to dissuade a romantic youth from sincerity and constancy: the coterie poet aimed at variety of circumstances, logical arguments, and attitudes, using an assortment of verse forms and meters. One poem is in five six-line stanzas, rhyming *aabbcc*; the other has twenty-six lines in heroic couplets. Part of the expected background for the "humor" of the poems is the Renaissance cliché that men are sincere and honest lovers, always constant, and that women are fickle, inconstant, schemingly untruthful. The untitled poem beginning "There never yet was woman made" is called "Womans Constancy" by Clayton, for the male poetic voice warns that "womens hearts like straw do move, / and what we call / Their sympathy, is but love to jett in general."

A typical love game poem is "Loving and Beloved":

> There never yet was honest man
>   That ever drove the trade of love;
>   It is impossible, nor can
>   Integrity our ends promove;
> For Kings and Lovers are alike in this
> That their chief art in reigne dissembling is.

Here "honest" calls up virginal, "drove" implies sexual intercourse, "the trade of love" indicates some kind of unmarried lovemaking, even prostitution, "integrity" suggests the coupling of two bodies posteriors and "promove" movement forward and downward. The thesis is that once into one, with "ends" equating "love" enters the picture, friendship, or "Honour," dies; the speaker asks the "God of Desire" to "Give me my honesty again." The punning and humor extend even to items of serious and factual import, such as "A Ballade. Upon a Wedding," which celebrates the union of John Lord Lovelace and Lady Anne Wentworth on 11 July 1638 and is addressed to Richard Lovelace, the poet, a distant kinsman of the groom. (The occasion and the identity of Richard have both been questioned.) This epithalamion (though much different from the kind of poem that Edmund Spenser wrote but not so different from Donne's lampoon of Spenser or Donne's questionable taste in his two other epithalamia) has John and Anne "doing" that

which was "no more / Then thou and I have done before / With *Bridget,* and with *Nell.*"

Suckling's poems include epithalamia, encomia ("On New-years day 1640. To the King," for example), poems on love themes, satire, songs and sonnets (by which is meant little songs), occasional verse ("To my Lady E. C. at her going out of England," for example), and a verse epistle; and he employs iambic tetrameter and iambic pentameter couplets, stanzaic forms, the quatrain, even fourteeners (if "Love and Debt alike troublesom" is indeed his). A major and imitated poem is "A Sessions of the Poets," also called "The Wits," written around 1637, probably before Jonson's death. It sets up a trial ("A Sessions") of various poets, who are named and epitomized in satiric terms, for the granting of the bays (that is, "The laurel" for poetry "that had been so long reserv'd, / Was now to be given to him best deserv'd"). The poem is in four-line stanzas of basically iambic pentameter (but with variations) in *aabb* rhyme, with some linkages between stanzas ("And," "But"). Some of the poets are uncertainly identified, but most, like Davenant, whose nasal deformity as a result of syphilis is alluded to, or Lucius Cary, Lord Falkland, whose flirting with Socinianism removes him from being both Apollo's priest and poet, are directly named. Jonson is accused of presumption (after all he called his 1616 collection *Workes*), not praised for merit. Apollo gives the crown to an alderman because "'twas the best signe / Of good store of wit to have good store of coyn." The alderman will forfeit the laurel if he lends any of his coin to "any Poet about the Town."

Suckling's poetry is considered to present the height of libertine cynicism, enjoyable excursions into a world of carefree abandonment, reveling in wine, women, and gambling, a male world of conquest and gratifications; but, as a line in "An Answer to some Verses Made in his praise" suggests, perhaps beneath all the humor and one-upmanship is a person evidencing unhappiness with himself and the frustrations of his life, who believed that "He shows himself most Poet, that most feigns."

Biographies:

Herbert Berry, "A Life of Sir John Suckling," Ph.D. dissertation, University of Nebraska, 1953;

Thomas Clayton, "An Historical Study of the Portraits of Sir John Suckling," *Journal of the Warburg and Courtauld Institute,* 23 (1960): 105–126;

John Freehafer, "Brome, Suckling, and Davenant's Theater Project of 1639," *Texas Studies in Literature and Language,* 10 (Fall 1968): 367–383;

Enid Madoc-Jones, "Mary Bulkeley: The Aglaura of the Poet Suckling," *Anglo-Welsh Review,* 18 (July 1970): 196–203;

Clayton, Introduction to *The Works of Sir John Suckling. The Non-Dramatic Works* (Oxford: Clarendon Press, 1971), pp. xxvii–lxxv;

Judith K. Gardiner, "Jonson's Friend Colby," *Notes and Queries,* 22 (July 1975): 306–307;

Allan P. Green, "An Unnoticed Fact of the Life of Sir John Suckling," *Notes and Queries,* 24 (May-June 1977): 205;

Clayton, "Sir John Suckling's Poems and Life, c. 1629," *Notes and Queries,* 26 (October 1979): 425–427;

Michael P. Parker, "Suckling in Paris," *Notes and Queries,* 34 (September 1987): 316–318.

References:

Raymond A. Anselment, "'Men Most of All Enjoy, When Least They Do': The Love Poetry of John Suckling," *Texas Studies in Literature and Language,* 14 (Spring 1972): 17–32;

Peter Beal, "Suckling's Verses in the Hopkinson Manuscripts," *Notes and Queries,* 24 (December 1977): 543–544;

Lester A. Beaurline, "The Canon of Sir John Suckling's Poems," *Studies in Philology,* 57 (July 1960): 492–518;

Beaurline, "An Editorial Experiment: Suckling's *A Sessions of the Poets,*" *Studies in Bibliography,* 16 (1963): 43–60;

Beaurline, "New Poems by Sir John Suckling," *Studies in Philology,* 59 (October 1962): 651–657;

Beaurline, " 'Why So Pale and Wan': An Essay in Critical Method," *Texas Studies in Literature and Language,* 4 (Winter 1962): 553–563;

Beaurline and Thomas Clayton, "Notes on Early Editions of *Fragmenta Aurea,*" *Studies in Bibliography,* 23 (1970): 165–170;

Allen R. Benham, "Sir John Suckling, *A Sessions of the Poets,*" *Modern Language Quarterly,* 6 (March 1945): 21–27;

Herbert Berry, ed., *Sir John Suckling's Poems and Letters From Manuscript* (London, Ontario: Humanities Departments of the University of Western Ontario, 1960);

Thomas Clayton, " 'At Bottom a Criticism of Life': Suckling and the Poetry of Low Seriousness,"

in *Classic and Cavalier: Essays on Jonson and the Sons of Ben,* edited by Claude J. Summers and Ted-Larry Pebworth (Pittsburgh: University of Pittsburgh Press, 1982), pp. 217–241;

Fletcher Orphin Henderson, "Traditions of *Précieux* and *Libertin* in Suckling's Poetry," *ELH: A Journal of English Literary History,* 4 (December 1937): 274–298;

David C. Judkins, "Recent Studies in the Cavalier Poets: Thomas Carew, Richard Lovelace, John Suckling, and Edmund Waller," *English Literary Renaissance,* 7 (Spring 1977): 243–258;

Michael H. Markel, "John Suckling's Semi-Serious Love Poetry," *Essays in Literature* (Western Illinois University), 4 (Fall 1977): 152–158;

Earl Miner, *The Cavalier Mode from Jonson to Cotton* (Princeton: Princeton University Press, 1971);

Michael P. Parker, "'All are not born (Sir) to the Bay': 'Jack' Suckling, 'Tom' Carew, and the Making of a Poet," *English Literary Renaissance,* 12 (Autumn 1982): 341–368;

Timothy Raylor, "Samuel Hartlib's Copy of 'Upon Sir John Suckling's Hundred Horse,' " *Notes and Queries,* 36 (December 1989): 445–447;

Hugh M. Richmond, *The School of Love: The Evolution of the Stuart Love Lyric* (Princeton: Princeton University Press, 1964);

Robert L. Sharp, *From Donne to Dryden* (Chapel Hill: University of North Carolina Press, 1940);

A. J. Smith, "The Failure of Love: Love Lyrics after Donne," in *Metaphysical Poetry,* edited by Malcolm Bradbury and David Palmer (London: Arnold, 1970), pp. 41–71;

Charles L. Squier, *Sir John Suckling* (Boston: Twayne, 1978);

Joseph H. Summers, *The Heirs of Donne and Jonson* (New York & London: Oxford University Press, 1970);

John Wilders, "Rochester and the Metaphysicals," in *Spirit of Wit: Reconsiderations of Rochester,* edited by Jeremy Treglown (Hamden, Conn.: Shoe String, 1982), pp. 42–57;

Warren W. Wooden, "The Cavalier Art of Love: The Amatory Epistles of Sir John Suckling," *West Virginia University Philological Papers,* 24 (November 1977): 30–36.

Edmund Waller

(3 March 1606 – 21 October 1687)

M. L. Donnelly
Kansas State University

BOOKS: *An Honorable and Learned Speech made by Mr. Waller in Parliament, against the Prelates innovations, false doctrin, and discipline* (London: Printed for Richard Smithers, 1641);

Mr. Waller's speech in Parliament, at a conference of both Houses in the Painted Chamber. 6. Iuly 1641 (London: Printed by J. N. for Abel Roper, 1641);

A Speech made by Master Waller Esquire in the honorable House of Commons, concerning Episcopacie, whether it should be committed or rejected (London, 1641);

A Worthy Speech Made in the Hovse of Commons This Present Parliament, 1641. 1. That Parliaments are the onely way for advancing the King's Affaires. 2. That the restoring of the property of goods and the freedome of the subject is a chiefe meanes to maintaine religion and obedience to His Majestie. By Mr. Waller (London: Printed for John Nicholson, 1641);

A vindication of the King, with some observations upon the two Hovses, possibly by Waller (Oxford: Printed for William Webb, 1642);

Mr. Waller's speech in the House of Commons, on Tuesday the fourth of July, 1643. Being brought to the Barre, and having leave given him to say what he could for himselfe, before they proceeded to expell him the Hovse (London: Printed by G. Dexter, 1643);

The Workes of Edmond Waller Esquire, Lately a Member of the Honourable House of Commons, In this present Parliament (London: Printed for Thomas Walkley, 1645); republished as *Poems, &c.* (London: Printed by Thomas Walkley for Humphrey Moseley, 1645; authorized edition, London: Printed for Henry Herringman, 1664; eighth edition, enlarged, London: Printed for Jacob Tonson, 1711);

A Panegyrick to My Lord Protector, of the present greatness and joynt interest of His Highness, and this nation (London: Printed for Richard Lowndes, 1655); also published as *A Panegyrick to My Lord Protector, by a gentleman that loves the peace, union, and prosperity of the English nation* (London: Printed by Thomas Newcomb, 1655);

A Lamentable Narration of the sad Disaster of a great part of the Spanish Plate-Fleet that perished neare St. Lucas, where the Marquiss, his Lady, and Children and many hundreth of Spanyards were Burnt and sunke in the bottom of the Sea, by the Valour and Prowess of the two brave Generals Montague and Blake in the yeare, 1657. being their first Victory obtained against the Spanyard in that Voyage (London: Printed by T. F. for N. B., 1658); republished in Samuel Carrington, *The History of the Life and Death of his most Serene Highness, Oliver, late Lord Protector* (London: Printed for N. Brook, 1659);

The Passion of Dido for Æneas. As it is Incomparably exprest in the Fourth Book of Virgil. Translated by Edmund Waller & Sidney Godolphin, Esq$^{rs.}$ (London: Printed for Humphrey Moseley, 1658);

Upon the Late Storme and of the death of His Highnesse ensuing the same, by Mr. Waller (London: Printed for H. H., 1658); republished in *Three poems Upon the Death of his late Highnesse Oliver Lord Protector of England, Scotland, & Ireland* (London: William Wilson, 1659);

To the King, upon His Majesties happy return (London: Printed for Richard Marriot, 1660);

On the Park at St. Jamese's (London: Printed for Tho. Dring, 1660); republished as *A Poem on St. James's Park as lately improved by His Majesty* (London: Printed for Gabriel Bedel & Thomas Collins, 1661);

To My Lady Morton on New-Years-Day, 1650 (London: Printed for Henry Herringman, 1661);

To the Queen, upon Her Majesties birth-day (London: Printed for Henry Herringman, 1663);

Pompey the Great, a Tragedy. Translated out of French, by Certain Persons of Honour, Pierre Corneille's *Mort de Pompée* translated by Waller, Charles Sackville, Charles Sedley, Edward Filmër, and Sidney Godolphin (London: Printed by Henry Herringman, 1664);

Edmund Waller (portrait by Cornelis Janssens; from The Poems of Edmund Waller,
edited by George Thorn-Drury, 1893)

Vpon Her Majesties new buildings at Somerset-House
(London: Printed for Henry Herringman,
1665);

*Instructions to a painter, for the drawing of a picture of the
state and posture of the English forces at sea, under
the command of His Royal Highness in the conclusion
of the year 1664* (London, 1665); enlarged as *Instructions to a painter, for the drawing of the posture
& progress of His Maties forces at sea, under the command of His Highness Royal. Together with the bat-
tel & victory obtained over the Dutch, June 3, 1665*
(London: Printed for Henry Herringman,
1666);

Of the Lady Mary, &c. (London: Printed by T. N. for
Henry Herringman, 1677);

*A Poem on the Present Assembling of the Parliament. March
the 6$^{th.}$ 1678* (London, 1679);

Divine Poems (London: Printed for Henry Herringman and sold by Jos. Knight and Fran. Saunders,
1685);

*A Poem on the Present Assembly of Parliament, November
9$^{th.}$ 1685* (London: Printed for George Powell,
1686);

The Maid's Tragedy Altered (London: Printed for
Jacob Tonson, 1690);

*The second part of Mr. Waller's poems. Containing His Al-
teration of the Maids Tragedy, and Whatever of His
Is Yet Unprinted* (London: Printed for Tho.
Bennet, 1690).

Editions: *The Works of Edmund Waller, Esqr. in Verse
and Prose,* edited by Elijah Fenton (London:
Jacob Tonson, 1729);

*The Works of Edmund Waller, Esq. in Verse and Prose.
To which is prefixed, the Life of the Author, by Percival Stockdale* (London: Printed for T. Davies,
1772);

*The Poetical Works of Edmund Waller and Sir John
Denham,* edited by George Gilfillan (Edinburgh: James Nichol, 1857);

The Poems of Edmund Waller, edited by George Thorn-Drury (London: Lawrence & Bullen / New York: Scribners, 1893).

OTHER: "To the King, On His Return From Scotland," in *Rex Redux, sive musa Cantabrigiensis voti damnas de felici reditu regis Caroli* (Cambridge: ex. acad. Cantab. typog., 1633).

Edmund Waller today is chiefly remembered, by those who remember him at all, for one of three things: his craven behavior in connection with the exposure of an abortive Royalist conspiracy, known as "Waller's Plot"; his sharing with Sir John Denham the most precipitous collapse and lasting eclipse of the most celebrated contemporary reputation in the annals of English literature; or his poem "Go, Lovely Rose," inevitably cited in practically every anthology as an example of the perfect Cavalier lyric. Paradoxically, however, Waller's contemporaries and the critics of the eighteenth century who heaped praises on his poetic gifts never mention this poem. Instead, they admire and comment on the political panegyrics, poems of compliment to noblemen and great ladies, and the poetry of social occasions – the poems that to readers from the Romantic period until recently have seemed the least susceptible to resuscitation of all Waller's literary efforts. In the last thirty years literary scholars have begun again to discover in Waller a significant transitional figure, and a subtle and skilled minor poet.

Edmund Waller was born on 3 March 1606 at the Manor-House, Coleshill (then in Hertfordshire, today in Buckinghamshire). He was baptized 9 March 1606 at the parish church in Amersham as the eldest son of Robert Waller and Anne Hampden Waller. His mother was the sister of John Hampden, the famous republican who vigorously opposed the royal prerogative in the Ship-Money Case. She was also a cousin by marriage to Oliver Cromwell. Important as these family connections were to be in Waller's public career, even more decisive was the inheritance that came to him at the death of his father on 26 August 1616, when Edmund was ten years old. Robert Waller's death left his eldest son the heir to between two thousand and thirty-five hundred pounds a year, a significant fortune in those days. Moreover, his father's departure from the scene left him to the guidance of his mother, by all accounts a formidable woman with a good head for business, who took a keen interest in her son's success throughout her long life. Following preparation of varying quality from a series of schoolmasters, Waller was sent by his mother first to Eton College, and then up to Cambridge, where he was admitted as a fellow-commoner of King's College on 22 March 1620. Apparently he did not take a degree. Despite the familiarity with the law Waller displays in his speeches, he specifically declared in *Mr. Waller's speech in Parliament* (1641) that "it has not beene my happiness to have the Law a part of my breeding." Edward Hyde, first Earl of Clarendon, later reported that Waller was "nursed in parliaments," and although there is some uncertainty about which parliament was his first, Waller himself asserted that he first held a seat when he was only sixteen.

In his twenty-sixth year Waller materially advanced his fortunes by carrying off as his bride Anne Banks. The only daughter and heiress of a wealthy London citizen and mercer who had died on 9 September 1630, Anne was at the time of her marriage a ward of the Court of Aldermen. Gaining the girl and her fortune was a particularly impressive coup since, with the help of relatives who were citizens of London, Waller secured her hand without the permission of her guardians and initially against the pretensions of Mr. William Crofts, later Baron Crofts of Saxham, whose aspirations were backed by the royal court. Waller married Anne on 5 July 1631 at Saint Margaret's, Westminster, and she was spirited out of the jurisdiction of the city authorities. To gain control of her fortune Waller faced a fine out of his wife's portion imposed by the Court of Aldermen, and it was only through the favor and influence of King Charles I that he was able to retire securely with his prize to his house at Beaconsfield. It is characteristic of Waller's whole career that although he had frustrated the plans of the Caroline court, not only did no permanent odium attach to him as a result, but he quickly secured royal favor in patching up the irregularity of his proceedings. In his study of Waller, Jack G. Gilbert suggests that, given the king's desperate need of cash during this period, "there is a suspicion of some *quid pro quo,* but no helpful records remain." Indeed, the eight thousand pounds that came to Waller as his wife's portion, combined with his own considerable inheritance, pleasant manners, plausible conversation, and eloquence in Parliament made him a man whose acquaintance anyone, even a king, might be glad to make.

A son, born 18 May 1633, was later tutored by Thomas Hobbes and admitted to Lincoln's Inn 15 June 1648, but no further records concerning him have been found, and he does not seem to have lived to adulthood. Anne Banks Waller died giving birth to their second child, a daughter who was bap-

Lady Dorothy Sidney, whom Waller addresses as "Sacharrisa" in sixteen poems of courtship (portrait by Anthony Van Dyck; from Van Dyck: Des Meisters Gemälde, *edited by Gustav Glück, 1931)*

tized on 23 October 1634. Waller did not remarry for nearly a decade, during which time Simonds D'Ewes recorded with an air of scandal in his parliamentary diary that Waller was "extremely addicted and given to the use of strange women" to such a degree that his complexion and countenance were altered by his dissipations.

Clarendon wrote that Waller, "at the age when other men used to give over writing verses, (for he was near thirty years of age when he first engaged himself in that exercise, at least that he was known to do so,) surprised the town with two or three pieces of that kind; as if a tenth muse had been newly born, to cherish drooping poetry." Waller himself told John Aubrey that "when he was a brisque young sparke, and first studyed Poetry; methought, sayd he, I never sawe a good copie of English verses; they want smoothness; then I began to essay." Though some of Waller's poems have as their subjects things that happened in the late 1620s

and early 1630s, they may have been written later, or reworked sometime after the event. Certainly Clarendon's remarks imply that Waller did not cultivate the muse until after the death of his first wife, when he undertook a course of study guided by Dr. George Morley, who had studied at Christ Church, Oxford, and was afterward bishop of Winchester. Waller took Morley to live with him and oversee his reading at Beaconsfield. Morley was a member of the "college" of serious-minded intellectuals collected by Lucius Cary, Viscount Falkland, at his country house, Great Tew. According to Clarendon, it was Morley who introduced Waller into that company. Morley's influence may be reflected in Waller's cultivation of a cool, balanced Augustan classicism in virtually all his poetry. Whether Morley's guidance simply heightened a temperamental affinity or formed the poet's mind more decisively, the larger Great Tew influence shows itself in Waller's consistent stance in favor of peace, moderation, tolerance, and programs of economic and intellectual improvement, no less than in his rational opposition to all radical innovations, whether from the left or the right, in society, church, or state.

Waller's "essays" at verse may be categorized in three main groups: public panegyrics, poems of compliment to private individuals, and love lyrics. First in the early collections, and in the esteem of contemporaries, are the panegyrics, poems of compliment with a political or larger public aspect. The second category, poems of compliment addressed to nonroyal personages or private friends, includes commendatory verses for publications by other writers and occasional poems ranging from remarks on significant honors or trifling occurrences that befall the recipient to poems occasioned by illnesses, and from celebrations of marriages and births to funeral elegies and epistles of consolation. Lastly, the love lyrics embrace various Cavalier songs and the group of poems to "Sacharissa."

Classification by purpose and type of occasion seems more satisfactory for Waller than an attempt to impose formalistic generic categories. Waller's habitual social manner tends to smooth away formal generic distinctions such as epigram, elegy, epistle, and song. The panegyrics aspire to a higher style, but the plain, urbane style of polished, sophisticated polite discourse often associated with Horatian epistles is Waller's characteristic manner in most of his productions. Irony and a fondness for a neat turn are frequently cultivated, but they are as likely to appear in a song as in a poem that looks formally more like a Jonsonian epigram. The writer of the anonymous life for the 1711 edition of Waller's poems describes the poet's range and concerns aptly: "Mr. Waller was not for things of Toil or Breath. He imitated the Noble Wits of the Ancients, Tibullus, Ovid, and others, who wrote for the Entertainment of Themselves, their Mistresses, and their Friends, which included the Great and the Fair. . . ."

Lines concluding "The Story of Phoebus and Daphne, Applied" assert that Waller's reputation as a poet was first made by the poems of courtship that he addressed to Lady Dorothy Sidney, under the name of "Sacharissa." Sacharissa certainly ranked among "the Great and Fair." Her father was Robert Sidney, second Earl of Leicester, one of the greatest peers of the realm. Her mother was Lady Dorothy Percy, daughter of Sir Henry Percy, ninth Earl of Northumberland, who was confined to the Tower on suspicion of complicity in the Gunpowder Plot. Other members of Sacharissa's old and distinguished maternal Percy clan were recipients of po-

etic praise from Waller during the last half of the decade of the 1630s.

On her father's side, Lady Dorothy's great-uncle was the famous Sir Philip Sidney. Waller refers specifically to Sidney's *Arcadia* (1590) in one of the sixteen Sacharissa poems; in two others he invokes Sidney's name and nobility, and in the last poem of the series, in mock exasperation and despair, he charges that Sacharissa's imperviousness to love and poetry deny her participation in Sir Philip's lineage. Sacharissa's connection with the author of the admired prose romance elicits many comparisons between nature and art suggested by Sir Philip Sidney's personal genius and hereditary nobility. All of Waller's explicit references to Sidney are to *Arcadia,* but implicitly behind the whole project of the Sacharissa poems lies the first great English sonnet cycle of the Renaissance, Sidney's *Astrophel and Stella* (1591), which likewise celebrated an unsuccessful lover's aspiration. In the Sacharissa poems, the poet establishes himself in the line of descent from the great relative of his indifferent mistress. Waller maintains that his claim to descent is better than hers because it is validated both by his poetry and by his devotion to love.

Perhaps the most complex and perfectly achieved of the Sacharissa poems, "The Story of Phoebus and Daphne, Applied," makes explicit the compensatory reward of fame for the artful, but unsuccessful, lover:

> Yet what he sung in his immortal strain,
> Though unsuccessful, was not sung in vain;
> All, but the nymph that should redress his wrong,
> Attend his passion, and approve his song.
> Like Phoebus thus, acquiring unsought praise,
> He catched at love, and filled his arm with bays.

The versification and rhetoric here show at its best the art that won Waller adulation as a poet. Limpid smoothness and a graceful forward movement of the lines are achieved through careful deployment of mainly one-syllable nouns modified by words of rarely more than three syllables; the lines pivot neatly on the balance point of the caesura; sound and sense alike work parallelism, repetition, and contrast: "Yet what he sung" – "was not sung"; "Attend – passion, approve – song"; qualification and paradox are strategically inserted: "Though unsuccessful – was not in vain"; "All, but the nymph, . . . Attend . . . approve"; "acquiring unsought praise"; "He catched at *x,* and filled with *y.*" This is not vatic poetry, or confessional meditation, or the spontaneous overflow of powerful feelings; as trifles are made precious, caught in pieces of amber, so Waller's verse civilizes and preserves the conflicts and games played out in human social interaction. What rejected lover would not relish being able to say what Waller says here to the disdainful object of his quest? Who could have found the device to say it so aptly and fully, without sounding smug, or bitter, or as if he were speaking a little too loudly, and with too much emphasis, just to show how well things really were with him?

Waller concluded this episode in the second of his two poems titled "At Penshurst." He exclaims (now in the first person) over Sacharissa's un-Sidneian imperviousness to love and poetry – poetry which makes *him,* the Orphic singer, the cynosure of the listening deer and the central focusing point giving order to the surrounding woods (as *she,* in her beauty, had been in the first "At Penshurst"). In a striking recognition of the actual psychological pattern of Petrarchan poetry, the suffering lover has replaced the coveted object of his desire at the center of the poetic world he created; but she is still unmoved by love or song, Orphic though it may be. Waller extricates himself from his erotic impasse by having his versified laments provoke the intervention of Apollo, who here, as in John Milton's *Lycidas* (1637), invades the poem to resolve the troubled poet with his authoritative words. In this case the words come in the form of advice to hang up the lute, go to sea, and divert the mind with wonders. Waller's good nature, so amply displayed in his graceful abandonment of his poetic suit, owes not a little to his vanity; he thought so well of himself and was so well satisfied with the returns on his investments of every sort in the world's markets that, at this stage at least, being a good and graceful loser was easy for him, because in his own eyes he was not a loser at all.

Waller himself asserts in "The Story of Phoebus and Daphne, Applied" that his courtship of Dorothy Sidney brought him recognition as a poet. That recognition came about this time is confirmed by mention of him in Sir John Suckling's "Session of the Poets" (1637). His poetic gifts were also recognized in solicited contributions of verse to *Jonsonus Virbius* (1638), the collection of tributes to Ben Jonson that opens with a poem from Viscount Falkland, and commendatory verses for the *Paraphrase Upon the Divine Poems* published in 1638 by George Sandys, also of the Great Tew circle. All three instances of Waller's recognition as a poet share connections to Falkland's circle, suggesting that entrée into that group was at least as important as the famous

courtship of Sacharissa in the sudden publicity given to his poetic gifts in the later 1630s.

When, years later, his Sacharissa, now dowager countess of Sunderland, asked Waller when he would write such beautiful verse to her again, the poet answered, in a reply worthy of Restoration comedy if not of his famous gallantry, "When, Madam, your Ladyship is as young and handsome again." If under the pretty compliments and graceful mythological "applications," Waller's love poems and lyrics are often surprisingly characterized by just such a wry, unillusioned awareness of the way of the world, his Royalist panegyrics in contrast achieve a kind of apotheosis of idealism and incarnate virtue that is scarcely ever violated by the brutal facts of the-way-things-are. "Of the Danger his Majesty (being Prince) escaped in the road at St. Andero" turns a retrospectively minor incident from Charles I's abortive courtship of the Infanta of Spain while Prince of Wales into a miniature heroic poem of 170 lines, imbedding a historical romance complimenting Henrietta Maria, who became the Infanta's replacement in Charles's state-marriage project. The slender plot of this occasion affords Waller the opportunity to celebrate both his royal master and Charles's consort in language gracefully lifted and adapted from Torquato Tasso, Claudian, Ovid, Virgil, and Homer, and in a series of mythological allusions virtually all of which would be available to the least learned of his courtly audience.

The elevation of his subject in apt mythological applications and witty compliment was a task Waller evidently found congenial from the beginning of his poetic career. His first known publication had been a Latin epigram, "To the King, On His Return From Scotland," which appeared in *Rex Redux,* a Cambridge collection congratulating Charles on his return from his coronation as king of Scotland at Edinburgh in 1633. Even in this slight effort, Waller's characteristic manner is evident: balance, antithesis, witty paradox, an appeal to admiration or wonder (the characteristic baroque aesthetic), and, finally, an ironic questioning of the reader's assumptions and acceptance of received notions. In translation it declares,

Wandering from his wonted seats, attended
  with an unarmed troop of followers,
And bearing a single crown, Behold!
King Charles returns, circled
  with two diadems at once:
Where naked pomp yields these things,
  what will arms give?

To the final question, which rhetorically *seems* to confirm the superior power and worth of "arms" to "naked pomp," a thoughtful answer might be, "what more *could* they give (that a beneficent and paternal monarch would wish to take)? What use of arms against a brother nation?" The pacific subtext is perfectly in keeping with Waller's views throughout his long career, despite the fact that panegyric must often celebrate martial glory. A champion of Britain's naval might, Waller obviously preferred that his country's fleet should cow potential antagonists without the necessity of actual engagements. The only warfare he seems to have contemplated with unmixed enthusiasm, anachronistic as it may seem, was a crusade against the Turkish infidels.

During the 1630s Waller presumably wrote and polished his other political panegyrics commemorating and moralizing contemporary events of the reign of Charles I. "Of His Majesty's receiving the news of the Duke of Buckingham's death," "Of Salle," "To the King, on his navy," and "Upon His Majesty's repairing of Paul's" comprise Waller's contributions to Caroline Royalist panegyric. The occasion of the first mentioned was Charles's reception of the news that his favorite and friend, George Villiers, first Duke of Buckingham, had been murdered by the knife of an assassin on 23 August 1628. The news was brought to the king while he was attending Morning Prayer, and he famously refrained from any reaction or show of emotion until the service was over, when he retired to his chamber and wept bitterly. Two notable conceits mark Waller's commemoration of this display of heroic self-control. One, an allusion to a famous classical painting outdone by the king's real-life self-possession, embodies the heightened connoisseurship and awareness of the visual arts and architecture of the Stuart court, both of which figure in many other poems early and late in Waller's career. The other is a device complimenting Charles by awarding him an oxymoronic combination of virtues within one person that virtually identifies him with divinity: the poem in fact asserts that Charles's behavior transcends the ancient pagan conceptions of the divine.

In a similar way, the poem in praise of Charles's fleet engages in a glorification of military power that would delight the most chauvinistic advocate of English mastery of the sea, but the power and force praised are subordinated to peaceful ends: the suppression of piracy and the brutal rule that "Ships heretofore in seas like fishes sped, / The mighty still upon the smaller fed." God allows

Charles such invincible power because his piety and virtue assure that he will not misuse it.

Perhaps more flawed than either of the preceding panegyrics, but also more influential, was Waller's poem "Upon His Majesty's repairing of Paul's." In *Harmony from Discords* (1968), Brendan O Hehir credits the influence of this poem in particular on the most famous topographical poem of the seventeenth century, Sir John Denham's *Cooper's Hill* (1642). Waller makes Charles's continuation of his father's project to repair, restore, and beautify the dilapidated structure of the cathedral in London an emblem of restoration and reformation of the church as an institution. However, it is a singular feature of the poem that, while the substance of its praise is couched in terms of concrete architectural accomplishments, most of the specific concrete detail in the poem consists of illustrative allusions, comparisons, images, and conceits, and the action of the king is presented either as an act of mind, or a kind of magnetic attraction that draws others to do what he conceives and wills. The reader is made to see vividly Amphion's music causing the stones of Thebes to leap into place, Saint Paul shaking off the poisonous viper (an allusion to Acts), the aged oak relieved of the clinging ivy, the queen of Sheba moved to admiration of Solomon's magnanimity and greatness figured in his fleet and temple, and Laomedon building the walls of Troy with the divine help of Neptune and Apollo; but in the poem's sixty-four lines, only three architectural facts about the actual building of Saint Paul's Cathedral are mentioned. The whole project is characterized, vaguely, by "beauty": this reconstruction with stones and mortar is but

> an earnest of his grand design,
> To frame no new church, but the old refine;
> Which, spouse-like, may with comely grace command,
> More than by force of argument or hand.
> For doubtful reason few can apprehend,
> And war brings ruin where it should amend;
> But beauty, with a bloodless conquest, finds
> A welcome sovereignty in rudest minds.

These lines articulate Waller's ethos as well as any he ever penned, speaking for his irenicism, his advocacy of a path of moderation, defending old tradition and established, civilized values, and identifying beauty with the good.

Such values faced hard going in the 1640s. From the opening skirmishes of the Long Parliament through his appeal for his life after the discovery of what has since been known as Waller's Plot, the poet's political position has seemed a mystery to some, a contradiction to others. His kinship to John Hampden, republican hero of resistance to the royal prerogative in the Ship-Money Case, as well as his position as a wealthy grandee and a member of Parliament, placed him in the center of the national crisis. Moderate though his views and instincts were, it was not a role from which he shrank. In the positions he adopted and the actions he undertook as a member of the Long Parliament, the pressures and interests of family, wealth, and status are easily traced. Waller sat for Amersham in both the Short Parliament (met 13 April 1640, dissolved before the end of May, the first Parliament to be held in eleven years), and the Long (met for the first time 3 November 1640). From the outset he participated vigorously in the attack on high-handed exercise of the royal prerogative. In July 1641 he delivered to the House of Lords the impeachment of Sir Francis Crawley, justice of the court of common pleas who in 1636 had been one of the twelve judges to endorse King Charles's right to levy ship-money throughout England and had joined in sentencing Waller's cousin John Hampden for his resistance to the ship-money as an illegal tax. Classically eloquent, full of apt illustrations from Roman history, patriotic scorn, and righteous indignation, *Mr. Waller's speech in Parliament* was reported to have sold twenty thousand copies in one day.

No friend to novel High Church views espoused by Laudian clerical meddlers in affairs of state, Waller steadfastly opposed radical innovation in the church, let alone in the social, political, and economic order; but he wished to reform the abuses of the ecclesiastical establishment, not root out the hierarchy. Waller's positions were essentially moderate, centrist positions: he feared popular agitation, and the central recurring theme in the speeches and fragments of parliamentary discourse that have survived is the defense of the traditional order, and of the liberties and property of the subject. Increasing polarization of factions and the logic of events left no space in the middle for the moderate to work; like Hyde and Viscount Falkland, Waller – having started out to curb the threat represented by the arbitrary power of the king's advisers, Thomas Wentworth, first Earl of Strafford, and Archbishop William Laud – found that John Pym and the high-flying partisans of parliamentary privilege and reform had become the real danger to the ancient constitution as he envisioned it.

Waller split with Pym's leadership over the bill of attainder against Strafford, for which he was favorably noticed by friends of the king; but he was disciplined by the House of Commons on 5 November 1641 for comparing Pym's counsel to Parliament to Strafford's advice to the king. Whether or not he sent the king "a thousand broad pieces," as alleged, when the king raised his standard at Nottingham, Waller continued to speak "upon all occasions with great sharpness and freedom" "against the sense and proceedings of the House," according to Clarendon. After the parliamentary defeat at Edgehill, the Commons made Waller one of the parliamentary commissioners to treat with the king in February 1643. Within a few months, however, Waller was involved as a central figure, not in an official negotiation for peace, but a conspiracy.

It is impossible to trace the inception of what has come to be known as Waller's Plot. On the mildest construction, the plot aimed simply to collect an influential and numerous party in the two houses and the city who would effectually resist arbitrary taxation and other measures in support of the war effort by Parliament, orchestrate focused verbal opposition, and effect a peaceful settlement, with restoration of the Crown and Crown rights. Waller was collecting names of the favorably disposed from parliamentary members; Nathaniel Tomkins, his brother-in-law, was performing the same function among the citizens. Other principals included Richard Chaloner, Tomkins's friend, and Chaloner's acquaintances, Algernon Percy, tenth Earl of Northumberland, and Jerome Weston, second Earl of Portland, and Lord Edward Conway and some of his noble connections. Waller was the chief conduit through which information traveled back and forth between the king and his advisers, notably Hyde and Falkland, in Oxford, and the plotters in London. However, eventual arrangements looked much more like plans for a coup de main than the scheme just outlined. On 29 May 1643 the London conspirators felt that they had their men and their plans in order. According to the modern editor of the poems, George Thorn-Drury, Waller drew up a declaration of the conspirators' cause, which was to be printed and posted, proclaiming that the rising was "to maintain the true reformed Protestant Religion against all Papists and Sectaries, the Laws of the Land, Privilege of Parliament, and Liberty of the Subject, and to oppose all illegal Taxations, Assessments, and the like." However, various indiscretions and leaks from those concerned in the plot had come to the attention of the authorities in London, and brought Waller and Tomkins under scrutiny. Pym took steps to get the whole story, then set about exposing the plot in the most sensational and alarming manner he could contrive, to be sure of winning over a frightened public.

Waller and Tomkins were arrested the night of 31 May 1643. The upshot of a committee investigation was Pym's initiative on 6 June recommending that everyone in the government and clergy be made to swear to the Solemn League and Covenant. This loyalty oath in effect served as a Rubicon which, once passed, allowed no turning back from the divisive course of civil war and forced moderates in public positions to align themselves with the extremists or be branded themselves as seditious, factious subverters of the Protestant religion and English liberties. In a word, the outcome of the Royalist plot in which Waller had become involved assured that the kind of moderation and opposition to extreme courses he had always hitherto espoused would be made an impossible stance for any public man.

What promises or threats were presented to Waller by his interrogators we cannot know. Clarendon, Percival Stockdale, and Samuel Johnson are all as severe as the sternest moralist could wish in their judgments on Waller's behavior. It was his betrayal of others who were complicit that provokes the strongest terms of reprobation. Tomkins and Chaloner, after trial by a military tribunal, were executed, hanged on 5 July in front of their own doors, Tomkins at the Holborn end of Fetter Lane, Chaloner in Cornhill. Tomkins, particularly, is recorded as having died with firmness and courage. The day before Tomkins and Chaloner were executed, Waller himself was brought before the bar of the House of Commons to say what he could in his own defense before being expelled from Parliament (the privileges of which protected him against prosecution while he was still a member) and remanded to a court-martial. In his apologia, Waller groveled and appealed to his judges' interests in not setting too disgraceful and dangerous a precedent in the punishment of one of their own. He also attempted to save himself by hypocritically submitting to the spiritual assistance of nonconformist ministers, whose very language he in part adopted in his confession, and for whose "ghostly assistance" he appealed also by considerable presents and gifts. The leading members of the house were similarly solicited. Aubrey recorded that "He . . . sold his Estate in Bedfordshire, about 1300 pounds per annum, to Dr. Wright, M.D., for about 10,000 pounds (much under value) which was procured in 24 hours time or els he had been hanged: With which money he Bribed the whole House, which was the first time a house of Commons was ever bribed." Whether Waller actually bought the judgment of his peers for such staggering amounts, or not, his contemporaries apparently thought he had. Certainly Parliament was in great need of the money to recruit new troops. What Waller undeniably did buy — whether with his pathetic eloquence, his tactics of delay, his friends, or ready cash — was time, and thus eventually his life: after several preparations for court-martial, followed by interruptions and delay, finally, on 23 September 1644, a petition is recorded from "Edm. Waller, prisoner in the Tower" hoping that the house will accept his offer of payment of a fine of ten thousand pounds and banishment from the realm. This was the judgment in fact finally handed down on 4 November 1644, giving Waller twenty-eight days from the 6th of November to leave England, not to return on pain of such punishment as both houses of Parliament should think fit. Thus ended the episode that, more than any other in his life, has caused posterity to heed his former friend Clarendon's coldly damning summation of his character: Waller "preserved and won his life from those who were most resolved to take it, and in an occasion in which he ought to have been ambitious to have lost it."

Aside from a handful of occasional pieces, Waller's poems first found their way into print during his exile. Four editions came out in 1645. The first edition, published by Thomas Walkley, was unauthorized and solely the result of Walkley's enterprising attempt to cash in on the notoriety of the recent parliamentary orator, principal in a state trial, and exile. Walkley's title, *The Workes of Edmond Waller Esquire, Lately a Member of the Honourable House of Commons, In this present Parliament,* certainly seems to promise something more germane to current affairs than the title of *Poems, &c.,* adopted by Humphrey Moseley in the subsequent editions of 1645. Walkley's edition does include three previously printed parliamentary speeches, which the second Moseley edition omits. In any case, even had Waller been in England at the time, he would have thought that offering his own works like a common hack to a printer, as opposed to circulating them among his friends and acquaintances in manuscript, would compromise his social standing. Moreover, the considerable body of Royalist panegyric included would have done him no good with the currently ascendant party, though it might have gone some way toward redeeming him with the party he had renounced and condemned at his trial. Apparently Waller from exile or his representatives on the scene pressured Walkley, for he surrendered the unsold sheets of his edition to Humphrey Moseley, who immediately republished the very sheets printed by Walkley, uncorrected, with an entirely new title, two inserted leaves comprising new poems not in Walkley's collection, and two leaves with a table of contents, as well as "An Advertisement to the Reader" warning that this edition corrects "an adulterate Copy, surreptitiously and illegally imprinted to the derogation of the Author, and the abuse of the Buyer." Moseley also added in his edition a dedication "To my Lady," which creates the impression that his text comes directly from a manuscript prepared by the poet for the unnamed lady. This edition by Moseley sold out immediately, and he set up another edition, omitting the speeches in Parliament and correcting the worst and most obvious printer's errors from the edition inherited from Walkley. When this sold out, Moseley produced still another edition within the year 1645, with changed format and style, reduced page size, and including the speeches again. The warning to the reader was also retained, with the result that it now applied to Moseley's own previous editions. It is worth reflecting on the impression that this publication would have made on the reading public. However disgraceful and cringing the poet's behavior in the effort to save his life might appear, the image of Waller as a man who had cultivated the arts of civilized life, who had revered his king and queen, and who had suffered for his loyalty and commitments can only have been enhanced by the wide circulation of his poems so soon after he played so principal a role in the Royalist plot that bears his name.

Waller's exile, as Gilbert has remarked, "was perhaps more an inconvenience than an ordeal." Sometime before Waller left England, he had remarried, taking as his bride Mary Bresse, from a family of Thame, in Oxfordshire. He spent much of his time in Rouen, Normandy, where his daughter Margaret was born. She was his favorite daughter and became his amanuensis when grown. Only scattered vignettes survive from this period. Two letters remain to witness the correspondence between Waller and Thomas Hobbes. Waller offered to translate into English Hobbes's *De Cive* (1642; translated, 1651), with which he was much impressed, but according to Aubrey, he asked Hobbes to make a trial of it first, and having seen Hobbes's translation, "would not meddle with it, for that nobody els could doe it so well." In 1646, leaving his wife in France, Waller traveled through Italy and Switzerland with John Evelyn, the connoisseur and diarist. At some time before 1658 he produced a loose translation of lines 455 to 585 of book 4 of the *Aeneid,* completing or perfecting the work begun by his friend from Great Tew,

POEMS,
&c.

WRITTEN BY
Mr. ED. WALLER
of *Beckonsfield*, Esquire ; lately a
Member of the Honourable
House of Commons.

All the Lyric Poems in this Booke
were set by Mr. HENRY LAVVES Gent.
of the Kings Chappell, and one of his
Majesties Private Musick.

Printed and Published according to Order.

LONDON,
Printed by *T.W.* for *Humphrey Moseley*, at the
Princes Arms in *Pauls* Church-
yatd: 1645.

Title page for the third 1645 edition of Waller's poems, the second of three editions published by Humphrey Moseley in that year. Thomas Walkley published the first edition without permission from Waller, who was in exile because of his part in a Royalist plot.

"Little Sid" (Sidney Godolphin), another casualty of the Civil War. The translation was published by Humphrey Moseley in 1658 as *The Passion of Dido for Æneas. As it is Imcomparably exprest in the Fourth Book of Virgil.* It was reprinted in 1679.

By the end of 1649 Waller and his wife had settled in Paris, where, in contrast to the poverty and distress of most of the Royalist exiles, he reportedly kept the most sumptuous table among the English exiles after Henry Jermyn, who was Henrietta Maria's de facto prime minister and favorite. Aubrey reports Waller's assertion that he had dined with Pierre Gassendi and René Descartes, as well as Hobbes, at the table of the "Lord Marquisse of Newcastle," William Cavendish, who was, on Waller's testimony, patron to all three. Waller had taken his new wife's jewels into exile and sold them off to support his by no means abstemious lifestyle, which brought him to the point that, he joked to friends and acquaintances, "he was at last come

Page from a letter (9 September 1657) to Thomas Hobbes in which Waller discusses the political climate and mentions Oliver Cromwell (Maggs Bros. catalogue no. 480) to the *Rump Jewel*." Machinery was set in motion (it is not clear exactly how; early biographers asserted that his sister's husband, Col. Adrian Scroope, interceded for him with Cromwell), and on 27 November 1651 the House of Commons responded to "the humble petition of Edmond Waller" by revoking his sentence of banishment and ordering a pardon to be prepared for him. On 13 January 1652 he took his leave of Evelyn in Paris, and by August, living on his diminished fortune in a house he built at Hall-barn, he was settled back near his mother, who continued to live at Beaconsfield until her death in April of 1653. Waller's depleted resources, according to Stockdale, still produced fifteen hundred pounds a year. He ingratiated himself with his distant kinsman, the lord protector, writing in 1652, the year of his return to England, perhaps his best political poem, *A Panegyrick to My Lord Protector, of the present greatness and joynt interest of His Highness, and this nation* (1655), a production which has given his subsequent biographers, mostly orthodox Royalists, considerable trouble and indignation, as they must allow the poetic art while condemning the sentiments. Waller seems to have sincerely admired the protector's abilities and character.

In addition to the *Panegyrick to My Lord Protector,* Waller wrote two other poems voicing views favorable to the protector's government, or promoting his success and greatness: "Of a War with Spain, and a Fight at Sea," and *Upon the Late Storme and of the death of His Highnesse ensuing the same* (1658), an elegy on the death of Cromwell. All three were suppressed in editions of Waller's works published after the Restoration. All three also share with several of the poems written before the fall of the monarchy and with speeches delivered throughout Waller's parliamentary career a highly developed interest in England's sea power as the chief means to her greatness. Perhaps in recognition of this interest, Waller was appointed one of the commissioners for trade in December 1655. His *Panegyrick to My Lord Protector* articulates an essentially Hobbesian political philosophy, in which Cromwell's sovereignty is justified, not by abstract right, but by the interest of all the ruled in the suppression of anarchy and civil war. Waller blandly adopts some of the standard tropes of prerevolutionary Royalist panegyric, including the oxymoronic union of opposites in the character of the ruler, and finally borrows the analogy with Augustus which had been so dear to the Stuart kings earlier in the century:

As the vexed world, to find repose, at last
Itself into Augustus' arms did cast;

So England now does, with like toil oppressed,
Her weary head upon your bosom rest.

When he turns to direct narration of a battle-piece, in "Of a War with Spain, and a Fight at Sea," Waller celebrates virtue, love, courage, and generosity of spirit in friend and foe alike and deplores the human cost of war, as emphasized by the title of the broadside version, *A Lamentable Narration of the sad Disaster of a great part of the Spanish Plate-Fleet that perished neare St. Lucas* (dated in manuscript on the title page "Aprill 13, 1658"). The poem is most memorable for the way the baroque excess, with which the deaths of the enemy marquis (Don Francisco Lopez de Zuniga, Marquis de Baydes) and his wife are described, is balanced by the homely moralization occasioned by the pity their deaths and their children's fate evoke in their enemies. It was reprinted, incorrectly described as "that never till now published & incomparable Poem of the English Virgil of our times, Mr. Edmund Waller," in Samuel Carrington's *History of the Life and Death of his most Serene Highness, Oliver, Late Lord Protector,* in 1659.

On 3 September 1658, in actuality the third day after the great storm his elegists took according to the pathetic fallacy as nature's lament for the passing of so great a man, the lord protector died. Waller's poem on the occasion, *Upon the Late Storme and of the death of His Highnesse ensuing the same,* was "Printed for H. H." as a broadside in 1658 and as one of *Three poems Upon the Death of his late Highnesse Oliver Lord Protector of England, Scotland, & Ireland,* printed by William Wilson in 1659. The other contributors to the latter publication were John Dryden and Thomas Sprat, who was later historian of the Royal Society. In Waller's poem Cromwell's end is compared to that of Romulus, the founder of Rome; the trees of his funeral pyre and glory of his deeds suggest Hercules. The highest praise is given to Cromwell's expansion of English power through the command of the ocean, and his uniting of Britons to direct their warlike energies on foreign foes:

The ocean, which so long our hopes confined,
Could give no limits to his vaster mind;
Our bounds' enlargement was his latest toil,
Nor hath he left us prisoners to our isle;
Under the tropic is our language spoke,
And part of Flanders hath received our yoke.
From civil broils he did us disengage,
Found nobler objects for our martial rage;
And with wise conduct, to his country showed
Their ancient way of conquering abroad.

The protector's death precipitated a succession crisis: no adequate mechanism for the transi-

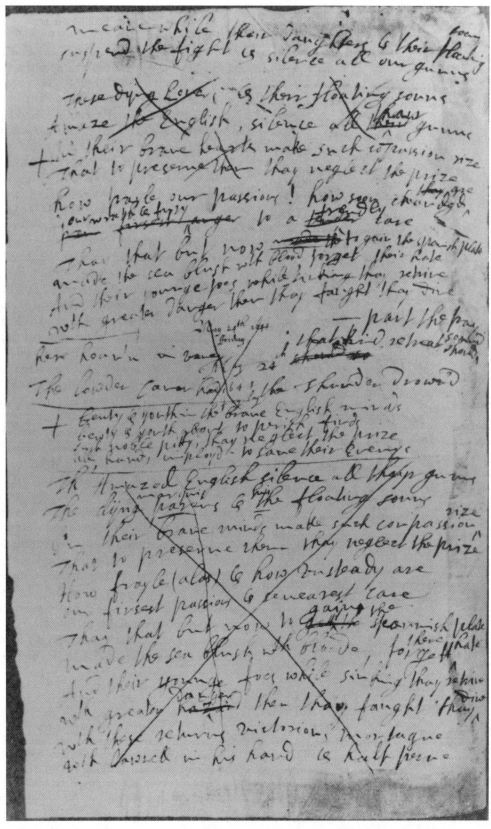

Rough draft for revisions Waller made in the 1659 version of his poem celebrating a 1656 British naval victory, "Of a War with Spain, and a Fight at Sea," first published in 1658 (Folger Shakespeare Library, MS. x. d. 309)

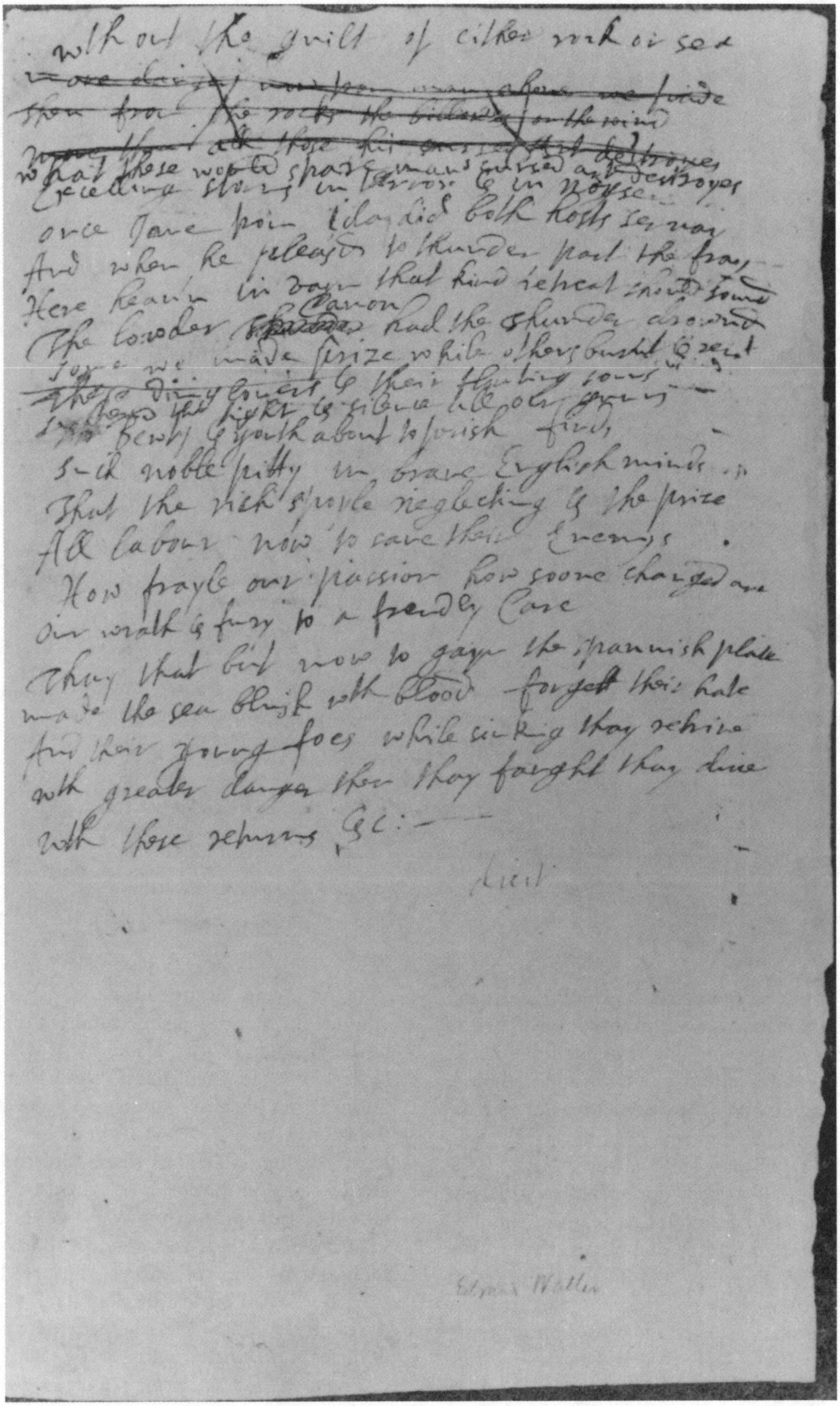

Waller circa 1685 (copy of a portrait by John Riley; National Portrait Gallery, London)

tion in power had been devised by the Protectorate. Cromwell's mantle was wishfully handed down to his son, Richard, anyway, but "Tumbledown Dick" proved quite inadequate to the task, and resigned. With enthusiastic demonstrations of relief, the nation threw itself at the feet of Charles II, who landed at Dover 25 May 1660, brought back by the army led by Gen. George Monck. Waller, like Dryden, who had also lamented the death of the lord protector, hastened into print a poem, *To the King, upon His Majesties happy return* (1660). An altogether slighter poem than Waller's efforts for the lord protector, this piece occasioned the most famous witty reply of Waller's career. When Charles twitted Waller on having written for him a poem much inferior to his panegyric for the usurper, Waller replied without hesitation, "Poets, Sire, succeed better in fiction than in truth."

As usual, Waller landed on his feet, for his conversation and pleasing manners ingratiated him in the Carolean court, a society of wits and elegant ladies who imagined themselves as embodying the pinnacle of polish, elegance, and style. According to the anonymous 1711 "Account of the Life and Writings," Waller dabbled in writing for the theater, and "had a hand in the *Rehearsal* with Mr. Clifford, Mr. Cowley, and some other Wits" at a stage in its development when it was conceived as a mock commentary on several plays, before Buckingham turned it into a burlesque play itself (1672). Waller particularly valued Pierre Corneille's plays, joining Charles Sackville and others in translating Corneille's *Mort de Pompée* (1642) as *Pompey the Great* (1664).

The 1664 edition of *Poems, &c.,* which claims to be the first authorized edition, closed with two lines from Horace's epistles voicing Waller's intention to hang up his harp and devote his life solely to serious matters. Nevertheless, as his eighteenth-century editor Elijah Fenton puts it, "he soon relaps'd into poetry" and continued to write verse to the end of his life. Workmanlike but uninspiring occasional pieces make up the bulk of the later compositions, and the graceful Cavalier love lyrics almost entirely disappear (appropriately enough, in Waller's sense of decorum, for a poet nearing sixty). Two poems written after the Restoration, however, deserve a place among Waller's best panegyrics. One, *On the Park at St. Jamese's* (1660), is a skillful instance of the topographic poem. In 1665 Waller set about the other, a composition of his own in a new genre he had commended in 1658, in lines "To His Worthy Friend, Sir Thos. Higgons, upon the Translation of 'The Venetian Triumph.' " These were commendatory verses to an English rendering of the poem by Giovanni Francesco Busenello purporting to direct the painter Pietro Liberi in executing a panoramic heroic portrayal of the Venetians' recent naval victory over the Turks. Waller's effort in this genre was *Instructions to a painter, for the drawing of a picture of the state and posture of the English forces at sea* (1665). Through the neglect or ineptitude of James, Duke of York, who failed to follow up the success at Lowestoft commemorated in the 1666 edition of the poem, the fruits of victory were lost. Events following the battle exposed both the poor maintenance and preparation of the English fleet and leadership that was incompetent or worse. More even than most panegyrics, Waller's *Instructions to a painter* was clearly seen as having excluded and glossed over facts that did not fit its vividly described heroic vision – as having succeeded "better in fiction than in truth." Consequently, the poem proved a fruitful provocation of imitations, the majority of them satiric, of which Andrew Marvell wrote the best, *The last Instructions to a Painter*. What this particular episode tells about the fate of the poet as Pollyanna may, like Waller's choice of "Sacharissa" to designate his poetic mistress, reveal a major problem in his poetic achievement. The very politeness, the persistent optimism and unfailing pleasantness that we are told characterized his conversation and social manner ultimately weaken the picture of the world he presents in his verse.

Such considerations did nothing to abate Waller's popularity with his contemporaries. His *Poems, &c.* went through ten editions by the end of the century. *The second part of Mr. Waller's poems* was published twice in 1690 and then incorporated in editions of *Poems, &.* in 1705, 1711, 1712, and 1722.

Divine Poems came out in 1685. Meanwhile, the poet was elected a member of the newly formed Royal Society and dabbled as a gentleman dilettante in questions concerning the habits of toads, the infections of sage, the growth in his beech woods, verjuice as a sauce, and the sound and heat of a candle burning in the socket of an iron candlestick. After the plague in 1665, however, Waller's connection with the society was negligible, and he was probably retained on the books as a member simply because of his wealth, court connections, and prominence as a poet and member of Parliament.

After the Restoration, Waller once again served in the House of Commons, representing Hastings in the Long Parliament of Charles II (1661 to 1679), remaining a member until the time of his death. He delighted in adopting the role of Nestor, lecturing his younger colleagues on the customs, rules, and practices of the house, and recalling for their edification instructive instances from his experiences before the revolution. The Whig bishop Gilbert Burnet in his *History of My Own Times* (1724, 1734) reported that "Waller was the delight of the House: and even at eighty he said the liveliest things of any among them." Burnet added, "He was only concerned to say that which should make him applauded. But he never laid the business of the House to heart, being a vain and empty, tho' a witty, man." Nevertheless, Burnet does implicitly include Waller among "the chief men who preserved the nation from a very deceitful and practising court, and from a corrupt House of Commons." Waller persistently spoke on religious affairs in favor of toleration, unity, and moderation, the old broad church principles of Great Tew. He particularly defended toleration of the Quakers, a sect which was the object of much fear and persecution at the time. In secular affairs he urged the king to rely on Parliament and Englishmen to concentrate on government, the fleet, and trade. He served after the Restoration on the Councils of Trade and Foreign Plantations, but failed in his pursuit of the provostship of Eton College, for which he appealed to royal favor when it became vacant in 1665. Clarendon, who was keeper of the Great Seal, refused to put the seal to the grant, on the grounds that the provost of Eton had to be in holy orders. Waller repaid his fellow alumnus of Falkland's "college" at Great Tew by taking a leading part in the impeachment of Chancellor Clarendon in the late summer and fall of 1667.

On the death of his second wife, who was buried 2 May 1677 at Beaconsfield, Waller retired from society to his house at Hall-barn for a time, disconsolate, and would not even receive his great friend Saint-Evremond; but he soon returned to his accustomed roles as gracious host and favorite guest. When James II succeeded his brother, Charles II, Waller continued to enjoy the royal presence, and wrote two panegyric poems, "A Presage of the Ruin of the Turkish Empire. Presented to His Majesty on his Birthday" and "To His Majesty, upon his Motto, Beati Pacifici, occasioned by the taking of Buda, 1686," in both of which he urges James to use the warlike virtues he demonstrated as duke of York to unite the European Christian powers, end internecine strife, and launch a crusade to free Greece and the Holy Land from the Ottoman yoke. It would appear that Edward Fairfax's *Jerusalem Delivered* (1600) influenced his ideas, as well as his versification. He was probably aware of the negotiations that resulted in the Glorious Revolution of 1688, bringing in William of Orange as king, with Mary, James's sister, as joint ruler. However, having learned well the lesson of Waller's Plot, the aged poet is reported to have warned his people to have nothing to do with the plots and plans until the prince of Orange had actually landed in England. His purported advice about when to declare one's change of allegiance was successfully followed by his son and heir.

In his last years Waller spent more and more time among the woods and prospects of his property in Buckinghamshire. Past eighty, his thoughts turned more and more to pious reflections. In an era characterized by Dryden as "lubrique and adult'rate," Waller's poetry had been throughout unusually chaste and decorous. Knightly Chetwood, in his "Life of Virgil," which prefixed Dryden's translation of Virgil's works (1697), cites Virgil's belief that poetry should teach virtue, and parallels "the Principle too of our Excellent Mr. Waller, who us'd to say that he wou'd raze any Line out of his Poems, which did not imply some Motive to Virtue." Waller resolved, however, that the last activity of his pen should be explicitly pious, and produced six cantos "Of Divine Love" and two "Of Divine Poesy," in addition to two poems occasioned by a verse paraphrase of the Lord's Prayer written by his neighbor, Anne Wharton, and the pious sentiments recorded in "Of the Last Verses in the Book." These efforts occasioned Dr. Samuel Johnson's strictures in *The Lives of the English Poets* (1779–1781) that "poetical devotion cannot often please." Nevertheless, one or two passages from the lines written by the octogenarian poet have continued to be quoted with particular approval by his commentators. Especially fine is the conceit in "Of the Last Verses," in which Waller looks forward to his bodily dissolution:

Clouds of affection from our younger eyes
Conceal that emptiness which age descries.
The soul's dark cottage, battered and decayed,
Lets in new light through chinks that time has made;
Stronger by weakness, wiser men become,
As they draw near to their eternal home.
Leaving the old, both worlds at once they view,
That stand upon the threshold of the new.

Waller had bought a small house at Coleshill, his birthplace, in the hope of dying there; according to Thorn-Drury, he said, "A stagge, when he is hunted, and neer spent, always returns home." In the summer of 1687, finding his legs beginning to swell, he sought out Sir Charles Scarborough, the king's physician. Informed, "Why sir, your blood will run no longer," Waller reportedly repeated some lines out of Virgil suitable to the situation, and went home to Hall-barn to die. He received the sacrament surrounded by his children, and died 21 October 1687; he was buried in Beaconsfield churchyard. Saint-Evremond, Sir Robert Cotton, Sir Thomas Higgons, Aphra Behn, George Granville, Thomas Rymer, and others contributed to *Poems to the Memory of That Incomparable Poet Edmond Waller,* a memorial volume published in 1688; Rymer wrote the Latin epitaph for the monument erected in 1700 in Beaconsfield, placing Waller "easily first among the poets of his day."

Aubrey had called Waller "one of the first refiners of our English language and Poetrey." The high opinion of Waller's importance continued for over half a century after his death. The fashionable men and women of mode depicted in the Restoration plays of Sir George Etherege and William Congreve quote Waller with fluent ease; Dryden habitually praised Waller's "sweetness" as his defining characteristic and remarked that "he first made writing easily an art"; he further asserted that the great Elizabethans could show "nothing so even, sweet, and flowing, as Mr. Waller," and added, "unless he had written, none of us could write." Alexander Pope repeated Dryden's characterization of Waller as "even, sweet, and flowing," and Denham as "majestic" and "correct" when he praised "the easy vigor of a line, / Where Denham's strength and Waller's sweetness join." The author of the anonymous life published in 1711 declared that "Mr. Waller was certainly the Father of our English Versification." Johnson pronounced less sweepingly that "it cannot be denied that he added something to our elegance of diction, and something to our propriety of thought." Later critics took these judges at their word, and when the neatness and artifice of the neoclassical couplet fell into disfavor, Waller's stock, too, fell. Later nineteenth-century literary scholars spent a good deal of time trying to make out just exactly what Waller's contribution to the development of the heroic couplet had been, an enterprise that has continued into our own day.

Clearly pentameter couplets, even some closed pentameter couplets, had been written in English back to Geoffrey Chaucer's time. Ben Jonson had a marked predilection for rhymed couplets, and Sir John Beaumont, George Sandys, and Waller's declared model and inspiration, Fairfax's *Jerusalem Delivered,* had all used closed couplets that were occasionally as metrically correct, balanced, and pointed as Waller's. In fact, Waller's contribution was not strictly a refinement of prosody in isolation from rhetoric, but rather smoothness of number combined with simplicity, clarity, and neatness of diction, and a rhetorical economy that highlighted emphasis, wit, and a peculiar combination of poignancy and irony. His early admirers often cite the propriety of his diction, and mention more frequently than any other rhetorical feature of his verse his adept use of the "turn," a term that, as used by Waller and his contemporaries, seems to cover a range of tropes and figures, from antimetabole through ploce and polyptoton to a broader identification of a "turn" with a "trope" — a figure that changes the meaning of a word and appeals not only to the ear, but also to the intellect. What distinguishes Waller and evoked the praise of his contemporaries and successors is the way all the elements in his poetry cohere: he avoids the vulgar as well as the pedantic or arcane; his allusions, comparisons, and mythopoesis are invariably familiar but apt and uniformly elevating; and he balances with grace and neatness the gallantry of his address in his lyrics. Finally central to the tone of his verse is an objectivity, conveyed in his cool mastery of all these elements, that may shade into a slight hint of irony.

Waller was quite conscious of the nature, purposes and functions, and effects of art, even when ostensibly writing about something else. He has several poems that address the art of poetry specifically, which, taken together, provide a clearer picture of his own conception of his enterprise. In both "To Mr. Henry Lawes, who had then newly set a song of mine in the year 1635" and "Upon the Earl of Roscommon's Translation of Horace," Waller asserts that harmonious sound is central to the ability of poetry to move its audience. Thus the music of poetry is inextricably intertwined with its power to persuade and instruct in virtue, as the myths of Orpheus and Amphion attest. Orphic song is not lightly achieved, as Waller's "Prologue to the *Maid's Tragedy*" (1690) reiterates. When he calls there for

"patience . . . to cultivate our thoughts," Waller preaches what was apparently his own practice of laborious polishing. The air of spontaneous facility about Waller's verse would seem to have been the effect of effort, conscious art, and the studious application of censoring judgment. In "Upon the Earl of Roscommon's Translation of Horace," Waller cautions that

> Though poets may of inspiration boast,
> Their rage, ill-governed, in the clouds is lost.
> He that proportioned wonders can disclose,
> At once his fancy and his judgment shows.
> Chaste moral writing we may learn from hence,
> Neglect of which no wit can recompense.

The poet's commitment to the labor of perfecting his medium and polishing his performance is particularly affecting in view of his skeptical awareness, not perhaps of shifts in taste, but of linguistic change, which erodes that very medium. In his lines "Of English Verse," he shares the anxiety of Dryden over the lack of fixity in English, and the rapid linguistic change in the living language that defaces the poet's meaning:

> But who can hope his lines should long
> Last in a daily changing tongue?
> While they are new, envy prevails;
> And as that dies, our language fails.
> . . . .
> Poets that lasting marble seek,
> Must carve in Latin, or in Greek;
> We write in sand, our language grows,
> And, like the tide, our work o'erflows.

The reader familiar with both the Cavalier and the Metaphysical verse of Waller's immediate predecessors and near contemporaries will still find pleasure in recognizing familiar themes and conventions handled always in Waller's particularly polite, elegant, smooth, and coolly distant manner. Waller's economy and felicity in rhyming create the simplicity and directness of "Go, Lovely Rose!," which surely must be one of the most subdued evocations of the carpe diem theme from the period. The poem, articulating a situation from courtship or seduction, paradoxically achieves an almost perfect impersonality:

> Small is the worth
> Of beauty from the light retired;
> Bid her come forth,
> Suffer herself to be desired,
> And not blush so to be admired.

The rueful recognition of "How small a part of time they share / That are so wondrous sweet and fair!"

applies pressure only to come forth and be the cynosure of admiring eyes, not specifically to accept a lover's importunity. A similar sense of the evanescence of youth and beauty, the changeability of the heart's affections, and the imperative to seize the present moment informs the more direct invitation "To Phyllis," which urges that even if youth and beauty would stay, "Love hath wings, and will away." Such mutability, indeed, is not unmixed with blessings for the experienced lover and his no less veteran mistress; ask no questions about those loved yesterday or what tomorrow may bring, "For the joys we now may prove, / Take advice of present love." Among Waller's other Caroline lyrics, "To a Very Young Lady" ("To my young Lady Lucy Sidney" in the 1645 edition) may be compared to Marvell's "To Little T. C., in a Prospect of Flowers" or "Young Love" for the central conceit (Waller's poem turns on the expression of abstract ideas and relationships, Marvell's on more concrete, specific images and conceits). Waller's "A la Malade," to a lady in ill health, is less frigid in its conceits than Thomas Carew's "Upon the Sickness of E. S.," and in its last ten lines it achieves an extraordinary mingling of delicacy, voyeurism, desolation, and spiritual exaltation at the near approach of death.

Other lyrics that gracefully address conventional themes include "To a Lady in a Garden" ("To a Lady in retirement" in the 1645 edition), which is closer to Marvell's "To His Coy Mistress" than most Waller lyrics, but still lacks both the wildly farfetched imaginative reach of the former's opening conceits, and the emotional urgency and violence of its climactic appeal; and "For Drinking of Healths," a decidedly well-bred and decorous championing of old social tradition in comparison to Robert Herrick's and Jonson's lighthearted poems on sack (Waller was reportedly a teetotaler). Also suggesting models and inspiration like Herrick's are two lyrics often favorably cited even by those Romantic and Victorian critics who severely deprecate Waller: "On a Girdle" and "Behold the Brand of Beauty Tossed." The first belongs among poems celebrating an object or intimate article of apparel belonging to the beloved; in Waller's changes of his verbs from the present tense to the past in revising from the 1645 edition, he subtly shifts the implied context to suggest a celebration of the trophy of an achieved conquest. In the second, Waller displays much more metrical variety and virtuosity than usual in a form that recalls some of Jonson's stanzaic experiments, such as "A Celebration of Charis: 4. Her Triumph" or his "Song. 'Slow, slow, fresh fount.'"

In "An apology for having loved before," Waller builds his poem on a smoothly polished elabora-tion of an apology John Donne made "To the Countess of Salisbury" for having perhaps praised other potential patronesses in language much resembling what he then applied to her. In his "Song: Stay, Phoebus, Stay," Waller's clinching argument for the lady being the only thing worth looking at under the sun impresses into service the Copernican theory, though Waller's handling of this characteristically "Metaphysical" conceit is so smooth and polished and translucent that few reading it would think of Donne, much less John Cleveland. If one characteristic of Metaphysical poetry is the display of wit in definition and dialectic, the poem "To Amoret: 'Fair! that you may truly know'" affords as elegantly discriminated and aptly illustrated a definition of the kinds of love a man may owe two different women as may be found among the poems of the period. Waller's "Epitaph on the Lady Sedley" is a perfect Jonsonian commemoration of a virtuous exemplar. In an occasional piece like "The Fall," Waller ventures just to the boundary of the risqué, but is not so ill-bred as to follow Carew, Richard Lovelace, or Sir John Suckling and venture over; of poems such as "Of a Tree Cut in Paper" or "To a Lady, from whom he received a silver pen," occasioned by the trivial events of social intercourse, the reader can judge whether or not such memorialization of the mundane and trifling is or is not an appropriate province for poetry — though a knowledge of the concerns of some contemporary verse may make one less inclined to enter fully into Johnson's high-serious censure that "of these petty compositions, neither the beauties or faults deserve much attention," or that in the love po-etry, "little things are made too important," so that "such books . . . may be considered as shewing the world under a false appearance."

If Waller shows the world under a false appearance, it is owing to his relentless determination to employ his muse in the praise of virtue, beauty, and nobility, and in the glorification of the interests and endeavors of his nation. While his elegant compliments are sometimes tinged with the irony of unillusioned worldliness and his generally upbeat tone not seldom modulates into a sweet melancholy, for him the proper function of poetry was praise, not blame.

> The Muses' friend, unto himself severe,
> With silent pity looks on all that err;
> But where a brave, a public action shines,
> That he rewards with his immortal lines.
> Whether it be in council or in fight,
> His country's honour is his chief delight;

Praise of great acts he scatters as a seed,
Which may the like in coming ages breed.

While Waller showed the way for the great Augustans who followed him in so many ways, he provided no immediate model in satire. Aubrey records Waller's distaste for satirical writing and adds, "All his writings are free from offence." In only two instances does he appear to have attempted a kind of delicate raillery verging toward mock-heroic, and one of these is "The Battle of the Summer Islands," a production in three cantos sufficiently odd to puzzle as learned a critic as Johnson. One thing does seem clear, and that is that the martial and heroic pretensions of the Bermudans, whose world seems more Hesperidean than Homeric, are mocked and ironized, and man's violence, pretensions, and greed are deplored rather than glorified in the fable. The other poem of raillery is "The Triple Combat." Here Waller depicts the rivalry of competing mistresses of Charles II – Hortense Mancini, Duchess of Mazarin; Louise Renée de Kéroualle, Duchess of Portsmouth; and the English Chloris (either Barbara Villiers, Duchess of Cleveland, or Nell Gwyn) – chiefly in the language of a military combat, but also through an epic simile recalling the Judgment of Paris. Instead of biting satire or crude lampoon on the susceptibilities that occupied the throne, however, Waller's light exercise in witty gallantry ends in a commendation of "our golden age; / Where Love gives law, Beauty the sceptre sways, / And, uncompelled, the happy world obeys." If this ending is intended ironically, the irony is so diffuse that it is impossible to conclude exactly who or what is ironized.

The judgment of his contemporaries and biographers of the next century, who continually mention Waller in the same breath with Virgil and even Homer, must seem wildly extravagant today; but the minor theme toward which the author of the anonymous life gestures on several occasions – that Waller was an English, and Christian, Petronius Arbiter – is attractive enough to hold our attention. Waller was a refiner of taste, an appreciator of the good life who at the same time recognized the limits of human pride and human pretension (at least in others). Aubrey's account of Waller's conversation, set down from firsthand experience, may well stand for his verse, as well: "He is something magisteriall, and haz a great mastership of the English Language. He is of admirable and gracefull Elocution and exceeding ready." In his verses, and apparently in his conversation as well, he served as an arbiter of wit and propriety for his age, an age which, interrupted by the social, religious, and political catastrophe that came so near to destroying Waller himself, and cursed throughout by violent political faction and religious fanaticism, acutely felt the need for refinement and a restored civility. Waller persistently emphasized the value of a poetry of praise. His panegyric assimilation of his often flawed and limited heroes and their relatively trivial deeds and limited successes to the most elevated classical and Christian types and models held up a standard for an increasingly unchivalrous and unheroic age, attempting to arouse emulation and glorify virtue. If his range is limited and his gifts of urbanity, polite irony, and superficial ease of social manner have not been the chief effects that later ages have sought from poetry, Waller nevertheless deserves a secure place among the foremost of the minor poets of his century, a century that has been the most prolific of memorable poems and poets that England has so far seen.

Bibliographies:

Beverly Chew, "The First Edition of Waller's Poems," *Bibliographer* (New York), 1, no. 7 (1902): 296–303; reprinted in Chew's *Essays and Verses About Books* (New York, 1926);

Thomas James Wise, *The Ashley Library,* 11 volumes (London: Privately printed, 1922–1936), VII: 183–196;

"A Catalogue of a Collection of the Works of Edmund Waller," in *The Oldenburgh House Bulletin,* no. 1 (Tunbridge Wells: Courier, 1934);

David C. Judkins, "Recent Studies in the Cavalier Poets: Thomas Carew, Richard Lovelace, John Suckling, and Edmund Waller," *English Literary Renaissance,* 7 (Spring 1977): 255–258;

Jack G. Gilbert, "Selected Bibliography," in his *Edmund Waller* (Boston: Twayne, 1979), pp. 152–156.

Biographies:

George Thorn-Drury, Introduction to *The Poems of Edmund Waller,* 2 volumes (London: A. H. Bullen / New York: Scribners, 1901);

Margaret Deas Cohen, "A Study of the Life and Poetry of Edmund Waller," Ph.D. dissertation, Cambridge University, 1931;

James Arthur Steele, "A Biography of Edmund Waller," Ph.D. dissertation, University of London, 1965.

References:

Richard Aldington, "Notes on Waller's Poems," *Living Age,* 312 (21 January 1922): 179–181;

Alexander Ward Allison, *Toward an Augustan Poetic: Edmund Waller's "Reform" of English Poetry* (Lexington: University of Kentucky Press, 1962);

Francis Atterbury, "Exhumations III: Atterbury's Preface to Waller," *Essays in Criticism,* 15 (July 1965): 288–293;

F. W. Bateson, "A Word for Waller," in his *English Poetry: A Critical Introduction* (London & New York: Longmans, Green, 1950), pp. 116–122;

Henry Charles Beeching, "Atterbury on Waller," in his *Provincial Letters and Other Papers* (London: Smith, Elder, 1906);

Beeching, "A Note on Waller's Distich," in *An English Miscellany Presented to Dr. Furnivall,* edited by W. P. Ker, A. S. Napier, and W. W. Skeat (Oxford: Clarendon Press, 1901), pp. 4–9;

Ronald Berman, "The Comic Passions of *The Man of Mode,*" *Studies in English Literature,* 10 (Summer 1970): 459–468;

John Buxton, "Edmund Waller," in his *A Tradition of Poetry* (London: Macmillan, 1967), pp. 87–101;

John Chalker, "Paysage Moralisé: Denham, Waller, Pope," in his *The English Georgic: A Study in the Development of a Form* (Baltimore: Johns Hopkins University Press, 1969), pp. 66–89;

A. B. Chambers, *Andrew Marvell and Edmund Waller: Seventeenth-Century Praise and Restoration Satire* (University Park: Pennsylvania State University Press, 1991);

Warren L. Chernaik, *The Poetry of Limitation: A Study of Edmund Waller* (New Haven: Yale University Press, 1968);

Chernaik, "Waller's *Panegyric to My Lord Protector* and the Poetry of Praise," *Studies in English Literature,* 4 (Winter 1964): 109–124;

James E. Congleton, "The Effect of the Restoration on Poetry," *Tennessee Studies in Literature,* 6 (1961): 93–101;

William Dighton, ed., *The Poems of Sidney Godolphin* (Oxford: Clarendon Press, 1931), pp. xxxix–xlii;

M. L. Donnelly, "Caroline Royalist Panegyric and the Disintegration of a Symbolic Mode," in *"The Muses Common-weale": Poetry and Politics in the Seventeenth Century,* edited by Claude J. Summers and Ted-Larry Pebworth (Columbia: University of Missouri Press, 1988), pp. 163–176;

Jack G. Gilbert, *Edmund Waller* (Boston: Twayne, 1979);

Paul H. Hardacre, "A Letter from Edmund Waller to Thomas Hobbes," *Huntington Library Quarterly,* 11 (August 1948): 431–433;

Charles S. Hensley, "Wither, Waller and Marvell: Panegyrists for the Protector," *Ariel: A Review of International English Literature,* 3 (January 1972): 5–16;

Edward Hyde, *Selections from the History of the Rebellion and the Life,* edited by Gertrude Huehns (Oxford & New York: Oxford University Press, 1978);

Paul J. Korshin, "The Evolution of Neoclassical Poetics: Cleveland, Denham, and Waller as Poetic Theorists," *Eighteenth-Century Studies,* 2 (December 1968): 102–137;

Korshin, "Figural Change and the Survival of Tradition in the Later Seventeenth Century," in *Studies in Change and Revolution: Aspects of English Intellectual History, 1640–1800* (Menston, Yorkshire: Scolar, 1972), pp. 99–128;

Charles Larson, "The Somerset House Poems of Cowley and Waller," *Papers on Language and Literature,* 10 (Spring 1974): 126–135;

F. R. Leavis, *Revaluation: Tradition and Development in English Poetry* (London: Chatto & Windus, 1936; New York: Stewart, 1947), pp. 29–36, 38–39;

J. B. Leishman, *The Art of Marvell's Poetry* (London: Hutchinson, 1966);

George deForest Lord, ed., *Poems on Affairs of State,* volume 1 (New Haven: Yale University Press, 1963), pp. 1660–1678;

Lauro Martines, *Society and History in English Renaissance Verse* (London: Blackwell, 1985);

Earl Miner, *The Cavalier Mode from Jonson to Cotton* (Princeton: Princeton University Press, 1971);

Ruth Nevo, *The Dial of Virtue: A Study of Poems on Affairs of State in the Seventeenth Century* (Princeton: Princeton University Press, 1963);

Brendon O Hehir, *Expans'd Hieroglyphicks: A Critical Edition of Sir John Denham's Coopers Hill* (Berkeley & Los Angeles: University of California Press, 1969);

O Hehir, *Harmony from Discords: A Life of Sir John Denham* (Berkeley & Los Angeles: University of California Press, 1968);

O Hehir, Review of Warren L. Chernaik's *The Poetry of Limitation, Modern Philology,* 68 (August 1970): 100–105;

M. T. Osborne, *Advice-to-a-Painter 1633–1856* (Austin: University of Texas Press, 1949);

George Parfitt, *English Poetry of the Seventeenth Century* (London & New York: Longman, 1985);

Annabel M. Patterson, *Marvell and the Civic Crown* (Princeton: Princeton University Press, 1978);

William B. Piper, *The Heroic Couplet* (Cleveland: Case Western Reserve University, 1969);

L. Proudfoot, *Dryden's Aeneid and its Seventeenth-Century Predecessors* (Manchester: Manchester University Press, 1960);

H. M. Richmond, "The Fate of Edmund Waller," *South Atlantic Quarterly,* 60 (Spring 1961): 230–238;

Richmond, "The Intangible Mistress," *Modern Philology,* 56 (May 1959): 217–223;

Richmond, *The School of Love: The Evolution of the Stuart Love Lyric* (Princeton: Princeton University Press, 1964);

J. W. Saunders, "The Social Situation of Seventeenth-Century Poetry," in *Metaphysical Poetry,* edited by Malcolm Bradbury and David Palmer (London: Edward Arnold, 1970; Bloomington: Indiana University Press, 1971), pp. 237–259;

Duncan Crooks Tovey, "Edmund Waller," in his *Reviews and Essays in English Literature* (Port Washington, N.Y.: Kennikat Press, 1970), pp. 88–114;

Hugh Trevor-Roper, "The Great Tew Circle," in his *Catholics, Anglicans and Puritans: Seventeenth Century Essays* (London: Secker & Warburg, 1987; Chicago: University of Chicago Press, 1988), pp. 166–230;

Ruth C. Wallerstein, "The Development of the Rhetoric and Metre of the Heroic Couplet, Especially in 1625–1645," *PMLA,* 50 (March 1935): 166–209;

C. V. Wedgwood, *Poetry and Politics Under the Stuarts* (Cambridge: Cambridge University Press, 1960);

Philip R. Wikelund, "Edmund Waller's Fitt of Versifying: Deductions from a Holograph Fragment, Folger MS. X. d. 309," *Philological Quarterly,* 49 (January 1970): 68–91;

George Williamson, *The Proper Wit of Poetry* (London: Faber & Faber, 1961);

Williamson, "The Rhetorical Pattern of Neo-classical Wit," *Modern Philology,* 33 (August 1935): 55–81; republished in Williamson's *Seventeenth-Century Contexts* (London: Faber & Faber, 1960), pp. 240–271.

Appendix

Second-Generation Minor Poets of the Seventeenth Century

Second-Generation Minor Poets of the Seventeenth Century

Ernest W. Sullivan, II
Texas Tech University

The seven poets discussed below represent only a few of the many lesser-known poets of their generation. All are "minor" in the sense that they have attracted very little critical attention and are very little read at present. Even so, a fuller understanding of seventeenth-century poetics will come about with further attention to such poets, because present scholarship focuses on lyric verse, often overlooking the diversity of seventeenth-century poetry and its cultural role. The particular authors selected have suffered the vagaries of twentieth-century critical prejudices: some are little thought of as poets because their other accomplishments overshadowed their verse; others are neglected because their work was not published until the nineteenth or twentieth century, and then only in editions of chiefly antiquarian interest; poets who failed to conform to the prevailing religious orthodoxy often had their works suppressed; yet most of these minor poets are ignored because they wrote in genres (historical narrative, heroic romance, religious verse, epigram, verse translation, epitaph, verse letter) little valued today. There are no great individual talents among them, but these poets are working within the traditions that inform and shape the verse of their generation.

Patrick Hannay
(? – 1629?)

BOOKS: *A Happy Husband. or, Directions for a Maide to choose her Mate. As also, A Wives Behaviour towards her Husband after Marriage. To which is adioyned the Good Wife; together with an Exquisite discourse of Epitaphs* (London: Printed by J. Beale for R. Redmer, 1619 [i.e., 1618]);

Two Elegies, on the late death of our Soueraigne Queene Anne. With Epitaphes (London: Printed by N. Okes, 1619);

The Nightingale. Sheretine and Mariana. A happy Husband. Elegies on the Death of Queen Anne. Songs and Sonnets (London: Printed by J. Haviland for Nathaniel Butter, 1622).

Edition: *The Poetical Works of Patrick Hannay,* edited by David Laing (Glasgow: R. Anderson, 1875).

OTHER: William Lithgow, *The totall discourse, of the rare adventures, of long nineteene yeares travayles,* commendatory verses by Hannay (London: Printed by N. Okes, 1632).

John Dunbar's *Epigrammaton Joannis Dunbari Megalo-Britanni Centuriæ Sex* (1616) mentions Patrick Hannay. *Philomela, The Nightingale* (1622), a poem in sixteen-line stanzas, is dedicated to Frances Stuart, Duchess of Lennox and has commendatory verse by his cousin Robert Hannay and from John Marshall and William Lithgow. *Philomela* is a long romance about Philomela, the fairer daughter of Pandion, King of Athens. Philomela is raped by Tereus, the husband of her sister, Progne. Tereus removes Philomela's tongue to prevent her from reporting the rape, but she weaves a tapestry describing the rape. Progne then revenges the rape by killing their son and serving his flesh to Tereus to eat. The two sisters and Tereus are then turned to birds. *Sheretine and Mariana* (1622), a narrative poem in six-line stanzas, is dedicated to Lucy Harrington, Countess of Bedford, and

Title pages for Hannay's imitation of Sir Thomas Overbury's Wife *(top) his elegies for the wife of James I (bottom left), and the collection that includes his narrative poems (bottom right)*

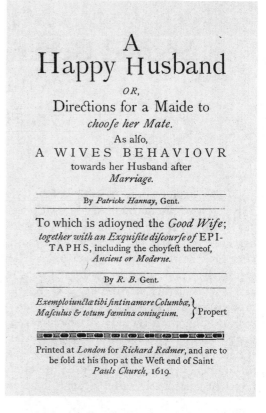

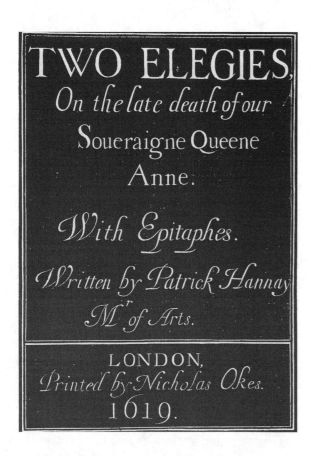

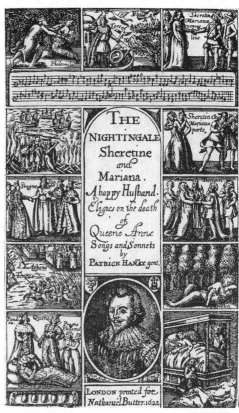

comes with a short prose history of Hungary to aid the reader in following the poem. *A Happy Husband* (1619) is Hannay's equivalent of Sir Thomas Overbury's *Wife* (1614). The elegies to Queen Anne (1619) are dedicated to Prince Charles. The sonnets, not all of fourteen lines, deal in Petrarchan terms with unrequited love. Some songs, like "A Paradox," on the inconstancy of women show the influence of John Donne.

Hannay may have been the third son of Alexander Hannay of Kirkdale in Kirkcudbright.

Donald Hannay of Sorbie would have been his grandfather. Hannay and his cousin Robert (created a baronet of Nova Scotia in 1629) were received favorably in the court of King James I. About 1620 they received grants of land in the county of Longford, Ireland. After Hannay returned from a 1621 visit to Sweden, he became a clerk in the Irish privy council in Dublin. In 1627 Hannay became master of chancery in Ireland and may have died at sea in 1629.

Thomas May

(1595 - 13 November 1650)

See also the May entry in *DLB 58: Jacobean and Caroline Dramatists.*

BOOKS: *The Heire, An Excellent Comedie* (London: Printed by B. Alsop for T. Jones, 1622);

Barclay His Argenis: or, The Loves of Poliarchus and Argenis, verse translations by May and prose translations by Kingesmill Long (London: Printed by G. Purslowe for H. Seile, 1625); May's verse translations republished in *John Barclay His Argenis,* prose translations by Sir Robert Le Grys (London: Printed by Felix Kyngston for Richard Meighen & Henry Seile, 1628);

Lucan's Pharsalia: Or, The Civill Warres of Rome, Betweene Pompey the Great, and Julius Caesar. The Three First Bookes, translated by May (London: Printed by J. Norton & A. Mathewes & sold by M. Law, 1626);

Lucan's Pharsalia. . . . The Whole Ten Bookes, translated by May (London: Printed by A. Mathewes for T. Jones & J. Marriott, 1627);

Virgil's Georgicks, translated by May (London: Printed by H. Lownes for T. Walkely, 1628);

Selected Epigrams of Martial, translated by May (London: Printed by H. Lownes for T. Walkley, 1629);

A Continuation of Lucan's Historicall Poem Till the Death of Julius Caesar (London: Printed by J. Haviland for J. Boler, 1630); republished in May's original Latin as *Supplementum Lucani* (London, 1640);

The Mirrour of Mindes, or, Barclay's Icon Animorum, translated by May (London: Printed by J. Norton for T. Walkley, 1631);

The Tragedy of Antigone (London: Printed by T. Harper for B. Fisher, 1631);

The Reigne of King Henry the Second, Written in Seaven Bookes. By his Majestie's Command (London: Printed by A. Mathewes & J. Beale for Benjamin Fisher, 1633);

The Victorious Reigne of King Edward the Third. Written in seven books. By his Majesty's Command (London: Printed by J. Beale for T. Walkley & B. Fisher, 1635);

The Tragedie of Cleopatra (London: Printed by T. Harper for T. Walkley, 1639);

The Tragedy of Julia Agrippina (London: Printed by R. Hodgkinsonne for T. Walkley, 1639);

Observations on the Effects of Former Parliaments (London, 1642);

A True Relation from Hull of the Present State and Condition It Is in (London: Printed by G. Dexter for John Bull, 1643);

The History of the Parliament of England, Which Began November the third, M.DC.XL. With a Short and Necessary View of Some Precedent Years (London: Printed by Moses Bell for George Thomason, 1647);

Historiae Parliamenti Angliae Breviarium, tribus partibus explicitum (London: Printed by Charles Sumpter & sold by Thomas Bruster, 1650); translated into English as *A Breviary of the History of the Parliament of England* (London: Printed by B. White for T. Brewster & O. Moule, 1650);

The Old Couple. A Comedy (London: Printed by J. Cottrel for Samuel Speed, 1658).

Edition: *The Old Couple,* edited by Sister M. Simplicia Fitzgibbons (Washington, D.C.: Catholic University of America Press, 1943).

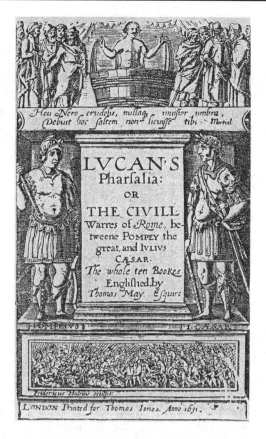

Title page for May's translation of the only surviving work by the first-century Latin poet Lucan (top). May later wrote a continuation of Lucan's poem in English and translated it into Latin. The copy below includes May's inscription to Dutch poet and scholar Daniël Heinsius (Sotheby's auction catalogue, sale number 2006, 17 July 1990)

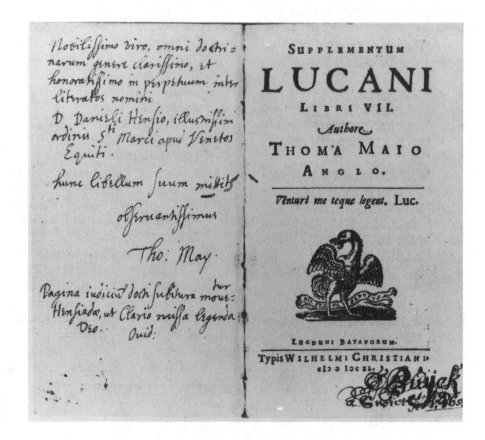

OTHER: *The Tournament of Tottenham,* prefatory verse by May (London, 1631);

Charles Aleyn, *The Battailes of Crescey and Poictiers,* second edition, enlarged, prefatory verse by May (London: Printed by T. Harper for T. Knight, 1633);

Ionsonvs Virbivs, includes an elegy by May (London: Printed by E. Purslow for H. Seile, 1638);

James Shirley, *Poems &c.,* prefatory verse by May (London: Printed for Humphrey Moseley, 1646);

The Lord George Digby's Cabinet and Dr. Goff's Negotiations, prefatory "Observations" by May and Thomas Sadler (London: Printed for Edward Husband, 1646);

"A Breviary of the History of the Parliament of England, 1655," in volume 1 of Francis Maseres's *Select Tracts Relating to the Civil Wars in England,* 2 volumes (London: R. Wilks, 1815).

PLAY PRODUCTIONS: See *DLB 58.*

Thomas May's "supplement of Lucan," writes Edward Hyde, Earl of Clarendon, in his *Life* (1857), "being entirely his own, for the learning, the wit, and the language, may be well looked upon as one of the best dramatic poems in the language." In *Athenæ Oxoniensis* (1691, 1692) Anthony Wood describes May's *Supplementum Lucani* (1640) as "written in so lofty and happy Lat. hexameter, that he hath attained to much more reputation abroad, than he hath lost at home."

Thomas May was the eldest son of Sir Thomas May of Mayfield, Sussex, who had married a daughter of the Rich family of Horndon-on-the-Hill in Essex. Young Thomas entered Sidney Sussex College, Cambridge, on 7 September 1609 as a fellow commoner and took the degree of B.A. in 1613 after distinguishing himself as a classical scholar. May was admitted to Gray's Inn on 6 August 1615. Prevented by a speech defect from practicing law, May turned to literature. His comedy *The Heire* was performed by the Revels Company in 1620 and praised in commendatory verses by Thomas Carew when it was published in 1622. After little success with another comedy and three tragedies, May tried translation, producing *Lucan's Pharsalia* (1626), *Virgil's Georgicks* (1628), and *Selected Epigrams of Martial* (1629). May followed his successful translation of Lucan with original continuations in Latin and English that continue the story to the death of Caesar. Ben Jonson's praise of the first translation of Lucan evidently gave May's work vis-

ibility: *A Continuation of Lucan's Historicall Poem* (1630) was dedicated to Charles I. Two command performance narrative poems on the reigns of Henry II (1633) and Edward III (1635) further suggest May's stature with Charles. The Texas Tech University copy of the first edition of *The Reigne of King Henry the Second* has extensive corrections, deletions, and emendations in a contemporary hand throughout the text of the poem; if the hand is May's, he may have been preparing a second edition. The verse "Argument of the first Booke" suggests the allegorical nature of the poem, though it does not adequately represent the relatively high quality of the verse:

> *The happy part of* Henry's *reigne is showne.*
> *His first Triumphant yeares and high renowne.*
> *His peace and power* Enyo *grieves to see;*
> *And to disturbe his long tranquillity*
> *Descending downe to* Lucifer *below*
> *She craves some Vices aide, to overthrow*
> *The causes of it: there these tragike times*
> *Of* Stephens *reigne, and* Englands *civill crimes*
> *So lately past,* Enyo *does relate;*
> *And shewes with griefe King* Henry's *present state.*
> *The Fiend foretells what suddaine change shall be*
> *Of* England's *peace, and his felicity.*

May, as Lucan's translator, is mentioned by Sir John Suckling as a candidate to succeed Jonson as poet laureate in 1637; and Charles, Sir Edward Sackville, fourth Earl of Dorset, and Philip Herbert, fourth Earl of Pembroke, recommended him for chronologer to the city of London. May's failure to receive either post may have caused him to side with Parliament during the civil wars. According to Wood, "Though he had received much countenance and a considerable donative from the king, upon his majesty's refusing him a small pension, which he had designed and promised to another very ingenious person, whose qualities he thought inferior to his own, he fell from his duty." The House of Commons appointed May and Thomas Sadler on 19 January 1646 to write a vindication "to the world the honour of the parliament, in this great cause of religion and liberty undertaken and maintained by the parliament." May thus published the *History of the Parliament of England* (1647) and *Historiae Parliamenti Angliae Breviarium* (1650, translated as *A Breviary of the History of the Parliament of England*). Even so, May was not a stereotypical Puritan: "he became a debauchee *ad omnia* (in all things), entertained ill principles as to religion, spoke often very slightly of the *Holy Trinity,* kept beastly and atheistical company," Wood wrote. Two accounts of the poet's death suggest his fondness for food and drink: Wood reported that May, "going well to bed, was therein found next morning dead ... occasion'd, as some say, by tying his night-cap too close under his fat chin and cheeks, which choak'd him, when he turned on the other side." In his *Miscellaneous Poems* (1681), Andrew Marvell claimed May died "As one put drunk into the packet-boat, / Tom May was hurried hence and did not know't." May was buried in Westminster Abbey but was removed by a warrant dated 9 September 1660 and, according to Wood, "buried in a large pit in the yard belonging to S. Margaret's church in Westminster." In 1670 his monument in Westminster Abbey was removed and replaced by that of Dr. Thomas Triplet.

Biography:

Allan Griffith Chester, *Thomas May: Man of Letters, 1595–1650* (Philadelphia: University of Pennsylvania, 1932).

References:

Leo Miller, "Milton's Patriis Cicutis," *Notes and Queries,* 28 (February 1981): 41–42;

Christine Rees, " 'Tom May's Death' and Ben Jonson's Ghost: A Study in Marvell's Satiric Method," *Modern Language Review,* 71 (July 1976): 481–488.

Papers:

Manuscripts for verse by Thomas May are at the British Library (Add. MS. 24492, f. 13^v and MS. Royal 18 c vii) and the Leeds Archives Department (MS. 237, ff. 85^v– 87^v.

James Shirley

(3 September 1596 – October 1666)

See also the Shirley entry in *DLB 58: Jacobean and Caroline Dramatists.*

BOOKS: *The Wedding* (London: Printed by J. Okes for J. Grove, 1629);

The Gratefull Servant. A Comedie (London: Printed by B. Alsop & T. Fawcet for J. Grove, 1630);

The Schoole of Complement (London: Printed by E. Allde for F. Constable, 1631); republished as *Love Tricks* (London: Printed for R. T., sold by Thomas Dring, Jr., 1667);

Changes: or, Love in a Maze. A Comedie (London: Printed by G. Purslowe for W. Cooke, 1632);

A Contention for Honour and Riches (London: Printed by E. Allde for W. Cooke, 1633);

The Wittie Faire One. A Comedie (London: Printed by B. Alsop & T. Fawcet for W. Cooke, 1633);

The Bird in a Cage. A Comedie (London: Printed by B. Alsop & T. Fawcet for W. Cooke, 1633);

The Triumph of Peace. A Masque (London: Printed by J. Norton for W. Cooke, 1633);

The Traytor. A Tragedie (London: Printed by J. Norton for W. Cooke, 1635);

Hide Park. A Comedie (London: Printed by T. Cotes for A. Crooke & W. Cooke, 1637);

The Lady of Pleasure, A Comedie (London: Printed by T. Cotes for A. Crooke & W. Cooke, 1637);

The Young Admirall (London: Printed by T. Cotes for A. Crooke & W. Cooke, 1637);

The Example (London: Printed by J. Norton for A. Crooke & W. Cooke, 1637);

The Gamester (London: Printed by J. Norton for A. Crooke & W. Cooke, 1637);

The Dukes Mistris (London: Printed by J. Norton for A. Crooke, 1638);

The Royall Master (London: Printed by T. Cotes, sold by J. Crooke & R. Serger, 1638);

The Ball. A Comedie (London: Printed by T. Cotes for A. Crooke & W. Cooke, 1639);

The Tragedie of Chabot Admirall of France, by George Chapman, revised by Shirley (London: Printed by T. Cotes for A. Crooke & W. Cooke, 1639);

The Maides Revenge. A Tragedy (London: Printed by T. Cotes for W. Cooke, 1639);

The Coronation: A Comedy (London: Printed by T. Cotes for A. Crooke & W. Cooke, 1640);

The Night-Walker, or The Little Theife, by John Fletcher, revised by Shirley (London: Printed by T. Cotes for A. Crooke & W. Cooke, 1640);

Loves Crueltie. A Tragedy (London: Printed by T. Cotes for A. Crooke, 1640);

The Opportunitie: A Comedy (London: Printed by T. Cotes for A. Crooke & W. Cooke, 1640);

James Shirley (engraving by W. Marshall from the 1646 edition of Shirley's Poems &c.*)*

The Humorous Courtier. A Comedy (London: Printed by T. Cotes for W. Cooke, sold by J. Becket, 1640);

A Pastorall Called The Arcadia (London: Printed by J. Dawson for J. Williams & F. Eglesfeild, 1640);

The Constant Maid. A Comedy (London: Printed by J. Raworth for R. Whitaker, 1640); republished as *Love Will Finde Out the Way* (London: Printed by Ja: Cotterel for Samuel Speed, 1661);

St. Patrick for Ireland. The First Part (London: Printed by J. Raworth for R. Whitaker, 1640);

Poems &c. (London: Printed for Humphrey Moseley, 1646); facsimile published as *Poems, 1646: To-*

gether with Poems from the Rawlinson Manuscript (Menston: Scolar Press, 1970);

Via ad Latinam Linguam Complanata; The Way Made Plaine to the Latine Tongue, the Rules Composed in English and Latine Verse (London: Printed by R. W. for John Stephenson, 1649); republished as *Grammatica anglo-latina. An English and Latine grammar* (London: Printed for Richard Lowndes, 1651);

Cupid and Death. A Masque (London: Printed by T. W. for J. Crook & J. Baker, 1653);

Six New Playes, viz. The Brothers. The Sisters. The Doubtful Heir. The Imposture. The Cardinall. The

Iacobus Shirlæus:

G Phenik pinx: R. Gaywood fecit 1658

Engraving by R. Gaywood after a portrait by G. Phenik (from the 1659 edition of Honoria and Mammon)

The Court Secret (London: Printed for Humphrey Robinson & Humphrey Moseley, 1653);

Grammaticae latinae institutiones (London: Printed by F. L. for R. L., 1654);

The Gentleman of Venice: A Tragi-Comedie (London: Printed for Humphrey Moseley, 1655);

The Polititian, A Tragedy (London: Printed for Humphrey Moseley, 1655);

[Eisagogae]; sive, introductorium Anglo-Latino-Graecum (London: Printed by J. G., sold by J. Crook, 1656);

The rudiments of grammar (London: Printed by J. Macock for R. Lownds, 1656); enlarged as Manductio; or, A Leading of Children by the Hand through the Principles of Grammar (London: Printed for Richard Lowndes, 1660);

No Wit, No Help Like a Woman's, by Thomas Middleton, possibly revised by Shirley (London: Printed for Humphrey Moseley, 1657);

Honoria and Mammon . . . Whereunto Is Added The Contention of Ajax and Ulisses, for the Armour of Achilles (London: Printed for John Crook, 1659);

An Ode upon the Happy Return of King Charles II. To His Languishing Nations, May 29, 1660 (London, 1660);

The True Impartial History and Wars of the Kingdom of Ireland, possibly by Shirley (London: Printed for Nicholas Boddington, 1692);

An Essay Towards an Universal and Rational Grammar; Together with Rules for Learning Latin, in English Verse, edited by Jenkin Thomas Philipps (London: Printed by J. Downing, 1726).

Editions: The Dramatic Works and Poems of James Shirley, edited by William Gifford and Alexander Dyce, 6 volumes (London: John Murray, 1833) — comprises Love Tricks, or, The School of Compliment; The Maid's Revenge; The Brothers; The Witty Fair One; The Wedding; The Grateful Servant; The Traitor; Love's Cruelty; Love in a Maze; The Bird in a Cage; Hyde Park; The Ball; The Young Admirall; The Gamester; The Example; The Opportunity; The Coronation; The Lady of Pleasure; The Royal Master; The Duke's Mistress; The Doubtful Heir; St. Patrick for Ireland; The Constant Maid; The Humorous Courtier; *The Gentleman of Venice; The Politician; The Imposture; The Cardinall; The Sisters; The Court Secret; Honoria and Mammon; Chabot, Admiral of France; The Arcadia; The Triumph of Peace; A Contention for Honor and Riches; The Triumph of Beauty; Cupid and Death; The Contention of Ajax and Ulysses for the Armour of Achilles;* and *Poems;*

The Poems of James Shirley, edited by Ray Livingstone Armstrong (New York: King's Crown, 1941).

OTHER: *Wits Labyrinth,* edited by Shirley (London: Printed for M. Simmons, 1648);

Robert Chamberlain, *The Harmony of the Muses,* includes a poem by Shirley (London: Printed by T. W. for William Gilbertson, 1654).

PLAY PRODUCTIONS: See *DLB 58.*

James Shirley was born on 3 September 1596 and baptized in London on 7 September 1596. He attended the Merchant Taylor's school from 1608 to 1612 and then entered Saint John's College, Oxford. By 1615 he had entered Catherine Hall, Cambridge, where he received the B.A. in 1617 and may have received the M.A. two years later. He married Elizabeth Gilmet in 1618, became an Anglican priest, and accepted a living at Wheathampstead in Hertfordshire. By 1621 he had, according to Anthony Wood, converted to Catholicism and become headmaster of a grammar school in Saint Albans. In 1624 he moved to London. By 1634 he was at Gray's Inn, and from 1636 to 1640 he wrote plays in Dublin. During the Interregnum, Shirley lived in Whitefriars, where he taught school and devoted his writing talents to producing Latin textbooks. After the great fire of 1666, Shirley and his second wife, Frances, moved to the parish of Saint Giles in the Field of Middlesex, where he and his wife died on the same day and were buried in Saint Giles on 29 October 1666.

Shirley's substantial talent as a dramatist has overshadowed his work as a poet, and many of his poems appear in, or as prologue or epilogue to, his plays. Even so, many of the verses in his *Poems &c.* (1646) rival those of Thomas Carew's in their Cavalier wit; his poem "One that loved none but deformed Women" echoes John Donne's "Elegie: The Anagram"; and his verse letters, critical poems on dramatic productions, verses on mortality, and poems on drinking, such as "To Gentlemen that Broke Their Promise of a Meeting, Made When They Drank Claret," mark him a "son" of Ben Jonson. Shirley is perhaps the most talented of the minor poets; among the Cavalier poets, only Jonson and Robert Herrick deserve more attention. No copies of his 1618 "Echo, or The Infortunate Lovers" survive; however, the work may be the lengthy poem *Narcissus* in his 1646 *Poems &c.* This erotic poem about a fatal unrequited love resembles William Shakespeare's *Venus and Adonis* (1593).

Bibliography:
Ruth K. Zimmer, *James Shirley: A Reference Guide* (Boston: Hall, 1980).

References:
George Bas, "Two misrepresented biographical documents concerning James Shirley," *Review of English Studies,* new series 27 (August 1976): 303–310;

R. G. Howarth, "Some Unpublished Poems of James Shirley," *Review of English Studies,* 9 (January 1933): 24–29;

Ben Lucow, *James Shirley* (Boston: Twayne, 1981);

Arthur Huntington Nason, *James Shirley, Dramatist* (New York: Privately printed, 1915);

Stephen J. Radtke, *James Shirley: His Catholic Philosophy of Life* (Washington, D.C.: Catholic University of America, 1929);

Felix E. Schelling, "Poems of James Shirley attributed to Carew and Goffe," *Modern Language Notes,* 11 (May 1896): 273–277.

Papers:
The Bodleian Library has a manuscript volume of poems (MS Rawl. poet, 88) thought to be in Shirley's hand. A manuscript for an early version of *The Court Secret,* in the hand of a scribe with later revisions in another hand, is at Worcester College, Oxford (MS 1200). The British Library has a manuscript for *Cupid and Death* (Add. MS 17799), and Shirley's will, in his own hand and dated July 1666, is at Somerset House.

Christopher Harvey the Younger
(1597–1663)

BOOKS: *The Synagogue, or The Shadow of the Temple. Sacred Poems and Private Ejaculations. In Imitation of George Herbert* (London: Printed by J. Legat for Philemon Stephens & C. Meredith, 1640;

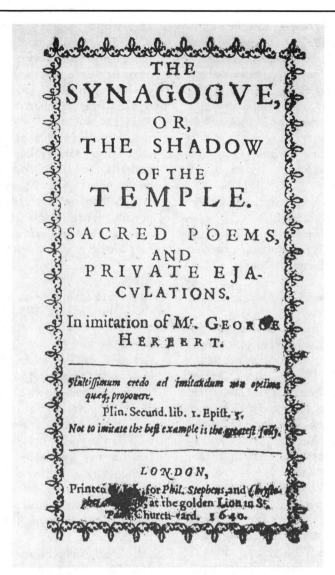

THE
SYNAGOGVE,
OR,
THE SHADOW
OF THE
TEMPLE.
SACRED POEMS,
AND
PRIVATE EJA-
CVLATIONS.

In imitation of Mr. GEORGE
HERBERT.

*stultiſſimum credo ad imitandum non optima
quæq; proponere.*
Plin. Secund. lib. 1. Epiſt. 5.
Not to imitate the beſt example is the greateſt folly.

LONDON,
Printed ... for *Phil. Stephens,* and *Chriſto-*
pher ... at the golden Lion in St.
Paul. Church-yard. 1640.

Title page for the poems in which Harvey, imitating George Herbert's The Temple, *depicted a sinner entering a church and undergoing salvation*

second edition, revised, London: Printed by J. Legat for Philemon Stephens, 1647; third edition, revised, London: Printed for Philemon Stephens, 1657; fourth edition, revised, 1661; fifth edition, revised, 1667; sixth edition, revised, London: Printed for Robert Stephens, 1673; seventh edition, revised, London: Printed by S. Roycroft for R. S., sold by John Williams, Jr., 1679);

Schola Cordis or the Heart of it Selfe, gone away from God; brought back againe to him; & instructed by him. In 47 Emblems (London: Printed for H. Blunden, 1647); republished as *The School of the Heart* (London: Printed for Lodowick Lloyd, 1664);

Αφηνιαστης: *or, The Right Rebel. A Treatise discov-* *ering the true Use of the Name by the Nature of Rebellion* (London: Printed for R. Royston, 1661); republished as *Faction Supplanted: or, A Caveat against the ecclesiasticall and secular Rebell* (London: Printed for R. Royston, 1663).

Editions: *The Synagogue,* in *The Poetical Works of George Herbert,* edited by George Gilfillan (Edinburgh: J. Nichol, 1853);

The Complete Poems of Christopher Harvey, edited by Alexander B. Grosart (London: Robson & Sons, 1874).

OTHER: Thomas Pierson, *Excellent encouragements against afflictions, or, Expositions of four select Psalmes: the XXVII, LXXXIV, LXXXV, and*

LXXXVII, edited by Harvey (London: Printed by John Legatt for Philemon Stephens, 1647).

Christopher Harvey's *Synagogue* (1640) consists of a series of twenty-two short poems beginning with "The Church-yard" and "The Church-porch" and moving on to "Travels at home." The poems, like those in George Herbert's *The Temple* (1633), show a sinner entering the church and experiencing the psychological and spiritual stages of salvation. A few of the poems, like "Confusion," connect physical and intellectual structure and show a sense of paradox, though the use of extended metaphor and shape is not as complex or logical as in Herbert. Izaak Walton contributed commendatory verses to the fourth edition of *The Synagogue* (1661) and quoted a poem from Harvey's collection in the 1655 edition of *The Compleat Angler*. Harvey adapted the emblems in his *Schola Cordis* (1647) from Benedictus van Haeften's 1629 work of the same title.

Harvey was the son of the Reverend Christopher Harvey of Bunbury in Cheshire. He attended Brasenose College, Oxford, in 1613; graduated B.A. on 19 May 1617; and was licensed M.A. on 1 February 1620. By 1630 he was rector of Whitney in Herefordshire. At Michaelmas in 1632 he became headmaster of Kington grammar school but returned to Whitney on or before the following 25 March, when a new headmaster was appointed. Between 1630 and 1639 five of his children were baptized at Whitney. Sir Robert Whitney obtained for him the vicarage of Clifton on Dunsmore, Warwickshire, which Harvey assumed on 14 November 1639. On 4 April 1663 he was buried at Clifton.

Reference:

Ilona Bell, "Herbert and Harvey: In the Shadow of the Temple," in *Like Season'd Timber: New Essays on George Herbert* (New York: Lang, 1987), pp. 255–280.

Thomas Washbourne

(1606 – 6 May 1687)

BOOKS: *Divine Poems* (London: Printed for Humphrey Moseley, 1654);

A Sermon Preached at the Funerall of Charles Cocks (London: Printed for Henry Twyford & John Place, 1655);

The Repairer of the Breach; a Sermon Preached at the Cathedral Church of Glocester May 29, 1661. Being the Anniversary of His Majesty's Birth-day, and Happy Entrance into His Emperial City of London (London: Printed for William Leak, 1661);

Edition: *The Poems of Thomas Washbourne,* edited by Alexander B. Grosart (Blackburn: C. Tiplady, 1868).

OTHER: Samuel Egerton Brydges, volume 4 of *The British Bibliographer,* includes poems by Washbourne (London: Printed for R. Triphook by T. Bensley, 1814).

John Milton's nephew Edward Phillips prefixed verses to Thomas Washbourne's *Divine Poems* (1654). Many of the *Divine Poems* are on specific biblical verses and resemble the poems found in emblem literature. The poems are frequently straightforward and didactic, though the very best poems attain a meditative quality (in "To the Reader," Washbourne refers to his poems as "meditations") much like those of George Herbert. The first two stanzas of "What Is Man" support this comparison:

> LORD, what is man that Thou
> So mindful art of him? Or what's the Son
> Of man, that Thou the highest heaven didst bow
> And to his aide didst runne?
> He is not worthy of the least
> Of all Thy mercies at the best.
>
> Man's but a piece of clay
> That's animated by Thy heavenly breath,
> And when that breath Thou tak'st away,
> Hee's clay again by death.
> He is not worthy of the least
> Of all Thy mercies, at the best.

Not all of the poems are meditations: there are pastoral dramatic dialogues, memento mori poems (such as "Upon a Passing Bel" and "Upon the Setting of a Clock-larum"), and verse letters. Washbourne's debt to Herbert is obvious, but occasionally the influence of Henry Vaughan appears in a poem, such as "Upon His Walking One Day Abroad, When Sometimes the Sun Shone and Sometimes the Winde Blew Cold on Him";

and sometimes Washbourne reaches (generally unsuccessfully) for the wit of John Donne, as in "To One that Married a very Rich, but a very Deformed Woman."

Thomas Washbourne was the younger son of John Washbourne of Wichenford, Worcestershire, by his second wife, Elenor, daughter of Richard Lygon of Madresfield, ancestor of the earls Beauchamp. Washbourne entered Balliol College, Oxford, as a commoner in 1622 and graduated with a bachelor of arts degree on 13 February 1626, a master of arts degree on 25 June 1628, and a bachelor of divinity degree on 1 April 1636. In 1639 he was made rector of Loddington, Northamptonshire, and in 1640 of Dumbleton, Gloucestershire. In 1643 he was nominated to a prebend in Gloucestershire Cathedral and is said to have been installed in the night because of the Civil War. The status of his livings during the Commonwealth remains uncertain. At the Restoration he was formally presented to his prebend on 23 July 1660, admitted on 7 August, and created doctor of divinity at Oxford on 16 August. From 1660 to 1668 he was vicar of Saint Mary's, Gloucester, where he is buried.

Papers:

A letter dated 7 January 1650 from Washbourne to Robert Sanderson, bishop of Lincoln, is preserved at Lincoln College, Oxford.

Sir Aston Cokayne

(December 1608 – February 1684)

BOOKS: *The Obstinate Lady: a New Comedy* (London: Printed by W. Godbid for Isaac Pridmore, 1657);

Small Poems of Divers Sorts Written by Sir Aston Cokain (London: Printed by Wil. Godbid, 1658); enlarged as *A Chain of Golden Poems, embellished with wit, mirth, and eloquence, together with two most excellent comedies, viz. The Obstinate Lady and Trappolin suppos'd a Prince, written by Sir Aston Cokayn* (London: Printed by W. Godbid, sold by Isaac Pridmore, 1658); enlarged as *Poems, with The Obstinate Lady and Trappolin supposed a Prince, by Sir Aston Cokain, Baronet; whereunto is now added The Tragedy of Ovid* (London: Printed for Phil. Stephens, Jr., 1662); republished as *Choice Poems of Several Sorts, With Three New Plays* (London: Printed for Francis Kirkman, 1669);

The Tragedy of Ovid (London: Printed for Philomen Stephens, Jr., 1662).

Edition: *The Dramatic Works of Sir Aston Cokain*, edited by James Maidment and William H. Logan (Edinburgh: W. Paterson / London: H. Sotheran, 1874).

OTHER: Giovanni Francesco Loredano, *Dianea: An Excellent New Romance,* translated by Cokayne (London: Printed for Humphrey Moseley, 1654).

Nahum Tate's *Duke and No Duke* (1684) and Robert Drury's *The Devil of a Duke: or, Trapolin's vagaries. A (farcical ballad) Opera* (1732) both derive from Sir Aston Cokayne's *Trappolin suppos'd a Prince* (1658). In *Athenæ Oxoniensis* (1691, 1692) it is noted that *Tyrannical Government anatomized, or a Discourse concerning evil Counsellors: being the Life and Death of John the Baptist* (1642) has been attributed to Cokayne, but Anthony Wood doubts his authorship. This work, retitled *Baptistes, a sacred Dramatic Poem*, was published as John Milton's in 1740 by Francis Peck.

Cokayne's verse has an unusually large autobiographical and biographical component: much of what is known about his life comes from his poems, and the *Dictionary of National Biography* notes that "For genealogical purposes . . . these numerous poems and epitaphs are invaluable, the number of persons and facts therein mentioned being probably without parallel." Cokayne incorporated line 65 of John Donne's *Second Anniversary* (1612) in lines 25 and 26 of "An Epitaph on Elizabeth the Lady Reppington, who deceased at Ammington, about the 50. year of her age, and lies buried at Tamworth" (1658). Thomas Bancroft, his neighbor, wrote of Cokayne in his 1639 *Two Bookes of Epigrammes and Epitaphs:* "He that with learning vertue doth combine, / May, tho' a laick, passe for *a divine / Piece of perfection;* such to all men's sight / Appeares yourselfe." Bancroft also prefixed a poem "To His Noble Friend Sir Aston Cokain on his Poetical Composures" to *A Chain of Golden Poems* (1658). "The Authors Epistle" to Cokayne's translation of Giovanni Francesco Loredano's *Dianea* (1654) is dated 25 October 1635; the work may

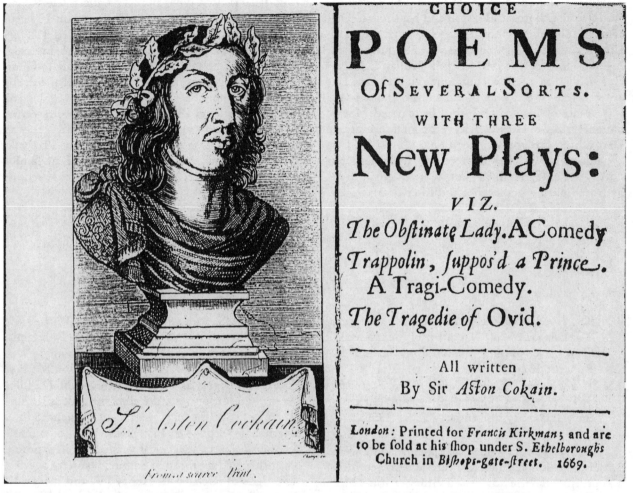

CHOICE
POEMS
OF SEVERAL SORTS.

WITH THREE

New Plays:
VIZ.

The Obſtinate Lady. A Comedy

Trappolin, ſuppos'd a Prince.
A Tragi-Comedy.

The Tragedie of Ovid.

All written
By Sir *Aſton Cokain.*

London: Printed for *Francis Kirkman*; and are
to be ſold at his ſhop under S. *Ethelboroughs*
Church in *Biſhops-gate-ſtreet.* 1669.

Frontispiece and title page for the last seventeenth-century edition of Sir Aston Cokayne's poems and plays

have been published as early as 1643, as suggested by the editor of *Athenæ Oxoniensis* (1813–1820), Philip Bliss, but no copy printed earlier than the 1654 edition survives. Wood says that Cokayne "was esteemed by many an ingenious gent. a good poet and a great lover of learning, yet by others a perfect boon fellow, by which means he wasted all he had."

Cokayne in "To my honoured friend Major William Warner" sums up the diversity of his literary output:

Playes, Eclogues, Songs, a Satyre I have writ,
A remedy for those 'ith amorous fit,
Love Elegies, and Funeral Elegies,
Letters of things of divers qualities,
Encomiastick Lines to works of some,
A Masque, and an Epithalamium,
Two Books of Epigrams: All which I mean
Shall (in this volume) come upon the Scene;
Some divine Poems, which (when first I came
To *Cambridge*) I writ there, I need not name;

Of *Dianea*, neither my Translation,
Omitted here as of another fashion.
For heavens sake name no more you say, I cloy you:
I do obey you; Therefore (friend) God b'wy you.

Cokayne's epigrams are most often personal, sometimes in appreciation of other poets (Geoffrey Chaucer and Edmund Spenser in book 3, epigrams 36 and 37), and occasionally bawdy and witty.

Cokayne came from an ancient family long seated at Ashbourne in Derbyshire which by marriage with the heiress of the family of Herthull had acquired large estates in several midland counties, including the lordship of Pooley (in Polesworth), Warwickshire. Cokayne's parents were Thomas Cokayne – the son and heir of Sir Edward Cokayne, the youngest son but eventually heir of Sir Thomas Cokayne – and Anne Stanhope Cokayne, half sister of Philip Stanhope, first Earl of Chesterfield, daughter of Sir John Stanhope of Elvaston, Derbyshire, by his second wife, Dorothy, daughter of Thomas Trentham of Rocester, Staffordshire. Born at Elvaston and baptized 20 December 1608 at Ashbourne, Aston was educated at Chenies school, Buckinghamshire, of which Peter Allibond was rector. He went to Trinity College, Cambridge, as a fellow commoner about 1624. He entered one of the Inns of Court and about 1642 was created M.A. at Oxford. He married Mary, daughter of Sir Gilbert Knyveton of Mercaston, Derbyshire. His son was born on 8 May 1636. On 26 January 1639 Cokayne succeeded, by his father's death, to Pooley Hall, but not to the estate of Ashbourne, held by his mother until her death on 29

August 1664. Cokayne, a loyal Anglican and Royalist, was created a baronet by Charles I on 10 January 1642, but the patent was never enrolled. His fortunes declined dramatically during the Interregnum: in 1671 he sold the Ashbourne estate to Humphrey Jennings, and he sold Pooley after the death of his wife there in May of 1683. He was buried next to his wife on 13 February 1684 at Polesworth. His only son having died childless, Cokayne was succeeded by his daughters Mary Lacy and Isabella Turville; and the male representation of the family apparently devolved on Bryan Cokayne, Viscount Cullen.

George Daniel

(29 March 1616 – September 1657)

BOOKS: *The Poems of George Daniel, Esq., of Beswick, Yorkshire (1616-1657)*, edited by Alexander B. Grosart, 4 volumes (Boston, Lincolnshire: R. Roberts, 1878);

The Selected Poems of George Daniel of Beswick 1616-1657, edited by Thomas B. Stroup (Lexington: University of Kentucky Press, 1959).

George Daniel's surviving poems (some were evidently destroyed in a fire) are in a signed folio manuscript in the British Library (Add. MS. 19255). The manuscript volume is enriched with several oil paintings (some of which – including a full-length, nude study of a nymph – may be by Daniel himself), four of which are portraits of Daniel, one hand in hand with his brother Thomas. In his "A Vindication of Poesie," Daniel calls Ben Jonson "Of English Drammatickes the Prince," and he speaks slightingly of "comicke Shakespeare." On the death of Jonson in 1637, Daniel wrote a panegyric "To the Memorie of the best Dramaticke English Poet, Ben Jonson." His *Occasional Poems* and *Scattered Fancies* were completed respectively in 1645 and 1646. He celebrated the charm of tobacco in "To Nicotiana, a Rapture." *Chronicles* and *Polylogia; or, Several Eclogues*, as well as the paraphrase *Ecclesiasticus* probably date from 1638 to 1648. He wrote *Trinarchodia* in 1649 and "Idyllia" in 1650, revising the latter in 1653. His poems circulated individually in manuscript among his friends.

Daniel considered himself a "son of Ben" but was influenced by a wide variety of contemporary poets – Sir Philip Sidney, Edmund Spenser, Francis Beaumont, John Fletcher, William Shakespeare, Michael Drayton, Samuel Daniel, George Wither, Sir John Suckling, Thomas Carew, Thomas Randolph, George Herbert, John Ogilby, George Sandys, William Habington, Thomas Stapleton, Thomas May, Sir Kenelm Digby, and James Shirley – though John Donne and Jonson were the chief influences. Unfortunately, Daniel's poems were more influenced than original (except for his poems on hawking). *Trinarchodia*, is an allegorical verse chronicle (probably influenced by those of Samuel Daniel) covering the reigns of Richard II, Henry IV, and Henry V. *Vervicensis*, dated 1639, is a complaint of Richard Neville, Earl of Warwick. *The Genius of this Great and glorious Isle*, dated 1637, defends Charles I. Daniel's *Scattered Fancies* consists of fifty-nine odes in a variety of forms. *Polylogia; or, Several Ecloges* are five long pastorals with significant political allegory and satire. *Idyllia: The Distemper* is a series of five "Idyls" (more satire) followed by six poems about painting that satirize the enemies of Charles I. *Love Platonicke*, dated 1642, is a series of eight odes. The remaining poems are personal and occasional.

Daniel, born in Beswick – a chapelry and estate in the parish of Kilnwick, Yorkshire, East Riding – was the second son of Sir Ingleby Daniel by his second wife, Frances, daughter and heiress of George Metham of Pollington, in the parish of Snaith. William Daniel, the eldest son, died unmarried and was buried at Saint Michael's Ousebridge, Yorkshire, 4 May 1644. George and the third son, Thomas, later Sir Thomas Daniel, captain in the foot-guards, were close friends. George seldom left home and his books. He had two sisters, Katharine (who married John Yorke of Gowthwaite and died

Four self-portraits in oil included in a manuscript volume of George Daniel's poems (British Library, Add. MS. 19255). In the first (top left) Daniel is shaking hands with his brother Thomas. The Daniel coat of arms is included in the second (top right). In the third (bottom left), painted after the execution of Charles I, Daniel is wearing the beard he grew to commemorate the death of his sovereign, while in the fourth (bottom right) he depicted himself as a Roman pastoral poet.

in March 1644) and Elizabeth. After the death of King Charles I in 1649, Daniel lived in retirement and let his beard grow in memory of 30 January, the date of Charles's execution. Daniel married Elizabeth, daughter of William Ireland of Nostell, Yorkshire, and Elizabeth, daughter and coheiress of Robert Molyneux of Euxton, Lancashire. The property Daniel's wife brought revived his failing fortunes. Their only son, a second George Daniel, died in infancy and was buried in Saint Giles in the Fields, London. The mother's wealth descended to three daughters, Frances, Elizabeth, and Girarda; the latter two married, but Girarda alone left issue, Elizabeth, in whom the direct line from George Daniel ended. Daniel himself was buried on 25 September 1657 in the churchyard of All Saints, Kilnwick.

Reference:

Raymond A. Anselment, "George Daniel and the Celebration of Caroline Peace," *Essays in Literature,* 12 (Spring 1985): 27–39.

Checklist of Further Readings

Aers, David, Bob Hodge, and Gunther Kress. *Literature, Language and Society in England 1580–1680*. Dublin: Gill & Macmillan / Totowa, N.J.: Barnes & Noble, 1981.

Alden, Raymond M. *The Rise of Formal Satire in England Under Classical Influence*, Publications of the University of Pennsylvania Series in Philology, Literature, and Archaeology, 7, no. 2. Philadelphia: University of Pennsylvania, 1899.

Allen, Don Cameron. *Doubt's Boundless Sea: Skepticism and Faith in the Renaissance*. Baltimore: Johns Hopkins University Press, 1964.

Ashley, Maurice. *England in the Seventeenth Century*, revised. New York: Barnes & Noble, 1980.

Aubrey, John. *Aubrey's Brief Lives*, edited by Oliver Lawson Dick, third edition, revised. London: Secker & Warburg, 1958.

Baker, Herschel C. *The Wars of Truth: Studies in the Decay of Christian Humanism in the Earlier Seventeenth Century*. Cambridge, Mass.: Harvard University Press, 1952.

Bennett, Joan. *Five Metaphysical Poets: Donne, Herbert, Vaughan, Crashaw, Marvell*, third edition. Cambridge: Cambridge University Press, 1964.

Bethell, Samuel Leslie. *The Cultural Revolution of the 17th Century*. London: Dobson, 1951.

Bradbury, Malcolm, and David Palmer, eds. *Metaphysical Poetry*. London: Arnold, 1970.

Bush, Douglas. *English Literature in the Earlier Seventeenth Century 1600–1660*, second edition, revised. Oxford: Clarendon Press, 1962.

Cain, T. G. S., and Ken Robinson, eds., *"Into Another Mould": Change and Continuity in English Culture, 1625–1700*. London & New York: Routledge, 1992.

Carlton, Charles. *Charles I, the Personal Monarch*. London & Boston: Routledge & Kegan Paul, 1983.

Chambers, A. B. *Transfigured Rites in Seventeenth-Century English Poetry*. Columbia: University of Missouri Press, 1992.

Colie, Rosalie L. *Paradoxia Epidemica: The Renaissance Tradition of Paradox*. Princeton: Princeton University Press, 1966.

Colie. *The Resources of Kind; Genre-Theory in the Renaissance*, edited by Barbara K. Lewalski. Berkeley: University of California Press, 1973.

Cook, Elizabeth. *Seeing Through Words: The Scope of Late Renaissance Poetry*. New Haven: Yale University Press, 1986.

Cruttwell, Patrick. "The Metaphysical Poets and their Readers," *Humanities Association Review*, 28 (Winter 1977): 20–42.

Cruttwell. *The Shakespearean Moment and its Place in the Poetry of the 17th Century*. London: Chatto & Windus, 1954.

Davies, Horton. *Worship and Theology in England*, 5 volumes. Princeton: Princeton University Press, 1961–1975.

Eliot, T. S. "The Metaphysical Poets," in *Selected Essays*, third edition, enlarged. London: Faber & Faber, 1951, pp. 281–291.

Ellrodt, Robert. *L'Inspiration personelle et l'esprit du temps chez les poetes metaphysiques anglais*, 3 volumes. Paris: J. Corti, 1960–1973.

Ezell, Margaret J. M. *The Patriarch's Wife: Literary Evidence and the History of the Family*. Chapel Hill: University of North Carolina Press, 1987.

Fish, Stanley E. *Self-Consuming Artifacts: The Experience of Seventeenth-Century Literature*. Berkeley: University of California Press, 1972.

Fowler, Alastair. *A History of English Literature*. Cambridge: Harvard University Press, 1987.

Fowler, ed. *The New Oxford Book of Seventeenth Century Verse*. Oxford & New York: Oxford University Press, 1991.

Fraistat, Neil, ed. *Poems in Their Place: The Intertextuality and Order of Poetic Collections*. Chapel Hill: University of North Carolina Press, 1986.

Fraser, Russell A. *The War Against Poetry*. Princeton: Princeton University Press, 1970.

Freeman, Rosemary. *English Emblem Books*. London: Chatto & Windus, 1948.

Goldberg, Jonathan. *James I and the Politics of Literature: Jonson, Shakespeare, Donne, and Their Contemporaries*. Baltimore: Johns Hopkins University Press, 1983.

Gordon, D. J. *The Renaissance Imagination: Essays and Lectures*, edited by Stephen Orgel. Berkeley: University of California Press, 1975.

Gottlieb, Sidney, ed. *Approaches to Teaching the Metaphysical Poets*. New York: Modern Language Association of America, 1990.

Grant, Patrick. *The Transformation of Sin: Studies in Donne, Herbert, Vaughan and Traherne*. Montreal: McGill-Queen's University Press / Amherst: University of Massachusetts Press, 1974.

Grierson, H. J. C. *Cross Currents in English Literature of the XVIIth Century: or, the World, the Flesh, & the Spirit, Their Actions and Reactions*. London: Chatto & Windus, 1929.

Halewood, William H. *The Poetry of Grace; Reformation Themes and Structures in English Seventeenth-Century Poetry*. New Haven: Yale University Press, 1970.

Hammond, Gerald. *Fleeting Things: English Poets and Poems, 1616–1660*. Cambridge: Harvard University Press, 1990.

Harris, Victor. *All Coherence Gone*. Chicago: University of Chicago Press, 1949.

Haselkorn, Anne M., and Betty S. Travitsky, eds. *The Renaissance Englishwoman in Print: Counterbalancing the Canon.* Amherst: University of Massachusetts Press, 1990.

Haydn, Hiram C. *The Counter-Renaissance.* New York: Scribners, 1950.

Helgerson, Richard. *Forms of Nationhood: The Elizabethan Writing of England.* Chicago: University of Chicago Press, 1992.

Hill, Christopher. *Puritans and Revolution: Studies in Interpretation of the English Revolution of the 17th Century,* edited by Donald Pennington and Keith Thomas. Oxford: Clarendon Press, 1978.

Hill. *Society and Puritanism in Pre-Revolutionary England.* London: Secker & Warburg, 1964.

Holden, William P. *Anti-Puritan Satire, 1572–1642.* New Haven: Yale University Press, 1954.

Hollander, John. *The Untuning of the Sky: Ideas of Music in English Poetry 1500–1700.* Princeton: Princeton University Press, 1961.

Joseph, B. L. *Shakespeare's Eden: The Commonwealth of England, 1558–1629.* London: Blanford Press, 1971.

Kahn, Victoria. *Rhetoric, Prudence, and Skepticism in the Renaissance.* Ithaca, N.Y.: Cornell University Press, 1985.

Kay, Dennis. *Melodious Tears: The English Funeral Elegy from Spenser to Milton.* Oxford: Clarendon Press / New York: Oxford University Press, 1990.

Keast, William R., ed. *Seventeenth-Century English Poetry; Modern Essays in Criticism.* New York: Oxford University Press, 1962.

Kernan, Alvin B. *The Cankered Muse: Satire of the English Renaissance.* New Haven: Yale University Press, 1959.

Knights, L. C. *Drama and Society in the Age of Jonson.* London: Chatto & Windus, 1937.

Lamont, William M. *Godly Rule: Politics and Religion, 1603–60.* London: Macmillan / New York: St. Martin's Press, 1969.

Lecocq, Louis. *La Satire en Angleterre 1588 a 1603.* Montreal, Paris & Brussels: Didier, 1969.

Lee, Maurice, Jr. *Great Britain's Solomon: James VI and I in His Three Kingdoms.* Urbana: University of Illinois Press, 1990.

Lee, ed. *Dudley Carleton to John Chamberlain, 1603–1624; Jacobean Letters.* New Brunswick: Rutgers University Press, 1972.

Leishman, J. B. *The Metaphysical Poets: Donne, Herbert, Vaughan, Traherne.* Oxford: Clarendon Press, 1934.

Lewalski, Barbara K. *Protestant Poetics and the Seventeenth-Century Religious Lyric.* Princeton: Princeton University Press, 1979.

Lovejoy, Arthur O. *The Great Chain of Being; A Study of the History of an Idea.* Cambridge: Harvard University Press, 1936.

Low, Anthony. *Love's Architecture: Devotional Modes in Seventeenth-Century English Poetry.* New York: New York University Press, 1978.

Lyons, Bridget Gellert. *Voices of Melancholy: Studies in Literary Treatments of Melancholy in Renaissance England.* London: Routledge & Kegan Paul, 1971.

Lyons, John D., and Stepen G. Nichols, Jr., eds. *Mimesis, from Mirror to Method, Augustine to Descartes.* Hanover: University Press of New England, 1982.

Mahood, Molly M. *Poetry and Humanism.* London: Cape, 1950.

Manley, Lawrence. *Convention, 1500–1750.* Cambridge: Harvard University Press, 1980.

Martines, Lauro. *Society and History in English Renaissance Verse.* Oxford: Blackwell, 1985.

Martz, Louis L. *The Poetry of Meditation: A Study in English Religious Literature of the Seventeenth Century.* New Haven: Yale University Press, 1954.

Martz. *The Wit of Love.* Notre Dame: University of Notre Dame Press, 1969.

Mazzaro, Jerome. *Transformations in the Renaissance English Lyric.* Ithaca, N.Y.: Cornell University Press, 1970.

Mazzeo, Joseph A. *Renaissance and Revolution: Backgrounds to Seventeenth-Century English Literature.* New York: Pantheon, 1967.

Mazzeo. *Renaissance and Seventeenth-Century Studies.* New York: Columbia University Press, 1964.

McCanles, Michael. *Dialectical Criticism and Renaissance Literature.* Berkeley: University of California Press, 1975.

McClung, William Alexander. *The Country House in English Renaissance Poetry.* Berkeley: University of California Press, 1977.

Miner, Earl. *The Cavalier Mode From Jonson to Cotton.* Princeton: Princeton University Press, 1971.

Miner. *The Metaphysical Mode from Donne to Cowley.* Princeton: Princeton University Press, 1969.

Miner, ed. *Seventeenth-Century Imagery: Essays on Uses of Figurative Language from Donne to Farquhar.* Berkeley: University of California Press, 1971.

Mulder, John R. *The Temple of the Mind: Education and Literary Taste in Seventeenth-Century England.* New York: Pegasus, 1969.

Neale, J. E. *The Age of Catherine de Medici and Essays in Elizabethan History.* London: Cape, 1943.

Nevo, Ruth. *The Dial of Virtue: A Study of Poems on Affairs of State in the Seventeenth Century.* Princeton: Princeton University Press, 1963.

Nicolson, Marjorie Hope. *The Breaking of the Circle: Studies in the Effect of the "New Science" upon Seventeenth-Century Poetry,* revised edition. New York: Columbia University Press, 1962.

Owens, W. R., ed. *Seventeenth-Century England: A Changing Culture,* volume 2. London: Ward Lock Educational, in association with the Open University Press, 1980.

Parfitt, George. *English Poetry of the Seventeenth Century.* London & New York: Longman, 1985.

Parry, Graham. *The Seventeenth Century: The Intellectual and Cultural Context of English Literature, 1603–1700*. London & New York: Longman, 1989.

Patrides, C. A., and Raymond B. Waddington, eds. *The Age of Milton: Backgrounds to Seventeenth-Century Literature*. Manchester: Manchester University Press / Totowa, N.J.: Barnes & Noble, 1980.

Patterson, Annabel. *Censorship and Interpretation: The Conditions of Writing and Reading in Early Modern England*. Madison: University of Wisconsin Press, 1984.

Praz, Mario. *Studies in Seventeenth-Century Imagery*, 2 volumes, second edition, enlarged. Rome: Edizioni di storia e letteratura, 1964, 1974.

Ricks, Christopher, ed. *English Poetry and Prose, 1540–1674*. London: Barrie & Jenkins, 1970.

Rivers, Isabel. *Classical and Christian Ideas in English Renaissance Poetry: A Students' Guide*. London & Boston: Allen & Unwin, 1979.

Ross, Malcolm M. *Poetry and Dogma: The Transfiguration of Eucharist Symbols in Seventeenth Century English Poetry*. New Brunswick: Rutgers University Press, 1954.

Røstvig, Maren-Sofie. *The Happy Man: Studies in the Metamorphoses of a Classical Ideal*, 2 volumes, revised. Oslo: Norwegian Universities Press, 1962, 1971.

Selden, Raman. *English Verse Satire, 1590–1765*. London & Boston: Allen & Unwin, 1978.

Sharp, Robert L. *From Donne to Dryden: The Revolt Against Metaphysical Poetry*. Chapel Hill: University of North Carolina Press, 1940.

Sharpe, Kevin, and Steven N. Zwicker, eds. *Politics of Discourse; The Literature and History of Seventeenth-Century England*. Berkeley: University of California Press, 1987.

Shawcross, John T. *Intentionality and the New Traditionalism: some liminal means to Literary Revisionism*. University Park: Pennsylvania State University Press, 1991.

Singleton, Marion White. *God's Coutier: Configuring a Different Grace in George Herbert's "Temple."* Cambridge: Cambridge University Press, 1987.

Smith, A. J. *Metaphysical Wit*. Cambridge & New York: Cambridge University Press, 1991.

Smith. *The Metaphysics of Love: Studies in Renaissance Love Poetry from Dante to Milton*. Cambridge & New York: Cambridge University Press, 1985.

Smith, James. "On Metaphysical Poetry," *Scrutiny*, 2 (December 1933): 222–239.

Spingarn, J. E., ed. *Critical Essays of the Seventeenth Century*, 3 volumes. Bloomington: Indiana University Press, 1957.

Stewart, Stanley. *The Enclosed Garden; The Tradition and the Image in Seventeenth-Century Poetry*. Madison: University of Wisconsin Press, 1966.

Stone, Lawrence. *The Causes of the English Revolution, 1529–1642*. New York: Harper & Row, 1972.

Stone. *The Family, Sex and Marriage in England, 1500–1800*. New York: Harper & Row, 1977.

Summers, Claude, and Ted-Larry Pebworth, eds., *"Bright Shootes of Everlastingnesse": the Seventeenth-Century Religious Lyric.* Columbia: University of Missouri Press, 1987.

Summers and Pebworth, eds., *"The Muses Common-Weale": Poetry and Politics in the Seventeenth Century.* Columbia: University of Missouri Press, 1988.

Summers, Joseph H. *The Heirs of Donne and Jonson.* New York: Oxford University Press, 1970.

Swardson, H. R. *Poetry and the Fountain of Light: Observations on the Conflict Between Christian and Classical Traditions in Seventeenth-Century Poetry.* London: Allen & Unwin, 1962.

Tayler, Edward William. *Nature and Art in Renaissance Literature.* New York: Columbia University Press, 1964.

Thomas, P. W., "Two Cultures? Court and Country under Charles I," in *The Origins of the Civil War,* edited by Conrad Russell. New York: Macmillan, 1973, pp. 168–193;

Thomson, Elizabeth M., ed. *The Chamberlain Letters; A Selection of the Letters of John Chamberlain Concerning Life in England from 1597 to 1626.* New York: Putnam's, 1965.

Tuve, Rosemond. *Elizabethan and Metaphysical Imagery; Renaissance Poetic and Twentieth-Century Critics.* Chicago: University of Chicago Press, 1947.

Vickers, Brian. *Classical Rhetoric in English Poetry.* London: Macmillan / New York: St. Martin's Press, 1970.

Wallerstein, Ruth C. *Studies in Seventeenth-Century Poetic.* Madison: University of Wisconsin Press, 1950.

C. V. Wedgwood. *Poetry and Politics Under the Stuarts.* Cambridge: Cambridge University Press, 1960.

Wedgwood. *Seventeenth-Century English Literature,* second edition. London: Oxford University Press, 1950.

Willey, Basil. *The Seventeenth Century Background; Studies in the Thought of the Age in Relation to Poetry and Religion.* London: Chatto & Windus, 1934.

Williamson, George. *The Donne Tradition; A Study in English Poetry from Donne to the Death of Cowley.* Cambridge, Mass.: Harvard University Press, 1930.

Wilson, F. P. *Elizabethan and Jacobean.* Oxford: Clarendon Press, 1945.

Wilson, Katharina M., and Frank J. Warnke, eds. *Women Writers of the Seventeenth Century.* Athens: University of Georgia Press, 1989.

Wood, Anthony. *Athen Oxonienses,* 5 volumes, edited by Philip Bliss. London: Printed for F. C. & J. Rivington, 1813–1820.

Contributors

Raymond A. Anselment...*University of Connecticut*
James Applegate...*Wilson College*
Joan S. Applegate...*Shippensburg University of Pennsylvania*
Meg Lota Brown...*University of Arizona*
M. L. Donnelly...*Kansas State University*
Charles Clay Doyle...*University of Georgia*
Jack D. Durant...*North Carolina State University*
Robert Thomas Fallon ....*La Salle University*
Dennis Flynn..*Bentley College*
Sidney Gottlieb...*Sacred Heart University*
Charles A. Huttar...*Hope College*
Daniel P. Jaeckle...*University of Houston-Victoria*
George Klawitter ....*Viterbo College*
Charles M. Kovich...*Rockhurst College*
Kari Boyd McBride...*University of Arizona*
Edmund Miller...*C. W. Post Campus, Long Island University*
Michael P. Parker ....*United States Naval Academy*
Graham Roebuck...*McMaster University*
Roger B. Rollin...*Clemson University*
Maureen Sabine ....*University of Hong Kong*
John T. Shawcross...*University of Kentucky*
Elizabeth Skerpan...*Southwest Texas State University*
Gary A. Stringer...*University of Southern Mississippi*
Ernest W. Sullivan, II...*Texas Tech University*
Claude J. Summers...*University of Michigan – Dearborn*
Linda V. Troost...*Washington and Jefferson College*

311

Cumulative Index

Dictionary of Literary Biography, Volumes 1-126
Dictionary of Literary Biography Yearbook, 1980-1991
Dictionary of Literary Biography Documentary Series, Volumes 1-10

Cumulative Index

DLB before number: *Dictionary of Literary Biography,* Volumes 1-126
Y before number: *Dictionary of Literary Biography Yearbook,* 1980-1991
DS before number: *Dictionary of Literary Biography Documentary Series,* Volumes 1-10

A

C

D

E

F

G

H

J

K

M

O

Q

R

Cumulative Index

S

U

V

ISBN 0-8103-5385-7

90000

8961

1860, edited by Catharine Savage Brosman (1992)

120 *American Poets Since World War II,* Third Series, edited by R. S. Gwynn (1992)

121 *Seventeenth-Century British Nondramatic Poets,* First Series, edited by M. Thomas Hester (1992)

122 *Chicano Writers,* Second Series, edited by Francisco A. Lomelí and Carl R. Shirley (1992)

123 *Nineteenth-Century French Fiction Writers: Naturalism and Beyond, 1860-1900,* edited by Catharine Savage Brosman (1992)

124 *Twentieth-Century German Dramatists, 1919-1992,* edited by Wolfgang D. Elfe and James Hardin (1992)

125 *Twentieth-Century Caribbean and Black African Writers,* Second Series, edited by Bernth Lindfors and Reinhard Sander (1993)

126 *Seventeenth-Century British Nondramatic Poets,* Second Series, edited by M. Thomas Hester (1993)

Documentary Series

1 *Sherwood Anderson, Willa Cather, John Dos Passos, Theodore Dreiser, F. Scott Fitzgerald, Ernest Hemingway, Sinclair Lewis,* edited by Margaret A. Van Antwerp (1982)

2 *James Gould Cozzens, James T. Farrell, William Faulkner, John O'Hara, John Steinbeck, Thomas Wolfe, Richard Wright,* edited by Margaret A. Van Antwerp (1982)

3 *Saul Bellow, Jack Kerouac, Norman Mailer, Vladimir Nabokov, John*

Updike, Kurt Vonnegut, edited by Mary Bruccoli (1983)

4 *Tennessee Williams,* edited by Margaret A. Van Antwerp and Sally Johns (1984)

5 *American Transcendentalists,* edited by Joel Myerson (1988)

6 *Hardboiled Mystery Writers: Raymond Chandler, Dashiell Hammett, Ross Macdonald,* edited by Matthew J. Bruccoli and Richard Layman (1989)

7 *Modern American Poets: James Dickey, Robert Frost, Marianne Moore,* edited by Karen L. Rood (1989)

8 *The Black Aesthetic Movement,* edited by Jeffrey Louis Decker (1991)

9 *American Writers of the Vietnam War: W. D. Ehrhart, Larry Heinemann, Tim O'Brien, Walter McDonald, John M. Del Vecchio,* edited by Ronald Baughman (1991)

10 *The Bloomsbury Group,* edited by Edward L. Bishop (1992)

Yearbooks

1980 edited by Karen L. Rood, Jean W. Ross, and Richard Ziegfeld (1981)

1981 edited by Karen L. Rood, Jean W. Ross, and Richard Ziegfeld (1982)

1982 edited by Richard Ziegfeld; associate editors: Jean W. Ross and Lynne C. Zeigler (1983)

1983 edited by Mary Bruccoli and Jean W. Ross; associate editor: Richard Ziegfeld (1984)

1984 edited by Jean W. Ross (1985)

1985 edited by Jean W. Ross (1986)

1986 edited by J. M. Brook (1987)

1987 edited by J. M. Brook (1988)

1988 edited by J. M. Brook (1989)

1989 edited by J. M. Brook (1990)

1990 edited by James W. Hipp (1991)

1991 edited by James W. Hipp (1992)